THE BATTLE OF PEACH TREE CREEK

Endowed by
TOM WATSON BROWN
and
THE WATSON-BROWN FOUNDATION, INC.

THE BATTLE OF
PEACH TREE CREEK

Hood's First Sortie, 20 July 1864

Robert D. Jenkins, Sr.

MERCER UNIVERSITY PRESS
MACON, GEORGIA

MUP/ H858

© 2013 Mercer University
Press 1400 Coleman Avenue
Macon, Georgia 31207
All rights reserved

First Edition, second printing 2014

Books published by Mercer University Press are printed on acid-free paper that meets the requirements of the American National Standard for Information Sciences—Permanence of Paper for Printed Library Materials.

Mercer University Press is a member of Green Press Initiative (greenpressinitiative.org), a nonprofit organization working to help publishers and printers increase their use of recycled paper and decrease their use of fiber derived from endangered forests.

Library of Congress Cataloging-in-Publication Data

Jenkins, Robert D., 1964-
 The Battle of Peach Tree Creek : Hood's first sortie, 20 July 1864 / Robert D. Jenkins, Sr. -- First edition.
     pages cm
  Includes bibliographical references and index.
  ISBN-13: 978-0-88146-396-5 (hardback : alk. paper)
  ISBN-10: 0-88146-396-5 (hardback : alk. paper)
 1. Peachtree Creek, Battle of, Ga., 1864. 2. Atlanta Campaign, 1864. I. Title.
  E476.7.J46 2013
  973.7'371--dc23
                    2013030163

To Aunt Elaine

CONTENTS

Acknowledgments
Preface
1. The Final Summer ... 1
2. The Plan ... 5
3. A Rich Man's War and a Poor Man's Fight ... 37
4. Cannonade Atlanta without Mercy ... 41
5. Old Reliable ... 52
6. The Bloody Magnolias ... 63
7. With One Foot over the Creek ... 75
8. There'll Be Trouble out There ... 93
9. Here They Come Boys, By God a Million of Them ... 97
10. A Straggling, Haphazard Kind of Hide and Seek Affair ... 104
11. Now You May Give It to Them, Captain ... 112
12. An I Give a Dare Affair ... 143
13. We Must Carry Everything...the Fate of Atlanta Depends on Us ... 161
14. Bailey Be a Good Boy ... 172
15. They Fought Like Very Devils ... 189
16. The Fight for Collier Mill ... 200
17. Holding onto Collier Ridge ... 252
18. Thickets Were Literally Cradled by Bullets ... 278
19. A Square Stand-up Fight for Three Hours ... 301
20. That Is Where but Little Fun Came ... 322
21. It Was Chickamauga Again ... 331
22. No, No, General, I Did Not Lose Any Men ... 349
23. We Will Have to Fight to Get Atlanta ... 359
24. Be on the Lookout for Breastworks ... 369
25. It Was the Saddest Day I Ever Saw ... 389
26. A Negative Victory Plainly Won ... 401
27. Fresh Tidings from the Battlefield ... 411
28. Epilogue: Peach Tree Creek National Military Park? ... 417

Roster of Confederate and Federal Losses at Peach Tree Creek 425
Bibliography 513
Index 533

ACKNOWLEDGMENTS

When I first decided to take on this project some twenty years ago, I never imagined all of the places that it would take me: from libraries to museums; national, state and local parks and monuments; cemeteries; archives; descendants' homes, and the like. It has been a pleasure just learning so much more about our nation's rich and deep history and meeting so many people. In fact, as I write these acknowledgments, it is impossible to list everyone who helped me along the way or who contributed to this work, and I am sure that in my efforts to thank each one, I will invariably miss somebody.

I should first thank my Lord and Savior, Jesus Christ, for blessing me, my family, and my home, and in whom I have all hope and peace for my life. It has been fascinating for me to see how our pioneers and pilgrim families who settled this country placed their faith strongly in God. During the Civil War, the soldiers, both North and South alike, spent much of their time in revivals, meetings, fasting (sometimes without option), and prayer. Perhaps the struggles that they faced drew them nearer to their faith. The more that I learn about our predecessors, the more I realize that they were just like you and me, ordinary Americans, only they were faced with extraordinary challenges.

When I first began this work, my plan was to write the regimental history on the 31st Mississippi Infantry as this glorious unit has never been given its place on the shelves of history. But, as I wrote the chapter on the Battle of Peach Tree Creek, I found myself trying to tell the story of this little known, but important, battle that was part of the struggle for Atlanta during the Georgia campaign of 1864. By the time I had completed a first draft of the Peach Tree chapter, it was seventy-six pages long. Moreover, no work has ever covered the battle in book level detail and the Battle of Peach Tree Creek has been unnecessarily abstruse. It became obvious to me that Peach Tree Creek and the events that led up to this battle needed to be covered more thoroughly. Thus, my work on the 31st Mississippi, "The Bloody Magnolias" as I have chosen to call them, would have to wait. I had to tell the story of Peach Tree Creek and replace the wide gap on the shelves of Civil War history on this important battle. In my estimation, history's shelves for this battle have heretofore been sparsely filled with a lot of inaccurate, misunderstood, and untold stories of the drama that was the inaugural military test of a new Southern commander and the beginning of the end for Confederate Atlanta and the Confederacy as a whole. In fairness, however, I must applaud the coverage provided by Albert Castel's *Decision in the West*, and Russell Bond's *War like the Thunderbolt*, which give a good chapter-length general history of the battle. For a study on the Atlanta Campaign, I highly recommend both books.

I am indebted to a number of people who graciously provided invaluable information to me for this work. I should also inform you that this book should perhaps have been written by someone who came along before me like the prominent Atlanta historians Wilbur G. Kurtz, Colonel Allen P. Jullian, and Franklin W. Garrett. Each of these three men spent over a half century uncovering details of Atlanta history including performing countless interviews of eye-witnesses to important events, making multiple field trips to sites throughout Georgia, and writing and compiling boxes and boxes of useful material.

Unfortunately, while all three of these men had much to tell us about Peach Tree Creek, and all three generously gave of their time and knowledge to any caller or group, with each man serving as regular speakers on related Atlanta history subjects, all three failed to begin or complete a manuscript on Peach Tree Creek. Moreover, all three men took much knowledge of the battle or of unit placements and individual soldier's stories to their graves. But, many of their working files and notes survive, particularly Kurtz's writings, which were deposited at the Keenan Research Center located at the Atlanta History Center by Kurtz's family. I am indebted to these men who have gone before me, and who have, at least in part, paved the way for my work. I am also indebted to Gordon Jones and the staff at the Atlanta History Center for granting me unfettered access to these and many other records.

To Chief Historian James Ogden of the Chickamauga-Chattanooga National Parks, thank you for encouraging me. Thank you, Jim, for sharing your invaluable knowledge and insights, and for pointing me in directions that always led to important information. To Dr. William Blackman, of Dalton, thank you, Bill, for encouraging me to turn my chapter into a full-sized work on Peach Tree Creek. To Dr. Timothy Smith of Shiloh National Battlefield Park, thank you, Tim, for all of your runs to libraries, museums, and battle sites and for kindly sharing so many of your records and so much of your knowledge with me. Your work on Champion Hill is a model for my work on this battle.

To Bob Lurate, formerly of Lexington, Virginia, thank you for your support and encouragement when I needed to hear it. To Grady Howell and the folks at the Mississippi Department of Archives and History, thank you for helping me find the most obscure records and resources. Nobody does it better than you folks. To Mercer University, Georgia Southern University, the University of Georgia, Ole Miss (The University of Mississippi), Mississippi State University, the University of Southern Mississippi, the University of North Carolina at Chapel Hill, Emory University, the University of Wisconsin, and Louisiana State University, and to the National Archives, and the state archives of Alabama, Georgia, Mississippi, Tennessee, Wisconsin, and every county, city, and local library and museum along the way, and the staffs, libraries, and special collections departments, thank you for all of your assistance and support.

To Gary Abrams, Doyle Calvi, Bill Clayton, David Cleutz, Jim Taylor, Robert Avent, cousin Howell Jenkins, James Drane, Lee White, Keith Bohannon, Rex Riner, Jerry and Nancy Dickey, Marilyn Knight Clark, Rob Hodge, Pete Christopher, and a host of others who freely shared research, family stories, photos, diaries, and letters, thank you for your help and contributions. With the advent of the internet, research for this book has been greatly broadened, permitting me to connect with hundreds of folks who have a shared interest in a particular regiment or subject.

To Thomas Cartwright, David Fraley, Tim Burgess, Sam Gant, Jamie Gillum, Robert Hicks, Sam Huffman, Eric Jacobson, the late David Logsden, Heath Matthews, Joe Smyth, Gregg Wade, and all of the "Tennessee Gang" who tirelessly work to preserve and promote the Spring Hill, Franklin, and Nashville battles and all of our nation's rich history in middle Tennessee, thank you for your encouragement and support and for freely sharing your wisdom, insights, research, and resources; thank you for your help and for your friendship.

To Greg Biggs, Ken Legendre, the late Howard Michael Madaus, and Hugh Simmons, thank you for sharing your knowledge about battle flags. I have learned volumes about this fascinating subject from each of you. Also, thank you, Hugh, for generously sharing your knowledge of the 12th Louisiana, a gallant regiment. To Fred Kimbrell, thank you for sharing your research on the brave 33rd Mississippi, who, as part of Featherston's Mississippi brigade, were massacred on Collier Ridge at Peach Tree Creek.

To Rick Reeves of Tampa, Florida, whose artwork is displayed on the cover of this work, thank you for sharing your talent so that others can gain a glimpse through your brush of just how a July day in 1864 looked for the boys in blue and gray. To my friend Dave Helton, whose graphics skills are unmatched, thank you for turning my rough maps into polished ones.

To Bill Scaife of Atlanta who passed away in summer 2009, thank you for letting me use your wonderful maps as a reference and resource for my projects. Bill was so generous to allow me and many others to freely use his maps in our works. Bill's understanding of topography and the landscape of battlefields and how it affects and changes battle plans is unmatched and, in many instances, not given proper weight when studying battles. To Steve Davis, Richard McMurry, Henry Howell, Dr. Linton Hopkins, Betty and George Heery, Russell Bonds, Charlie Crawford, and many others in and around Atlanta who have shared your knowledge, resources, and family stories, thank you. Charlie, I cannot tell you enough how much I appreciate your scrupulous review of my work and your willingness to offer your keen insights and deep knowledge of the war to help make my work as accurate and detailed as it can be.

To Joan and Murray Scripture of Greenville, South Carolina, who have tirelessly edited my poor English skills into a polished work, thank you. Joan, who has such a strong and deep background in grammar, having taught English for years, thank you for your discerning red ink pen. Murray, who like me is a student of the war, having read and studied it all of his life, thank you for your wisdom and guidance. I know of no one who has read more about the war than Murray, who also has a unique interest in this battle as his own ancestor fought opposite mine in it. Murray's relative served with the 136th New York Infantry in Hooker's XX Corps, which fought desperately to take back the ridge and works on it along Collier Road from the 31st Mississippi in which my great-great grandfather fought. A member of the 136th New York captured the flag of the 31st Mississippi, and a photograph of this flag, which has never been published before, is included in this book. It is a blessing to have friends who read, re-read and re-re-read to ensure the work is the best that it can be. So, thank you to Joan for editing my grammar, and Murray for editing the content, to make my rambling thoughts and nonsense into some kind of sense. Any errors in grammar or content that remain are strictly my own.

To my wife, Kathy, and my children, Katie Beth and Robby, who have endured countless "field trips" to libraries, museums, parks, and battlefields, thank you for your love, patience, and support. Without Kathy's love and support, I could not take on these heartfelt projects as I attempt to balance family, work, church, high school and Georgia Southern football, Atlanta Braves and Falcons, and Civil War research, among other interests. God has blessed me with a wonderful family and I am truly grateful for each of you.

To my mother and late father, Joy and Bob Jenkins, and to my extended family of grandparents, aunts and uncles, many of whom have passed on, thank you for giving me such a rich and loving upbringing with all the support that a child and young adult could ever hope for, and with the encouragement to inspire me to fulfill any dream, thank you. Thank you, also, for teaching me the importance of history and for allowing me to explore it.

Finally, to my late Aunt Elaine McIntire of Choctaw County, Mississippi, a school teacher, cook-book writer, genealogist, quilt-maker, Sunday school teacher, family historian and history writer, and my inspiration for writing this book, thank you. Some twenty years ago after her husband, Uncle Jerry McIntire, died, Aunt Elaine took the time to go to the state archives in Jackson, Mississippi, and dig up the Civil War records of our ancestor, Caradine "Jerry" Jenkins. Family tradition had it that he fought during the war but was home a great deal as he had a wife, a number of small children, and a small farm to tend. It was speculated that he was a grown man and too old for the service and thus was likely in a home guard unit. Aunt Elaine discovered his compiled service records, which had heretofore eluded the family because we knew him only as "Jerry Jenkins," revealing much about him and our family. Acting on a hunch, Aunt Elaine followed a lead on the unusual family name that she had once heard an elderly relative mention, and Caradine "Jerry" T. Jenkins was discovered. The military records had him listed only as Caradine Jenkins.

As it turns out, Jerry Jenkins was a private in Company E, of the 31st Mississippi Infantry, he was thirty-three when the war broke out and thirty-seven at its end. He had been a veteran of the Mexican War like so many Mississippi Confederates; he was married to a descendant of German immigrants, Martha Caroline Whisenant; he had four children at the start of the war, would have two more children during the war, and five more following the war for a total of eleven children. He was home often because he was twice AWOL, which was common among Civil War soldiers. He returned to the regiment in time to suffer all the hardships of the Georgia and Tennessee campaigns of 1864 under Johnston and Hood. His story is typical of many a Yank and Reb.

I would perhaps never have deepened my childhood interest in the war and American history had it not been for Aunt E. M.'s discovery, or for her pressing me for details on where the 31st Mississippi traveled during the war. It then became a quest for me to retrace my ancestor's steps across the Civil War map as I put my own knowledge of the war to the test and quickly realized that I had only touched the surface. To Aunt Elaine, I also thank you for living your life as a Christian example. Thank you Aunt Elaine for your love, for your support, and for your encouragement to write this book. I dedicate it to you.

Author's note: I have included quotes from many of the soldiers. Some of the material quoted contains grammatical and spelling errors. I have included them as originally written.

PREFACE

One hundred and fifty years ago, our nation was immersed in the most terrible, bloody, and fatal conflict, testing, as Abraham Lincoln so eloquently stated, "whether that nation or any nation" conceived in liberty, could "long endure."

By May 1864, many Southerners in Georgia, which had until that point been relatively insulated from the war's devastation, had a rude awakening. While the possibility of Yankee invasion into the Peach State had been the topic of conversation among Georgian civilians for three years, there had developed a kind of security, or feeling of isolation from the war, because it had mostly been fought far away in Virginia, Tennessee, and Mississippi. Perhaps the best depiction of the naive impressions that some Georgians held were embodied in the character "Aunt Pitty Pat" in *Gone With the Wind* when, upon hearing cannon fire for the first time, she exclaimed, "Yankees in Georgia! How did they ever get in?" Many Georgians who had not seen the war's effects had even developed a form of false hope that they would remain out of its path and that the Confederacy would somehow win the war, much the way that the nation had won its independence during the Revolutionary War with the other side eventually giving up. Spring 1864 brought the reality of the war to Georgia, which proved to be devastating both to the state and to the Confederacy.

The action for control of Georgia, known popularly as the Atlanta Campaign, is probably better described as the Georgia Campaign because it eventually encompassed almost all of the Empire State of the South, reaching from Chattanooga to Savannah. From the Southern viewpoint, the campaign's principal villain was Federal commander William Tecumseh Sherman. To this day the very name "Sherman" evokes a deep and painful passion in the Deep South, particularly in Georgia, South Carolina, and Mississippi, where Sherman's torches lit the way to victory for the North and the end of the terrible war. Sherman's "total war" policies brought the South to its knees. Sherman bragged that he would "make Georgia howl." The year before, the Vicksburg Campaign had split the Confederacy in two as the South lost control of the Mississippi River. The Georgia Campaign became important because it once more divided the South and drained most of the Confederacy's remaining resources. It was, in the estimation of many scholars, the turning point of the war.

In all of my studies of the Civil War, I have found the battles, leaders, and soldiers of the Western armies have been too much overlooked, particularly those from the Deep South, perhaps because they did not share the same notoriety as their counterparts in Virginia and the border states. Maybe it was because most did not come from major cities or urban regions like those of the eastern coast. But, for whatever reason, there is a void of material on the Confederate Army of Mississippi, its leaders, battles, and units. For example, a series of regimental histories exists in Virginia that covers every single unit that donned the gray for the Old Dominion. But in Alabama, Georgia, Mississippi, and Louisiana, only a few units have been given such treatment, and among these works, at least half of the regiments covered served with the Army of Northern Virginia.

No work has ever concentrated on the Battle of Peach Tree Creek, or for that matter, any of the battles around Atlanta until recently. Because at the time of the battle, Peachtree Creek was generally referred to as "Peach Tree" Creek, I have chosen to use the 1864 spelling of the creek and battle. When reference is made to a current Peachtree site, then the modern version is given. The Atlanta name "Peachtree" has been used so often for streets, places, and events in Atlanta over the past several generations, that residents often confuse one Peachtree street or place for another when giving or receiving directions. In fact, the over-usage of the popular name has become so epidemic that local governments and postal authorities refuse to allow any new street or subdivision to use "Peachtree" in any part of a name in the Metro-Atlanta area.

A number of battles around the Gate City were called the Battles for Atlanta, but the fighting on 20 July was known as battle of Peach Tree Creek. Cleburne's division fought during the night of 20 July against a portion of McPherson's Army of the Tennessee called the Battle of Bald Hill, or Leggett's Hill, which became a prelude to a battle on 22 July called the Battle of Atlanta. That action was fought on 22 July between Atlanta and Decatur could also have been called the Battle of Decatur. The Battle of Ezra Church that occurred on 28 July, was also called the Battle of Lickskillet Road and the Battle of the Poor House, particularly by Southern troops who fought there. Ezra Church, Utoy Creek on 6 August and Jonesboro on 31 August and 1 September, joined Peach Tree Creek and Decatur to be known collectively as the Battles for Atlanta, although none of these engagements actually took place within the corporate limits of the city. Further, there were a number of cavalry actions throughout Georgia during summer 1864 that also affected the situation in Atlanta. Many books have been written about this campaign that culminated in the fall of Atlanta, including the social and political picture that gripped Atlanta at the time.

The Battle of Peach Tree Creek marked the beginning of the end for the Confederacy, for it turned the page from the patient defense displayed by General Joseph E. Johnston to the bold offense called upon by his replacement, General John Bell Hood. Until this point in the Georgia Campaign, the Southern Army of Tennessee had fought primarily in the defensive, from behind earthworks, forcing General Sherman to either assault fortified lines or go around them in flanking moves. At Peach Tree Creek, the roles would be reversed for the first time as Confederates charged Federal lines.

Peach Tree Creek is important because it is the last planned battle by Confederate General Joseph E. Johnston who was so popular among his men, but who was held in such contempt by his president in Richmond. The battle is important because it is the first of the new Southern commander John Bell Hood's many offensive exploits as he attempted both to impose his bold will on the Rebel army and to repel Sherman's legions from Georgia through aggressive and hard offensive tactics. Peach Tree Creek offers a clue as to what was in store for these Confederates under Hood's leadership. It was the first of many bloody contests under Hood that so decimated the army that the Confederacy would, by the following spring, be brought to her knees. From the wooded ridges and ravines along Peach Tree Creek's southern banks to a quiet solemn cemetery in Franklin, Tennessee, lie the graves of Southern soldiers who suffered 150 days of slaughter in battles from Atlanta to Nashville where they fought at such a disadvantage and at such long odds.

The Battle of Peach Tree Creek is important because it was the beginning of the end for the Deep South and the Confederacy. Peach Tree Creek would be the first in a series of defeats and set-backs from which the South would not recover. Before Peach Tree Creek, there remained some semblance of hope for victory and Southern Independence. After Peach Tree Creek and the defeats at Decatur and Ezra Church that quickly followed, there could be no more hope of a military victory by the Confederacy. After Peach Tree Creek, and its companion battles for Atlanta, the alert Southerner could hear the death throws of the Confederacy.

Peach Tree Creek was the first battle in which General Hood commanded an army, and it was the first of three battles in eight days where Hood led the Confederates to desperate, but unsuccessful, attempts to repel the Federal armies encircling Atlanta. The Confederacy's aggressive plan to sweep a portion of the Northern invaders into the creek and Chattahoochee River beyond and force the Yankees to retreat, would demonstrate reasonably good skill in its planning by Johnston and Hood. But, it would also display a failure to grasp the logistical requirements needed to make it a success, an inability to account for and adjust to changes in circumstances during the attack, a breakdown in the chain of command and in communications between the commanding general and his field commanders and between the various unit commanders, and a piecemeal and mixed effort in its execution, all common threads in each of Hood's future battles. Peach Tree Creek started the South on its downward spiral from which she would never recover. This battle was, in my view, the first nail in the coffin of the Confederacy.

Understanding why it was fought, how it occurred, and what resulted makes this work a challenge, as there is, unfortunately, a lack of published material, particularly regarding many units in the Confederate Army. Many diaries, letters, and narratives exist, however, that provide a picture of the carnage that befell the ridges, fields, and woodlands just south of a creek that gave its name to the bloody battle. Hopefully, by trying to leave no stone unturned, this book will better inform the reader about this little-known, but very important battle. Also, by placing the battle into perspective within the Civil War and by introducing its principal actors on a more detailed level, I hope that the participants and the events in this struggle will be better understood.

But this book was also written for more selfish reasons. In my quest to find my own ancestor's role in the war, I found that nothing had been written about his regiment, the 31st Mississippi, or its men and boys who came from the small farms of Choctaw, Chickasaw, Calhoun, and Pontotoc counties in northeastern Mississippi. Finding that their regimental losses along the ridge above Collier Mill during the Battle of Peach Tree Creek rivaled and surpassed those of many other legendary Northern and Southern units from fields far more familiar, their story, as well as the accounts of their comrades who charged with them on a hot summer day in July, had to be told.

In addition, the valiant defense made by their Northern counterparts needed to be remembered. These men from the hapless IV, XIV, and XX corps in the Federal Army of the Cumberland have also been neglected by much of the print and praise after the war. The Army of the Cumberland's veterans certainly fought well enough during the Georgia Campaign to earn their place on history's shelf. It was due to the efforts of these Federal soldiers who rallied and stood their ground in the face of the surprising Rebel assault that the attack was repelled.

As President Lincoln so aptly described the sacrifice of soldiers on another field in the Gettysburg Address where this same XX Corps fought as the XI and XII corps, these men who fought and died along Peach Tree Creek, both North and South, also gave "their last full measure of devotion." I thought they should be remembered.

Major General Samuel Gibbs French, although born in New Jersey, he commanded a Confederate Division.

Major General William Brimage Bate of Tennessee. His Division got lost during the action in today's Ansley Golf Club and Sherwood Forest Subdivision.

General Clement Hoffman Stevens, was mortally wounded along the Buckhead Road while leading his Georgia Brigade.
He died 25 July, 1864.

General Winfield Scott Featherston, commanded Mississippi Brigade.

Major General William Wing Loring of Florida, lost an arm during the Mexican War and commanded a Confederate Division.

Major General John Newton, commanded a Division which held the heights known today as Cardiac Hill against Hardee's attacks. Photo courtesy Library of Congress.

General Edward Asbury O'Neal, commanded a Brigade in Walthall's Division. He was later Governor of Alabama.

Lieutenant General Alexander Peter Stewart, commanded the Army of Mississippi, later called Third Corps, Army of Tennessee.

Flag of 33rd Mississippi captured at Peach Tree Creek. Flag is in possession of the Mississippi Dept. of Archives and History. Special consideration has been paid by the author to obtain permission to display the flag in this book.

Photo of sign reflecting location of Howell Battery along Buckhead Rd., first published in Martin, Thomas H. Atlanta and Its Builders, 1902, at Vol. 1 p. 397; copy at Harvard Library

General Benjamin Harrison of Indiana became 23rd President of the United States. His brigade reversed Confederate fortunes at Collier's Mill.

General Joseph Farmer Knipe, commanded a brigade in Williams' Division. Photo courtesy Library of Congress.

Hubert Dilger, a German immigrant, commanded a battery in Palmer's XIV Corps. He was awarded the Medal of Honor for his conduct at Chancellorsville.

Major General 'Fighting Joe' Hooker, commanded the XX Corps which turned back Stewart's attack. Photo courtesy of Library of Congress.

Coat worn by John E. Johnson, 29th Alabama, who was mortally wounded at Peach Tree Creek. Courtesy, Atlanta History Center, permanent display, contributed by Henry De Ramus.

Fighting at Collier's Mill, watercolor by Wilbur G. Kurtz, courtesy Atlanta History Center.

Captain John P. Seeman, 26th Wisconsin, Killed at Peach Tree Creek. Photo courtesy U. S. Army Military History Institute, Carlisle Pa.

General Daniel Harris Reynolds circa 1900. He commanded an Arkansas Brigade. Photo courtesy the Butler Center for Arkansas Studies, Central Arkansas Library System.

Major General Alpheus Starkey Williams, a War Democrat from Detroit, Mich, commanded a Division which turned back O'Neal's surprise assault. Photo courtesy Library of Congress.

Lieutenant Stephen Pierson, 33rd New Jersey, became a physician after the war.

General John Bell Hood, newly appointed commander of the Confederate forces defending Atlanta.

Captain Evan P. Howell, commanded a Georgia Battery at the Buckhead Road during the Battle. Sketch by Wilbur G. Kurtz, courtesy Atlanta History Center.

Colonel Douglas Hapeman, commanded the 104th Illinois. He received the Medal of Honor for leading the repulse of Reynolds' attack along the Howell Mill Road.

Lieutenant General William J. Hardee (Old Reliable), Commanded a Corps in the Army of Tennessee. Photo courtesy Library of Congress.

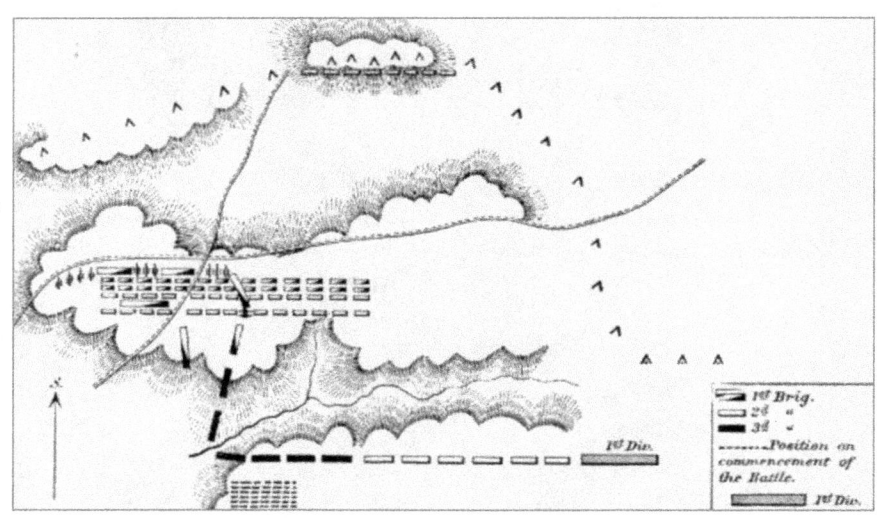

Sketch of Geary's position at Peach Tree Creek drawn by Geary.
O.R., Serial 73, p. 139.

Sketch of General Hooker overlooking Collier's Mill during battle, by Theodore Davis, Century Magazine.

BATTLE OF PEACH TREE CREEK,

July 20th, 1864.

Composed by John Hughes, Com. E,   ★   29th P.V., 20 A.C., Com. by Joe Hooker

It was on the Twentieth of July, Hood said unto his men,
This day we'll charge those Yankee lines, and drive them back again;
Their dead shall rot upon the field and their wounded men shall die,
And their living beg for quarters on this Twentieth of July.
    Chorus—Hurrah! hurrah! for Fighting Joe, hurrah!
        Hurrah for the battle-flag that bears a single Star.

Their well-laid plans did not succeed, as you shall quickly know,
For eagle-eye Joe Hooker kept watch upon the foe,
And though they charged us heavily we bravely met the shock,
And hurled our haughty foemen back like waves dashed from a rock.

They came again in columns with Battallions closed Enmasse,
Their bayonets glittered in the sun like dew upon the grass;
Our foemen far outnumbered us, our gallant boys well knew,
But still there was no waver in that solid line of blue.

They charged with desperation, our ranks they fiercely pressed,
Whilst volley after volley we poured into their breasts,
And yankee grape and canister into their Ranks did pour,
And many a reb lay cold and dead in front of Hooker's Corps.

They charged upon our right and left but found it all in vain,
And when they tried our centre were driven back again;
They formed their ranks upon the flanks, but found it would not do,
For we made them smell Greek fire from those yankee lines of Blue.

Our Rebel foes their ranks did close, they formed and came again,
And with a firm defiant tread on came those southern men;
But the prospects that was ahead of them, it made them heave a sigh,
As they fell before Joe Hooker's Corps on the 20th of July.

Go back unto your rebel friends and tell your Gen'l Hood,
Two thousand of his bravest men lies weltering in their blood;
Two thousand of his gallant men has fell to rise no more,
His rebel braves have found their graves, in front of Hooker's Corps.

Our rebel foe fell back again as night was drawing nigh,
They left their dead upon the field and their wounded for to die;
They left their dead behind them, and their wounded men also,
All to the tender mercies of their hated Yankee Foe.

We carried off their wounded and buried all their dead,
You look with pity on us now, a wounded rebel said;
You may pity all, but cant recall the deeds done by your corps,
For in yonder vale lies cold and pale, two thousand men or more.

Yes many of their bravest men that day was stricken down,
They once so bold now dead and cold, their life's blood stains the ground;
For yankee ball both great and small, had done their duty well,
As many a wounded rebel by experience can tell.

Then three cheers for brave Joe Hooker, our gallant fighting Joe,
Beloved by all his soldiers, a terror to his foe;
And likewise to that lone bright Star, the badge we truly love,
The motto of that gallant corps, it proudly waves above.

Printed at Johnson's Card and Job Printing Office, 7 North 10th st., Philada.

Sung to the tune of "The Yellow Rose of Texas!"

Major General William T. Ward, Commander Third Division, XX Corps, Army of the Cumberland. Photo courtesy the Library of Congress.

Major General Edward Cary Walthall, circa 1899, commanded a Confederate Division.

Major General John White Geary, much of his Division was routed by portions of Scott's and O'Neal's Brigades before order was restored. Photo courtesy of Library of Congress.

Private Hiram Nail, 31st Mississippi and relative of author, killed at Peach Tree Creek. Photo courtesy of author's cousin Howell Jenkins.

Flag of 33rd New Jersey, captured at Peach Tree Creek. Photo courtesy of State of New Jersey Dept. of Military and Veteran Affairs.

*Flag of 31st Mississippi captured at Peach Tree Creek.
Courtesy of the Mississippi Dept. of Archives and History. Special consideration
has been paid by the author to obtain permission to display the flag in this book.*

General George Thomas, the 'Rock of Chickamauga,' again showed his steadiness at Peach Tree Creek. Photo courtesy Library of Congress.

Lieutenant Colonel James Drane, commanded 31st Mississippi at Peach Tree Creek. Was wounded five times atop Collier Road but survived. Photo courtesy the Drane House, French Camp, MS.

General William T. Sherman

General Joseph E. Johnston

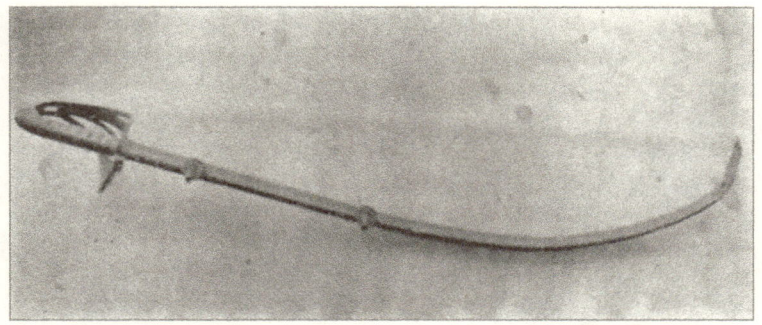

Photo of Colonel Silas Colgrove's US 1850 officer's sword carried by him when he was struck by a solid shot from Preston's Battery at Peach Tree Creek.

General Hooker riding along his lines on the morning of July 21, 1864. Sketch by Theodore R. Davis, Harper's Weekly, Aug. 13, 1864.

Key's Battery goes into action along the Buckhead Road, sketch by Wilbur G. Kurtz. Courtesy Atlanta History Center.

Photograph of Peach Tree Creek battlefield taken by George Barnard, 1864. Photo is taken from Collier Road facing north at site of Featherston's breakthrough.

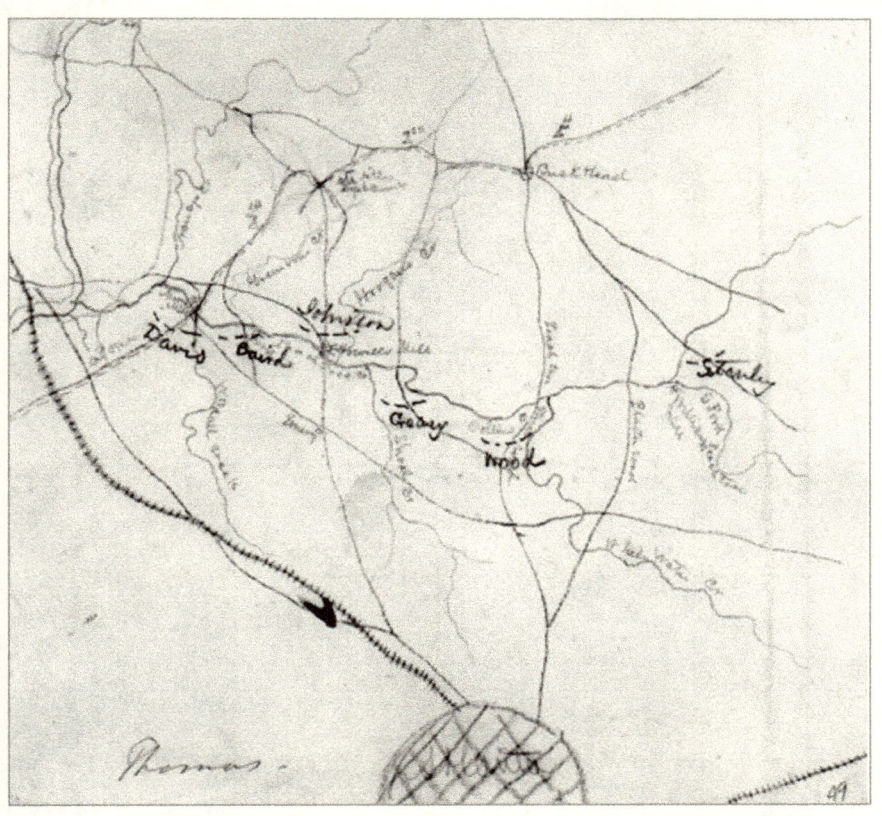

Sketch prepared by General Thomas on evening of 19 July, 1864, to show Sherman his troop positions. Courtesy of Official Atlas.

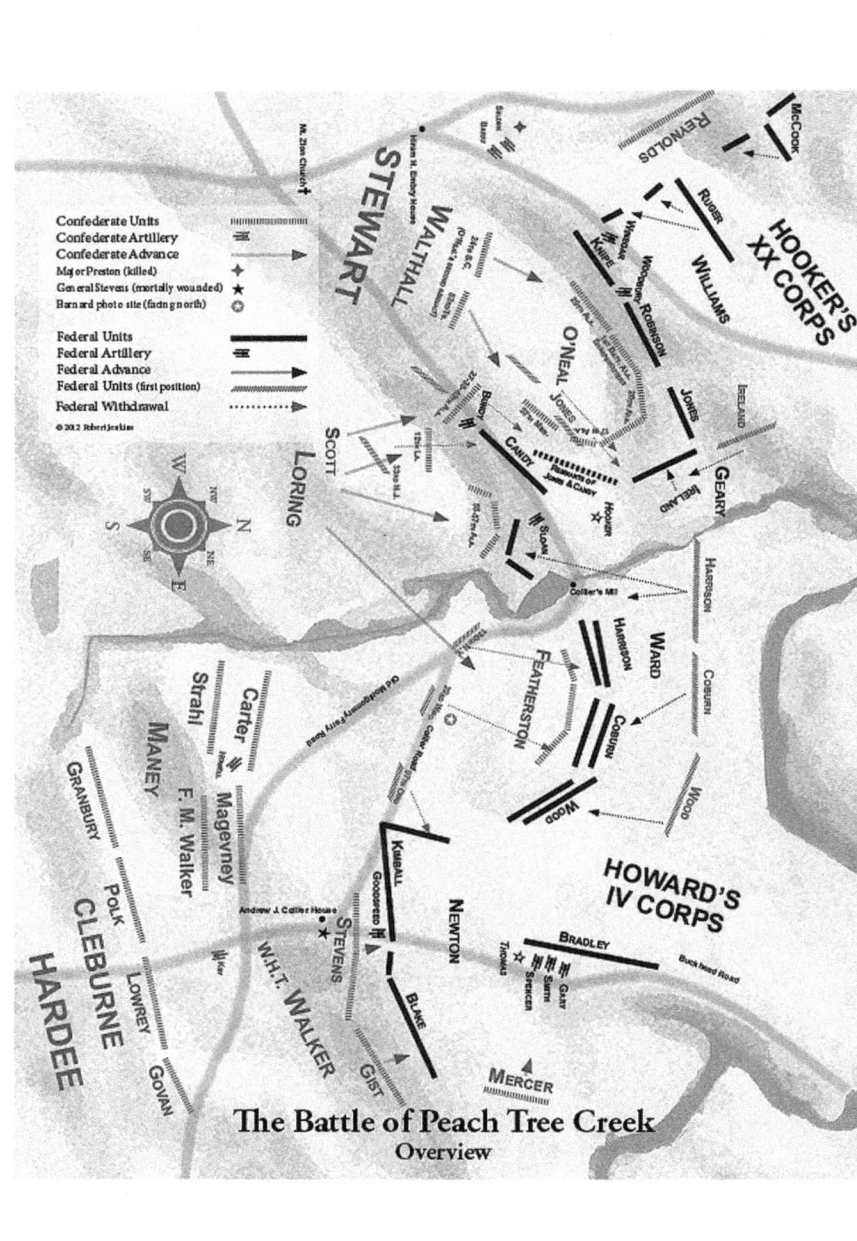

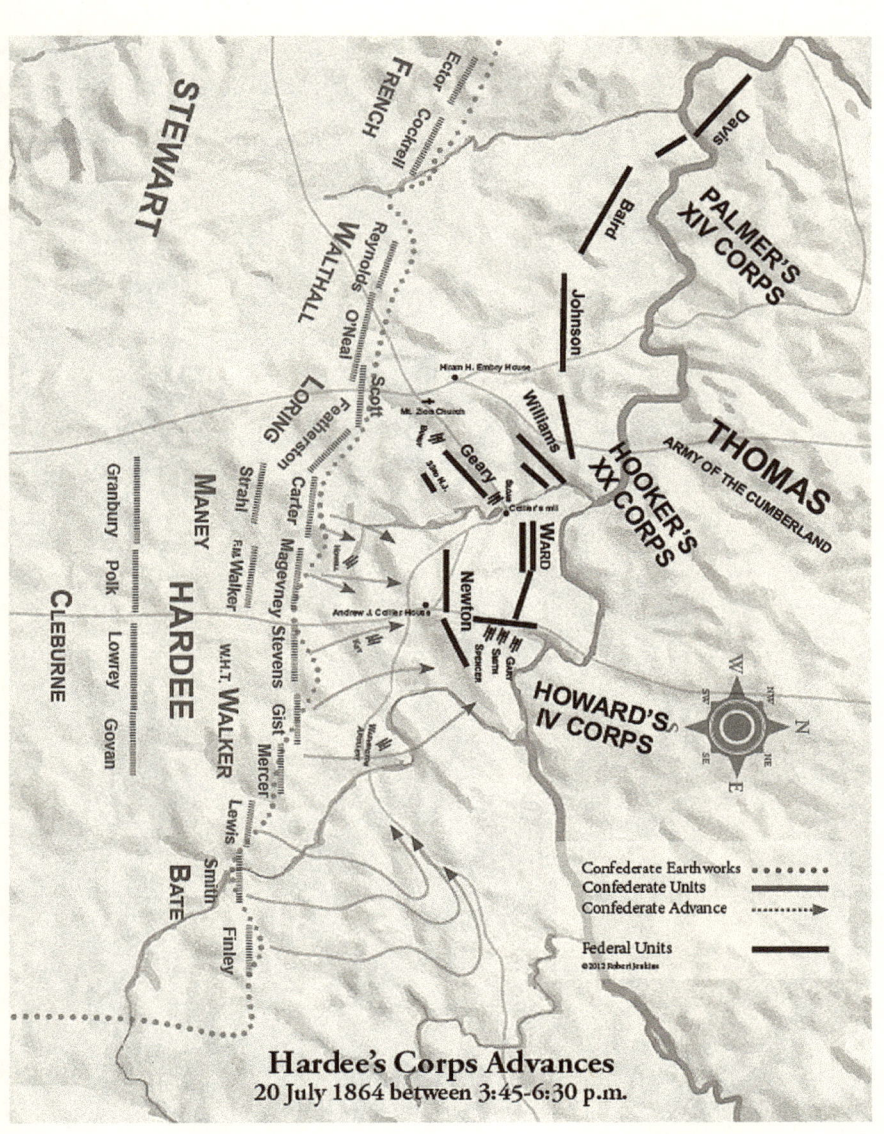

Hardee's Corps Advances
20 July 1864 between 3:45-6:30 p.m.

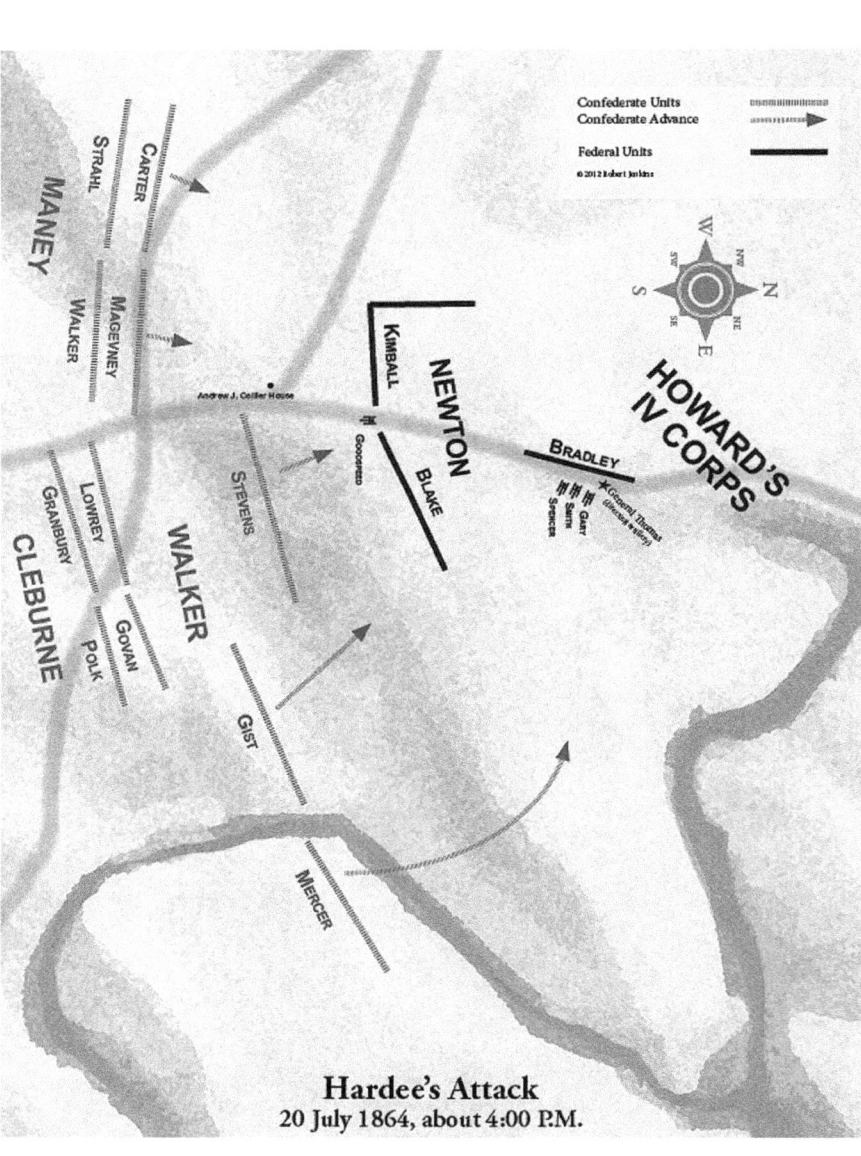

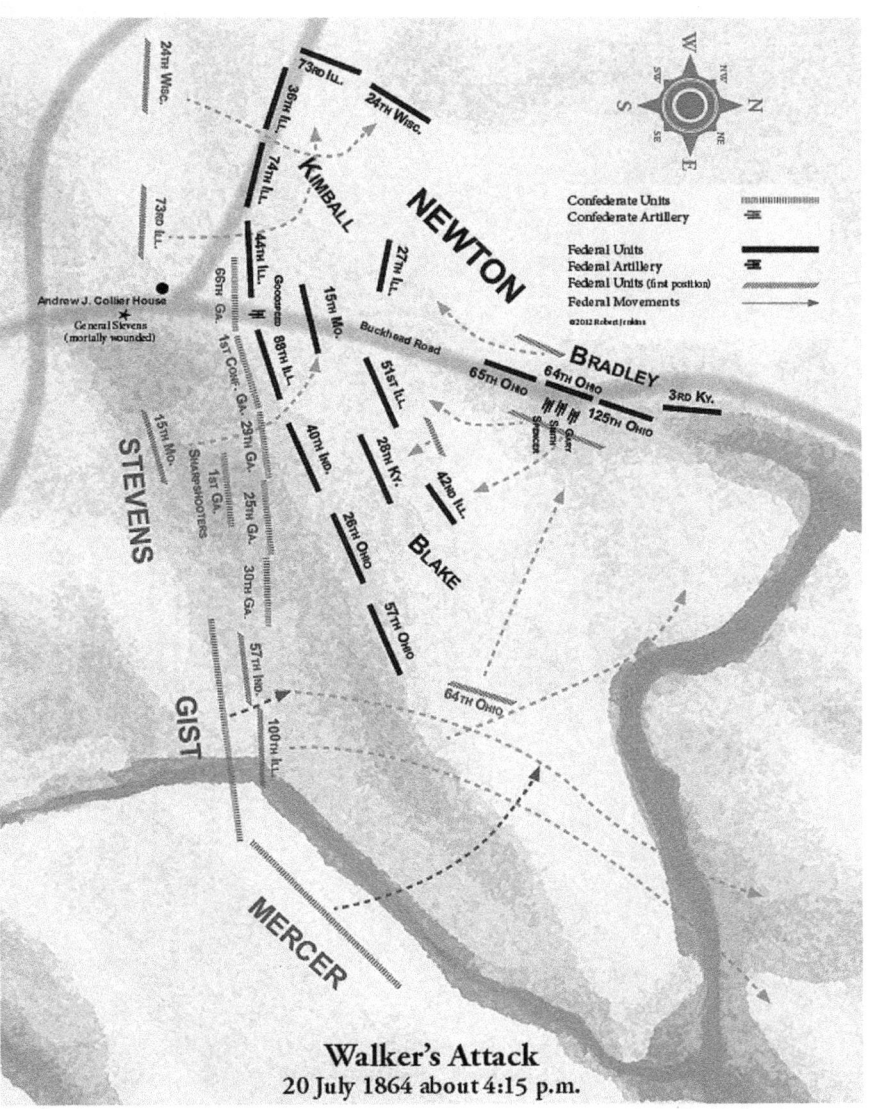

Walker's Attack
20 July 1864 about 4:15 p.m.

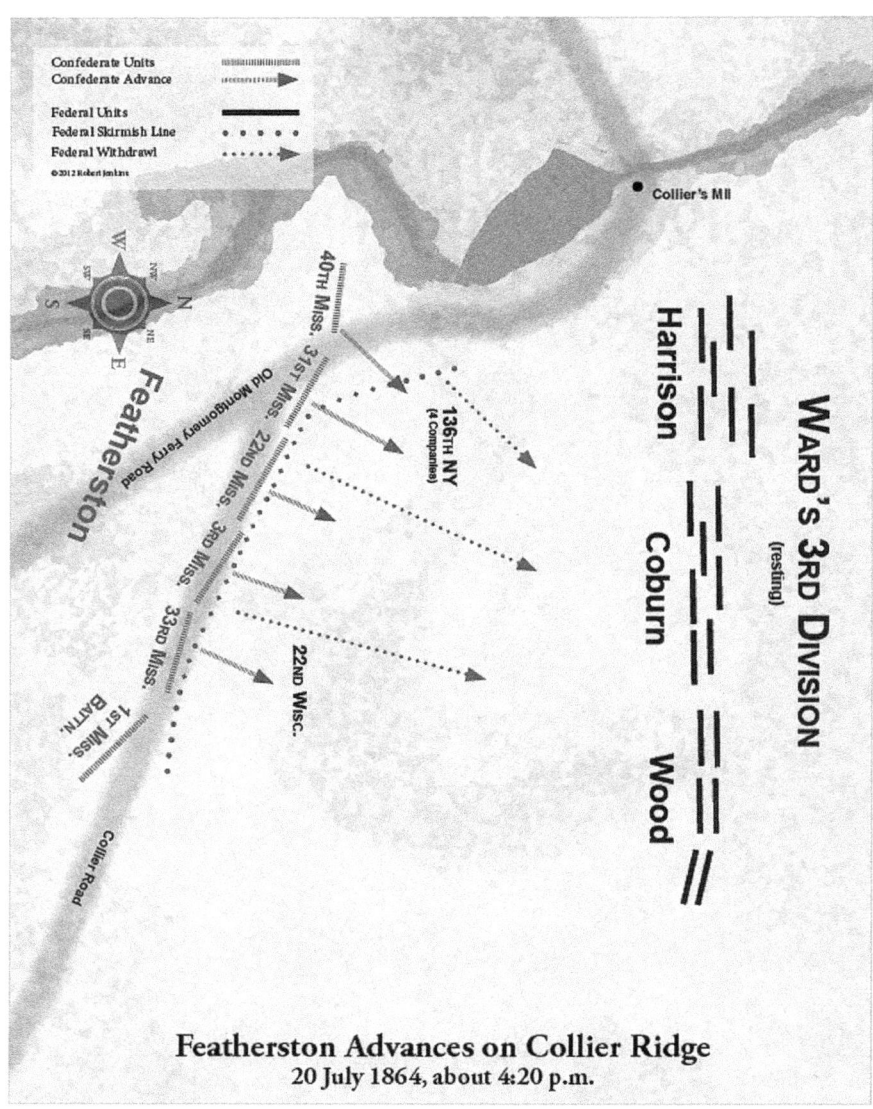

Featherston Advances on Collier Ridge
20 July 1864, about 4:20 p.m.

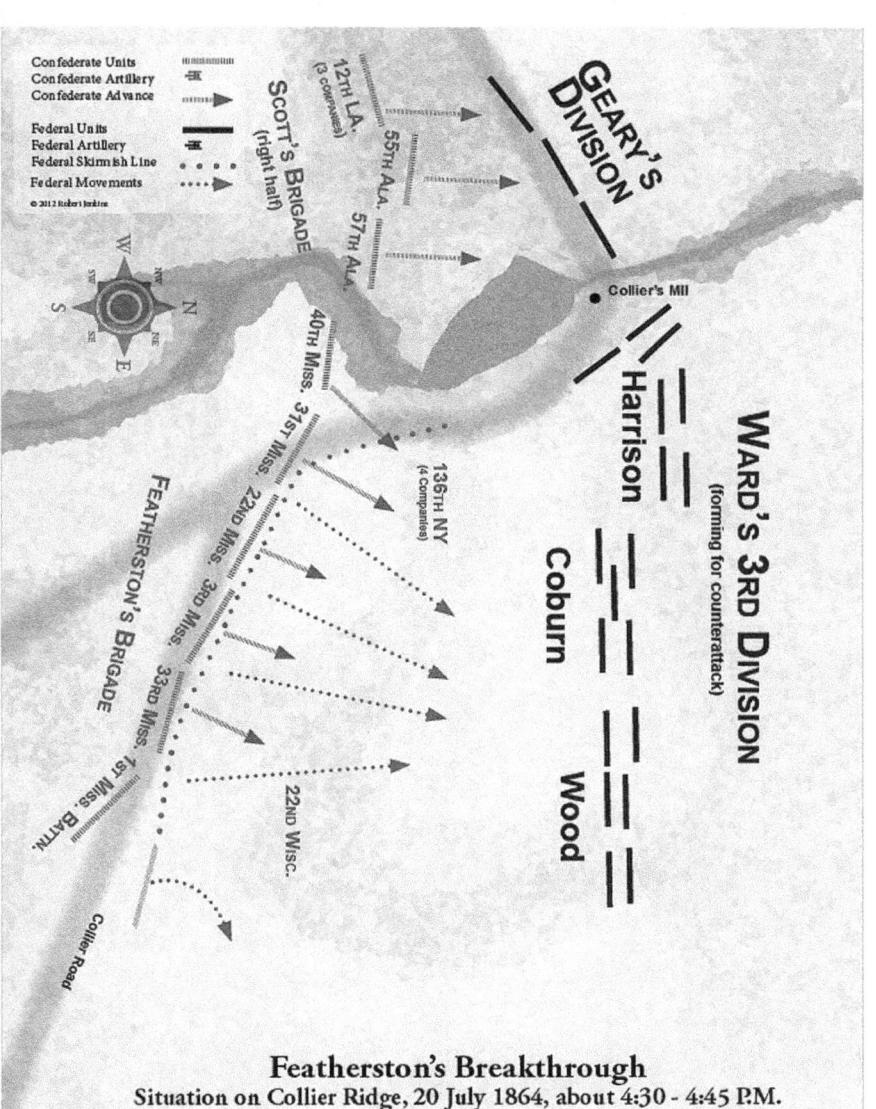

Featherston's Breakthrough
Situation on Collier Ridge, 20 July 1864, about 4:30 - 4:45 P.M.

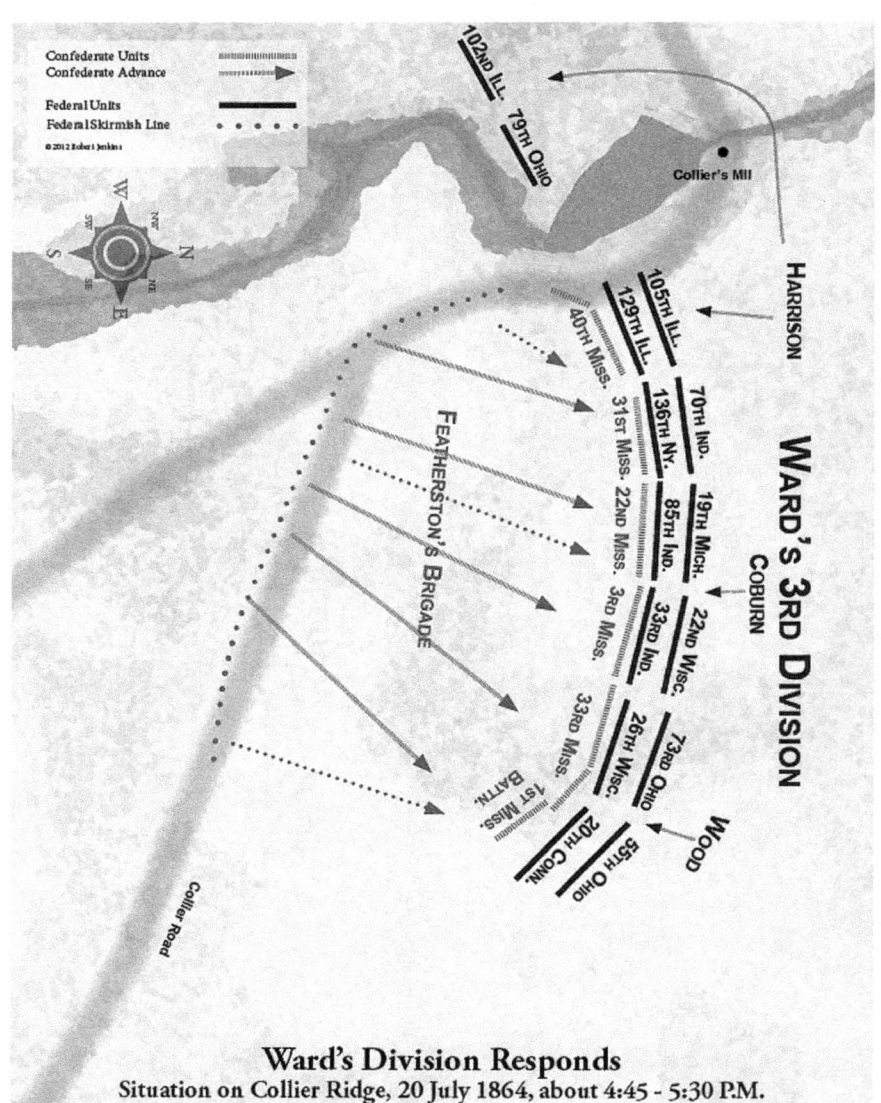

Ward's Division Responds
Situation on Collier Ridge, 20 July 1864, about 4:45 - 5:30 P.M.

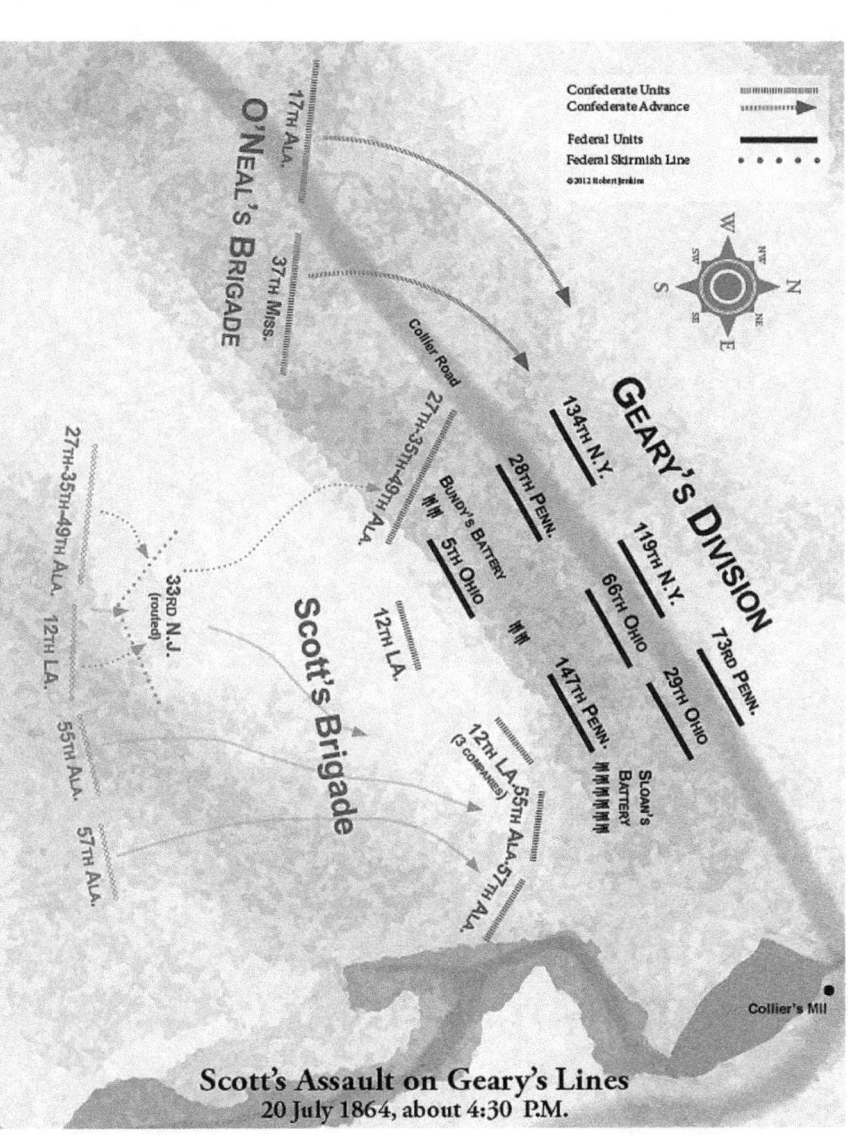

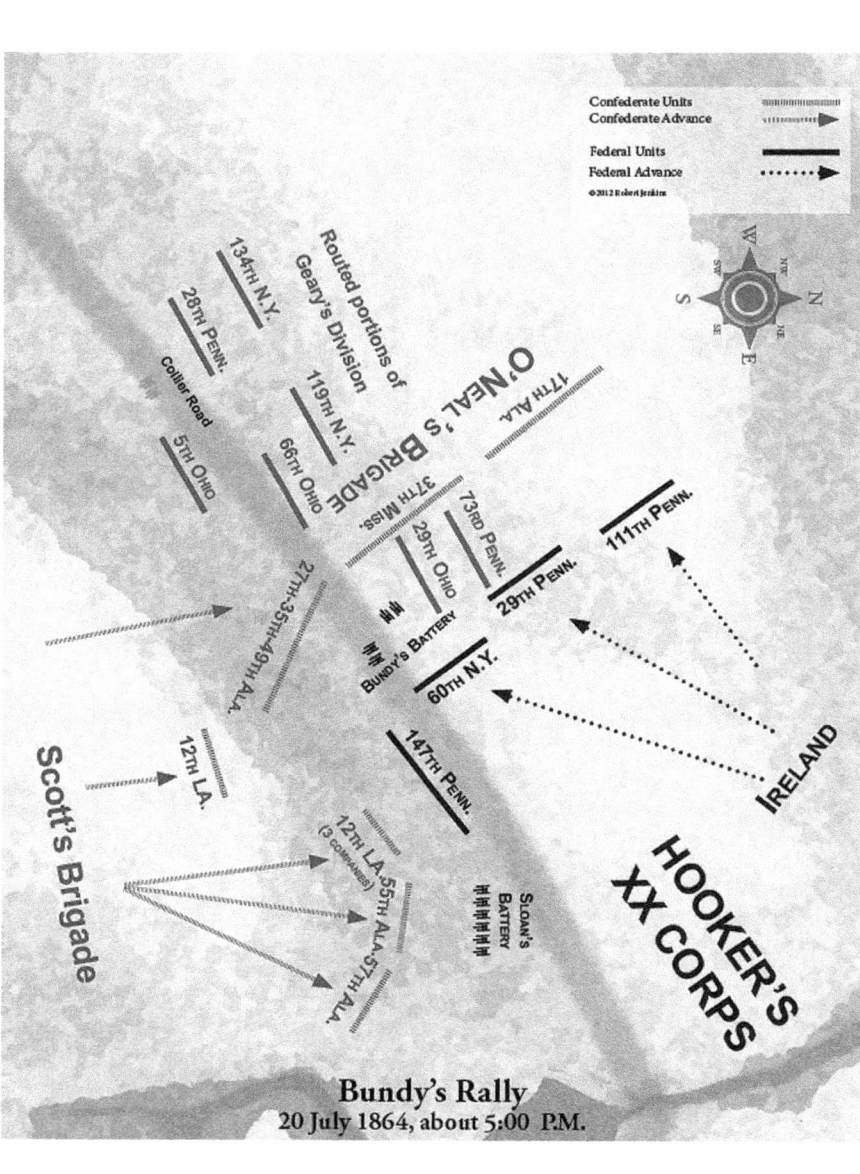

Bundy's Rally
20 July 1864, about 5:00 P.M.

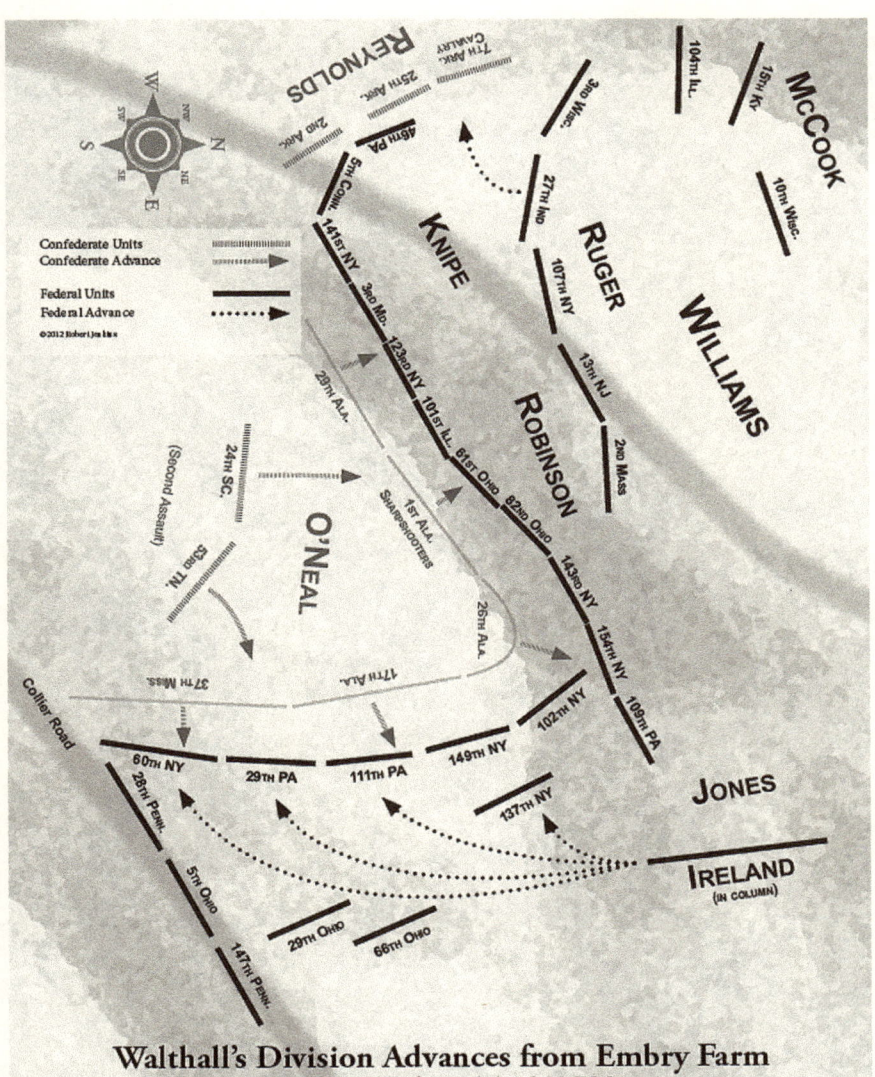

Walthall's Division Advances from Embry Farm
20 July 1864, about 4:45-6:30 P.M.

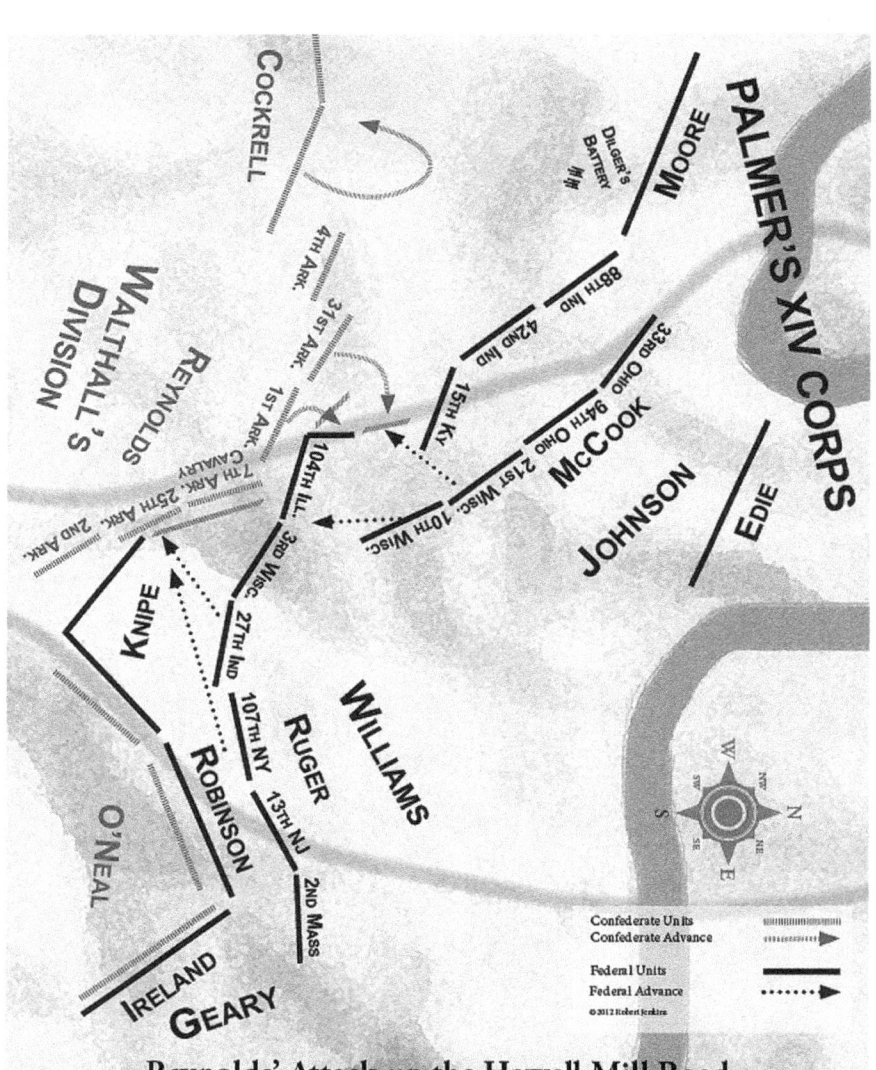

Reynolds' Attack up the Howell Mill Road
20 July 1864, about 5:00 P.M.

1

THE FINAL SUMMER

"I feel assured that the war will end this year."[1]

The morning of Wednesday, 20 July 1864, broke warm, promising another sultry summer day. Most of the men of Company C, from the 31st Mississippi Infantry Regiment of Volunteers of Featherston's brigade, were off on picket duty to the west. Nicknamed the "Chickasaw Guards," they had been out all night since being ordered to guard the fords on the Chattahoochee River the evening before.

After three years of marching and shooting, drilling and digging, freezing and sweating, the hardened survivors of the 31st Mississippi had come to Georgia, some 300 or so of them. They had buried their own at such places as Corinth, Grenada, Vicksburg, Holly Springs, Oxford, Coffeeville, Canton, the Delta, Jackson, Lauderdale Springs, and Meridian, in Mississippi; Baton Rouge, Port Hudson, Camp Moore, and Greenwell Springs, in Louisiana; Demopolis, and Montevallo, in Alabama; and Resaca, New Hope, Lost Mountain, Noon Day Creek, and Kennesaw, in Georgia. It wasn't hard to follow their trail of graves that had now led them to the outskirts of Atlanta, just below a winding creek named Peach Tree where it was downright hot. One Federal soldier simply recorded in his diary entry for 20 July: "hot enough."[2]

The veterans were used to the hot summer days in the Georgia heat but that didn't make it any easier to bear. Many in each army built "arbors of brush" to shelter themselves from the sweltering heat and bright sun.[3] Aside from a few afternoon "popcorn showers" that provided a brief respite to the men from the high humidity and oppressive sun, it had hardly rained in a month since the

---

[1] Solomon M. Thornton to wife Sarah F. Thornton, 7 March 1864, Special Collections, Mitchell Memorial Library, Mississippi State University, Starkville, Mississippi.

[2] George H. Cutter, diary, 90, Special Collections, Hargrett Library, University of Georgia, Athens, Georgia.

[3] Nathaniel Cheairs Hughes, Jr., *The Pride of the Confederate Artillery, The Washington Artillery in the Army of Tennessee* (Baton Rouge: Louisiana State Press, 1997) 194.

steady rains of June. It rained so much during the month of June, however, that Confederate Major General Samuel G. French wrote in his diary that "It rained forty days and it rained forty nights, And the ark it rested on the Kennesaw heights."[4] The June rains had caused real inconveniences for the armies of both sides while they marched toward Atlanta, as trenches turned into muddy streams and roads became quagmires. By July, the roads and trenches of Georgia had turned dusty and dry.[5] One violent lighting storm, however, cleared the Georgia air in its brief appearance. On the evening of 10 July, "a sudden and terrific thunderstorm broke over the camp." According to one Federal soldier from the 85th Illinois in the XIV Corps, "The lightning played most vividly and several trees were struck in the immediate vicinity, two men being killed by a single bolt in a regiment nearby." The soldier explained that "the men were badly used up and glad when it was over."[6]

Over two months had passed since the men of the 31st Mississippi and the other veterans of the Army of Mississippi that became the third corps of the Confederate Army of Tennessee, had jumped off of the trains at Resaca in May, and not a day had gone by without the threat of being hit by a bullet or a shell from the enemy. Nevertheless, the men were ready to settle the score with the Yankees once and for all.[7] There remained a general feeling that they could whip the Federals in a fair fight and that one Southerner was worth two or three of their foe in battle. Furthermore, most of these men from the Army of Mississippi had not been through the Chattanooga campaign defeats and morale setbacks of the officer in-fighting found in the Army of Tennessee. They were not yet resigned to the thought of ultimate defeat that was beginning to be talked about, and many genuinely believed that they could still win the war on the field of battle. This difference between them and the battle-weary veterans of the rest of the Army of Tennessee would soon become evident.

While the men understood the odds were against them and that Sherman's army was two to three times larger than theirs, they still believed that they could make a difference. Additionally, many of the men of the Army of Mississippi

---

[4] S. G. French, *Two Wars* (1901; repr., Huntington WV: Blue Acorn Press, 1999) 202.

[5] Chuck Brown, Weather Conditions during the Atlanta Campaign, May 7–September 3, 1864, Pickett's Mill State Historical Park and Museum, Dalton GA, 125 (copy with author).

[6] Henry J. Aten, *History of the Eighty-Fifth Regiment, Illinois Volunteer Infantry* (Hiawatha KS: Regimental Association, 1901) 196.

[7] Brown, Weather Conditions; United States War Department, comp., *Official Records of the Union and Confederate Armies in the War of the Rebellion*, 128 volumes (Washington, DC: Government Printing Office, 1880–1901) vol. 29, pp. 874–75.

Hood's First Sortie, 20 July 1864

continued to feel the stigma of not having been in some of the biggest battles of the war like their counterparts in the armies of Northern Virginia and Tennessee, and they had something to prove. In a letter to his wife Sarah from their camp near Demopolis, Alabama, on 7 March 1864, Captain Solomon M. Thornton, commander of Company B, 31st Mississippi, wrote: "I feel assured that the war will end this year. I have seen some soldiers from Virginia and some from Dalton, Ga., and they seem in good spirits and they say they are not whip[p]ed. I am of the opinion that this is the only army in the Confederacy that is whip[p]ed and not all of us. It is only that [some were] not true to their cause."[8]

In any event, three months of daily fighting in the red clay ditches of Georgia had not settled the contest with Sherman's legions and the men of the Army of Mississippi were ready to get it over with. Many of them had concluded that it would be better to decide the issue in one grand battle rather than have to continue the daily trench-style warfare replete with its own privations. Lack of shelter and clean clothes had taken its toll. For most, the crossing of and subsequent time spent on picket duty around the Chattahoochee River during the past two weeks was the first time they had taken a bath or washed their clothes since boarding the trains in Rome on 10–12 May.[9] Many officers and men of the Confederate Army lost their appetite. According to Major Thomas J. Burnett of the 17th Alabama, the men were served a daily diet of coarse beef and "coarse cold corn bread & bacon [that] absolutely sickens me to look at, for we have had it so long without variation."[10]

After ninety days of constant fighting, the Confederate soldiers looked more like ragged ditch diggers than soldiers, but there was an air of confidence among them. According to Lieutenant Colonel Walter A. Rorer of the 20th Mississippi Infantry:

> Our marches have nearly all been made in the night and many times in the rain and mud, when the darkness was so intense nothing could be seen. Still, the army would drag its slow length along passing over four or five miles during the night. The morning light would reveal the most haggard and

---

[8] Solomon M. Thornton to wife Sarah, 7 March 1864, Special Collections, Mitchell Memorial Library, Mississippi State University, Starkville, Mississippi.

[9] H. Grady Howell, Jr., *To Live and Die in Dixie, A History of the Third Mississippi Infantry, C.S.A.* (Jackson MS: Chickasaw Bayou Press, 1991) 292.

[10] Thomas J. Burnett to wife, 18 June 1864, Pearce Civil War Collection, Navarro College, Corsicana, Texas; Illene D. and Wilbur E. Thompson, *The Seventeenth Alabama Infantry: A Regimental History and Roster* (Bowie MD: Heritage Books, Inc., 2001) 84.

hungry looking set of wretches you ever saw, dragging themselves along through mud half a leg deep and numbers of them bare footed, the mud being so adhesive as to pull a shoe to pieces, but on they would go being sure "Old Joe" was taking them to the right place.[11]

---

[11] Walter A. Rorer, to "Cousin Susan," 9 June 1864, vertical files, Carter House, Franklin, Tennessee.

2

THE PLAN

> "While we have not the same confidence in [Hood's] generalship that we had in General Johnston, we have resolved that if there is a failure, it shall not be our fault!"[1]

By the morning of Wednesday, 20 July, every newspaper had fled the Gate City, except for the *Atlanta Appeal,* which had decided to brave it out. Fittingly, the editor of the *Atlanta Appeal* wrote what seemed more like a prayer than an editorial in the 20 July edition after news of Hood's replacement of Johnston had become widespread and the approach of Sherman's legions. "God defends the right. His hand is the buckler and shield of the soldier who bravely maintains such a cause as ours." The editor explained that while other papers fled to the safety of Griffin or Macon further south, the *Atlanta Appeal* would remain to "encourage the troops until the enemy reaches the gates." Following President Davis's opinion that replacing Johnston for his timidity for risking battle against the superior foe was now necessary to save Atlanta and preserve the Confederacy, the editor asserted "it is time perhaps that Stonewall Jacksonism had usurped the place of caution and strategy. There is a limit to prudence."[2]

During the week of 11 July, Sherman had begun the process of consolidating his three armies to strike Atlanta. Over the next several days, as the Confederates withdrew to a new line south of Peach Tree Creek, the lines grew eerily silent. By Monday, 18 July, Sherman had his armies on the move as he prepared to cut Atlanta's communication from Richmond and destroy the

---

[1] J. P. Cannon, *A History of the 27th Regiment Alabama Infantry. "Bloody Banners and Barefoot Boys,"* ed. Noel Crowson and John V. Brogden (Shippensburg PA: Burd Street Press, 1997) 84.

[2] Waverly, *Atlanta Appeal,* 20 July 1864; quoted in the *New York Times,* 29 July 1864; Erol Clauss, "The Atlanta Campaign, July 18, 1864" (Ph.D. diss., Emory University, 1965). A number of papers sojourned on in Atlanta during the campaign, including the *Knoxville Register,* the *Chattanooga Daily Rebel,* and the *Memphis Appeal,* as well as papers that called Atlanta home: the *Atlanta Appeal,* the *Intelligencer,* the *Southern Confederacy,* the *Revielle,* the *Commonwealth,* and the *Georgia Journal & Messenger.*

The Battle of Peach Tree Creek

railroad linking the Gate City east to Augusta. As his forces awaited orders to advance between 11 July and 17 July, Sherman continued to ponder on how to best strike a blow at the Rebels and take Atlanta. Meanwhile, his men sat—and waited. During the lull, one Illinois officer in McPherson's army penned in his journal, "In a few hours we will know if it is to be a fight. If the army marches right into Atlanta, I'll think it damned mean, but if there is a fight will not feel so badly, unless we can get a big battle out of [the Rebels]. I want to help in that."[3]

Considering Johnston's constant fall backs over the previous three months, and now facing a strange quietness since crossing the Chattahoochee River, Sherman began to believe that the Confederates were withdrawing again, and that they may even give up Atlanta without a fight. Then, on Tuesday, 19 July, Sherman learned of the transfer of command from Johnston to Hood. Sherman understood that Hood's appointment could only mean more aggressive action from the Confederates. Sherman, upon receiving news of the transfer, remarked: "No officer or soldier who ever served under me will question the generalship of Joseph E. Johnston."[4] He would not write as favorably about his new adversary.

When news of the transfer hit the Federal high command, General Schofield told Sherman that he knew Hood well, and that he knew him to be a fighting man. Schofield had been classmates with Hood at West Point, as had generals McPherson and Howard. They were all intimately familiar with Hood's courage and zest for fighting. They were also aware that he was rash in his judgment. Schofield, the Army of the Ohio's commander, told his chief to be on the lookout as Hood would most certainly attack. General Granville M. Dodge recalled hearing Schofield tell Sherman, upon learning of Hood's appointment: "This means a fight, Hood will attack you within twenty-four hours." Dodge explained that after discussing the matter with Schofield, "Sherman sat down on a stump by the roadside and issued his orders calling McPherson immediately to us and closing us all in toward Thomas."[5]

---

[3] Clauss, "The Atlanta Campaign, July 18, 1864," 68–69; Kellogg, 283; United States War Department, comp., *Official Records of the Union and Confederate Armies in the War of the Rebellion*, 128 volumes (Washington, DC: Government Printing Office, 1880–1901) ser. 1, vol. 38, pt. 5, serial 76, p. 195 (hereafter *OR*).

[4] James Rabb, *W. W. Loring, Florida's Forgotten General* (Manhattan KS: Sunflower University Press, 1996) 162.

[5] Granville M. Dodge, "The Late Gen. J. M. Schofield," *Confederate Veteran*, vol. 14 (October 1907): 461.

Hood's First Sortie, 20 July 1864

General Thomas, who had served with Hood in Texas before the war, agreed that the Southern commander would attack soon. Another Federal officer, a colonel from a Kentucky regiment, told Sherman that he had "Seed Hood bet $2,500 with nairy a pair in his hand." In light of Hood's appointment, Sherman issued a general order to his forces on the evening of 19 July to be prepared to accept an offensive action from the Rebels. General Sherman must have understood that Hood's promotion meant action from the Confederacy. In his orders to General Thomas on the morning of 20 July, Sherman wrote, "In advancing this morning of course we will bring on a heavy battle, and should be as fully prepared as possible." Sherman wrote after the war that "The character of a leader is a large factor in the game of war, and I confess I was pleased."[6]

John Bell Hood was not a man of great intellect. He was stubborn, brave, and bold, even to the point of rashness, in the opinion of most of his peers and subordinates. While commanding a corps under General Johnston during the Georgia Campaign, he and one of his division commanders, Major General Thomas C. Hindman, often butted heads. In one such exchange, Hood came up to his subordinate and said, "Gen. Hindman, when you see the enemy crown that eminence take your division and charge them off." Hindman then replied, "Let me take my division and post them there, and the enemy will not crown that eminence." Scorned by Hindman's insubordinate, but intelligent response, Hood continued, "General Hindman, why is it that I can never give an order but that you have some suggestion to make?" Hindman quipped, "Because you never gave me an order with any sense to it."[7]

Even as the Richmond administration placed its faith in the young commander, there were clearly fears about his ability to handle the daunting task. Secretary of War James A. Seddon wrote to General Hood on the evening of 17 July as soon as the dispatch relieving Johnston was delivered. In it, he admonished Hood to "Be wary no less than bold." The Confederate war secretary explained to his new army commander, "You are charged with a great trust. You will, I know, test to the utmost your capacities to discharge it." He also gave some unsolicited advice on how to confront Sherman" "It may yet be

---

[6] Lloyd Lewis, *Sherman, Fighting Prophet* (Lincoln: University of Nebraska Press, 1993) 383 *OR*, ser. 1, vol. 38, pt. 5, serial 76, p. 193; Stanley F. Horn, *The Army of Tennessee* (Norman: University of Oklahoma Press, 1953) 346.

[7] J. C. Higdon, "Hindman's Reply to Hood," Brace TN, *Confederate Veteran* 8/69; Chuck Carlock, *History of The Tenth Texas Cavalry (Dismounted) Regiment, 1861–1865* (North Richland Hills TX: Bibal Press, 2001) 156.

practicable to cut the communication of the enemy or find or make an opportunity of equal encounter whether he moves east or west."[8]

The recent replacement of beloved General Joseph Johnston with General John Bell Hood had been met with disbelief, shock, and outright anger among the men. General Hood was called by some of his men Old Wooden Head, referring to both his hard-headed nature and his perceived lack of intellect.[9] While no one questioned General Hood's bravery, few could understand how a man like Old Joe with his experience, leadership, ability, and concern for his men could be removed.

Originally General Johnston's idea, the defense of Atlanta was simple enough. As the Federal armies crossed the Chattahoochee River and spread out over the northern and eastern approaches to Atlanta, the Confederates would spring out of the trenches guarding Atlanta and attack a portion of Sherman's army. Johnston hoped to catch the Yankees as they crossed Peach Tree Creek, driving them back over the creek and against the Chattahochee River behind them. To accomplish this, two of the three Confederate corps would come out of the woods and trenches above Atlanta to lie in wait to attack. The gray lines would swing counterclockwise like a gate sweeping everything between them and the river. Then, unable to retreat across the Chattahoochee River, Sherman's men would be crushed in the vise.[10] One private described the river as "very difficult river to cross. It is not a very wide or a very deep stream, but is swift, muddy, with great large limestone rocks scattered all thro. it. The banks are steep descending into deep water very abruptly, and covered with a thick growth of cane."[11]

Prior to his removal on 17 July, General Johnston had wanted to spring the trap sometime in the next two or three days, depending on when the bulk of Sherman's men crossed the Chattahoochee River and when they would be the most spread out. The change in Confederate command followed by Sherman's rapid march beginning the same day would change the timing of the attack

---

[8] *OR*, ser. 1, vol. 38, pt. 5, serial 76, p. 885; John Cannan, *The Atlanta Campaign, May–November, 1864* (Conshohocken PA: Combined Publishing, 1991) 111.

[9] "Valley of the Shadow of Death," Episode 6 of *The Civil War: A Film by Ken Burns*. But Hood was not without intelligence; otherwise, he would have never risen to division and corps command, let alone command of an army.

[10] William R. Scaife, *The Campaign for Atlanta* (Atlanta: self-published, 1993) 83–84; Franklin Garrett, *Atlanta and Its Environs*, 2 vols. (Athens: University of Georgia Press, 1954) 1:610–12.

[11] Henry Campbell, "Three Years in the Saddle" (diary), 6 July 1854, Special Collections, Wabash College, Crawfordsville, Indiana.

drastically. General McPherson with the Army of the Tennessee and its XV, XVI, and XVII corps, Sherman's favorites, had already reached the Augusta Railroad east of Atlanta early on the afternoon of 18 July. While "The Transfer" paralyzed the Confederate Army as John Bell Hood took the reigns of command during the day, McPherson's army was just 2 miles from Stone Mountain and 7 from Decatur by that afternoon, and he was poised to strike at Atlanta, which was only 6 miles west of Decatur. McPherson's way into Atlanta was open, at least for the moment. In addition, General Schofield with the Army of the Ohio and its XXIII Corps was pressing from the northeast faster than expected, and he was already at Cross Keys and moving to the north fork of Peach Tree Creek.[12]

In his first move as the new Confederate army commander, Hood issued an address to his men:

> Soldiers: In obedience to orders from the War Department I assume command of this army and department. I feel the weight of the responsibility so suddenly and unexpectedly devolved upon me by this position, and shall bend all my energies and employ all my skill to meet its requirements. I look with confidence to your patriotism to stand by me, and rely upon your prowess to wrest your country from the grasp of the invader, entitling yourselves to the proud distinction of being called the deliverers of an oppressed people.[13]

Hood's forces were deployed on a line from west to east at the Western & Atlantic Railroad on the Chattahoochee River, then "extending east for about six miles, it crossed the high ground north of the present Crestlawn Cemetery, known as Casey's Hill; Howell Mill Road; the valley of Tanyard Branch, also known as Shoal Creek; Peachtree Road at Spring Street; and the valley of Clear Creek." The outer entrenchments reached the northernmost point of today's Piedmont Park along Piedmont Avenue before turning south "at the present intersection of North Highland Avenue and Zimmer Drive," and "paralleling Highland Avenue and Moreland Avenue until it reached the Georgia Railroad, near the present Moreland Avenue crossing, at the De Kalb-Fulton line. From this point," explained Garrett, "it extended roughly south and southeast to the present East Atlanta business section at Glenwood and Flat Shoal Avenues."[14]

---

[12] Jacob D. Cox, *Atlanta* (1903; repr., Dayton OH: Morningside Press, 1987) 150, 153; Scaife, *The Campaign for Atlanta*, 83, 93.

[13] *OR*, ser. 1, vol. 38, pt. 5, serial 76, p. 889.

[14] Garrett, *Atlanta and Its Environs*, 1:610.

The Battle of Peach Tree Creek

It is difficult to piece together the events that occurred at the Confederate headquarters from the evening of Sunday, 17 July, when Johnston received the news of his removal and the beginning of the Battle of Peach Tree Creek just before 4:00 P.M. on Wednesday, 20 July. Johnston's writings do not provide any details concerning his activities of the afternoon of Monday, 18 July as he and his wife departed Atlanta. Hood's reports of the events given in both his official report, which was written on 15 February 1865, after the Confederate army had been virtually destroyed during the Tennessee campaign and he had resigned in disgrace, and in his writings after the war, which were published after his death in *Advance and Retreat: Personal Experiences in the United States and Confederate States Armies*, contain a series of distorted facts, half-truths and, in some instances, complete misstatements of events as Hood sought to defend his tarnished reputation. But, in fairness, any post-war memoir of a soldier must be examined with caution. Johnston published his own version of events in his *Narrative of Military Operations Directed DURING the Late War between the United States* in 1874, which slants history to his view.

Although Hood was given Johnston's plans for a future offensive, Hood wrote after the war about the plan to attack Sherman at Peach Tree Creek as if he had conceived it.

> Accordingly, on the night of the 18th and morning of the 19th I formed line of battle facing Peach Tree Creek; the left rested near Pace's Ferry road, and the right covered Atlanta. I was informed on the 19th that Thomas was building bridges across Peach Tree Creek; that McPherson and Schofield were well over toward, and even on, the Georgia railroad, near Decatur. I perceived at once that the Federal Commander had committed a serious blunder in separating his corps or armies by such a distance as to allow me to concentrate the main body of our army upon his right wing, whilst his left was so far removed as to be incapable of rendering timely assistance. General Sherman's violation of the established maxim that an army should always be held well within hand, or its detachments within easy supporting distance, afforded one of the most favorable occasions for complete victory which could have been offered; especially as it presented an opportunity, after crushing his right wing, to throw our entire force upon his left. In fact, such a blunder affords a small army the best, if not the sole, chance of success when contending with a vastly superior force.[15]

---

[15] John Bell Hood, *Advance & Retreat* (1880; repr., New York: Da Capo Press, 1993) 167; Ned Bradford, ed., *Battles and Leaders of the Civil War* (New York: The Fairfax Press,

Hood's First Sortie, 20 July 1864

While General Hood subsequently denied that the idea of a surprise attack at Peach Tree came from Johnston, there is support from independent sources to suggest otherwise. Hood explains in his official report that he conceived the plan of battle, "Finding it impossible to hold Atlanta without giving battle, I determined to strike the enemy while attempting to cross this [Peach Tree Creek] stream...My object was to crush Thomas' [The Army of the Cumberland] before he could fortify himself, and then turn upon Schofield and McPherson." However, on Sunday, 17 July, at 10:30 A.M., a circular order from General Hardee's headquarters to his division commanders was delivered as follows: "By direction of General Johnston, the command will be held in readiness to move, if necessary, at a moment's notice."[16]

Plans for an imminent attack were evident in Hardee's circular order because this type of order had always preceded some offensive action. When given such an order from the commanding general, officers refused to grant furloughs or sick leaves for those only slightly sick, so they could have as many men available for duty as possible for an anticipated action. But there were no details on just what Johnston had in mind or if he had in fact matured plans for an attack. Private John Kern of the 45th Mississippi in Lowrey's brigade of Cleburne's division recorded in his diary on 17 July, "Ret'd [returned to camp] & found we had orders to be ready to move." Kern had previously served as sergeant-major and understood the significance of the order. A battle was about to be waged.[17]

Also, on Sunday morning, 17 July, Johnston called Stewart to his headquarters to inform him of his plan for an attack against Sherman as his divided forces attempted to cross Peach Tree Creek. Johnston ordered Stewart to draw his corps south of Peach Tree Creek, find suitable artillery positions to defend from, and cut down trees to create fields of fire. Stewart then rode off with three of his staff officers to deliver the news to his three divisions and begin the work. Late that evening, Stewart returned to Johnston's headquarters to report on his progress and expected to find his commander working out the details of his

---

1979); Hood, considering the plight of Atlanta's citizens during the siege, explained, "It was painful yet strange to mark how expert grew the old men, women, and children in building their underground forts" (514).

[16] Hood, *Advance & Retreat*, 167; *OR*, ser. 1, vol. 38, pt. 5, serial 76, p. 887.

[17] John Kern, diary, 17 July 1864, Old Courthouse Museum, Vicksburg, Mississippi; David Williamson, *The Third Battalion and the 45th Mississippi Regiment* (Jefferson NC: McFarland & Company, Inc., 2004) 214.

The Battle of Peach Tree Creek

planned attack. Instead, he found Old Joe in the act of transferring command and composing his farewell address.[18]

Stewart implored the general to ignore the order until he had made his planned attack, but Johnston refused. Stewart then rode to Hardee's headquarters to try and gain support for a mutiny against President Davis's order, but Hardee was more interested in whether he had been given command. When Old Reliable discovered that his former subordinate, John Bell Hood, had been given the job, he suggested that Stewart take it up with Hood. By this time, it was getting late. Stewart sent a note to Hood asking to meet him early the next morning to discuss the issue and Hood agreed. Meanwhile, Stewart asked Hardee to keep a lid on the news.[19]

The next morning, Stewart and Hood met on the way to Johnston's headquarters about daylight. Hardee joined the two officers at Johnston's headquarters where they discussed Stewart's proposal to suspend the order. While Johnston would not endorse the petition, he allowed his three corps commanders to send a note to the president explaining that they each believed that the order should be suspended until the fate of Atlanta was decided because battle was imminent. The order was sent by General Hood as the commander and was endorsed by Stewart and Hardee. The request must have taken the Confederate president by surprise as there was no immediate reaction from Richmond. In fact, the officers waited all day for a reply as Hood asked Johnston to remain with him. Hood issued all orders to the troops throughout the day under Johnston's name while the officers waited. Davis finally replied at 5:20 P.M., declining to reverse his decision and explaining that he could not undo what had already been done without making the situation worse than it was already. Shortly thereafter, Johnston and his wife departed for Macon.[20]

Other accounts support the conclusion that Old Joe had planned something for Sherman's legions as they crossed Peach Tree Creek, including General Arthur Middleton Manigault's journal of the war in which he recorded that as

---

[18] Sam Davis Elliott, *Soldier of Tennessee, General Alexander P. Stewart and the Civil War in the West* (Baton Rouge: Louisiana State Press, 1999) 200; John Witherspoon DuBose, *General Joseph Wheeler and the Army of Tennessee* (New York: The Neale Publishing Company, 1912) 357–58; Robert M. Hughes, *General Johnston*, Great Commanders series (New York: D. Appleton and Company, 1893) 335.

[19] Elliott, *Soldier of Tennessee*, 200; DuBose, *General Joseph Wheeler and the Army of Tennessee*, 358; Albert Castel, *Decision in the West: The Atlanta Campaign of 1864* (Lawrence: University Press of Kansas, 1992) 362–63.

[20] *OR*, ser. 1, vol. 38, pt. 5, serial 76, p. 888; Elliott, *Soldier of Tennessee*, 200; Castel, *Decision in the West*, 363.

he rode into Atlanta from camps on Sunday morning, 17 July, to hear Bishop Ley of Arkansas preach, he "noticed an unusual stir amongst the train of wagons, and the movement of considerable bodies of troops.... Returning to camp later in the day" the general "found that orders had been received a short time before to hold ourselves in readiness to march at any moment." Moreover, all of the transportation and equipment wagons, except for those carrying ammunition and the ambulances had been sent away and the "surgeons looked mysterious, and had received orders to prepare for the reception in Atlanta of a large number of wounded." Manigault also witnessed that large masses of troops that had been in camps west and northwest of Atlanta, were on the move to the east and north of the city. Then, "About 5 P.M., the bugles sounded for the men to fall in, and in less than fifteen minutes after, the division had taken the route step, moving in a north-easterly direction." He overheard a number of his men "speaking freely among themselves, remarking that Old Johnston was waking up again" and that a battle was imminent.[21]

Colonel Irwin Walker, of the 10th South Carolina from Manigault's brigade, wrote enthusiastically, "Johnston's dispositions made us all feel the general engagement of the campaign was now to be fought, and everything was to be risked to save Atlanta. The crossing at Peach Tree Creek was to be disputed and made the great battle ground." Explained the South Carolina colonel, "our retreating was done and we had the enemy where we wanted him."[22]

Eight days after the Battle of Peach Tree Creek, General William Wing Loring, commanding a division in Stewart's corps, spoke bitterly at a Confederate hospital in Atlanta while he recovered from a wound he received at the Battle of Ezra Church on 28 July. At the hospital, Chaplain J. R. McNeilly witnessed the conversation between Loring and a number of other Southern officers from Stewart's Army of Mississippi in which it was apparently understood that Johnston had intended a strike at the divided Federal forces astride Peach Tree Creek on 19 July, the day before Hood's attack.[23]

---

[21] Lockwood Tower, ed., *A Carolinian Goes to War: The Civil War Narrative of Arthur Middleton Manigault, Brigadier General* (Columbia: University of South Carolina Press, 1964) 198–99.

[22] C. Irvine Walker, *Rolls and Historical Sketch of the Tenth Regiment So. Ca. Volunteers in the Army of the Confederate States*. Charleston SC: Walker, Evans, & Cogswell, 1881) 112; Scaife, *The Campaign for Atlanta*, 83–84.

[23] James H. McNeilly, "A Day in the Life of a Confederate Chaplain," *Confederate Veteran*, vol. 26 (1918): 471.

The Battle of Peach Tree Creek

In his report of 20 October 1864, Johnston explained that when he was relieved from command, he relayed his plans to Hood as follows, "First, to attack the Federal Army while crossing Peach Tree Creek. If we were successful great results might be hoped for, as the enemy would have both the creek and the river to intercept his retreat." Old Joe continued, "Second, if unsuccessful, to keep back the enemy by intrenching, to give time for the assembling of the State troops [the Georgia Militia] promised by Governor Brown; to garrison Atlanta with those troops," he explained, "and when the Federal approached the town attack it on its most exposed flank with all the Confederate troops." Hood adopted Johnston's first plan for the Battle of Peach Tree Creek. Also, Hood's plan for his second attack at Decatur on 22 July that became known as the Battle of Atlanta might have been taken from Johnston's second idea.[24]

Shortly after war ended, Sherman and a group of officers were on their way down the Mississippi River to New Orleans when he learned that his old rival and friend General Joseph Johnston was about to take a boat from Memphis to St. Louis. Sherman and his staff quickly changed plans and secured a place on the St. Louis-bound vessel. After supper, Sherman asked Johnston if he objected to visiting with him about their war experiences and when the old Southern leader accepted, the two sat down and discussed the campaign from Dalton to Atlanta. "So Sherman spread his maps on the cabin table and, surrounded by a throng of listeners, they began. Sherman would ask about his line at a certain place, and Johnston would explain how his move was made. Sherman would point to his map and say," according to one Southern veteran from Arkansas who witnessed the encounter, "'How in the world did you get away from me here?' They talked all night. Johnston needed no map. He had been in the very thick of battle for 74 days; the map of campaign was burned into his brain, and he knew every foot of the ground. His retreat was a wonder to Sherman and to the world," exclaimed the Arkansas veteran. "Yet this great military genius was thrown out on the eve of his final and greatest assault upon Sherman." Clearly, it was widely understood by the soldiers of the Army of Tennessee that Johnston was close to launching some kind of offensive against Sherman as the Yankees neared Peach Tree Creek.[25]

---

[24] *OR*, ser. 1, vol. 38, pt. 3, serial 74, p. 618.
[25] William E. Bevens, *Reminiscences of a Private: William E. Bevens of the First Arkansas Infantry, C.S.A.,* ed. Daniel E. Sutherland (Fayetteville: University of Arkansas Press, 1992) 185–87.

Another source reveals that General Johnston had given an address to the entire army on 17 July similar to the one he had published before the planned assault at Cassville. According to Colonel Ellison Capers, who commanded the 24th South Carolina Infantry, Johnston "announced that he would attack General Sherman's army as soon as it should cross the Chattahoochee."[26] This address to the army was characteristic of Johnston and he had given similar ones prior to plans for offensive movements during the Peninsular Campaign in Virginia in 1862, the Vicksburg Campaign in 1863, and at Cassville in May 1864. The offensive in Virginia would be the only one that Johnston actually carried out, while at Vicksburg, his plan came too late to relieve the beleaguered city. Ironically at Peach Tree Creek, as had occurred at Cassville, Johnston would again not have an opportunity to carry out his planned attack, and Hood would be the reason.[27]

Oliver Otis Howard, commanding the Federal IV Corps, wrote after the war that "Johnston had planned to attack Sherman at Peach Tree Creek, expecting just such a division between our wings as we made." Federal division commander Jacob Cox of Schofield's Army of the Ohio, also credited Johnston with planning the Confederate attack, but recognized that Hood had to adopt it and mature the plan for battle.[28]

Another source reveals that Johnston had conceived of the plan to strike Sherman from the Peach Tree Creek defensive line as early as three weeks earlier when Confederate forces were still in and around Marietta. Senator Louis T. Wigfall, admittedly a Johnston supporter, reported that after he informed Johnston that the Richmond government was growing weary of his fallbacks and demanded offensive measures from him, Old Joe continued to explain that Sherman had double his number of troops, and that his "plan of operation must therefore, depend upon that of the enemy." This response is the same that Johnston had been giving President Davis for months. When Joe's close and

---

[26] Scaife, *The Campaign for Atlanta*, 84.

[27] See John Witherspoon DuBose, *General Joseph Wheeler and the Army of Tennessee*, 358–60, 370; Hughes, *General Johnston*, 335; and Craig L. Symonds, *Joseph E. Johnston, a Civil War Biography* (New York: W. W. Norton & Company, 1992) 328–30; and Johnston's own *Narrative of Military Operations during the Late War Between the States* (New York: D. Appleton & Company, 1874) 350–51, 358. A number of other officers and soldiers also wrote after the war that an offensive at Peach Tree Creek had been planned by Johnston. Moreover, biographers for each of the principal participants have all concluded that Johnston indeed intended such a move.

[28] O. O. Howard, "'The Very Woods Seemed to Moan and Groan'": The Struggle for Atlanta," in Bradford, ed., *Battles and Leaders of the Civil War*, 504; Cox, *Atlanta*, 144–49.

The Battle of Peach Tree Creek

trusted friend, Senator Wigfall, pressed him at Marietta in early July after Johnston had fallen back from Kennesaw Mountain, Old Joe finally opened up to say that "he intended to look for opportunities to sally forth from prepared field fortifications to defeat Federal detachments one by one." Wigfall explained that Johnston added "that if the Federal army were still largely intact by the time he had withdrawn close to Atlanta, he would attack and cripple Sherman's army as it was divided while crossing Peachtree Creek."[29]

In his post-war memoirs, Hood acknowledged Johnston's idea to strike an offensive blow, referring to Johnston's plan "to attack the enemy as they crossed Peach Tree Creek," but he added that "Johnston evidently had little faith in this plan, since he was unwilling to await thirty-six hours to test its feasibility." Hood also denied that Johnston gave any further details or contingency plans should the Peach Tree Creek attack fail. This claim is probably at least partially true as there is no record that Johnston had matured any plans beyond Peach Tree Creek except to try to turn either flank of Sherman's army, a very basic strategy of war. In any event, it is clear from the 17 July address that Johnston planned some kind of an attack once Sherman's men crossed the Chattahoochee River, and it is equally apparent that he kept the details of his plans to himself.[30]

Evidence exists, however, that at least some of the details of Johnston's plan were known to some of his junior officers. Confederate cavalry veteran John Witherspoon Du Bose wrote that Joe Johnston was preparing for his surprise attack against an exposed portion of the Federal armies along Peach Tree Creek when he sent for Lieutenant General A. P. Stewart. According to Du Bose, Johnston told Stewart to "Go find the best position on our side of Peachtree Creek for our army to occupy. Do not entrench. Find all the good artillery positions and have them cleared of timber."[31] Du Bose witnessed the scene as Stewart left:

> Immediately mounting his high-bred bay mare and calling three staff officers to accompany him, the general rode away at full speed up the river. In an hour he rode back alone, at full speed. The staff had been left to superintend

---

[29] Robert, R. Long, "A Brief History of the Battle of Peachtree Creek, July 20, 1864," in author's personal papers, Dalton, Georgia, 8; United States Department of the Interior, Atlanta Campaign .

[30] Hood, *Advance & Retreat*, 144.

[31] DuBose, *General Joseph Wheeler and the Army of Tennessee*, 357–58.

the disposition of the troops, as ordered by him. The longed for event approached; the great battle was to be precipitated.

Knowing General Sherman as he did, and his manner of handling his army, General Johnston expected him to scatter it in motion. He was sure Sherman would cross Peachtree Creek with a fragment, while the other parts moved to more or less remote points. The plan was to attack these fragments at their different points of crossing and capture or drive them into the fork of the creek and the river. That done, the army would be thrown in full strength upon the other parts. Hardee and Hood received orders to be in readiness to move forward at a moment's notice.[32]

Evidently, some of Hardee's command knew of Johnston's plan for attack at Peach Tree Creek as well. After the war, Captain I. A. Buck, adjutant general for General Cleburne and his division, recorded that "Johnston proposed to push a corps" into the gap created between Thomas and Schofield while Sherman's divided forces crossed Peach Tree Creek. Buck also confirmed that at Peach Tree Creek, "Hood attempted to carry out the plan decided upon by Genl. Johnston."[33] Thus, Johnston planned to exploit the gap with one of his corps, presumably Hardee's corps, his largest and most veteran corps, while holding his left with Stewart's force and his right with Hood's corps. Hood's plan would adopt the same concept of throwing Hardee's corps into the breech and sweep to the left everything in his path, but Hood would add Stewart's corps to the attack, providing additional punch for the offensive. Whether the Johnston plan intended to include Stewart in the initial assault is unclear from Buck's account, but from the surviving accounts from Stewart's Army of Mississippi, including the conversation between General Loring and a number of officers in this part of the Confederate force, it was clear that they were expecting to be a part of the attack.

By the evening of 18 July, leading elements of the Federal forces under General McPherson were nearing Decatur and were busy tearing up the railroad between Decatur, Stone Mountain, and beyond. General Hood and the Confederate high command were apparently never aware that McPherson's Army of the Tennessee had arrived that quickly. According to General Hood's orders and his after-action reports, he thought that McPherson's force arrived in the vicinity of Stone Mountain and Decatur on Tuesday, 19 July, and that the destruction to the Augusta railroad occurred then. According to Hood, he only

---

[32] Ibid., 358.
[33] I. A. Buck, "Cleburne's Division at Atlanta," 1–2, subject file PW-5, vertical files, Kennesaw National Battlefield Park, Kennesaw, Georgia.

learned after the war in reading Sherman's memoirs that McPherson's Army was so close to Atlanta on Monday 18 July.[34] With Decatur only some 6 miles east of the Gate City, McPherson had an opportunity to race into the city through the back door as the Decatur Road was unguarded at the time. But as he had done at Resaca at the beginning of the Campaign, McPherson failed to capitalize on his opportunity and instead waited until he had torn up the Augusta railroad and had support from other portions of Sherman's armies before advancing. Unlike Resaca, McPherson was ordered to get to the Augusta railroad and cut and destroy the track and telegraph lines as far to the east toward Augusta as possible so as to stop any communication or use of the railroad from the east. Sherman did not plan for McPherson to take Atlanta alone, merely to destroy the Augusta railroad from further use by the Confederates during the campaign for Atlanta. In this effort, McPherson totally succeeded.[35]

After the war General Hood accused Johnston of knowing that McPherson's forces were close to Atlanta, but did not tell Hood about it: "[I]f I was regarded as chief in command [on that day, his first as commander], this important movement was not made known to me at headquarters by our cavalry, which was, generally, very prompt in reporting all such information." Hood continued, "I cannot but think, therefore, that General Johnston was cognizant before 4 o'clock that day, and before his departure for Macon, of the enemy's presence on the Augusta railroad, within six or eight miles of Atlanta." Where Hood came up with the idea that Johnston, who had been deposed from command the night before, would somehow learn between 2:00 P.M. and 4:00 P.M. that Sherman's forces were tearing up the Augusta railroad 8 or 10 miles east of Atlanta, appears to be based purely upon his imagination as there is not a scintilla of evidence to support his supposition. Hood's next remark on the subject comes nearer to the truth than any other reasonable conclusion. "If such is not the case, our cavalry, stationed upon the right, neglected most unpardonably its duty—which supposition I am not inclined to admit." This supposition that Joe Wheeler's cavalry failed to keep in close contact with McPherson's lead forces on the flank and did not learn that the railroad was under destruction for twenty-four hours, is probably correct. During this time, Wheeler's cavalry had been dispersed along the southern banks of the Chattahoochee River across a 40-mile front from McAfee's Bridge north of

---

[34]. Hood, *Advance & Retreat*, 163.
[35] Ibid., 164–67.

Atlanta to Sandtown Road and Campbellton west of the city. Unsure of Sherman's intentions, Wheeler was posted near the center of his force at Buckhead. Perhaps Wheeler should have anticipated Sherman's buildup below Roswell and Ishom's Ford as a threat on the Augusta railroad and shifted his cavalrymen northeastward to parry it. But until Hood ordered him east to cover Decatur and the Augusta railroad on the afternoon of 19 July, Wheeler was still north of Atlanta on Buckhead Road. That Hood was not prepared to admit Wheeler's failure is not surprising as Hood was fond of Wheeler.[36]

While the Confederate high command may have been ignorant of McPherson's activity east of Atlanta on Monday, 18 July, the civilian population was apparently made acutely aware of it. When the Augusta train returned to Atlanta, being unable to get past Stone Mountain, the Gate City was abuzz with news from the depot. In the *Georgia Journal & Messenger* of 20 July, a passenger who had just arrived from the Atlanta train reported, "on Monday, the Georgia Railroad was cut somewhere between Atlanta and Stone Mountain—that a train went out nine miles and returned—that a body of three thousand cavalry was sent to meet the raiders, but no report from them." The article added, "the main body of the enemy were across the river and our army in line of battle four miles from Atlanta extending from the Chattahoochee to the Georgia Railroad."[37] In fact, by 18 July, the entire body of Sherman's army was east of the Chattahoochee in the act of executing a grand right wheel with Thomas's army of the Cumberland positioned at the hub, the apex of Peach Tree Creek and the Chattahoochee River; McPherson's Army of the Tennessee marched at the end of the wheel, 8 to 10 miles east, and Schofield's Army of the Ohio kept time in the center.

An examination of the orders given by Hood during the interval between Johnston's removal and the Battle of Peach Tree Creek reveals the best explanation of the circumstances surrounding Hood's actions. In his first dispatch to the secretary of war, the new commander revealed his understanding of the location of his troops as well as the whereabouts of Sherman's legions: "The enemy advanced to-day on all the roads leading from Isham's Ford and Roswell, and established his line on Peach Tree Creek, his right resting on the Chattahoochee in the vicinity of the railroad, his left at Buck Head; our army about four miles from Atlanta, the creek intervening between the armies."[38] By

---

[36] Ibid., 164–65.
[37] Joseph Clisby, "News from the Front," *Georgia Journal & Messenger* [Macon GA], 20 July 1864.
[38] Hood to "Hon. Secretary of War," 18 July 1864, in *OR*, ser. 1, vol. 38, pt. 5, serial

noon on his first day, Hood continued to carry out Johnston's plan to have Wheeler's cavalry fall back across Peach Tree Creek and then burn all the bridges while having his infantry close at hand preparatory to an offensive operation the next day.[39]

Monday, 18 July, was an awkward day for the Confederate army. Hood essentially found himself in command of an army that respected his gallantry and service to the Southern cause for independence, but overwhelmingly did not want him as their commander. The next ranking officer, General Hardee, threatened to resign, while the lone remaining corps commander, General Stewart, lead the effort to get President Davis to reverse the decision to remove Johnston. While Hood, Hardee, and Stewart awaited a reply from the president, Johnston packed. He had already prepared his farewell address to the soldiers. During the day, as the Confederate high command lay in a state of paralysis, Hood tried to assess the situation. According to Dr. J. W. Worsham of the 19th Tennessee Regiment, "Early on the morning of the 18th, General Hood rode to General Johnston's headquarters and remained with him all day for the purpose of getting his plans for the battle, then hourly expected."[40]

By 9:30 that night, as the reality of his new responsibility set in and hours after Johnston had left the scene, John Bell Hood considered his options. At this point, he still did not know where Sherman's lines were located. Moreover, the young commander did not even know where his own lines reached. He later admitted that nightfall on Monday, 18 July, when he really took command of the army after Johnston's departure, he found himself in the embarrassing position of not even knowing where the troops of the other two infantry corps, Hardee's and Stewart's, were located. In a sound move, he then ordered Wheeler to move to the right of his infantry line and find where the Confederate right reached, and also ascertain Sherman's position.[41] In light of his circumstances, much credit is due to the new commander in both his quick appreciation of the circumstances, and in his rapid preparation for considering offensive operations, either by taking Johnston's plan, or proceeding otherwise.

76, p. 889.

[39] W. W. Mackal to Wheeler, 18 July 1864, in *OR*, ser. 1, vol. 38, pt. 5, serial 76, pp. 889–90.

[40] J. W. Worsham, reminiscences of the battle around Atlanta, in *Confederate Reminiscences and Letters, 1861–1865*, vol. 3 (Atlanta: United Daughters of the Confederacy, 1996) 75–80.

[41] *OR*, ser. 1, vol. 38, pt. 5, serial 76, p. 890.

Hood's First Sortie, 20 July 1864

Clearly, on Monday, 18 July, Hood assumed that Sherman's entire force lay between Buckhead and the Chattahoochee River, an assumption apparently shared by Johnston given he had dispatched the bulk of the Confederate cavalry along the Nancy Creek and Peach Tree Creek lines north of Atlanta. In fact, Sherman's forces were at that moment spread out along a wide arc northeast of Atlanta from the Chattahoochee River to the Augusta railroad 7 miles east of Decatur and 4 miles east of Stone Mountain.[42] The distance between the flanks of Sherman's armies was over 18 miles. By Tuesday evening, 19 July, Sherman's forces had begun to constrict their lines as they drew closer to Atlanta, and by Wednesday, 20 July, McPherson's troops were at Decatur and the right wing of Thomas's Army of the Cumberland rested at Howell's Mill on Peach Tree Creek, but Sherman's flanks were still 9 miles apart, with gaps between each army of up to 2 miles.

Terrain south of Peach Tree Creek would play a key role in the ensuing battle. "South of the creek, the ground is very broken and irregular, being cut up into knolls and gullies by numerous little streams, dry in summer, running into the creek," remembered one Northern veteran.[43] This land provided a shield for Hood's attackers and made it possible for fighting to be isolated into regimental and brigade level, where the shock of his surprise attack could tilt the contest in his army's favor against a numerically superior foe. His strategy was bold. The new Confederate leader had been put in command to stir things up and be aggressive. The plan displayed sound reasoning, and provided some hope for victory, but whether Hood could take the necessary measures to ensure its success remained to be seen.

While the young Confederate commander spent the day learning of the relative locations of the forces for both sides, his cavalry leader would fail to reveal the eastward progression of Sherman's legions until late morning on Tuesday, 19 July. Wheeler had spent 17 and 18 July opposing the advance of Thomas's Army of the Cumberland, and he would spend 19 and 20 July resisting the push for the Gate City by McPherson from the east.[44] Hood had assumed that only Yankee cavalry had roamed as far to the east as the Augusta railroad or Stone Mountain and that McPherson and Schofield were behind

---

[42] Ibid., 168.

[43] Henry Stone, "From the Oostanaula to the Chattahoochee," in *The Mississippi Valley, Tennessee, Georgia, Alabama, 1861–1864*, ed. Military Historical Society of Massachusetts, 439–40, vol. 8 of *Papers of the Military Historical Society of Massachusetts* (Wilmington NC: Broadfoot Press, 1990).

[44] *OR*, ser. 1, vol. 38, pt. 3, serial 74, p. 951.

them. Believing that Thomas's foot soldiers were isolated, Hood determined to strike while they crossed Peach Tree Creek during the day on Tuesday, 19 July.[45] He assumed that Thomas's men would be in the act of crossing the creek having just arrived by midday on Tuesday, so the attack was planned for 1:00 P.M. This was apparently the original date for the planned attack by Johnston as communicated to him by Old Joe on Monday during their exchange. But, other than the general concept of attack, it is unclear just how far Johnston had matured the plan or how much of its detail he had relayed to Hood. The new Confederate commander had to consider implementing Johnston's plan of a surprise attack along Peach Tree Creek and adjust it to fit the changing circumstances he faced, or reach a different plan of offense. So, while the concept originated from Johnston, the battle and its details should be considered Hood's plan for he had to adopt and revise it to fit the situation he faced. By the evening of 18 July, Hood was learning of the troop strength under his command, the disposition of his force, and the wherabouts of Sherman. Hood was following President Davis's orders to take to the offense and try and wrest the initiative from his foe.

A captured document entitled "Estimated Strength of Hood's Army" captured by one of Thomas's men from a Confederate cavalry camp around dusk at Pace's Ferry on Monday, 18 July, the day that Hood took over, it was reported that Hood had available about 44,400 infantry in his three corps. The figures from that document were quickly turned over to Generals Thomas and Sherman so that the Federal high command knew as much about the effective infantry strength as General Hood did within the first day or two of his command.

18 July 1864, in Estimated Strength of Hood's Army
Hardee's Corps
First Division, Cheatham's
Maney's brigade	1,200
Strahl's brigade	1,000
Wright's brigade	1,400
Vaughan's brigade	<u>1,200</u>
	4,800

Second Division, Cleburne's
Polk's brigade	1,000

---

[45] Henry Stone, "1st Wisconsin Volunteer Inf.," in Sydney C. Kerksis, comp., *The Atlanta Papers* (Dayton OH: Morningside Bookshop, 1980) 110.

Hood's First Sortie, 20 July 1864

Govan's brigade	1,200
Lowrey's brigade	1,500
Granbury's brigade	<u>1,200</u>
	4,900
Third Division, Walker's	
Mercer's brigade	2,000
Stevens' Brigade	1,500
Jackson's brigade	1,000[46]
Gist's brigade	<u>1,200</u>
	5,700
Fourth Division, Bate's	
Lewis' Brigade	700
Finley's brigade	1,000
Tyler's brigade	<u>1,300</u>
	3,000
Total for Hardee's corps	18,400
Hood's corps	
First Division, Hindman's	
Deas' Brigade	1,200
Manigault's brigade	1,200
Tucker's brigade	1,000
Walthall's brigade	<u>1,200</u>
	4,600
Second Division, Stevenson's	
Cummings's brigade	1,500
Brown's brigade	800
Baker's brigade	1,000
Reynolds's brigade	<u>1,200</u>
	4,500
Third Division, Stewart's	
Gibson's brigade	800
Stovall's brigade	1,200
Clayton's brigade	1,500
Moore's brigade	<u>1,000</u>

---

[46] Jackson's Brigade was broken up and the majority of its regiments were temporarily attached to Gist's brigade OR, ser. 1, vol. 38, pt 3, serial 74, 655.

	4,500
Total for Hood's corps	13,600
Stewart's corps	
First Division, Loring's	
Featherston's brigade	1,500
Adams's brigade	1,500
Scott's brigade	1,200
	4,200
Second Division, French's	
Cockrell's brigade	2,000
McNair's brigade	1,000
Sears's brigade	1,200
	4,200
Third Division, Walthall's	
Cantey's brigade	2,000
Reynolds's Arkansas Brigade (incorrectly listed as Ector's brigade)	1,000
Quarles's brigade	1,000
	4,000
Total for Stewart's corps	12,400
Total	44,400[47]

Even though Sherman's force outnumbered the Confederate army by two to one, Hood calculated that he could send two of his three corps to attack a portion of Sherman's force and destroy it before the remainder of the Federal armies could respond. This was Johnston's basic plan of action and, quickly grasping the strategic command situation, Hood was preparing to proceed with it sending a confidential order to his cavalry commander, Major General Joseph Wheeler, on Tuesday morning: "unless circumstances now not seen should prevent, Generals Hardee and Stewart have been ordered to attack the enemy at 1 P.M. to-day. General Cheatham, on the right, is ordered to hold in check any force of the enemy that may advance in that direction, and you are desired to give all the aid in your power to General Cheatham to carry out this part."[48]

---

[47] *OR*, ser. 1, vol. 38, pt. 5, serial 76, pp. 178–79.
[48] Ibid., 892–93.

Hood's First Sortie, 20 July 1864

Hood's decision to send Wheeler east to help Cheatham hold off any Federal counter-thrust while he attacked with Hardee and Stewart had far-reaching consequences. First, almost immediately upon arriving east of Atlanta, Wheeler's horsemen discovered just how far east McPherson's Federal forces had advanced. Second, Wheeler dispatched this news to Hood by mid-day and before his intended attack at 1:00 P.M. on Tuesday, 19 July. Third, upon receiving Wheeler's news, Hood determined not to attack while he considered his options and awaited more news from Wheeler. Moreover, Hood had also dispatched an order to his corps commanders, Hardee and Stewart, to watch the Peach Tree Creek crossings closely and to report with detail the location and troop strength of all Federal crossings. By 1:00 P.M., no Northern troops had reached the south side of Peach Tree Creek, so Hood had to wait to spring his trap. Fourth, while he would not realize it at the time, Hood's decision to send Wheeler east on the morning of 19 July would prove to be a key move in protecting the Gate City's exposed eastern flank and keep McPherson's legions from entering Atlanta without a fight and trapping Hood's army north of the city.

Alarmed by Wheeler's dispatch that McPherson was east of the Gate City, and realizing that Thomas's slow-moving Army of the Cumberland had not yet crossed over Peach Tree Creek by the forenoon of Tuesday, 19 July, Hood could not proceed with the planned attack. Additionally, he needed to find out just what kind and strength of Yankee force was operating east of town. Hood quickly fired off another dispatch to Wheeler: "General Hood directs me to acknowledge the receipt of your note in which you express the opinion that the extreme left of the enemy's infantry is moving toward Decatur. It is important to get exact information of the state of affairs in that vicinity at night-fall. He therefore requests you to send your best scouts close in, so as to ascertain whether the left of the enemy's infantry crosses Peach Tree Creek, where it rests, and what is its strength, and notify him of the result."[49]

Probably, Hood assumed the force was enemy cavalry on a raid to destroy his rail lines east to Augusta, but he needed confirmation. Clearly from his dispatch to Wheeler, Hood believed that all of Sherman's infantry was north of Peach Tree Creek, or were just beginning to cross it. He had no idea that McPherson's infantry was already many miles south and east of the creek. During the afternoon of 19 July, after receiving a dispatch from Wheeler that the Yankees were pressing Ferguson's brigade of cavalry below Nancy's Creek

---

[49] Ibid., 893.

The Battle of Peach Tree Creek

as Ferguson's troopers fell back toward Moore's Mill, Hood maintained the belief that Sherman's entire infantry force lay north of him, just above Peach Tree Creek.[50] At 3:30 P.M., Hood had his adjutant send his third dispatch in four hours to his cavalry commander: "Your dispatch about the force pressing Ferguson is received. General Hood directs that you will hold the enemy in check as much as possible, and strike him as you think best."[51]

While Hood continued to look to Wheeler for more information on Sherman's whereabouts, he directed his infantry divisions to be ready to contest the Peach Tree Creek line while he contemplated his next move. Hood also assumed, as the Army of the Cumberland had failed to cross Peach Tree Creek by midday on Tuesday that Thomas's army would take until midday on Wednesday, 20 July, to reach the south side of Peach Tree Creek. His assumption would prove to be fatal for in the twenty-four hours that elapsed between the two planned attacks, Thomas's massive Army of the Cumberland would secure three bridgeheads and gain important ridges and high grounds south of the creek prior to the attack. Thomas's three corps, the IV at Buckhead, the XX at Howell's Mill and along today's Northside Drive, and the XIV at Moore's Mill, would all send one division across the creek and establish bridgeheads by dusk on 19 July. In a circular order delivered to all of his three infantry corps commanders during the moring of Tuesday, 19 July, Hood continued his preparations: "[Y]ou will cause the banks of Peach Tree Creek to be thoroughly examined in front of your division; place a strong skirmish line there, and cause the best defenses that can be made to be placed there. The object is to enable a small force to resist the enemy's crossing for some time."[52]

Interestingly, the order included the endorsement of General Hardee to his men urging his subordinates to follow Hood's directives. Possibly, dissension in the ranks and junior officers was so great that orders from Hood might not have been carried out unless the next commander in line, in this case Hardee, also endorsed it. Hood was learning quickly that it is lonely at the top. General Stewart even had to call on his brigade and division commanders to prevent a near-revolt in the camps of his corps.[53]

---

[50] Allen P. Julian, "Operations through the Present Ridgewood Community, July 1864," 110, MSS 130, box 4, folder 4, Wilbur G. Kurtz Collection, Kenan Research Center, Atlanta History Center.

[51] *OR*, ser. 1, vol. 38, pt. 5, serial 76, 893.

[52] Ibid., 894.

[53] J. C. Thompson to A. P. Stewart, 8 December 1867, box 1, folder 5, Joseph E. Johnston Collection, Earl Gregg Swem Library, College of William & Mary, Williamsburg,

Hood's First Sortie, 20 July 1864

Sherman launched his offensive on Sunday, 17 July, but it was not until Monday that many of his units began moving. It was correctly assumed by both Johnston and Hood that Sherman's infantry force was between Roswell to the north and Paces Ferry to the west. However, once Sherman's troops began advancing on Atlanta during that day, contact with the extreme left flank of Sherman's force, which consisted of McPherson's Army of the Tennessee, was lost. It appeared to Johnston, and believed by Hood, throughout Monday and into Tuesday, that Sherman's eastern flank was traveling south from Roswell toward Buckhead, or just east of Buckhead, and not southeast toward Stone Mountain. Only on the afternoon of 19 July did Hood first learn from Wheeler that Federal troops were moving on Decatur.[54]

Confederate cavalry commander Joseph Wheeler posted his brigades along the Chattahoochee River from McAfee's Bridge near today's city of Duluth to the north of Atlanta, and Campbellton southwest of Atlanta, a distance of some 40 miles. To cover this vast area, Wheeler had available just 11 brigades totaling barely 10,000 men. Moreover, Sherman's legions could force a crossing in any one of a number of fords and ferries that dotted the Georgia countryside.

From the first crossings over the river near Roswell on Friday and Saturday, 8 and 9 July, Wheeler's cavalry anxiously awaited evidence of further crossings or of any massing of infantry signaling Sherman's next move. For a week, the two armies opposed each other with the river between them as Johnston had removed his infantry to the south side of the Chattahoochee River. On 9 July, Sherman feigned a move to the southwest by sending a cavalry force under General Stoneman toward Newnan via Campbellton while Sherman shifted his infantry to the northeast to launch his strike on the Georgia and Augusta Railroad east of Atlanta with the Army of the Tennessee. To do this, Sherman sent McPherson's three corps from the extreme right of the Federal line below Pace's Ferry to the left of the northern line at Roswell.[55]

Johnston continued to wait on information from Wheeler. Reports came in from Lieutenant Colonel J. F. Gaines commanding Hannon's Alabama Cavalry Brigade around 5:00 P.M. on Friday, 8 July, that Sherman appeared to be forcing a crossing over the river at McAfee's Bridge (Holcomb Bridge) above Roswell Factory. By 9:00 A.M. the next morning, news came that Federal infantry that had crossed below Soap Creek at Isham's Ford (also called Isom's Ferry and

---

Virginia.
[54] Johnston, *Narrative*, 349–50; Hood, *OR*, ser. 1, vol. 38, pt. 3, serial 74, p. 630; *OR*, ser. 1, vol. 38, pt. 5, serial 76, pp. 889–93.
[55] *OR*, ser. 1, vol. 38, serial 76, pp. 98–99, 101–108, 877–90.

The Battle of Peach Tree Creek

Cavalry Ford) the day before, had erected a pontoon bridge and been reinforced. Johnston decided to withdraw his infantry to the southeast side of the Chattahoochee River that evening. By Sunday afternoon 10 July, reports from General John S. Williams commanding a Kentucky brigade of cavalry revealed that the body of Northern infantry at Isham's Ford was not substantial and did not appear to be advancing, while General J. H. Kelly in command of the division of cavalry assigned to the northern perimeter of Johnston's defensive cavalry screen sent a message at 6:00 P.M. on 10 July explaining that the force that had crossed at Roswell the day before was only cavalry and that it was entrenching, not apparently preparing to advance.[56]

While it first appeared that the Federal crossings at Roswell and Soap Creek were preparatory to an advance on Atlanta via Buckhead and Cross Keys, the lack of supporting infantry or of any sign of advancing Federal cavalry to clear the way coupled with Sherman's launching of Stoneman's Cavalry toward Newnan confused Johnston. Uncertain of the whereabouts of Sherman's infantry, Old Joe could only fall back below the river, place his force in a defensive position below Peach Tree Creek so that he could cover a Federal advance on the Gate City from the north or the west, and wait.

While Sherman shifted his infantry toward the northeast preparatory to a move on Decatur and the Georgia and Augusta Railroad, he shrewdly hid his intentions while anxiously awaiting results of Stoneman's raid. Meanwhile, Johnston and his legions continued to wait as the citizens of Atlanta and the Confederate officials in Richmond hung on every slight change in the news. As cavalry pickets reported no change along the banks of the Chattahoochee River on Monday and Tuesday, 11 and 12 July, President Davis lit up the wires with dispatches to Johnston asking for details of both the latest news and of Old Joe's plan to repel Sherman. Coolly, Johnston replied on 11 July that the Federal prisoners in Andersonville should be removed immediately. Johnston was tracking Stoneman's cavalry raid and was concerned they could reach as far as the southern prisoner of war camp, but his telegrams did not explain his reasons for recommending the precaution and only served to confirm to Davis that Johnston had no intention of holding Atlanta.[57]

On 14 July, Johnston was aware that at least three of Sherman's seven corps of infantry were established on the southeast side of the river, from Power's Ferry to Roswell, but Johnston showed no sign of moving to counter

---

[56] Ibid., 869–74.
[57] Ibid., 874–81.

Hood's First Sortie, 20 July 1864

Sherman's deployment over the Chattahoochee. By Friday, 15 July, President Davis believed that Sherman was massing his infantry force at Roswell for an apparent strike on the rail line linking Atlanta with Augusta, meaning that his communication with Johnston and the Confederate forces in Atlanta could be cut off at any moment. Thus, on Saturday, 16 July, Davis sent a telegram to Johnston expressing his concern that the railroad might be severed and asking his commander to tell him his plan for operations. Johnston's reply was less than encouraging as he defended his performance over the past three months by explaining that as Sherman's force was larger than the Southern force opposing it Johnston must be on the defensive and that his decisions "depend upon that of the enemy." Johnston also indicated that he was trying to "put Atlanta in a condition to be held for a day or two by the Georgia militia" so that his army could perhaps be used in an offensive movement on Sherman. This reply pushed Davis to fire Johnston the following day.[58]

On Saturday, 16 July, around 9:00 P.M., Johnston learned that all of Sherman's infantry was north of the railroad bridge that linked Atlanta with Chattanooga and that the majority of the Federal forces were several miles further north and across the river. This information led Johnston to finally mobilize his infantry as they began to shift to the east and northeast to cover Atlanta from the north and east below Peach Tree Creek during the afternoon of Sunday, 17 July. A circular order from Hardee's headquarters to his division commanders was issued at 10:30 that morning indicating that a movement preparatory to an attack was imminent. Later in the day, Hood's corps was moved northeast of Atlanta while Hardee's corps followed and deployed along the south banks of Peach Tree Creek. Stewart's corps also shifted to the east from its position and stretched to cover the area from the river to Hardee's left.[59]

By the afternoon of Monday, 18 July, Old Joe retired from headquarters where he had been Hood's nominal mouthpiece all day and was quietly packing his bags and making arrangements to leave for Macon. John Bell Hood had asked Old Joe to stay on throughout the day on Monday, and allow Hood to continue to send orders to the army through Johnston's name to help with making the transfer a smoother transition. Johnston agreed to the task for the day while the suspension of his order of removal was being considered by President Davis, but by the end of the day when Davis's reply came, Old Joe was ready to quietly depart from Atlanta. Hood blamed Johnston for promising

---

[58] Ibid., 880–85.
[59] Ibid., 884–89.

to support him, but then leaving town without helping him or telling the new leader that he was departing.[60]

On the evening of Tuesday 19 July, probably around midnight, after Hood's first full day in sole command of the army, Hood summoned his corps commanders and prepared for his inaugural battle as commander of the Army of Tennessee.[61] Present were generals Hardee, Stewart, and Benjamin Cheatham, just placed in temporary command of Hood's old corps until a new corps commander could be assigned. Also present was General G. W. Smith who was in command of the Georgia State Militia. Hood ordered Generals Hardee and Stewart with their two corps to assault the exposed Federal forces that had become separated by about 3 or 4 miles from McPherson's Army of Tennessee that was now at Decatur, some 6 miles east of Atlanta.[62]

Interestingly, Sherman was also aware of and concerned about the gap between Thomas's men and the rest of his force. On the morning of 19 July, Sherman cautioned Thomas about the deployment of his troops and sent General Coarse to spell out his wishes. "I think you have too much of your force [on] the other side of Nancy's Creek. One Division, [instead of Palmer's entire XIV Corps] would be ample there, and all the rest in a general line, with Buck Head as a center." Thomas's force was at that point entirely west of Buckhead, and not where Sherman desired. Sherman added "Howard's [IV] Corps should then feel to the left and cross the forks of the Peach Tree, toward Pea Vine Creek." Accordingly, then Thomas sent two of Howard's three divisions toward Pea Vine Creek during the evening of 19 July and morning of 20 July, as requested by Sherman, but the move still did not stretch out the remainder of Thomas's force sufficiently to cover the 2 mile gap as Sherman had hoped. Sherman then correctly predicted, "I take it for granted all the main crossings of Peach Tree in that quarter are well covered, but can be turned by the left." Thomas responded twice to assure Sherman that his orders were being carried out and that his entire force was now between Nancy's Creek and Peach Tree

---

[60] Hood, *Advance & Retreat*, 164–67; Symonds, *Joseph E. Johnston*, 330. In fairness to Johnston, Symonds points out that it was only prudent for the general to leave Atlanta to give the new leader space to exercise his own command over the army.

[61] Castel, *Decision in the West*, 366. Note that Hood indicated that he summoned his corps commanders for a war council on the evening of Tuesday, 19 July, around midnight. Stewart's report explained that Hood's orders were received on the morning of Wednesday, 20 July, at about 7:00 A.M. Hood must have met with his lieutenants on 19 July, revealed his plan to attack the next day, and the next morning reiterated his plan by issuing specific orders of attack. Compare *Stewart's Report, OR*, ser. 1, vol. 38, pt. 3, serial 74, p. 871.

[62] Hood, *Advance & Retreat*, 167.

Creek.[63]

It was also during this time that Sherman learned of Johnston's removal and Hood's promotion. In his dispatch to Thomas, Sherman recorded, "I have seen an Atlanta paper of the 18th, containing Johnston's farewell order to his troops. From its tone and substance I infer he has been relieved by Jeff. Davis, who sent Bragg to Atlanta to bear the order. I also infer it is not for the purpose of getting another command. Hood succeeds." Just twenty-four hours before, the Northern commander had pondered whether Johnston would make a stand at Atlanta.[64]

For all of Sherman's correct assumptions and predictions, he was totally blind concerning where Hood was preparing to attack. Sherman assumed a move would be made on McPherson's force east of Atlanta and not on Thomas. The fight that Hood would make on 22 July at Decatur was precisely what Sherman feared, and he continued to press Thomas to hurry across Peach Tree Creek so that he could reunite his force before Hood had time to strike. The Federal commander admonished Thomas, "You must get across Peach Tree either by moving direct on Atlanta, or, if necessary, leave a force to watch the bridge in possession of the enemy and move by the left. This is very important, and at once, as we may have to fight all of Hood's [Army] from east of Atlanta."[65]

It is interesting to note that had Thomas's Army of the Cumberland moved with the speed that Sherman desired over Peach Tree Creek, Thomas's men might well have been attacked on 19 July instead of 20 July and without any of his troops entrenched on the south side of the creek. Of course, this assumes that Hood would have been able to launch a coordinated attack on his second day of command and that his corps and division commanders would be able to time their strike on the Yankees at the moment where they were most vulnerable as they crossed the creek but had not yet begun to dig in. Moreover, it assumes that the various Federal brigades assigned with the task of crossing would all reach the south side of the creek at or near the same time. The XX Corps and XIV Corps of Thomas's command would have found themselves isolated from the rest of the Northern troops. The IV Corps would have been out of position at Buckhead, or at the Peach Tree Creek crossing on the Buckhead Road, and they would have had to either backtrack along the country lane in the woods west of Buckhead (along today's West Pace's Ferry Road) to the Chattahoochee River

---

[63] Ibid., 183–84.
[64] Ibid., 183, 170.
[65] Ibid., 183.

The Battle of Peach Tree Creek

to avoid being cut off and to come to the aid of the other two corps, or cut their way across the jungle-like terrain southwest of Buckhead and attempt to launch an attack into the right flank of the charging Confederates. It is impossible to predict the potential outcome of such a move, but had things gone wrong for the Army of the Cumberland, the remainder of Sherman's forces would be from 5 to 12 miles away from the scene of the attack and by the time that they could come to Thomas's aid, his men would be bottled up against the Chattahoochee River west of Nancy Creek, just as Johnston had predicted.

At 7:00 P.M. on 19 July, Sherman remained convinced that if Hood attacked it would be east of the city against McPherson. In a dispatch to Thomas at that hour, Sherman asked for details of the location of his forces, to place his units on a map, and if there was a fight east of the city, to seek whether or not Thomas's force could be in a position to "take part in the battle if offered outside of Atlanta." The Yankee commander added that if Hood fought outside of the city's defensive works, "we must accept battle."[66] At 8:10 P.M. on 19 July, stewing on his earlier dispatch to Thomas, Sherman added, "With McPherson [Army of the Tennessee], Howard [IV Corps], and Schofield [Army of the Ohio], I would have ample [men] to fight the whole of Hood's army, leaving you [the XX Corps, the XIV Corps, and one division of the IV Corps of the Army of the Cumberland] to walk into Atlanta, capturing guns and everything. But with Schofield and McPherson alone, the game will not be so certain."[67] Sometime between 8:00 P.M. and midnight, Sherman received Thomas's sketch map showing the location of his various commands. Also, Thomas likely forwarded a dispatch sent to headquarters by General Joseph Hooker of the XX Corps, informing that Hooker had captured Rebels in his front from two of the three Confederate corps were facing him along Peach Tree Creek, miles away from Decatur and McPherson's troops. Hooker's dispatch of 6:00 P.M. on 19 July indicated that he had crossed Geary's division to the south side of Peach Tree Creek (at today's present Northside Drive crossing) and had Williams's division in close support, but that they had captured Confederates in front of Geary's force and learned of the change in command:

> Prisoners state that the order was published last night relieving Johnston and putting Hood in command of their army. They do not know that any portion of the forces have been sent to our left. They say that Stewart's [Polk's] corps is on the left of Hardee's which latter is in our front. They state further

---

[66] Ibid., 185.
[67] Ibid., 186.

that their main line of defense is three miles from Atlanta in front of me, and about two and a half miles in the direction of the Chattahoochee. They state that the assignment of Hood gives great dissatisfaction in Hardee's Corps.[68]

Hooker had by dusk on the evening of 19 July almost perfect intelligence on the location of the Confederate Army, its disposition, its fortifications and defenses, and its state of morale concerning the change in commanders. Thus, the Federal high command had in its hands accurate intelligence on the condition of the Confederate forces before them, with essentially as much information as Hood himself had at that time about his own force. Moreover, a critical element in Hooker's dispatch was that there was no evidence that any Rebel troops had moved to the east in the direction of Decatur or that the Confederates were aware that McPherson was that far east, and two of Hood's three corps were apparently accounted for in front of Hooker or between Hooker and the Chattahoochee River to the west, and not east of Atlanta. Whether Sherman actually received a copy of Hooker's dispatch from Thomas, or whether the substance of Hooker's intelligence was included in Thomas's evening report to Sherman is unclear.

What is clear is that at 1:55 A.M. on the morning of 20 July, Sherman was still up, he was certain that 20 July would bring on a decisive battle, and he was still guided by the belief that Hood would attack his left at Decatur. At 1:55 A.M., Sherman sent the following dispatch to Thomas, "I am now in possession of your sketch, which is perfectly clear and plain. In advancing this morning, of course we will bring on a heavy battle, and should be as fully prepared as possible. I think as your troops are now disposed your right will be too strong as compared with your left."[69] The Federal commander added, "I wish you to strengthen your left and risk more to your right, for the reason that as Atlanta is threatened the enemy will look to it rather than the river."[70] It is probable that Sherman discounted the information obtained by Hooker because Sherman did not think much of Fighting Joe or that Hood had planted false evidence via the captured troops to mask his plan to attack McPherson.

Since crossing the Chattahoochee River at Roswell Factory and Soap Creek, McPherson's three corps and Schofield's Army of the Ohio with its XXIII Corps had been allowed to pretty much roam free north and east of Atlanta, with little or no resistence by portions of Wheeler's cavalry. When

---

[68] Ibid., 190.
[69] Ibid., 195.
[70] Ibid., 195.

The Battle of Peach Tree Creek

McPherson's corps started for Atlanta on the morning of 20 July, Wheeler's men began to sound the alarm early and often all day, until Hood finally had shifted his entire army to the right to cover the city, and, by dusk, he would have to dispatch Cleburne's division to support Wheeler. Hood's plans to attack Thomas's Army of the Cumberland were, therefore, frustrated by both McPherson's approach on Atlanta and by Thomas's tardy crossing of Peach Tree Creek.

Wheeler's warnings forced a change in Hood's plans. Needing to block the threats from the east, Hood ordered General Cheatham, who had just taken command of Hood's old corps, to march further east and south to connect with Wheeler's cavalry force of some 2,500 to 3,500 troopers that were opposing McPherson's 25,000 men. When Schofield's advance to support McPherson was detected, Hood needed to fill the gap created by Cheatham's southeastward move and thus cover northeast Atlanta. Thus, by late morning on 20 July, he ordered generals Hardee and Stewart to move their corps to the right by half a division width prior to making their attack. The attack was to have been made at 1:00 P.M. It would now have to wait until the shift to the right had been completed.[71]

Hood would turn to Old Reliable, General William J. Hardee, and his 18,400-man infantry corps of veterans whom Hood had regarded as "the best in the army," a distinction that was debatable, but certainly they had that reputation in the army. Together with Stewart's corps to support the attack, Hood would be able to throw two-thirds of his infantry force against the exposed Federal right flank.[72]

Thomas's men were just beginning to reach Peach Tree Creek on the morning of Tuesday, 19 July. By late afternoon many units were beginning to cross and fortify on the southern side. At nightfall, Thomas's Army had three established bridgeheads south of the creek. At dusk on 19 July, Palmer's XIV Corps was almost entirely across the creek and posted along the heights near the Howell Mill Road after a short, but hard, fight between Davis's 2nd Division and Reynolds's Arkansas Brigade and elements of Adams's Mississippi Brigade at the mouth of Green Bone Creek at Peach Tree Creek. About a mile to the east, Geary's 2nd Division of Hooker's XX Corps crossed where Northside Drive today crosses Peach Tree Creek and crowned the heights just south of

---

[71] Cox, *Atlanta*, 153; Web Garrison, *Atlanta and the War* (Nashville: Rutledge Hill Press, 1995) 149; Jim Miles, *Fields of Glory* (Nashville: Rutledge Hill Press, 1995) 137; Castel, *Decision in the West*, 371.

[72] Hood, *Advance & Retreat*, 164–71; Scaife, *The Campaign for Atlanta*, 88–89.

there. Further to the east, another mile away, units of Howard's IV Corps secured heights south of Peach Tree Creek at the Buckhead Road (today's Peachtree Road).[73]

But, only one of Howard's three divisions, Wood's, was in position on the Buckhead Road south of the creek while the two remaining divisions were en route. Similarly, in Hooker's corps, Williams's 1st Division was coming up in rear of Geary's division, while Ward's 3rd Division was still on the north side of the creek and following a circuitous route behind the IV Corps. Should Hood have attacked on the afternoon of 19 July he would have likely surprised and routed one division each from Thomas's three corps, who were separated by a mile from each other and not in supporting distance to each other. Moreover, the second and third divisions of each of Thomas's three corps would be found in rear of the lead divisions, with one division in each corps south of the creek, another in the act of crossing, and the final division of each corps still in column, or line of march, on the north side of the creek.[74]

Had the Rebel assault struck on Tuesday, 19 July, the Confederacy might well have pulled off another Chancellorsville-like surprise and routed Thomas's Army of the Cumberland. For support of this position, one could consider the effect of the unexpected counterattack made by Reynolds's Arkansans and parts of two Mississippi regiments under Colonel Mike Farrell of the 15th Mississippi against Dilworth's 3rd Brigade of Davis's 2nd Division. With an undersized brigade of only 400 men in Reynolds's Arkansas Brigade, plus about 250 men in Farrell's 15th Mississippi and another 40 or so men from two companies of the 6th Mississippi, barely 700 Confederates in two uncoordinated assaults surprised and pushed back about 2,000 Yankees in Dilworth's large brigade, and another 2,000 Federal troops of Mitchell's 2nd Brigade of the same 2nd Division were tied up in dealing with and throwing back the unexpected threat.[75]

By dusk on Tuesday, 19 July, over half of Thomas's men were across, and by noon on the next day, all of his force would be south of Peach Tree Creek,

---

[73] Hood, *Advance & Retreat*, 164–71; Scaife, *The Campaign for Atlanta*, 88–89; Thomas L. Connelly, *Autumn of Glory, The Army of Tennessee, 1862–1865* (Baton Rouge: Louisiana State Press, 1971) 422–25; *OR*, ser. 1, vol. 38, pt. 1, serial 73, p. 201; Julian, "Operations through the Present Ridgewood Community, July 1864."

[74] Hood, *Advance & Retreat*, 164–71; Scaife, *The Campaign for Atlanta*, 88–89; Julian, "Operations through the Present Ridgewood Community, July 1864."

[75] James Willis, *Arkansas Confederates in the Western Theater* (Dayton OH: Morningside House, 1998) 508–12, H. Grady Howell, Jr., *Going to Meet the Yankees, A History of the "Bloody Sixth" Mississippi, C.S.A.* (Jackson MS: Chickasaw Bayou Press, 1981) 227–28.

and various parts of his command would be well entrenched. The new Southern leader waited until the afternoon of 20 July to attack; its delay would give Thomas's men the time needed to receive it.

With Hood in command, the men knew that a fight was eminent. One soldier explained: "Skirmishing was heavy all the morning, and everything indicated that a battle would be fought during the day. We all know that General Hood was placed in command of this army for the express purpose of making a desperate effort to hold Atlanta. While we have not the same confidence in his generalship that we had in General Johnston, we have resolved that if there is a failure, it shall not be our fault."[76]

The renowned German military strategist, Karl Von Clausewitz, explained that it does not take "great intelligence to devise a sound battle plan, but that a general needs something very close to genius to overcome the inertia of his army and successfully execute the scheme."[77] Von Clausewitz wrote of a certain zealousness for offensive fighting that some generals acquired when he recorded, "War is the province of danger, and therefore courage above all things is the first quality of a warrior." Von Clausewitz added, "Usually, before we have learnt what danger really is we form an idea of it which is rather attractive than repulsive. In the intoxication of enthusiasm, to fall upon the enemy at the charge—who cares then about bullets and men falling?"[78] During his military career, Hood seemed to be under that "intoxication of enthusiasm" that Von Clausewitz described. Whether the battle-scarred warrior possessed the "genius to overcome the inertia of his army" would remain to be seen.

---

[76] Cannon, *History of the 27th Regiment Alabama Infantry,* 84.

[77] Richard M. McMurry, *John Bell Hood and the War for Southern Independence* (Lexington: University Press of Kentucky, 1982) 128.

[78] Karl von Clausewitz, *On War,* trans. James John Graham (London: N. Trübner, 1873) 44, 49.

3

A RICH MAN'S WAR AND A POOR MAN'S FIGHT

> Now the question is, had I better go as a volunteer for three years and get the bounty of two hundred dollars, and the honor of going as a volunteer? ...Or go as a draftee? ...and have the disgrace of being drafted.[1]

The Army of the Cumberland was the North's unwanted step-child. With the nation's focus on the Army of the Potomac in the Eastern Theater, and with all of the successes of the Federal Army of the Tennessee from the capture of Forts Donelson and Henry, to Shiloh and Vicksburg, it was hard for the officers and men of the Army of the Cumberland to live up to expectations. Battles they had won such as Perryville and Stones River were nearly always tactical draws. While they were strategic, albeit unimpressive, victories where in both cases the Rebels had been turned back, they did not appear to gain anything for the North. But at the Battle of Chickamauga in September 1863 in which the army was caught unawares in Northwest Georgia, where it could have been destroyed in detail, it was embarrassed, and nearly undid all of the good that Gettysburg and Vicksburg had done that summer for the Northern cause. After two days of fighting, former Commander William Rosecrans was routed and then bottled up in the confines of Chattanooga with a river at his back and surrounded by mountains. There, the army had to be rescued by Grant and Sherman and the successful Army of the Tennessee.

Many in the North, therefore, looked upon the Army of the Cumberland as inept, poorly led, unreliable, and unlucky. The IV and XIV corps grew so sick of the mistreatment by their counterparts, that when they were finally given a chance to make an assault on the Confederate lines after Sherman's men had struggled at Missionary Ridge, the men of the Army of the Cumberland took Orchard Knob in a gallant frontal assault and did not stop until the Confederates were on their way back to Georgia.[2]

---

[1] John Michael Priest, ed., *John T. McMahon's Diary of the 136th New York, 1861–1864* (Shippensburg PA: White Mane Publishing Company, 1993) 23.

[2] Peter Cozzens, *The Battles for Chattanooga, The Shipwreck of Their Hopes* (Champaign: University of Illinois Press, 1994) 126–35.

The Battle of Peach Tree Creek

In addition to the IV and XIV corps, the cast-offs of the Army of the Potomac, the former XI and XII corps that contained a number of German and Irish immigrants, had been sent west to supplement the ranks of the Army of the Cumberland. These corps had been revamped into the new XX Corps, and many men and officers in it felt they had something to prove. They were tired of hearing about their failures at Fredericksburg and Chancellorsville, and the first two day's battle at Gettysburg.

Formed on 4 April 1864, the XX Corps retained the badge of the old XII Corps that was broken up along with parts of the XI Corps to make the new unit, which was assigned to General Joseph Hooker, the ill-fated commander of the Army of the Potomac at Chancellorsville a year before. The badge, a five point star, was colored red for the 1st Division, commanded by General Alpheus Starkey Williams, white for the 2nd Division led by General John White Geary whose middle name was fortuitous, and blue for the 3rd Division under General William Ward who replaced General Daniel Butterfield during the Georgia Campaign. These three divisions of the XX Corps each contained three brigades, consisting in total, "52 regiments of infantry and 6 batteries" of artillery. A fourth division was assigned to the XX Corps led by General Lovell H. Rousseau, but it remained on garrison duty in Tennessee and most of the men in the corps were never even aware of its existence. When the XX Corps began the Georgia Campaign, it numbered 21,280 officers and men present for duty. By the time they crossed Peach Tree Creek, only about 14,600 remained.[3]

136th New York, The Iron Clads. The 136th New York Infantry, nicknamed the "Iron Clads,"[4] and the 33rd New Jersey Infantry were typical of the units that had been shipped west from the Army of the Potomac. The men of the 136th New York came by and large from the finger lakes region of New York state. In August 1862, President Lincoln had called for 300,000 men to volunteer by 15 August for three years to put down the rebellion. A $200 bounty would be paid together with $16 per month to all who volunteered. Moreover, there was talk that another 300,000 men would be drafted for nine months at only $11 per month and no bounty. In the news came reports that General Lee had turned things around in Virginia for the South while General

---

[3] www.civilwararchive.com/CORPS/20thhook.htm (7 May 2006); United States War Department, comp., *Official Records of the Union and Confederate Armies in the War of the Rebellion*, 128 vols. (Washington, DC: Government Printing Office, 1880–1901) ser. 1, vol. 38, pt. 1, serial 72, p. 115 (hereafter *OR*).

[4] "Union Regimental Histories," www.civilwararchive.com/Unreghst/unnyinf9.htm (7 May 2006).

Hood's First Sortie, 20 July 1864

Bragg had done the same in Tennessee. Invasion into Maryland and Kentucky appeared imminent as the North felt the threat of war on her doorsteps for the first time. Thus, many citizens in the Northern states experienced the threat to their homelands like the people in Mississippi had felt when Grant and his blue-clad army was at Shiloh six months before. It is easy to see why there was a great fervor that spread throughout the North to preserve the Union during this time. According to one member of the 136th New York, "Now the question is, had I better go as a volunteer for three years and get the bounty of two hundred dollars, and the honor of going as a volunteer? …Or go as a draftee? …and have the disgrace of being drafted."[5] It was in this climate that the 136th New York was formed.

The Northern victory at Gettysburg was important for many of these previously untested regiments, or units that had not experienced success before. The 136th New York and her sister regiments in what was then in the 2nd Brigade under Colonel Orland Smith of the 2nd Division of the XI Corps arrived on Cemetery Hill on 1 July and did not participate in the first day's fighting at Gettysburg, but the New Yorkers and their comrades made their presence felt the next two days as they helped to repel numerous Confederate assaults in their portion of the battlefield. At Gettysburg, the 136th New York, under the direction of Colonel James Wood, Jr., lost 17 men killed, saw 88 wounded, and another 3 men were missing or captured for a total loss of 108 men. Joining the New Yorkers were the 33rd Massachusetts, the 55th Ohio, and the 73rd Ohio at Gettysburg where the brigade suffered 62 men killed, 261 wounded, and 22 men missing or captured for a total loss of 345 men as they helped to repel various Rebel parries including Lee's famous Pickett's Charge. For the first time in the war these regiments and others that eventually merged into the XX Corps were successful. By the time that the 136th New York and her sister regiments reached the Army of the Cumberland at the start of the Atlanta Campaign, they had become the 3rd Brigade of the 3rd Division of the XX Corps. The 20th Connecticut was added to their number and Colonel Wood of the 136th New York became their brigade commander.[6]

---

[5] Priest, *John T. McMahon's Diary*, 23.

[6] *OR*, ser. 1, vol. 25, pt. 2, serial 40, pp. 26–27; *OR*, ser. 1, vol. 25, serial 39, pp. 66–67; *OR*, ser. 1, vol. 27, serial 43, pp. 723–25; *Supplement to the Official Records of the Union and Confederate Armies* (Wilmington NC: Broadfoot Publishing Company, 1995–2001) pt. 2, vol. 36, serial 58, pp. 772–73 (hereafter *Supplement to* OR); William R. Scaife, *The Campaign for Atlanta* (Atlanta: self-published, 1993) 156.

The Battle of Peach Tree Creek

33rd New Jersey, The Mutinous Regiment. Mixed in with the regiments in the XX Corps were several new regiments that were created as the Conscription Act of 1863 drafted single and married male citizens and immigrants between the ages of twenty and forty-five. Draft riots broke out during this time, particularly in New York, and eventually 20,000 soldiers had to be dispatched to restore order. When the rioting was curtailed, 105 people had been killed. In the midst of this turmoil, a number of men, including men of the 33rd New Jersey, volunteered to avoid being drafted.[7] While a number of the men who joined the 33rd New Jersey were immigrants, chiefly from Ireland and Germany, the majority of the volunteers were native New Jersians whose main motivation for joining was economic. With the continued, rapid, and unchecked immigration in the eastern coastal cities of the North, finding work for a reasonable wage became increasingly difficult. By the time that the 33rd New Jersey was formed in spring 1863, "combined Federal and State bounties ranged from $174 for a single man without experience to $618 for married veterans." Moreover, a volunteer's monthly pay was $13 while a draftee's monthly pay would be $11 with no bounty. With the average annual wage at just over $300, joining a Federal regiment and receiving a bounty became not just a symbol of courage but a means of economic survival. It also became way to fleece the government as the temptation for "bounty-jumping," in which someone volunteered for a new unit, received his bounty in the form of an up-front cash payment, and then skipped town only to repeat the process in the next city, grew. During this time, "the city of Newark [New Jersey] paid out almost $80,000 in such bounties."[8] It was in this climate that the 33rd New Jersey was organized and nicknamed the "Mutinous Regiment" by its historian.

---

[7] John G. Zinn, *The 33rd New Jersey in the Civil War, The Mutinous Regiment* (Jefferson NC: McFarland & Company, 2005) 5–12.

[8] Ibid., 11.

4

CANNONADE ATLANTA WITHOUT MERCY

Each army commander will accept battle on anything like fair terms, but if the army reach within cannon-range of the city without receiving artillery or musketry fire he will halt, form a strong line, with batteries in position, and await orders. If fired on from the forts or buildings of Atlanta no consideration must be paid to the fact that they are occupied by families, but the place must be cannonaded without the formality of a demand...[for surrender].[1]

During the day on Tuesday, 19 July, Sherman learned of Johnston's removal and of Hood's appointment to command the Confederate forces opposing him through a copy of the 18 July edition of the *Atlanta Daily Appeal*, one of Atlanta's many newspapers, captured by a spy in General Greenville Dodge's XVI Corps. Fearing an attack to his left, Sherman had ordered Thomas to send two divisions of Howard's IV Corps east to connect with Schofield.[2]

Hood's target, however, was Thomas, not McPherson, and Sherman's order to hasten Thomas's advance and move two divisions to Schofield, would actually weaken Thomas at the very point of Hood's attack and push Thomas's men into the Confederate trap quicker. Hood was unaware of the threat posed by McPherson's forces at Decatur, just 6 miles from Atlanta, while he concentrated on his offensive strike against Thomas. Hood was not considering or appreciating the need for a defensive plan against the Federal forces advancing toward the Gate City from the east. For his part, Sherman was not considering the need for a defensive plan in the event that Thomas's forces were attacked. On the eve of the Battle of Peach Tree Creek neither commander was

---

[1] United States War Department, comp., *Official Records of the Union and Confederate Armies in the War of the Rebellion*, 128 vols. (Washington, DC: Government Printing Office, 1880–1901) ser. 1. vol. 36, pt. 2, 672 (hereafter *OR*); James M. McPherson, *Battle Cry of Freedom: The Civil War Era* (New York: Ballantine, 1988) 730.

[2] *OR*, ser. 1, vol. 38, pt. 5, 169–75; Albert Castel, *Decision in the West: The Atlanta Campaign of 1864* (Lawrence: University Press of Kansas, 1992) 366–69.

aware or concerned about the threat to their right flank, instead focusing on advancing their left flank to force the issue against the other side.

Hood, under pressure to make a bold offensive in the hopes of lifting the Yankee grip on Atlanta, no doubt questioned his own inexperience and looked to Johnston's plan of attack and to his chief of staff, Brigadier General William W. Mackall, for direction. Hood would also rely heavily on his most experienced General, Lieutenant General William J. Hardee, for leadership in the field command of his first attack. Hood would continue to depend on Old Reliable throughout the battles around Atlanta during the next forty days, beginning with Peach Tree Creek and again on each of the successive field operations that would follow.

On the morning of 20 July, General Howard accompanied Stanley's and Wood's divisions of his IV Corps as they probed southeast of Buckhead along the north and south forks of Peach Tree Creek. According the general, "About 8:30 A.M. we were at the south fork of Peach Tree Creek, where the enemy met and resisted us with infantry skirmishers. This point was about a mile to the right of (west of) Schofield's main column, but the roads for Schofield and Stanley advancing were now converging toward Atlanta."[3] General Hazen, commanding the 2nd Brigade of Wood's division was in the rear of the line of march. Hazen reported that his men were wakened at 3:00 A.M., and they remained in their position along the Buckhead Road just south of Peach Tree Creek until they were relieved by Bradley's brigade of Newton's division at 8:00 A.M. At that time, they recrossed Peach Tree Creek, "[j]oined the 1st and 3rd brigades, and marched up the creek on the north side, following Stanley's Division." Hazen recalled that there was "considerable skirmishing in [his] front during the afternoon" that caused the column to move very slowly. He added that his brigade "[c]rossed both branches of Peach-tree Creek, and finally went into camp in reserve between the two branches, about a quarter of a mile in rear and right of Stanley's line, about 4 miles from Atlanta. Several were wounded by stray shots while waiting to get into position," explained the veteran Federal commander.[4]

Stanley's division with Wood's division following marched generally along today's Lenox Road while the van of Schofield's XXIII Corps followed the course of Briarcliff Road to Johnson Road south to near its juncture with

---

[3] O. O. Howard, *Autobiography of Oliver Otis Howard*, vols. 1 and 2 (New York: The Baker & Taylor Company, 1907) 1:609–10.

[4] William B. Hazen, *A Narrative of Military Service* (Boston: Ticknor and Sons, 1885) 272.

Hood's First Sortie, 20 July 1864

Lenox Road at Highland Avenue where the main Rebel works were located. Wood's division remained in column as they followed Stanley's men along today's Lenox Road and Old Cheshire Bridge Road. During the day, pioneers from Howard's divisions erected two bridges across the North Fork, and late in the afternoon, they completed a bridge across the South Fork. From their position below the South Fork of Peach Tree Creek and as they converged on Atlanta, Wood's and Stanley's division exchanged skirmish fire with elements of Cheatham's corps. General Howard explained, "We had found the bridge over the South Fork burned. While our skirmishers were wading the creek and driving those of the enemy back, our bridge men were vigorously employed rebuilding. By ten o'clock the bridge was done and Stanley moved his skirmishers beyond it."[5]

Howard continued, "A little more than half a mile from the bridge the firing became more lively and exciting; the enemy resisted from behind piles of rails and other barricades. Soon the main Confederate works were uncovered." Here, portions of Stevenson's division of Cheatham's corps stiffened their resistance: "A battery of artillery slowly opened its annoying discharges against Stanley's advance." Howard had just received a dispatch from Sherman ordering him to "move forward and develop the enemy;" and to "see whether he is in force." Stanley's division captured some Confederates during their advance across the two forks of Peach Tree Creek. "From some prisoners taken I ascertained that I was again engaging Stevenson's division," exclaimed Howard. "We put in our batteries, covering them by slight epaulements and supporting them by infantry regiments. Then we proceeded in the usual way to carry out Sherman's brief order, moving forward a strong line till we received such resistence as made us more careful."[6]

About 2:00 P.M. General Sherman came up to Howard's position. According to Howard, Sherman believed that "the enemy was withdrawing or would withdraw from my front to meet McPherson, for, up to that time, from his last accounts, McPherson had encountered nothing but artillery and cavalry."[7] Sherman continued to remain convinced that Hood would attack McPherson's exposed left flank despite the reconnaissance provided by Howard and McPherson's apparent lack of contact with any Rebel infantry, and the

---

[5] Howard, *Autobiography*, 610.
[6] Ibid., 610.
[7] Ibid., 610.

The Battle of Peach Tree Creek

Federal leader could not be dissuaded from believing that little or no Confederate troops remained to block Thomas's easy advance into Atlanta.

According to Howard, "About 3:30 P.M. we succeeded by change of position in driving the Confederates from a strongly constructed line of skirmish rifle pits. In this advance we captured some fifty prisoners." This was located along a line of hills near today's Wildwood Park to the west, Lenox-Wildwood Park to the east, and Sussex Park to the Southeast, on which Stevenson anchored his defenses. "A little later, Stevenson, leaving his works, made a charge upon us along Stanley's front; but his impulsive effort was bravely met and quickly repelled."[8]

Stevenson's division was assigned the task of covering the northeast side of Atlanta's defenses from the area north of Piedmont Park's northern boundary at today's intersection of Piedmont Avenue and Westminster Drive, to the intersection of today's North Highland Avenue and Zimmer Drive to the east. From this point, the remainder of Cheatham's (Hood's) corps continued southward along a line parallel with Highland Avenue. Just to the north of the intersection of Zimmer Drive and North Highland Avenue was a mill located on the South Fork of Peach Tree Creek named Durand's Mill. The mill was owned by Samuel A. Durand which he operated on old Briarcliff Road at the creek. Just west of the mill, Stanley's and Wood's divisions of Howard's IV Corps crossed the creek around 8:30 A.M. on 20 July, and began feeling their way south through the Georgia woodlands for the main Confederate lines. As a precaution, Howard's Yankees erected a line of entrenchments to protect their bridgehead throughout the midday. To check their advance, a little before 4:00 P.M., Stevenson ordered Brigadier General Edmund W. Pettus's Alabama Brigade to attack Stanley's skirmishers. This occurred at the same time as Bate's division was getting under way just west of the large ridge at Piedmont Park that separated the two divisions (Bate's and Stevenson's) from viewing each other.[9]

Stevenson's counterattack, which at first caught Stanley's skirmishers off guard, southwest of Durand's Mill, quickly ran out of steam and into Federal works that had been erected at the Federal bridgehead west of the mill at today's Wildwood Park located to the northeast of the intersection of today's Wellbourne Drive and Wildwood Road where portions of the Federal works are still

---

[8] Ibid., 610–11.
[9] *OR*, ser. 1, vol. 38, pt. 5, pp. 169–75; Howard, *Autobiography*, 610–11; http://wikimapia.org/10578799/Durand-s-Mill-site (8 August 2009); www.waymarking.com/waymarks/WM1YK8 (8 August 2009).

visible today. In Pettus's Alabama Brigade, which spearheaded the attack, the 30th Alabama lost one man killed, eight men wounded, including one mortally, with one of the wounded also being captured, for a total of nine casualties.[10]

Morgan Leatherman of Company C., 18th Tennessee in Brown's brigade of Stevenson's division, wrote his parents shortly before the battle informing them that he had been having "quite a heavy time for the last two or three months." He added, "We have not the whole time been two or three days out of the hearing of cannon and small arms and the most of the time have been in range of them." Leatherman explained, "Although I am not very fond of fighting, I am anxious to see the decisive battle of this campaign come off." Perhaps the Tennessee soldier had a particular sense of anxiety for the impending battle for it would be his last. Leatherman, who ended his letter prophetically "Though we may never meet no more below can we not try to meet in a better world?," would be killed during the fighting on 20 July.[11]

Another Tennessee casualty at Peach Tree Creek occurred when Private William H. Marshall was captured along the banks of the creek. Marshall, from Company G, 18th Tennessee Infantry from Sumner County, had been captured at Fort Donelson, then exchanged, later wounded at Chickamauga, 20 September 1863, where his "left arm [was] broken by [a] minie ball. Ball left in, lodged between bones of lower arm. Pieces of bone worked out of arm. In hospital 4 months. Rejoined regiment at Dalton, Ga."[12] After Marshall was captured at Peach Tree Creek, he was "Sent to Camp Douglass, Ill. Guard stuck bayonet into left hip in attempt to escape on way to prison. Paroled on oath at Camp Douglass one month before end of war. Had chronic diarrhea."[13] Marshall had seen a lot of the war, and for him, Peach Tree Creek would be the last of his service to the South, but it would not be the end of his suffering.

"Before night set in we had succeeded in my part of the line in gradually working up Stanley's Division till we occupied the position lately held by the

---

[10] Larry D. Stephens, *Bound for Glory, A History of the 30th Alabama Infantry Regiment, Confederate States of America* (Ann Arbor MI: Sheridan Books, 2005) 259.

[11] James Lee McDonough and James Pickett Jones, *War So Terrible, Sherman and Atlanta*, (New York: W. W. Norton & Company, 1987) 211–12; *Tennesseans in the Civil War, A Military History of Confederate and Union Units with Available Rosters of Personnel*, 2 vols. (Nashville: Civil War Centennial Commission, 1964–1965) 2:246.

[12] Edwin L. Ferguson, *Sumner County, Tennessee in the Civil War*, ed. Diane Payne (Tompkinsville KY: self-published, 1972) www.rootsweb.com/~tnsumner/sumnfg15.htm (1 March 2008).

[13] Ferguson, *Sumner County,* www.rootsweb.com/~tnsumner/sumnfg15.htm (1 March 2008).

enemy's skirmishers, so connecting us with Schofield's army upon our left" (along today's Highland Avenue), explained Howard. "Wood's Division had gone the same as Stanley a little farther to Stanley's right," along a line at today's Rock Springs Road. Howard, adroitly described his army's mission. "This business of approaching prepared parapets, from the rough nature of this wooded country, was perplexing and dangerous."[14] His men were becoming quite adept at it as, Stanley's report reflected, "Colonel Suman, 9th Indiana, of Grose's Brigade, charged their picket-line, farther to our right, and took 43 prisoners without losing a man."[15] The Federal skirmish line that made the capture was commanded by Lieutenant Drullinger of the 9th Indiana together with sergeants Kennedy and Chids and twenty men.[16] According to John Obreiter of the 77th Pennsylvania, "the fortified position of the enemy was attacked and his rifle-pits carried on the twentieth." He added that his "brigade captured 43 prisoners and the regiment had two men wounded," during the skirmishing along the North and South Forks of Peachtree Creek on 20 July.[17] One man in the 75th Illinois was killed, however, while the two wounded men came from the 77th Pennsylvania.[18] By 4:00 P.M., Stanley's 1st Brigade, led by Colonel Isaac M. Kirby, connected with and relieved the skirmishers of the XXIII Corps of Schofield's Army of the Ohio, brought up the 5th Indiana Battery and entrenched.[19]

While Howard's IV Corps was busy engaging portions of Hardee's corps and Stevenson's division, Schofield's XXIII Corps had their hands full with more Georgians under Stovall's Georgia Brigade of Clayton's division throughout the afternoon and evening of 20 July. Falling in the day's fighting were Captain Julius H. Barclay of Company G, 52nd Georgia, and nine others in the 52nd Georgia who were wounded and killed.[20] Colonel Edward M. Galt, of the 1st Georgia State Line troops that had just joined the brigade on 28 May, was wounded while directing his men.[21] The remaining division of Hood's

---

[14] Howard, *Autobiography*, 611.

[15] *OR*, ser. 1, vol. 38, pt. 1, serial 72, 225.

[16] Ibid., 276–78.

[17] John Obreiter, *The Seventy-Seventh Pennsylvania at Shiloh, History of the Regiment* (Harrison PA: Harrisburg Publishing Company, 1908) 210.

[18] *OR*, ser. 1, vol. 38, pt. 1, serial 72, pp. 268, 288.

[19] Ibid., 225, 233, 236–39.

[20] Gary Ray Goodson, Sr., *Georgia Confederate 7,000, Army of Tennessee, Part II: Letters and Diaries* (Shawnee CO: Goodson Enterprises, 2000) 76.

[21] *OR*, ser. 1, vol. 38, pt. 3, serial 74, p. 657; William R. Scaife, *The Campaign for Atlanta* (Atlanta: self-published, 1993) 180.

Hood's First Sortie, 20 July 1864

corps was Hindman's division led by General John C. Brown. It was also busy checking the advance of Schofield's XXIII Corps that had advanced along Briarcliff Road and was reaching to the North Decatur Road (along the Clifton Road corridor at Emory University). Further, Brown's men were watching the ominous gathering of McPherson's forces at Decatur beyond their right flank.[22] Meanwhile, on the extreme right of Brown's lines was Captain C. H. Mathews of the 39th Alabama of Deas's brigade. Mathews was killed while rallying his men to retard the advance of the Yankees under Logan's XV Corps near the Troup Hurt House along the Decatur Road.[23]

Sherman's Controversial Order. On the morning of 20 July, General Sherman moved his headquarters to the northwest intersection of Old Williams Road (the present North Decatur Road) and Briarcliff Road. There, Sherman pitched his tent and issued the following order: "Each army commander will accept battle on anything like fair terms, but if the army reach within cannon-range of the city without receiving artillery or musketry fire he will halt, form a strong line, with batteries in position, and await orders. If fired on from the forts or buildings of Atlanta no consideration must be paid to the fact that they are occupied by families, but the place must be cannonaded without the formality of a demand...[for surrender]."[24]

The Confederate attack that was supposed to begin at 1:00 had been delayed because of the pressure created from General James B. McPherson's Army of The Tennessee and its three veteran corps that were closing in on Atlanta from the east. Hood had hoped to launch his first assault as the newly appointed Southern commander shortly after noon and before the Yankees could strike at him. However, the first blows at Atlanta would be struck by the Northerners instead. Ironically, at 1:00, instead of the start of a Confederate attack, a Federal battery set its sights on the Gate City.[25]

Captain Francis De Gress, commanding Battery H, 1st Illinois Light Artillery, had been trading shots with Confederate artillerists all day. The Southerners were contesting his advance on Atlanta as De Gress supported the

---

[22] Scaife, *The Campaign for Atlanta*, 178–79.

[23] Willis Brewer, *Alabama: Her History, Resources, War Record, and Public Men, from 1540 to 1872* (Montgomery AL: Barrett & Brown, 1872) 649.

[24] William Key, *The Battle of Atlanta and the Georgia Campaign* (New York: Twayne Publishers, 1958) 49; Samuel Carter III, *The Siege of Atlanta, 1864* (New York: St. Martin's Press, 1973) 200.

[25] *OR*, ser. 1, vol. 38, pt. 3, serial 74, 3–12, 264–66, 358–59, 369; Scaife, *The Campaign for Atlanta*, 93.

advance of the XV Corps. This corps, commanded by Major General John A. Logan was moving along the Augusta railroad from Decatur. Logan's corps numbered about 10,000 infantry, plus artillery, a cavalry escort, and some staff. To Logan's left, the Army of the Tennessee's XVII Corps under Major General Francis P. Blair with about 8,000 infantry marched southwest from Decatur covering Logan's flank and heading toward a prominent hill known locally as Bald Hill. Since the war, this hill has been called Leggett's Hill, named after Federal general Mortimer Leggett whose 3rd Division, XVII Corps, Army of the Tennessee, together with General Giles A. Smith's 4th Division of the same corps, attacked and, after fierce fighting, drove Major General Patrick R. Cleburne's Confederate Division from the prominent hill on 21 July. General Leggett was wounded in the action but his men had accomplished their task of seizing the high ground. Leggett's successful attack precipitated General Hood's assault on the Federal left on 22 July near Decatur, in what has come to be called the Battle of Atlanta. Behind Logan's corps, the XVI Corps of Major General Grenville M. Dodge and his 10,000 veteran infantry followed in support. Thus, McPherson's three corps of the Army of the Tennessee, some 28,000 Infantry, pushed ever closer to Atlanta.[26]

Following Sherman's instructions to cannonade Atlanta if fired upon very loosely, De Gress unlimbered his 20-pounder Parrott rifled guns on a height overlooking Atlanta near the Troup Hurt House some 2 1/2 miles east of the city. The location is prominently featured in the famous painting at the Atlanta Cyclorama located in Grant Park and is close to where a tower was erected creating the vantage point where the Cyclorama was painted. Sherman's order, which said that if any Federal artillery unit got within range of Atlanta and received opposing fire from the city's forts or buildings, permitted his artillerists to return fire on the city regardless of civilian life. The eager De Gress could not wait to claim the honor of firing the first shells on the Gate City. His report stated that his battery "Advanced on the 20th, taking up position several times during the day and engaging rebel batteries. At 1 o'clock fired three shells into Atlanta at a distance of two miles and a half, *the first ones of the war* [emphasis added])." Major Thomas Davies Maurice proudly reported that Battery H, 1st Illinois Artillery "fired three shells into Atlanta, a distance of two and one-half miles, the first shells thrown in the town."[27] There was no mention of any Rebel

---

[26] *OR*, ser. 1, vol. 38, pt. 3, serial 74, pp. 3–12, 264–66, 358–59, 369; Scaife, *The Campaign for Atlanta*, 93.

[27] Scaife, *The Campaign for Atlanta*, 93, 103; Key, *Battle of Atlanta*, 49; Carter, *Siege of Atlanta*, 200; *Supplement to the Official Records of the Union and Confederate Armies*,

fire coming from the city or its forts in De Gress's report, but he justified his decision to fire on Atlanta by including that his men had been compelled to unlimber and trade fire with Rebel batteries. The Rebel batteries that De Gress was referring to were four guns attached to Wheeler's cavalry that had been desperately trying to hold off the Federal advance.

A Southern war correspondent, writing for the *Chattanooga Daily Rebel*, contributed this report of the state of affairs in Atlanta, "There are no inhabitants in Atlanta, save those whose poverty prevents the possibility of their removal… We hear no church bells to-day. The steady roar of heavy field pieces, the unsteady shriek of rifled shells, the anxiety of the poor people shut up here for no crime of theirs…"[28] By the time the newspaper writer penned this article, the Gate City was under siege, or at least a semi-siege, with sporadic shelling.

An often-told Atlanta Civil War story about the siege and bombardment of the city goes something like this: At about one o'clock that day (20 July) the City of Atlanta felt the first pains of Sherman's order as Federal artillery fire reached her streets for the first time. A man by the unusual name of Er Lawshe witnessed a child and her parents standing before Frank P. Rice's lumber yard as he passed the corner of Ivy and Ellis streets. The golden-haired girl had gone out into the dusty road in front of her parents' temporary home followed by a playful puppy. The "first shell fell at the intersection of East Ellis and Ivy streets, where it exploded and killed" the little girl and puppy. The two lay lifeless in a pool of blood on the northeast corner of the intersection of Ellis and Ivy (today called Peachtree Center Avenue) before her shocked and disbelieving father who had been knocked off of his feet on the front porch. Next to him lay his wife, mortally wounded from the blast. Their identity would never be known, except that they had sought refuge in Atlanta away from the war's path of destruction which had ravaged Tennessee and North Georgia. They were the first of many victims to Sherman's missiles on the Gate City. They would not be the last.[29] In the post-war reconstruction, bitter Southerners who talked about

---

(Wilmington NC: Broadfoot Publishing Company, 1995–2001) pt. 1, vol. 7, serial 7, pp. 44–48 (hereafter *Supplement to* OR).

[28] *Chattanooga* [Griffin GA] *Daily Rebel*, 27 July 1864, Tennessee State Library and Archives, microfilm 1045, roll 1, Nashville.

[29] Web Garrison, *Atlanta and the War* (Nashville: Rutledge Hill Press, 1995) 71; Carter, *Siege of Atlanta*, 200–201; A. A. Hoehling, *Last Train from Atlanta* (New York: Thomas Yoseloff, Printer, 1958) 113; Phil McCall, ed., "Private Isaiah Crook, 37th Ga., Smith's Brigade, Bate's Division, Hardee's Corps," vertical files, Kennesaw Mountain Battlefield Park Library, Kennesaw, Georgia; Castel, *Decision in the West*, 378; but see,

how dastardly the Yankees had been retold stories like this one about the little girl and her mother. Whether it is based on a true witness account or whether it is merely Southern folk lore hasn't mattered to inhabitants of Atlanta for over a hundred years since the "damned Yankees" came and destroyed their city, a curse word permitted by an otherwise lingually pure society.

During the first shelling, three of De Gress's shells fell on Atlanta's streets. These huge shells that may have killed the refugee girl and her mother and puppy came from De Gress's 20-pounder Parrott Battery that had taken up a position on a hill near today's Highland Avenue, a prominent height east of Atlanta where the Jimmy Carter Presidential Library stands today. Later, during the siege of Atlanta, one of the Yankee missiles struck a lamp post and exploded killing a well-known and -liked free black man named Solomon Luckie, a local barber. According to an account by historian Wallace Reed, Atlanta's first biographer with his *History of Atlanta* published in 1889, "Sol Luckie, a well-known barber, was standing on the Jame's Bank corner, on Whitehall and Alabama, when a shell struck a lamppost, ricocheted, and exploded. A fragment struck Luckie and knocked him down. Mr. Tom Crusselle and one or two other citizens picked up the unfortunate man," explained Reed, "and carried him into a store. He was then taken to the Atlanta Medical College, where Dr. [Noe] D'Alvigney amputated his leg. The poor fellow was put under the influence of morphine, but he never rallied from the shock, and died in a few hours."[30]

The lamppost that had deflected the shell fragment that fatally wounded Luckie became a symbol, ironically, of the Old South. In 1919, the United Daughters of the Confederacy (UDC) erected a memorial sign at the site explaining "the lamp post, shot down from this spot 15 August 1864, was replaced by the city and remains one of the few standing relics of your brave fight to save Atlanta." Later, the UDC placed a bronze tablet on the lamppost

---

Stephen Davis, "How Many Civilians Died in Sherman's Bombardment of Atlanta?," *Atlanta History: A Journal of Georgia and the South* 45/4 (2003): 6, that refutes the authenticity of this story. In Wallace P. Reed's *History of Atlanta, Georgia* (1889), Reed wrote of a little girl's death and added that its veracity was "confirmed by Col. Samuel Williams" who commanded Confederate artillery east of the city during the siege. Williams was Lt. Colonel Samuel C. Williams who indeed commanded a battalion (3 batteries) of artillery for Cheatham's (Hood's) corps during this time. Reed explains that Lawshe and Williams both witnessed the fall of the shell that killed the girl, her mother, and her puppy. See Wallace Putnam Reed, *History of Atlanta* (Syracuse NY: D. Mason & Company, 1889) 175; Scaife, *The Campaign for Atlanta*, 185.

[30] Reed, *History of Atlanta*, 191–92.

dedicating the place to Andrew J. West, a local veteran. Solomon Luckie's name was nowhere to be found. Amid the excitement surrounding the opening of the motion picture *Gone With the Wind*, on 14 December 1939, replete with old guardsmen wearing bearskin hats, a high school band playing "Dixie," and a grand speech by Mayor William B. Hartsfield, whose legacy would be his claim that Atlanta was "a city too busy to hate" during the turbulent Civil Rights and race riots in the 1950s, the UDC unveiled a new plaque designating the lamppost as the "Eternal Flame of the Confederacy." The post has since been moved to its current location in Underground Atlanta, a local tourist attraction, "below the Alabama and Peachtree entrance, very near its original site."[31] A street was later renamed Luckie Street after the popular barber who had not been lucky.[32] For the next forty days Atlanta would feel the pains of war on her streets, homes, churches, businesses, her citizens and refugee visitors.[33]

---

[31] Davis, "How Many Civilians Died," 6–8.
[32] McCall, "Private Isaiah Crook," 3; Garrison, *Atlanta and the War*, 200-201; Carter, *Siege of Atlanta*, 200–201; Hoehling, *Last Train*, 113.
[33] For an excellent discussion about civilian casualties during the bombardment of Atlanta and about the Southern correspondents who covered the siege, see Stephen Davis, "How Many Civilians Died in Sherman's Bombardment of Atlanta?," *Atlanta History: A Journal of Georgia and the South* 45/4 (2003): 4–23.

OLD RELIABLE

I am Brigade-officer-of-the-day today. And as it has been my luck heretofore to have trouble with the Yanks every time I am officer of the day—I suppose we will have a Muss of some sort. The Yanks have crossed the river above us and are coming, in fact they are shooting away to our right now, and have been since yesterday.[1]

William Joseph Hardee, the son of Major John Hardee of Pitt County, North Carolina, and the former Miss Sarah Ellis of Savannah, Georgia, was born 12 October 1815 at a place called Little Satilla Neck, Georgia, near the Georgia-Florida line. William Joseph, the youngest of seven children, would be destined to follow his family's military tradition. His father, John, earned the title of major during his service in the Georgia Militia during the War of 1812 after previously serving for two decades immediately following the Revolution. John's father, Joseph Hardee, came to Camden County, Georgia, just before hostilities broke out with the British and became a captain in the Georgia Militia during the Revolutionary War. From Native American raids and run-ins with outlaws in the nearby Okefenokee Swamp whose vast expanses harbored every element, to clashes with the Spanish and then the British, Camden County, Georgia, was the border for America during her first few decades and served as an outpost for the fledgling nation. It also proved to be a training ground for young William Joseph Hardee.[2]

After trying unsuccessfully for four years, William Joseph was finally granted admission to the United States Military Academy and only after intervention on his behalf by Georgia's governor, Wilson Lumpkin. Other than the career service of his father who had been a state legislator and militia leader, Hardee did not have much to offer the academy. His only schooling in Little Satilla Neck had come from tutoring by local attorney William J. Gipson who

---

[1] Samuel T. Foster, *One of Cleburne's Command, The Civil War Reminiscences and Diary of Captain Samuel T. Foster, Granbury's Texas Brigade, C.S.A.*, ed. Norman D. Brown (Austin: University of Texas Press, 1980) 107.

[2] Nathaniel Cheairs Hughes, Jr., *General William J. Hardee: Old Reliable*, 3–8.

had taken the fourteen-year-old under his wing and taught him the fundamentals of "English, education, reading, writing, grammar, arithmetic, 'moral philosophy,' and 'the elements of Euclid.'" Gipson even found time to introduce Hardee to Latin and French before sending the boy north to New York at the age of nineteen. Perhaps wondering whether his pupil would measure up at West Point, Gipson remarked that Hardee was 5', 4" tall "and free from any bodily defect" at the time of his departure. For the next four years, Hardee would make the most of his opportunity. Graduating twenty-sixth out of forty-five in the class of 1838, Hardee's West Point career could be described as mediocre at best. Considering that he had come from the rural outpost of South Georgia and did not have the benefit of formal preparatory schools like most of his fellow cadets, however, young Hardee had done well.[3]

Hardee spent the next eighteen years in the United States Army in various roles, including serving as a lieutenant in the 2nd Dragoons (cavalry) during the Second Seminole Indian War. He was also selected to attend a prestigious French cavalry school in Paris for a year, and he later observed British military tactics in England for several weeks. By age twenty-seven, Hardee had acquired all of the best military knowledge and training that America, France, and England had to offer. At the time, France was regarded as having the best-trained army in the world while England continued to enjoy the reputation of owning the finest navy on the high seas. It was little wonder, then, after successful stints during the Mexican War and service on the Texas frontier, that Hardee would be destined to write a new series of tactics, to become published and adopted by the United States Army, and called *Hardee's Rifle and Light Infantry Tactics*, or simply, *Hardee's Tactics*, and used by officers of both armies during the Civil War.[4]

When war clouds descended on the country, Hardee tendered his resignation as a lieutenant colonel in the United States Army and joined the Confederate cause, serving with distinction during the early part of the war in raising and training troops. Up until the Georgia Campaign, Hardee's war record could be best described as competent, but not brilliant. His first significant Civil War combat service was at Shiloh where he earned the moniker Old Reliable by his men. At Shiloh, Hardee effectively brought his men into action during the first day despite being given an unwieldy plan of attack by commanding general Albert S. Johnston. Hardee was wounded in the arm

---

[3] Ibid., 9–13.

[4] Ibid., 14–50; William J. Hardee, *Hardee's Rifle and Light Infantry Tactics*.

during the second day's fighting as his men strove to stave off disaster by the reinforced Yankees. Hardee had ignored warnings during the previous night from General Nathan B. Forrest about the reinforcing by the enemy.[5]

After the Confederate army fell back to Corinth following their defeat at Shiloh, Hardee continued his service as a corps commander under Generals P. G. T. Beauregard and Braxton Bragg. While Hardee may have tolerated working under Bragg for a season, by October 1862, after the withdrawal from Kentucky following the Confederate defeat at the Battle of Perryville, he became one of the most outspoken officers against Bragg. During this time, Hardee and Polk became allies and Polk's disdain for Bragg began to affect Hardee. After the Perryville battle, Hardee became a leader in the anti-Bragg revolution among the officers in the Army of Tennessee. As a mentor to junior officers, it was his temperament to "enjoy criticism of Bragg's operations, yet he disliked responsibility himself," according to historian Thomas Connelly, who added, "Hardee specialized in frank conversations with his staff, division and brigade officers. In an atmosphere resembling a military academy classroom, he combined direct criticism and innuendo to demolish Bragg's reputation with the junior officers of [Hardee's] Second Corps."[6] It is little wonder then, when Davis offered him the command of the army in December 1863, that Hardee refused it. Perhaps Old Reliable knew that he was not up to the task of being the commander of an army, only of second-guessing one. One could hardly blame Davis, then, for looking past Hardee in July 1864 for Johnston's replacement. Now, Hardee had to take orders from his one-time junior officer, John Bell Hood.

The day of 20 July found Hardee contemplating how to carry out his new commander's order to attack while his sweat-soaked men baked in the hot summer sun. Hardee had at Peach Tree Creek approximately 17,973 infantry men, 1,201 artillerists, and 287 staff and escort troops, for a total force of 19,461 men available for the attack. He also had another 300 men from the 24th South Carolina Infantry who would be detached from his corps to serve with

---

[5] James Lee McDonough and James Pickett Jones, *War So Terrible, Sherman and Atlanta*, (New York: W. W. Norton & Company, 1987) 209. James Lee McDonough, *Shiloh, in Hell before Night* (Knoxville: University of Tennessee Press, 1977) 70, 194–95; O. Edward Cunningham, *Shiloh and the Western Campaign of 1862* (New York: Savas Beatie, 2007) 191, 200, 234, 334, 364, 402; Larry J. Daniel, *Shiloh, The Battle that Changed the War* (New York: Simon & Schuster, 1997) 149, 272–73.

[6] Thomas L. Connelly, *Autumn of Glory, The Army of Tennessee, 1862–1865* (Baton Rouge: Louisiana State Press, 1971) 21–22, 288–92.

Hood's First Sortie, 20 July 1864

Walthall's division during the battle. Thus, Hardee's corps mustered some 19,761 strong on the morning of 20 July.[7]

Hardee's men were to be the hammer and heaviest part of the assault, with Stewart's Army of Mississippi to join in and press just as hard once Hardee's boys got things going. From right to left, Hardee aligned Major General William B. Bate's division with his three brigades on the right, Major General William H. T. Walker's division of three brigades in the center, and the division of Major General Benjamin F. Cheatham commanded by Brigadier General George E. Maney (hereinafter referred to as Maney's division) on the left with four brigades. Maney took over the division on 19 July after Cheatham had taken over temporary command of Hood's corps. A fourth division, commanded by Major General Patrick R. Cleburne with four brigades, was held in reserve to be used to exploit any gain that was made.[8]

Bate's division mustered some 3,275 men present on 10 July, with Walker's division numbering 5,559 men. Maney's division listed 4,733 men present and Cleburne's division return showed 5,478 men on that day. Including his artillery corps of 1,201 men and his staff and escort of 287 men, Hardee had 20,533 aggregate present on 10 July. Also, according to the 10 July report, Hardee had forty-seven pieces of cannon accompanying his corps. Removing the artillerists and escort staff from Hardee's attacking force for purposes of evaluating the size and strength of the infantry available for Hardee's charge, there were just over 19,000 infantry present for duty. Taking into consideration some loss of men due to illness and some minor skirmishing during the 10 days from the date of the 10 July report and the morning of 20 July, it is reasonable to assume that Hardee had about 18,500 infantry available to him on 20 July for the attack.[9]

The effective strength of Hardee's corps on 20 July is further evidenced by a memorandum found by Federal forces at an abandoned Confederate camp on 18 July 1864 that listed the estimated strength of Hardee's corps on that date at

---

[7] "Abstract of Returns of the Army of Tennessee," 10 July 1864, in United States War Department, comp., *Official Records of the Union and Confederate Armies in the War of the Rebellion*, 128 vols. (Washington, DC: Government Printing Office, 1880–1901) ser. I, vol. 38, pt. 3, p. 679 (hereafter *OR*); "Compiled Service Records of Confederate Soldiers Who Served in Organizations from the Union and Confederate States of America during the War of the Rebellion," RG 269, National Archives, Washington, DC.

[8] Ibid. OR series I, 38, pt3, serial 74, 679; William R. Scaife, *The Campaign for Atlanta* (Atlanta: self-published, 1993) 173–78.

[9] "Abstract of Returns of the Army of Tennessee," 10 July 1864, in *OR*, ser. [#?], vol. 38, pt. 3, serial 74, p. 679; Scaife, *The Campaign for Atlanta*, 173–78.

The Battle of Peach Tree Creek

18,400. In that document, the estimated strength of Hardee's divisions is listed as follows: Bate's division, 3,000; Walker's division, 5,700; Maney's division, 4,800; and Cleburne's division, 4,900. Hardee's corps was nearly twice the size of either of the other two Confederate corps at Atlanta. Hardee, therefore, probably had in his control some 18,500 infantry for the attack, over 40 percent of Hood's total available mobile force from all three corps.[10]

On the far right of the attacking column, Bate lined up his division from right to left as follows: on the right, Finley's Florida Brigade, in the center Smith's Georgia and Tennessee Brigade, and on the left, Lewis's Kentucky "Orphan" Brigade.[11] General Jesse J. Finley's Florida Brigade numbered about 1,000 strong. In Finley's brigade were the 1st and 3rd Florida Cavalry Consolidated (dismounted), the 1st and 4th Florida Infantry Consolidated, the 6th Florida and the 7th Florida regiments. General Thomas B. Smith's brigade of Georgians and Tennesseans consisting of about 1,300 men dressed off to Finley's left. This brigade had been previously commanded by General Bate, the division commander, and then by Brigadier General R. C. Tyler, who was severely wounded and rendered incapacitated at Missionary Ridge on 25 November 1863. Smith's brigade consisted of the 4th Georgia Sharpshooters, 37th Georgia, 20th Tennessee, 30th Tennessee, and the 15th and 37th Tennessee consolidated regiments.[12] General Joseph H. Lewis's famous Kentucky Orphan Brigade, which had been reduced from 1,512 men on 7 May at the beginning of the campaign to 1,002 men fit for duty by 20 July, was on the left of Bate's attacking column.[13] Lewis's Orphans included the 2nd, 4th, 5th, 6th, and 9th Kentucky regiments. Thus, Bate's division totaled some 3,302 men in line for the attack.

In order for Hood's plan to succeed, Bate's veterans would need to strike the end of the exposed Federal line, turn its left, and begin rolling up the Yankee line. Then, as additional Confederate troops joined in the battle,

---

[10] *OR*, ser. I, vol. 38, pt. V, serial 76, pp. 178–79.

[11] Scaife, *The Campaign for Atlanta*, 88–93; Wilbur G. Kurtz, map, Special Collections, Atlanta Historical Society Museum.

[12] *OR*, ser., vol. 23, pt. V, chap. 50, pp. 178–79; "Abstract of Returns of the Army of Tennessee," 10 July 1864, in *OR*, ser. I, vol. 38, pt. 3, serial 74, 679; Scaife, *The Campaign for Atlanta*, 173–78; *Tennesseans in the Civil War, A Military History of Confederate and Union Units with Available Rosters of Personnel*, 2 vols. (Nashville: Civil War Centennial Commission, 1964–1965) 1:218; John Berrien Lindsley, ed., *Military Annals of Tennessee, Confederate*, 2 vols. (Wilmington NC: Broadfoot Publishing Company, 1995) 1:452–53.

[13] William C. Davis, *The Orphan Brigade: The Kentucky Confederates Who Couldn't Go Home* (Baton Rouge: Louisiana State University Press, 1980) 227–29.

Hood's First Sortie, 20 July 1864

Newton's division would be destroyed on the south bank of Peach Tree Creek. "Bate's Division had a key role. It would be the enveloping element, attacking the enemy left and starting the process of rolling up the Union line...," according to biographer Nathaniel Cheairs Hughes.[14] It was critical that Bate and his brigadiers reconnoiter and determine what Federal force was located in their front. Because Hardee and his corps had to move to the right over a mile and a half before mounting their assault, his subordinate commanders had failed to scout the Federal positions in front of them, even though there was ample time to investigate the ground during the three hours it took to change position. Why this was not done remains a mystery. One explanation is that Hardee did not consider it. He did not order his division commanders to perform a reconnaissance, and his chief concern appears to have been linking up with Cheatham's corps to his right rather than with preparing for an assault.

In the center of Hardee's corps, General Walker lined up his veterans: General Hugh Mercer's Georgia Brigade was on the right with about 2,000 men. Mercer's brigade was made up of the 1st, 54th, 57th, and 63rd Georgia regiments. General Clement H. Stevens's Georgia Brigade formed on the left being guided by the Buckhead Road on its left with some 1,500 "Georgia Crackers," which included the 1st Georgia Confederate, 25th, 29th, 30th, and 66th Georgia regiments, and the 1st Georgia Sharpshooters. General States Rights Gist made up the center of Walker's division with his brigade of about 1,200 Georgians and South Carolinians together with some 1,000 Mississippians and Georgians from the newly arrived regiments of General John R. Jackson's brigade that had been broken up and temporarily attached to Gist. These regiments included the 2nd Georgia Sharpshooters, the 65th Georgia, and the 8th Mississippi.[15] Gist's brigade included the 8th Georgia Battalion, 46th Georgia, 16th South Carolina, and the 24th South Carolina, and the remnants of Jackson's old brigade.[16] The 24th South Carolina would wind up joining

---

[14] Hughes, *The Pride of the Confederate Artillery: The Washington Artillery in the Army of Tennessee* (Baton Rouge: Louisiana State University Press, 1997) 196.

[15] Ray Roddy, *The Georgia Volunteer Infantry, 1861–1865* (Kearney NE: Morris Publishing, 1998) 63, 285; *OR*, ser. 1, vol. 35, pt. 1, serial 65, pp. 70, 125, 128; Scaife, *The Campaign for Atlanta*, 177. The 5th Georgia had been serving guard duty at Andersonville, and, on 4 July 1864, they were sent to Savannah. The 47th Georgia was also sent to Savannah on 4 July, where they participated in the defense of Charleston Harbor and Burden's Causeway in South Carolina from 7–10 July.

[16] *OR*, ser. I, vol. 38, pt. V, chap. 50, pp. 178–79; "Abstract of Returns of the Army of Tennessee," 10 July 1864, in *OR*, ser.I, vol. 38, pt. 3, serial 74, 679; Scaife, *The Campaign for Atlanta*, 173–78; Walter Brian Cisco, *States Rights Gist: A South Carolina General of the*

Walthall's division during the attack, supporting O'Neal's brigade near the Mt. Zion Church along Howell Mill Road. During the pre-assault shift to the right down the Confederate trenches, the 24th South Carolina was ordered to shield the movement by placing a screen, or skirmish line, and after Hardee's corps had shifted to the right, the South Carolinians were located a mile or two west of the balance of Gist's brigade. Thus, Gist's brigade, minus the 300 veterans of the 24th South Carolina, would line up for the assault, some 1,900 strong.

On Walker's left, Stevens's brigade stepped off in battle line, its left resting astride the Buckhead Road (today's Peachtree Street) with General Stevens in command. General Clement Hoffman Stevens was born in Norwich, Connecticut, on 14 August 1821. Before the war, he was a banker and inventor. After hostilities began, he used his talents as an inventor to design the ironclad battery that served in Charleston Harbor. Nicknamed "Rock" by his men, Stevens served with Generals Barnard Bee and States Rights Gist at the Battle of First Manassas, where Rock was wounded.[17] Stevens next raised and commanded the 24th South Carolina Volunteers beginning in 1 April 1862. Subsequently, Stevens served as a brigade commander in the Army of Tennessee where he was severely wounded in the breast and arm at Chickamauga on September 20, 1863, but he recovered in time to return to duty by the new year.[18]

Stevens's brigade of veterans from the Peach State lined up with Colonel James Cooper Nisbet and his 66th Georgia on the left of the brigade. Colonel Nisbet's regiment contained about 325 men, which included the three companies of the 26th Georgia Battalion that he had raised in addition to the ten companies that comprised the 66th Georgia, which Nisbet had also formed. Nisbet had seen much action during the war in General Lee's Army of Northern Virginia. After this time, he obtained a commission to raise a new regiment in Georgia that he called the "Bloody 66th."[19] Nisbet placed the 26th Georgia

---

Civil War (Shippensburg PA: White Mane Publishing Company, 1991) 126.

[17] www.geocities.com/BourbonStreet/Square/3873/gist.html (1 March 2008).

[18] Eugene W. Jones, Jr., *Enlisted for the War: The Struggles of the Gallant 24th Regiment, South Carolina Volunteers, Infantry, 1861–1865* (Highstown NJ: Longstreet House, 1997) 405. Clement H. Stevens's mother was Ann Bee Stevens of the Pendleton District in South Carolina, and his brother-in-law was General Bernard E. Bee, the famous South Carolinian who said, "Look, there stands Jackson [referring to Virginia general, Thomas J. "Stonewall" Jackson] standing like a stone wall. Rally behind the Virginians!" on the First Manasas battlefield just before General Bee was killed.

[19] Bell Irvin Wiley, foreword to *4 Years on the Firing Line* by James Cooper Nisbet, ed. Bell Irvin Wiley (Jackson TN: McCowat-Mercer Press, 1963) ix–xx.

Battalion under the command of his brother, Major John W. Nisbet. Colonel Nisbet dressed the left of his unit on the Buckhead Road as they prepared for the charge.[20]

To Nisbet's right, the 1st Georgia Confederate Regiment under the command of Colonel George A. Smith formed in battle formation. Consisting of about 250 men, mostly from Northwest Georgia, these Georgia crackers were veterans of Chickamauga and Chattanooga, and most of them had seen their homes overrun by the invading Yankees in the 1864 campaign during Johnston's withdrawals, causing many to be in despair. The balance of Stevens's brigade dressed to the right of the 1st Georgia Confederate, namely the 29th Georgia, 25th Georgia, and 30th Georgia with the 1st Georgia Battalion Sharpshooters out front as skirmishers.

To the right of Stevens's brigade, Gist's brigade of veterans from Georgia, Mississippi, and South Carolina lined up. Given the unusual name States Rights Gist, he was born on 3 September 1831 in the Union District of South Carolina. Attending what later became the University of South Carolina and Harvard, Gist "practiced law and became involved in politics and the militia. He was a brigadier in the militia prior to the war and served as Inspector General of the State of South Carolina after secession."[21] States Rights Gist assumed command after the death of General Barnard Bee at First Manassas. Gist subsequently was promoted to brigadier on 20 March 1862 and assigned to South Carolina. After serving briefly in Wilmington, North Carolina, and Mississippi during the first Vicksburg Campaign, Gist's brigade was assigned to Bragg's Army of Tennessee where he served during the battles around Chattanooga and where he "was wounded at Chickamauga and rendered valuable service in the retreat from Missionary Ridge."[22]

---

[20] Nisbet, *4 Years on the Firing Line*, ix–xx, 209.

[21] Gist was a member of South Carolina's aristocracy. Gist's brother Joseph also served the Confederacy as a brigadier general of the militia after previously serving as a major in the 15th South Carolina. William Henry Gist, a cousin, became governor of South Carolina during the war. www.geocities.com/BourbonStreet/Square/3873/gist.html. (1 March 2008).

[22] Gist would be wounded again in the Atlanta campaign, and he would be killed leading his troops forward in the suicidal charge at Franklin. The South Carolinian general with the peculiar name is buried at Trinity Episcopal near his friend, the bishop and general Ellison Capers. www.geocities.com/BourbonStreet/Square/3873/gist.html. (1 March 2008).

The Battle of Peach Tree Creek

To the left of Walker's 4,900 veterans, General Maney placed his all-Tennessee division in the following order: on the right of the division was Mageveny's brigade (formerly Vaughan's brigade) with its 1,200 "Volunteers" commanded by Colonel Michael Magevney, General Alfred J. Vaughan, Jr., having been wounded on 7 July near Vining Station.[23] Magevney's brigade consisted of the 11th, the 12th and 47th consolidated, the 27th, and the 13th and 154th consolidated Tennessee regiments. To Mageveny's left, General Otho F. Strahl's "Volunteers" came next with some 1,000 veterans from the 4th and 5th consolidated, the 19th, 24th, 31st, and the 33rd Tennessee regiments. To Strahl's left was Maney's old brigade commanded by Colonel Francis M. Walker consisting of 1,200 "Volunteers" from the 1st and 27th consolidated, 4th Confederate, 6th and 9th consolidated, 41st, and the 50th Tennessee regiments. On the left of Maney's division, Colonel John H. Anderson of the 8th Tennessee Regiment led Wright's Tennessee brigade and its 1,400 "Volunteers" from the 8th, 16th, 28th, 38th, and the 51st and 52nd consolidated Tennessee regiments.[24] Thus, Maney's Tennessee division stepped off to meet their foe some 4,800 strong.[25]

In reserve, Hardee placed Cleburne's four brigades behind the center of his corps and in position to exploit any breakthrough accomplished by his initial assault. Cleburne's lined up his brigades along the Buck Head Road behind Maney's and Walker's divisions. On the far left, behind Strahl's brigade, was General Lucius Polk's brigade of 1,000 Arkansans and Tennesseans which included the 1st and 15th Arkansas Consolidated, the 5th Confederate, the 2nd Tennessee, and the 35th and 48th Tennessee Consolidated. Next, left, behind Walker's brigade, was General Hiram M. Granbury's Texas brigade of 1,200 men, including the 6th and 15th cavalry (dismounted), 7th, 10th, 17th and 18th

---

[23] Scaife, *The Campaign for Atlanta*, 174.

[24] Colonel Anderson previously led the brigade briefly after the Battle of Missionary Ridge when General Wright was assigned to duty at Atlanta as a district or post commander. But, during their encampment in winter quarters from November 1863 to May 1864 at Dalton, Colonel John C. Carter of the 38th Tennessee was placed in command of the brigade when his regiment returned from duty at Charleston, Tennessee. Colonel Carter, who would be mortally wounded on his boyhood farm on 30 November 1864 during the Battle of Franklin, led the brigade throughout the Georgia campaign until the army arrived at the doorsteps of Atlanta, and on 7 July1864, he was promoted to brigadier general. For reasons that are unclear, during the battle of 20 July Wright's brigade was led by Colonel Anderson.

[25] *OR*, ser. I, vol. 38, pt. V, serial. 50, pp. 178–79; "Abstract of Returns of the Army of Tennessee," 10 July 1864, in *OR*, ser. I, vol. 38, pt. 3, serial 74, p. 679; Scaife, *The Campaign for Atlanta*, 173–78.

Hood's First Sortie, 20 July 1864

Cavalry (dismounted), and the 24th and 25th Cavalry (dismounted) Texas regiments, which made Cleburne's force some 4,971 strong.[26] General Lowery's brigade was placed behind Steven's brigade, which would occupy the hottest part of Hardee's line.[27] From his position along the Buckhead Road, General Mark P. Lowrey, commanded some 1,500 Alabamians and Mississippians from the 16th, 33rd, and 45th Alabama and the 32nd and 45th Mississippi regiments. His brigade spearhead any supporting attack from Cleburne's division. On the far right and behind Gist's brigade was General Daniel C. Govan's brigade of 1,211 Arkansans made up of the 2nd and 24th Arkansas Consolidated, 5th and 13th Arkansas Consolidated, 6th and 7th Arkansas Consolidated, 8th and 19th Arkansas Consolidated, and the 3rd Confederate regiments.[28]

In Granbury's Texas brigade, one Captain predicted misfortune on 20 July: "I am Brigade-officer-of-the-day today. And as it has been my luck heretofore to have trouble with the Yanks every time I am officer of the day—I suppose we will have a Muss of some sort. The Yanks have crossed the river above us and are coming, in fact they are shooting away to our right now, and have been since yesterday."[29] The Texas captain, Foster, would find a "muss of some sort" as his brigade would watch the carnage sustained by some of the Southern units in Hardee's corps in front of his Texans, but at least twenty men from Granbury's brigade would also become casualties, mostly from shelling and grape shot.[30]

During the morning of 20 July, the 16th South Carolina and the 46th Georgia of Gist's brigade, which had been posted on picket duty near the Howell Mill the day before, rejoined their brigade as they prepared to assault the Yankees. According to one South Carolina captain, "Wednesday moved out

---

[26] *OR*, ser. I, vol. 38, pt. V, chap. 50, pp. 178–79; "Abstract of Returns of the Army of Tennessee," 10 July 1864, in *OR*, ser. I, vol. 38, pt. 3, serial 74, p. 679; Scaife, *The Campaign for Atlanta*, 173–78; Foster, *One of Cleburne's Command*, 107.

[27] Lowrey reported losing forty-five men in "a little skirmishing" at Peach Tree Creek. Lowery, *OR*, ser. 1, vol. 38, pt. V, p. 733.

[28] Govan's brigade strength is derived by adding the effective total of his brigade on 23 July 1864, which was 722 men, plus the casualties of the 22 July battle at Decatur, which totaled 489 troops. No casualties were reported by Govan's brigade at Peach Tree Creek, although it is possible that the brigade sustained a few men slightly wounded based upon both the returns of her sister brigades and the location of the brigade during the action (*OR*, ser. 1, vol. 38, pt. 3, 741).

[29] Foster, *One of Cleburne's Command*, 107.

[30] *OR*, ser. 1, vol. 38, pt. 3, 741.

on the same road [Howell Mill Road] a half mile or more in front of entrenchments at day break—remained for some hours, left 24th So. Car. on picket and went to our bivouac of two preceding nights, had only been here [briefly] when we had 60 rounds of cartridges [issued] & moved out to attack the enemy."[31]

During the evening of 19 July, Major T. R. Hotchkiss's Artillery battalion, which included Key's Arkansas battery, was camped in a field west of the Huff House. "Major Hotchkiss established his headquarters at the Huff house about the same time Cleburne was at the Whitehead house." Sarah Huff, an eight-year-old child, remembered just before the battle "when orders came to move this outfit up toward Peachtree Creek—recalled the shouting of orders—the trample of horse's hoofs—the 'hitching up' of the steeds and the rumble of the heavy guns down the road."[32]

---

[31] "The Letters and Papers of Charles Manning Furman," http://batsonsm.tripod.com/letters/letters9.html (1 March 2008).

[32] The home of Jeremiah Huff was located at today's 70 Huff Road, about three-quarters of a mile due east of the Whitehead House which was the home of Archibald Whitehead located at the old Marietta Road near Johnson Road. Wilbur G. Kurtz, Sr., "Captain Thomas J. Key's Battery which was at the Battle of Peachtree Creek, July 20, 1864" (letter to members of the Atlanta Civil War Roundtable, 19 May 1955), MSS 130, scrapbook 28, Wilbur G. Kurtz Papers, Kenan Research Center, Atlanta History Center.

6

THE BLOODY MAGNOLIAS

It is a fearful thing to charge an enemy in his works, especially when outnumbered two or three to one, but feeling that it had to be done we nerved ourselves up to this point to do our whole duty. So when orders came to form in front of the breastworks we were ready.[1]

On 20 July, Stewart prepared the three divisions of his Army of Mississippi[2] for the pending attack with Loring on the right, Walthall in the center, and French on the left. Loring's division was to strike first from Stewart's corps as he was directed to continue Hardee's attack, and the other two divisions were to support Loring's movement. Hood's orders to Hardee and Stewart called for the assault to be made "in echelon by division leaving 200-yard intervals between each division" and "to attack the enemy, drive him back to the creek, and then press down the creek to the left."

An echelon attack meant that as each brigade or division moved forward, the next one followed suit by moving forward to support the flank of the first unit. As synchronizing watches or marking an exact time for an attack or action was a concept that had not yet arrived, an attacking force during the Civil War often times was directed to make an attack in sequence to ensure that each unit moving forward did so in conjunction with the other attacking units. At Peach Tree Creek, Hood's attackers were spread out along a 4-mile front in wooded and hilly terrain from the northern tip of today's Piedmont Park to near Crestlawn Cemetery. They could not see when other units moved forward or attacked, but could only see the movements of the units located immediately to their left or right. By ordering an attack "in echelon by division" with each of

---

[1] J. P. Cannon, *A History of the 27th Regiment Alabama Infantry. "Bloody Banners and Barefoot Boys,"* ed. Noel Crowson and John V. Brogden (Shippensburg PA: Burd Street Press, 1997) 84.

[2] Stewart's corps was known as the Army of Mississippi, until 26 July 1864 when General Hood merged Stewart's corps into the Army of Tennessee. Special Field Orders 58, in United States War Department, comp., *Official Records of the Union and Confederate Armies in the War of the Rebellion*, 128 vols. (Washington, DC: Government Printing Office, 1880–1901) ser. 1, vol. 38, pt. 5, serial 76, p. 912 (hereafter *OR*).

The Battle of Peach Tree Creek

Hardee's and Stewart's divisions being no more than 200 yards apart, Hood was hopefully guaranteeing that all of his force would strike the Federal positions at approximately the same time and that none of his attacking units would be isolated in their attack. Unfortunately, this plan would not be adhered to by Hardee and his units, which would lead to disaster to Stewart's men.[3]

General Loring received his orders from General Stewart at an early hour on the morning of 20 July that an attack was to be made against General Thomas's Army of the Cumberland. Thomas's men, within his IV, XIV, and XX corps, were stretched across the few bridges and fords over Peach Tree Creek in that area. They were exposed to an attack as their backs were to the creek and they were too far away to receive support from McPherson and Schofield, just as Johnston had previously planned.

With two of his brigade commanders, Loring examined the ground over which his men were to charge. General Adams and his Mississippi Brigade were on picket duty guarding the approaches and fords on the Chattahoochee River to the west, leaving Loring's division with only the two brigades of Featherston's Mississippians and Scott's Alabamians and Louisianans to make the assault. They numbered only about 2,700 men present for duty. Loring and his brigadiers confirmed that the Federals were crossing Peach Tree Creek and were about 2 miles away.

Major General William Wing Loring was a unique character. Already a veteran of two wars, he was respected for his tenacity in battle. While much admired by his men and many of his peers, Loring had quite a temper. Frequently he quarreled with other officers, including those who outranked him, which needless to say impaired his chance for advancement. Born in Wilmington, North Carolina, on 14 December 1818, the second son of Reuben and Hannah Kenan Loring, William Wing Loring was named for an original Plymouth colony family. After Florida became an American territory free from

---

[3] Ordering an attack in echelon provided another potential advantage for the attackers, as well, as often times when a defending party receives an attack in one part of its line, it will move troops from another area to reinforce the area being threatened, thus weakening or creating a gap in the defenses in front of the attack. This situation occurred at the Battle of Chickamauga where the attacking Confederates broke through the Federal lines after a mistake in orders created an unnecessary movement of a part of the Northern defenders just before that same part of the line was struck. Some historians have argued that this is the reason that Hood ordered an attack in echelon by division at Peach Tree Creek, though nothing in the record suggests it. Apparently, Hood's sole plan was to ensure that his attacking columns worked in conjunction with each other and that they would catch the Federals off guard as they crossed the creek and before they had time to entrench.

Hood's First Sortie, 20 July 1864

Spanish control in 1821, the Lorings settled in St. Augustine in 1823 where William Loring grew into manhood. It seemed that Loring was destined to be a career soldier. At the age of fourteen Loring volunteered for the Florida Militia in the 11th Regiment, 2nd Brigade, where he was known as the "Boy Soldier." By the age of seventeen, Loring had been promoted to sergeant. During this time, the Seminole War erupted and Loring got his first taste of battle. The Seminole War lasted from 1835 to 1842 and by the time that the war had ended, young Loring had become a seasoned veteran at the age of twenty-three.[4]

Described as a volatile man with a great gift for profanity, Loring, it was said, could cuss an artillery piece or wagon up a muddy hill, almost without assistance of a horse. Many were afraid of him for he chafed and roared like a lion, especially in a crisis. Loring could come out with big oaths and will men to do more than they believed possible. Profanity was not only Loring's trademark, it was a way of life. He was a master craftsman in a particular linguistic art, working in words the way that another artisan worked with clay or paint. It was his true medium.

Loring's long black hair had curled up at the end but was now thinning and gray. Earlier in the war he had been called "Old Ringlets" because of his hair. Now, most of his division called him "Old Blizzards."[5] In a battle at Fort Pemberton during the Yazoo Pass Expedition in the Mississippi River Delta during spring 1863, Loring displayed one of his usual verbal outbursts when his cotton-battery fort was being attacked by Federal gunboats and ironclads. At 5 feet, 11 inches tall, the man had a considerable amount of fire in him. Being short of ammunition, and realizing that if the Federal boats were not turned back Loring's men would have to retreat and the way to Vicksburg from the north would be open, the one-armed general paced across the top of the cotton bales defiantly waiting until the gunboats got in close, when he began prancing back and forth "shouting and cursing purple oaths, his spittle flying, encouraging his men, 'Give them blizzards, boys! Give them Blizzards!' The name would stick around, but the Federal gun boats did not. After several days of trying to break

---

[4] James Rabb, *W. W. Loring, Florida's Forgotten General* (Manhattan KS: Sunflower University Press, 1996) 1–3; Sam Davis Elliott, ed., *Doctor Quintard Chaplain & Second Bishop of Tennessee, The Memoir and Civil War Diary of Charles Todd Quintard* (Louisiana: Louisiana State University Press, 2003) 47-49.

[5] Walter A. Rorer to "Cousin Susan," 2 February 1864, vertical files, Carter House, Franklin, Tennessee.

the Confederate cotton battery without success, the badly crippled gunboats withdrew.[6]

Beginning near today's Loring Height Subdivision, Loring placed General Featherston's brigade on the right and General Scott's brigade to the left of Featherston. With the absence of General Adam's Mississippi brigade as well as parts of Featherston's and Scott's brigades serving picket duty to the west, Loring would have to make the most of his attack at something less than two-third strength. While Loring's division was about 4,500 men, only 1,230 troops in Featherston's brigade and 1,450 troops in Scott's brigade would be available for the attack. Adams's 1,500 Mississippians would not be available for Loring. He would have to make do with just 2,700 men.[7]

Featherston lined up his veterans for the attack, 1,230 strong. The 40th Mississippi led by Lieutenant Colonel George P. Wallace was on the far left. Next, the 31st Mississippi commanded that day by Lieutenant Colonel James Drane formed the left center of the brigade. In the middle, Featherston placed the 22nd Mississippi under Major Martin A. Oatis. Forming the right center of the brigade, the 3rd Mississippi under the command of Colonel Thomas A. Mellon lined up. On the extreme right of the brigade, the 33rd Mississippi directed by Colonel Jabez L. Drake, was placed. In front, the 1st Mississippi Battalion Sharpshooters led by Major James M. Stigler, together with a few companies from Featherston's regiments including Company F, the "Calhoun Tigers" of the 31st Mississippi from Calhoun County, were deployed forward of the brigade as skirmishers.

To Featherston's left, Brigadier General Thomas M. Scott's brigade of Alabamians and Louisianans formed. Scott, a native Alabamian, moved to Louisiana prior to the war and commanded the 12th Louisiana before being promoted to brigade command. Scott was a "tall, slim, sharp visaged gentleman, with sandy hair and beard." He was about forty years old and described as "neat in appearance and of a soldierly bearing."[8]

Scott lined up his brigade left to right, or west to east, with the consolidated regiment of the 27th Alabama under Colonel James Jackson, the 35th Alabama with Colonel Samuel S. Ives, and the 49th Alabama and Lieutenant Colonel John D. Weeden was placed on the left and led by Colonel

---

[6] Rabb, *W. W. Loring*, 94–97, 111.

[7] *OR*, ser. I, vol. 38, pt. 5, serial 76, pp. 178–79; *OR*, ser. I, vol. 38, pt. 3, serial 74, pp. 876–84.

[8] Walter A. Rorer to "Cousin Susan," 22 March 1864, vertical files, Carter House, Franklin, Tennessee.

Ives. In the center, Scott placed his old command, the 12th Louisiana, under the direction of Colonel Noel L. Nelson. This veteran regiment was described as a "fine one…composed of Louisiana's best young men, such men as never desert nor run away."[9] One major from another brigade said of the 12th Louisiana, a twelve-company regiment, "they will live on a pound of poor beef and a pound of coarse corn meal per day and fight the enemy indefinitely."[10] The same could be said of most of the regiments in the Confederate Army by this point in the campaign. To the right of the 12th Louisiana, Scott placed the 55th Alabama led by Colonel John Snodgrass on the right center. The 57th Alabama led by Lieutenant Colonel William C. Bethune formed the extreme right of the brigade.

To Loring's left, Major General Edward C. Walthall's and Major General Samuel G. French's divisions were also getting ready. Walthall's division mustered about 4,000 officers and men present for duty on 10 July, while French's division mustered only about 3,300 officers and men.[11] According to a captured memorandum of the estimated strength of Hood's Army, Walthall's force on 18 July was 4,000 men while French's division numbered 4,200 men. The reason for the discrepancy in the returns for French's division was that his brigades had been covering the rear of the army as it withdrew below Peach Tree Creek and had been in the closest contact and in heavy skirmishing with Sherman's forces. Also, as General French noted, quite a number of men had been reported as sick after two months of exposure in the trenches.[12]

These two divisions, like Loring's, were each missing a brigade as they had also been detached to guard the approaches to Atlanta from the north and west. General Walthall placed his brigades in line with O'Neal's Alabama-Mississippi Brigade on the right and Reynolds's Arkansas Brigade on the left. Walthall's third brigade under General William A. Quarles had relieved Reynolds's brigade on picket duty during the morning and was posted along the Peach Tree Creek line opposing Federal Major General John M. Palmer's XIV Corps and part of General Alpheus S. Williams's 1st Division of Major General Joseph Hooker's XX Corps. Thus, Quarles's brigade was unavailable for the attack, except to support Walthall's other two brigades. In that capacity, Quarles

---

[9] Ibid.

[10] Ibid.

[11] "Abstract of Returns of the Army of Tennessee," 10 July 1864, in *OR*, ser. I, vol. 38, pt. 3, serial 74, p. 679.

[12] Samuel G. French, *Two Wars* (1901; repr., Huntington WV: Blue Acorn Press, 1999) 210–16.

The Battle of Peach Tree Creek

had been ordered to wait until the attack had developed and the other two brigades had passed him, and then his men were "to form immediately in its rear and keep within easy supporting distance."[13]

Walthall's three brigades numbered, at least on paper, some 4,000 men with O'Neal's (previously Cantey's) brigade 2,000 men; Reynolds' brigade 1,000 men; and Quarles's brigade 1,000 men.[14] But, O'Neal's brigade had perhaps 1,500 men available, while Reynolds's brigade, which had been undersized for some time and had been additionally depleted during the fighting at Moore's Mill the day before, mustered only 540 men for the attack.[15] With Quarles's brigade in reserve to be used only in the event of a breakthrough in support of the initial assaulting line, Walthall had only about 2,000 men available to begin the attack in his portion of the field.

Forming the right of Walthall's attacking force, Colonel Edward Asbury O'Neal, a lawyer from Lauderdale County, Alabama, commanded Cantey's brigade of Alabamians and Mississippians. Wounded during the Seven Pines battle near Richmond, Virginia, in spring 1862 and again at Bonesboro, Maryland, during the Army of Northern Virginia's Maryland campaign in the fall of the same year, Colonel O'Neal led the 26th Alabama for two years in the Eastern Theater. Colonel O'Neal was wounded a third time while leading the 26th Alabama as part of Stonewall Jackson's famous flank attack at Chancellorsville. After fighting in the battles during the Seven Days Campaign east of the Confederate capital, and at Antietam, Fredericksburg, Chancellorsville, Gettysburg, and Mine Run, O'Neal and his veteran 26th Alabama headed to Dalton where O'Neal was placed in command of Cantey's brigade that included O'Neal's seasoned regiment.[16]

Joining the 26th Alabama were the 17th Alabama, veterans of Shiloh and other campaigns in the Western Theater. Also in O'Neal's brigade, was the 29th Alabama, which had served chiefly on the Gulf Coast at Pensacola, Florida, and Mobile, Alabama, until the Georgia Campaign, when the 29th Alabama was put to the test at Resaca where they lost about a hundred men. As they looked northward from their trenches, these men could hardly know that they were about to be "cut to pieces," according to one participant. The 37th Mississippi

---

[13] *OR*, ser. 1, vol. 38, pt. I, serial 74, p. 930.
[14] *OR*, ser. 1, vol. 38, pt. 5, serial 76, pp. 178–79.
[15] *OR*, ser. 1, vol. 38, pt. 3, serial 74, pp. 924–26, 938.
[16] Willis Brewer, *Alabama: Her History, Resources, War Record, and Public Men, from 1540 to 1872* (Montgomery AL: Barrett & Brown, 1872) 302–303, 630–31.

was additionally placed in O'Neal's Alabama brigade, making it conspicuous as the only Mississippi regiment in all of Walthall's division.[17]

O'Neal prepared his men. O'Neal's brigade formed up in the rear of the trenches and to the right of the Pace's Ferry Road as O'Neal placed his men in line of battle. Colonel O. S. Holland with his 37th Mississippi was put on the far right. The 17th Alabama commanded by Major T. J. Burnett was placed next, second from the right. O'Neal's veteran 26th Alabama held the center under the command of Major D. F. Bryan. The 1st Corps (Alabama) Sharpshooters was placed on the left center where it was commanded by the very capable Captain Sidney "Sid" B. Smith who had previously served with distinction while commanding the skirmish line of O'Neal's brigade at Kennesaw Mountain. At Kennesaw, Major Smith had led a small skirmish line that held off a superior Federal assault and prevented the Federals from reaching the main line and inflicted some forty or fifty casualties on the enemy while incurring none killed and only eight wounded. Finally, the 29th Alabama commanded by Colonel John F. Conoley was on the extreme left of the brigade.[18]

To the left of the Paces Ferry Road and just west of Mt. Zion Church, Walthall placed Reynolds's Arkansas Brigade. General Daniel H. Reynolds and his tiny brigade mustered just 540 men for the attack. Already undersized, Reynolds's brigade had been heavily engaged at the Battle of Moore's Mill on 19 July where they sustained fifty-nine casualties. Moreover, the 9th Arkansas was on duty on the skirmish line and would not join in the charge, but remained in close proximity with portions of Palmer's XIV Corps along the Bohler Road corridor where they kept up a hot fire. Behind Reynolds's brigade, Walthall's artillery battalion led by Major Preston, would support the attack.[19] While the 53rd Tennessee would join in a supporting attack on the right of O'Neal's line along the Collier Road and wooded ridge late in the engagement where they assisted the 37th Mississippi, the remainder of Quarles's brigade would not participate in the assault.[20]

---

[17] Brewer, *Alabama*, 617, 636; *OR*, ser. 1, vol. 38, pt. 3, serial 74, p. 660; Dunbar Rowland, *Military History of Mississippi, 1803–1898,* ed. H. Grady Howell, Jr. (Spartanburg SC: The Reprint Company, Publishers, 1978) 324–30. At the battle of Shiloh, the 17th Alabama lost 125 men. During the Georgia Campaign from Resaca to Love Joy's Station (7 May–September 1864), the 17th Alabama would lose 586 men to enemy fire.

[18] *OR*, ser. 1, vol. 38, pt. 3, serial 74, p. 941.

[19] Ibid., 938.

[20] Edwin H. Rennolds, *A History of the Henry County Commands which Served in the Confederate States Army* (Jacksonville FL: Sun Publishing Company, 1904) 188–89; Edward Young McMorries, *History of the First Regiment Alabama Volunteer Infantry, C.S.A.*

The Battle of Peach Tree Creek

French's division, on the left of Stewart's corps, had, on paper, 4,200 men, according to a memorandum containing the number of troops in the Confederate Army that was created on Monday, 18 July, in General Hood's first day as the army's new commander. That list showed Cockrell's Missouri Brigade with 2,000 men, Ector's Texas and North Carolina Brigade with 1,000 men, and Sears's Mississippi Brigade with 1,200 men.[21] In reality, French's division mustered only about 3,000 men and another 300 officers for a total effective strength of about 3,300 officers and men as a fourth of the division was out sick or on detail duty.[22]

One of French's three brigades, Sears's Mississippi Brigade, commanded by Brigadier Claudius Sears, had been in almost constant skirmishing with units of Federal General Palmer's XIV Corps for the past three days. With Sears's brigade still guarding the crossings along the Chattahoochee River and its confluence with Peach Tree Creek, Sears's men would be unavailable for the ensuing attack.

French's other two brigades, Ector's brigade of Texans and North Carolinians, and Cockrell's Missouri Brigade, were both veteran units filled with hard fighters, but they had very different reputations when it came to discipline. Brigadier General Mathew D. Ector was short and heavy, with dark hair and dark eyes. He had been wounded at Lost Mountain on 2 July, and was still suffering from its effects. His very capable subordinate, Colonel William H. Young, of the 9th Texas Infantry, served in his absence.[23] Ector's brigade included the 29th and 39th North Carolina and the 10th, 14th and 32nd Texas Cavalry along with the 9th Texas Infantry. They had no horses, but the Texans in the three former cavalry units still referred to themselves as cavalrymen, because, they would tell you, whoever heard of a cowboy from Texas without a horse. This brigade was described by one observer as consisting of "wild Texas and Arkansas boys, they are good in a fight but are wild and reckless and troublesome, hard to manage."[24]

(Montgomery: Brown Printing Company, 1904) 76.

[21] *OR*, ser. 1, vol. 38, pt. 4, serial 76, 178–79.

[22] *OR*, ser. 1, vol. 38, pt. 3, serial 74, 679–80.

[23] Walter A. Rorer to "Cousin Susan," 22 March 1864, vertical files, Carter House, Franklin, Tennessee; William R. Scaife, *The Campaign for Atlanta* (Atlanta: self-published, 1993) 182.

[24] Walter A. Rorer to "Cousin Susan," 22 March 1864, vertical files, Carter House, Franklin, Tennessee.

Hood's First Sortie, 20 July 1864

Cockrell's brigade, on the other hand, had the reputation of being the finest in army. Described by Major Rorer as "fair fancied," the Missouri brigade "are the brag men of this or any other army, they fight better, drill better and look better than any other men in the army, clean clothes, clean faces, and all in Uniform and every man in the step."[25] One veteran from this brigade wrote that he believed that the Atlanta Campaign had been the "hardest campaign we ever saw. We have been fighting the Yanks every day for three months. We fought them from Dalton to Atlanta. We are shooting at each other every day, [and] now and then a Missourian falls."[26] James A. Kennerly, of the 1st Missouri Regiment, added: "I think we get at least five for one. Our brigade...," the Missourian exhorted, "is the best in the Confederate Army. It has not yet been whipped" Kennerly added, "I do not want to go home until we are victorious. I would consider myself disgraced to be conquered by the Yanks."[27] Proudly, Kennerly asserted, "We conquer or die."[28] Included in this brigade was the 1st and 4th Missouri Infantry, the 2nd and 6th Missouri Infantry, the 3rd and 5th Missouri Infantry, and the 1st and 3rd Missouri Cavalry.[29]

So, Stewart's corps would be making the assault at only two-thirds strength, but that would not stop them from giving it their best effort. General Stewart went down the line and met with each brigade as they formed up. "We were going to assault the enemy in his works," he said, "and we must carry everything, allowing no obstacle to stop us; that the fate of Atlanta probably depended on the result of this battle." One man in Scott's brigade would later write in his diary about that day. "It is a fearful thing to charge an enemy in his works, especially when outnumbered two or three to one, but feeling that it had to be done we nerved ourselves up to this point to do our whole duty. So when orders came to form in front of the breastworks we were ready.[30]

As General Loring recalled, General Stewart:

> informed me that the movement was to be made at 1pm in echelon by division, at 200 yards distance, [Hardee's] corps on my right to take the advance. At 1 o'clock the Lieutenant-General notified me that General Hardee would move to the right the distance of half a division front, and I

---

[25] Ibid.

[26] James A. Kennerly to sister, 8 August 1864, vertical files, James Kennerly Papers, Wilson's Creek National Park Library, Republic, Missouri.

[27] Ibid.

[28] Ibid.

[29] Scaife, *The Campaign for Atlanta*, 182.

[30] Cannon, *History of the 27th Regiment Alabama Infantry*, 84–86.

must follow the movement with my division and connect with his left. The order was obeyed, but instead of General Hardee's Corps halting at the distance indicated, he had proceeded further to the right, requiring Loring's Division to continue a full division front, or about a mile to the east. It seems that one of Hardee's Divisions had gotten lost, and failed to participate in the attack.[31]

General Hardee posted Staff Officer Major Samuel L. Black on the Confederate line near today's Howell Mill Road to "wait at the point where his left flank should be. Black went to his station and showed one of Stewart's staff where Hardee's left would rest. Then to his surprise, Hardee's left brigade [Carter's] moved farther and farther to the right and finally out of sight." Acting on his own initiative, Black "ordered the brigade to stop. The brigade commander refused, because his division commander [newly appointed General George Maney] had sent orders for him to continue moving." Concerned that there had been a mistake, Black "galloped to General Hardee and reported that I had halted his left at the point designated, but that it was then moving still further to the right. He replied that his orders were to connect with General Cheatham, who was continually moving to the right." Black continued, "The interval could have been quickly closed, if it had been created by one instead of repeated moves of Cheatham's Corps." Instead, "one corps would move a short distance to the right, halt, face and prepare for action, when it would again become necessary to close to the right," remembered Hardee's staff officer. "In this matter," reasoned Black, "General Cheatham was not to blame, for I suppose his orders were simply to prevent the enemy from overlapping or turning his flank." Afterward, Black would record, "I know that General Hardee expressed his impatience at the delay, and his annoyance at the repeated movements to the right."[32]

Stewart ordered his men to follow Hardee. His instructions were "to move forward and attack the enemy; if found to be entrenched, to fix bayonets and carry his works; to drive him back to the creek and then press down the creek; that we were to carry everything in our front on our side of the creek.... The

---

[31] Loring, report, in *OR*, ser. 1, vol. 38, pt. 3, serial 74, 876–78; Thomas L. Connelly, *Autumn of Glory, The Army of Tennessee, 1862–1865* (Baton Rouge: Louisiana State Press, 1971) 443; Carter, *Siege of Atlanta*, 206–207.

[32] Nathaniel Cheairs Hughes, Jr., *General William J. Hardee: Old Reliable*, 220–21; S. L. Black to Thomas Benton Roy, 31 May 1880, in Roy's "General Hardee and the Military Operations around Atlanta," *Southern Historical Society Papers* 8/ (August/September 1880): 347–50.

instructions given were obeyed promptly and with alacrity," recorded Stewart. By the time that they stopped, Loring's division was along today's Northside Drive while Walthall's division was astride Howell Mill Road, called the Pace's Ferry Road by some of the Confederate Officers. Both divisions had traveled over a mile and a half to the east, three times farther than Hood had anticipated.[33]

In Featherston's Mississippi Brigade, Colonel M. D. L. Stephens was absent sick from the 31st Mississippi Regiment after having endured three months of combat during the Campaign. Thus, Lieutenant Colonel James W. Drane commanded the regiment as they were led down the trenches to the right. Born in Georgia, Drane's family had moved to Choctaw County, Mississippi, when he was only three. There, his parents cleared a place in the wilderness in the south part of the county where his father had killed a 110 deer the first year. His father, James L. Drane, had a successful career in politics and had once considered a run for the governor's office of Mississippi. His father and grandfather had both served with distinction in the Continental Army during the American Revolution. Now, the thirty-one year old Drane found himself in command of the regiment for the first time in battle.

Drane watched as the gray and butternut veterans of his regiment continued on with solemn resolve. It seemed that they would never stop moving through the maze-like walls of the earthen clay. Like a dirty gray snake, the regiment zig-zagged through the trenches following the regiment in front of it. Surely they had gone far enough. They were only supposed to go about a half mile. It seemed they had gone twice that far. When they finally halted it was nearly 3:00 P.M. Another hour would pass as they waited on Hardee's corps to their right to begin the attack. Soon enough, however, the Mississippians would be in motion toward the unsuspecting blue lines. By the time that darkness would fall upon the Collier Ridge, Drane's 31st Mississippi would earn the right to the sobriquet, the "Bloody Magnolias."

After the movements, General Loring discovered that his division was in the most exposed portion of the line and that much of his division's attack would have to be made across an open 700-yard field up a ridge to a line that showed clear signs of Federal occupation. Across the field, a fresh line of Georgia red clay could be seen, chilling evidence of recent earthworks, plus fence posts lined the earthworks, creating a formidable defensive position. Loring reported, "The enemy was in plain view about 700 yards distant on the

---

[33] *OR*, ser. I, vol. 38, pt. 3, serial 74, p. 871.

opposite side of the field, occupying a ridge running east and west, and marked by a line of red earth, which plainly told the work that was before us." While Loring's veterans prepared themselves for the work that lay ahead, his trusted General Featherston listened to his right for signs of Hardee's advance, and with it, his cue to attack.[34]

On the Federal side, "there were positive indications," according to Corporal Edmund R. Brown in the 27th Indiana, "as we moved across the creek and up the opposite slope, that we had come about as far as we were to be permitted to come without vigorous opposition."[35] Williams's Red Star Division, the 1st Division of Hooker's XX Corps, crossed Peach Tree Creek during the morning of 20 July behind Geary's White Star, or 2nd, Division of the same corps, at the present day Northside Drive location. "There was brisk firing on the skirmish line," added the Indiana corporal, "and a rebel battery was dropping shells wherever it could in such a timbered region, endeavoring thus to hinder and delay our progress."[36]

---

[34] Ibid., 876–78.
[35] Edmund R. Brown, *A History of the 27th Indiana* (Monticello IN: Edmund R. Brown, 1899) 517.
[36] Ibid.

WITH ONE FOOT OVER THE CREEK

Tomorrow night...will give us Atlanta, or there will be a fair start for a new graveyard near the town.[1]

Newton's Division. Federal troops in various sectors had been crossing the creek all evening and into the following morning and had begun throwing up breastworks and heavy skirmish lines along a high ridge south of Peach Tree Creek. This ridge ran generally east to west beginning from the eastern most point of the Federal line (along today's Brighton Road east of Peach Tree Road), where the men of General Newton's division from Howard's IV Corps had been working to create a good line of earthworks.[2] Newton would hold the Federal left flank that day, and according to their bold, if not rash commander, they consisted of just "3,200 bayonets." Moreover, Newton's division would actually field only "2,700 men in line" when the attack came.[3] They were about to be tested by General Hardee's corps of nearly 20,000 veterans of the Army of Tennessee. First Sergeant John W. Hagan of the 29th Georgia Infantry wrote, "the grate storm is gathering. heavy Skirmishing going on in our front & the enimy crossing in heavy force."[4]

Sergeant W. H. Newlin of the 73rd Illinois of Kimball's brigade in Newton's division recorded "weather pleasant on the morning of July 20. The rebels—Cleburne's Division close in our front, throwing balls over our heads from their skirmish line. Had orders to march at 5 A.M. Some hopeful ones

---

[1] Robert, R. Long, "A Brief History of the Battle of Peachtree Creek, July 20, 1864," in author's personal papers, Dalton, Georgia; *Soldier, Including a Day by Day Record of Sherman's March to the Sea: Letters and Diary of the Late Charles W. Willis* (Washington, DC: Globe Printing Company, 1906).

[2] United States War Department, comp., *Official Records of the Union and Confederate Armies in the War of the Rebellion*, 128 vols. (Washington, DC: Government Printing Office, 1880–1901) ser. 1, vol. 38, pt. 5, serial 76, 199 (hereafter *OR*).

[3] See ibid.; but compare, *OR*, ser. 1, vol. 38, pt. 1, serial 72, 290.

[4] Samuel Carter III, *The Siege of Atlanta, 1864* (New York: St. Martin's Press, 1973) 201; Janet B. Hewett, ed., *The Roster of Confederate Soldiers, 1861–1865*, 16 vols. (Wilmington NC: Broadfoot Publishing Company, 1995) 336.

thought Atlanta would be ours by nightfall of the 21st."[5] With three months of constant withdrawals by Confederate forces, it was hard for the Federal veterans to imagine a Rebel offensive against them. Newlin added, "At 6 A.M. we changed position, and relieved the 3rd [Wood's] Division again; 3rd Division moved to the left. Our lines lacked nearly a half a mile of connecting on our right with the left of XX Corps. The space was filled at noon," remembered Newlin, "or partially so, and a forward movement made by our division, in connection with XX Corps at 12:45 P.M., driving the rebels from their works. At 2:15 P.M. our brigade moved forward about 3/4 of a mile, halted a short time, and then the 15th Missouri and 73rd Illinois were ordered forward," explained the Illinois Sergeant, "with instructions to go as far as we could."[6]

Newton and his division had been aggressive on the morning of 20 July, taking one ridge after another as they forced the Rebel skirmishers back toward their earthworks encircling Atlanta. A biographer of the 15th Missouri in Kimball's brigade described the advance: "Newton's division moved out, away from the south bank of Peach Tree Creek, across open country of sedge grasses and rushes. Once in a while they crossed a soft ridge of thickets and woods cut by deep hollows."[7] According to Lieutenant Colonel Wilbur F. Hinman of the 65th Ohio, "During the early part of the day we did a good deal of wild maneuvering, evidently in search of a place where we would be expected to do something. At length we seemed to have found it, and our brigade was formed in mass for a charge upon the Confederate works, which," Hinman explained, "were on high ground some four hundred yards distant, the intervening space being open, with no cover."[8]

With Kimball's brigade in front, Newton's men hop-scotched over the series of hills and ridges ahead. "Late in the morning, the division advanced, about a mile along the road and the adjacent fields when it began to run into gray skirmishers. Around noon, Thomas arrived on the scene."[9] In front of them was a low ridge about 600 yards away on which was a line of entrenchments

---

[5] W. H. Newlin, *The Preacher Regiment, 1862–65, History of the 73rd Illinois Volunteer Infantry* (Springfield: Regimental Reunion Association of Survivors of the 73rd Illinois Infantry Volunteers, 1890) 324.

[6] Ibid., 324.

[7] Donald Allendorf, *Long Road to Liberty, The Odyssey of a German Regiment in the Yankee Army: The 15th Missouri Volunteer Infantry* (Kent OH: Kent State University Press, 2006) 205.

[8] Wilbur F. Hinman, *The Story of the Sherman Brigade* (Alliance OH: Press of Daily Review, 1897) 57–58.

[9] Allendorf, *Long Road to Liberty*, 205.

manned by enemy troops. Understanding the need to take the high ground in his front, Thomas ordered Newton to seize the ridge. Newton subsequently ordered General Nathan Kimball to advance his 1st Brigade and take the heights. Accordingly, Kimball lined up his regiments: on the left was the 36th Illinois, in the center came the 74th Illinois, and on the right was the 88th Illinois that made up the first line under the command of Colonel Wallace W. Barrett of the 44th Illinois. They were supported by a second line led by Colonel John Q. Lane and his 97th Ohio on the left and the 28th Kentucky under Major George W. Barth on the right.[10] These two regiments were from Colonel John W. Blake's 2nd Brigade.[11]

"The skirmish line advanced at noon and quickly drove the rebels from their pits, capturing a number of prisoners," explained Kimball.[12] Falling in the attack was Nicholas Kessler, killed, of the 15th Missouri who had been detached to join the skirmish line of the attackers as a sharpshooter.[13] Kimball's men "took possession of the Confederate trench works on the first ridge when they discovered another, wooded and crowned with a number of cedars, about a quarter of a mile away."[14] The second ridge commanded the position just taken according to Kimball, so he sent Colonel Barrett and the same line forward to take it. Barrett wasted no time leading the Illinoisans over the 400 yards and took the heights before the Rebels knew what had hit them, "taking prisoner a surgeon and 2 privates, with an ambulance and team."[15] By just after noon, Kimball's men had taken the ridge on which Piedmont Hospital is now located. "The possession of this hill," according to Kimball, "proved of the most vital importance in the action which followed."[16]

General John Newton explained that the events in his front had an "ugly look," so he ordered log barricade to be immediately erected to cover the high ground along the Buckhead Road that his men had seized.[17] The work of his men in seizing the high ground and preparing defensive works would prove to

---

[10] *OR*, ser. 1, vol. 38, pt. 2, serial 72, pp. 297, 305, 320–21; William R. Scaife, *The Campaign for Atlanta* (Atlanta: self-published, 1993) 147–48; & Allendorf, *Long Road to Liberty*, 206.

[11] Scaife, *The Campaign for Atlanta*, 147.

[12] *OR*, ser. 1, vol. 38, pt. 2, serial 72, 305.

[13] Allendorf, *Long Road to Liberty*, 206.

[14] Ibid.

[15] *OR*, ser. 1, vol. 38, pt. 2, serial 72, 305.

[16] Ibid., 305.

[17] Thomas B. Buell, *The Warrior Generals, Combat Leadership in the Civil War* (Pittsburgh: Three Rivers Press 1997) 371.

be a key reason for the success of Newton's division during the battle. Kimball replaced his skirmish line by placing the 15th Missouri forward to the left, the 73rd Illinois to cover the center, and the 24th Wisconsin under the command of Major Arthur MacArthur to the right. This skirmish line, led by Colonel Joseph Conrad of the 15th Missouri, spread out and moved forward to explore what lay ahead while shielding the remainder of the Federal line, which began preparing a defensive line. Kimball posted the remainder of his brigade atop the hill from left to right as follows: the 88th Illinois to the left of the Buckhead Road (Peachtree Street), to the right of the Buckhead Road was the 44th Illinois, next the 74th Illinois, and on the far right was the 36th Illinois, which stretched down the Collier Ridge along Collier Road. Kimball also posted four of Captain Wilbur F. Goodspeed's Napoleon guns from the 1st Ohio Light Artillery Battery A along the Buckhead Road between the 88th and 44th Illinois.[18] These two sections of Battery A were led by Lieutenant Charles W. Scovill as Captain Goodspeed had been promoted in June to command the division's artillery, but Goodspeed would be present to lead his old battery on the Buckhead Road when the attack began.[19]

Colonel John W. Blake's 2nd Brigade continued Kimball's line to the left and down toward Clear Creek, following the military crest of the cedar-lined ridge through today's Brookwood Hills Subdivision. This line generally followed the course of today's Brighton Road facing south and southeast toward Camden Road. Blake sent two regiments out on skirmish to link up with Kimball's skirmishers. The 100th Illinois led by Major Charles M. Hammond went to the left, and the 57th Indiana under Lieutenant Colonel Willis Blanch moved to the right and connected with the left of the 15th Missouri. While his skirmishers felt their way forward in the dense woodlands below, Blake's remaining regiments lined up along the southeastern slope of the ridge (along Brighton Road) and began to dig in and cut down trees in their front to create a field of fire. Blake placed, from left to right, the 40th Indiana, the 26th Ohio and the 97th Ohio along the line that connected with the left of the 88th Illinois. He also posted the 28th Kentucky in reserve to support any breach in his line. The left-most regiment, the 40th Indiana under the command of Lieutenant Colonel Henry Leaming, refused its line, or bent the left half of it back, to protect its left flank, there being no troops to the left of it.[20]

---

[18] *OR*, ser. 1, vol. 38, pt. 2, serial 72, pp. 305–306.
[19] Scaife, *The Campaign for Atlanta*, 148.
[20] *OR*, ser. 1, vol. 38, pt. 2, serial 72, pp. 337–38; J. Britt McCarley, *The Atlanta Campaign: A Civil War Driving Tour of Atlanta-Area Battlefields* (Atlanta: Cherokee

Finally, the 3rd Brigade in Newton's division, led by General Luther P. Bradley, lined up in column (or line of march) along the Buckhead Road behind the Yankee line, so that Newton's three brigades made a "T" when formed. Bradley's brigade contained the 27th Illinois, the 42nd Illinois, the 51st Illinois, the 79th Illinois, the 3rd Kentucky, the 64th Ohio, the 65th Ohio, and the 125th Ohio. The 79th Illinois led by Lieutenant Colonel Henry E. Rives was posted to the left of the crossing on the northern bank on picket and did not participate in the battle, except that one man, a stretcher-bearer, was wounded.[21]

Hooker's XX Corps. To Newton's right, along Collier Road (where Piedmont Hospital is today located), the Federal line continued west along the ridge to Collier's grist Mill. From the mill, the line continued west across Tanyard Branch (or Early's Creek), a tributary that flowed beside Collier's Mill into Peach Tree Creek. Tanyard Branch flows generally east to west below Collier Ridge and on the south side of a large old field before the branch turns sharply northward by the grist mill and deposits into Peach Tree Creek. Atop the ridge ran the Collier Road, which was lined with fences. The attacking Confederates would have to cross Tanyard Branch prior to moving through the open 700-yard field, then seize the ridge, which was crowned with the slightly sunken Collier Road and fences manned by Federals. The headwaters for Tanyard Branch come from a spring now located in Centennial Olympic Park, but Atlanta's growth and development have long since buried most of the branch under her streets.[22]

Ward's 3rd Division had been ordered to march at daylight and about 7:00 A.M. they moved out. "The time was occupied principally in shifting from one position to another, marching along poorly constructed roads and through dense forests until Peach Tree Creek was finally reached at about 10 o'clock A.M."[23] One veteran of the 19th Michigan in Coburn's brigade remembered, "The entire corps moved over swiftly and was only partially prepared when the Confederate attack came."[24] According to John McBride of the 33rd Indiana in Coburn's 2nd

---

Publishing Company, n.d.) 24–26.

[21] *OR*, ser. 1, vol. 38, pt. 2, serial 72, pp. 355–56, 364.

[22] Dave Kaufman, "Riverchat," *Upper Chattahoochee Riverkeeper* (Fall 2002): pages 1-4.

[23] John R. McBride, *History of the 33rd Indiana Veteran Volunteer Infantry* (Indianapolis: Wm. B. Burford, Printer, 1900) 128.

[24] Terry L. Jones, "'The Flash of Their Guns Was a Sure Guide': The 19th Michigan Infantry in the Atlanta Campaign," in Theodore P. Savas and David A. Woodbury, eds., *The Campaign for Atlanta & Sherman's March to the Sea*, 160. (Savas Campbell CA: Woodbury Publishers, 1994).

The Battle of Peach Tree Creek

Brigade, "After the brigade and division had successfully crossed the creek skirmishers were thrown out to cover each brigade front—the 22nd Wisconsin performing that duty for the 2nd Brigade."[25] Actually, only the 22nd Wisconsin and just four companies of the 136th New York of Colonel Wood's 3rd Brigade were needed to cover the skirmish line for Ward's 3rd Division front as both Newton's division of the IV Corps to the left and Geary's 2nd Division to the right were angularly pushed forward along ridges, which pinched Ward's position so that his front was narrower than his rear.

From Tanyard Branch the Federal line extended westward another mile or so past Howell's Mill reaching toward Moore's Mill (located along today's Moore's Mill Road, just west of Interstate 75). All three mills were located along Peach Tree Creek, which in that area resembled a river more than a creek. "Peach Tree Creek is a narrow and muddy stream, about forty feet wide and very deep, varying from four to twelve feet, and impassable, except by bridges," wrote Colonel John Coburn.[26] Further, virtually all of the Federal troops of Thomas's Army of the Cumberland were south of Peach Tree Creek, with their backs to the large steep-banked and stony stream. Colonel Benjamin Harrison, a lawyer from Indianapolis before the war who raised the 70th Indiana Regiment and who was now commanding the 1st Brigade in Ward's division, described the danger of having his back to Peach Tree Creek, "The creek in our rear at this place, ten feet deep, with a very miry bank and bed, had not been bridged, and to attempt to retire across it would have been utter destruction."[27] Harrison, a staunch Republican who would become the twenty-third president of the United States, was only thirty-one at the time of the Battle of Peach Tree Creek.[28] The future president certainly had the lineage for leadership. Young Benjamin was the grandson of President William Henry Harrison from Ohio, and the great-grandson of a signer of the Declaration of Independence from Virginia.[29]

Along the ridge occupied by the Federals ran a very well-traveled road from east to west (today's Collier Road between its intersection with Peach Tree Street, across the railroad behind Piedmont Hospital), and continuing west to Collier's Mill. The road was lined with a rail fence that would be put to use by the Federals. Along this road and ridge overlooking the open field and Tanyard

---

[25] McBride, *History of the 33rd Indiana*, 128.
[26] *OR*, ser. 1, vol. 38, pt. 2, serial 73, 389.
[27] Ibid., 344–45.
[28] Paul Hinde, "Benj. Harrison, 23rd President, in Battle of Peachtree Creek," *Inn Dixie Magazine* (January 1937): 5.
[29] Hinde, "Benjamin Harrison," 5.

Hood's First Sortie, 20 July 1864

Branch below, the 22nd Wisconsin on the east and, to their right, four companies of the 136th New York had been deployed as skirmishers. Down the old field to the south, Tanyard Branch flowed through a small skirt of trees that somewhat screened the Confederate advance. As the gentle brook meandered at the bottom of the long field some 700 yards away, the Federals looked ominously southward, wondering just how far away, hidden behind the woods and marsh on the other side of Tanyard Branch, was the illusive Confederate Army they had been chasing since May. Many surely wondered when they would next clash. It had been relatively quiet the last several days since they had crossed the Chattahoochee River. Surely the Rebels would not give up Atlanta without a fight.

Down the field, across the branch, and over the distant wooded hill, the veterans of the 31st Mississippi waited quietly. Some 215 of them would be in the assault. For the record, they would be without Company C (nicknamed the "Chickasaw Guards" or "Old Chickasaw"), although some of these men were just coming back into camp after being out all day and the previous night on picket duty when they learned that the order to form had been given. Many of the men from Old Chickasaw could not resist joining their comrades.

The men of the 22nd Wisconsin and 136th New York continued to dig. The New Yorkers, veterans of Chancellorsville, Gettysburg, and Chattanooga were still looking for respect from their western counterparts from Sherman's forces. While they had performed well during the Georgia Campaign including the fights at New Hope and Resaca, where they were instrumental in capturing a four-gun Confederate Battery, they continued to bear the albatross of the failures of other sister units on battlefields in the Eastern Theater. Having Hooker as their corps commander and the drunkard Ward in charge of their division did not help matters. Under this leadership, the New Yorkers could never hope for proper recognition from Sherman. Perhaps if they led the assault to capture Atlanta, they would finally get their due and, together with the remainder of the Army of the Cumberland, join the Army of the Tennessee as "Sherman's Pets."

The Wisconsin boys of the 22nd Regiment had different worries. A year before, this Wisconsin unit had been surprised and routed by a band of Confederate marauders who had sacked Brentwood and Thompson's Station, Tennessee. Embarrassed by running from a lesser attacking force in Tennessee, the Wisconsinites did not want to be badgered again. They needed to prove that

The Battle of Peach Tree Creek

they were worthy soldiers.[30] Many of these men had performed well throughout the Georgia Campaign, but they had not been "tested" in the same manner as they had been in Tennessee the previous year. While they tried to improve their line along the Collier Road by taking down the wooden fence that ran along the northern side of the road and by piling up the rails along the southern side of the road that had been cut into somewhat of a trench by rain and erosion, many of the Wisconsin men reflected on their prior performance and on their present crisis. They quickly realized that with the remainder of Ward's division a half mile in the rear along the creek with another ridge between them, they were isolated atop the Collier Ridge. It was further apparent that this ridge would be the key to the entire region should they become under attack. To lose it would mean that all of Ward's division would be swept into the creek at their backs. But if they were attacked, what would the Wisconsin men do? Would they run again? Each man considered what he would do as well as what his comrade might do if it got bad. What if the others bolt? Would you stay or run, too? Why were they chosen to have to be on skirmish? Why didn't the rest of the Division come up? Why had their commander, General Ward, not given them proper support to adequately cover this important ridge with sufficient troops to hold it? Whatever happens, the Wisconsin veterans singly and in small groups vowed to do their duty.

They had been on the ridge since mid-day and had been trading fire with the Rebel skirmishers for several hours. One Federal veteran in rear of the 22nd Wisconsin remembered, "The skirmish line kept up a lazy 'wood chopping' as it has been aptly compared to—from our position [on the bluff on the north side of Peach Tree Creek just west the Buckhead Road] we could see the white puffs of smoke from their guns."[31] This was the most prominent point in the entire area and offered a commanding view of what would become the center and hottest spot on the battlefield. To the south of the 700-yard field descending down to the branch, its wooden canopy concealed the butternut and gray clad foe. Captain Francis Mead directed the "Racine Boys" of the 22nd Wisconsin as they prepared their lines.[32]

---

[30] Racine Boy to Friend T., 21 July 1864, 16-17, subject file PW-4, Kennesaw Mountain National Battlefield Park, Kennesaw, Georgia.

[31] Harvey Reid, *Uncommon Soldiers: Harvey Reid and the 22nd Wisconsin March with Sherman*, ed. Frank L. Byrne (Knoxville: University of Tennessee Press, 2001) 172.

[32] *OR*, ser. 1, vol. 38, pt. 2, serial 73, 424–28; Reid, *Uncommon Soldiers*, 172.

Hood's First Sortie, 20 July 1864

Earlier in the day, the 22nd Wisconsin served as the skirmish line for Ward's 3rd Division as they crossed Peach Tree Creek just after daybreak behind Newton's division of the IV Corps. Ward's division stacked up along the southern side of Peach Tree Creek (in the area of the eastern part of the Bobby Jones Golf Course south of Peachtree Creek). "We now lay on a flat, beyond which lay two high ridges, the first covered by timber and occupied by the enemy's skirmishers," remembered Lieutenant Colonel Edward Bloodgood, commander of the 22nd Wisconsin. "The second ridge was bare, a rail fence running along the top parallel to our lines." The 22nd Wisconsin was deployed as skirmishers between the right of the IV Corps and the left of the 2nd Division of the XX Corps. Four companies of the 136th New York were added to the right of the line to connect with the 22nd Wisconsin and Geary's 2nd Division of the XX Corps. Three Companies, A, C, and F, were held as a reserve.[33]

To the north of the high ridge, the land sloped down to a ravine that included some dense underbrush and then back up to a smaller ridge. The smaller ridge was covered by scrub pine and sassafras trees and shielded the land and Peach Tree Creek behind it. Between the smaller ridge and Peach Tree Creek was a corn field. It was occupied by the rest of Ward's three Federal brigades that made up the 3rd Division of General Hooker's XX Corps. The cornfield ran some 200 yards wide along the southern side of Peach Tree Creek and was screened from view by the scrub-laden ridge. (This cornfield was located where that portion of today's Bobby Jones Golf course south of Peach Tree Creek is situated.)

Harvey Reid, a brigade clerk in Coburn's 2nd Brigade of Ward's division, who was with the supply wagons north of Peach Tree Creek, had a bird's eye view of the valley occupied by his comrades of Ward's division south of the creek:

> A battery was in position in a corn field on the edge of the bluff [north of the creek near the Buckhead Road crossing] and I walked up there to see the position of the troops. There they lay just below us. The creek ran just at the foot of the bluff on which we stood—on the other side was a flat valley of about 80 rods [about 1,320 feet] in width, then another bluff or steep bank not as high as the one on the north side from the top of which was a gentle

---

[33] *OR*, ser. 1, vol. 38, pt. 2, serial 73, pp. 424–28; Reid, *Uncommon Soldiers*, 172; Racine Boy to Friend T., 21 July 1864, 16-17, subject file PW-4, Kennesaw Mountain National Battlefield Park, Kennesaw, Georgia.

slope to the top of the hill. Our Division lay in the valley just at the foot of the opposite bluff I speak of while the skirmishers were on its top [along the Collier Road from today's railroad bridge to the Collier Mill]. On our front was an open space for at least half a mile but further to the right, in front of the right of Geary's [2nd] Division, the woods extended down the bank of the creek. In this point of woods Geary had stationed a battery [on the ridge overlooking the Tanyard Creek parking lot] which had commenced throwing shells towards the rebel skirmish line. To our left also the woods extended nearly to the creek, so that the troops on that part of the line could not be seen, and here too a battery was belching forth flame and smoke, shelling the woods at irregular intervals.[34]

The battery in Geary's division was actually two batteries, Sloan's (Knap's) Battery E of the Pennsylvania Light Artillery with its six 3-inch ordnance rifles, and the six Napoleons of Bundy's 13th New York Light Artillery, which commanded the Tanyard Branch valley and today's parking lot and park of Tanyard Creek Park.[35] The battery to the left contained two sections, or 4 guns, of Goodspeed's Battery A of the 1st Ohio Artillery of Newton's division, which was posted along the Buckhead Road sweeping the woods to the south.[36]

General William Ward had lost the respect of many of his men. Reputed to be a drunk, he was viewed as a leader who only wished to gain laurels in battle by leading his men to the front without regard to the lives and safety of his men. Ward, a lawyer from Kentucky, had fought in the Mexican War as major of the 4th Kentucky Infantry Regiment. A member of the old Whig party, Ward served first in the Kentucky legislature and then in Congress where he represented the Bluegrass State. When the Whig party folded, he became a Republican, saw eye to eye with President Lincoln politically speaking, and found favor with the president who commissioned him to the rank of brigadier general although Ward had done nothing on a battlefield to earn the position.[37] Nicknamed "Old Falstaff" by one of his sergeants, Ward had taken the place of Major General Daniel Butterfield. According to Sergeant George F. Cram of the 105th Illinois, Ward "hungered for the heat of battle" to get his name in the papers at the

---

[34] Reid, *Uncommon Soldiers*, 171–72.
[35] *OR*, ser. 1, vol. 38, pt. 2, serial 73, 200.
[36] *OR*, ser. 1, vol. 38, pt. 2, serial 72, 297.
[37] Eric Foner, *Free Soil, Free Labor, Free Men: The Ideology of the Republican Party before the Civil War* (New York: Oxford University Press, 1995) 270–71; http://bioguide.congress.gov/scripts/biodisplay.pl?index'W000145 (23 August 2013).

sacrifice of his men, and Cram once exclaimed in a letter home to his mother, that "Ward [is] a regular old Falstaff whose sheer delight is to swill whiskey, etc." The not so flattering moniker "Falstaff" was in reference to the Shakespearean character that was described as a drunken, swaggering, brazen soldier without scruples.[38]

Ward not withstanding, Federal troops in the 22nd Wisconsin and 136th New York prepared their lines. The men sweated in the Georgia sun as they looked southward. They took down pieces of the wood rail fence that lined the sides of Collier Road and used it on top of their works and in places where the trenches were not very deep. By this time in the war a veteran unit could dig in a formidable line of works in about two hours. Given a day or overnight, they could build works that were nearly impregnable. The Yankees on Collier Road would have less that two hours to prepare, and there were not enough of them to build sufficient defenses in the time allotted. Moreover, Ward had not ordered his men to entrench as he believed that the Federals would be moving toward Atlanta later in the day. Experience had taught his men, however, that the prudent thing to do first when they halted was to erect a defensive line. The veterans of the 22nd Wisconsin and the 136th New York understood the danger, and, ignoring Ward's directive, they began to improve their position along the Collier Road by pulling down the fences and piling up the rails along the south side of the road, which was slightly depressed.

"The rest of the division stacked arms in the edge of a cornfield, and, like all good soldiers when opportunity offered, kindled fires and boiled coffee, little dreaming of the storm that was about to burst upon us," remembered George Newton of the 129th Illinois in Harrison's brigade.[39] They were in no hurry to move up to the ridge and help. Besides, General Ward, their division commander, had given them no orders to advance. Many of Ward's men were in the Peach Tree Creek, washing clothes and bathing, while they waited for orders to advance.[40] Some of the men went out to pick blackberries. They were the last of the Federal troops to get across Peach Tree Creek because they had to follow the two other divisions of Hooker's XX Corps. Ward had chosen to take

---

[38] George F. Cram to mother, 23 April 1864, in George F. Cram, *Soldiering with Sherman: The Civil War Letters of George F. Cram*, ed. Jennifer Cain Bornstedt (DeKalb: Northern Illinois University Press, 2000).

[39] George A. Newton, "Battle of Peach Tree Creek," in Sydney C. Kerksis, ed., *The Atlanta Papers*, 396 (Dayton OH: Morningside Books, 1980).

[40] Jean M. Cate, ed., *"If I Live to Come Home": The Civil War Letters of Sergeant John March Cate* (Pittsburgh: Dorrance Publishing Company, 1995) 195–96.

The Battle of Peach Tree Creek

a detour by crossing Peach Tree Creek at the bridge behind Newton's division of the IV Corps near Peach Tree Road rather than follow his own corps across the creek at the ford below Collier's Mill. He thought it would be easier for him to get into his assigned place at the left of the XX Corps line this way.[41]

Perhaps Ward did not want to disturb the men's opportunity to clean up and refresh along the creek's banks as they endured the hot Georgia sun. In any event, it was not sound military logic to fail to have the high ground in his front sufficiently covered, but the only forces in position to defend in his division during the afternoon were the 22nd Wisconsin and four companies of the 136th New York. Thus, only a regiment and a half, some 300 men, were preparing to meet any assault mounted by the enemy that day. One of the clerks of Coburn's 2nd Brigade watched as his former regiment, the 22nd Wisconsin, performed their duties on the skirmish line: "When we arrived in their vicinity the [enemy] skirmishers were not more than 40 rods [about 660 feet] from the stream, and we got there just in time to see our boys advance with loud cheers and drive them up the slope into a strip of woods [at Ardmore Road and Collier Road] about 3/4 of a mile from the stream.... Our wagons were then driven to the edge of the bluff, or north bank of the stream, and word was sent to the brigade that we were ready to issue."[42]

West of Ward's position, the divisions of Geary and Williams had crossed Peach Tree Creek near today's Northside Drive bridge over the creek. At the time of the Civil War, Peach Tree Creek was about 40 feet wide and up to 12 feet deep in and around the Bobby Jones Golf Course (or Atlanta Memorial Park), Howell's Mill, and today's Northside Drive. "It was virtually impassible, except by bridges," according to historian Robert Long. "It flowed through a valley about 200 yards wide, generally level and cleared of timber. The hills to the south of it, about 400 yards away, rose about 70 feet."[43]

Over to the far right of the Federal line, along the Howell Mill Road, General Richard W. Johnson met up with Colonel Andrew J. Mackay of General Thomas's staff. "We are going to have a hard battle today," explained Mackay. The division commander asked why Thomas's assistant quartermaster thought so. Mackay, who had fought Native Americans with Hood in Texas before the war, replied, "I have just seen an Atlanta paper which contains an

---

[41] *OR*, Report of Major Henry L. Arnold, 136th N.Y; Report of General William T. Ward, 3rd Division, XX Corps; John Michael Priest, ed., *John T. McMahon's Diary of the 136th New York, 1861–1864* (Shippensburg PA: White Mane Publishing Company, 1993).

[42] Reid, *Uncommon Soldiers*, 171.

[43] Long, "A Brief History of the Battle of Peachtree Creek," 10.

order placing Hood in command and relieving Johnston; and, a man who will bet a thousand dollars without having a pair in his hand will fight when he has the troops with which to do it."[44]

Along the sector between the Collier Mill and Howell Mill Road, elements of Geary's White Star Division and Williams's Red Star Division began to deploy and feel their way southward as Southern resistance stiffened. Geary's men fanned out along the ridges just west of the Collier Mill and Tanyard Branch, which flowed west and then north into Peach Tree Creek near the left of Geary's lines. Geary's division had forced a crossing of Peach Tree Creek during the evening of 19 July at the present day Northside Drive location amid light resistance. There, Geary's pioneers bridged the crossing and they built several other bridges over the creek, so that by daylight on 20 July, five bridges across Peach Tree Creek had been spanned in his sector. Williams's men crossed the creek behind Geary's division during the forenoon of 20 July, and found "quite a strip of marshy land [in the area of today's Bobby Jones Golf course and the Bitsy Grant Tennis Center between Northside Drive and Peach Tree Creek], and after passing this, the ascent to the higher ground beyond [moving toward today's Collier Road and southwest toward Howell Mill Road] is gradual."[45]

As Williams's division passed Geary's lines and filed to the right, they found an old country lane that ran to the southeast toward Howell Mill Road and the Hiram Embry House where the Rebel skirmish line was located. "From near the point where we crossed the creek, a narrow country road angled to the right, passing diagonally up the slopes and across the ravines on the south side, and uniting with a more prominent road, leading from Howell's Mills to Atlanta, about a half a mile beyond."[46] While Geary's division had fanned out across the ridges to the left, Williams's division took this lane as it proceeded from today's Northside Drive crossing of Peach Tree Creek south, then southwest, toward the Embry House, generally along the course of Norfleet Road.

Around noon, after Williams's division came up to the right of Geary's rear lines, the 74th Ohio, which had been on picket in the woods between today's Northside Drive and Howell Mill Road along today's McKinley Road,

---

[44] R. W. Johnson, *A Soldier's Reminiscences in Peace and War* (Philadelphia: J. B. Lippincott Company, 1886) 280; *OR*, ser. 1, vol. 38, pt. 5, serial 76, 436, 1075.

[45] Edmund R. Brown, *A History of the 27th Indiana* (Monticello IN: Edmund R. Brown, 1899) 517.

[46] Ibid.

The Battle of Peach Tree Creek

returned to its brigade. That morning, part of the 74th Ohio had been ordered to advance on a Rebel skirmish line "strongly posted behind piles of rails and in an old log house." Striking from the Confederate right flank, the Yankees gained a "cross fire on the rail piles, causing the Johnnies to leave "in a hurry." One Ohioan, Walter Collins, "captured one prisoner, who was behind a tree near him, and had his gun loaded, but he dropped it when Walter leveled his gun at him and told him to surrender." After halting at the edge of the woods near the confluence of today's McKinley Road and Belvedere Drive, a portion of the 74th Ohio together with the 21st Ohio and the 5th Connecticut of Knipe's brigade, "built [a] slight protection with sticks and stones, such as we could gather by dogging from one big tree to another," according to one veteran. From their position, about a "hundred yards from the rebel's [rifle] pits," which was located along today's Howell Mill Road at its intersection with Collier Road on the Embry Plantation, the Yankee skirmishers could observe the Southern lines. "The bullets flew about us pretty fast and close," and several men were wounded, including three men from the 5th Connecticut, and "a Lieutenant in the 21st Ohio [who] had two fingers shot off."[47]

Sergeant Rice Cook Bull of the 123rd New York in Knipe's brigade of Williams's division remembered after his division crossed Peach Tree Creek over the bridges that had been laid by Geary's division pioneers, "By this time it was noon and we were notified that we would halt long enough for our dinner. The Generals had their lunch prepared under the trees nearby. We made our little fires, fried our pork, boiled our coffee, and ate our hardtack. It was a bright day, though hot," the New York Sergeant remembered. "[A]fter we had our meal we made ourselves as comfortable as we could. Some were soon sleeping, others reading books or papers, a good many were having a friendly game of cards using the greasy pack that always was handy when we halted. Thus things went on until 3 in the afternoon."[48]

One veteran of Williams's division remembered, "All of the land in our front or near us was wooded, except some small patches around a cluster of vacant cabins, slightly in advance of where the 27th [Indiana] halted. To our right, and a little behind us, was a division of the XIV Corps [Johnson's division]."[49] According to Corporal Brown, "the time until after 3:00 P.M., was

---

[47] Theodore W. Blackburn, *Letters from the Front: A Union "Preacher" Regiment (74th Ohio) in the Civil War* (Dayton OH: Press of Morningside House, 1981) 214–15.

[48] Rice C. Bull, Diary, in Henry Woodhead, ed., *Voices of the Civil War—Atlanta* (Richmond: Time-Life Books, 1997) 76.

[49] Brown, *History of the 27th Indiana*, 518.

spent in crossing the troops over the creek and moving into position. The indications at that time were that we were about ready for a farther advance."[50] Therefore, the men did not entrench. Some units that had begun constructing earthworks were quickly halted as orders came down the line to prepare to move forward again shortly. Lieutenant Colonel Edwin S. Salomon of the 82nd Illinois in Robinson's brigade recorded that William's division arrived on the right flank of Geary's 2nd Division about 10:00 A.M. and they "were ordered to halt until our position would be assigned to us. It was very hot; the place where my regiment had stacked arms was without shade, and the men suffered severely from the heat."[51]

Sergeant Bull described the scene in Williams's division during the afternoon of 20 July. "There had been so far no sign of the enemy, not a warlike sound broke the stillness; and were it not for the distant sound of cannonading far to our left, we might have felt we were on a pleasure trip in the most peaceful of lands." The New York sergeant remembered, "While we were resting the rumor spread that the enemy was on the retreat, and we were marking time and in all probability would enter Atlanta the next day. The attitude of our Generals, who were near us, would seem to confirm this opinion."[52] Perhaps the constant Confederate withdrawals under Old Joe Johnston had lulled the Federal army into a belief that the Southerners were either unwilling or incapable of initiating an offensive against them.

Palmer's XIV Corps. Palmer's XIV Corps, General Johnson's 1st Division was nearest to and connected with Hooker's XX Corps along the Howell Mill Road corridor. There, his 3rd Brigade under Colonel Marshall F. Moore deployed along a wooded ridge east of the road while his 1st Brigade led by General Anson G. McCook continued the Federal line across the Howell Mill Road to Moore's right. Johnson's remaining brigade, the 2nd US Regulars commanded by General John H. King, formed a reserve line to the right and rear of McCook and linked up with the left of the 3rd Division directed by General Absalom Baird as the meanderings of Peach Tree Creek turned toward Moore's Mill where Davis's 2nd Division continued to tangle with Sears's Mississippi Brigade.[53]

---

[50] Ibid.
[51] *OR*, ser. I, vol. 38, pt. 2, serial 73, pp. 99–100.
[52] Bull, *Atlanta*, 76.
[53] *OR*, ser. I, vol. 38, pt. 1, serial 72, pp. 601–602; Blackburn, *Letters from the Front*, 214–15.

The Battle of Peach Tree Creek

According to Corporal John H. Forbes of the 74th Ohio of Moore's brigade, "At 3 o'clock [A.M.] we moved to the left, and just at daybreak crossed Peach Tree Creek (a stream of considerable size), formed in line, and after marching and countermarching for some time, we halted and cooked breakfast." There, "One company from each regiment in our brigade was ordered out on the skirmish line. Our Company was on the extreme left of our line, and joining the 20th [Hooker's] Corps skirmishers. At eight o'clock the line was ordered to advance. In front of us, about 200 yards distant," remembered the Federal corporal in a letter written to his cousin Kate the next day, "the rebels [were] strongly posted behind piles of rails and in an old log house. Our left swung round, getting a cross fire on the rail piles, and the Johnnies left in a hurry. We followed them half a mile, driving them into their rifle pits."[54]

Forbes noted that three men from the 3rd Connecticut of Hooker's corps were wounded during the Federal advance. About noon, the skirmishers of Moore's brigade which had made the advance that morning were relieved by men from General Williams's 1st Division of Hooker's corps, and the remainder of Moore's brigade retired to the right and formed on the right of McCook's brigade thus extending Johnson's line while King's brigade continued to serve in reserve behind Moore's new line. To strengthen the Federal defenses, Captain Hubert Dilger's Battery I, 1st Ohio, with its four 10-pounder Parrott Rifles, was added to Moore's line.[55]

With McCook's 1st Brigade deployed along Howell Mill Road at today's Beaverbrook Drive in which the 104th Illinois was pushed forward atop a knoll at today's Glenbrook Drive and Radcliffe Drive, Moore's 3rd Brigade formed to its west along a ridge on which today's Northcliffe Drive rests from which the brigade could overlook the plain over which today's I-75 and Tennyson Drive pass. King's 2nd Brigade rested behind Northcliffe Drive and Moore's brigade near today's Dean Drive and Wellesley Drive straddling Howell Mill Road in supporting distance.

To Johnson's right, Baird's 3rd Division found the events of 19 July both frustrating and fruitless as General Absalom Baird found no place to cross Peach Tree Creek or to deploy his force. To his left, Johnson's 1st Division found the crossing at Howell Mill "strongly disputed" by Rebel forces, while to his right, Davis's 2nd Division was being pressed by a surprising Confederate

---

[54] Blackburn, *Letters from the Front*, 214–15.
[55] Blackburn, *Letters from the Front*, 214–15; *OR*, ser. I, vol. 38, pt. 1, serial 72, pp. 507, 524, 742–43.

counterattack above Moore's Mill. Baird's men were posted along today's Peachtree Battle Circle and Peachtree Battle Avenue north of the creek and between today's Bohler Road and Howell Mill Road. By now, it was getting late into the afternoon of the hot July day. After finding no place to effectively cross around Howell Mill, "the character of the ground admitted of such easy defense that to have forced a passage must have been hazardous and attended with much loss," according to General Baird; he sent his 1st Brigade led by Colonel Moses B. Walker to cross over behind and support Dilworth's and Mitchell's brigades of Davis's division, which had formed a lodgement at today's Bohler Road.[56]

By this time in the early evening, Geary's division of Hooker's XX Corps had forced a passage over the creek along today's Northside Drive, which relieved the hitch on Johnson's division and forced the opposing Confederates at nearby Howell Mill to retire. Thus, Baird began to move his remaining two brigades "soon after dark," and, supported by Johnson's men, crossed his 2nd and 3rd brigades over at Howell Mill. By midnight, Baird's engineers erected two bridges spanning the creek that Johnson's division crossed at daylight and relieved Baird's men. Baird then moved his 3rd Brigade led by Colonel George P. Este forward to connect on its left with Johnson's division continuing the Federal line along the ridge at today's Norcliffe Drive. His 1st Brigade under Colonel Walker remained just east of today's Bohler Road and to the left of Davis's division along today's Elysian Way and Cross Creek Parkway.[57]

After linking his 1st and 3rd brigades along the low ground occupied by today's I-75 passes just east of today's Arpege Way, Baird "pushed the two out and took possession of an important range of wooded hills half a mile to the front of my first location." This was located along today's La Parc as it meanders over three wooded hills. To support his advance position, Baird placed his two batteries, the 7th Indiana Light Battery with its four 10-pounder Parrott Rifles commanded by Captain Otho H. Morgan, and the 19th Indiana Light Battery containing four Napoleons and two three-inch ordnance rifles under Lieutenant William P. Stackhouse, "at a point on Brigadier General Johnson's front, from which they would have a cross-fire upon the wooded ground over which the troops [of the enemy] must pass" to reach his lines.

---

[56] *OR*, ser. I, vol. 38, pt. 1, serial 72, pp. 742–43.
[57] Ibid.

Thus, Baird's two batteries were posted along the ridge where today's Northcliffe Drive is found.[58]

As portions of Thomas's Army of the Cumberland relaxed and began to make coffee and dinner, others wondered when and if the "Johnnies" would stick their heads out of the woods to give them a contest. Many of the Federal regimental and brigade officers speculated that the Confederates would not offer battle and their countenance clearly projected a false sense of security among the men. Meanwhile, the Rebels prepared for the battle that had long been dreamed—the battle that would redeem the South, repel the Yankee invaders, and lead to Southern Independence. Just as Old Joe Johnston had hoped, Thomas's Army of the Cumberland was spread out, without support, and now had one foot over Peach Tree Creek. His men were vulnerable to an attack during the morning and midday of 20 July, but with each passing hour, as portions of his lines advanced to take new heights and entrench upon them, his position grew stronger. Expecting great results, General Hood was described by one observer as having eyes flashing "a strange and indescribable light."[59] Hood and his staff anxiously looked to Hardee and Stewart to give him a startling and staggering victory over Sherman, and begin to reverse the tide for the South in Georgia. For Charles W. Wills of Illinois, the approach of Sherman's forces toward Atlanta was foreboding. On 19 July, he adroitly predicted in his diary, "Tomorrow night...will give us Atlanta, or there will be a fair start for a new graveyard near the town."[60]

---

[58] Ibid.; Scaife, *The Campaign for Atlanta*, 153.

[59] Long, "A Brief History of The Battle of Peachtree Creek," 12; Donald H. Bailey, *The Civil War: Battles for Atlanta, Sherman Moves East* (Alexandria VA: Time-Life Books, 1985) 92.

[60] Long, "A Brief History of the Battle of Peachtree Creek," 12; Mary E. Kellogg, ed., *Army Life of an Illinois Soldier, Including a Day by Day Record of Sherman's March to the Sea: Letters and Diary of the Late Charles W. Willis* (Washington, DC: Globe Printing Company, 1906) 244.

8

THERE'LL BE TROUBLE OUT THERE

The woods were ominously still; even the birds seemed to have stopped singing.[1]

Around three o'clock, General Featherston ordered his men out of the chalky red clay trenches. He had waited until General Maney's division to his right advanced the requisite 200 to 300 yards. "Owing to the dense forest, rugged ground, and abatis in front of our works, I moved by the right of companies to the front until I reached our line of skirmishers," explained Featherston. There he formed the men for the attack. The heart rates of the men in the 31st Mississippi began to rise.

Featherston continued to look to the wooded hill up on the right. Had Maney's division advanced? He had not seen them since they left the trenches. He couldn't hear any evidence of their advance; it seemed too quiet for such a large scale attack. The men in the lines began to fidget. They had been waiting nearly an hour. Presently, some of the men from Company C of the 31st Mississippi who had just gotten off picket duty came rushing forward from camp with their rifles, swords and pistols in hand to join their comrades. Because they had been on picket since the evening before and had not had rest or a meal in over twenty-four hours, the Chickasaw Guards had been excused from the attack. However, when they learned it was to be a general assault, many of them quickly gulped down a bit of food, grabbed their weapons, and took off down the trenches to find their regiment. They were not to be denied a chance to whip the Yankees.

Featherston continued to wait. Surely Hardee's men had gone forward? Maybe they had encountered no opposition? Maybe the dense woods muffled the familiar roar of a general engagement? In any event, he had waited the requisite time. He was the right flank of Stewart's entire corps. His advance

---

[1] Larry M. Strayer and Richard A. Baumgartner, eds., *Echoes of Battle: The Atlanta Campaign* (Huntington WV: Blue Acorn Press, 1991); Stephen Pierson, "From Chattanooga to Atlanta in 1864–A Personal Reminiscence (1907)," *Proceedings New Jersey Historical Society*, vol. 16 (1931): 209.

would start their right to left attack. Besides, what if Hardee's men had gone forward and there was now a gap between the two corps? His supporting role and that of Stewart's corps would now be needed to help relieve pressure off of Hardee and the main assault, and to help sweep any gains made by Hardee's corps. There were no staff officers from General Hood or General Stewart around to tell him when to go. If his men were to do any good that day, it was time. It was almost 4:00 o'clock.

The 33rd New Jersey Infantry in General John Geary's division, also in Hooker's XX Corps, had been ordered forward of the main line to a high point below Tanyard Branch to prepare a place for a battery. First Lieutenant Stephen Pierson, adjutant of the regiment, was reading a letter just received from his father. "The woods were ominously still; even the birds seemed to have stopped singing. Col. Jackson of the 134th New York rode up alongside of me, put out his hand and said: 'Good-bye, Adjutant.' I laughed at him, but he said, 'There'll be trouble out there.' He was right. There was to be trouble and plenty of it."[2] Pierson continued, "With no opposition we advanced to the knoll and were about to stack arms preparatory to making a place ready for the battery. The woods were dense; our skirmishers in front had made but small progress."[3]

It was a homecoming of sorts for Third Lieutenant Richard Nicholas Ivy of the 31st Mississippi. He was born just north of Atlanta before the city even existed. He was the son of Hardy Ivy and Sarah Todd Ivy, the first white settlers in the area. His parents' old home place was just beyond the ridge to the north along a street he preferred to call Ivy, originally named for his family. It has been changed since then to Peachtree Center Avenue in downton Atlanta, which merges with the now more recognizable name Peach Tree Street on its way north out of town. Yankees presently occupied the ancestral Ivy place. The war had gotten personal for Lieutenant Ivy and it was time to take back the family home. His mother was buried at Oakland Cemetery in Atlanta. Soon, many Mississippians trying to take back Ivy's old home would be added to the silent roles at Oakland Cemetery.[4]

Major Francis Marion Gillespie drew his sword. Perhaps his thoughts drifted to his fiancee back home. Lieutenant Colonel Drane, and each of the

---

[2] Ibid.

[3] Pierson, "From Chattanooga to Atlanta," 289.

[4] "Compiled Service Records of Confederate Soldiers Who Served in Organizations from the Union and Confederate States of America during the War of the Rebellion," RG 269, microfilm rolls 231-236, National Archives, Washington, DC; Ivy family memoirs, author's personal papers, Dalton, Georgia.

company captains and lieutenants likewise drew their swords and waited for the signal. For Drane, it was the first time that he had been given the opportunity to lead the regiment in an all-out assault. Sure, he had commanded the regiment on a number of occasions, including drilling, in camps, and even in defense in the Georgia Campaign, but this was different. His thoughts no doubt turned to his Choctaw County home and to his family. How would he do this day? Would this be another empty order to attack, with much marching about but no real action?

To the east, Hardee's men were supposed to be underway, but no sounds of advance were heard. Three hours had passed since the attack should have commenced. Finally, from the distant woods to the right could be heard the sound of battle. It was time for Featherston to advance. "Having reached our line of skirmishers, and being in sight of the enemy, my brigade was at once formed in line of battle for the attack." It was now after 4:00 P.M. The Mississippi brigadier formed his line "in an old field some 400 yards wide and a half a mile long. On the edge of the field, about 300 yards in my front, was a tortuous creek [Tanyard Branch]; just beyond the creek was a narrow strip of woodland running from the west to the center of my brigade." Beyond the woods, Featherston saw the Federal line [the 136th New York and 22nd Wisconsin] on an elevated ridge [today's Collier Road]. "Between the strip of timber in my front and the timber on the right of my brigade was an open space of about 150 yards, which furnished a fine view of the enemy's position, and enabled him to see my brigade, formed in line of battle 600 or 700 yards in his front."

By now, Featherston's Mississippians were prepared to attack, and on the other side of the ridge, the Federals were scrambling to meet him. Looking to his right and expecting to see Hardee's corps beginning to engage the enemy, Featherston saw that they had not gone forward. "Having formed my line of battle, I discovered the left of General Cheatham's [Maney's] division on my right—not in advance of, but on a line with me. I waited several minutes for it to advance 200 or 300 yards to the front, in accordance with the order of battle." The delay would provide time for Ward's division to assemble. Featherston added, "[Maney] moved first farther to the right, throwing the left of his division in the woods on my right, and then moved to the front. Having waited long enough, as I supposed, for him to get 200 or 300 in advance of me, and engage the enemy as soon, if not sooner than I could…I immediately ordered my brigade to move upon the enemy."[5]

---

[5] United States War Department, comp., *Official Records of the Union and Confederate Armies in the War of the Rebellion*, 128 vols. (Washington, DC: Government Printing Office, 1880–1901) ser. 1, vol. 38, pt. 3, serial 74, 868–71.

9

HERE THEY COME BOYS, BY GOD A MILLION OF THEM

Here they come, boys! By God, a million of them.[1]

> Well we saw a hot time...you may be shore.... We charged the yankees and we whipped them but I think that we got the most men killed.... I can tell you I run out a mong the yankes an a shooting at me. 2 or 3 of them said surrender or I will kill you. I told them no and I went to shooting at them. I don't see what cept them from killing me.[2]

The skirmishers of General John Newton's division cautiously moved from their position atop the large hill through the wooded ravine east of the Buckhead Road and down past the A. J. Collier outbuildings and garden skirting the road. They were under the command of Colonel Conrad of the 15th Missouri. As the Yankee skirmishers advanced toward the wooded ridge to the south (along today's Palisades Road), all of a sudden a growl came from a number of the men. When the five Federal regiments that had fanned out in a skirmish line to explore the next ridge began to peer over the new found height, they could not believe their eyes. It seemed as if Hood's entire army was before them, and what's more, the gray-clad legions were formed for an attack and were marching straight for them. From this point, Conrad's skirmishers could see the entire valley below Peach Tree Creek all the way to the Rebel's outer defenses of the city. The massed columns of Walker's division from Hardee's corps were fully in view. In the distance could be seen more columns of Confederate troops as the remainder of Hardee's lines stretched out along the plain.

Back on the hill to the east of the Buckhead Road (along today's Brighton Road) Corporal John Raper of the 26th Ohio Infantry described the scene as Conrad's skirmishers began to return: "The enemy came en masse, and our skirmishers lost no time getting back to the main line. The first one [of our skirmishers] I saw emerge from the woods seemed to be making strides about

---

[1] William R. Scaife, *The Campaign for Atlanta* (Atlanta: self-published, 1993) 90.
[2] Angus McDermid, "Letters from a Confederate Soldier," ed. Benjamin Rountree, *Georgia Review* Vol. 18, no. 3, Fall (1964): 266–67.

The Battle of Peach Tree Creek

15 feet, and as he came in sight of our line he called out at the top of his voice: 'Here they come, boys! By God, a million of them.'"[3] By 4:00 P.M., the prominent hill that was crowned by the A. J. Collier farm, had been secured and fortified by Newton's division. The hill earned its modern moniker "Cardiac Hill" by athletes who have to run up its long, grueling slope from the north along Peachtree Road in Atlanta's annual Peachtree Road Race, which occurs every Fourth of July.[4] While Cardiac Hill was not known by that name at the time that Hardee's corps attacked Newton's Federal division, many veterans, North and South alike, who had to fight along its slopes on 20 July would have surely agreed with the name.

While the remainder of Newton's men prepared a defensive line, Colonel Conrad moved the skirmishers forward. "Having advanced about 400 yards," recorded Conrad, "my right met the enemy's skirmishers in a hollow, where they had rifle pits, out of which we drove them."[5] Conrad continued, "My regiment was nearly on the summit of a very commanding ridge in front of us [just south of today's Palisades Road at its intersection with Peachtree Street] when the 73rd Illinois, with which we connected on our right, came to a halt."[6] The Missourian considered his options. "I also ordered a halt, the same time refusing my left in order to protect my left flank. I then ordered a few men to go on the top of the ridge to ascertain if any enemy in force was near us."[7]

Maurice Marcoot, one of Conrad's Missourians who had been sent to reconnoiter, recorded that his regiment had "advanced in skirmish line about a half a mile in advance of our main line. We had passed the hollow in which the confederates had dug their skirmish pits, while just on the hill beyond their main works had been erected. We thought these works were vacated from their appearances."[8] Marcoot, merely a nineteen-year old boy with German immigrant roots, volunteered to go forward. "At my request," he explained, "I was permitted to crawl up the hill and ascertain, but was cautioned to be very

---

[3] Scaife, *The Campaign for Atlanta*, 90.

[4] Ibid., 92c; Steve Davis, "So Much for Historical Accuracy: The Misplacement of the Howell Battery Marker," 3, www.atlantatrackclub.org/am-coursemap.pdf (10 Feb 2008).

[5] United States War Department, comp., *Official Records of the Union and Confederate Armies in the War of the Rebellion*, 128 vols. (Washington, DC: Government Printing Office, 1880–1901) ser. 1, vol. 38, pt. 2, serial 72, 326 (hereafter *OR*).

[6] Ibid.

[7] Ibid.

[8] Donald Allendorf, *Long Road to Liberty, The Odyssey of a German Regiment in the Yankee Army: The 15th Missouri Volunteer Infantry* (Kent OH: Kent State University Press, 2006) 207.

careful, as we had no orders to go further forward than the hollow."[9] Conrad remembered, "They came back in a few minutes reporting to me that the enemy was approaching in heavy columns on our left and also in our immediate front. Their reports proved to be true," added the colonel.[10] Marcoot was more specific, and graphic:

> Proceeding forward, I soon gained a position were I commanded a view of the works, and vicinity beyond them and found that their troops were marching toward our left…Soon [our] bugler in the center—far to our left—blew "retreat" but we were in no hurry as we saw nothing to retreat from, and I still continued to watch the "Johnies…" Suddenly they came to a halt, then in quick succession came the command, "front, forward, double quick, march!" and over their works they jumped with a yell toward us. The fun was suddenly all over for me—for as soon as I started to run for my command, I was discovered and then was the bullets rattled around me for a few moments was not slow, and I could not make up my mind to heed their friendly intimation to "surrender, you d–d [Yankee]."[11]

Conrad and his Missourians and the others on his skirmish line including the 73rd Illinois, the "Preacher Regiment," had "stumbled onto half of Hood's army."[12] Conrad recorded, "A few minutes afterward the enemy appeared in heavy force right in our front, on our left and right, firing and yelling, demanding to surrender, &c. Seeing the impossibility to hold my ground, I ordered the men to fall slowly back, which was done in good order," continued Conrad, "the men running from tree to tree, always keeping firing up, until we came near our works."[13]

Whether Conrad's men retired in good order was certainly debatable. Many Yankees took off for safety to the rear, some not stopping until they were well behind the newly erected Federal works and a couple hundred yards up the Buckhead Road toward the bridge that had just been completed over Peach Tree Creek. A number of Federals in the reserve brigade that was posted along the road began to call out to their comrades to stop, and their entreaties began to take hold of the unnerved skirmishers who then almost as a whole began to form up and return to the defense line on the hill. Most of Conrad's men,

---

[9] Ibid.; Maurice Marcoot, *Five Years in the Sunny South* (St. Louis: Missouri Historical Society, 1890) 69–73.
[10] *OR*, ser. 1, vol. 38, pt. 2, serial 72, 326.
[11] Allendorf, *Long Road to Liberty*, 207–208.
[12] Ibid., 208.
[13] *OR*, ser. 1, vol. 38, pt. 2, serial 72, 326–27.

however, upon reaching the earthworks, stopped, turned, and quickly positioned themselves to receive the Rebel blow. Some of the blue-clad skirmishers were not so fortunate to reach the Northern works, however. Over to the left of Conrad's line, portions of the 57th Indiana were pushed all the way toward and over Peach Tree Creek near the mouth of Clear Creek in the wake of the onrushing Rebels. Others were trapped in the wooded ravines along the western edges of Clear Creek (along today's Huntington Road and Wakefield Drive) and captured. While the surprised Federal skirmishers were fraught with sudden fear, a different response came from the Confederates almost as suddenly. "At the same moment a cheer arose—a wild, tumultuous, shrill cry, from thousands of throats—falling on the ear like a sudden and unsuspected clap of thunder."[14]

According to one Northern correspondent, "Our skirmishers commenced firing and falling back at the same moment." It didn't slow the Confederate advance. "With lightning-like celerity heavy columns of rebels appeared in front of, or rather tumbled out of the forests, their columns seeming to be endless, and carrying themselves with a certain indescribable verve in the onset which made every one who beheld it from our lines tremble."[15] To many of the Yankees atop the hill, it appeared that all was lost. "'How will that fearful wave be broken?' was the piercing fear that filled every bosom, which was not allayed by seeing our lines in apparent confusion—the confusion of men grasping their muskets, taking the touch of the elbow and facing to the front." As Walker's heavy columns drew closer, the risk to Newton's isolated line seemed most perilous. "Words cannot describe the crushing suspense of the first five minutes of the charge," wrote one witness. "Newton's lines were so thin they looked, in some places, like skirmish deployments."[16] The newspaperman observed the return of the skirmishers. "The curtain of pickets guarding the interval in our lines came rushing along, bedaubed with mud and bedraggled with water, having barely escaped the rebel rush with their liberty." In summing up the situation, he added, "it [was] confounded scaly."[17]

The German Missourian Marcoot remembered his race to Federal line: "our troops had already thrown up considerable earthworks, not formidable at

---

[14] D. Van Nostrand, "How We Fight in Atlanta," in Frank Moore, ed., *Rebellion Record. A Diary of American Events*, vol. 11, comp. G. P. Putnam, 250.

[15] *Cincinnati Commercial*, 28 July 1864; Erol Clauss, "The Atlanta Campaign, July 18, 1864" (Ph.D. diss., Emory University, 1965) 78.

[16] Nostrand, "How We Fight in Atlanta," in Moore, ed., *Rebellion Record*, 11:250.

[17] Ibid.

all, but something for the boys to stand by."[18] Young Marcoot recalled sadly that one of his comrades may have been killed by friendly fire: "As soon as we had returned from the skirmish line, our command opened fire, and I fear that Comrade Phister fell from a bullet from a musket of one of our own men, as I had passed him completely fagged some thirty yards from the line in my own wild race for life."[19] Samuel Phister, a thirty-five-year-old shoemaker from Switzerland, had been "hit in the shoulder and left leg, which was soon amputated," the wound causing his death at a hospital in Chattanooga six weeks later.[20]

General O. O. Howard, leader of the IV Corps, afterward said that "John Newton could never be surprised,"[21] but Conrad's Missourians had fled the skirmish line so quickly that when they reached the Federal lines, they had split such that half of the regiment, the 1st Battalion, came in "on the main Atlanta Road" (Peachtree Street), which Conrad posted on the right of the 88th Illinois alongside Goodspeed's Battery along the road, while the 2nd Battalion "having to make a detour, came in the works of the Second Brigade [Blake's], where they remained fighting with the rest of said brigade until toward evening."[22] To his credit, however, Newton and his division had wisely begun to prepare defensive works along the heights along the Buckhead Road so that by the time Hardee's men advanced, Newton's men had a good line of works from which to fight. Marcoot, who had fallen back with the 2nd Battalion of the 15th Missouri to Blake's line east of the road, recorded the action of Goodspeed's Battery posted on the Buckhead Road: "Our cannon…had been brought up quickly and took their position on our right a little to the front of our line, so that they could shoot down in front and parallel with our lines."[23] Marcoot added, "When [the] Confederates had advanced so near us that our officers were firing upon them with their revolvers, it was the grape and cannister fired by those two guns that saved the day. The carnage however was fearful,"[24] remembered the Missouri veteran. "The enemy seemed determined to stay and were literally mowed down again and again before they would yield."[25]

---

[18] Allendorf, *Long Road to Liberty*, 208.
[19] Ibid.
[20] Ibid.
[21] O.O. Howard, *Autobiography* (New York: The Baker & Taylor Co, 1907) I:613.
[22] *OR*, ser. 1, vol. 38, pt. 2, serial 72, p. 327.
[23] Allendorf, *Long Road to Liberty*, 209.
[24] Ibid., 209.
[25] Ibid.

Walker's Division. Walker's division advanced up the wooded ridge: "Massed in enormous columns...[they came] on without skirmishers and with yells whose volume exceeded those of any battle-shout I ever heard." The correspondent added that the Confederates "poured forth from their concealment ...with the celerity of lightning." While Newton's blue-clad forces scrambled to find cover, Walker's men pressed closer. "The Johnnies were charging by the acre," a Yankee exclaimed, adding that "our troops were in confusion."[26]

Walker's Georgians appeared over a hill so quickly that the Federals darted for their guns, casting aside shovels and axes that had occupied them moments before. As both sides began to fire at each other, almost instantly the southern slope of the hill exploded in a violent and mind-numbing crescendo of battle noise. On the road, Goodspeed's artillery began to fire in earnest, causing one cannoneer to describe the sound of battle as "something like the heavens and earth had suddenly come together."[27]

Walker's division, largely Georgia troops, struck the Federal lines without any support. In the meantime, Bate's division, which led off the attack, marched aimlessly off into a boggy, cane- and pine-laden plain along the southern side of Peach Tree Creek and, failing to find the Federal left flank, got lost in the process. As Walker's veterans moved up astride the Buckhead Road, they struck Newton's division. According to one Federal officer, Walker's Georgians and the rest of Stewart's corps down the line "came surging on through the woods...with noise and fury like Stonewall Jackson's men at Chancellorsville."[28]

In the rear of Newton's lines there was much activity. "A stream of non-combatants commenced flowing across the bridge over Peach Tree Creek. Pack-mules, imprudently taken close to our lines by fortuitous darkies, came scampering back, the latter turned tawny-brown with fright and perspiration," remembered one Northern correspondent. "Ambulances tumbled over the bridge in demoralized columns. A few armed stragglers stalked sheepishly

---

[26] [*New York Tribune*, 27 July 1864; Clauss, "The Atlanta Campaign, July 18, 1864," 78.

[27] Castel, *Decision in the West*, 376.

[28] O. O. Howard, "'The Very Woods Seemed to Moan and Groan': The Struggle for Atlanta," in Ned Bradford, ed., *Battles and Leaders of the Civil War* (New York: The Fairfax Press, 1979) 504; Glenn W. Sunderland, *Five Days to Glory* (South Brunswick NJ: A. S. Barnes, 1970) 158.

along, the consciousness that everybody who met them would fathom their meanness imprinted on their faces and in their movements."[29]

---

[29] Nostrand, "How We Fight in Atlanta," in Moore, ed., *Rebellion Record*, 11:250.

10

A STRAGGLING, HAPHAZARD KIND OF HIDE AND SEEK AFFAIR

On the 20th the battle of Peach Tree Creek was fought and given a prominence in excess of the facts as the writer saw it; a straggling, haphazard kind of hide and seek affair, magnified into a battle.[1]

Bate's Division. General Bate ordered his division out of the trenches for the attack. While Walker's men were drawing the attention of Newton's division along the Buckhead Road, Bate's men marched out from around the northern end of today's Piedmont Park over a mile and a half away. Bate's veterans headed toward Peach Tree Creek across today's Ansley Park Golf Course. Bate's three Brigades had drawn the key assignment of being the enveloping force, by starting the attack and then rolling up the Federal line. Unfortunately, Bate's men would lose their way and "flounder about," unable to find the enemy. "Knowing that they were expected to attack, these blind gropings, these senseless stop-and-start tactics, exasperated the troops of the division."[2]

Bate's division moved forward and out of sight from Hardee and his staff. Finding no Federal infantry in their front, Bate's legions continued north until they ran into a tangle of "heavy woods, thickets and ravines."[3] Having failed to perform a reconnaissance of the area they were to attack, Bate's men were blindly marching forward in battle formation, in search of the Federal lines. Not having been ordered to scout the area he was to attack by General Hardee, perhaps because they did not have time in light of the eastward shift, Bate did

---

[1] L. D. Young, *Reminiscences of a Soldier of the Orphan Brigade, June 26, 1916* (Paris KY: Louisville Courier-Journal Job Printing Company, 1918) 90.

[2] Nathaniel Cheairs Hughes, Jr., *The Pride of the Confederate Artillery, The Washington Artillery in the Army of Tennessee* (Baton Rouge: Louisiana State Press, 1997) 196–97; Thomas L. Connelly, *Autumn of Glory, The Army of Tennessee, 1862–1865* (Baton Rouge: Louisiana State Press, 1971) 440–41; Albert Castel, *Decision in the West: The Atlanta Campaign of 1864* (Lawrence: University Press of Kansas, 1992) 372–78.

[3] Phil McCall, ed., "Private Isaiah Crook Diary, 37th Ga., Smith's Brigade, Bate's Division, Hardee's Corps," 3, vertical files, Kennesaw Mountain Battlefield Park Library, Kennesaw, Georgia.

not know what lay ahead of his men. He could not know that there was no Federal force directly in front of him, and that his division was actually positioned to exploit a gap of almost 2 miles in the Federal lines. What happened next seems almost unbelievable: "The right division under Bate, scheduled to strike the entrenchments first, did not even find Thomas. Bate's men spent the afternoon stumbling through the thick underbrush in search of Thomas's line. Suddenly, Bate simply disappeared from sight, and Hardee did not find him until after 6 P.M., when he sent a staff officer who located the general still searching for Thomas's line in a forest of thick timber."[4]

Bate's division had moved north and northwest from the northern edge of today's Piedmont Park and across today's Ansley Golf Course and into the swampy cane-laden ground along the southern bank of Peach Tree Creek east of the Clear Creek Branch of the creek. Bate's division marched and countermarched in the pocket created by the two creeks for the next two or three hours. They did not find any Federal force before them save a few skirmishers to their left, which they pushed back across the creek. Instead of crossing Peach Tree Creek and sweeping to the left or west along the northern bank of the creek, Bate's men changed direction and marched to the west to the sound of the battle where their comrades in Walker's division could be heard in action. By failing to perform an adequate reconnaissance of their place of attack, Bate and his men never knew that they were in a position to turn and flank Newton's division and to get in the Federal rear without having to face a fixed or entrenched Yankee line. They were positioned to deliver a surprise rear or flank assault, but Bate and his troops had failed to realize it. But having failed to perform any reconnaissance, Bate's staff had failed to discover that the terrain they were to cross would prove to be impenetrable to a battle line formation. Instead, by the time that they were located and redirected into the fight, it was too late for them to render any effective assistance to Walker's division, or to Featherston's Mississippians and the remainder of Stewart's corps who would make vigorous assaults farther down the line.

When he had not heard from Bate, and after nearly two hours of Bate's absence without hearing any sound of battle from his front, Hardee had staff officer W. D. Pickett find General Bate and his "lost" division and connect them with Walker's right. Pickett found them in today's Sherwood Forest. They had veered off course in the cane brush that forms the bottom of today's Ansley Golf Course and were slowed so much by the thick underbrush that they had

---

[4] Connelly, *Autumn of Glory*, 443.

ground nearly to a halt. At some point, Bate and his staff realized that they had been veering to the north and northeast and that the cane brush was preventing them from maneuvering toward the Federal line in time for any attack. When he found Bate and his men, Pickett wrote this dispatch to Hardee:

> General: On reaching General Bate, I found that he had swung his division around, and was moving in a direction to strike the enemy's flank. Under the circumstances I thought his movement the best, and did not change it. He is now moving slowing onward, but it is necessarily slow, as the undergrowth is in places dense. I fear he will not be able to strike the enemy's flank much before dark. I sent Captain—with an order to Walker to swing around, and thought it best to come to Bate.[5]

Hearing the sounds of fighting to his left and having failed to gain any appreciable ground in nearly two hours of struggling through the cane, Bate ordered his division to change front to the southwest to move out of the cane thicket and back toward the wooded low ridges that formed the southern boundary of the cane-covered bottoms. This ground was the old home place of George W. Collier, father of A. J. Collier, and one of the oldest white settlers in the area, the area long known as the Collier Woods (and also called Land Lot 104). Portions of Old Montgomery Ferry Road wound through the woods and provided an escape from the Sherwood Forest for Bate and his men. By the time Bate's division filed out of the Collier Woods and into the Atlanta-Buckhead Road (Peachtree Street) from the area near today's Robin Hood Road, NE, dusk was imminent, too late to mount any attack. Thus, some 3,000 veterans, including the Kentucky Orphan Brigade with about 1,002 men left in their number, who were to be the trigger of the Southern attack, were effectively put out of action without even firing a shot.[6] Moreover, while they couldn't see the Federal lines, the now-alerted Yankees on the Buckhead Road along the ridge behind the Federal works could see them and began directing artillery fire on them. Bate's division had Finley's Florida Brigade on the right, Smith's Georgia Brigade in the center, and Lewis's Kentucky Brigade on the left.[7]

---

[5] United States War Department, comp., *Official Records of the Union and Confederate Armies in the War of the Rebellion*, 128 vols. (Washington, DC: Government Printing Office, 1880–1901) ser. 1, vol. 38, pt. 5, serial 76, p. 897 (hereafter *OR*).

[6] William C. Davis, *The Orphan Brigade: The Kentucky Confederates Who Couldn't Go Home* (Baton Rouge: Louisiana State University Press, 1980) 229.

[7] William R. Scaife, *The Campaign for Atlanta* (Atlanta: self-published, 1993) 92c.

Hood's First Sortie, 20 July 1864

After getting untangled, Bate's men skirted around the left of the cane thicket, trying to locate the left of the Federal position. Instead, they found the wrath of Thomas's guns on the ridge overlooking the Buck Head crossing of Peach Tree Creek. According to one Federal officer, "whole battalions went far east of [Newton's division] into the gap... [General] Thomas, behind the creek, was watching; he turned some reserved batteries upon those Confederate battalions, and fired his shells into the thickets that bordered the deep creek, sweeping the creek's valley as far as the cannon could reach. This was sufficient; in his own words, "it relieved the hitch." The hostile flankers broke back in confusion."[8] It has been widely believed that they "attacked east of present day Peach Tree Road near Piedmont Hospital, but made no headway against the Federals arrayed on higher ground. After two hours, the Battle of Peach Tree Creek [in that part of the field] ground to a halt...."[9] However, this was Mercer's Georgia brigade's attack.

Lewis's Kentucky Orphan Brigade. According to Johnny Green of the Orphan Brigade, "A short sharp fight we had at Peach Tree to day. Lost seve[r]al men killed & wounded. The army is massed around Atlanta now. We were slowly moving from one position to another nearly all night..."[10] Green's comrades in the 9th Kentucky lost four men wounded, all from Company A.[11] The 5th Kentucky lost three men wounded while in the 6th Kentucky Private A. Jeff Henderson who was merely a boy, "but hardy, courageous, and faithful...lost a finger" during the assault. Another veteran from the Orphans remembered that the role played by the Kentuckians and her fellow members of Bate's division in the Battle of Peach Tree Creek was a futile waste of time and men. Lieutenant L. D. Young recorded: "On the 20th the battle of Peach Tree Creek was fought and given a prominence in excess of the facts as the writer

---

[8] O. O. Howard, "'The Very Woods Seemed to Moan and Groan'": The Struggle for Atlanta," in Ned Bradford, ed., *Battles and Leaders of the Civil War* (New York: The Fairfax Press, 1979) 504.

[9] McCall, ed., "Private Isaiah Crook," 3. This was actually Georgia's Brigade attack.

[10] A. D. Kirwan, ed., *Johnny Green of the Orphan Brigade* (Lexington: University of Kentucky Press, 1956) 147.

[11] Courtesy of James Ogden, chief historian. Subject file, Kentucky Confederate Regiments, Chickamauga and Chattanooga National Parks, Research Library, vertical files [; Wounded were 1st Corp. E. E. Dunn, Prvt. R. Boone Chastain, and Prvt. Moses H. Hester, a teamster, and Drummer Benjamin White, all in Company A, from Russellville, Logan County, Kentucky. Corp. Dunn had been wounded before at Chickamauga, and he would recover in time to receive his third wound, which would prove to be fatal, at Jonesboro a month later.

saw it; a straggling, haphazard kind of hide and seek affair, magnified into a battle."[12]

One Orphan remembered, "a slight engagement took place on Peach Tree Creek, on the afternoon of July 20, in which the Kentucky Brigade participated, and suffered some loss, mainly in skirmishe[r]s under [Lieutenant] Colonel [George W.] Connor, who charged those of the enemy and drove them across the creek."[13] Therefore, the Kentucky Orphans lost a total of eight men wounded during the attack at Peach Tree Creek while they failed to reach the Federal line.

Finley's Florida Brigade. Private Washington M. Ives experienced the battle from Brigadier General Jesse J. Finley's Florida Brigade, which formed the extreme right of the assault. The private noted in his diary:

> July 19—Last night we began building breastworks. Completed works this morning, sprinkle of rain last night. Very warm brisk skirmishing during the day. Marched out to meet the enemy but returned to the works.
>
> July 20—At 11:00 A.M. Hardee's Corps moved 1 1/2 miles east along the works and at 1:00 P.M. [actually, about 4:00 P.M.] it crossed the works and charged the enemy. Bates Division on the right did not become engaged. Walker and Cheatham [Maney] suffered most.[14]

While Ives did not see any action, some of the remainder of Finley's Floridians fell victim to General Thomas's artillery as Finley's men attempted to cross through the cane thicket. The Floridians lost six men along Peach Tree Creek during 19 and 20 July, with one man being wounded on the 19th. The Florida Brigade saw five of its men fall to the Federal artillery fire that harassed the right of Bate's charge along the creek. With two men killed during the advance and three wounded, the frustrated Floridians did not get the chance to return fire or get close enough to make any difference in the assault.[15]

Smith's Brigade. In Brigadier General Thomas B. Smith's Georgia and Tennessee Brigade, Sergeant Isaac V. Moore of Carlton, Madison County,

---

[12] Young, *Reminiscences of a Soldier,* 90.

[13] Ed Porter Thompson, *History of the Orphan Brigade 1861–65* (Cincinnati: Caxton Publishing House, 1868) 261, 724–25, 777, 809–11, 815.

[14] Washington Ives, *Civil War Journal and Letters of Serg. Washington Ives, 4th Florida C.S.A.,* trans. and ed. Jim R. Cabaniss (Tallahassee: self-pubished, 1987) 14.

[15] Jim Thomas, "Soldiers of Florida," vertical files, Chickamauga National Military Park Library, Chickamauga, Georgia.

Georgia, who served in the 37th Georgia, recorded in his diary: "We fell back to our breastworks and made a charge." It was telling, perhaps, that Moore gave no other details of his regiment's charge, it being as nondescript as the results of his brigade's assault. Sergeant Moore also noted that three men were wounded in Company H.[16] The total casualties in the 37th Georgia were two killed, four wounded, and one captured, for a total of seven men, with one of the killed and the captured occurring on 19 July.[17]

Only one casualty was reported in the 20th Tennessee Infantry Regiment as Private Nathan E. Morris of Company H fell wounded,[18] while the lone casualty in the 30th Tennessee Infantry was 3rd Sergeant F. M. Browning of Company H who was wounded in the leg.[19] The remaining units in Smith's brigade, the 4th Georgia Sharpshooters, the 15th and 37th Tennessee regiments, did not report any casualties on 20 July. Thus, Smith's total losses at Peach Tree Creek were six wounded, one captured, and two killed, but only seven men were casualties during the attack, six wounded and one killed.[20]

One war correspondent, Albert Roberts, editor for the *Southern Confederacy*, went by the pen name of "John Happy" for his contributions to the *Chattanooga Daily Rebel*, a refugee newspaper that had fled Chattanooga to Atlanta, and then to Griffin, Georgia, where it issued a paper on Wednesday, 27 July 1864.[21] In that edition "John Happy," who had attached himself to Smith's brigade, formerly known as Tyler's brigade (and still referred to as Tyler's

---

[16] I. V. Moore, diary, vertical files, Chickamauga National Military Park Library, Chickamauga, Georgia.

[17] ftp://ftp.rootsweb.com/pub/usgenweb/ga/muscogee/military/k37.txt (26 July 2008).

[18] W. J. McMurray, *History of the Twentieth Tennessee Regiment Volunteer Infantry, C.S.A.* (Nashville: Elder's Bookstore, 1976) 168.

[19] http://freepages.genealogy.rootsweb.ancestry.com/~providence/cw_chap8k.htm (26 July 2008).

[20] ftp://ftp.rootsweb.com/pub/usgenweb/ga/muscogee/military/k37.txt (26 July 2008); *Tennesseans in the Civil War, A Military History of Confederate and Union Units with Available Rosters of Personnel*, 2 vols. (Nashville: Civil War Centennial Commission, 1964–1965) I:207, 255; John Berrien Lindsley, ed., *Military Annals of Tennessee, Confederate*, 2 vols. (Wilmington NC: Broadfoot Publishing Company, 1995) I:334–35, 503–505; "Compiled Service Records of Confederate Soldiers Who Served in Organizations from the Union and Confederate States of America during the War of the Rebellion," RG 269, National Archives, Washington, DC, microfilm roll 192. Browning had previously been captured at Fort Donelson, exchanged, and later shot through both thighs at Chickamauga; his wounding at Peach Tree Creek ended further active duty with the army.

[21] Stephen Davis, "How Many Civilians Died in Sherman's Bombardment of Atlanta?," *Atlanta History: A Journal of Georgia and the South* 45/4 (2003): 5–23.

The Battle of Peach Tree Creek

brigade by many of its members), wrote of the brigade's experience during the Battle of Peach Tree Creek. "On the afternoon of Wednesday, Hardee's Corps advanced on the enemy. At three o'clock the firing was general along our whole line. While Walker's and Cheatham's Divisions, and a part of Stewart's Corps, advanced on the enemy's front, Bate's Division was wheeling on its left, and," according to John Happy, "drove the enemy in its front across the creek."[22]

What Happy was referring to was the small line of skirmishers posted there from Newton's IV Corps, including the 100th Illinois and perhaps a portion of the 57th Indiana.[23] The Federal skirmishers in front of Bate's division scattered and withdrew to the northern side of Peach Tree Creek after firing a few scattering shots at the advancing Confederates. John Happy continued, "Bate who was on our right [of the Confederate attack], swung around on his left and moved steadily forward till nightfall, when he was ordered to halt, which he did when he had gained the Buckhead Road."[24] In other words, Bate had failed to find the enemy's flank, and his division had failed to deliver a blow against Newton's division. By dark, Bate's tired brigades crept out of the Collier Woods and, using portions of the old Montgomery Ferry Road as a guide to get out of the cane thickets where they had spent the past three hours, filed their way onto the Buckhead Road (between today's Robin Hood Road and The Prado) where they fell back to Atlanta's trenches.

The casualties in Bate's division were tellingly light. Lewis's Kentucky Orphans lost eight men wounded, Finley's Floridians lost three wounded and two killed (another man was wounded on 19 July), and Smith's Georgia and Tennessee Brigade lost six wounded and one killed (with one man captured and one killed on 19 July) while squandering the day in the cane thicket east of Clear Creek. Thus, some 3,300 men were effectively kept out of action while 17 men were wounded and 3 men killed in either light skirmishing with a couple of Federal units or from Federal artillery fire.

Members of Wood's and Stanley's Federal divisions of Howard's IV Corps, which had stopped for the day and begun to entrench, watched Hardee's attack from their vantage point on the distant heights between the North and South Forks of Peach Tree Creek (along today's La Vista Road and Briar Vista School). "At 4 o'clock we heard the sound of battle some distance on our right

---

[22] *Chattanooga* [Griffin GA] *Daily Rebel*, 27 July 1864, Tennessee State Library and Archives, microfilm 1045, roll 1, Nashville.

[23] *OR*, ser. 1, vol. 38, pt. 3, serial 72, 297.

[24] *Chattanooga* [Griffin GA] *Daily Rebel*, 27 July 1864, Tennessee State Library and Archives, microfilm 1045, roll 1, Nashville.

on Newton's and Hooker's fronts. From our line of works we had a very good view of the valley and could follow the course of the contending forces by the smoke of their guns," remembered Adjutant Cope of the 15th Ohio in Wood's division. Cope added that "the fighting continued until dark when it suddenly ceased."[25]

---

[25] Alexis Cope, *The 15th Ohio and Its Campaigns, War of 1861–5* (Columbus OH: Alexis Cope, 1916) 525.

NOW YOU MAY GIVE IT TO THEM, CAPTAIN

> I have never forgotten a mere boy, belonging to a Georgia regiment, whom we brought in and laid upon a blanket under a tree. He was helpless, a bullet having crushed his thigh. We gave him food and water, and did what else we could to mitigate his suffering. The tears gathered in his eyes as he said, "They told us that you-all would kill us if you took us prisoners. I didn't think you'd be so kind to me!"[1]

Walker's Division, Stevens's Georgia Brigade. While Bate's men were hopelessly mired in the dense underbrush and cane thickets to the east, Walker's division reached the Federal lines atop the heights where Buckhead Road and Collier Road adjoined at the home of A. J. Collier. The first brigade from Walker's division to reach the heights was Stevens's Georgia Brigade.

Reaching the fences surrounding the Collier's home and garden, the left of Stevens's brigade closely followed portions of Kimball's skirmishers as they retreated into the Federal works. Unable to fire until the front was cleared of friendlies, Goodspeed's four guns held until men from the 15th Missouri, 73rd Illinois, and 24th Wisconsin scurried into the works. No sooner had Kimball's troops been recovered than Goodspeed's guns blasted out their noisy greeting to Stevens's men. Hordes of Rebels gained the outer works atop the hill along the Buckhead Road and curtilage surrounding the Collier home as the 66th Georgia under Colonel James C. Nisbet and the 1st Confederate Georgia led by Colonel George A. Smith swarmed the heights. For a moment it seemed that Newton's division would be routed from the works, but Kimball's veterans then unleashed a scathing fire all along their front, causing the Georgia lines to crumble before them. Exposed in the open around the Collier homestead, the 1st Confederate Georgia and 66th Georgia were slaughtered in just a few minutes.

Seeing the repulse of their comrades, the right half of Stevens's brigade checked up about twenty paces from the Federal works and began to fire from

---

[1] Wilbur F. Hinman, *The Story of the Sherman Brigade* (Alliance OH: Press of Daily Review, 1897) 580.

the cover of the wooded ridge in that sector. To their right and rear, Gist's brigade came up and also checked its advance, choosing instead to take up a line along side the right of the remainder of Stevens's brigade in the woods (extending east along today's Camden Road). When it became clear that breaching the Yankee works in their front (along today's Brighton Road) would be extremely costly if not fatal, Gist's men began sliding to the right, covered from Federal fire by a ravine toward Clear Creek as they explored a place from which to attack the Federal flank or rear. Meanwhile, Maney's Tennesseans having taken longer to arrive due to the tangled briars and vines to the southwest of Stevens's brigade, (below today's Ardmore Park), found that the left of Stevens's brigade was hopelessly exposed to a solid Federal line behind works. After reaching this conclusion, Maney's men begin to lie down and exchange rifle fire from a couple of hundred yards away (around today's 28th Street between Wycliffe Road and Ardmore Road).

Isolated and exposed, the ranks of the 1st Confederate Georgia and 66th Georgia rapidly thinned. In less than ten minutes, the two regiments were wrecked. Nearly 100 men from each regiment fell in that time. Colonel George A. Smith of Macon, Georgia, was killed as he led the 1st Confederate Georgia, while Lieutenant Colonel Algemon S. Hamilton and Major Robert Newton Hull of the 66th Georgia were wounded. Seeing the disintegration of his two left regiments and realizing that Maney's Tennesseans were not coming up, General Stevens rode to his left front to recall his men.

1st Confederate Georgia. Falling with Colonel Smith in the 1st Confederate Georgia was Samuel Fields, of Bibb County, Georgia, where Macon is located. Samuel, the son of John Fields, was killed as he carried the regiment's flag. After the color-bearer of the 1st Confederate Georgia was "shot down, young Fields seized the standard, but had not borne it five minutes before he, too, received a mortal stroke."[2] The *Macon Daily Telegraph* reported on Friday, 22 July, that "Several of the wounded of this regiment arrived by the noon train of yesterday," making for a mournful reunion for those in the city known as the Heart of Georgia.[3] In the 30th Georgia, also in Stevens's brigade, Orderly Sergeant Joseph Jolley of Company I was shot in the arm, which he subsequently lost.[4]

---

[2] "From the Front," *Macon* [GA] *Daily Telegraph*, 22 July 1864, 1.
[3] Ibid.
[4] After the war, Jolley became the clerk of the superior court of Butts County and later the clerk of the board of commissioners for that county. A. P. Adamson, *Brief History of the 30th Georgia Regiment* (Jonesboro GA: Freedom Hill Press, 1987) 126.

Captain Russell J. Jones of Company D, 1st Georgia Confederate Infantry Regiment led his men into the fray. Company D was made up of men and boys from Catoosa and Walker counties in Northwest Georgia, and Jones was from the little railroad town of Ringgold, Georgia, near where the Andrews Raid, or better known as the Great Locomotive Chase had ended two years earlier. Captain Jones had been wounded the year before while leading his company at Chickamauga, but had returned to carry his men through the North Georgia campaign. As they approached the Federal works, a bullet struck Captain Jones. Desperately, his men struggled to carry him from the field, where a surgeon successfully stopped the bleeding. But the war for Russell J. Jones was over. He would later die from his wound at Peach Tree Creek, more than thirty years later. An 1896 *Walker County Messenger* published his obituary: "Russell J. Jones, one of the oldest and most prominent residents of Ringgold, Ga. died Saturday evening about 7 o'clock at his home in Ringgold. His death was caused from a bullet wound which he received in the war." The article continues by explaining that he was the Catoosa County clerk, had previously been the ordinary (probate judge) for Catoosa County, and "was well known by every man, woman and child in Ringgold, and his death has cast a gloom over the community." Jones was about sixty years old, and had suffered for years before succumbing to the wound.[5] The massive casualties sustained by the 1st Georgia Confederate Infantry bore testament to the severity of the fighting along the Buckhead Road. The 1st Georgia Confederate lost twenty-six men killed, forty-nine wounded (with two who were wounded and then captured), and seventeen captured (one of whom was captured on 19 July) for a total casualty list of ninety-two men.[6]

29th Georgia. To the right of the 1st Georgia Confederate, the 29th Georgia led by Captain J. W. Turner added three more men killed, with nine wounded and one of the wounded men was captured, for a total of twelve losses as their advance along the wooded ravine and up the slope of the hill just to the east of the Buckhead Road was checked by Newton's men. Among the killed from the 29th Georgia was Private Elias Lastinger who owned a farm in Bulloch County, Georgia leaving his eleven-year-old daughter, America

---

[5] "Obituaries," *Walker County* [La Fayette GA] *Messenger*, 6 August 1896; Lillian Henderson, ed., *Georgia Confederate Pension and Record Office. Roster of the Confederate Soldiers of Georgia, 1861–1865*, 7 vols. (Hapeville GA: Longino & Porter, 1955–1958) 1:1–113.

[6] Henderson, *Roster of the Confederate Soldiers of Georgia*, 1:1–113; *Macon* [GA] *Daily Telegraph*, 22 August 1864; *Macon* [GA] *Daily Telegraph*, 25 August 1864.

Hood's First Sortie, 20 July 1864

Lastinger (later Davis), to work and plow the fields with her mother.[7] Private Angus McDermid of the 29th Georgia from Adel, Georgia, was just seventeen when he enlisted in 1861. Now, at twenty, he was a seasoned veteran. McDermid wrote home on 21 July about the Battle of Peach Tree Creek: "I hav bin spared to live this long and fought the Yanks twice. Well we saw a hot time yesterday you may be shore. I was in a nother Battle yesterday. We charged the yankees and we whipped them but I think that we got the most men killed," he explained. "Father I can tell you I run out a mong the yankes an a shooting at me. 2 or 3 of them said surrender or I will kill you. I told them no and I went to shooting at them. I don't see what cept them from killing me."[8]

66th Georgia. To the left of the 1st Georgia Confederate, Colonel James Cooper Nisbet, led the 66th Georgia to the federal works. Wounded two years earlier at Gaines Mill, near Cold Harbor during the Seven Days Battles in Virginia, Nisbet was a veteran of Lee's Army of Northern Virginia where he had served as a captain of Company H, 21st Georgia.[9] When Nisbet was well enough to return to service, General Howell Cobb granted him permission to raise a regiment, the 66th Georgia, and he was commissioned its colonel.[10]

According to Colonel Nisbet on 20 July:

> Stevens' Brigade moved out of the works on the Peach Tree Road. We were told that the enemy had just crossed Peach Tree Creek that morning and were unfortified. My regiment formed into line of battle on the left of the Brigade with my left resting on the Peach Tree Road.
>
> We advanced, and drove in the enemy's skirmishers. There was a considerable gap on my left. I protested against advancing until this gap was filled; but the order was given—and the line went in with a rush—right up to well-constructed earthworks!
>
> My regiment and that on my right, the 1st Georgia Confederate Infantry, captured the works in our front. But we were not supported. The enemy on my left, not being assaulted, continued to enfilade my line. Seeing

---

[7] Willa Davis Johnson, "Reminiscences of the Sixties," in *Confederate Reminiscences and Letters, 1861–1865*, ed.: Georgia Division, United Daughters of the Confederacy, 1996–2000) 11:34.

[8] Angus McDermid, "Letters from a Confederate Soldier," edited by Benjamin Rountree, *Georgia Review* 18, Fall, no. 3 1964): 266–67.

[9] James Cooper Nisbet, *4 Years on the Firing Line*, ed. Bell Irvin Wiley (Jackson TN: McCowat-Mercer Press, 1963) 64–65; Ray Roddy, *The Georgia Volunteer Infantry, 1861–1865* (Kearney NE: Morris Publishing, 1998) 367.

[10] Nisbet, *4 Years on the Firing Line*, 64–67; Roddy, *The Georgia Volunteer Infantry*, 367.

The Battle of Peach Tree Creek

fresh troops being rushed up against us, I was certain we could not hold the position. This was near the bridge crossing Peach Tree Creek. Our brigade commander, General Stevens, rode in, ordered me to fall back and was killed as he gave the order. I ordered the regiment to fall back. Captain Briggs Moultrie Napier and Captain Charles J. Williamson both received wounds in carrying General Stevens' body from the field. Lieutenant Charles W. Gray was wounded. Captain Thomas Parks of the Newton County Company was killed. He was a noble, efficient, brave soldier. Never was I under a heavier fire than there....[11]

Captain Parks was Henry F. Parks of Covington, Georgia who had been killed during the assault.[12] William Reed of the 66th Georgia, wrote his sister on 21 July telling her that when she read his letter, it would bring tears. "We have again had ourselves exposed to a most terrific fire," he wrote. "God in His kind providence has again spared me, even to having allowed a minie ball to strike my pants and yet not injure my leg. But He saw fit to take a leg from our dear friend Captain B. H. Napier." Reed went on to explain that Briggs Napier with one leg was worth a dozen two-legged ones. "He was shot...in a dreadful charge up over the enemy's breastworks. Being repulsed, Briggs among the wounded was left on the field of wounded and dead. Night came on and my company was sent forward on picket duty. In deploying, I heard in an excited tone, 'Halt!,'" noted the Georgia veteran. Reed continued, "In feeble answer, 'I am a wounded man!' 'Are you a Rebel or Yankee?' 'A rebel!' Then says the picket, 'Lieutenant Reed, there is a wounded man in our front.'" The Georgia officer explained, "I not knowing who it was, but for the sake of humanity, had one of the litter bearers of our brigade to bear him off the field. I never thought any more of it. Wounded men were all too common there. On being relieved and returning to our breastworks," said Reed, "I was sent for by Briggs and to my great astonishment found he was the poor sufferer I had heard that came so near to being left in the hands of the enemy and who perhaps would have been shot again by them. I took his head on my breast, brushed the hair off his forehead," explained the Lieutenant, "and made him as comfortable as possible. Briggs acted like a man, stood up to his post with credit."[13]

---

[11] Nisbet, *4 Years on the Firing Line*, 209.
[12] Ibid., 136.
[13] William Reed to sister, 21 July 1864, in Mills Lane, ed., *"Dear Mother: Don't Grieve about Me. If I Get Killed, I'll Only Be Dead": Letters from Georgia Soldiers in the Civil War* (Savannah GA: Beehive Press, 1977) 318.

Hood's First Sortie, 20 July 1864

General Clement Hoffman Stevens. As General Clement H. Stevens rode up to the 66th Georgia and the 1st Georgia Confederate Infantry to withdraw his men, he was, according to one account, shot fatally in the head. The minnie ball entered his skull just behind the right ear as the general turned his head to face the 66th Georgia. According to another account, Stevens was mortally wounded by an artillery round fired just as he turned to face the 66th Georgia, knocking him from his horse and also fatally wounding the animal, which "made its way to the front of the line of battle before collapsing."[14] One Federal account places Stevens in front of the 40th Indiana, which fought along the right of Blake's position (where Brighton Road today joins Peachtree Street).[15]

Willie Reed, also of the 66th Georgia, wrote his sister about the falling of her boyfriend, Briggs Hopson Napier, and of Stevens: "I also carried General Stevens off the field; he was shot through the temple and in his delirium gave his martial orders to his last breath."[16] Stevens was carried off the field to a hospital where he died on 25 July. According to Captain Furman of the 16th South Carolina, "General Clement Hoffman Stevens, former commander of the 24th South Carolina and first commander of the Gist Brigade, Stevens was called 'Rock' by his men."[17] Brother to Colonel P. F. Stevens of the Holcombe

---

[14] Arthur W. Bergeron, Jr., and Clement Hoffman Stevens, "The Confederate General," in William C. Davis, ed., *The End of an Era*, 6 vols. (Garden City NY: Doubleday, 1984) 4:4–5.

[15] Albert Castel, *Decision in the West: The Atlanta Campaign of 1864* (Lawrence: University Press of Kansas, 1992) 376. It is probable that Stevens and his horse were fatally wounded from a canister round fired by Goodspeed's battery posted on Buckhead Road, or that he and the horse were hit by a combination of rifle and artillery fire (with his wounding at today's Peachtree Street in front of Ted's Montana Grill). However, the Georgia Historical Marker erected by the late historian Wilbur Kurtz place Stevens's wounding near the intersection of Wycliff Road and 28th Street, which would put him in front of the approach of Maney's Tennessee division that was supposed to support Stevens's Georgians. While that location makes sense if Stevens was trying to encourage Maney and his division to help, Stevens's officers state that he was in the act of trying to extract the left regiments of his brigade (the 1st and 66th Georgia) from the Federal lines along Buckhead Road when he was hit. Moreover, Stevens's horse was also killed in the incident and some Northern veterans gave accounts of Stevens's horse remaining on the Buckhead Road for several days after the battle, a gruesome reminder of the Georgia brigade's attack and of Stevens's mortal wounding.

[16] Willie Reed to sister Elizabeth Adele Jones "Bessie" Reed, later Mrs. Briggs Hopson Napier, in *Confederate Reminiscences and Letters, 1861–1865*, edited by GA Division of UDC, 58–61. Volume 6. (Atlanta: United Daughters of the Confederacy, 1997.

[17] "The Letters and Papers of Charles Manning Furman," http://batsonsm.tripod.com/letters/letters9.html (1 March 2008).

Legion of South Carolina, the beloved general was initially buried at the Magnolia Cemetery in Charleston, South Carolina, on 27 July but his body was reinterred at the St. Paul's Cathederal in Pendleton, South Carolina, where he was buried next to his wife and two sons.[18]

Colonel Nisbet described the action along the Buckhead Road atop Cardiac Hill. "I thought I would certainly see my 'Valhalla' that day. I lost one-fourth of all of my officers and men engaged. The firing from both the front and flank was terrific. We abandoned the works and fell back a short distance, as ordered."[19] Lieutenant William Ross of the 66th Georgia led his Company forward. Willie Ross from Macon was just nineteen and was engaged to Emma Jane Kennon of Oxford, Georgia. While the 66th Georgia advanced, a bullet ripped the tip of his sword off as he directed his men with it.[20]

By this point, Goodspeed's Battery was inflicting a devastating toll on Stevens's and Gist's brigades along the southern approaches to the Northern position. One Federal soldier observed, "the dusky, gray columns slackened their pace and began to waver and lose their careful arrangement. In a few minutes they had come to a standstill, in partial confusion, and firing heavily but wildly." The Yankee witnessed Southern officers bravely ride up on horseback with swords drawn, urging their men forward, and color-bears bravely leading their regiments on, only to be cut down by Federal fire. "Color-bearer after color-bearer went down underneath the crash of our canister.[21]

Colonel Nisbet summarized the fruitless assault: "It will be seen that the enemy had crossed Peach Tree Creek the evening before and fortified, and that Hood was acting on *misinformation*. The fight was a miserable affair on his part, from start to finish."[22] Had Hardee properly coordinated his brigades and

---

[18] Eugene W. Jones, Jr., *Enlisted for the War: The Struggles of the Gallant 24th Regiment, South Carolina Volunteers, Infantry, 1861–1865* (Highstown NJ: Longstreet House, 1997) 405; www.geocities.com/BourbonStreet/Square/3873/gist.htm (1 March 2008).

[19] Nisbet, *4 Years on the Firing Line*, 210.

[20] Unscathed, Willie managed to return to the safety of the Atlanta trenches to fight in the Battle of Atlanta where he would again be spared. But his good luck would not continue for on 6 August the young lieutenant would be struck by three bullets, paralyzing his legs and leaving him mortally wounded. He would die before his fiancé could be summoned to his side.

Lee Kennett, *Marching through Georgia: The Story of Soldiers & Civilians during Sherman's Campaign* (New York: Harper-Collins Publishers, 1995) 196–97.

[21] "Assault on Newton's Division," *New York Tribune*, 28 July 1864; Erol Clauss, "The Atlanta Campaign, July 18, 1864" (Ph.D. diss., Emory University, 1965) 81–82.

[22] Nisbet, *4 Years on the Firing Line*, 210 (emphasis original).

divisions, Nisbet believed his spearhead attack could have been successful. Instead, the failure to strike the Federal lines by more than Walker's lone division, which made three disjointed assaults by its three brigades, would result in their easy repulse by Newton's blue-clad veterans who were heavily outnumbered by Hardee's corps.

Gist's Brigade. Gist's brigade had found portions of Newton's division exposed on a wooded ridge a couple of hundred yards in front of the main line of works, and, after a couple of wild shots were fired by the surprised Yankees, began chasing them toward Peach Tree Creek. Kimball had posted from east to west the 15th Missouri east of the Buckhead Road, the 73rd Illinois, astride it, and the 24th Wisconsin. The skirmish line was commanded by Colonel Joseph Conrad of the 15th Missouri, but the screen created by the three regiments under Conrad did not extend far enough to the left or east to cover the Federal position to the Peach Tree Creek or the Clear Creek branch that flowed into it east of Newton's lines.[23] To cover that gap, the 100th Illinois and the 57th Indiana were sent forward, but the ground that they were ordered to cover was a series of hollows and hills that spread out the two units into small bands not fit for any defensive deployment in the event of attack.

Just at that moment, the woods in front of them filled with Rebels. For a brief moment, the surprised Yankees looked at the surging gray lines to confirm their first suspicions, fired a shot into the woods before them, and then ran like deer for their lines. Those that were too far downhill and nearer Clear Creek found themselves trapped along its banks. Here, several Yankee wounded and trapped men surrendered to some of the attacking units of Gist's brigade that began to sweep into the area between today's Camden Road and Clear Creek as parts of Blake's and Bradley's brigades formed along today's Brighton Road and prepared to receive them.

Veteran Lewis (or Lucius) Q. C. Askew, of Company F, 46th Georgia in Gist's brigade, wrote about his experience along Clear Creek on the far east of the battlefield.

> I received a slight wound and went to a small spring branch to quench my thirst and wash my wound. There I met a sight that I can never forget. Many of the wounded who were able to get to the water, and many others carried there by friends to quench their thirst and wash and dress their wounds, were

---

[23] United States War Department, comp., *Official Records of the Union and Confederate Armies in the War of the Rebellion*, 128 vols. (Washington, DC: Government Printing Office, 1880–1901) ser. 1, vol. 38, pt. 3, serial 72, 305–306 (hereafter *OR*).

lying there with their heads in the water dead. Poor fellows, those who were mortally wounded, some of them managed to get to the water, and died in it, while many of them were bathing their wounds. The water was bloody, and no chance to get a drink without drinking their comrades' blood. I was so very thirsty that I was forced to quench my thirst with water that was red with blood from the dead and dying comrades. After washing my wound I got a wounded comrade to tie my handkerchief over my wound, and sought a place away from this sad scene, using my gun as a crutch, and as I was hobbling on my way I discovered a Federal crouched in a gully. On the spur of the moment I was about to surrender to him, but as I stood looking at him, and he making no effort to capture me or make his escape, the thought popped into my mind that he mistook me for a friend, as I had on a Federal cavalry jacket. I at once took advantage of his mistake, and called on him to get out and shoot the Confederates, as they could plainly be seen pressing their enemy before them. And, to my surprise, he jumped up looking in the direction I pointed, and I discovered for certain that he had mistaken me for a friend, and I told him that my gun was unloaded, and if he would let me have his gun I would show him how good a shot I was. I was not surprised at him handing me his gun; but I assure you I surprised him. I treated him kindly, and would suffer no one to take anything he had or to mistreat him in any way. We became good friends, and before I turned him over to the guards who took him to prison, he gave me his watch, gold ring and other things he was sure would be taken from him after I left him. Each of us exchanged addresses, promising to write after the war was over. But when I was captured in October after that and taken to prison at Camp Douglas, Ill., everything was taken from me, even my diary which had his address.[24]

Mercer's Georgia Brigade. In Bigadier General Mercer's brigade, after running through the woods east of the Buckhead Road and up and down the hollows, hills and ravines, the men were exhausted by the time they reached the Federal works. The some 2,000 Georgia "Crackers" were in a position to flank the left of the Yankee lines and to seize the Federal escape route across Peachtree Creek, but they faced an unexpected obstacle: a stream known as Clear Creek. According to historian Scott Walker, "Mercer's brigade charged into a

---

[24] Askew, L. Q. C., Monday, 3 August 1908 -Historic Templeton McCanless P Dowisetrriecdt by Mambo, www.historictempletonmccanlessdistrict.com (generated 15 June 2008, 18:40).

morass of wooded, vine-entangled swamp, only to find no Union troops in front of them. They had unknowingly flanked the left end of the Union line."[25]

The 100th Illinois and part of the 57th Indiana of Brigadier General George D. Wagner's 2nd Brigade (commanded by Colonel John W. Blake because Wagner was absent sick from 10 July to 25 July) arced in front of Mercer's brigade in a wide skirmish line.[26] The 100th Illinois and the 57th Indiana had been sent forward on a reconnaissance to the left of the skirmish line established by Kimball's brigade and were covering the extreme left of Newton's position (along today's Ottley Drive and Armour Drive) east of Clear Creek.[27]

Clear Creek and its plain northeast of Atlanta was a significant geographic challenge to Hood's plan of attack, which has been little understood and little considered by historians as it was not considered by Hood and Hardee before launching his attack across the Clear Creek Valley. Although Newton's division and the remainder of Howard's IV Corps were separated by nearly 2 miles before the attack, they were fortuitously protected by the winding stream and its swampy, cane-filled bottom, which covered this gap. While not impassable, it posed a significant obstacle for Hardee's attackers and provided no north-south roads for infantry units or supporting artillery batteries. Only old Native American trails, animal trails, and the Old Montgomery Ferry Road, which meandered generally east to west, were found in Bate's front or in front of the right of Walker's division where Mercer advanced. Today, the Sherwood Forest Subdivision and the Ansley Golf Club are hidden in the valley of Clear Creek, which still protects them from any major roads or thoroughfares of Atlanta and serves as a buffer between Peachtree Street to the west, Interstate 85 to the north, Piedmont, Cheshire Bridge Road and Monroe Drive to the east, and downtown Atlanta to the south.[28]

Clear Creek would serve as a buffer for Newton's exposed left flank during the Battle of Peach Tree Creek as it deflected Bate's division away from the Federal lines and shielded them from view. While Bate's men were

---

[25] Scott Walker, *Hell's Broke Loose in Georgia, A History of the 57th Georgia* (Athens: University of Georgia Press, 2005) 153.

[26] William R. Scaife, *The Campaign for Atlanta* (Atlanta: self-published, 1993) 147; *OR*, ser. 1, vol. 38, pt. 3, serial 72, 337.

[27] *OR*, ser. 1, vol. 38, pt. 3, serial 72, 337.

[28] David R. Kaufman, *Peachtree Creek: A Natural and Unnatural History of Atlanta's Watershed* (Athens: University of Georgia/Atlanta History Center, 2007); http://preservemidtownatlanta.org/MidtownHistory.html (30 November 2008).

wandering in the wilderness of the Clear Creek valley, Mercer's brigade crossed the creek near where Interstate 85 and the Southern Railway intersect. Next, Mercer's brigade had to cross the stream again between today's Clayton Road and Armour Drive before crossing the Camden spur east of Brighton Road on its way up the hill to meet Thomas's artillery and Bradley's reserve brigade.

Colonel Charles H. Olmstead, commander of the 1st Georgia Infantry Regiment in Mercer's brigade, described their advance. "[Mercer's brigade] advanced over very difficult ground, first through a thick wood, then across a boggy valley through which a small water course meandered tortuously. It turned and twisted so much that we had to wade it two or three times in pressing forward." Olmstead and the remainder of Mercer's brigade finally got over Clear Creek a second time and formed to attack (along the Camden Road spur east of Brighton Road), but Stevens's and Gist's men had already been repulsed and their assault was stillborn. A few well-placed rounds from Thomas's guns confirmed Mercer's decision to call off the attack but not before he lost approximately forty men. Colonel Olmstead explained, "Indeed we never got fairly into action as the attack had failed in other parts of the field and the [brigade] was withdrawn before it reached a point of close touch with the enemy."[29]

Only a few minutes before the attack, Newton's men grew suspicious of the "quietness in front" and "the ease with which this position was secured," which "excited suspicion" that the Rebels were about to attack them. Therefore, Blake's veterans and Kimball's men to their right, "commenced a line of works a short distance in front of the line on which they had stacked arms." According to one member of the 26th Ohio, Corporal John T. Raper, "A barnyard's numerous cross fences and buildings furnished abundant material." The corporal continued, "Stakes were driven, rails piled in between them and the whole line took up the work thus begun," explained Raper. "Very little earth had been thrown against this rail barricade when the enemy began his advance; but it was sufficient protection from the musketry, and the heavy woods in front shielded it from the view of the rebel artillerymen."[30]

Blake's (Wagner's) Brigade. Colonel John W. Blake had been in command of General Wagner's 2nd Brigade for the past ten days because Wagner was sick. Forming to the left of Kimball's brigade, Blake lined his brigade up (along today's Brighton Road starting at its intersection with Peachtree Street) with the

---

[29] Walker, *Hell's Broke Loose in Georgia*, 153.
[30] Scaife, *The Campaign for Atlanta*, 90.

Hood's First Sortie, 20 July 1864

40th Indiana on the right under the command of Lieutenant Colonel Henry Leaming next to the 88th Illinois of Kimball's brigade, which was posted just east of the Buckhead Road and in support of Goodspeed's four guns. Next, the 26th Ohio led by Lieutenant Colonel William H. Squires formed the center of Blake's line, while the 97th Ohio under Colonel John Q. Lane made up the left. Colonel Blake refused the left of his line (opposite the intersection of today's Wakefield Drive with Brighton Road), meaning that he placed a part of his force at a 90-degree angle to cover his exposed left flank, because there was no supporting force to connect with his left. Blake had earlier ordered the 57th Indiana commanded by Lieutenant Colonel Willis Blanch to cover his front in a skirmish line and also the 100th Illinois under Major Charles M. Hammond was sent out on skirmish to cover the left flank of the brigade. Finally, Blake held the 28th Kentucky, led by Major George W. Barth, in reserve behind his line (just north of today's Brighton Road).[31]

Corporal Raper of the 26th Ohio Infantry was serving as the acting ordnance sergeant in charge of keeping "the regiment supplied with ammunition." He would have a front row seat to the approach of Walker's division against his regiment and those around him and to the Federal batteries as they deployed and prepared to defend Newton's left flank and rear and the division's escape route over the Buckhead Road bridge over Peach Tree Creek. The Ohioan had heard that the Rebels were coming as the Missouri skirmish line clamored over the works and into the protection of the Federal lines. As soon as the Rebel lines approached, "The men in the works immediately set up the cry, 'Ammunition, ammunition!' I knew that they had 40 rounds or more; but in the Atlanta campaign they had come to think that 40 rounds were hardly enough to commence a fight with, much less to complete it," explained the ordnance sergeant. Moreover, he and his men "knew it was nearly three-quarters of a mile back to the bridge which was without a floor, and therefore the ammunition wagons could not cross it. The cry for ammunition and this knowledge made me uneasy, for I took a good deal of pride in the fact that while it had been my duty to supply them," Raper explained, "they had never called in vain nor withdrawn from a line of battle, however long the engagement, to replenish their [cartridge] boxes. I didn't know how it was going

---

[31] Scaife, *The Campaign for Atlanta*, 147; Castel, *Decision in the West*, 376; Raper, 213.

to be with the closest wagon three-quarters of a mile away, and a 'million' rebels in front." Raper "started off with all speed to the bridge."[32]

By the time that Mercer's Georgians caught up to and lapped over the left of Blake's lines, Stevens's and Gist's brigades had already delivered their blow against the Federal regiments under Kimball and Blake atop the hill along the Buckhead Road corridor. General Bradley's 3rd Brigade had first deployed to meet Gist's attack, and then re-deployed to meet Mercer's parry, once Gist's assault had been diffused. From their position on the spiny ridge along the Buckhead Road, the men of the 3rd Brigade could observe the attack. Stevens's brigade had struck the Federal line along the Buckhead Road and wrapped around the southern slopes of the ridge in the Brookwood Hills neighborhood to the east (today's Brighton Road) and the home and garden of the A. J. Collier house to the west (near the southwest corner of today's intersection of Peach Tree Street and Collier Road), while Gist's brigade came up in support to the east of the road. Meanwhile, to the far east, or in the wooded ridges and ravines east of the Buckhead Road and between it and Clear Creek, Mercer's Georgia Brigade made their way toward the Federal lines, pushing back and chasing elements of Kimball's and Blake's skirmishers as they went.

Ten or fifteen minutes after Stevens's Georgians had first struck Newton's lines along the Buckhead Road corridor, Featherston's Mississippi Brigade began its attack. "At this time Hooker's XX Corps became heavily engaged at some distance to our right. Sherman's line was much attenuated and broken, McPherson and Schofield being six or eight miles to the left," exclaimed Lieutenant Colonel Hinman of the 65th Ohio. Significantly, Hinman recorded, "It was Hood's evident purpose to burst through the Union center and disrupt the line. The roar of musketry and artillery upon our right indicated fierce fighting."[33] The Ohio colonel's remarks indicate that the fighting to the west in front of Ward's division and beyond was much more desperate than that witnessed in his front.

Concerning the action before the 1st and 2nd brigades (Kimball's and Blake's), Hinman explained that the two brigades "halted and began to throw up intrenchments. They had not half finished their work, when a large mass of the enemy, in three successive lines, emerged from the woods and charged them, with blood-curdling yells." Hinman was most likely describing the three brigades of Walker's division as they attacked Newton's position. "The Union

---

[32] John Raper, "General Thomas at Peach Tree Creek," 214.
[33] Hinman, *The Story of the Sherman Brigade*, 578.

soldiers withheld their fire until the rebels were within fifty yards and then delivered a volley so destructive that the assailants recoiled and fled in disorder."[34]

Gist's brigade reformed, and, after probing the Federal lines for a weakness, turned to strike at the vulnerable Federal left flank that lay exposed along the spiny ridge on which the Buckhead Road lay. According to one historian, "Brigadier General States Rights Gist's Georgians, South Carolinians, and Mississippians, taking advantage of a sheltering ravine, bypass the Union left and head for the bridge over Peachtree."[35] This was in the area between today's Camden Road the west bank of Clear Creek, which turns northeast around the ridge spur on which sits today's Brighton Road where the Federal line was formed.

At first, Bradley's 3rd Brigade advanced to line up with and extend Blake's brigade line to the east and northeast along today's Brighton Road to meet Gist's parry. However, after reaching this point, it became evident that the Yankees were being flanked by the Georgians of Mercer's brigade. According to Lieutenant Colonel Hinman, "at the left of the 2nd Brigade [Blake's] was a deep ravine which was not occupied by our troops. It was soon discovered that a column of the enemy (Mercer's brigade) was moving through this ravine for the apparent purpose of gaining our rear." This ravine is located east of today's Brighton and Camden Roads and between them and Clear Creek, and then swings north and west around the elbow of a ridge on which Brighton Road sits. "Our brigade was instantly dispatched to check this movement," explained Hinman.[36]

"We formed line of battle to the left of the road and parallel to it, and advanced. Reaching the crest of a low ridge [the eastern portion of Brighton Road facing southeast] our skirmishers came upon those of the enemy, not more than thirty yards distant," as remembered by Lieutenant Colonel Hinman. "In their rear we could see a heavy line [some 2,000 men of Mercer's Georgia Brigade] advancing upon us. Our position was not advantageous for defence, and our single brigade was evidently greatly inferior in strength to the force we must encounter." Colonel Emerson Opdycke wrote his wife the day after the battle, "There was a gap of a mile upon our left, and the enemy soon began passing a heavy column through it."[37]

---

[34] Ibid., 578.
[35] Castel, *Decision in the West*, 376.
[36] Hinman, *The Story of the Sherman Brigade*, 578–79.
[37] Emerson Opdycke to Wife Lacy Opdycke, 21 July 1864, in Glenn V. Longacre and

The Battle of Peach Tree Creek

Bradley's brigade (a/k/a The Sherman Brigade). According to one veteran of the old Sherman Brigade, which was now a part of the 3rd Brigade of Newton's division, commanded by General Luther P. Bradley, "the stress of the fighting fell upon the XX Corps, but we got enough of it to make it decidedly interesting."[38] Earlier, before the Confederates launched their surprise attack, Bradley's brigade had been lined up to assault the Confederate lines. Lieutenant Colonel Hinman remembered, "With a vivid recollection of our experience at Kennesaw, we did not relish the prospect before us, and no regrets were expressed when, after a more careful survey of the ground, the plan was changed and the order to assault was revoked."[39]

Bradley's 3rd Brigade of which Hinman's 65th Ohio was a part, mustered barely 1,000 men, but over half of the brigade had already been detached and sent to various sectors along the Federal front line, including the 51st Illinois, which was sent to support the 88th Illinois just east of and at the Buckhead Road; the 27th Illinois, which was moved forward to support Kimball's refused line on the right along the grounds of today's Piedmont Hospital; and the 42nd Illinois, which was pushed up along with the other Illinois regiments at the onset of the assault by Walker's division. According to Colonel Opdycke, "The 3rd [Bradley's] Brigade was in reserve but some portions of it were sent to brace up the front line."[40] The 42nd Illinois supported the 97th Ohio of Blake's brigade along the middle of the Brighton Road sector of the Federal line east of Buckhead Road. Additionally, the 79th Illinois had already been sent to the left, north of Peach Tree Creek, and east of the Buckhead Road on picket duty. When fighting broke out, General Bradley went forward with the three Illinois regiments to the front line to survey the situation. He left the remaining four regiments, the 3rd Kentucky, and the 64th, 65th, and 125th Ohio regiments, under the command of Colonel Emerson Opdycke of the 125th Ohio. Therefore, Opdycke's force, merely a half-brigade strength, watched as Mercer's 2,000 Georgians moved through the wooded ravine below them and around their left flank and into the field that approached the road and bridge over Peach Tree Creek behind them.

Opdycke described the scene. "My four regiments were formed in a single line, two ranks, obliquely to the rear, from the left of our front line; and I then

---

John E. Haas, eds., *"To Battle for God & the Right": The Civil War Letters of Emerson Opdycke* (Champaign: University of Illinois Press, 2007) 200–201.

[38] Hinman, *The Story of the Sherman Brigade*, 577.
[39] Ibid., 578.
[40] Opdycke to wife Lucy Opdycke, 21 July 1864, 200–201.

advanced them some distance under fire, taking 18 prisoners [apparently from Grist's brigade]; was doing first rate, when I received orders from General Newton to return with haste." Opdycke explained that he was to "take another position facing a field and farther to my left. We withdrew in not very good order, except the 125th Ohio." Opdycke praised the Ohioans (his old regiment): "It maneuvered as well under fire as at any time, and went to its position with ranks perfectly closed; then the other regiments rallied upon it. God bless the 125th Ohio. Their discipline and courage are conspicuous and glorious."[41] While various shirkers and non-combatants of Newton's division began to beat a hasty retreat up the Buckhead Road, the 125th Ohio held its position along the side of the road awaiting orders. Colonel Bradley of the 51st Illinois and Colonel Opdycke "vainly tried to stop these men," remembered First Lieutenant Ralsa C. Rice of the 125th Ohio. Then, Opdycke rode by the Ohioans, and after "observing our line, remarked, 'I always know where to find my boys.'"[42]

Opdycke first sent Colonel Moore and the 125th Ohio to the woods to the left flank of Blake's brigade, but seeing Mercer's Georgians advancing around the low field to the left and rear and on its way toward the bridge over Peach Tree Creek, reversed the Ohioans quickly back to their original spot along the Buckhead Road. There, the Ohioans along with the balance of Bradley's brigade that had not been sent to reinforce other parts of Newton's hotly contested lines, prepared to give the Georgians a warm reception.[43]

At this time, Bradley returned to his four regiments along the low ridge (at the eastern part of today's Brighton Road), and, seeing the danger that faced his men, [by Mercer's brigade] quickly ordered them to withdraw back to the Buckhead Road and their original position atop the spiny ridge. According to General Bradley, "Returning from the front line soon after I found the enemy working around to our left, and immediately withdrew Colonel Opdycke and," his reduced force "formed on the Atlanta road, facing east."[44] All that stood between the Buckhead Road bridge crossing over Peach Tree Creek and disaster were the some 500 men of Opdycke and Bradley's little command and a few artillery pieces that had been brought up when the attack began.

---

[41] Opdycke to wife Lucy Opdycke, 21 July 1864, 201.
[42] Ralsa C. Rice, *Yankee Tigers, through the Civil War with the 125th Ohio*, ed. Richard A. Baumgartner and Larry M. Strayer (Huntington WV: Blue Acorn Press, 1992) 127.
[43] Ibid., 127.
[44] *OR*, ser. 1, vol. 38, pt. 1, serial 72, pp. 355–56.

Lieutenant Colonel Hinman received new orders: "We were instantly ordered to 'about face' and move back to the road, which was upon high ground and a good place to fight. We made our change of base at double-quick, and the rebels, supposing us to be in full retreat, followed swiftly, with loud cheers." Hinman continued, "Our officers were cautioned not to permit their men to keep on running after regaining the road, but to halt them there, face about and confront the enemy. There was little need for caution; our soldiers were too well schooled in war." The Ohio leader proudly boasted, "There seemed to be scarcely a man in the ranks who did not comprehend, as well as those who wore shoulder straps, the situation of affairs and the need of the moment."[45]

According to Colonel Opdycke, "The rebel column was in fair view, crossing the field along my new front, just as we were ready for them."[46] Hinman explained, "At the road the men turned by a common impulse, and, partly covered by a fence, faced the foe. The rebel skirmishers were almost at our heels and the main body was not more than two hundred yards away. Our men poured into them a staggering volley and immediately began to 'load and fire at will,' each man working with the energy of desperation. Never did soldiers stand more bravely to their work. There was scarcely a laggard or a skulker," exclaimed Hinman. "The rebels halted and delivered a volley, but they were upon much lower ground than ourselves and most of their shots passed harmlessly over our heads."[47] As for Mercer's Georgians who attempted to turn the Federal left and get into their rear, Opdycke explained, "Our fire, and that of a portion of Goodspeed's Battery, soon sent them back again in utter disorder. The officers exerted themselves to rally and charge again, but did not succeed."[48]

1st Lieutenant Rice of the 125th Ohio remembered:

> Our next formation was in line facing the creek, our regiment on the right of this line which reached nearly to the bridge. The road at this point was along

---

[45] Hinman, *The Story of the Sherman Brigade*, 579.
[46] Opdycke to to wife Lucy Opdycke, 21 July 1864, 201.
[47] Hinman, *The Story of the Sherman Brigade*, 579.
[48] *OR*, ser. 1, vol. 38, pt. 1, serial 72, pp. 202–203, 298, 500–501, and serial 73, 474, 484; Scaife, *The Campaign for Atlanta*, 157; Opdycke to to wife Lucy Opdycke, 21 July 1864, 201. One section of Goodspeed's battery along with the six Napoleons of Battery C from the 1st Ohio Light Artillery and the six 10-pounder Parrott rifles of the 1st Michigan Light Battery, for a total of fourteen guns were trained on Mercer's Brigade as they attempted to turn the Federal left at the bridge. The 1st Ohio Light and the 1st Michigan Light Batteries were actually from Ward's 3rd Division of Hooker's XX Corps, but were in park on the north side of the bridge immediately prior to the Confederate assault.

the crest of high ground that descended rapidly to low, flat ground along the creek. This low ground from the woods to the bridge was under pretense of cultivation—stunted corn and weed, with the later predominating—surely not good footing for men on the run. We were in position only momentarily when a column of the enemy came out of the woods into the field. They were in a solid column, company front. I saw no skirmishers or flankers.[49]

Rice witnessed a conversation between General Thomas at the bridge and a courier from General Newton with an urgent message. Newton, from the front line, called for reinforcements. Thomas, who had no additional troops nearby, calmly told the messenger, "Go back and tell Newton that I will reinforce him personally." Thomas then crossed over to the southern side of the creek and began directing the artillery that had been in reserve to cover the exposed left flank.[50]

Back along the Buckhead Road at the hill, a Northern reporter witnessed the action as Goodspeed's Battery repelled Walker's attack. "There are some things [that] happen in battles which go to show that Providence does not always favor the largest battalions," he wrote. "It falls to the lot of some men to do the lucky things at the lucky moment; and…Goodspeed…, twenty minutes before the charge, ordered ten guns from the north to the south bank of Peachtree Creek, he probably little thought," said the correspondent, "that he was to contribute so much toward crushing the rebellion—to the repulse of what many think the most reckless charge the enemy has made during the war."[51]

Along the Buckhead Road behind Newton's division and overlooking the Federal bridgehead over Peachtree Creek, were six guns from Newton's division and two more batteries of Ward's division that Goodspeed and General Thomas had brought over from the north side of Peachtree Creek when the fighting commenced.[52] The six guns of Newton's division consisted of the 1st Illinois Light Artillery, Battery M, a four-gun battery of 3-inch ordnance rifles (which had an effective range of 1,830 yards, or just over 1 mile at 5 degrees of elevation) commanded by Captain George W. Spencer, and one section of two guns from the 1st Ohio Light Battery A, which used 12-pounder Napoleon guns (which could fire 1,600 yards effectively at the same elevation). Ward's batteries, the 1st Michigan Light Artillery, Battery I consisting of six 10-

---

[49] Rice, *Yankee Tigers*, 127.
[50] Ibid., 127.
[51] Frank Moore, "How We Fight in Atlanta," in, *Rebellion Record. A Diary of American Events*, vol. 11, comp. G. P. Putnam (New York: G. P. Putnam, 1868) 251.
[52] Castel, *Decision in the West*, 376.

The Battle of Peach Tree Creek

pounder Parrot rifles (which had a range of 1,900 yards), was led by Captain Luther R. Smith, while the other battery commanded by Lieutenant Jerome B. Stephens, was the 1st Ohio Light Artillery, Battery C, containing six Napoleons. Together, the two batteries of Ward's division artillery were led by Captain Marco B. Gary who had his men and guns in parc on the north side of Peach Tree Creek awaiting further orders from General Ward to advance over to the south side of the creek and take up a position along his front.[53]

Corporal Raper, who was on his mission back to the north bank of Peach Tree Creek to retrieve additional ammunition for his regiment, was nearing a bridge that had just been completed when "a mounted orderly dashed across the road in front of me. He reined up his horse suddenly at a pile of rails on which an officer was sitting, his elbows resting on his knees which were drawn well toward his body," observed the acting Ordnance Sergeant, "and field binoculars in his hands directed toward the corner of the woods to left and rear of the position held by Wagner's [Blake's] Brigade. As the orderly reined up, the officer took the glasses from his eyes, turned his face and I saw it was General George H. Thomas." Thomas was looking intently at the exposed left flank of the Federal line located along the end of today's Brighton Road where it curls back toward Camden Road. The Federal commander had come across the creek at the first sounds of firing, and taken up a command position along the Buckhead Road near today's Peachtree Park Drive.[54]

Raper continued, "The orderly saluted and said, 'Gen. Thomas, Major McGraw [of the 57th Indiana] presents his compliments and says to inform you that the enemy is moving on him en masse, and it will be impossible to hold his position.'" The orderly had just come from the threatened area on the Federal left flank. "'Orderly, return to Major McGraw, give him my compliments and tell him to hold his position. I will attend to those fellows as soon as they can get out from behind the woods,' was the reply, with which Gen. Thomas again turned his glasses to the corner of the woods."[55]

The Ohioan forgot his mission for the moment. "From the direction taken by the orderly and Gen. Thomas's fixed attention to the corner of the woods, I inferred that Major McGraw, who commanded the 57th Indiana, was along the

---

[53] *OR*, ser. 1, vol. 38, pt. 1, serial 72, pp. 291, 493, 500; *OR*, ser. I , pt. 2, vol. 38, serial 73, pp. 474, 484; Jack Coggins, *Arms & Equipment of the Civil War* (Garden City NY: Doubleday, 1962) 66, 77; Scaife, *The Campaign for Atlanta*, 148, 157; Raper, "General Thomas at Peach Tree Creek," 213–14.

[54] Raper, 214.

[55] Ibid., 214.

creek in front of the advancing column of rebels. So I stopped to see the result." The 57th Indiana was, indeed, in front of the advancing Rebels, but they were under the command of their lieutenant colonel, Willis Blanch. According to Blanch, "My line, after the brigade had moved into position [Blake's brigade along today's Brighton Road] and began construction of works facing the south, was about 600 yards disconnected from the brigade. At about 3:30 P.M. while the lines remained in this position," explained Blanch, "a desperate assault was made upon them by the enemy coming in massed columns, coming from the south. This assault struck my right flank squarely, and in consequence I was forced to change my line to the rear on its left. By so doing," the officer continued, "I occupied the crest of a slight elevation of ground from which a deliberate fire was given the still advancing foe by the whole line."[56]

Blanch was describing the advance of Mercer's and Gist's brigades on his right front and flank, which was just east of Stevens's brigade along the Buckhead Road. The width of Walker's division front forced Mercer's brigade to cross Clear Creek twice before reaching the Federal flank. Blanch's 57th Indiana had reached the area of today's north-south part of Huntington Road with his men facing east. When he retreated the right half of his regiment from its advance position, near the curve in today's Huntington Road, the Indianans fell back to near the Camden Road, but Gist's men were right behind them and Mercer's were flanking them from across Clear Creek. Blanch explained that "[h]aving but a thin skirmish line, and being advanced upon by a massed column of the enemy, with my right flank entirely unprotected, I retired my line a second time to a line of rifle-pits formerly used by the enemy, probably 20 yards, where I formed and where the regiment delivered a second fire." The rifle pits that Blanch described were those used by the 20th Tennessee (of Smith's brigade, Bate's division) and the 2nd Tennessee (of Polk's brigade, Cleburne's division) during the night before and the morning of 20 July after Wood's division had crossed. The rifle pits were probably located near the Camden Road spur, east of Brighton Road.[57]

Gist's and Mercer's men kept coming, chasing the Yankees back toward Peach Tree Creek. "At this place I remained until on the right I was thoroughly flanked, when I gave the order to fall back again," explained the 57th Indiana's beleaguered leader. "This retirement brought me to Peach Tree Creek, and owing to a bend in the creek it was absolutely impossible for a part of the

---

[56] Ibid., 214; *OR*, ser. 1, vol. 38, pt. 1, serial 72, 348.
[57] Ibid., 348.

regiment to escape capture unless they waded it. For this cause the regiment was here divided, a part of it going to the north side of the creek, where," Blanch explained, "during the engagement it rendered valuable service in aiding to repel two advances of the enemy from the east, while the other part remained south side of the creek where it defended a point against the advances of the enemy." During this split, Major McGraw commanded one part of the 57th Indiana, presumably the part that remained south of the creek, while Blanch continued to lead the other. The left half of the 57th that crossed over to the north side of Peach Tree Creek was instrumental in firing into the flank of Mercer's brigade, which advanced a few minutes later from east of the Clear Creek. Also, at about early dusk, this portion of the 57th Indiana fired into a portion of Bate's division which finally arrived on the scene.[58]

Meanwhile, back on the Buckhead Road where General Thomas studied the Confederate threat, "The orderly had scarcely turned his horse when the first rebel line appeared, followed by another and another. The mounted officers were in their positions in rear of the several lines," observed Corporal Raper, "which were advancing at quick time, each step bringing their left flank closer in line with the point where Gen. Thomas still quietly sat, his eyes riveted to his glasses. Only once did he take the glasses from his eyes. Bradley's brigade was occupying the road, and," the Ohioan explained, "for some reason there was momentarily considerable confusion in the ranks which was heightened in Gen. Thomas's vicinity by Col. Opdycke's horse becoming unmanageable and making a scatterment of the men to keep them from being trampled on." Raper turned back to the general. "For just a moment he took his glasses down and looked over his right shoulder. When he looked the disorder was at its height, but he turned back to his glasses as if it did not concern him."[59]

"The advancing rebel column was now almost to the creek, its left flank nearly opposite to Gen. Thomas and half a mile in the rear of the left of Wagner's [Blake's] brigade, in which were my friends and comrades," said Raper. Mercer's brigade was now in full view by Thomas and the rest of the men along the Buckhead Road. Gist's brigade had by now been checked by Blake's men along the Brighton Road, while Steven's brigade was being roughly handled along the Buckhead Road just below its intersection with today's Brighton Road. Mercer's Georgians were still proceeding north as they cleared the edge of the woods near the end of today's Brighton Road. "I

---

[58] Ibid., 348–49.
[59] Raper, "General Thomas at Peach Tree Creek," 214–15.

commenced to think it was high time for Gen. Thomas to 'attend to those fellows,' and I saw no way in which he was going to do it. Bradley's brigade was not so strong enough to rout that column, even though it was fairly on its flank, and no other troops were at hand that I could see." With Bate's division absent from the field, Mercer's assault on the Federal flank would be unsupported.[60]

"But Gen. Thomas also seemed to think the time had come. He took the glasses from his eyes, turned his head over his left shoulder, nodded it forward, at the same time saying, slowly, deliberately and distinctly, 'Now you may give it to them, captain.'" Raper was relieved. "'Fire!' rang out a clear and sharp command, and a dozen or more cannon, which had heretofore been concealed or overlooked by me…sent their charges of shot, shell and canister tearing straight down the enemy's lines." The Ohio Corporal witnessed that "Load after load as fast as the artillerymen could handle their pieces followed—a continuous shower of murderous iron. No troops on earth could stand that long, for they were taken at a disadvantage, could not reply and were in an open field at point-blank range." Raper explained that "A heroic effort was made to maintain lines [by Mercer's brigade], but in a minute or less it was apparent that they would go to pieces under the unmerciful pounding of our artillery."[61]

Raper went on to say that "All this transpired in less time than it takes me to tell it; but I had now regained my wind and must be off. It was an intensely exciting scene from which it was almost impossible to tear one's self. But my duty to keep my regiment supplied with ammunition was imperative." Raper proceeded to the creek, "on the banks of which a pile of ammunition boxes had been carried across the still incomplete bridge. Taking one of the boxes—1,000 rounds—on my shoulder, and forcing a straggler from my regiment, whom I had found on the way back, to take another, we started for the regiment," which was "nearly three-quarters of a mile up the road and along Bradley's line of battle, which was facing eastward." Raper and the straggler watched as "The pounding of the rebel column by our artillery still continued, and the confusion created in their lines increased. The Johnnies were game, however, and threw out a line of skirmishers in the new direction indicated by our artillery, attempting to change front forward on their left." Raper was appalled at the carnage being tolled on the Southerners. "But they went to pieces in the movement," he explained. "At the same time Bradley's men leaped over their barricades and

---

[60] Ibid., 215.
[61] Ibid.

charged the tangled mass." This effort routed Mercer's isolated Georgians from the field, and sent them back across the Clear Creek from the direction in which they came putting them out of the action for the remainder of the battle.[62]

"As I passed the edge of the woods with my box of cartridges on my shoulder," Raper continued, "the enemy was disappearing in rout where they had first appeared and Bradley's brigade was in pursuit." Concerning his mission, Raper wryly remarked, "Before I had reached the line of my own brigade the floor of the bridge was completed, Bradley's advance had made the road safe and the ammunition wagons crossed, making an abundant supply a certainty."[63]

Impressed with his commander's performance, Raper described the calm and deliberate nature in which "Pap Thomas" went about his work.

> Until an intervening obstruction hid Gen. Thomas from view I could still see him sitting in the same position, watching the result of the conflict. I did not notice any of his staff present, but two or three staff officers or orderlies reported to him and dashed off again with orders apparently given in the same quiet way as those I overheard given to the orderly from Major McGraw. The particular business he had in hand just then was to crush and drive back the rebel column, for it had wedged its way through our lines where an interval of nearly two miles existed. His orders were given as deliberately and pleasantly as he might request his orderly to bring him a drink of water; their execution was the breaking of an overwhelming cyclone. Nothing could withstand it; confusion, destruction, death and defeat to the enemy marked its pathway.[64]

Lieutenant Colonel Hinman described the destructive fire of the Federal artillery on Mercer's lines. "In the meantime two or three batteries had been brought up, on the other side of Peachtree creek, and so posted as to completely enfilade the rebel line. The guns opened with canister, and scarcely a dozen shots had been fired, when the Confederates broke and fled in dismay to the cover of the ravine, from which they had debouched before forming for the charge. They seemed to be satisfied for that day, as they did not re-appear to renew the attack."[65]

---

[62] Ibid.
[63] Ibid., 215–16.
[64] Ibid., 216.
[65] Hinman, *The Story of the Sherman Brigade*, 579.

Hood's First Sortie, 20 July 1864

In addition to the Federal artillery, Bradley's infantry made its presence known to Mercer's Georgians. First Lieutenant Ralsa C. Rice of the 125th Ohio recorded the action.

> We began firing by volley on the first appearance of the Johnnies. "Battalion ready—aim, fire, load!" shouted Colonel Moore in regular cadence. The shock of our broadside was terrific. We were evening up matters with June 27 (Kennesaw) in mind. The range was no more than 100 yards and every shot was telling. The charging rebel column had cleared the woods when the artillery at the bridge opened fire. The enemy's momentum carried them nearly half way from the timber line to the bridge. We fired five volleys in all, our guns sending such a shower of death that the destruction seemed like a massacre. The foremost rebels faltered, and with a charge of grapeshot from the cannons they scattered and ran for the woods.[66]

Captain Charles T. Clark also from the 125th Ohio remembered that the Rebel column "had made its way through the thickets to the edge of the timber and were ready to rush for the apparently unsupported batteries and the bridge. A skirmish line emerged from the timber closely followed by a column massed, company or, possibly, division front, moving double quick," explained the Northern Captain, "and headed for the bridge. Our men opened fire so quickly that most of them heard no order to begin. The artillery also opened. The impetus of the movement carried the enemy's head of column some distance into the open, but with all those guns firing grape and canister into their faces," exclaimed Clark, "and an infantry line, at the distance of a few rods, sending showers of minnie balls into their ranks at just the proper angle to work the utmost possible havoc, continued progress was simply impossible. The leading companies, or what was left of them, surged backwards upon those in the rear," added the Federal veteran, "they in turn broke, and then all went in wild disorder back to the friendly cover of the timber. The 125th Ohio fired five rounds per man, and probably hit more men than upon any other occasion in the same length of time." Clark proudly recalled that "The return fire of the enemy was light and wild, only the men on their flank could fire. Opdycke's demi-brigade did its part in preventing Hood from taking everything south of the creek at all hazards, with a trifling loss." Only two men from the 125th Ohio were wounded, and no one had been killed.[67]

---

[66] Rice, *Yankee Tigers*, 128.

[67] Charles T. Clark, *Opdycke Tigers, 125th O. V. I.: A History of the Regiment and of the Campaigns and Battles of the Army of the Cumberland* (Columbus, Ohio: Spahr & Glenn,

The Battle of Peach Tree Creek

In less than ten minutes' time, Mercer's Georgians had been scattered along the eastern slope of the Buckhead Road within sight of the bridge. The crisis to the Yankee left flank had been averted by the good work of the Federal soldiers and artillerists and the quick thinking of General Thomas and his subordinate officers. According to General Bradley, "We had a sharp fight here of half an hour's duration, and successfully repulsed the attack on our part of the line."[68] With the initial assault by Stevens' and Gist's brigades lasting about 20 minutes, and the supporting attack on the Federal left by Mercer's brigade being suppressed within ten minutes after it reached the exposed flank and rear, Newton's undersized Division had successfully held its portion of the line. For the remainder of the afternoon, his force would continue to trade shots with Walker's Georgians and Maney's Tennesseans. Bradley reported that he lost 24 men during the day's action, and he provided a casualty report with his after-action battle report. However, his list failed to include the stretcher-bearer wounded from the 79th Illinois, and it missed 3 additional casualties in the 64th Ohio and 1 from the 65th Ohio during the fight, but it is remarkable that Bradley's brigade lost only 29 men during the day's action.

According to Lieutenant Colonel Hinman, "our loss was singularly small, the killed and wounded in our brigade numbering less than thirty, while that of the rebels in our front, judging from the dead and severely wounded left upon the field, was more than ten times that number."[69] It is unclear from Hinman's statement whether he is referring to the Confederate losses solely along the eastern slope of the Buckhead Road which his regiment helped to repel, or whether he includes all of the Rebels found in front of Newton's division after the attack. One point made by Hinman suggests that he included most or all of Walker's division attack. Hinman explained, "As we did not move immediately, details were sent out to care for the rebel wounded. Sixty or more were brought in and received the attention of our surgeons."[70] This is about the total of Walker's divisional losses sustained in the battle, both in terms of the number of wounded or captured on the field at about 60 or so, and the total losses incurred by the division, that number being just under 300.

Among the sad episodes of the day's carnage came one encounter which Lieutenant Colonel Hinman forever lamented. "I have never forgotten a mere boy, belonging to a Georgia regiment, whom we brought in and laid upon a

---

1895) 292.
[68] *OR*, ser. 1, vol. 38, pt. 3, serial 72, p. 356.
[69] Hinman, *The Story of the Sherman Brigade*, 579–80.
[70] Ibid., 580.

blanket under a tree. He was helpless, a bullet having crushed his thigh. We gave him food and water, and did what else we could to mitigate his suffering." The boy, one of Walker's Georgians who had spilled his blood that day to defend his home state, was overcome with emotion. "The tears gathered in his eyes as he said, 'They told us that you-all would kill us if you took us prisoners. I didn't think you'd be so kind to me!'"[71]

Mercer's Georgia Brigade. Seventeen year old Private Robert Braswell of the 57th Georgia in Mercer's brigade was relived that he was not among the Rebel casualties. The 57th Georgia lost sixteen men during the day's action. While Braswell contemplated his good fortune, however, his thoughts surely turned to the fate of his two brothers, Sergeant Major William Braswell and Private Samuel Braswell, who made the charge along the Buckhead Road with the 1st Confederate Georgia Infantry Regiment in Stevens's brigade. Unfortunately, his brothers would not be so lucky. Both fell killed in front of Newton's lines just east of the Buckhead Road.[72]

First Lieutenant Ralsa C. Rice of the 125th Ohio, which had defended the bridge from the Confederate charge, reflected on Mercer's attack. "This maneuver of the enemy may have been scientific warfare but, in my judgment, had they come out of the woods in line of battle and used their muskets on us the result would have been far different." Losing only two men wounded, Rice and the Ohioans were relieved to survive the near disaster. His men were then called out to form a picket line "along the edge of the woods and over the battlefield" from where the Georgians had first appeared. Rice described the carnage:

> After establishing our line of posts, I went to the place where the enemy had come out of the woods. I found their trail and followed it to the end. Dead and dying rebels lay strewn over the ground—a harrowing, pitiful sight. The dead did not have that angry look which we ascribe to men fighting for their lives, but rather a sorrowful, frightful one of death by violence. I followed a trail of blood through the weeds to the creek. Here I found a young man in the agonies of death; grapeshot had torn across his body, disemboweling him. In his pain he had sought the creek and let himself down into the water. Poor fellow, I could do nothing to help him.

---

[71] Ibid., 580.
[72] Walker, *Hell's Broke Loose in Georgia*, 156.

One of our pickets reported hearing strange sounds near his post. We made a search and in a ravine found a youth of 17, wounded. We took him to the reserve and found that a bullet had passed through his leg above the knee. We gave him hot coffee and food, and I learned his address, age, etc. as soon as he revived I sent him to the hospital. Though he died soon after, I had the satisfaction of knowing that he had been treated with the utmost kindness on our part.[73]

Mercer reported that his brigade sustained out of his 2,000 men a total of 3 men killed, 15 men wounded, and 5 men missing or captured, as follows: 1st Volunteer Georgia: 1 killed and 3 wounded; 54th Georgia: 5 wounded and 5 missing; 57th Georgia: 2 killed and 4 wounded; and the 63rd Georgia: 3 wounded.[74] After just ten minutes, Mercer's brigade took flight which prevented their casualty rolls from being greater.

Gist's Brigade, 46th Georgia. In Gist's brigade, the 46th Georgia "suffered many casualties that day before falling back to Atlanta," according to one company's historian. "There were three killed and three wounded from Company H alone."[75] However, contemporary accounts from the regiment just after the battle reveal that casualties were fairly light as the regiment did not engage as much as did Stevens's brigade.[76] Captain T. E. Sullivan of Company A reported that the regiment "was in support to Stephens' Brigade." Company A reported no casualties. Company B's Captain Robert J. Redding wrote, "had a skirmish with the enemy of 19 July at Peachtree Creek. Also on 20 July on the same creek." Company B reported no casualties. In Company C, known as the Muscogee Volunteers from Muscogee County, four men were wounded, while in companies D and E, only one man was wounded from each company.[77]

Captain Robert M. Dixon of Company F, the Webster County Invincibles, explained, "Had a picket skirmish July 19. Next day, July 20, further on the right, attacked the enemy." Company F lost one man killed, Private William P. Davis who was accidentally killed, and three men wounded, including James D.

---

[73] Rice, *Yankee Tigers*, 128–30.

[74] *OR*, ser. 1, vol., 38, pt. 3, serial 74, 756. Research by the writer, however, reveals a total of forty-two to forty-five casualties in Hugh Mercer's Georgia Brigade.

[75] George W. Wright, "Sgt. James E. Wright," *Confederate Veteran* (March–April 1993): 38.

[76] www.rootsweb.ancestry.com/~gamarion/military/coh46reg.html (5 January 2009).

[77] *Supplement to the Official Records of the Union and Confederate Armies*, 100 volumes (Wilmington NC: Broadfoot Publishing Company, 1995–2001) pt. 2, serial 18, 744–68 (hereafter *Supplement to* OR). Parker was also wounded at Franklin TN, 30 November 1864.

Shepherd. Company I sustained just one man wounded. Captain Abe Miles of Company K, taking a cue from Dixon's report, stated, "Had a picket skirmish on July 19. Next day, July 20, further on the right." Captain Miles's company sustained only one casualty, Private George H. Phillips who was wounded in the leg.[78] Tellingly, nine of the ten company reports fail to mention that they attacked the enemy on 20 July, while many of them indicate that they participated in a "skirmish" with the enemy on 20 July or "supported Stephens' Brigade." The 46th Georgia lost twenty-nine men during the two days along Peach Tree Creek, with five killed, thirteen wounded, and eleven missing or captured.[79]

16th South Carolina. Seven men were killed in Company D of the 16th South Carolina. This company was from the upper end of Greenville County, South Carolina, which was made up of "highlanders" from the Greer and Mountain View portions of Greenville County. The 16th South Carolina was led by Colonel James McCullough.[80] One soldier of Gist's brigade described the attack as a "badly-handled offensive." While Walker's division "initially threw [the Yankees] back...Hardee allowed his troops to attack piecemeal, some never coming into contact with the enemy at all." The veteran explained, "There was none of the precise timing called for in the commanding General's textbook-perfect plan."[81] While the left regiments of Stevens's brigade struck the Federal works straight on along the Buck Head Road, Gist's brigade turned to the northeast as it approached Newton's line. One veteran remembered that Gist's attack began to fizzle as they climbed the slope, "turning [their] attack to the right to compensate for a bulge in the Federal line. This was the beginning of the end, as the attack began to fall apart."[82] Many of Gist's men witnessed

---

[78] Shepherd was subsequently captured at Taylor's Ridge GA on 16 October 1864 and sent to Camp Chase. Phillips, born at Indian Springs GA on 30 August 1844, was subsequently placed on light duty as a shoemaker in the quartermaster department at Columbus GA until 1 May 1865 when the war concluded.

[79] *Supplement to* OR, pt. 2, serial 18, 744–68. Only fourteen casualties have been verified from the 46th Georgia on 20 July with two men killed, eleven wounded, and one captured. But, during the skirmishing of 19 July along the creek south of the crossings below Howell Mill, the 46th Georgia saw three men killed, two men wounded, and ten men captured, or fifteen total casualties for 19 July and twenty-nine for both days.

[80] "Taylors's Rosters and Notes, Co. D, 16th South Carolina," www.geocities.com/BourbonStreet/Square/3873/franklin7d.html (31 December 2007).

[81] Walter Brian Cisco, *States Rights Gist: A South Carolina General of the Civil War* (Shippensburg PA: White Mane Publishing Company, 1991) 127.

[82] "Taylors's Rosters and Notes, Co. D, 16th South Carolina," www.geocities.com/BourbonStreet/Square/3873/peachtree.html. (1 March 2008).

The Battle of Peach Tree Creek

the fatal wounding of beloved General Clement Stevens, "and the attack continues to unravel."[83] After the war, Colonel Ellison Capers lamented the events of the day. Tellingly, Capers noted that only one of Hardee's four divisions participated in the battle. "In this fight Walker's Division made a gallant but unsuccessful assault and suffered considerable loss."[84]

According to Captain Charles M. Furman of the 16th South Carolina, "Steven's brigade moved first, we followed. Stevens' men attacked the enemy and drove in his skirmishes. We were not [brought] into action. Though somewhat [exposed to] the enemy's fire—one man of my company was wounded in the arm the only casualty in the Regt—Genl Stevens was wounded I fear mortally."[85] So, much if not all of Gist's brigade failed to get farther than rifle range of the Federal works, leaving Stevens's brigade alone at the Federal works along the Buckhead Road. Captain Furman explained, "Several of our Brigade were wounded. The troops retired to breast-works an hour or two after dark."[86] With seven men killed from Company D, the losses confirmed for the regiment of eight men killed, two wounded, and one captured for a total of eleven casualties from the 16th South Carolina reflect the unevenness of the fighting.[87]

Historian Bill Scaife accurately described the uneven fighting and explained the rough treatment received by Stevens's Georgians that, due to the topography of the area and to the advance deployment of Newton's division on the heights along the Buckhead Road, first struck the Federal line: "Walker's division, on Bate's left, because of a bulge in the Federal line, made contact with the enemy before Bate, and the classic movement en echelon began to fall apart before it even started."[88] Bate's division would continue to struggle in the cane thickets to the east, getting lost in the process for the next two hours. "After driving some distance, Walker's Division was repulsed, and Brigadier General Clement H. Stevens was killed while leading his brigade. When Walker was repulsed, Maney's Division hesitated on his left and the next Division in

---

[83] Ibid.

[84] Ibid.

[85] "The Letters and Papers of Charles Manning Furman," http://batsonsm.tripod.com/letters/letters9.html (1 March 2008).

[86] "The Letters and Papers of Charles Manning Furman," http://batsonsm.tripod.com/letters/letters9.html (1 March 2008).

[87] "Taylors's Rosters and Notes, Co. D, 16th South Carolina," www.geocities.com/BourbonStreet/Square/3873/franklina.html (6 December 2008).

[88] Scaife, *The Campaign for Atlanta*, 89.

line [Loring's] moved out ahead of Maney—disrupting even more the text book, en echelon movement."[89]

The 1st Georgia Confederate and the 66th Georgia of Stevens's brigade were making their charge along the Buckhead Road and the grounds surrounding the Collier Farm, which contained some crops and outbuildings near the road, making their approach to the Federal works more open than the remaining units in Hardee's attack. By charging across the open area created by the road and the surrounding farm, Nisbet's 66th Georgia and Smith's 1st Georgia Confederate were more exposed to the Federal fire, but they also had a straighter and shorter line of attack, which enabled them to reach the Federal outer works as the surprised Yankees briefly fell back to receive the shock of the attack. As a result, these two Georgia regiments, the oldest and the newest by regimental number designation, lost some two thirds of Walker's total division loss during the battle.

The other units in Stevens's brigade to the east were somewhat protected by the sloping and heavily forested downhill lands that fell sharply into a ravine before the Federal line. For example, the lone casualty in the 2nd Georgia Battalion Sharpshooters, which had recently joined the brigade from Jackson's brigade, was Private William C. P. Huffman of Company D, who fell wounded during the charge.[90] Additionally, the Federal works fell back sharply to the northeast as they followed the contour of the ridge along today's Brighton Road. Across this deep ravine, the remainder of Stevens's brigade as well as Mercer's and Gist's brigades had to travel before reaching the Federal lines. Similarly, to the west of the Buckhead Road, the ground also drops off severely into a wooded ravine which Maney's supporting Tennessee division had to traverse. In just three or four hours, Newton's veterans had taken, cleared, and entrenched the highest ridge, the Collier Ridge, in the area, which served as the anchor of the ground south of Peach Tree Creek along the Buckhead Road. This aggressive and well-executed work would prove pivotal in the battle for the Buckhead Road crossing of Peach Tree Creek.

In both the eastern and western wooded approaches to Newton's lines, the Northerners were not severely tested. According to one Federal officer, "Walker's Division of Confederates, coming straight up on both sides of the road, was without protection. They were cut down like grass before the scythe,

---

[89] Ibid., 89.
[90] Roster of the 2nd Ga. Battl., S.S., *Georgia Journal Magazine* 35/1-2 (Winter/Spring 1995): 1-2, vertical files, Chickamauga National Battlefield Park Library.

as Newton's men had been at Kennesaw less than a month before."[91] They had prepared fairly sturdy works in the short time they had occupied the ridge and they were able to cut down a number of trees in their front to create a killing field of fire that compelled any attacking force to make their way across a criss-cross section of cut logs and tree tops while at the same time being subjected to both artillery and rifle fire from the Federal lines above them. Thus, any Rebel force that attempted to attack them would be peppered mercilessly by Federal rifle and artillery fire while they could only lie down and try to return sporadic fire. The only option for them was to try to turn one flank or the other, or to rush overwhelming numbers down the road in support of Stevens's brigade.

---

[91] Howard, *Autobiography*, 615.

AN I GIVE A DARE AFFAIR

Some of the Southern troops advanced at the double-quick for perhaps a half-mile, so that when they finally reached the Northern lines they were completely winded; they were so tired and it was so hot they could only walk."[1]

Maney's (Cheatham's) Tennessee Division. On the left of Hardee's corps, Cheatham's division, which was led that day by General George Maney, began its advance. One of the officers in Granbury's Texas Brigade, which was posted in rear of Maney's lines, watched Maney's Tennesseans disappear into the Collier Woods before them. The Texas captain recorded that "Cheatham's Div. in front of our Div. [Cleburne's] advanced through the woods until we found the Yanks, behind breastworks."[2] The critical point in his note was that Maney's Tennesseans found the enemy *behind breastworks*, which was unexpected, and that at that point the Tennesseans stopped any further advance without seriously testing the strength of the Federal works or the number of its defenders.

The days' marching and counter-marching to get into position to strike the Yankees had also taken a toll on Hardee's men. One Federal observer on Newton's front noted that the hot July sun had tired the attackers. "Some of the Southern troops advanced at the double-quick for perhaps a half-mile, so that when they finally reached the Northern lines they were completely winded."[3] One of the Yankees on the picket line watched as the Confederates approached: "they were so tired and it was so hot they could only walk."[4]

The veterans of Kimball's brigade prepared to receive the blow from Maney's large force as the Tennessee division approached. "As the attackers

---

[1] Lee Kennett, *Marching through Georgia: The Story of Soldiers & Civilians during Sherman's Campaign* (New York: Harper-Collins Publishers, 1995) 187.

[2] Samuel T. Foster, *One of Cleburne's Command, The Civil War Reminiscences and Diary of Captain Samuel T. Foster, Granbury's Texas Brigade, C.S.A.*, ed. Norman D. Brown (Austin: University of Texas Press, 1980) 107.

[3] Kennett, *Marching through Georgia*, 187.

[4] Ibid.

approached, some obstacles they encountered—a fallen tree, a ravine or streambed—slowed their movement for other reasons. Men dropped down behind the cover they afforded to take a drink from their canteens or to examine an arm or leg grazed by a bullet," explained the Yankee observer, "others coming along needed no further inducement to follow their example. Once down, they found it hard to move forward again, though the call of an officer would usually bring them back into the open."[5] One of the Confederate officers explained that his unit "was making good progress when it encountered a fence-row only thirty or forty steps from the enemy's works: 'Our line halted and it was fatal to them, for never did they advance again...'"[6] The fence was around the A. J. Collier home and garden along the Buckhead Road where General Stevens was mortally wounded.

Maney's Tennesseans saw Walker's division to their right front being roughly handled, cooling the advance of the Tennessee Volunteers. Nevertheless, the right brigade of General Maney's division pressed forward toward what appeared to be an opening in the Federal line. Opposing them was Kimball's brigade of Newton's division. Watching the great numbers of Confederates sweeping the wooded valley below them, and seeing Featherston's Mississippians advancing up and over the Collier Ridge and road to their right, the 73rd Illinois formed at right angles to the right side of Kimball's brigade to cover the exposed flank.[7] The Tennesseans appeared poised to strike a massive blow against the exposed flank of Kimball's refused line and into the gap created by the failure of Ward's division to reach and deploy along the Collier Ridge to Kimball's right. Maney's four brigades were approaching the Federal position in this manner: Magevney's (formerly Vaughan's) Brigade on the front right of the column was roughly between today's Wycliff Road on the right and Anjaco Road on the left; to their left, Carter's brigade was more or less between today's Anjaco Road on the right and Ardmore Road on the left; behind Magevney's men, Walker's brigade followed in support, while Strahl's brigade was behind Carter's veterans.

The new division commander from Franklin, Tennessee, George Maney was given a tough first assignment: lead four brigades uphill toward an enemy of unknown strength who was posted behind works and who was ready for him.

---

[5] Ibid.

[6] Ibid.

[7] United States War Department, comp., *Official Records of the Union and Confederate Armies in the War of the Rebellion*, 128 vols. (Washington, DC: Government Printing Office, 1880–1901) ser. 1, vol. 38, pt. 1, serial 72, p. 306 (hereafter *OR*).

Hood's First Sortie, 20 July 1864

Only two of Maney's four brigades managed to make any kind of impact. These were Magevney's brigade on the right of the division, which was nearest to and supporting Stevens's Georgia brigade to its right, and Carter's brigade, which was on the left of the division, but which turned to the right, or northeast, as it approached the sound of firing. Due to the ground that the four brigades had to cover, the Tennesseans were slowed in their march. "The dense underbrush along Peachtree Creek [actually Tanyard Branch] slowed the progress of Maney's Tennesseans."[8] When they did not find any Federals in their front as they disappeared into the woods, Carter's brigade turned to the right as it climbed the wooded hill located along today's 28th Street. Coming out of the woods they were surprised to find the Yankees entrenched and ready to receive them. They had to advance about a half a mile in this fashion before reaching the outskirts of the Collier Farm just south of the Federal works. Moreover, when Maney's men saw Walker's division being repulsed by the Yankees, they simply laid down and refused to advance any further. One man in Maney's division even called it a "I give a dare affair!"[9]

Historian Albert Castel described the timid advance by Maney's Tennesseans, as "a belated and tentative attack by Vaughan's [Magevney's] and Carter's Brigades against Newton's right and Ward's left soon ceases when the Tennesseans—who, as they feared, find the enemy 'posted behind breastworks,' —start taking too many casualties to 'make it pay,'" according to one of Maney's veterans. The two supporting brigades in Maney's division, Strahl's on the left in rear of Carter's, and Walker's on the right in rear of Magevney's, "merely advance a short distance, then lie down below the crest of a hill," explained Castel.[10] This position was located along today's Ardmore Road to the left, Anjaco Road to the center, and Wycliff Road to the right.

Companies D, I, F, H, G, and K of the 5th Tennessee of Strahl's brigade were thrown out as skirmishers in front of Carter's brigade. The skirmish line was under the command of Captain B. F. Peeples, while Lieutenant J. L. Lemonds commanded companies D and I in front of the left flank of the brigade.[11] With the 5th Tennessee in front as skirmishers, followed by Carter's

---

[8] John D. Fowler, *Mountaineers in Gray: The Nineteenth Tennessee Volunteer Infantry Regiment, C.S.A.* (Knoxville: University of Tennessee Press, 2004) 152.

[9] Sam R. Watkins, *Co. Aytch* (Columbia TN: Times Printing Company, 1882) 173.

[10] Albert Castel, *Decision in the West: The Atlanta Campaign of 1864* (Lawrence: University Press of Kansas, 1992) 377.

[11] Edwin H. Rennolds, *A History of the Henry County Commands which Served in the Confederate States Army* (Jacksonville FL: Sun Publishing Company, 1904) 88. The 5th

brigade, and then Strahl's brigade in support, the Confederates advanced toward the Federal works in three lines. One veteran of the skirmish line manned by the 5th Tennessee described the attack by Maney's Tennessee division: "About 3 or 4 o'clock P.M. we advanced half a mile, Lieut. J. W. Howard leading the charge, cap in hand, leaping the fences like a deer. We charged up to within about sixty or seventy-five yards of the enemy's works and halted in a ravine and sought protection behind trees, etc. When Carter's Brigade came up they halted also, securing all the protection possible, and all the efforts of their officers failed to induce them to go further. A continuous fire was kept up on both sides till dark."[12] During the action, sixteen men of the 5th Tennessee would become casualties, constituting all but five of the casualties sustained in Strahl's entire brigade. "Lieut. Lemonds, though severely wounded, refused to leave his command till compelled by loss of blood and severe pain to do so."[13] The 5th Tennessee also lost Private Aaron M. Pinson who was killed.[14] He was listed as the lone fatal casualty from Strahl's brigade that day, according to the surgeon's report of casualties in Cheatham's division at Peach Tree Creek, but three more would later die from their wounds.[15]

Howell's Georgia Battery. As the advance of Maney's Tennessee division stalled, a Confederate battery under Captain Evan P. Howell, who grew up in the area, positioned itself along a ridge just west of the Buckhead Road, between where 28th Street and 26th Street are located today, and engaged the Federal artillery posted along the ridge to the west of Collier Mill and Tanyard Branch in Geary's division. The Rebel battery, consisting of four 12-pounder Napoleons, had an effective range of three-quarters of a mile, more than enough to strike the Yankees near Collier's Mill. Howell's battery helped to soften the Federal position as Scott's Alabamians and Louisianans made their approach on these Federal lines, but Featherston's Mississippians had already taken the ridge east of the mill when Howell became engaged.[16] Drawing the attention of the

---

Tennessee was from Paris, Henry County, Tennessee, and, although they were from Strahl's brigade, they would lead Carter's brigade into the maelstrom.

[12] Rennolds, *History of the Henry County Commands*, 88–89.

[13] Ibid., 89.

[14] John Berrien Lindsley, ed., *Military Annals of Tennessee, Confederate*, 2 vols. (Wilmington NC: Broadfoot Publishing Company, 1995) 203.

[15] F. Rice, Report of F. Rice, Chief Surgeon, Cheatham's division, B. F.Cheatham Papers, Tennessee State Library and Archives, Nashville.

[16] Steve Davis, "So Much for Historical Accuracy: The Misplacement of the Howell Battery Marker," 1–8, author's personal papers, Dalton, Georgia; Howell, Henry, Family Information and Notes. There is located on the crest of Cardiac Hill, where the former J. J.

Hood's First Sortie, 20 July 1864

Rebel artillerists was Sloan's battery of Geary's 2nd Division on the low ridge west of Collier's Mill. One Yankee observer claimed that Sloan's battery came near killing General Cleburne. One of Cleburne's staff was killed by a shell from one of the Federal guns, most likely one of Goodspeed's on Newton's front. "Now Gen. Cleburne's presence riding north on Peachtree Road proves that the battery [Sloan's] was left oblique," the Federal veteran asserted. However, the presence of Featherston's Mississippians and Scott's Alabamians

---

Spalding estate Deerland once stood, in front of Piedmont Hospital, an historical tablet honoring Captain Evan P. Howell and his artillery battery. The marker was placed there by the Atlanta chapter of the United Daughters of the Confederacy and dedicated on 10 October 1919. Unfortunately, the marker describes the location of the battery as being on "the Confederate line." Some unnecessary controversy and confusion has since occurred as the southern crest of Cardiac Hill was in fact the line of Newton's Federal division during the height of the Confederate assault, and thus, it could not have been the location of Howell's battery during the conflict. However, it is likely that the battery saw service on the northern slope of Cardiac Hill the day before and early on the morning of 20 July as Confederates contested the crossing of Peach Tree Creek by elements of Howard's IV Corps. By the afternoon of 20 July, however, all Confederate batteries had vacated the area and been replaced by Newton's Federal division as they continued to press southward. At least two Confederate batteries, Howell's Georgia Battery and Key's Arkansas battery, saw action in support of Hardee's attack along the Buckhead Road (Peachtree Street) corridor. Howell's battery supported Walker's division attack by following it up the Buckhead Road until some point near the 26th Street intersection, where the battery went to the left of the road, protected by the crest of the hill on which the 28th Street lies, and proceeded along an old road at that time known as the Old Montgomery Ferry Road, which ran northwest from the Buckhead Road to the Collier Mill. From that position, Howell's battery gained the heights along the left, or western slope of the hill overlooking Ardmore Park, along today's Ardmore Circle and the western reaches of 28th Street, and went into action against elements of Geary's and Ward's division opposing Scott's and Featherston's brigades on the Collier Road and ridge overlooking today's Tanyard Creek Park. During the lull after Walker's division had been repulsed, and as Cleburne's division was forming to renew the attack, Key's battery attempted to run a section up the Buckhead Road to engage the Federal position and soften their lines prior to Cleburne's assault, but the effort was quickly abandoned as futile when Goodspeed's Federal battery responded. An example of confusion that has been unnecessarily created is the relocation of the four markers that once stood along Collier Road at the railroad bridge just west of Piedmont Hospital to Ardmore Park, a couple of hundred yards south. The present location of the signs (Ardmore Park) provides a safer, more solemn place to read about Featherston's Mississippi brigade attack and the defense and counterattack by Coburn's and Wood's brigades and to reflect on the action. However, the markers give specific references to points including courses and distances, such as "about .8 miles south of this location," etc…that, because the signs were moved, are no longer accurate.

and Louisianans in the front and flank of Sloan's battery provided all the targets that these artillerists could handle.[17]

Kimball's Brigade. On the Federal side in front of Howell's Battery and the Tennesseans of Maney's division, Kimball's brigade, with its refused line, was occupied with firing into the right flank of Featherston's brigade as the Mississippians rolled over the Collier Ridge and toward Peach Tree Creek where Ward's division awaited them. The left portion of Kimball's line, the 88th Illinois, the 44th Illinois, and the 74th Illinois, together with the half of the 15th Missouri that had been out on the skirmish line before the attack, held off the hard-charging Georgians of Stevens's brigade. Next, portions of Maney's Tennessee division came into view in the broken woods with Collier's garden in front of them. This line of Confederates was composed of Magevney's brigade that, after seeing Stevens's Georgians repulsed, checked their advance. Pushing up the wooded hill behind them were the veterans of Walker's brigade, which also slowed their advance as they surveyed the Federal position.

Over on the right of Kimball's line, the men of 36th Illinois, who had refused their line by nearly 90 degrees, readied themselves for the approaching Tennesseans of Carter's and Strahl's brigades. One Yankee veteran of the 36th Illinois remembered that "when the barricades were scarcely completed, the enemy, without skirmishers and without warning broke upon us in masses...with the evident determination to break through and cut us off from retreat."[18] Carter's men had outmarched Magevney's brigade, which was slowed by their ascent up the hill in their front (today's Ardmore Circle). Carter's brigade initially dipped into the skirt of woods to their right (along and across the street from today's Ardmore Park). Finding no enemy in their front, as the right part of Kimball's line had withdrawn to cover their right after Featherston's men had passed by their flank, and hearing the sounds of fire in their front as Featherston's men were going at it on the other side of the ridge, Carter's Tennesseans moved forward into the open fields and broken timber in their front and swung right toward Kimball's refused line. There, the Yankees gave them a warm reception.

In what Major Arthur MacArthur, Jr., described as "a very brilliant affair," his 24th Wisconsin, together with the 73rd Illinois, which had both been on the forward skirmish line when the attack began, joined the 36th Illinois to protect

---

[17] Cyrus E. Custis to Wilbur G. Kurtz, 29 October 1932, MSS 130, Maps, Clippings, Notes and Files, Wilbur G. Kurtz Collection, Kenan Research Center, Atlanta History Center.

[18] L. G. Bennett and William M. Haigh, *History of the 36th Regiment Illinois Volunteers during the War of the Rebellion* (Aurora IL: Knickerbocker & Hodder, 1876) 614.

Newton's right flank.[19] The skirmish line had advanced about a quarter of a mile before the attack "to ascertain the strength and position of the enemy," explained one veteran of the 24th Wisconsin. From that position, the skirmishers had begun receiving fire from Rebels in rifle-pits, which checked their advance. The 24th Wisconsin, mostly men from Milwaukee, "counted fewer than 200 men in its ranks. The thin line of Wisconsin skirmishers waited nervously in front."[20] At once, the skirmishers began to form a line of breastworks, but were not able to get them ready before Hardee launched his attack. "When enemy skirmishers confronted the Milwaukee men, the blue soldiers loosed a shot or two, then sprinted back, informing [Major MacArthur]. While he ordered the regiment back some 200 yards, the 19 year old officer remained with a dozen men." There, MacArthur and his little band staved off the advancing Confederates. "When the main body had established a firm defensive line, MacArthur and his men pulled back; the leapfrog maneuver was repeated until the 24th [Wisconsin] was again safely inside the Federal defenses."[21]

One veteran of the 73rd Illinois recalled that "[p]art of the regiment held position in a garden. The striking of balls against the garden fence made quite a rattling, disagreeable noise. The firing on our left by the enemy became so severe that our forces were driven back."[22] The garden was part of A. J. Collier's farm. "Orders came for us [the 73rd Illinois] to fall back, which we did immediately, taking position on the extreme right of the 4th Corps, to protect its flank and fill or cover a space between us and the left of the 20th Corps."[23]

Seeing Featherston's Mississippians pour through the hole between the IV and the XX corps, the men of Kimball's Federal brigade were worried that they would be cut off from their line of retreat. "It was thought for a time that we would be compelled to fall back, as the rebels passed our right flank, but we held our position, delivering a destructive enfilading fire on the enemy, both as he advanced on Hooker and as he retreated across the open field in Hooker's

---

[19] MacArthur was the father of World War II General Douglas MacArthur. *OR*, ser. 1, vol. 38, pt. 1, serial 72, 329–30.

[20] William J. K. Beaudot, *The 24th Wisconsin Infantry in the Civil War: The Biography of a Regiment* (Mechanicsburg PA: Stackpole Books, 2003) 321.

[21] Beaudot, *The 24th Wisconsin Infantry*, 321.

[22] W. H. Newlin, *The Preacher Regiment, 1862–65, History of the 73rd Illinois Volunteer Infantry* (Springfield: Regimental Reunion Association of Survivors of the 73rd Illinois Infantry Volunteers, 1890) 324.

[23] Ibid., 324.

front."[24] Lieutenant Newlin of the 73rd Illinois explained, "The rebels were punished severely."[25] Another Yankee soldier, Maurice Marcoot of the 15th Missouri, who had fallen back to the Federal line before the battle and who had helped fight off Walker's attack from just to the left or east of Goodspeed's guns along the Buckhead Road, watched anxiously as Featherston's brigade threatened to get in behind Newton's position. "Hooker's men joined us on the right and as we watched them we feared lest they were compelled to give way, in which case we would have been flanked on the right as well as the left. At times they were actually mixed up with the rebels fighting hand in hand, but they never wavered," remembered Marcoot.[26]

General O. O. Howard observed the plight of Kimball's brigade: "Just as he began to worry about his right flank, Kimball caught glimpses of finely led brigades appearing at the crest of that height, 800 yards off. It was a refreshing sight," added Howard. "There were Ward's skirmishers. They did not retire at the prolonged yell of their opponents, nor at the brisk fire of the first rifle shots aimed against them. They kept their advanced positions till Ward could make his deployments behind them." Moreover, with their backs protected, Bradley's brigade posted along the Buckhead Road facing east "were thus quickly relieved" and with confidence, met and fended off Mercer's charging Georgians.[27]

Some of MacArthur's 24th Wisconsin veterans also ran to protect the crumbling left flank of Newton's exposed division. "We thought the fun was over, when all of a sudden, a tremendous noise broke loose in our rear and left," exclaimed Moritz Tschoepe, a German immigrant wagon-maker from Milwaukee. General Kimball's adjutant "rushed up and ordered the 24th back on its left flank." At that moment, "only a small skirmish line protected the Federals from the bridges across the creek." According to Tschoepe, "here the rebels were determined to break through, cut us off from the bridge and our army, and give us fits. We double-quicked back through a regular hail of shot and shell and reenforced that thin line behind a fence." This was along the Buckhead Road along the ridge overlooking the bridge crossings over Peach

---

[24] Ibid., 324–25.
[25] Ibid., 325.
[26] Donald Allendorf, *Long Road to Liberty, The Odyssey of a German Regiment in the Yankee Army: The 15th Missouri Volunteer Infantry* (Kent OH: Kent State University Press, 2006) 209; Maurice Marcoot, *Five Years in the Sunny South* (St. Louis: Missouri Historical Society, 1890) 71.
[27] Howard, *Autobiography,* 1:615–16.

Tree Creek. "On the road behind us ambulances, wagons and stragglers hurried to the rear."[28]

Witnessing the Rebel assault, Tschoepe explained, "They came without skirmishers and with yells whose volume exceeded any battle shout ever heard." One of the Wisconsin men described the Rebel yell as "that high yelping, keening screech from thousands of throats that likely fingered fear up many blue soldiers' spines." One newspaper reporter witnessing the plight of Newton's division as it tried to beat back thrusts from three sides at the same time wrote, "For the first few minutes everything hung trembling in the scale." The biographer for the 24th Wisconsin explained, "Newton's division had not fully completed erecting defensive breastworks, and they had barely enough time to grab rifle-muskets and fall into battle line before the attackers plunged upon them. Blood red flags snapped before them." Tschoepe remembered, "On came the enemy again and again, and I could not help admiring their bravery."[29]

Watching with relief, Tschoepe and the Wisconsinites saw the Federal artillery swing into position to parry the Rebel assault on the exposed left flank. "The gun carriages thundered up at the gallop; after their horses were unhooked and brass barrels swung forward, the guns trained on the running rebels. The artillerymen threw off their jackets and rolled up their sleeves and labored with a will over our heads. We repulsed every onslaught until the rest of our corps put in their appearance." The Federal guns began to take their toll as the advancing Confederate lines began to waver. "They had come to a stand still in partial confusion, and firing heavily and wildly. Color bearer after color bearer went down under the crash of our canister." Southern officers continued to urge their men on uselessly; within twenty minutes, Walker's attack had been broken. For the remainder of the afternoon, Hardee's men kept up the fighting, occasionally attempting another assault, but the effort would prove to be futile. "The battle raged until nearly dark, the enemy fighting with great desperation." The 24th Wisconsin lost Sergeant John Barrett from Wauwatosa, killed, and "three others were slightly wounded."[30]

Subsequently, over on the right of Newton's position the refused portions of Kimball's brigade, consisting of some of the 36th Illinois, and the 73rd Illinois, swung back into line with the remainder of the Brigade as Ward's division closed the gap. Next, the rejoined line exchanged fire with the retiring

---

[28] William J. K. Beaudot, *The 24th Wisconsin Infantry in the Civil War: The Biography of a Regiment* (Mechanicsburg PA: Stackpole Books, 2003) 321.

[29] Ibid., 321–22.

[30] Ibid., 322.

The Battle of Peach Tree Creek

Mississippians of Featherston's brigade and Maney's Tennesseans which by now had joined in the long-range fight. "The firing continued quite a while after the repulse of the rebels, but was less severe, being principally by their skirmishers and sharp-shooters."[31] Among the losses in Kimball's brigade were, from the 88th Illinois, three killed and five wounded, three mortally, for a total loss of eight men.[32] The 15th Missouri lost only one man killed, and two wounded, despite all of the regiment's activity of the day and their hurried retreat from the skirmish line.[33]

Falling during the action from the 73rd Illinois, the "Preacher Regiment," was Private George C. Daerfler of Company G who was killed during the early action at the garden. Among the wounded were First Lieutenant William H. Newlin and privates William Martin and Martin Moody who were both apparently hit by the same sharpshooter's bullet during the subsequent long-range fighting. Moody later died of his wounds on 28 July at Chattanooga. The 73rd Illinois lost a total of one killed and eight wounded during the action. Ironically, Joseph Jarvis of Company K died on 20 July at Andersonville Prison while his comrades were engaged in the battle of Peach Tree Creek.[34]

Sergeant Wormley of Company I, 36th Illinois, was wounded in the action, one of only seven men wounded in the regiment. None of their unit was killed. One Illinoisan gleefully wrote, "This was the first time that the 36th had been permitted to do justice to the masses of the enemy in front, while at the same time, both their flanks were protected, and the opportunity was improved to the utmost."[35] A veteran of the 36th Illinois remembered the actions of one of his fellow soldiers: "Scales, Co. K, had a Spencer Rifle, and finding a sheltered nook in advance of our line, took possession and went to work with a will. Soon a squad of Rebels came up and desired to surrender to him. 'Go to the rear,' replied Scales, 'and get out of my way. I have no time to take prisoners.' So excited did the men become, that they continued to fire long after the gray coat had disappeared."[36]

Carter's Tennessee Brigade. Carter's brigade approached the Federal lines. One of Carter's Tennesseans explained that when his regiment reached "the top of a hill we could see the Yanks in their trenches a little way from the foot of

---

[31] Newlin, *The Preacher Regiment*, 325.

[32] http://civilwar.ilgenweb.net/reg_html/088_reg.html (11 March 2012).

[33] Allendorf, *Long Road to Liberty*, 210.

[34] Newlin, *The Preacher Regiment*, 35, 38, 52, 64, 66, 324–25.

[35] Bennett and Haigh, *History of the 36th Regiment Illinois*, 615.

[36] Ibid., 615.

the hill."[37] The soldier, from the 16th Tennessee, continued, "The order to flank to the right was not heard by 2 or 3 of us and we pressed forward to the foot of the hill. Clark and Sam Worthington fired 60 rounds that evening, and fell back that night after silencing the enemy's battery with Ben Lack and Jim Martin."[38] Instead of going straight ahead and into the gap that had been breached in the Federal lines, the Tennesseans had swung to the northeast to conform to the Federal position. Moreover, after reaching a couple of hundred yards from Kimball's line and beginning to receive fire from the Yankees, the Tennesseans hit the ground. They could not or would not advance any further. In Carter's brigade between today's Ardmore Road and Anjaco Road a couple of hundred yards south of today's Collier Road, one man in the 16th Tennessee ran across a Federal officer who had been wounded on the original line before it had been refused and pulled back:

> I felt very sorry for a Yankee officer who had been wounded and was lying in an exposed position, and could not get to a place of safety. He was lying about ten steps inside of the works and just behind us, and the shells and minie [sic] balls were making it hot for us. He called to us and asked us to please come and get him down in the ditch where we were, so I started out to bring him in but one of our officers told me to come back and I had to let him lie in his dangerous position. I never knew how he came out. I ran upon a wounded Dutchman and he was doing a whole lot of Dutch talk. I offered him a drink of water from my canteen and he would shake his head. He might have been cussing me for all I knew. We held the works that we captured until after night but just across a draw further up their line they held part of their works. I ventured out in front of our line to see what I could find and run up on a dead Rebel and got me a good hat and a few shirts out of the Yankee knapsacks and then went back into our lines.[39]

Magevney's Tennessee Brigade. Magevney's brigade came out of the woods and, with bayonets fixed, gave the Rebel yell and charged the Federal line just to the west of the Buckhead Road along the Wycliff Road and Anjaco Road corridor. Waiting for Magevney's men, the 44th Illinois and the 74th Illinois fired volley after volley until the Tennesseans broke and fell back to the

---

[37] Jamie Gillum, *An Eyewitness History of the 16th Regiment, Tennessee Volunteers, May 1861–May 1865*, www.tngenweb.org/records/military/civilwar/16regtnvol.html, n.23. (11 March 2012).

[38] Gillum, *An Eyewitness History*, n.23.

[39] Ibid., n.31.

cover of the hillside and woods behind them. Falling in the attack from the 11th Tennessee were four killed and one wounded, mortally. Another four killed and two wounded, one mortally, from the 12th Tennessee, fell victim to the Federal fire.[40] The 47th Tennessee had been consolidated with the 12th Tennessee under the command of its old leader, Colonel William M. Watkins who fell wounded in the left thigh.[41] The colonel's wounding chilled any further advance by Magevney's brigade, but it apparently rekindled the reliance on faith by its men. Private James Sawyer of Company C, 47th Tennessee, wrote his wife after the battle: "I poot my trust in God. I went into the charge with the boolets a flying around us without hardly enney fear. I was not excited at all hardley."[42]

Also falling with Magevney's men was Private George Whited of the 25th Tennessee who was detached from his regiment, which was in Virginia fighting with the Army of Northern Virginia. Private Whited died from his wound later on the same day.[43] In the 13th Tennessee, which had been merged into the 154th Tennessee, seven men were casualties with three killed, two wounded, and two captured.[44] In the 154th Tennessee Infantry Regiment, Private Thomas B. Turley, of Company L, was wounded in the charge.[45] There were a total of 15 men killed and 107 men wounded for a loss of 122 men in Magevney's brigade at Peach Tree Creek.[46]

Carter's Tennessee Brigade. In Carter's brigade, which was led by Colonel John H. Anderson during the charge, the losses were virtually identical to Magevney's losses. Among the wounded were Colonel D. C. Crook and Captain W. C. Bryant of the 28th Tennessee. "At the Peach-tree Creek fight, Capt. W. C. Bryant, of Company C, was mortally wounded, and died in the

---

[40] Lindsley, ed., *Military Annals of Tennessee*, 1:302–305, 310–11, 602; *Supplement to the Official Records of the Union and Confederate Armies* (Wilmington NC: Broadfoot Publishing Company, 1995–2001) pt. 2, ser. 78, pp. 626–67 (hereafter *Supplement to* OR); *OR*, ser. I, vol. 38, pt. 3, serial 74, pp. 654–55; *Tennesseans in the Civil War, A Military History of Confederate and Union Units with Available Rosters of Personnel*, 2 vols. (Nashville: Civil War Centennial Commission, 1964–1965) 2:348.

[41] www.geocities.com/bsdunagan/47tn.html (5 July 2008).

[42] Kennett, *Marching through Georgia*, 173.

[43] Lindsley, ed., *Military Annals of Tennessee*, I:399; *OR*, ser. 1, vol. 31, pt. 3, serial 74, p. 891.

[44] Alfred J. Vaughan, *Personal Record of the Thirteenth Regiment, Tennessee Infantry, C.S.A.* (Memphis: S. C. Toof & Company, 1897) 40–67.

[45] Clement Anselm Evans, ed., *Tennessee*, vol. 10 of *Confederate Military History*, 19 vols. (1899; repr., Wilmington NC: Broadfoot Publishing Company, 1987) 760; *Tennesseans in the Civil War*, 2:408. Turley would later become a prominent lawyer in Memphis.

[46] Benjamin F. Cheatham Papers, Tennessee State Library and Archives, Nashville.

hospital at Griffin, Ga.; Col. D. C. Crook was also wounded, a Minie-ball entering the body just under the breast-bone, and passing through came out near the backbone."[47] Casualties among the regimental leaders seemed to hinder the advance of the Tennesseans throughout Maney's four brigades. In the 38th Tennessee, led by Lieutenant Colonel Andrew D. Gwynne, three were killed while two were wounded.[48]

The 8th Tennessee saw one killed and five wounded, with Private John Y. Blackwell of Company A wounded "by [a] minie ball just above left ankle shattering both bones." Blackwell remained "[o]n crutches fifteen years after the war."[49] The 16th Tennessee, led by Major Benjamin Randals, sustained four killed and two wounded including Lieutenant John Akeman who "was killed by four mortal wounds,"and "Lieutenant J. D. Brown [who] was wounded sevier in the grind," according to one comrade. Second Lieutenant John Jenkins of the 52nd Tennessee, who had transferred from the 154th Tennessee, was wounded, disabling his arm.[50] In Carter's brigade, 14 men were killed and 108 men were wounded, for a total casualty list of 122 men.[51]

Strahl's Tennessee Brigade. In Strahl's brigade, the 5th Tennessee, on skirmish line lost sixteen men, one killed, and two with mortal wounds. Five more men in Strahl's brigade were also wounded. The remainder of the brigade came up on Carter's men and could do nothing but halt behind them in the ravine located at and around today's Ardmore Park. In the 19th Tennessee, commanded by Major Deaderick because Colonel Walker had been dispatched to command Maney's brigade, the men were frustrated at being exposed to the enemy's fire without any apparent intent by the brigade in front of them to move forward. According to one source on the 19th Tennessee: "Encountering intense small arms and artillery fire, the front brigades [Carter and Magevney]

---

[47] Lindsley, ed., *Military Annals of Tennessee,* I:431.

[48] Lindsley, ed., *Military Annals of Tennessee,* I:508; J. D. Thomas, and L. F. Burks, Chairman His. Comm. Camp Rodes, 22 February 1897, Roll of the Tuscaloosa Plow Boys, Company G, 38th Tennessee Infantry Regiment.

[49] Thomas A. Head, *Campaigns and Battles of the Sixteenth Regiment, Tennessee Volunteers, 1861–1865* (Nashville TN: Cumberland Presbyterian Publishing House, 1885); Edwin L. Ferguson, *Sumner County, Tennessee in the Civil War,* ed. Diane Payne (Tompkinsville KY: self-published , 1972) 224; *Supplement to* OR, pt. 2, vol. 66, ser. 78, p. 580; Thomas A. Head, *Sumner County, Tennessee in the Civil War,* ed. Diane Payne (self-published, 1972).

[50] Lindsley, ed., *Military Annals of Tennessee,* I:341; Gillum, *An Eyewitness History*, n.27, n.28; Rennolds, *History of the Henry County Commands,* 17.

[51] Benjamin F. Cheatham Papers, Tennessee State Library and Archives, Nashville.

advanced to within one hundred yards of the enemy entrenchments but could go no further. When Strahl's and Walker's brigades came up, they could do little more than take cover behind the crest of a hill and exchange fire with the Yankees."[52] According to Dr. J. W. Worsham of the 19th Tennessee, "The battle ground was rough and uneven, and Stewart's men were the only ones engaged here and had to cross a ravine to reach the enemy's works." Moreover, added Worsham, "Hardee did not press the fight in front of him."[53]

Not willing to try to storm the Federal position, Carter's and Magevney's brigades fell back to and lay in the wooded ravine between today's Collier Road and 28th Street. Behind them, Strahl's and Walker's brigades huddled behind the wooded hill near 28th Street just west of Peachtree Street. A veteran from the 19th Tennessee explained that "The battle did not materialize as was expected."[54] The only known casualties sustained in the 19th Tennessee were Captain J. G. Deadrick of Company B, and Private Andy G. Johnson of Company K who were wounded.[55] About 10:00 P.M., Strahl's men, along with the rest of Maney's Tennesseans, withdrew. In summary, Strahl's brigade lost twenty-one men, with one killed and twenty wounded during the charge.[56] A veteran of the 5th Tennessee that engaged the enemy at Peach Tree Creek lamented, "The general attack having failed to accomplish anything, we retired after nightfall to our works and bivouacked, and at 3 A.M. on the 21st fell back within the fortifications of Atlanta."[57]

Walker's Tennessee Brigade. In Walker's (Maney) Brigade, which was commanded by Colonel Walker of the 19th Tennessee, only eleven men were wounded, and there were no men reported killed or missing.[58] One veteran in the 1st Tennessee in Walker's brigade described the brigade's role as supporting Magevney's brigade in the effort to dislodge the Yankee position. According to Private Sam Watkins, his regiment, the 1st Tennessee, was in support of the 154th Tennessee, which, he recalled "was pretty badly cut to pieces" and he

---

[52] Fowler, *Mountaineers in Gray*, 152.

[53] J. W. Worsham, reminiscences of the battle around Atlanta, in *Confederate Reminiscences and Letters, 1861–1865*, vol. 3 (Atlanta: United Daughters of the Confederacy, 1996) 76.

[54] J. W. Worsham, "The Old Nineteenth Tennessee Regiment, C.S.A.," in *Confederate Reminiscences and Letters, 1861–1865*, vol. 3 (Atlanta: United Daughters of the Confederacy, 1996) 128.

[55] Ibid., 205.

[56] Benjamin F. Cheatham Papers, Tennessee State Library and Archives, Nashville.

[57] Rennolds, *History of the Henry County Commands*, 89.

[58] Benjamin F. Cheatham Papers, Tennessee State Library and Archives, Nashville.

"remembered how mad they seemed to be, because they had to fall back."[59] Another veteran in Walker's brigade, from the 9th Tennessee, also recounted their experience while in support of the front line. "Here our brigade formed the supporting line and though under fire, was not brought into action. The position of the enemy was so strong and the loss of our front line so heavy that the attack was abandoned without bring[ing] up the reserves."[60]

For Martin Van Buren Oldham, of the 9th Tennessee, Wednesday, 20 July, would prove his prediction of the evening before that the fight would open on this day. He recorded after the battle the events of the day in Maney's division: "We moved last night reaching a position on the line at midnight. Here we remained in reserve until [11] o'clock when we moved to the right and short distance and advanced in two lines, Vaughan [Magevney] and Wright [Carter] in front. The boys at first did not like the idea of going outside the breastworks," Oldham explained, "but few failed to go. [Magevney] and [Carter] soon came up with the enemy posted behind breastworks. Getting within fifty or a hundred y[ards] and behind the crest of the hill the men remained here awaiting orders to storm the works which were very strong." The Tennessee veteran added, "At night we withdrew the lines and went back again to our position behind the works. We have attacked their line in several places today and captured a good many prisoners. Maj. Rogers is wounded. [Magevney] and [Carter] lost heavily." The major that Oldham referred to was Major H. A. Rogers of Company I, in the 9th Tennessee Infantry.[61]

According to Captain James I. Hall, commanding Company C of the 9th Tennessee, his unit had a "plain view" of the Federal position and the battle, and they "suffered considerable loss from the enemy's fire."[62] It soon became clear to Walker's brigade that Magevney's men were not having any success in reaching the Federal lines, let alone taking them. As the veterans of Walker's brigade hunkered down in the face of increasing shell fire from the Federal artillery, what happened next, according to Captain Hall, was nothing short of miraculous:

---

[59] Watkins, *Co. Aytch*, 173.

[60] James R. Fleming, *Band of Brothers, A History of Company C, 9th Tennessee Regiment*, 75; James R. Fleming, *The Confederate Ninth Tennessee Infantry* (Gretna LA: Pelican Publishing Company, 2006) 116–17.

[61] Martin Van Buren Oldham, *Civil War Diaries of Van Buren Oldham, Company G, 9th Tennessee, 1863–1864*, ed. and intro. Dieter C. Ullrich (Martin: University of Tennessee at Martin Library, 1998) www.utm.edu/departments/acadpro/library/departments/special_collections/E579.5%20Oldham/text/vboldham_indx.htm (29 November 2008).

[62] Fleming, *Band of Brothers*, 75; Fleming, *Ninth Tennessee*, 116–17.

While we were lying on the ground in the rear line, a cannonball from the enemy's batteries struck a pine tree under which we were lying, cutting the trunk almost in two about half-way up the tree. The top fell but was held by some splinters which prevented its falling to the ground. Being afraid that it would fall on us, I moved my company back twenty paces to the rear of the line where we again lay down. Immediately after this movement was made, a large shell struck the ground directly on the spot where we had been lying a minute before and exploded with terrific force, scattering earth and fragments of the shell in every direction. The warning given by the broken tree top had saved the lives of many if not all the company.[63]

Captain Hall went on to say that "nothing was accomplished" by the attack except to incur heavy losses to the army.[64] Inspection of the muster rolls for the 9th Tennessee Infantry, however, reveal that there were no known casualties by the regiment at Peach Tree Creek.[65]

"Walker on Bate's left met, it seems, with more obstinate resistance," John Happy, the newspaper man for the *Chattanooga Daily Rebel*, continued his account. The Tennessee war correspondent who accompanied Smith's Tennessee and Georgia Brigade, added "In the advance made by his Division Brig. General Stevens was severely if not mortally wounded." Tellingly, John Happy described the minimal role taken by the all-Tennessee division led by General George Maney: "Cheatham's division, commanded by Brig. Gen. Maney, met with the same success, driving the enemy into their works." In his glowing account of the performance by Maney's men, the Tennessee writer actually reveals the limited role that Maney's division played in the engagement. Maney and his men were ordered to "take the works" of the enemy, not push their skirmishers back to their entrenchments. In contrast, the writer explained that "Stewart took possession of the front line of the enemy's works, and captured many prisoners but could not hold them, because of the strength of [the Federal's] second line." John Happy was describing the counterattack made by the balance of Ward's division on Featherston's Mississippians as well as the response made by other portions of Hooker's XX Corps (Geary and Williams) against Walthall's attackers. The war corre-

---

[63] Fleming, *Band of Brothers*, 75; Fleming, *Ninth Tennessee*, 116–17.

[64] Fleming, *Band of Brothers*, 75–76; Fleming, *Ninth Tennessee*, 116–17.

[65] Ninth Tennessee Volunteer Infantry "Compiled Service Records of Confederate Soldiers Who Served in Organizations from the Union and Confederate States of America during the War of the Rebellion," Record Group 269, National Archives, Washington, DC; Fleming, *Ninth Tennessee*, 188–97.

spondent added "[Stewart's] loss was heavy, especially in Featherston's brigade."[66]

The total losses in Maney's Tennessee division were 277 according to a report from division surgeon F. Rice, with just 30 killed, 247 wounded, and none captured or missing.[67] According to General Ward's after-action report, among the 246 men captured from Featherston's Mississippi Brigade, one man from Cheatham's division was included, but in the official report of casualties from his division, no men were listed as captured in Maney's four brigades. Seemingly, very few of the Tennesseans managed to get to the Federal works. The only confirmed captured Southerners in Maney's division were two men from the 13th Tennessee, but, the 13th Tennessee, consolidated with the 154th Tennessee in Magevney's brigade, attacked the Federal works along the Collier Road. As the right half of Kimball's brigade had been refused to protect Newton's division from the threat posed by Featherston's Mississippians that had blown through Ward's skirmishers, Maney's Tennesseans entered combat in an oblique movement to the right, meaning that the left of Maney's division had much farther to travel than the right. Thus, the right brigade, Magevney's brigade, was the closest to, and was the only one that reached, or came nearer to, the Federal works. While the losses appeared to be futile and high, Maney suffered only about 277 men in killed and wounded, according to his return,[68] with 33 coming from Strahl and Wright's brigades and the rest, about 122 or 50% each, in Magevney's and Carter's brigades.[69]

On the other side, Federal losses in Kimball's brigade were almost miraculously light as compared to those of Maney's Tennesseans and some of Walker's Georgians who had charged them. In the 36th Illinois, only seven men were wounded, and none were killed. In the 73rd Illinois, one man was killed while eight were wounded. The few losses in the face of what seemed to be certain destruction to the men of Newton's division caused the men from the 36th Illinois to give thanks to God: "When all was over, it seemed more like a

---

[66] John Happy, "From the Front," *Chattanooga* [Griffin GA] *Daily Rebel*, 27 July 1864, Tennessee State Library and Archives, microfilm 1045, roll 1, Nashville.

[67] F. Rice, Surgeon's Report of Casualties in Cheatham's Division at the Battle of Peach Tree Creek, 20 July 1864, *Atlanta* (Macon GA) *Daily Intelligencer*, 6 August 1864, Benjamin F. Cheatham Papers, Tennessee State Library and Archives, Nashville.

[68] Castel, *Decision in the West*, 381; *OR*, ser. 1, vol. 31, pt. 3, serial 74; 877, 882–84.

[69] Castel, *Decision in the West*, 381; F. Rice, Surgeon's Report of Casualties in Cheatham's Division at the Battle of Peach Tree Creek, 20 July 1864, *Atlanta* (Macon GA) *Daily Intelligencer*, 6 August 1864, Benjamin F. Cheatham Papers, Tennessee State Library and Archives, Nashville.

The Battle of Peach Tree Creek

dream than a reality, and made not a few of us declare that our success was due to the good providence of God watching over and protecting us."[70]

General Hardee, sitting on his horse, waited for results with General Cleburne and their combined staffs "in a small grove of trees adjacent to the Atlanta Road [today's Peachtree Street] when a courier from Walker reported that his attack had been repulsed. Hardee ordered Cleburne to commit his Division."[71] It was now about 6:00 P.M. Walker's division of Georgians had been thrown back, and Maney's Tennesseans were checked. Hardee, concerned about not hearing the guns of Bate's division to his right had earlier sent a staff officer to locate Bate and his division. Unfortunately for Hardee and the Confederates, Bate's men had gotten lost in the cane thicket in the branch of Clear Creek which, together with Peach Tree Creek, had served to envelop Bate's men on three sides, causing Bate to misjudge his point of attack and location of the Federal position.[72]

Bate's men could not realize in their tangled march through the canes that they had detoured up the branch of Clear Creek, and were headed south, back toward the direction that they had begun the attack. Somewhere during the marching and countermarching in the cane thicket for two hours, one of Hardee's staff officers, W. D. Pickett, located Bate and got his division around Clear Creek and on the right flank of Walker's division. It was now after 6:00 P.M. Thus, at about 6:10 P.M. Hardee ordered Cleburne to renew the attack by replacing Walker's division with Cleburne's veterans. Joining Cleburne would be Bate's division to his right, hoped Hardee, between the Buckhead Road and Clear Creek. Unfortunately, Bate's slow-moving men would not be in position to threaten Newton's left until almost dusk.

---

[70] Bennett and Haigh, *History of the 36th Regiment*, 615.
[71] Craig L. Symonds, *Stonewall of the West, Patrick Cleburne and the Civil War* (Lawrence: University of Kansas Press, 1997) 224.
[72] *OR*, ser. 1, vol. 38, pt. 1, serial 72, pp. 348–49.

13

WE MUST CARRY EVERYTHING...
THE FATE OF ATLANTA DEPENDS ON US

Everything was as quiet as could be when the Rebs appeared in front of our men, first one line, then two, then three, till seven lines of battle had emerged from the woods. Our artillery opened on them. Still on they came, on and on with overwhelming force, as quick as a thought, almost. Our men were in the line and opened fire on them, still on they came. They fell with such iressistable force upon the 2nd (Gerrys) Division that they had to fall back.[1]

Major General William Wing Loring studied the Federal lines with his subordinates. Missing General John Adams's Mississippi Brigade, which had been detached to guard along the Chattahoochee River, Loring had only two of his three brigades on the field to make the attack. Loring instructed General Featherston to lead his Mississippi Brigade across the open field before it and take their works. Old Blizzards also ordered General Scott to take his Alabama and Louisiana Brigade and support Featherston by following it at an interval of about a hundred yards on the left. Loring's division was supposed to wait for Hardee's corps to open the ball before they were to advance. After waiting for Hardee's men to get started for what must have seemed like an eternity to the anxious men, Loring's veterans finally heard the unmistakable sound of war in the distant woods to their right. Loring had instructed his men and officers to press the Yankees, take their works, and push them all the way and into the creek and river behind them, and he rode along his line to ensure that these orders were understood by all.

Featherston lined up his regiments left to right as follows: the 40th Mississippi led by Lieutenant Colonel George P. Wallace, 31st Mississippi commanded that day by Lieutenant Colonel James Drane, 22nd Mississippi under Major Martin A. Oatis, 3rd Mississippi under the command of Colonel Thomas A. Mellon, and the 33rd Mississippi directed by Colonel Jabez L. Drake, with the 1st Mississippi Battalion Sharpshooters led by Major James M.

---

[1] Jean M. Cate, ed., *"If I Live to Come Home": The Civil War Letters of Sergeant John March Cate* (Pittsburgh: Dorrance Publishing Company, 1995) 196.

Stigler, together with Company F, the "Calhoun Tigers" of the 31st Miss., deployed forward of the brigade as skirmishers. With some 1,230 Mississippians, Featherston advanced.[2]

Over to the left of Featherston's line, General Scott's brigade of some 1,450 veterans moved up in support of Featherston's men. Scott's brigade was lined up left to right, or west to east for the assault, as follows: the consolidated regiment of the 27th Alabama under Colonel James Jackson, 35th Alabama with Colonel Samuel S. Ives, and the 49th Alabama and Lieutenant Colonel John D. Weeden was placed on the left and led by Colonel Ives, the 12th Louisiana was put in the center under the command of Colonel Noel L. Nelson, the 55th Alabama led by Colonel John Snodgrass next lined up on the right, and the 57th Alabama commanded that day by Lieutenant Colonel William C. Bethune was on the far right.[3]

It was now after 4:00. Featherston recalled that the fight was to be a general one; every possible effort by all engaged in the attack should be made. He explained that the order he had received "was to attack the enemy whenever his lines were reached, and if he was found behind works, to fix bayonets, charge, and take them if possible. The victory was to be made as decisive as possible." They were not to stop and that they were to press any advantage gained to the fullest. One Alabamian in Scott's brigade recorded that General Stewart made a speech to his brigades. "We 'were going to assault the enemy in his works, and we must carry everything, allowing no obstacle to stop us; that the fate of Atlanta probably depended on the result of this battle.'"[4] Featherston continued:

> These instructions were given to my regimental commanders and strictly obeyed by them. The whole command dashed forward with eagerness and rapidity, crossing the creek without difficulty, passing through the strip of woods on the left of the brigade, the open space on the right, and entering the field occupied by the enemy. No halt was made, but the movement was forward and rapid. After entering the field a volley was fired, and the enemy's lines were charged from the right to the left of the brigade. This

---

[2] United States War Department, comp., *Official Records of the Union and Confederate Armies in the War of the Rebellion*, 128 vols. (Washington, DC: Government Printing Office, 1880–1901) ser. 1, vol. 38, serial 74, 880–84 (hereafter *OR*).

[3] Ibid., 894–95.

[4] J. P. Cannon, *Inside of Rebeldom: The Daily Life of a Private in the Confederate Army* (Washington, DC: National Tribune, 1900) 154.

advance and this charge were made under a very heavy and destructive fire from the enemy's batteries and small-arms...[5]

As the men pressed forward for the charge they were observed by Adjutant Pierson of the 33rd New Jersey who was abruptly interrupted from reading the letter from his father:

> Suddenly and unexpectedly a volley was fired at them and, so close were they to us, that the bullets came on over into our line. Evidently they [Scott's brigade was in their front in the dense woods.] had not expected our presence at that particular point any more than we had expected theirs, for the firing ceased for a moment. Col. Fourat ordered me to ride out to the open on our left [overlooking the old field south of Tanyard Branch and the field before Featherston's brigade]. And there I saw a beautiful sight. Down through the great, open fields they were coming, thousands of them, men in gray, by brigade front, flags flying.... I stopped but a few moments to take it all in, and then rode back to report.[6]

Actually, the thousands that Pierson saw were the some 1,230 Mississippians of Featherston's brigade as they pressed forward across the old field and to the brook named Tanyard. Some 215 of that number represented the 31st Mississippi, who had come from Calhoun, Chickasaw, Choctaw, and Pontotoc counties. Observing Loring's division in the assault, Federal General John Geary described the battle as being quite remarkable for its desperateness. Geary explained, "The field everywhere bore marks of the extreme severity of the contest, and recalled to my mind, in appearance, the scene of conflict where the same division fought at Gettysburg. Not a tree or bush within our range...[escaped] the scars of battle," explained the Pennsylvania general. "The appearance of the enemy as they charged upon our front across the cleared field was magnificent." Geary went on to say that "rarely [had] such a sight been presented in battle" and that "the rebel troops also seemed to rush forward with more than customary nerve and heartiness in the attack."[7]

General Loring ordered his two brigades forward. Crossing a branch of one of the Peach Tree Creek tributaries called Tanyard, named for a tanning

---

[5] *OR*, ser. 1, vol. 38, serial 74, 880–84.

[6] Larry M. Strayer and Richard A. Baumgartner, eds., *Echoes of Battle: The Atlanta Campaign* (Huntington WV: Blue Acorn Press, 1991); Stephen Pierson, "From Chattanooga to Atlanta in 1864–A Personal Reminiscence (1907)," *Proceedings New Jersey Historical Society*, vol. 16 (1931): 209.

[7] *OR*, ser. 1, vol. 38, serial 73, 136–41.

warehouse to the south, the butternut veterans had to move by the right of companies to step over the creek and get through the tangled undergrowth that lined the Tanyard Branch. On they went "with alacrity and great spirit." Federal General John Geary witnessed the attack of Featherston's Mississippi brigade from his vantage point near Collier's Mill as the Southerners came out of the woods skirting Tanyard Branch: "Pouring out from the woods they advanced in immense brown and gray masses (not lines) with flags and banners, many of them new and beautiful, while their general and staff officers were in plain view, with drawn sabers flashing in the light, galloping here and there as they urged their troops to the charge."[8] The Federal pickets were encountered after marching about half a mile. They fired a few scattering shots that did the Mississippians no harm and then fled to their works on the ridge. The Mississippi Brigade was then halted and the lines rectified in the open field. On the opposite side of the field, up on the ridge some 700 yards away, the enemy was in plain view behind "a line of red earth, which plainly told the work that was before us," explained Loring who added:

> Perceiving the left of Cheatham's division [commanded by Maney], on my right, to be advancing through the woods with less than the prescribed 200 yards distance between us my command was still delayed for that division to get its full distance. It was again ordered forward, and the men moved with bold confidence and resolute step in face of the enemy's works and his two lines of battle, when, arriving within 400 or 500 yards of the enemy's works, a terrible fire from his batteries and small-arms opened upon us, but the command moved forward with quickened step and a deafening yell, driving the enemy from his position and not stopping until our colors were planted on different points of the breast-works from right to left in a distance of half a mile, and capturing a number of prisoners.... This brilliant charge of my gallant Division was made so rapidly and with such intrepidity that up to this time we had sustained but comparatively a small loss. As the enemy fled in confusion from his works the steady aim of the Mississippi, Alabama, and Louisiana marksmen of my command produced great slaughter in his ranks.[9]

Featherston's and Scott's brigades moved so quickly upon the unsuspecting Yankees that they had seized the ridge splitting the Federal line for about half a mile. To their right, General Kimball's brigade occupying the right of Newton's division of the IV Corps not finding any opposition in its

---

[8] Ibid.
[9] *OR*, ser. 1, vol. 38, serial 74, pp. 876–78.

Hood's First Sortie, 20 July 1864

front where General Hardee's men were supposed to be coming from, but seeing the unchecked Rebel assault succeeding in taking the ridge to their right and putting Newton's division in danger of being cut off from the rest of the Federal troops, refused its line so that it faced west instead of south, to protect its now opened right flank and to fire upon the newly arrived Mississippians on the Collier Road and ridge.

In Coburn's brigade, of Ward's division, Private Henry E. Crist of Company I from the 33rd Indiana had decided to go forward from his lines earlier that afternoon after his unit had halted and been allowed to stack arms and rest. The private was on a mission in search of blackberries, and in mid-July, they were ripe for the picking. Crist had spotted some really nice blackberry bushes in the wooded canopy that screened the Tanyard Branch across the field in front of the Federal line of skirmishers that had deployed on Collier Ridge. There, the private "rambled nearer the forest, picking and eating. Suddenly a flash of light dazzled his eyes. He blinked. It was the sun striking on gun barrels of gray-coated men pouring out of the forest—six lines of them, muskets at right-shoulder shift. Cist screamed murder, Rebels, help, get ready, and bounded homeward through the briers, berry stains on his open lips. His comrades dropped their noonday meals, cannon boomed, musket volleys crashed—and the fight was on."[10] The six lines of Rebel soldiers that Crist saw were the six regiments of Featherston's Mississippi Brigade which included the 1st Battalion Sharpshooters and the 3rd, 22nd, 31st, 33rd, and 40th Mississippi infantry regiments as they crossed over the small hill that had previously concealed them from Crist and into the valley that held the Tanyard Branch of Peach Tree Creek. According to one veteran who heard Crist recount his story, "as he passed the skirmishers in his hasty retreat, he told them the enemy was coming, and in force; and so it proved to be."[11]

Watching Featherston's Mississippians advance out of the woods, many of the Yankee veterans had visions of another Chancellorsville disaster, one which a number of them had witnessed firsthand as part of the Army of the Potomac's old XI and XII corps. Newton's position had been overlapped on the right, threatening their rear. "They came surging on through the woods, down the gentle slope, with noise and fury like Stonewall Jackson's men at Chancellors-

---

[10] Lloyd Lewis, *Sherman, Fighting Prophet* (Lincoln: University of Nebraska Press, 1993) 383; Newton, 129th Illinois, 396; John R. McBride, *History of the 33rd Indiana Veteran Volunteer Infantry* (Indianapolis: Wm. B. Burford, Printer, 1900) 128.

[11] Newton, *129th Illinois*, 399.

ville. As to our men [Newton's], some of them were protected by piles of rails, but the most had not had time to barricade."[12]

> Everything was as quiet as could be when the Rebs appeared in front of our men, first one line, then two, then three, till seven lines of battle had emerged from the woods. Our artillery opened on them. Still on they came, on and on with overwhelming force, as quick as a thought, almost. Our men were in the line and opened fire on them, still on they came. They fell with such iressistable force upon the 2nd (Gerrys) Division that they had to fall back.[13]

A Northern war correspondent, impressed with Loring's division as it swept forward recorded, "the thickets fairly wilted and disappeared under their feet, so closely were they packed, and so irresistible their progress. They came on without skirmishers and, as if by instinct, struck [the Federal] flank."[14] The 1st Mississippi Battalion Sharpshooters and the remaining companies on skirmish, including the Calhoun Tigers, Company F of the 31st Mississippi, retired upon reaching the Federal skirmish line and joined the rest of the brigade, thus giving the impression that there were no skirmishers. Along the Federal skirmish line in Colonel Bloodgood's 22nd Wisconsin, veteran C. H. Dickinson recorded in his diary the advance of Featherston's Mississippians as they drew closer to him: "Never before in the war had we been able to see so long a line of battle…" explained Dickinson. "And now to see that whole plain covered with troops, each one standing out plain and distinct under that bright July sun, their burnished arms and gleaming bayonets flashing in the sunlight and when in motion seemed instilled with life. It was a magnificent sight…"[15] Another veteran of the 22nd Wisconsin remembered that they were met there by the "rebels in force, who charged down upon them in three different lines of battle at least twenty men deep; but our advanced line of skirmishers, under command of Captain Mead gave the order to 'rally on the reserve.'"[16]

Before the surprise attack, Federal General John Geary lined up his division along the hills and ridges just west of the Collier Mill in the area along

---

[12] O. O. Howard, "'The Very Woods Seemed to Moan and Groan'": The Struggle for Atlanta," in Ned Bradford, ed., *Battles and Leaders of the Civil War* (New York: The Fairfax Press, 1979) 504.

[13] Cate, *"If I Live to Come Home,"* 196.

[14] "Assault on Ward's Division," *New York Tribune*, 28 July 1864, 1.

[15] Lee Kennett, *Marching through Georgia: The Story of Soldiers & Civilians during Sherman's Campaign* (New York: Harper-Collins Publishers, 1995) 174–75.

[16] Racine Boy to Friend T., 21 July 1864, p. 15, subject file PW-4, Kennesaw Mountain National Battlefield Park, Kennesaw, Georgia.

today's Collier Road as it approaches Northside Drive. According to General O. O. Howard, "Our Geary had been compared to Napoleon's Marshal Ney, from his large proportions, his cheerful deportment, and his unfailing energy."[17] Howard was quite generous in his depiction of the Pennsylvanian. Geary was competent as an officer and was recognized as a very good and effective administrator, which would serve him well as governor of Pennsylvania in 1867. While he was a Democrat before the Civil War, and was part of the "War Democrat" wing of the party before and during the war, a party which was split in its support of the war. Geary became a Republican after the war and served as governor until his death in 1873. As for his military career, however, he was at best a mediocre general. Tragically, he would lose one of his two sons who fought under him during the war.[18]

Born on 30 December 1819, at Mt. Pleasant, Pennsylvania, Geary studied at Jefferson College "when the death of his father forced him to begin adult life early," according to his biographer. Before the war, he was a lawyer and served with distinction as colonel of the 2nd Pennsylvania Infantry during the Mexican War. After that, Geary organized the postal service in California and briefly served as mayor of San Francisco before being made the territorial governor of Kansas, a position which the staunch abolitionist had to resign for his views were even too much for the fledgling anti-slavery state. When the Civil War broke out, Geary organized the 28th Pennsylvania and served in the Eastern Theater during the first three years of the war. He received a brigadier general's commission on 25 April 1862 and was wounded in the foot and shoulder during the Battle of Cedar Mountain. He subsequently led a division in the XII Corps of the Army of the Potomac and his unit was part of the Federal force that was routed at Chancellorsville. There, Geary yelled out to General Hancock's II Corps to cover his division's retreat as his own men ran streaming by. Geary imprudently called out to Hancock's men to "Charge, you cowards, charge!" Then, "two of Hancock's men were so insulted they lowered their bayonets toward Geary until an adjutant stepped in." Shortly thereafter, the Pennsylvania General "was struck in the chest by a cannonball and knocked unconscious. When he came to, he was able to talk only in whispers for weeks."[19]

---

[17] Howard, *Autobiography*, 1: 616.

[18] *OR*, ser. 1, vol. 38, pt. 2, serial 73, pp. 136–41,151–52; Garold L. Cole, *Civil War Eyewitnesses: An Annotated Bibliography of Books and Articles, 1955-1986* (Columbia: University of South Carolina Press, 1988) 38.

[19] www.civilwarhome.com/gearybio.htm (20 August 2005). www.gdg.org/Research/OOB/Union?July1–3/jgeary.html (7 May 2006).

The Battle of Peach Tree Creek

During one battle, Geary reportedly "caught a soldier he thought was a skulker and threatened him with the flat of his sword. When the private replied, 'Put up your sword or I'll shoot you,' Geary apparently concluded that such combativeness was inconsistent with cowardice and apologized."[20] John White Geary was "hard working, reliable, and a meticulous administrator." He was "intense and passionate," as well, who was "renowned for a short temper and a sharper tongue." Despite his flaws, Geary was a "determined and aggressive fighter." Sergeant Charles W. McKay of Company C, 154th New York Infantry, described Geary fondly: "The General was a man of large stature, fine black eyes, very robust physique, and when mounted upon his horse was a figure of commanding presence. He was a strict disciplinarian, withal a warm-hearted, emotional man, and although some of the men feared him, they all respected him." McKay thought that Geary's stern discipline had made his White Star Division the crack unit of Sherman's Army. Not all of Geary's soldiers were as fond of him, however. Lieutenant Lloyd wrote, "General Geary, the bastard, is our division commander."[21]

At Gettysburg, he blundered on the second day of the battle, leading his division completely off the field and out of the fight as his division had been called to reinforce the Federal line. He was not heard from until after 9:00 P.M. that day. Perhaps the staff officer who led his unit astray should be found mostly at fault, but nevertheless, Geary's men were completely missing during the fighting of 2 July. On 3 July, however, on the third day of the battle, his command fought resolutely to restore a part of the Federal line lost the evening before on Culp's Hill.[22]

During the Battle of Lookout Mountain, Geary's men received for him the highest notoriety of his Civil War career when they swept up the slopes of the indomitable mountain and took the heights "above the clouds." Perhaps with visions of Lookout Mountain on their minds, Geary led his unfortunate division up the slopes of Dup Gap Mountain, near Dalton, Georgia, six months later where they were met with disaster when he had been ordered merely to "demonstrate," that is, to hold the attention of the Confederates along Dug Gap Mountain while the main effort was to have McPherson's Army of the Tennessee flank the Rebel position through Snake Creek Gap and to Resaca below Dalton. At the Battle of Dug Gap Mountain, Geary lost nearly 400 of his

---

[20] Ibid.

[21] www.civilwarhome.com/gearybio.htm (20 August 2005); www.gdg.org/Research/OOB/Union?July1–3/jgeary.html (7 May 2006); Doug Cubbison, notes on Geary.

[22] www.civilwarhome.com/gearybio.htm (20 August 2005).

men shot or killed and failed to take the gap, but he did accomplish his primary objective, however; his force held the attention of Johnston at Dalton while McPherson gained the Confederate rear.[23]

While he was not a brilliant strategist, his self-portrayals of his behavior and that of his command in battles in letters written to his wife, Mary at Philadelphia, would have one believe that he carried the Federal army to victory single-handedly. Chancellorsville was not a bright spot in his service, and, but for the relief which would be rendered by others around him during the surprise assault at Peach Tree Creek, Geary's imprudence in placing his command so far in advance of the other divisions around him and in sticking the right flanks of two of his brigades "in the air," or exposed to an attack, would have been more revealed. John White Geary would subsequently write home to Mary and include in his after-action report about how he and his division beat back thousands and thousands of screaming Confederates and that he was "attacked by overwhelming numbers." He also estimated that there were some 2,500 Rebel casualties in his front, when in reality about 222 officers and 3,751 men of Geary's Division had been pushed back. He should have praised Hooker, Williams, Ireland, and Harrison and their commands for saving him and two of his brigades from disaster.[24]

Geary's 1st Brigade commanded by Colonel Charles Candy was posted along a ridge south of today's Collier Road and between that road and Spring Valley Road facing southeast. Candy's right extended to the west as far as today's Northside Drive but only a few yards west of it. Along today's Spring Valley Road was a small cornfield in front of the right of Candy's line beyond which was a wooded knoll that seemed to command the area to the south beyond. Geary determined to take and fortify this knoll so he ordered the 33rd New Jersey of Jones's 2nd Brigade to take it, dig in, and prepare a place for a gun battery (the knoll being on the north side of Greystone Drive just west of its intersection with Meredith Drive). He also ordered the 119th New York, also of Jones's 2nd Brigade, forward to support the 33rd New Jersey, but the order was soon countermanded and the 119th New York held its position in line behind Candy's 1st Brigade.[25]

Candy's 1st Brigade was placed into position with the 147th Pennsylvania on the left and the 5th Ohio on the right of the first line located along the

---

[23] Ibid.; www.gdg.org/Research/OOB/Union?July1–3/jgeary.html (7 May 2006).

[24] *OR*, ser. 1, vol. 38, pt. 2, serial 73, 136–41,151–52; Cole, *Civil War Eyewitnesses*, 38.

[25] *OR*, ser. 1, vol. 38, pt. 2, serial 73, 138–40; 212–14, 236.

heights overlooking today's Tanyard Branch Park and parking lot along Collier Road on the east and just south of Collier Road as the Federal line reached west to near today's Northside Drive. The 29th Ohio was formed in a second line behind the 147th Pennsylvania, on the heights just north of Collier Road, and the 28th Pennsylvania continued the second line west from the 29th Ohio's line to reach Northside Drive at its intersection with Collier Road. The 66th Ohio formed a third line in reserve behind the second line and on the top of the slope perpendicular to today's Cottage Lane and Evergreen Lane. As the hot afternoon of 20 July wore on, Geary ordered that new uniforms, which had recently arrived, be issued to his men. His men, like the remainder of the army, "needed a new issue of clothes. The men were fatigued and lice ridden," according to one historian of the 66th Ohio. "Many were undernourished, and some had scurvy, but their goal was before them. After Peachtree Creek there would not be many more streams to ford." After some of the other troops were moved further forward, the 66th Ohio, and the 28th Pennsylvania to their front right in the second line, were exposed to an attack to their right flanks that were "in the air," from the woods below the present-day intersection of Collier Road and Northside Drive.[26]

Geary also posted artillery along Candy's front by placing Sloan's Pennsylvania Light Artillery Battery E with its six 3-inch ordnance rifles along the line occupied by the 147th Pennsylvania, and Bundy's 13th New York Battery of Artillery with its six Napoleon 12-pounders along the works erected by the 5th Ohio. Two of Sloan's pieces were placed on the left of the 147th Pennsylvania while the other four pieces were put in line with that regiment, while four of Bundy's guns were posted between the right of the 147th Pennsylvania and the left of the 5th Ohio and the remaining two pieces in Bundy's battery were placed on the right of the 5th Ohio. All of Candy's and Jones' regiments and the artillery of the division were thus facing southeast, toward today's Tanyard Branch Park.[27]

The remainder of Geary's 2nd Brigade under Colonel Patrick H. Jones was placed in two lines, with three regiments, the 73rd Pennsylvania on the left, the 119th New York in the center, and the 134th New York on the right, posted along the reverse slope (or northern side) of the ridge along Collier Road (between today's Overbrook Drive and Collier Road). The balance of Jones's

---

[26] David T. Thackery, *A Light and Uncertain Hold, A History of the 66th Ohio Volunteer Infantry,* 200–201.

[27] *OR,* ser. 1, vol. 38, pt. 2, serial 73, pp. 138–40, 212–14.

Hood's First Sortie, 20 July 1864

Brigade was posted on the ridge behind the Collier Road ridge along the area at the entrance to the Bitsy Grant Tennis Center and connected with the left of Williams's division (Robinson's 3rd Brigade), on the right and overlooking the ravine between the tennis center and Overbrook Drive to the south. These regiments included the 33rd New Jersey, which had originally been posted in the area where the tennis courts and clubhouse are today before being sent to take the knoll in front of Candy's brigade, which was originally on the left. The 109th Pennsylvania was in the center, along the drive, and the 154th New York was on the right, on the knoll at the entrance to the tennis center and Northside Drive.[28]

Geary's 3rd Division, led by Colonel David Ireland, and was placed in column in rear of today's Bitsy Grant Tennis Center along the eastern slope of the ridge and overlooking Peach Tree Creek. From south to north, the two columns were: first on the left the 29th Pennsylvania, on the right the 60th New York, in the center on the left the 111th Pennsylvania and to its right the 102nd New York, and in the rear on the left the 137th New York and to its right the 149th New York.[29]

---

[28] Ibid.
[29] Ibid., 138–40, 273.

14

BAILEY BE A GOOD BOY

The order to "fix bayonets, forward, double-quick, march," was given. We raised the old Rebel yell and rushed on the works, but the yell was soon drowned by the roar of musketry and thunder of cannon, canister, and minieballs mowed great gaps in our ranks, but on we went until it seemed a hand-to-hand conflict was inevitable...[1]

As General Scott's Alabama and Louisiana veterans stepped off through the forest and briers ahead of them, they quickly stumbled onto Lieutenant Colonel Enos Fourat's 33rd New Jersey Regiment that had been posted by General John Geary on a high wooded ridge in front of his main line to prepare an artillery position. It was a difficult march for the veteran Confederate troops as they entered the combat zone. After the proper distance between each division had been gained, "the command was given 'By the right of companies to the front, march,' and it was well that such was the order, for we could never have gone through that tangled mass of timber and brush in line-of-battle." The Alabamian described the terrain as "a heavy timbered section and [where] the trees had been felled, lapped and crossed until they presented an almost impassable barrier; but we finally made our way through the worst of it," he explained, "and were then halted and wheeled by the left flank into line-of-battle, being then under fire of the pickets."[2]

Geary was with the surprised New Jerseans when firing broke out. With Geary was Colonel Patrick H. Jones, commander of his 2nd Brigade. Geary and Jones and their startled staffs quickly rode off in the direction of their main body while Fourat tried to form his line of defense. Fourat's men were some 500 yards in advance of Geary's division and were without support. "Meantime," remembered Adjutant Pierson of the 33rd New Jersey, "the force

---

[1] J. P. Cannon, *A History of the 27th Regiment Alabama Infantry. "Bloody Banners and Barefoot Boys,"* ed. Noel Crowson and John V. Brogden (Shippensburg PA: Burd Street Press, 1997) 84.

[2] J. P. Cannon, *Inside of Rebeldom: The Daily Life of a Private in the Confederate Army* (Washington, DC: National Tribune, 1900) 154.

Hood's First Sortie, 20 July 1864

in the woods [Scott's men] in our immediate front had sized us up as to numbers and on they came."[3] According to Fourat, "The position was an isolated one, the ground intersected in all directions by deep ravines."[4] General Geary and Fourat's men had no idea of the impending attack. Fourat explained:

> General Geary was with me, and from the feeble opposition made to our skirmishers and the statements of prisoners he was led to believe that no large force of the enemy was in close proximity. Scarcely had I made dispositions to build my works before the enemy, advancing in mass through the woods, drove back the skirmishers instantly and rushed down upon us with loud yells, pouring in volley after volley. We were without shelter, but my men kept their ground defiantly and returned the fire with vim. Almost immediately another overwhelming force came down upon our right flank.[5]

The men of the 33rd New Jersey had been at the knoll just fifteen minutes before they were overwhelmed by Scott's men who broke suddenly through the dense woods in their front and on both flanks. The approaching attackers to Fourat's right were the men of the Consolidated 27th-35th-49th Alabama and part of the 12th Louisiana. According to one veteran of the 35th Alabama, "Our regiment and part of the 12th Louisiana was advancing through the timber, while the rest of the brigade had 600 yards of open fields to cross. At this time, John E. Abernathy, from the old 27th Alabama, captured the colors of the 33rd New Jersey Regiment."[6]

Lieutenant Colonel Fourat's men had been caught off guard, many of them without their weapons loaded or within reach as they had been working on digging trenches and felling trees. "How the bullets did come in from the front! Our reply was vigorous, too. And for a time we held them," lamented Adjutant Pierson.[7] Fourat tried to protect his exposed right flank by throwing two of his companies to cover, but it was too late. "We fought as long as we could, the

---

[3] Stephen Pierson, "From Chattanooga to Atlanta in 1864–A Personal Reminiscence (1907)," *Proceedings New Jersey Historical Society*, vol. 16 (1931): 289.

[4] United States War Department, comp., *Official Records of the Union and Confederate Armies in the War of the Rebellion*, 128 vols. (Washington, DC: Government Printing Office, 1880–1901) ser. 1, vol. 38, pt. 2, serial 73, 225 (hereafter *OR*).

[5] Ibid.

[6] Leroy F. Banning, *Regimental History of the 35th Alabama Infantry, 1862–1865* (Bowie MD: Heritage Books, 1999) 51–52; Clement Anselm Evans, ed., *Alabama*, vol. 8 of *Confederate Military History*, 19 vols. (1899; repr., Wilmington NC: Broadfoot Publishing Company, 1987) 143.

[7] Pierson, "From Chattanooga to Atlanta," 289.

The Battle of Peach Tree Creek

most desperate bravery and heroic valor could not balance those tremendous odds," declared Fourat.[8] His surprised men were simply overwhelmed. Now, the left of the 33rd New Jersey was also being enveloped by more of Scott's men, compelling Fourat to order a hasty retreat. "But very soon they were wrapping around both our flanks and getting into our rear. The firing was fearfully hot. Our isolated position was no longer tenable and the order to retire was given. At first it was orderly enough, but, almost surrounded as we were, our line was soon broken," explained Adjutant Pierson, "and in confusion."[9]

"I have an indistinct recollection of crossing a little brook and wondering at the splashes made by the Rebel bullets as they struck the water," continued Pierson. "I remember, too, stopping for rest a moment behind the little line we had left."[10] Pierson was referring to the original line along the ridge overlooking today's Tanyard Branch Park and parking lot just west of the bridge over Tanyard Branch on Collier Road. Pierson's regiment had first occupied this entrenched line before being ordered to move forward to the wooded knoll in front. "I suppose I was still somewhat weak from my wound of a month before; anyway I could not keep up with the others. As I lay there to get breath, the Rebel advance came up, and a long, lank Johnny, seeing me said: 'Get out of that, you Yankee son of a gun.' I got out."[11] Pierson wasted no time in running from the abandoned Federal line. "Whether he fired at me or not I do not know. Perhaps he had a momentary spasm of pity, the mark was so easy. Perhaps he did fire and missed. Going back further I met the same New York Colonel who had bidden me good-bye."[12] This was Lieutenant Colonel Allan H. Jackson, commander of the 134th New York.[13] "He was coming up by the flank. 'Where are they, Adjutant?' 'Deploy quickly, Colonel, they are right here,' was my answer. Before he could give his order, he was wounded, and still further back we were all driven in great confusion and disorder."[14]

> Under these circumstances, with such an overwhelming force against us and on three sides of us, with such a withering fire from front, right, and left, and the enemy rapidly gaining our rear, to stand longer was madness, and I

---

[8] John Y. Foster, *New Jersey and the Rebellion* (Newark NJ: 1868) 633; Erol Clauss, "The Atlanta Campaign, July 18, 1864" (Ph.D. diss., Emory University, 1965) 87.
[9] Pierson, "From Chattanooga to Atlanta," 289–90.
[10] Ibid., 290.
[11] Ibid.
[12] Ibid.
[13] William R. Scaife, *The Campaign for Atlanta* (Atlanta: self-published, 1993) 155.
[14] Pierson, "From Chattanooga to Atlanta," 290.

reluctantly gave the order to retire fighting. As the men rose and commenced to retire, with a yell of exultation the enemy rushed upon us with his dense masses and pressed so close that he ordered the surrender of our colors. With this order we could not comply. The fire was terrific; the air was literally full of deadly missiles; men dropped upon all sides; none expected to escape. The bearer of our State colors fell; 1 of the color guard was killed and 1 or 2 missing. The enemy were too close upon us to recover the colors; it was simply impossible...[15]

The shattered remnants of Fourat's 33rd New Jersey fell back to Geary's main line before Scott's double envelopment swallowed them all whole. The 33rd New Jersey lost sixteen men killed, two officers and seventeen men severely wounded, and four officers and thirty-eight men missing and presumed captured or killed, for a total of seventy-seven men lost in less than five minutes.[16] Among the dead were nineteen-year-old Isaac Knight, an immigrant from England, killed by a cannon shell, and Irish-born James Fortune and Hugh Shields. Of the forty-two missing officers and men, only eleven men made it to the Confederate prison camp at Andersonville and three of these subsequently died.[17] Presumably, the remaining thirty-one missing officers and men were among the dead on the field. With one-third of his men out of action, Fourat's remaining soldiers managed to escape capture, and they tried to regain their composure as they helped to restore the Federal line along the Collier Road, many without their guns. But, on a positive note explained Adjutant Pierson, "Every moment they could be held was of importance, giving our main line time to be more ready."[18]

During the assault on the 33rd New Jersey, Corporal Joseph Nicholas Thompson of Company B, 35th Alabama, charged the Federal works with a couple of buddies that he had made a pact with: "Just prior to being wounded, he and two others went over the breastworks to 'capture or kill a Yankee each.' His comrades made their charge and killed their man, but Thompson's rifle had a bad cap and failed to fire. He recapped his gun and pursued his man, but as he fired, his enemy fell to his knees and begged for mercy. The man was taken

---

[15] *OR*, ser. 1, vol. 38, pt. 2, serial 73, 225.

[16] Ibid., 215.

[17] Compiled Service Records, New Jersey State Archives; John G. Zinn, *The 33rd New Jersey in the Civil War, The Mutinous Regiment* (Jefferson NC: McFarland & Company, 2005) 131.

[18] Pierson, "From Chattanooga to Atlanta," 289.

prisoner and turned over to the guard."[19] Corporal Thompson recovered from his wound in time to have his leg taken off by a cannonball during the charge at Franklin, Tennessee, where he fell in front of the Federal breastworks. Thompson would have to lay on the bloody field at Franklin where General John Adams's horse, Charlie, almost rode over him on his fateful ride to the Federal works where both horse and rider were killed.

As the routed men of the 33rd New Jersey and the 134th New York ran for the rear along with other shattered and surprised units from portions of Candy's and Jones's brigades, it appeared that the Confederates had won a surprising victory. Adjutant Pierson lamented, "I was very blue; it seemed to me that the day was lost. Just then was met [by] Hooker coming forward."[20] Over on the other side of the gap, to their left, General Joseph Hooker arrived on the scene near the Collier Mill. He was "mounted on a splendid horse" and was "magnificent in appearance," "...looking, as he was, the beau ideal of a soldier of the olden type." The 33rd New Jersey had been decimated, put on the run, and lost its flag. Now, with Federal soldiers from all over Geary's division falling back all around him, Pierson looked to General Hooker. "Boys, I guess we will stop here," Pierson heard him say. There, General John W. Geary with his 2nd Division of the XX Corps was frantically trying to reform his men. He had posted the 13th New York Independent Battery, consisting of three two-gun sections of Napoleon 12-pounders commanded by Captain Henry Bundy, on the height just west of and overlooking the valley in front of Collier Mill.[21]

J. P. Cannon, a soldier in the 27th Alabama exclaimed: "The order to 'fix bayonets, forward, double-quick, march,' was given. We raised the old Rebel yell and rushed on the works, but the yell was soon drowned by the roar of musketry and thunder of cannon, canister, and minie-balls [sic] mowed great gaps in our ranks, but on we went until it seemed a hand-to-hand conflict was inevitable..."[22]

Bundy's battery had been occupied in firing upon Featherston's Mississippians to their left front in an enfilade (or from the side), sweeping fire down the exposed field. They were about to turn the guns to the left to fire up the ridge upon the newly lost Federal line, when out of nowhere, Scott's brigade

---

[19] Banning, *Regimental History of the 35th Alabama*, 134.

[20] Pierson, "From Chattanooga to Atlanta," 290.

[21] Larry M. Strayer and Richard A. Baumgartner, eds., *Echoes of Battle: The Atlanta Campaign* (Huntington WV: Blue Acorn Press, 1991); Pierson, "From Chattanooga to Atlanta," 210; Scaife, *The Campaign for Atlanta*, 156.

[22] Cannon, *History of the 27th Regiment Alabama Infantry*, 84.

came crashing into their immediate front from the dense woods that had heretofore hidden their progress. The right section of this battery, consisting of two guns under command of Lieutenant Miller, twice lost its guns to the men of Scott's brigade until a combination of crossfire from the left section of the battery firing with canister, case shot, "dummies," and concentrated rifle fire from the reformed infantrymen of Geary's 2nd Division forced the Alabamians and Louisianans back into the thicket. Owing to this desperate effort and the personal exertions of Major J. A. Reynolds, commander of the Artillery Brigade for the XX Corps, who rallied the infantry to support the artillerymen and helped pull back the four right guns to safety, the guns were saved from capture. According to J. P. Cannon of the 27th Alabama, "Our boys began to waver and soon the line fell back under cover of a little hill, where we reformed our shattered columns and forward again with the same result."[23]

Pierson watched the erosion of part of Candy's and Jones's lines in the face of the advancing Confederates. Scott's brigade exploded from the woods in front of them. Featherton's Mississippi Brigade could be seen advancing across the field and up and over the Collier Ridge to their left, and over to the right, O'Neal's brigade could be heard sweeping the ravine behind them and racing for their crossings of Peach Tree Creek in their rear. "Just at the left of the gap, left in our lines when we were driven back, was our Division battery, Bundy's. It was just at the edge, too, of the open field, down which I had seen the enemy coming," explained Adjutant Pierson. "Through this gap, and the still longer one to our right, where connection had not get been made with Williams' Division, the Rebels swarmed, took Bundy's Battery in the flank and attempted to rush it. He wheeled two of his pieces to the right to meet the attack."[24] The attackers were from the 37th Mississippi and a part of the 17th Alabama of O'Neal's brigade.

"So hot was the Rebel infantry fire that many of the spokes of the wheels of his (Bundy's) pieces were almost cut in two by the bullets alone. But Bundy held his ground, drove them off and saved all his guns. That evening I walked over to the battery," remembered Pierson, "and an artillery Sergeant, still black and grimy from the fight, told me the story, and, as he told it, he leaned against his piece, one arm thrown over it, patting it affectionately with his hand, as a mother might pat her child who had been in great danger, but had been saved. 'It was awful, Adjutant,' he said." The staff officer relayed the sergeant's

---

[23] Ibid., 84.
[24] Pierson, "From Chattanooga to Atlanta," 290–91.

desperate struggle, "'awful, but your stocking legs saved us.' It was our habit, when the powder in our cartridges became damp and spoiled, to break it off, throw it away, save the bullets, and, when we had enough to fill a stocking, to take them over to Bundy for use at close quarters."[25] These "dummies" were used with great effect that day in the struggle to push Scott's men back away from Collier's Mill.[26] "[Bundy] filled his guns with these, and then, at point blank range, poured it into them. The slaughter was terrible. 'It was awful, Adjutant,' said the Sergeant, and out yonder in the tangle, piled up, they lay," Pierson sadly reflected, "mute evidence of the truth of the of the sergeant's story."[27]

Because the 33rd New Jersey Regiment of General Geary's division had been posted in the wooded knoll in advance of the division, Scott's brigade hit it unexpectedly and began to swing around both sides of the smaller 33rd New Jersey. Lieutenant Colonel Fourat, commanding the 33rd New Jersey, reported that the regiment lost fifteen men killed, three officers and seventeen men wounded, six mortally, and three officers and thirty-three men lost to capture, for a total of seventy-one men lost in only five minutes. The complete surprise of both sides and the heavy wooded terrain probably spared men of the 33rd New Jersey from Scott's advancing forces.[28] "A total of 21 men had been killed during the battle or would die from their wounds."[29]

By the time that the survivors of the 33rd New Jersey could fall back out of the three-sided pocket their defense had created, Scott's brigade had largely gone past them in two masses, effectively splitting the Rebel brigade. The Consolidated Alabama Regiment (27th, 35th, and 49th Alabama) and the left nine companies of the 12th Louisiana (This regiment had twelve companies instead of the usual ten.) had swung left and headed up the hollow (toward Overbook Drive) to the west and center of Geary's division. Despite being outnumbered about four to one, this group was the portion of Scott's brigade that succeeded in twice capturing Lieutenant Miller's four guns of the left two-sections (if looking south from the Federal line) of Bundy's federal battery, before the hail of fire compelled Scott's men to withdraw.

---

[25] Ibid., 291.

[26] Strayer and Baumgartner, eds., *Echoes of Battle*, 210; Pierson, "From Chattanooga to Atlanta," 210; *OR*, ser. 1, vol. 38, pt. 2, serial 73, p. 482.

[27] Pierson, "From Chattanooga to Atlanta," 291.

[28] *OR*, ser. 1, vol. 38, pt. 2, serial 73, 215.

[29] Zinn, *The Mutinous Regiment*, 131.

Hood's First Sortie, 20 July 1864

One soldier of the 27th Alabama observed, "A four gun battery was immediately in our front and the enemy were massed in the ditch. Indeed it seemed like a forlorn hope to attempt to dislodge them, but having rested a short time we made the third charge and drove them from the works, captured the four cannon, the flag of the 33rd New Jersey [which had already been taken on the wooded knoll in front of the works], and planting our colors on the breastworks."[30] Scott's men thought the battle had been won, and began celebrating. But it was short lived. They were soon ordered to withdraw, giving up the ground gained, and they fell back in good order about 150 yards and into the woods from where they had mounted their assault, remaining there and exchanging fire for the remainder of the battle. After dark, they were ordered to fall back to the Confederate entrenchments taking with them their wounded and their prized captured flag of the 33rd New Jersey. The Alabamians later learned that Hardee's corps had failed to take the works to their right, causing their brigade and Featherston's brigade to their right to be unsupported and thus exposed to counterattack by the Federals.[31]

The 27th Alabama sustained nine men wounded in the charge on the Federal lines, with two of these soldiers falling and becoming captured. One of these men, Private William Molt of Company C, apparently later died at the Federal field hospital.[32] The 35th Alabama added twelve more men to the casualty rolls along the Collier Ridge including nine wounded, two captured, and one killed.[33] The 49th Alabama added fourteen more men to the casualty list with thirteen men wounded and one man killed. The consolidated 27th-35th-49th Alabama thus lost thirty-five men wounded, two captured, and two killed.[34] One veteran of the 27th Alabama wrote, "Sorrowfully the survivors retired to our breastworks, mourning the moss of many of our friends, but thankful that we had escaped." The next day, the same soldier recorded in his diary: "I have not learned our exact loss in yesterday's battle, but the loss in our consolidated regiment is about 25 percent, which is not as heavy as might have been expected, considering the short range at which we fought, and the

---

[30] Cannon, *History of the 27th Regiment Alabama Infantry*, 84.

[31] Ibid., 85.

[32] Harry V. Barnard, *Tattered Volunteers: The Twenty-Seventh Alabama Regiment, C.S.A.* (Northport AL: Hermitage Press, 1965) 94–158; Cannon, *History of the 27th Regiment Alabama Infantry*, 111–22.

[33] Banning, *Regimental History of the 35th Alabama*, 73–143.

[34] *OR*, ser. 1, vol. 38, pt. 3, serial 74, 895.

disadvantage we had in making three successive charges on the enemy in is works."³⁵

The right half of Scott's brigade had not been idle; instead, they were having a much rougher time in the ravine below the Tanyard Branch (around today's Tanyard Creek Park parking lot). This part of Scott's brigade included the three right companies of the 12th Louisiana that had become separated from the rest of its regiment because the file guides had dressed off of and continued to support the regiment to its right, the 55th Alabama. The 55th Alabama contained an unusual number of Hispanic Americans as Latino settlers along the Southern half of the "Yellowhammer State" flocked to this regiment during the second year of the war.³⁶

In this battle each unit was to be guided by the right flank. Each unit was to pay attention to the direction of the unit to its right and keep up with it and cover, or protect, its left flank or side. Unfortunately for the men of Scott's brigade, the main Federal line occupied a large wooded ridge that was shielded by a smaller tree-covered knoll in its front. Scott's Alabamians and Louisianans unwittingly found themselves smashing blindly across the bottom of a bowl and into the Federal lines on the ridge on the opposite side that was being defended by Geary's veteran division of Hooker's XX Corps. The knoll had hidden the ridge from view as the Southerners approached. On the advanced knoll the men of the 33rd New Jersey had quickly found themselves surrounded on three sides by the attackers. The topography of the area split Scott's brigade as it passed the wooded knoll occupied by the 33rd New Jersey and continue past it in the hollows on either side. Thus, when Scott's men assaulted the ridge and the main Federal position, the brigade was fragmented without support from either half.

To the right of the 55th Alabama was the 57th Alabama that guided Scott's entire brigade.³⁷ The 57th Alabama had to watch for and cover Featherston's brigade to its right. When Featherston's brigade continued up the large open field in front of and to the east of the Collier Mill, it necessarily changed front slightly to the right to match the topography of the ridge and Federal line on top so as to hit the line with the entire brigade at the same time. To avoid a large and potentially dangerous separation between the two brigades, the right of Scott's brigade continued to slide right to try and keep up its support of

---

³⁵ Cannon, *Inside of Rebeldom*, 155.
³⁶ "57th Alabama Infantry," www.managementaides.com/my_interests/hispanic_ america.htm (22 November 2008).
³⁷ Scrapbook 28, 13 ½, MSS 130, Wilbur G. Kurtz Papers, Kenan Research Center, Atlanta History Center.

Featherston, thus causing a gap of about 100 yards in the center of Scott's line. The right (or east) section of Scott's brigade hit the left part of Geary's division, including Candy's brigade and the six-gun Pennsylvania battery commanded by Lieutenant Thomas S. Sloan where General Hooker had taken charge of the defense. Also, the lay of the land had allowed part of Colonel Harrison's brigade on Ward's extreme left to fire on the right flank of Scott's brigade that had separated from Featherston's left.

Part of Harrison's brigade from Ward's 3rd Division also met and assisted in repulsing the right half of Scott's brigade that had advanced across the lower field where the parking lot of Tanyard Creek Park is now located. The right part of Scott's brigade, consisting of the 55th and 57th Alabama and three companies of the 12th Louisiana had continued to the northeast across the left edge of the field to the support of Featherston's Mississippians as they dressed off of Featherston's left by about 100 to 200 yards. "Between the two regiments on the right and those on the left of the 1st Brigade, there flowed a small stream which prevented the Rebels from coming as close to the right as they did to the left of the brigade, consequently the left bore the brunt of the fight," remembered George Newton of the 129th Illinois. The 79th Ohio and the 102nd Illinois were aligned to the west of the Tanyard Branch, while the 129th Illinois, and the two regiments in the second line, the 105th Illinois and the 70th Indiana, wheeled to the left, or east, across the Tanyard Branch behind and subsequently to the left flank of the 129th Illinois during their defense and counter-thrust to Featherston's attack. Thus, the 79th Ohio and the 102nd Illinois remained west of the Tanyard Branch throughout the fight and materially assisted Geary's division in repulsing Scott's brigade and its brief capture of the 2nd Division's guns as well as firing into the left and rear of Featherston's exposed flank. Describing Scott's advance on Geary's artillery, Newton explained, "Between the right of the 3rd Division and the left of the 2nd Division, the Rebels forced their way through our lines, and for a short time the battery of the 2nd Division was in their possession; but, with the assistance of the 102nd [Illinois], which was armed with Spencer rifles, it was soon retaken."[38] In the 102nd Illinois, there were four companies, C, E, G, and I that were armed with the Spencer rifles.[39]

For 1st Lieutenant Cyrus E. Custis of Company G, 79th Ohio, the Battle of Peach Tree Creek was memorable. While writing Atlanta historian and city

---

[38] Newton, *129th Illinois*, 400.
[39] Ibid.

planner, Wilbur G. Kurtz in 1932, Custis recalled that the sounds of battle began to ring from the front. His regiment, along with the rest of Harrison's brigade was moved forward as they rushed to meet the oncoming Rebels. Custis explained that his 79th Ohio crossed over a "hillside on which the tobacco was grown," and there was a "tobacco curing barn dismantled to the floor" located on the hill to the west of the Collier Mill and the Tanyard Branch on which General Hooker was posted during much of the fighting. His 79th Ohio proceeded south from the cornfield that grew along the plain on the southern side of Peach Tree Creek and then over a tobacco-laden hill and field with the Tanyard Branch flowing to the left of his regiment and the 129th Illinois next to the left was on the other side of the branch. "The 129th Illinois was not keeping in line with us with perhaps obstruction in crossing the Branch and climbing the hill. While we were crossing the little bottom cornfield below, the bulets [sic] of the skirmishers we stepped lively I tell you." The old soldier continued, "The right of the 102nd Illinois climed the hill from the branch up to the breastworks and beyond to the battery its men falling back behind the infantry, the 102nd [Illinois] opened fire the skirmishers disappeared, the battery returned to their guns and directed their fire to theirs." The firing "continued till the Confederates gave way."[40]

In another post-war letter, Custis added more details about the Yankee response to Scott's surprise attack. From the high bluff on the west side of Tanyard Branch opposite the Collier Mill, Custis could observe the entire field of battle in front of Ward's and Geary's divisions: the "Officer leading the 102nd Illinois located us on the west side of the branch, rode up to left end of 2nd [Geary's] Division breastworks, [and] just in a very few minutes the Confederate skirmish [line] opened fire on the battery [Sloan's Pennsylvania Light Battery E]." Custis remembered,"The officers [and gunners of the battery] ran…diagonally across our front to Brigade Headquarters. [Then, Harrison's] Brigade moved forward." From the 79th Ohio, "our Colonel's orderly was killed and fell from his horse." After crossing the Tanyard Branch, the 79th Ohio and the 102nd Illinois "crossed through the corn in line with the 102nd Ill. passing the breastworks of Second Division soon meeting the battery men who had left their guns in the hands of Confederates who were turning the guns" on

---

[40] Cyrus E. Custis to Wilbur G. Kurtz, 3 February 1932, 1–2, MSS 130, box 3, folder 7, Wilbur G. Kurtz Papers, Kenan Research Center, Atlanta History Center.

them. Custis relayed that "a volley from the 102nd [Illinois] cleared them out."[41]

Scott's men gallantly continued to charge up the slopes just west of the Collier Mill in the face of relentless fire from Geary's men and from the two regiments of Harrison's brigade that had cross the branch to support them. Bundy's men continued to fire "dummy" rounds and double cannister from their battery into the left half of Scott's brigade that included the 27th, 35th, and 49th Alabama, and the nine left companies of the 12th Louisiana, while Sloan's 3-inch ordnance rifles continued to do their damage on the 55th and 57th Alabama and the three remaining companies of the 12th Louisiana, until the overwhelming fire of it and Geary's three brigades of infantry broke the back of Scott's men. The number of dead and dying around the wooded hollows west of the Collier Mill bore tribute to the fierceness of Scott's attack. While they captured the flag of the 33rd New Jersey and about a third of its men while wounding another third, they suffered terribly. It was even reported that they lost the colors of the 12th Louisiana captured by the 105th Illinois of Col. Harrison's brigade on the slope of the ridge just southeast of the Collier Mill, but it appears that the flag lost there was that of the 40th Mississippi in Featherston's brigade as we will see later.[42] Scott's brigade casualties at Peach Tree Creek were heavy, especially in the 55th Alabama and 57th Alabama and the three companies of the 12th Louisiana, companies A, H, and M, that had charged along the edge of the open field in the face of the Federal artillery batteries.[43] But their losses occurred chiefly in front of Sloan's guns in the left part of Candy's brigade on the ridge overlooking the Tanyard Branch and today's parking lot and the grassy field below it in the Tanyard Creek Park as they attempted, unsuccessfully, to take the heights held by Harrison's 102nd Illinois and 79th Ohio, which had quickly come up and covered the crest of the ridge south of Collier's Mill overlooking the Tanyard Branch.

One Federal veteran of the 102nd Illinois on the right of Harrison's line west of the Tanyard Branch explained that his men poured a "perpetual sheet of flame" into the advancing Alabamians of the 55th and 57th Alabama. "Rebel flags waved defiantly in their front line, and were shot down," remembered the

---

[41] Cyrus E. Custis to Wilbur G. Kurtz, 9 March 1932, 1, MSS 130, box 3, folder 7, Wilbur G. Kurtz Papers, Kenan Research Center, Atlanta History Center.

[42] "Report of the Adjutant General of the State of Illinois," in *History of One Hundred and Fifth Infantry*, 5:686–88.).

[43] Hugh Simmons, personal correspondence and notes, in possession of the author, (RDJ) vertical files No. 396.

Illinois soldier. After the charge of the Alabama regiments had been broken, the fallen colors were "quickly taken up and carried forward to the line where waved the stars and stripes."[44] According to members of the 57th Alabama, they carried the flag of the "Clanton Rifles," from Company A, which was presented to the unit on 1 May 1863 as their regimental colors. One source from the Alabama State Archives reveals "This particular flag was used as the Regimental Colors during the entire period of the war. It was shot down several times during the battle of Peach Tree Creek and at Franklin. The flag was brought home by J. P. Wood in Feb. 1865. Wood donated the flag to the Alabama State Archives on Dec. 10, 1910." This flag remains in the collection at the Alabama State Archives.

The 55th Alabama carried 22 officers and 256 men into the fight at Peach Tree Creek, for a total of 278 men, and lost 14 officers and 155 men killed and wounded, more than half of its number. Included in the casualties were Lieutenant Colonel John H. Norwood of Jackson County, Alabama, who was wounded, Major J. H. Jones, also of Jackson County, who was killed, and Adjutant J. C. Howell of Cherokee County, Alabama, who was killed. Five of the regiment's captains were casualties, including Peter Nunnally of Calhoun County who was wounded, from Jackson County, J. M. Thompson of who was wounded, John W. Evans who was killed, J. H. Cowan, who was wounded, and Arthur B. Carter from Marshall County who was killed.[45] With 169 men lost out of 278 men in the battle, the 55th Alabama sustained over 60 percent casualties.

In the 57th Alabama Infantry Regiment, the story was much the same. One veteran said that the regiment was "cut to pieces" at Peach Tree Creek.[46] The double-cannister rounds from the Federal artillery took its toll on the Alabamians. Lieutenant Colonel R. A. Bethune of Pike County, fell wounded. Captain Faison was wounded. Major W. R. Arnold, also of Pike County, was killed, as was fellow Pike County resident, Captain Bailey M. Talbot.[47] First Sergeant Riley Barnes from Troy, Alabama, was in Company G in the 57th Regiment.[48] "The rank may be due to the facts that Riley could read and write.

---

[44] S. F. Fleharty, *A History of the 102nd Illinois Infantry Volunteers* (Chicago: 102nd Illinois Association, 1865) 90; Clauss, "The Atlanta Campaign, July 18, 1864," 84.

[45] Willis Brewer, *Alabama: Her History, Resources, War Record, and Public Men, from 1540 to 1872* (Montgomery AL: Barrett & Brown, 1872) 667.

[46] Ibid., 667; http://www.archives.state.al.us/referenc/alamilor/57thinf.html (19 March 2008).

[47] Brewer, *Alabama*, 669; Evans, ed., *Alabama*, 219; Simmons, Hugh, Historian for 12th Louisiana, personal correspondence and notes.

[48] "Compiled Service Records of Confederate Soldiers who Served in Organizations

Hood's First Sortie, 20 July 1864

He was a farmer, store keeper and school teacher." During the action Barnes was killed as his regiment tried to charge across the lower part of the old field in front of the guns of Geary's division. "Family oral history relates that he was killed by 'friendly fire'. His burial place is unknown."[49] But there was no friendly fire in the cauldron that his Alabamians found themselves. This sway in the ground was created by the turn of the Tanyard Branch. He was likely among the unknown buried on the field by the Northern troops, and later reentered at the Oakland Cemetery in Atlanta. The 57th Alabama's battle flag was "pierced with many balls" during the battle.[50]

The 12th Louisiana found itself split in the attack with its three right companies continuing to support the men of the 55th Alabama to their right as they crossed over the ground near the Tanyard Branch of Peach Tree Creek to the east of the knoll where the 33rd New Jersey had its position. Eight of the other nine companies of the oversized 12th Louisiana Regiment found themselves caught up in the pursuit of the fleeing New Jersians along with the 27th, 35th, and 49th Consolidated Alabama Regiment in the woods and tangles to the north and west over and around the left of the knoll. Many of the consolidated Alabama regiment and the left portion of the 12th Louisiana found themselves with either the task of securing Yankee prisoners and returning them to the Confederate trenches or pursuing the fleeing remainder of the 33rd New Jersey into the sway between the knoll just taken and the ridge occupied by Candy's brigade and two Federal batteries that were firing double rounds of cannister into the woods before them. Many chose the former option, explaining in part why their casualties, particularly in the consolidated Alabama regiment, were considerably lighter than the 55th and 57th Alabama and the right wing of the 12th Louisiana. Nevertheless, most of both portions of the 12th Louisiana and the Alabamians pressed their advantage beyond the knoll and attempted, at least twice, to take the ridge and Federal batteries but were met with a fierce counter-response. Taking 318 men into the attack, the 12th Louisiana lost 11 killed, 57 wounded, and 5 missing.[51]

---

from the State of Alabama," http://www.knology.net/~toniab/57th.rtf. (28 February 2008).

[49] www.auburn.edu/~barnejr/regiments/57th/index.html (28 February 2008).

[50] Brewer, *Alabama*, 667; object files, Civil War Flags, Alabama Department of Archives and History.

[51] Clement Anselm Evans, ed., *Louisiana and Arkansas*, vol. 10 of *Confederate Military History*, 19 vols. (1899; repr., Wilmington NC: Broadfoot Publishing Company, 1987)195; *OR*, ser. 1, vol. 38, pt. 3, serial 74, 894–99.

The Battle of Peach Tree Creek

A breakdown of the 12th Louisiana's losses by company reveals that the right three companies that accompanied the 55th and 57th Alabama across the lower Tanyard Branch field (near and including today's Tanyard Creek Park parking lot west of the branch), lost six of the regiment's eleven total men killed during the battle, while the other eight companies lost only five men killed in nearly three times the number of men engaged. Companies A, H, and M went to the right and charged across the open bottom. According to historian Hugh Simmons, "Company A reported 3 killed in action, and 1 mortally wounded, Company H reported 3 killed in action, 1 mortally wounded and 3 missing." Simmons explained that "one [was] left on the battlefield and presumed dead, [while] one who died in a nearby Federal field hospital. Company M reported 1 mortally wounded" and 1 missing.[52] As for the remaining nine companies of the regiment, "Company K was absent on picket duty on the Chattahoochee River," while "Companies C, D, E, I and L reported no casualties." In the remaining companies, "Company B reported 2 killed in action including Captain Joseph A. Bivin, Company F reported 1 killed in action, Company G reported 2 killed in action, 1 mortally wounded," while the "Field & Staff reported 1 mortally wounded."[53] Also falling in the attack were Lieutenant M. S. McLeroy who was killed along the front of the line, and Major H. V. McCain who was wounded.[54] In addition, the 12th Louisiana lost fifty-seven men wounded, mostly from her three right Companies, A, H, and M, and three men were captured and sent to Camp Douglas.[55]

The losses from the consolidated 27th, 35th, and 49th Alabama, which fielded some 524 men during the charge, were just 2 killed, 33 wounded, and 2 missing or captured for a total loss of 37 men. The 12th Louisiana, which sent 318 men into the fray, sustained 11 men killed, 57 wounded, and 5 missing or captured for a total of 73 men. The 55th Alabama brought 278 men to the Tanyard Branch and saw 169 men fall with 29 killed on the field, 63 wounded, and 77 missing or captured. The 57th Alabama had 330 men present for duty on 20 July, and lost 157 men with 13 killed on the field, 98 wounded, and 46 missing or captured. Scott's brigade thus took into the fight 1,450 men, and lost

---

[52] Hugh Simmons to author, 22 August 2007, 2, in author's personal papers, (RDJ vertical files No. 396), Dalton, Georgia.

[53] Ibid.

[54] Evans, ed., *Louisiana and Arkansas*, 195; *OR*, ser. 1, vol. 38, pt. 3, serial 74, pp. 894–99.

[55] Hugh Simmons to author, 22 August 2007, 2, in author's personal papers, (RDJ vertical files No. 396), Dalton, Georgia.

55 men killed, 249 wounded, and 132 missing or captured for a total loss of 436 men, or 30 percent of its force.

On the Federal side, Bundy's battery lost three men killed, two mortally wounded, and another seven wounded, for a total of twelve casualties.[56] Geary reported that his division buried 409 in his front alone.[57] However, this figure is unsubstantiated in the corresponding casualties of Scott's brigade. Geary's figure no doubt includes the losses in Featherston's brigade in front of Ward's division, and perhaps a portion of O'Neal's brigade who fell closest to Geary's division along today's Collier Road west of Tanyard Branch, or in the ravine north of Collier Road in front of the Bitsy Grant Tennis Center.

Scott's brigade was supported by O'Neal's attack on part of the flank of Geary's division, as the right of O'Neal's line struck the right of Geary's 1st Brigade under the command of Colonel Charles Candy. With O'Neal's brigade, Confederate forces thus attacked and pushed back an entire Federal division and inflicted greater casualties on the Yankees with only two brigades, despite being outnumbered.

A few days after the battle, Mary Talbot of Pike County, Alabama, received this letter written to her new-born son on the eve of the Battle of Peach Tree Creek:

Dear Son

For the first time I now write you a letter. Under some circumstances I would call it silly and uncalled for to address one so young as yourself by letter but under such circumstances which I write I am convinced that it will do no harm, but hope you may derive pleasure and benefit therefrom. I am not indifferent to the fact that it is very likely the fate that Southern people are now engaged in, may deny me the pleasure of ever seeing your face again.

In such an event you will lose the advice and experience of a Father. You will be reared by a widowed mother, whom my dear Boy I know you will duly obey, confide in, reverence, and appreciate. History will explain why I am absent from your mother, sister, and yourself today. Should I fall fighting for what history will tell you, my boy avenge the blood of your father. But now let us look at the other side of the picture. Let us hope soon to gain Southern Independence and I will be home with you, Mother, and Nettie. What a happy time. Grow fast. Next time I come home, hope it will not be

---

[56] www.dmna.state.ny.us/historic/reghist/civil/artillery/13thIndBat/13thIndBatTable.htm (13 April 2008).

[57] Pierson, "From Atlanta to Chattanooga," 291.

long, I want to hear you say Father. Now Bailey be a good boy, always be kind to your Mother and sister, and follow the advice of your Mother. May God protect you, make you a pious wise, useful, and honorable man…

The writer was Captain Bailey Montgomery Talbot, Commander of Company H, 57th Alabama. Captain Talbot was killed "at the Battle of Peachtree Creek near Atlanta while gallantly leading a charge against the enemy." He was only twenty-nine. Mary Mullins Talbot was left a widow to raise two small children at the age of twenty-four.[58]

---

[58] Bailey M. Talbot, letter to son Riley, 19 July 1864. www.geocities.com/Heartland/Pines/9703/bmtalbot.html (23 November 2008).

15

THEY FOUGHT LIKE VERY DEVILS

They fought like very devils.[1]

Running at the double quick, Featherston's Mississippians crossed the open field and reached the top of the ridge. Next, they wrestled the Federal entrenchments along the Collier Road from the troops of the 136th New York and 22nd Wisconsin of Ward's 3rd Division in the Federal XX Corps. According to Lieutenant Colonel Edward Bloodgood commanding the 22nd Wisconsin, the Mississippians came upon them "with the true rebel yell."[2] Bloodgood remembered that his regiment fired on the charging Mississippians from the moment that they had left the woods on the far side of the large open field, but there were too many Rebels and not enough time to react. The Wisconsin commander explained that the advancing line was within 30 feet of them when the Federals began receiving grape and cannister fire from friendly batteries, compelling the Wisconsin soldiers to retreat.

Presently, the overwhelmed Yankees went streaming back down the other side of the ridge toward Peach Tree Creek. As the blue-clad skirmishers ran, the Mississippians pursued. Featherston's men were determined to press their advantage rather than stop to reform at the top of the ridge. Up until then, they had lost relatively few men. It seemed that they had caught the Yankees off guard.

Actually, Featherston's braves had hit only about 300 Federal skirmishers on a line that had not yet fully deployed and were no match for the 1,230 Mississippians who had swept up the 700 yard field before the defenders could fire three volleys. Caught up in the melee in front of the 31st Mississippi were some 100 additional Federal riflemen armed chiefly with repeating Spencer rifles who had just been sent forward at the time of the Confederate charge.

---

[1] Jean M. Cate, ed., *"If I Live to Come Home": The Civil War Letters of Sergeant John March Cate* (Pittsburgh: Dorrance Publishing Company, 1995) 196.

[2] United States War Department, comp., *Official Records of the Union and Confederate Armies in the War of the Rebellion*, 128 vols. (Washington, DC: Government Printing Office, 1880–1901) ser. 1, vol. 38, pt. 3, serial 73, 44 (hereafter *OR*).

The Battle of Peach Tree Creek

They were under the command of Captain William N. Wilkerson and were from the 79th Ohio and the 102nd Illinois of Colonel Harrison's brigade and could fire eight shots before being reloaded. These men had been detailed to relieve the 136th New York from the advance line just before the attack was made and were rushing forward to try to help hold the blue line as they met their retreating companions. It was an irresistible tide of gray that had compelled the Federal veterans to turn back to their blue comrades who were having coffee and lunch near the ford over Peach Tree Creek. The Mississippians had broken through the Yankee line, and victory seemed to be at hand, at least for the moment.

To one of the non-combatants in Ward's division who watched the action from the brigade wagons located on a bluff north of Peach Tree Creek, it was an impressive sight: "Suddenly there seemed to be a wakening up. In the woods where the 4th Corps were stationed the firing commenced quicker and sharper—it extended along the line, and then the batteries opened two or three guns at a time, quicker and faster. The troops on the line who had been lying down behind their gun stacks sprang to their feet and horsemen at quick gallop commenced crossing the valley in different directions."[3] Harvey Reid, the witness from the division wagons, gazed to the Collier Ridge to the south with concern as he strained to follow the action. "Ah! Now we see them," he exclaimed. "Dark masses in the edge of the woods moving steadily forward—that battery on the right [Sloan's] is throwing shell into them—we see shell burst and men fall but still they keep right on."[4] Reid next described the Confederate attack on Sloan's guns as the right half of Scott's brigade tried to support Featherston's assault on the Collier Ridge. "Under cover of that projecting point of woods they have advanced close to those guns and then the charge is changed to cannister..."[5] The veterans of the 55th and 57th Alabama and three companies of the 12th Louisiana ran right into the teeth of these guns as they rained death and destruction into their ranks (in the sway along today's Tanyard Creek Park and parking lot).

To the north of the ridge the land sloped down to a ravine that contained a tangled jungle of vines and briars and some scrub pine and sassafras trees. To the other side of the ravine ran a small ridge that was also covered with pine and sassafras foliage. Beyond this ridge the land opened up to a long, narrow cornfield that was only about a hundred yards wide before reaching Peach Tree

---

[3] Harvey Reid, *Uncommon Soldiers: Harvey Reid and the 22nd Wisconsin March with Sherman*, ed. Frank L. Byrne (Knoxville: University of Tennessee Press, 2001) 172.

[4] Ibid.

[5] Ibid.

Creek. The crest of the second ridge was laden with pine and sassafras and hid the rest of the idle three brigades of Ward's division.

When General Ward learned of the Confederate attack at the onset of the charge from General Coburn, one of his brigade commanders, he initially claimed that he had no orders from General Hooker for an advance. Henry Crist, the hungry soldier from the 33rd Indiana who had been out picking blackberries when he discovered Featherston's legions approaching, reported his revelation to Coburn. "The Colonel at once mounted his horse and rode to General Ward, and asked permission to advance his brigade. He was told that General Hooker's orders were to remain where we were..."[6] According to one veteran, "Ward flatly refused to assume the responsibility, saying that General Hooker had ordered him to remain in the valley."[7] After hearing the firing and taking in the situation, however, Ward reluctantly ordered his division to form up in the field between the small piney ridge and Peach Tree Creek and move forward under cover of the trees and brush "to the high ground in our front." He didn't have to give the order, for his three brigades were already moving out toward the sound of the fire. They had not taken the usual precaution of securing the high ground and digging in as soon as they crossed the creek that morning, instead taking a leisurely pace across the wide creek and leaving the task of setting up trench works on the high ground to only a regiment and a half. The veterans of Ward's division seemed to appreciate that they were out of position, and that if they didn't act quickly, another Chancellorsville debacle, where some sister units had been routed, could be the result. Further, the Federals were not happy that their afternoon coffee and nap had been interrupted. Awakened like a nest of blue hornets, the Yankees wanted to make someone pay for disturbing them.

Featherston's brigade could not have seen the massing blue line forming behind the second wooded ridge to their front. His 1,230 Mississippians were less than 500 yards from Peach Tree Creek, but masked in the sassafras and pine between them and their goal were the 5,000 veterans of Ward's division forming to meet them.[8] The two sides continued to rush toward the inevitable

---

[6] Newton, *129th Illinois*, 399.

[7] John R. McBride, *History of the 33rd Indiana Veteran Volunteer Infantry* (Indianapolis: Wm. B. Burford, Printer, 1900) 128.

[8] *OR*, ser. 1, vol. 38, serial 76, 256–59; Federal reports for those present for duty on 25 July 1864 for Ward's Division reflect 386 staff officers and men, 219 field officers, and 4,233 men, for a total of 4,838 officers and men, after sustaining 551 casualties on 20 July during the Battle of Peach Tree Creek.

fiery clash. One veteran of the 136th New York remembered, "As events proved we were none too soon in getting into position, for we were hardly formed before the rebels made a terrible onslaught on our lines."[9] That soldier remembered that the Confederates made a number of charges that day that were all eventually "repulsed with great loss."[10]

The Mississippians were chasing the survivors of the 22nd Wisconsin and 136th New York like rabbits through the ravine several hundred yards past the ridge on Collier Road that had been the Federal line. They were following their orders to "press any advantage" that they gained and were pushing the fleeing Yankees toward the Peach Tree Creek and Chattahoochee River. They had no idea that they were running into disaster. Coburn recalled that as his men reached the crest of the low ridge below the cornfield, "we met the skirmishers—22nd Wisconsin—being driven in."[11]

W. P. Archer, a Confederate soldier, who thought they had caught the Yankees off-guard at mealtime, would regretfully write, "The Battle of Peach Tree Creek was on good and strong. At first the Federals seemed demoralized and panic-stricken and everything seemed to favor the Confederates, but this situation did not last long, for just over beyond the creek lay thousands of bluecoats, who came sweeping down like a thunderbolt upon the thin lines of Hood's Confederates. For two hours and thirty minutes the battle raged."[12] Private Archer witnessed Captain Evan P. Howell's light artillery battery set up along the western slope of the hill overlooking today's Ardmore Park and the Tanyard Branch Park where it began to send fire toward Geary's division lines on the heights below Collier's Mill in support of Featherston's assault. Howell's battery followed Walker's and Maney's division attack along the Buckhead Road and filed to the left behind the cover of the ridge spur near today's 26th Street. To Archer, it appeared that the Federal infantry that rallied to plug the hole along Collier Ridge came from north of Peach Tree Creek as he gazed northward to the Yankee positions.[13]

During the charge up to the ridge across the old field, the men of the 31st, 22nd, and 40th Mississippi were slowed a marshy bog in the middle of the old field, compelling them to go around the soggy ground in groups by companies,

---

[9] L.O.S. to Editor, 7 August 1864, L.O.S. letter, *Wyoming County Mirror*, 24 August 1864, Warsaw NY.

[10] Ibid.

[11] G. S. Bradley, *The Star Corps, 22nd Wisconsin* (Milwaukee: 1865) 133.

[12] A. A. Hoehling, *Last Train from Atlanta* (New York: 1958) 115.

[13] Janet B. Hewett, editor, Georgia Confederate Soldiers 1861–1865, vol. I, A-J, 22.

allowing the Federal artillerists to their left (Bundy's left section and Sloan's Pennsylvania light artillery) to train their guns on the gray surge. Also, because of the constant fire in their front and flank caused by Harrison's hundred or so Spencer riflemen and by the New Yorkers of the four companies of the 136th New York who donned their distinctive white felt hats, the Mississippians were unable to reform into neat lines. They continued forward in masses of men.

Rolling over the ridge, the Southerners did not stop to reform but pushed on after the fleeing Yankees. One Federal veteran remembered that the Rebels seemed to have risen from the infernal regions to assault them. "They fought like very Devils," he would remark.[14] Down the reverse slope they charged and into a small ravine where they believed a rout was on. The Mississippians poured fire into the backs of the fleeing Federal skirmish line. Here, they did considerable damage as most of the Confederates had not fired as they made their charge on the Collier Ridge until reaching the reverse slope of the ridge. They were now only 50 yards away from the blue line of Ward's men forming to meet them in the tangled undergrowth below. Now, the full lines of Ward's division came into view as the skirmishers began to halt and form with them. Still, the Mississippians pressed on. If the Mississippians could break this line, then only corn stalks stood between them and Peach Tree Creek.

The Calhoun Tigers, Company F, 31st Mississippi. Deployed as skirmishers, the Calhoun Tigers, Company F of the 31st Mississippi, began taking casualties, including Sergeant James Nelson, Fourth Sergeant James Wilson, Sr., and Third Corporal William J. Wilson who fell wounded and were subsequently captured; Nelson would die the next day, while Sergeant Wilson would die 17 September. Twenty-year-old Corporal Wilson, shot in the hip and back, would survive but sit out the war in a prison camp. The Calhoun Tigers thus lost three non-commissioned officers who would never fight again for their beloved Magnolia State.

According to Major M. A. Oatis, commanding the 22nd Mississippi, just right of the 31st Mississippi, once his unit hit the marshy ground "we were exposed to a murderous enfilade fire of both musketry and artillery from the left," that was "rendered far more destructive by the grouping of companies and the concentration of the line into masses in order to effect a passage of the marsh and the creek by the beaten paths and the open fords." Major Oatis lamented, "In effecting the passage of this marsh I lost many of my bravest and

---

[14] Cate, *"If I Live to Come Home,"* 196.

The Battle of Peach Tree Creek

best officers and men."[15]

At this point, Lieutenant Colonel James W. Drane fell while leading the 31st Mississippi forward. Drane was described as a naturally energetic man who was always attentive. Drane had been encouraging his men on while leading at the front of his regiment before the Federal works. A rather tall and large man, Drane made an easy target. Although wounded twice during the charge up the hill, he continued onward. After he was hit three more times at the crest of the ridge and the freshly won Federal line, he called over to Major Gillespie to take over command. Gillespie held up his bleeding arm, revealing that he, too, had been hit, but he willingly took on the position and moved the regiment forward. Drane's near lifeless body lay at the top of the partially erected works just gained. He had been wounded in the head when a bullet went through his right cheek. His left arm had been shattered by a minnie ball. Another ball had passed through his shoulder, a fragment of a shell tore into his side, and he had received a bullet wound through his right foot. His men feared that he would bleed to death from all of the wounds in the hot July sun.

The Jackson Rifles, Company I, 31st Mississippi. Drane's beloved Jackson Rifles followed him up the bloody ridge. After securing the ridge, many went on chasing the Yankees down the other side. Then, unexpectedly, they found themselves caught on three sides by the Northern crossfire. Brothers Myres W. and Sylvester P. Broomhall, both privates, were hit; Myres received a mortal wound and died on the field, while Sylvester was wounded in his hand and finger. Private George W. Butler fell with a gunshot wound to his right leg, was captured and sent to the hospital in Nashville where he died on 17 December 1864.

The Jackson Rifles also lost Fourth Sergeant Charles C. Cameron who fell wounded in the hip and was taken to the hospital to recover. Private Wiley Carpenter was not so lucky. He fell mortally wounded and was buried in the field by the Yankees. Private James R. Daves sustained gunshot wounds to his leg and hand. He was taken by the Yankees to Chattanooga where he died on 1 September.

The Jackson Rifles saw two turncoat Confederates emerge from the fighting. Twenty-nine-year-old Private Thomas J. Cockerham was wounded severely in the leg, but recovered sufficiently to serve with the regiment in the Tennessee campaign that fall; after his capture on 15 December 1864 at Nashville, he joined a Federal regiment, the 5th US Volunteer Infantry, on 18

---

[15] *OR*, ser. 1, vol. 38, pt. 3, serial 74, 887.

April 1865, by claiming that he had been conscripted in the Confederate service. Actually, he had volunteered with the Jackson Rifles on 8 March 1862, two months before the Conscription Act became effective. Joining him as a galvanized Yankee was Private Leroy Minter who was captured and who also enlisted in the 5th US Volunteer Infantry on 18 April 1865. Many Southerners at the end of the war would take the oath, become clad in Yankee blue and fight Native Americans out West in Federal regiments merely for survival. By joining the Federal army, they could get better food, a paying job, and they could get out of the horrible prisoner of war camps.

Also in Company I was thirty-three-year-old Private Robert E. Conn, who had been a hospital cook for much of the war, who was now surrounded by Federals, and captured. He was sent to Camp Douglas, Illinois, to cook for fellow prison-ers for the rest of the war. Twenty-year-old Private James Henry Cooper was wounded severely in the hand and he sat out the rest of the war at his home in Mississippi.

Corporal James M. Franks was shot at near point-blank range in the abdomen, but managed to escape capture. Private Pinkney Raspberry was shot in the hip, but was also able to get away. Corporal George B. Gray, only twenty-one years old, and Private James W. Ray were not so lucky. Both fell on the ridge, dead from Yankee bullets. The Jackson Rifles also lost privates Elizah D. Stewart, John J. Lever and Charles S. Wiltshire, who were killed, and George T. Smith who fell mortally wounded and was left on the field to die. All but Smith, who died 1 August, were left to be buried in unknown tombs along Collier Ridge by blue-clad strangers. Smith was buried in Nashville.

Private Jonathan Montgomery of Company I was wounded in the thigh, but would recover to fight another day. Hyrum Marion Nail (cousin of the author) also a private, would not fight again. The thirty-three-year-old was struck by a sharpshooter's bullet and died on the field. He left his wife Mary and three young sons to scratch out an existence on a small farm in the Choctaw hills.

Captain Cyrus Seymour White Richards led the Jackson Rifles forward from the trenches, and the thirty-four-year-old certainly had no idea where the day's events would take him. Richards led his men up and over the ridge and was caught chasing the Yankees down the other side and into the Federal lines. He fell wounded behind the lines and was taken prisoner. Captain Richards was sent to Chattanooga, and then to Nashville where he arrived on 27 July. He was then shipped to Louisville. On 29 July he was taken to Johnson Island, Ohio, where captured Confederate officers were kept. The captain was admitted to the hospital at Sandusky, Ohio, on 30 July with chronic dysentery. He remained there until 4 October when he was sent to Point Lookout, Maryland. On 6 October, the sickly Captain was transferred to Fort Monroe, Virginia, and was exchanged to the Confederate side on 11 October. On 15 October, Richards was admitted to Confederate General Hospital 4 at Richmond with "chronic diarrhea–dysenteria," and by 21 October, he was on his way home to Bankston, Mississippi. In order to get back to his Choctaw County, Mississippi home, Richards had traveled through fourteen states in less than three months.

Third Lieutenant John C. Hallum, at thirty-five, was one of the older Jackson Rifles. He led his men over the works before being shot in the bowels and legs and fell out of reach of his men. After the battle was over, the victorious Yankees could do nothing for him. Five days later, he was taken to the field hospital at Vining Station where he died on 31 July having suffered terribly for eleven days.

Captured were First Sergeant John C. Gregory and Private James R. Trussell (cousin of the author) who followed their captain down the hill and the met the blue counterattack fighting hand to hand until they were totally surrounded by men in blue. After some twenty-five minutes, and finding that most of the Jackson Rifles were wounded or dead, the remaining Jackson Rifles reluctantly surrendered to the massive blue tide that had enveloped them. Both were taken to Camp Douglas where Gregory died on 1 January 1865.

The Jackson Rifles would suffer twenty-four casualties that day, including thirteen who would die from their wounds or from exposure in a Yankee prison, while only three would return to fight for the Magnolia State. Losing eight men to capture, four of the Jackson Rifles would die in captivity. Company I also suffered eleven wounded, of which four were captured.

22nd Mississippi. To the right of the 31st Mississippi Infantry, the men of the 22nd Mississippi led by Major M. A. Oatis were being annihilated:

> Having passed the marsh it was impossible to halt long enough to restore order in the ranks by reason of the terrible and destructive fire that was poured upon us from the front and flanks, and we pressed upon the enemy in a broken line and with disordered ranks. Notwithstanding the great disadvantages under which the attack was made, the enemy in my front was speedily dislodged and driven from his position. A part of my regiment pursued the enemy forty or fifty yards beyond his temporary works, but the troops to the right and left of Featherston's brigade not coming to our support as I expected, and the enemy continuing to enfilade us from the flanks, firing now almost in our rear, we were forced to fall back to the line from which he had been expelled, where the temporary works afforded us

partial protection. But even here the fire from the left was very destructive to us.... The line of battle occupied by the enemy was along an old road which water and travel had cut into a ditch. On the farther side of the road there had been a rail fence running parallel with the road. The rails were transferred to the nearer side of the road, and these, with the advantage of the ditch, afforded ample protection against musketry.[16]

Falling in the action were Major Oatis and Ensign M. Neighbor who were severely wounded, and Adjutant Claudius Virginius H. Davis who was killed. One fellow Mississippian recorded, "The 22nd Regt. had three color bearers shot down, one was Claudy Davis, he was waiving the colors when he fell."[17] Adjutant Davis had recorded just two days before that General Johnston's removal from command "was received in absolute silence. Not a cheer was heard and...many unfavorable comments and direful forebodings were indulged in, for our boys felt that a fatal mistake had been made."[18] The 22nd Mississippi had fought alongside of the 31st Mississippi at Baton Rouge, and shared with them the distinction of having the highest casualties among the Confederates there. Today, they would again sustain one of the highest casualty rates among the Rebel army.

After Major Oatis fell, command of the 22nd Mississippi fell to Captain J. T. Farmby. Company G, commanded by Captain Standley, was deployed as skirmishers for the 22nd Mississippi. After the regiment had occupied the Federal rifle pits on the picket line, they advanced and were caught up by the terrible crossfire that was concentrated upon them. Yet they went on and drove the enemy from a line of rail works along Collier Road and down into the ravine, but were forced to retire to avoid capture. The 22nd Mississippi Infantry suffered twenty-four killed, sixty-four wounded, and five missing, for a total of ninety-three losses.[19]

"Ensign Michael Meagher, Private J. T. Longino, Company A, and Sergeant Harrison Bailey, Company B, all were shot down while carrying the colors." Adjutant Claudius "Claudie" Davis "ran forward with the rest of the

---

[16] Ibid., 886–88.

[17] Mathew Andrew Dunn, Letters, *Journal of Mississippi History* 1 (January–October 1939): 123–24; Gregg S.Clemmer, *Valor in Gray: Confederates who Received the Medal of Honor* (Staunton VA: Hearthside Publishing Co., 1998) 214–16.

[18] Larry M. Strayer and Richard A. Baumgartner, eds., *Echoes of Battle: The Atlanta Campaign* (Huntington WV: Blue Acorn Press, 1991); Davis, 220.

[19] Dunbar Rowland, *Military History of Mississippi, 1803–1898*, ed. H. Grady Howell, Jr. (Spartanburg SC: The Reprint Company, Publishers, 1978) 248.

regiment. As adjutant, he carried no musket for his job was to help Major Oatis coordinate the regiment's attack for maximum advantage. He knew that the deadliest part was getting across this short fatal space."[20] "But...under a terrible enfilading fire from the left [from Sloan's artillery battalion of Geary's division] both officers together with the company commanders yelled and motioned frantically as they sought 'beaten paths' and 'open fords' over the mire of boot-sucking mud. No obstacle, their orders had stated, was to stop them."[21]

"It was desperate going," remembered one survivor, "already a number of men were down, including Ensign Michael Meager with the regimental colors of the 22nd [Mississippi]. But Pvt. J. T. Longino of Company A bravely snatched them from the mud and with the regiment gathered about him, charged up the hill."[22] Longino next fell, wounded, as the Mississippians broke the Federal line atop the Collier Ridge. By now, Featherston's men were no longer in organized lines, having been reduced to "no more than a mob of armed men. Hitting the Federal line...they succeeded in driving their foe from a rail-fenced sunken road...but at a fearful cost."[23]

The 22nd Mississippi, together with the rest of the brigade, continued up and over the ridge. "In the center of the attack, Martin Oatis, 'Claudie' Davis and the few company officers still unhurt led the men as they stormed toward the top of the ridge. Sgt. Harrison Bailey of Company B had the flag now," remembered one veteran, "having grabbed it on the slope from the hands of a desperately wounded Pvt. Longino. But this honor, like Longino's, lasted just seconds. More bullets hit the charging Confederates and dropped Bailey and the regimental colors to the ground."[24] Claudie Davis then grabbed the colors at the top of the ridge and led the survivors of the 22nd Mississippi around him down the northern slope as they chased the Federal soldiers who had fled the ridge. According to one witness, "The breach widened as more of Featherston's Confederates poured into the road along the Union line. To save themselves, Federals raced for the rear. With his flag aloft, Claudie scampered after them, all the while calling for his compatriots to follow him forward."[25] The witness described Davis's heroism and the advance of the Mississippians. "Fifty yards beyond the enemy's works—and far in advance of his own men—he halted,

---

[20] *Valor in Gray*, 215.
[21] Ibid., 215.
[22] Ibid., 216.
[23] Ibid.
[24] Ibid.
[25] Ibid.

waving the standard for all to see...and drawing the attention to his form as the rallying point from which they might drive the fleeing enemy into Peach Tree Creek."[26]

Actually, the men of the 22nd Mississippi, together with the remainder of Featherston's brigade, traveled several hundred yards beyond the Federal line along Collier Road before being turned back by Ward's counterattack. The fellow Mississippians lamented Davis's demise and the breakup of the attack. "It was not to be," one veteran exclaimed. "Featherston's and Scott's attack had hit the Federal line unsupported. On the right and left, the Federal line was still intact. Hundreds of leveled Union muskets blasted into both flanks of the tenuous Southern toehold." As for the brave adjutant, "for a moment more, Claudie waved his flag then fell with fatal wounds through the head and left breast, hardly a munth past his 21st birthday."[27] After Adjutant C. V. H. Davis was killed, Lieutenant Lea, Company C, was able to recover the flag and held it during the rest of the engagement. In the struggle, "seven men were killed and wounded in saving their flag."[28] During the struggle, Major W. A. Oatis was wounded. With Davis killed and Oatis wounded, there were no other field officers present on the field for the 22nd Mississippi. Command structure fell apart as four of the regiment's captains were wounded, four lieutenants were killed, and another three lieutenants were wounded during the melee. It was impossible to determine which junior officer was now the ranking commander of the fast evaporating regiment. According to the *Official Records*, the 22nd Mississippi had 190 present for duty at Peach Tree Creek and lost 21 killed, 64 wounded, and 5 captured for a total loss of 90 men, but a review of the service records of the 22nd Mississippi reveals 26 men killed, 66 men wounded, and 5 men captured or missing for a total of 97 casualties.[29]

---

[26] Ibid.
[27] Ibid.
[28] Dunn, Letters, *Journal of Mississippi History*, 124.
[29] Microfilm 1045, roll 2, Tennessee State Library and Archives, Nashville; http://members.aol.com/missregt/Miss22G.html#Twenty-Second (10 January 2009); *OR*, ser., vol. 38, pt. 2, serial 74, p. 884.

16

THE FIGHT FOR COLLIER MILL

> First one would charge, then the other, soon the rebs began to break and fall back. Then out we charged.[1]

Just over the far ridge, General William T. Ward's three veteran brigades of the 3rd Division of the Federal XX Corps were forming. When Coburn received Private Crist's report from his blackberry reconnaissance, he immediately began to form his brigade, and as Coburn was getting the news from Crist, Harrison came up and he, too, put his brigade in motion. Simultaneously, Wood put his brigade in motion as he also learned of the Confederate advance and determined to advance his brigade to cover the high ground before the Rebels could arrive. Interestingly, all three brigade commanders reached the same conclusion on their own to advance without orders to try and reach high ground before the Southerners got there and took it first. From west to east on the far ridge, Ward's division lined up to meet Featherston's men. On the left near to and just north of the Collier Mill, Colonel Benjamin Harrison commanded the 1st Brigade, Colonel John Coburn and the 2nd Brigade were in the center behind the second ridge located north of today's Redland Road, and Colonel James Wood on the right (behind present day Piedmont Hospital) brought up the 3rd Brigade. In all, some 5,000 men in Ward's division were preparing to counterattack the 1,230 charging Mississippians. Aided by Newton's division on the heights to the east and Geary's division on the wooded ridge to the west beyond Collier's Mill, some 10,000 Federal troops in the area were prepared to receive the Southern blow with a massive response.

Just before the surprise assault, the balance of Ward's division had been resting in the cornfield next to Peach Tree Creek. "Ward's division was comfortably eating its dinner in the flat fields beyond the creek [on the south side], when the fire along the skirmish line became sharp, indicating there was trouble ahead and the division sprang to arms."[2] Coburn's 2nd Brigade and

---

[1] Jean M. Cate, ed., *"If I Live to Come Home": The Civil War Letters of Sergeant John March Cate* (Pittsburgh: Dorrance Publishing Company, 1995) 196.

[2] Adin B. Underwood, *33rd Massachusetts* (Boston: A Williams & Co., 1881) 226.

Hood's First Sortie, 20 July 1864

Harrison's 1st Brigade, being posted nearer the action, were the first to respond. But Wood's 3rd Brigade also sprang into action and quickly moved to the first ridge to the left of Coburn. As has been discussed, General Ward hesitated, explaining that he had no orders to move, but Coburn and Harrison ignored Ward, who subsequently relented. While Ward was contemplating what to do, his old command, the 3rd Brigade, commanded by Colonel James P. Wood, also sought approval to advance. But, as the sound of battle became more intense and the noise and smoke drew closer, it was evident that a forward move was appropriate. Private Charles Stamm from the 26th Wisconsin remembered, "we came to an old dead corn field and had stacked our arms with a view of getting some supper. The Kenosha members of the regiment had made it a custom to stick together and when we stacked arms George C. Limpert went out and got some wood to make a fire." The Wisconsin soldier added, "Charley Vollmer scouted out to get some water for the coffee and I was out gathering blackberries."[3]

Moreover, Lieutenant Colonel Frederick C. Winkler, commanding the 26th Wisconsin of Wood's brigade, also ignored orders to wait, and followed Coburn's brigade into the maelstrom ahead—in the nick of time. The 26th Wisconsin, nicknamed "The Sigel Regiment," after German Immigrant General Franz Sigel, was "composed primarily of German immigrants and Americans of German descent."[4] Winkler's men numbered some 260 muskets, according to its leader.[5] Had Ward's subordinates awaited his directive to advance, if it would have ever come, the whole of his division would have been bottled up on the low strip of land that was the cornfield with the large Peach Tree Creek to their back and surrounded by tangled wooded ridges on three sides. History will remember Ward's division for responding heroically during the crisis on Collier Ridge on 20 July, but it was the initiative and determination of his subordinates and soldiers, and not Ward, who would save the Federals from disaster on the ridge that day.[6]

---

[3] Charles Stamm, "Recall Famous Fight," *Kenosha News*, 20 June 1914; James S. Pula, *The Sigel Regiment: A History of the 26th Wisconsin Volunteer Infantry, 1862–1865* (Campbell CA: SAvas Publishing Co, 1998) 255–56.

[4] Pula, *The Sigel Regiment*, inside cover, dust jacket, and publisher's preface, iii.

[5] Russell Scott, "26th Wisconsin," www.russscott.com/~rscott/26thwis/26pgwk64.htm (7 May 2006).

[6] Reports of Ward's Division "Reports," in United States War Department, comp., *Official Records of the Union and Confederate Armies in the War of the Rebellion*, 128 vols. (Washington, DC: Government Printing Office, 1880–1901) Underwood,, 225–27.

The Battle of Peach Tree Creek

Coburn's Brigade. Opposing the center of Featherston's Mississippians was the brigade of Colonel John Coburn. With the 22nd Wisconsin engaged on the skirmish line with 18 officers and 315 men, the remainder of Coburn's brigade lined up to meet the center of Featherston's attack with the 33rd Indiana on the left led by Major Levin T. Miller with 10 officers and 380 men, and the 85th Indiana on the right under Lieutenant Colonel Alexander with 16 officers and 278 men. Behind them were the veterans of the 19th Michigan commanded by Major John J. Baker and Captain David Anderson with 300 men.[7] Coburn's brigade thus totaled some 1,317 men and officers plus Coburn's brigade staff.[8] One veteran remembered that the brigade went into the fight with 1,263 muskets.[9]

After Coburn had been informed of the approaching Rebels and he had confronted Ward to give him permission to advance to the ridges, Coburn "insisted that unless a forward movement was made quickly the division would be driven into the creek and overwhelmed with disaster. Finally, General Ward agreed that the advance should be made if Colonel Coburn would go out and see for himself that the rebels were coming."[10] Coburn elected to take his brigade to the first ridge as a reconnaissance in force and set his horse in motion for the first ridge when he came across Colonel Harrison of the 1st Brigade who was coming to confirm whether the Confederates were approaching and to find Ward as Coburn had done. Coburn "informed [Harrison] that General Ward desired both to move together if the enemy was coming. Colonel Harrison heartily concurred in the contemplated movement. In the meantime, Colonel Coburn had given the command to his brigade to fall in.[11] Coburn then rode up

---

[7] Terry L. Jones, "'The Flash of Their Guns Was a Sure Guide': The 19th Michigan Infantry in the Atlanta Campaign," in Theodore P. Savas and David A. Woodbury, eds., *The Campaign for Atlanta & Sherman's March to the Sea*, 160–62 (Savas Campbell CA: Woodbury Publishers, 1994).

[8] *OR*, ser. 1, vol. 38, pt. 2, serial 73, 378–428; William R. Scaife, *The Campaign for Atlanta* (Atlanta: self-published, 1993) 156; see also John R. McBride, *History of the 33rd Indiana Veteran Volunteer Infantry* (Indianapolis: Wm. B. Burford, Printer, 1900) 128–30, which shows that the 33rd Indiana had 10 officers and 380 men present for a total of 390, not 380. This number is given some credence by the calculation of the casualty count of 20 men killed and 71 officers and men wounded for a total loss of 91, and an effective present after the battle of about 300.

[9] McBride, *History of the 33rd Indiana*, 131.

[10] Ibid., 128.

[11] Ibid., 128–29.

to the crest of the first ridge to see what danger lie ahead telling Harrison that "if the enemy was there he would move forward at once," said McBride.[12]

Coburn "then went to the top of the ridge in front and, seeing the enemy approaching and near at hand, ordered the advance."[13] Adjutant McBride continued, "It was important to gain a certain commanding ridge before the enemy did, which could only be done by rapid movement and overcoming great difficulties in having to cross deep ravines and to pass through dense growths of pine and oak."[14] Seeing the advance of the veteran Mississippians, the 22nd Wisconsin was ordered to "rally on the reserve."[15] They needed no encouragement. The advancing Confederates were just 30 feet from their line atop Collier Ridge when the order was given. Lieutenant Colonel Edward Bloodgood, commander of the 22nd Wisconsin gleefully recorded that just then "[Coburn's] brigade came cheering over the first ridge and down into the ravine."[16] One veteran recorded: "Our men fell back slowly down the hill, disputing the ground slowly inch by inch, until they met the reserves, when they again rallied and drove the rebels up the hill the second time with tremendous slaughter. The balance of the brigade coming up at this moment," the Wisconsin veteran wrote, "we were enabled to maintain, finally, all the ground we had gained."[17] Actually, the overmatched Wisconsinites had been routed by Featherston's Mississippians and were relieved to see their comrades advancing to the rescue.

Ward's men, seeing the Rebels coming down the reverse slope after their blue-clad comrades, seemed inspired in coming to the rescue as they increased their pace to a run. In a rare moment of the war, both sides were charging each other full speed with neither party slowing. Having less ground to cover, many of the warriors in blue got to the ravine first, clashing with the scores of Rebels that had also reached the ravine. According to McBride of the 33rd Indiana, "These regiments had to cross an intervening ravine or ditch, and in doing so were met with a galling fire."[18] Looking to his right, McBride saw the advance of the 85th Indiana: "The 85th crossed with some difficulty and upon reaching

---

[12] Ibid., 129.

[13] Ibid., 129.

[14] Ibid., 129.

[15] *OR*, ser. 1, vol. 38, pt. 2, serial 73, p. 427.

[16] Ibid., 427.

[17] Racine Boy to Friend T., 21 July 1864, subject file PW-4, Kennesaw Mountain National Battlefield Park, Kennesaw, Georgia, 16-17.

[18] McBride, *History of the 33rd Indiana*, 129.

the opposite bank, and being partly protected by it, as the enemy came charging down the rise, poured a continuous and deadly fire into his ranks, who was then only about fifty feet away."[19]

"The advance of the 33rd Indiana was even more difficult and hazardous," according to McBride, "especially that of the right wing of the regiment, the left wing being more or less protected by an undergrowth of bushes. Though the right of the regiment, while crossing the ditch, was exposed to a deadly fire and not being able to return it, it did not waver," remembered the adjutant, "but unflinchingly crossed over, reformed its ranks and the united regiment and brigade poured a well-directed and effective fire into the ranks of the advancing foe, which checked and for a time dismayed the rebel front."[20] While the Federal forces enjoyed numerical superiority of at least three to one, their lines were disjointed, the three brigades having diverged from three sides, and the skirmish line had been thrown back.

Meanwhile, Featherston's Mississippians had breached the Federal line and were in possession of the high ground atop Collier Ridge. Continuing their charge down the long slope, the Mississippians began firing at the massive blue wave. Unfortunately for them, many of their shots fell over the heads of the Federal line as they overshot their targets in their run down the ridge and as they began to get winded. Empty, they continued on toward the blue throng with clubbed muskets in hand as the two lines melted into one in the ravine.

The Federal troops upon reaching the ravine, began firing into the charging Confederates as the Yankees continued their counterattack up the slope. The Federal fire was much more accurate as they were able to aim uphill at the Southerners bearing down on them. Further, the Mississippians coming down the ridge were silhouetted in the afternoon summer sun and made easy targets. Soon, however, the two lines clashed and brute force was the measure of the struggle. Federal troops had quickly formed up from the field where they were resting, some with stacked arms, and others not. Some of the Northern troops had their bayonets fixed, while many did not. Any orders to fix bayonets in the blue lines were only given in small groups. Thus, in the fight for Collier's Mill along the ravine, a few bayonets and swords of officers swung and found their mark, but most of the damage was done by the bullet and the musket turned club. One Federal soldier remembered that "over 20 of the Rebels were found

---

[19] Ibid., 129.
[20] Ibid., 129.

the next morning, killed by blows on the head."[21] A United States government report on the battle of Peach Tree Creek explained that "rarely did the opposing lines...come into actual [hand-to-hand] combat..., but when, as at Peachtree Creek, the lines did become comingled, the men fought individually in every possible style, more frequently with the musket clubbed than with the bayonet."[22]

The brutal struggle in the ravine around and between today's Golfview Drive and Dellwood Drive would last for about twenty minutes.[23] The small creek that ran through the bottom of the ravine ran red with the blood of the many, many casualties of both North and South. One Confederate drummer boy recalled years after the fight that a temporary field hospital or aid station was set up in the ravine just west of Golfview Drive where the wounded and dying of both sides crawled to as they looked desperately for water. A little spring also became tainted red from the wounded men. This was the last drink of water on earth for many of the "Bloody Magnolias" of Featherston's brigade. According to the drummer boy, doctors and surgeons began working on these men, while the fighting continued along the ridge only a few yards above them.[24]

From his view of the battle on the bluffs north of Peach Tree Creek, Clerk Harvey Reid described the counterattack by Ward's division: "By this time too the whole line [Ward's division] has advanced up the bluff and pour into [the Mississippians] a deadly fire of minies. They cannot stand it—they break and run, and then that bare slope looks like an ant hill swarming with dark objects hurrying back to the cover of the woods..."[25] By now, Scott's Alabama and Louisiana regiments had retired to the other side of the corner of the field below the Tanyard Creek Park and parking lot and were no longer a threat to Sloan's guns. The Pennsylvania battery then turned its guns onto Featherston's ranks as they tried to hold onto the pocket atop Collier Ridge. Reid continued: "and the puffs of dust covering the hill shows where the canister balls is falling among them. You can see men turning complete somersaults as those deadly missiles

---

[21] Cate, *"If I Live to Come Home,"* 196.

[22] Robert, R. Long, "A Brief History of the Battle of Peachtree Creek, July 20, 1864," author's personal papers, Dalton, Georgia, 19; United States Department of the Interior, Atlanta Campaign.

[23] Report of 85th Indiana, in *OR*, ser. 1, vol. 38, pt. 2, serial 73, 413.

[24] George and Betty Heery, interview by author, 27 March 2008, tape recording, author's personal papers, Dalton, Georgia.

[25] Harvey Reid, *Uncommon Soldiers: Harvey Reid and the 22nd Wisconsin March with Sherman*, ed. Frank L. Byrne (Knoxville: University of Tennessee Press, 2001) 172.

strike."[26] As Featherston's men retired from the ridge, Reid rejoiced at the sight of the advance of his comrades: "And now [our] line slowly advances in pursuit—firing at every step—and unbroken roar of musketry—forward they go and still forward until they too gain the woods..."[27] Federal soldiers of Harrison's, Coburn's, and Wood's brigade began to press their superiority in numbers as they struggled to regain control of the Collier Ridge from Featherston's Mississippians. "First one would charge, then the other, soon the rebs began to break and fall back. Then out we charged."[28] "One Regt. in our Brigade, the 26th Wisconsin, exhausted their ammunition, and so did the Rebs," remembered one veteran of Wood's brigade.[29]

One Northern correspondent witnessed the events in the ravine: "Portions of the hostile lines halted at close quarters and fought for a while, and on the right, so great was the momentum of the counter-charge, several regiments became commingled, the rebels in such cases exhibiting the greatest disorder, and submitting to capture without debate." This struggle continued for some twenty minutes in the ravine. "In front of [Ward's] division the slaughter of the rebels was very great. In riding over the ground next morning, I was astonished to see the long windrows of their dead collected for burial. Many of their severely wounded—of whom one hundred and fifty-four fell into Ward's hands," explained the reporter, "were still scattered over the field, though the ambulances were all engaged in carrying them to our hospitals." The newspaperman added, "[Ward] captured over three hundred prisoners. His victory was the most pronounced of any along the line, and his loss, though severe, is probably much less than it would have been had he not met the enemy half way." Ward's division had also "done the lucky thing at the lucky moment."[30]

Casualties on both sides began to mount up, many falling with multiple wounds. The Federal field hospital for the 3rd Division of the XX Corps had 345 wounded from the battle in their division and some 110 captured and wounded Southerners were treated. Surgeon William Grinsted would later exclaim, "The wounds received in this action were of a severe character, the enemy charging boldly. The rebels received were very severely wounded, many

---

[26] Ibid., 172–73.
[27] Ibid., 173.
[28] Cate, *"If I Live to Come Home,"* 196.
[29] Ibid., 196.
[30] Frank Moore, "How We Fight in Atlanta," in Frank Moore, ed., *Rebellion Record. A Diary of American Events*, vol. 11, (New York: D. Van Nostrand, 1868) 252.

having from three to five wounds, a single wound being the exception. Six died the same night they came in, and some 30 subsequently prior to their transportation."[31] According to one Yankee who survived the melee, "the ground was piled in heaps of dead and wounded and, strange to say, there were 3 Rebels to one of our men." The veteran continued, "We lost very light, only about 150 killed and wounded. We have buried very nearly 500 Rebs in from of our Division alone. Three Rebel colonels killed."[32]

Actually, both Featherston's brigade and Ward's division that squared off suffered significant casualties, with Featherston's brigade losing 679 out of 1,230 men engaged, and Ward's three brigades suffering 561 out of just under 5,000 men. Moreover, while Featherston's dead and dying were strewn thickly along the Collier Road on the high ridge overlooking Peach Tree Creek, there were not 500 of them to be buried there. There were about 200 or so Mississippians who were buried on the ridge along side of nearly as many Federal dead. Thus, one in three casualties in both sides who fought along the Collier Road were fatal casualties, a truly remarkable fact, particularly so when typically, one in five or six battlefield casualties were fatal during the Civil War.

33rd Indiana. The 33rd Indiana formed on the left front of Coburn's line in the center of Federal counterthrust with 380 men and officers. According to Adjutant McBride of the 33rd Indiana, "It was a race between the two lines as to which would first reach the top of this ridge, the key to the situation—the position that was necessary to the success of the line that could gain it and hold it."[33] Although their advance to the ravine had been checked, Featherston's brigade still held the Federal skirmish line atop Collier Ridge. "The enemy at this time was rather favored in position, but when the command 'Forward' rang along the Union line upon its being reformed, with a yell, heard above the roar of artillery and din of musketry," explained the Indianan officer, "the regiments of the brigade intermingled and as one command or organization dashed up the hill and drove the enemy from the coveted position, the temporary breastworks which had previously been erected by the skirmishers of the 22nd Wisconsin."[34] McBride proudly wrote that Ward's 3rd Division gained the coveted ridge and held it "but by severe fighting and under the most adverse circumstances."[35]

---

[31] *OR*, ser. 1, vol. 38, pt. 2, serial 73, 337.
[32] Cate, *"If I Live to Come Home,"* 196.
[33] McBride, *History of the 33rd Indiana*, 129.
[34] Ibid., 129.
[35] Ibid., 130.

McBride added, "All this time the enemy fought gallantly and with apparent confidence."[36]

The 33rd Indiana was on the left flank of Coburn's 2nd Brigade and, as Wood's 3rd Brigade was somewhat to the left and rear of their line and had farther to travel to reach Collier Ridge, the left of the 33rd Indiana was in danger of being turned. Captain Maze and Lieutenant Hollingsworth quickly turned companies G, K, and B to the left and "standing like a stone wall, sending the enemy back faster than they came."[37] According to McBride, "The position held by the enemy was obstinately contested by them, and at times the conflict was hand to hand; but the onslaught of Ward's 3rd Division was so terrific and well-directed that the enemy was overwhelmed, dismayed and demoralized."[38] He continued, "Three or four distinct charges were made by the enemy and as often he was gallantly repulsed."[39]

Color-bearer Albert H. Law of Company C, 33rd Indiana, "was among the first to be severely wounded, when Private William H. [Hank] Orner, of same company, grasped the colors and triumphantly carried them in the front line of battle until victory was won."[40] The adjutant proudly recorded that "[p]risoners and Enfield rifles were captured by the wholesale, and several battle flags were taken by the 2nd Brigade."[41] Concerning the battle flags, McBride explained, "Some of the men of the 33rd Indiana and 19th Michigan captured a rebel flag, but gave it to some officer unknown to them to take care of, but who the officer was never known, except that he was serving upon the division staff."[42] The 19th Michigan was led by Major Baker who performed handsomely. "The regiment fired volley after volley into the enemy ranks." According to Sergeant Hager of the 19th Michigan, "We slaughtered the confederates terribly." After failing to break the Federal lines, "the Confederates pulled back to a hill [Collier Ridge] with the Federals in close pursuit. At times hand-to-hand fighting broke out. Captain Frank Baldwin of Company D charged into the Confederate line and personally captured a Confederate battle flag and two officers."[43]

---

[36] Ibid., 130.
[37] Ibid., 130.
[38] Ibid., 130.
[39] Ibid., 130.
[40] Ibid., 130.
[41] Ibid., 130.
[42] Ibid., 130.
[43] Terry L. Jones, "'The Flash of Their Guns Was a Sure Guide': The 19th Michigan Infantry in the Atlanta Campaign," in Theodore P. Savas and David A. Woodbury, eds., *The Campaign for Atlanta & Sherman's March to the Sea* 157–95, at 188. 2 vols. (Savas

The 33rd Indiana lost twenty men killed and four officers and sixty-seven men wounded, for a total loss of ninety-one men. In comparison, "The 33rd Indiana captured 92 'Johnnies' and also 150 muskets..."[44] Second Lieutenant Hezekiah H. Lyon of Company E, 33rd Indiana, remembered the Battle of Peach Tree Creek as "A hard fight."[45]

85th Indiana. On the right of Coburn's brigade, the 85th Indiana, with a strength of some 294 men and officers, reached the ravine in front of portions of the 22nd Mississippi and 31st Mississippi of Featherston's brigade. To the 85th Indiana's right and silhouetted by the evening's sun were the men of the 40th Mississippi, which were coming down the north slope of the Collier Ridge where the Collier Road bent back toward the mill to support their fellow Mississippians. James H. Crabb of Company G, 85th Indiana, reported that "three lines of Johnnies broke from the cover [of the woods] and it looked as though the whole of Confederate army was racing toward them across the open field, guns belching, officers' swords flashing and bayonets looking mean and ugly." Observing the work of the skirmish line occupied by the 22nd Wisconsin and a part of the 136th New York, Crabb explained, "The skirmishers held their ground as the fierce looking column advanced and heard their own columns coming up at a double quick from the rear." After the skirmishers had fallen back to the main body and Featherston's brigade, which had pursued, them reached the ravine, Coburn's veterans nerved up for the work before them. "The two columns were within 14 feet of each other when the fighting began in earnest and [Crabb] was able to shoot ten times in a fierce, bloody hand to hand conflict, when knives, bayonets, pistols, clubbed guns, swords, and even fists were used."[46]

Captain William T. Crawford of Company H, 85th Indiana, remembered: "Though there was plenty of time for musketry fire as the Confederates were seen advancing, for some reason the fire was held and with crunching grind the two armies came together at bayonet points. Horrors of the field were sickening." Crawford explained, "Rash and fearless the Confederates threw

---

Campbell CA: Woodbury Publishers, 1994).

[44] McBride, *History of the 33rd Indiana*, 130–31.

[45] 2nd Lt. Hezekiah H. Lyon, margin notes in McBride, *History of the 33rd Indiana*, 128, in author's personal papers, Dalton, Georgia.

[46] James H. Crabb "Memories of the Civil War," *The Terre Haute* (IN) *Tribune*, 15 October 1911 1911, quoted in Frank J. Welcher and Larry Liggett, *Coburn's Brigade: 85th Indiana, 33rd Indiana, 19th Michigan & 22nd Wisconsin in the Western Civil War* (Carmel IN: Carmel Press, 1999) 239.

The Battle of Peach Tree Creek

themselves against the Union lines, bristling with bayonet points." One of the most gruesome moments of the entire war was witnessed in the fight between Featherston's Mississippians and Ward's division. "Crawford saw a Confederate and Yankee deliberately run toward each other with bayonets set, and both weapons took effect, passing entirely through the bodies of each fighter." The horrified Indianan could never erase the image from his mind. "The black muzzles of the guns stuck out at the back of the men, locked in death, and held together by the grewsome bonds."[47]

After the battle was over, the exhausted, but jubilant veterans of the 85th Indiana surveyed their casualties. "It was found that Company G had not lost a man, though it had held the hardest position. There was not one member of the company, however, who had not been struck by a bullet. Hats were shot through, guns bore the splotches of lead where the bullets had struck." The Indiana veteran continued, "Coats were shot through and such mementos of the flirts of death shown."[48] In fact, of the 294 officers and men of the 85th Indiana who had gone into the fight, it was discovered that only 3 men had been killed, 32 wounded, and 3 either captured or missing, for a total of 38 men. It was indeed a lucky, but hard fought, day for the Indianans, but some brave Indianans paid dearly.[49] "Among the killed were Sgt. Mitchell C. Purcell of Company C...and Sgt. Charles Ault of Company K."[50] But, with at least equal casualties in each of Ward's fourteen regiments that held off the enemy's five regiments and one battalion, the carnage was terrible.

According to one observer in the 33rd Indiana to the left of the 85th Indiana, "Private Thomas J. Williamson, of the 85th Indiana, picked up a rebel flag, waved it three times, and then threw it down."[51] A number of men of the 33rd Indiana and the 85th Indiana saw Williamson's bravery. When his commander, Lieutenant Colonel A. B. Crane asked him why he threw it down, Williamson replied, because "he could not carry it and fire his gun."[52] The flag's identity remains unclear, but it was most likely that of the 3rd Mississippi, which was directly in front of the 85th Indiana during the closest of

---

[47] Welcher, *Cogburn's Brigade*, 240.
[48] Ibid., 239.
[49] *OR*, ser. 1, vol. 38, pt. 2, serial 73, 414.
[50] Welcher, *Cogburn's Brigade*, 240.; J. E. Brant, *History of the Eighty-Fifth Indiana Volunteer Infantry, Its Organization, Campaigns and Battles* (Bloomington IN: Cravens Bros., 1902) 67.
[51] McBride, *History of the 33rd Indiana*, 130.
[52] *OR*, ser. 1, vol. 38, pt. 2, serial 73, 414.

the fighting. One veteran observed, "The battle was over, but...the real battle came when that field of horror was witnessed. Along the fighting line where the hand to hand conflict had been, the dead and dying soldiers, blue and gray lying side by side, were piled everywhere, and," the soldier continued, "directly on the firing line the dead made a low wall of human flesh." It was a terrible sight. All throughout the valley and spilling onto and over the Collier Ridge and road, the dead and dying covered the earth. "Pitiful groans and pleadings for water, the first craving of the dying or badly wounded, was heard on every side and contortions of their sufferings could be seen grotesquely through the haze of smoke which covered the battleground." While many men were beyond help, "The Union soldiers in charge of the field gave aid, indiscriminately, to all the wounded, and honorable burial for the dead."[53]

19th Michigan. The 19th Michigan, which was in the second line, went into the fight with 300 men. During the fighting in the ravine and along the Collier Ridge, the Michigan regiment lost four killed and thirty-five wounded, including Major Baker.[54] Sergeant Phineas A. Hager remembered, "We slaughtered the rebels terribly."[55] Hager also wrote his wife, telling her that "We have punished the rebels pretty severely. I don't see how they can have a particle of courage to hold out. They have to fall back every few days and their army must be getting smaller very fast." Private Henry Dean grasped the strategic situation. "The army in front of us has got to be whiped, & if Hood will fight it soon will be accomplished."[56] Also from the 19th Michigan Captain Frank Baldwin captured a battle flag and two officers, wining him the Congressional Medal of Honor.[57] During the remaining siege of Atlanta, the 19th Michigan Infantry suffered only two more men killed, and six men wounded.[58] " [Major] John J. Baker, commanding the 19th Michigan was wounded, and Captain David Anderson assumed command of the regiment."[59]

22nd Wisconsin. The 22nd Wisconsin's survivors, which had been up on the line just taken by the Mississippians, were mixed in with the rest of the

---

[53] Welcher, *Cogburn's Brigade*, 240.

[54] John Robertson, *Michigan in the War* (Lansing MI: W. S. George & Company, 1882) 395.

[55] Jones, "'The Flash of Their Guns,'" I:157–95, at 162.

[56] Albert Castel, *Decision in the West: The Atlanta Campaign of 1864* (Lawrence: University Press of Kansas, 1992) 385.

[57] Jones, "'The Flash of Their Guns,'" I:162; Joseph B. Mitchell, *The Badge of Gallantry* (New York: MacMillan Co., 1968) 12.

[58] http://hometown.aol.com/dlharvey/19thinf.htm (1 March 2008)

[59] Welcher, *Cogburn's Brigade*, 240.

Federal troops readying to form the countercharge. Slugging it out along the center of the gap in the ravine, Coburn's men took fearful losses. According to Lieutenant Colonel Bloodgood of the 22nd Wisconsin, the Wisconsin boys had been compelled to run from their line to avoid certain capture and he had ordered his men to "rally on the reserve" just as the rest of his "brigade came cheering over the...ridge and down into the ravine. Now the [Rebels] came pouring over the ridge we had just abandoned, and rushing down upon our lines in perfect crowds only to meet and fall before our fire. The fight raged in this way for nearly an hour, the [Rebels] coming to the charge time after time and was always repulsed." Coburn's men faced the brave veterans of the 22nd and 31st Mississippi and part of the 3rd Mississippi as they clashed along the Redland Road line.[60]

"The 22nd Wisconsin fought well and bravely," noted one veteran, "and it is a great wonder they were not all taken prisoners, for before Captain Mead gave orders to fall back on the reserve, the rebels were in their front, on both sides of them, and in three minutes longer would have been in the rear of them." The veteran continued, "They came down the hill after our men in swarms, but when they went up again their number was considerably lessened, for this morning I counted in front of our brigade 128 rebels, lying stark and stiff, in winrows, ready for the burial party." The next day the Wisconsin soldier remembered, "When I left the regiment, about 10 A.M., our boys were still bringing in bodies."[61]

In the 22nd Wisconsin, one veteran remembered that the regiment lost seven killed and thirty-five wounded, but the report given by Lieutenant Colonel Bloodgood was that the 22nd Wisconsin lost seven dead and thirty-seven wounded.[62] Harvey Reid of the 22nd Wisconsin recorded that it was "the first field fight of the campaign—the only one in which neither party had the shelter of breastworks."[63] Prisoners reported that "Hood made the remark ...that they should fight no more with spades and picks."[64] The carnage left behind on the Collier Ridge and the ravine beside the mill was truly awful. Wood's 3rd Brigade buried 420 men, while the 22nd Wisconsin of Coburn's Second

---

[60] John Michael Priest, ed., *John T. McMahon's Diary of the 136th New York, 1861–1864* (Shippensburg PA: White Mane Publishing Company, 1993) 104.

[61] Racine Boy to Friend T., 21 July 1864, p. 16, subject file PW-4, Kennesaw Mountain National Battlefield Park, Kennesaw, Georgia.

[62] Reid, *Uncommon Soldiers*, 171; *OR*, ser. 1, vol. 38, pt. 2, serial 73, pp. 426–27.

[63] Reid, *Uncommon Soldiers*, 173.

[64] Ibid.

Brigade buried by ten o'clock the following morning another 53 men. According to Reid, "There are more rebel wounded in our Hospital [Ward's 3rd Division] than our own."[65]

Adjutant McBride of the 33rd Indiana remembered that "[t]he fighting lasted about 4 hours and was the severest the regiment and brigade had participated in during the campaign."[66] According to McBride, "The loss in the brigade [Coburn's] was 33 men killed, 169 wounded, and 7 missing, for a total of 213," although the breakdown of casualties in Coburn's 2nd Brigade reveal 33 killed, 179 wounded, and 7 captured or missing, for a total loss of 219 men.[67]

The Palmetto Guards, Company G, 31st Mississippi. The men of Company G, the "Palmetto Guards," had been taking on casualties almost from the beginning of the charge. Named for the small village of Palmetto south of Tupelo, Mississippi, in Pontotoc County (now part of Lee County) where the Orr family from South Carolina had settled, the Palmetto Guards were catching shell fire from Yankee artillery to their left near the Collier Mill as the Guards crossed the open field. Corporal Francis M. Prather and Private Thomas R. Atkins were struck by a shell and fell wounded. Both were taken to the Ocmulgee Hospital in Macon.

1st Corporal Benjamin Franklin Rasberry was struck in the face. Another Rasberry was not so fortunate. Sergeant Joseph C. Rasberry was shot in the back during the hand-to-hand fighting. Captured and unable to walk, he was left by the Yankees to die. When he hadn't died, Joseph was carried to the US field hospital at Vining Station on 26 July. When he was well enough to be moved, the sergeant was sent to Camp Chase on 10 September, but pneumonia set in during the winter and on 27 March 1865 he died.

Fellow Palmetto Guards privates John T. McCully and Cullen Lark Pitts were both wounded in the foot and toe when a shell went off at their feet. Both limped to safety and were treated at the hospital in Macon where McCully, fittingly, requisitioned the quartermaster for a new pair of shoes. Both returned to duty and marched with the 31st Mississippi all the way to the surrender at North Carolina the following spring.

Captain John Franklin Manahan led the Palmetto Guards forward to the ridge. Following him in the charge were his son Private Thaddeus Aethelberg Manahan, and his nephews Private Adonoram Judson Manahan and Fourth

---

[65] Ibid.
[66] McBride, *History of the 33rd Indiana*, 131–32.
[67] Ibid., 132.

Sergeant William H. Biggers (a cousin of the author). It was Sergeant Biggers's last charge. A Yankee bullet found its mark and felled the twenty-five-year-old who was left by his cousins dead on the field. The forty-six-year-old captain, too, fell with a severe and painful gunshot wound to his thigh and was carried from the field. He was taken to the Ocmulgee Hospital in Macon to recover.

Caught in the crossfire on top of the ridge, the Palmetto Guards were inundated with shot and lead. Private Henry J. Easterwood was shot in the left hand while Private William Jefferson Evans was hit in the leg, which was later amputated. Both men were put out of action for the rest of the war. It was the last battle for Private Reuben T. Gray. The blue-eyed, twenty-three-year-old from Pontotoc was knocked down and captured by Federal troops rolling back up the ridge. He spent the rest of the war at Camp Chase. Second Lieutenant John C. McCullough was also surrounded by the Yankees and was forced to surrender. The gray-eyed "Nute" McCullough looked through the white smoke at the victorious blue lines and wondered at his fate. He would spend nearly a year in captivity in the Confederate POW camp on Johnson's Island, Ohio, before returning to his Pontotoc County home in Saltillo at the age of thirty-two.

Private Rufus C. Suggs was shot in the head with a bullet that penetrated his brain and was left on the field where he died two days later. Private William A. Morris was killed in the fighting that day when he fell mortally wounded and had to be left on the field by his comrades. Company G also lost Private Ezekiel McMarks for the rest of the war when he fell shot in the thigh. First Sergeant Samuel H. Robinson was also wounded, albeit slightly, but he kept fighting. The Palmetto Guards saw sixteen of its number fall that summer day, four of whom would never rise again. Only six would return to duty.

Wood's 3rd Brigade. To the far right opposing Featherston's brigade, the men of Colonel James Wood, Jr.'s brigade lined up behind the far ridge from east to west: 20th Connecticut and 26th Wisconsin in the front line, backed by the 55th Ohio (behind the 20th Connecticut) and 73rd Ohio (behind the 26th Wisconsin). The 73rd Ohio had originally been placed by Colonel Wood in the front line on the right of his Brigade, but in order to give room for the rest of the Division to deploy, Wood had been ordered to reduce his front line from three regiments to two. According to veteran E. B. Fenton of the 20th Connecticut, "By noon our whole right [Thomas's Army of the Cumberland] was across the creek. The men had stacked arms and were taking a little rest. Some prisoners, brought in from the skirmish line, gave the information that a strong line of entrenchments was about a mile in advance," he explained, "behind which the rebels were awaiting an attack."[68]

Wood's brigade joined the remainder of Ward's division on the plain south of Peach Tree Creek, stacked arms, and began to prepare dinner. There, they rested not expecting any further activity that day. After about three or four hours, the men were quickly summoned from their liberty. "At once the bugle sounded the assembly, the men rushed to their places, seized their arms and deployed into line." Fenton explained, "the rebels advanced to the attack, and our forces were immediately put in motion to meet the assault. Inclining a little to the right, the whole third division advanced in an open field and was soon hotly engaged." The 20th Connecticut was on the left of Wood's brigade. The men had been resting in the field just south of Peach Tree Creek at today's Colonial Homes condominiums, and as they proceeded south to meet the attacking Confederates, they crossed the area of today's Seaboard Coastline Railroad and met the Confederate line along today's Collier Road between the railroad's present location to the west and Anjaco Road to the east.[69]

As the 20th Connecticut proceeded south, it had the longest distance to cover. Therefore, this regiment lagged behind the remainder of the division during the counterchange. Moreover, a gap of up to a quarter mile on their left began forming (behind today's Piedmont Hospital and including the parking deck north of Collier Road) between the left of the 20th Connecticut and the refused right of Kimball's brigade. "For a short time our regiment was in an extremely critical condition, the rebels firing into it from the front, flank and rear." But the Connecticut boys were able to maintain its ground: "The bugle now sounded the charge, and the whole line pressed forward with loud cheers. Our regiment advanced over an open field under a heavy fire, with an almost perfect line, as if on parade, reserving our fire until within a few rods of the rebel line," explained the Connecticut Yankee. There, "we "delivered a volley, driving the rebels out of their position up to a crest of a hill in front, where the whole line of our division was halted."[70]

According to Colonel Wood, the crossing of Peach Tree Creek "by the division was effected about 11:00 A.M.…without opposition." At first, Wood's

---

[68] E. B. Fenton, "From the Rapidan to Atlanta. Leaves from the Diary of Commpanion E. B. Fenton, Late Twentieth Connecticut Volunteer Infantry. Read before the Commandery of the State of Michigan MOLLUS, Detroit, April 6th, 1893," in Sydney C. Kerksis, ed., *The Atlanta Papers*, 230–31. (Dayton OH: Morningside Books, 1980).

[69] Fenton, "From the Rapidan to Atlanta," 231.

[70] Ibid., 231.

The Battle of Peach Tree Creek

3rd Brigade was ordered to connect with the left of Geary's division near an old grist mill, Collier's Mill, and deploy skirmishers along a ridge overlooking the mill and Tanyard Branch, the stream which flowed by the mill and into Peach Tree Creek. Wood sent Lieutenant Colonel Lester B. Faulkner with his 136th New York Regiment forward to accomplish this task. The 136th New York had played a prominent role on a number of other battlefields throughout the war, but had often been overlooked for prasie. From Gettysburg to Resaca and New Hope, the "Iron Clads" of the 136th New York Infantry Regiment had fought valiantly. Today, they would again be found in the center of the storm.

While Faulkner marched off with the 136th New York, Colonel Wood received a new directive from General Ward: deploy at the base of the first ridge on the left of the division and connect with the right of Newton's division, which was about to move on the big hill (today's Cardiac Hill). According to Colonel Wood, he was informed by Ward that Coburn's 2nd Brigade had not yet crossed the creek and it was important to occupy the left position at once to support Newton's impending advance. There were still Rebel forces posted atop the hill in Newton's front, the 2nd Tennessee of Cleburne's division, in front of Newton while Confederate skirmishers remained along the larger Collier Ridge in prepared works in Ward's front. "Subsequently the 2nd Brigade [Coburn's] took position on my right, the 1st Brigade [Harrison's] on the right of the 2nd, connecting with Brig. Gen. Geary," explained Wood. This change placed the 136th New York in front of Harrison's 1st Brigade, while the 22nd Wisconsin was sent forward by Coburn to cover the front of the 2nd and 3rd brigades.[71]

At about 11:00 A.M. or noon, the 22nd Wisconsin commanded by Lieutenant Colonel Edward Bloodgood was ordered to take the first ridge (intersected today by Dellwood Drive) overlooking the cornfield (in the flats on the south side of Peach Tree Creek today's Bobby Jones Golf Course and Colonial Homes Subdivision). An hour later, the 22nd Wisconsin was ordered again to advance, this time taking the second ridge, the commanding Collier Ridge, which connected with the hill that contained Buckhead Road on the left. At some point after 1:00 P.M., the 22nd Wisconsin had secured the Collier Ridge, Collier Road running along the spine. The 136th New York, supporting this move, covered the right portion of the advance above the Collier Mill. By the time Bloodgood deployed his regiment as skirmishers connecting with right

---

[71] *OR*, ser. 1, vol. 38, pt. 2, serial 74, pp. 389, 426–27, 441–42; James Wood, *Report of the Operations of the 3rd Brigade, 3rd Division of the XX Army Corps The Atlanta Campaign of 1864*, 27, 44 (Albany: Weed, Parsons & Company, Printers, 1889).

Hood's First Sortie, 20 July 1864

of Kimball's brigade above Ardmore Road, his 22nd Wisconsin line reached most of the way down the ridge toward the Tanyard Branch. There was only room for four of Faulkner's white-hat-donned companies to fill the void. Thus, the 136th New York placed companies A, C, D, and G along the skirmish line, with Company G connecting on the left with the right of Bloodgood's Wisconsinites.[72]

After deploying his brigade at the foot of the first ridge in the cornfield (at today's Colonial Homes Subdivision) as ordered, Wood received orders from General Ward, who had established his headquarters in rear of Wood's line, "to have the men stack arms and make themselves as comfortable as possible; that a further advance was not at that time expected." Coburn's and Harrison's brigade followed suit, and by 2:00 P.M., the entire brigade was in leisure along the southern side of Peach Tree Creek except for the 22nd Wisconsin and four companies of the 136th New York. For the next couple of hours, men reclined, smoked, swam in the creek, picked blackberries, washed clothes, prepared small cooking fires, and enjoyed the time off until the rattle of skirmish fire, which had never completely ceased, began to grow. Wood "suggested to Gen. Ward that he had better advance the division to the top of the bluff. He declined, saying that he had orders from corps headquarters not to move until further orders, and he should stay where he was until he received orders to move."[73]

Ward obviously did not appreciate the growing danger before him, though his men and junior officers did. "The rapid discharge of musketry on our left, in front of Newton's division, the sudden retreat to the rear of non-combatants, ambulances, etc., of that division, the activity of our own skirmish line, indicated" trouble, said Wood. The New York brigade commander, James Wood, had just received word from a private sent from his old regiment, the 136th New York, on the skirmish line that "the enemy in force was advancing upon us." Wood explained, "I immediately, without orders, ordered my brigade to advance to meet and resist the threatened attack of the enemy. The skirmish line gallantly held out to the last, and gravely fought the enemy and materially checking his advance." Wood, looking to his right saw that Coburn and Harrison had reached the same conclusion as their brigades were moving forward. "Over the crest of the hill, down into the ravine on the other side, the

---

[72] Ibid., 27–28, 44–47.
[73] Ibid., 27–28.

brigade line advanced, and as it emerged from a fringe of trees or gushes, with which the bottom of the valley or ravine was lined, it met the enemy."[74]

Wood's brigade was proceeding south generally along a line with today's Dellwood Drive before meeting Featherston's Mississippians in the ravine just north of today's Redland Road. Wood's brigade commenced firing: "Cooly and deliberately the men poured into their line a well-directed, withering and destructive fire, which covered the ground with dead and wounded." Coburn's and Harrison's brigades were also meeting the Mississippians in the ravine and beginning to fire into them. "This checked his advance and caused him to recoil," explained Wood. "The line continuing its fire charged up the hill, gained the crest and drove the enemy into the valley on the other side."

On the left of Wood's line, a new threat appeared as his left regiment, the 20th Connecticut, had to travel a bit farther to reach the Collier Ridge (in the area of today's Seaboard Coastline Railroad as it approaches Collier Road and Ardmore Road). "The 20th Conn. on the left, by some misapprehension, halted before reaching the crest of the second hill, its commander being erroneously ordered to halt and cease firing," Wood recalled, "as our skirmishers were still in front" of that part of the line. "This misapprehension and error I at once rectified, and the regiment advanced to the crest just as a body of the enemy formed in double column were about to take advantage of the apparent gap in the line to attack Newton's Division on its right flank."[75]

This new threat was the late arrival of Maney's Tennessee division, which was massed in a two-brigade front with two additional brigades formed in rear. If Maney's Tennesseans reached the Collier Ridge and road before his men could come up and close the hole, it could spell disaster for Kimball's men and the rest of Newton's division. Moreover, if Maney's Tennesseans could wrestle the top of the ridge away from the left of Wood's line, the weight of this new, fresh, Confederate force could support the survivors of Featherston's brigade, which were still clinging onto the ridge in a hand-to-hand contest along the Collier Road. Outnumbered, Ward's division would be rolled up and forced back into the cornfield between Tanyard Branch and Peach Tree Creek, just as Hood had designed. "A well-directed and murderous volley from the 20th Conn. poured into this column," however, and "threw it into confusion and it broke and fled," explained Wood. "I ordered the 55th Ohio to reinforce the line

---

[74] Ibid., 28–29.
[75] Ibid., 29–30.

on the left, as there was a gap on the left of the 20th Conn., between it and the right of the 4th Corps."[76]

The Mississippians were left alone to slug it out with Ward's three brigades and then to retreat fighting in a futile effort to buy time before help could arrive. It would not come. The survivors of Featherston's gallant clan drew off down the valley to reform and try again.[77] After Featherston's men fell back, Wood "ordered forward the 73rd Ohio to relieve the 26th Wisc., which was nearly exhausted by the extreme heat of the day and the severe fighting in which it had been engaged." The 136th New York, which had fought with Harrison's 1st Brigade near the Collier Mill, then returned. Wood replaced the 20th Connecticut with the New Yorkers on the front line. "The enemy made one or two ineffectual attempts to renew the attack, but his troops would not or could not withstand the destructive fire which ours kept up upon them from our line." Sometime during the afternoon, Wood recalled seeing Colonel John Coburn come rushing up to him "in an excited state of mind and said something in reference to the state of affairs."[78] Coburn explained that more Rebels were advancing on Wood's left and that Wood needed to be ready to receive them.

Soon, Wood's men along with the remainder of Ward's division had secured the Collier Ridge and began to fortify the line along the Collier Road while still under fire. As the large mass of Confederates huddled below the left of Wood's line continued to remain in sight, the threat remained. Maney's Tennessee division had settled a couple of hundred yards south of the Federal line, and from this position the front ranks began to exchange fire with Kimball's men and a part of the left of Wood's line, (from today's Ardmore Park, Ardmore Road, and Anjaco Road areas). As this continued threat appeared great, Wood determined to reinforce the left of his line and "held the 55th Ohio and 73rd Ohio in reserve, to protect my left flank in case it should be exposed." Wood was happy to see the arrival at that time of General Thomas who noticed the mass of Confederates in Wood's left front. They made tempting targets for his cannoneers, and Thomas sent the 1st Ohio Light Artillery, Battery C, with its six Napoleons to support Wood's line and begin raking the woods. Thus, about 5:00 P.M., Stephens Ohio Battery, which had just assisted in repelling Mercer's brigade along the Buckhead Road near the bridge over Peach Tree Creek, "moved to the right and went into position on a rise of

---

[76] Ibid., 30.
[77] Ibid., 29; *OR*, ser. 1, vol. 38, pt. 3, serial 74, 880–91.
[78] Wood "Report of the Operations of the 3rd Brigade," 44.

ground in rear of Colonel Wood's brigade and opened upon the enemy with solid shot, firing over the heads of our troops, which I kept up until dark," explained Stephens.[79] (The hill on which Stephens's battery was placed was just north of today's Collier Road between Anjaco and Ardmore roads). Huddled in the woods, Maney's men showed no further interest in testing the Collier Ridge line.

Major Samuel H. Hurst, commander of the 73rd Ohio in Wood's second line, remembered:

> Our battalions at once sprang to arms, and, as soon as orders could be obtained, the first line of our brigade went forward. It reached the top of the first range of hills, just as our skirmishers began to retire from the second, three hundred yards in front. The line pushed forward two hundred yards to a ravine, where, meeting the retreating skirmishers, the battalions were halted, and the men lay down.
>
> On came the rebel lines, sweeping everything before them, shouting and cheering in the fullness of their enthusiasm. On they came, over the second hill and down almost to the ravine, —when our men suddenly rose up, and poured into their ranks a most murderous volley. Many of them fell, some tried to hide in the ditches on the hillside, and others fell back. Then our line charged up the crest of the hill, and continued to deliver a rapid and tolling fire on the retreating foe.[80]

Major Hurst next explained that the 73rd Ohio was ordered to relieve the first line and retake the lost ridge. "We went forward, amid a shower of balls from the enemy, and were welcomed with a shout by our comrades. We at once opened fire upon the enemy, who was now trying to take shelter in the woods to our right and left front."[81] Hurst's men continued to take and receive blows for the remainder of the afternoon as the fire from both sides continued to be heavy. One observer in Coburn's brigade to the right of Wood's brigade remembered, "After the crest was gained the 3rd Brigade [Wood's], by magnificent fighting, succeeded in filling the gap on the left, closing up to Norton's [Newton's] Division of the IV Corps."[82] When it was over, the Federals saw the wrecked

---

[79] Ibid., 29; Scaife, *The Campaign for Atlanta*, 157; *OR*, ser. 1, vol. 38, pt. 2, serial 73, 484.

[80] Samuel H. Hurst, *Journal-History of the Seventy-Third Ohio Volunteer Infantry*,139–40.

[81] Hurst, *Journal-History of the Seventy-Third Ohio*, 140.

[82] McBride, *History of the 33rd Indiana*, 130.

remainder of their brigade and the right wing of Featherston's brigade all around them. "The valley between the ridges was filled with dead and wounded rebels," remembered one veteran.[83] The carnage was so great that the Federal troops in Wood's brigade thought that the Rebels had lost 6,000 men. "The ground was literally strewn with their dead and wounded; and of one regiment, the Thirty-third Mississippi, there were left upon the field thirteen commissioned officers, and a proportional number of men killed and wounded."[84] Major Hurst reported that the 73rd Ohio lost 18 men killed and wounded, while Wood's brigade lost 143; Ward's division losses were 520, and Hooker's XX Corps lost 1,700, according to the Ohioan.[85] Among the casualties in the 73rd Ohio were First Lieutenant Rufus Hosler who was wounded, and Privates William May, killed, and Noble Lewis, mortally wounded.[86]

William Cline of the 73rd Ohio recorded in his diary the next day, "the Rebls made a charge on the 20 and 4 corps Bute [was] Repulste with Heavey loss the [73rd Ohio Volunteer Infantry] i loste 18 men in kilde and wounded then Hour Boyes charged the Rebes ande Drove them from ther position." According to Cline, "the Batel of the 20 ware foughte on verey Broken grounde." The fighting had been severe. Cline remembered, "i counted 114 shotes in one tree 3 feate." Cline noted six days later that "the 20 corps loste 19 Hundred in kilde ande wounded ande after the fighte Hour Boyes Buriede 900 of Rebels thate layede Before the 20 corps and [not] all Buriede yete there is a greate meney Rebels in Hour Horspitels wounded the woundede is Dying off ver faste." Thus, on 26 July, the Federal burial details were still busy finding and burying Confederate dead and those who continued to suffer and die as they lay for several days in the hot Georgia sun along the Collier Ridge and the neighboring woods and ravines. Cline explained on 26 July, "a greate meney of the Joneyes [not] Buried yete 2 squades Has volunteerde to 2 Dayes ande wente ande Buriede Rebels Bute [not] all Buried yete."[87]

The 33rd Massachusetts of Wood's brigade guarded the division wagon train and were on the north side of the creek, near the Buck Head crossing. From that vantage point, they observed Hardee's attack on Newton's division, and Featherston's assault on their own division. They watched as General Thomas moved two batteries from the left rear of Newton's division, where it

---

[83] Underwood, *33rd Massachusetts*, 226.
[84] Hurst, *Journal-History of the Seventy-Third Ohio*, 140–41.
[85] Ibid., 141.
[86] Ibid., 195, 208, 214.
[87] Cline, Diary, Special Collections, University of Notre Dame, 160–61, 164–67.

The Battle of Peach Tree Creek

had served to repel Bate's division and part of Walker's division from the exposed Federal flank, to the right rear of Newton's position where it was able to lob shells over Wood's men and into the field where Featherston's men had fallen back to after being driven from the ridge. "The artillery fire on our side was particularly effective; ten guns were got into position in the nick of time, by Thomas's personal directions."[88] Ward's division artillery also lobbed shells to the left of Featherston's lines and into Maney's Tennessee division, which had by then come up in line with Featherston. It was this rain of shell fire that Captain James I. Hall, commanding Company C of the 9th Tennessee (who were crouched or in a prone position on the side of the hill near today's Ardmore Park during the shelling) described as nearly destroying his entire company.

Wood's brigade opposed the 33rd Mississippi under Colonel J. L. Drake, and the 3rd Mississippi led by Colonel T. A. Mellon, together with most of the 1st Mississippi Battalion Sharpshooters commanded by Major J. M. Stigler. Upon meeting the Federal skirmish line, the 1st Mississippi Battalion formed in the rear and to the right of the 33rd Mississippi on the far right of Featherston's brigade. E. B. Fenton of the 20th Connecticut Infantry in General Wood's brigade, which was opposite the 33rd Mississippi Infantry Regiment of Featherston's brigade, exclaimed, "Four times during that afternoon the rebels tried to carry our line but were as often sent reeling back. From 3 o'clock until 8 o'clock we stood with no cover, and without assistance or relief.... In front of us were found the dead and wounded of...[three] Mississippi Regiments...." These were men from the 33rd Mississippi, the 3rd Mississippi, which was next to the left of the 33rd Mississippi, and most likely the 1st Mississippi Battalion Sharpshooters, which began the assault in front of Featherston's brigade as skirmishers, but when they reached the old field in front of the Federal line on the ridge, they moved over and formed on the right flank and rear of the 33rd Mississippi and supported Colonel Drake's regiment as they took the ridge and moved past it until check by Colonel Wood's Federal brigade of Ward's division. Fenton wrote that his regiment lost nearly half of its officers and men, quite remarkable for a defending unit in an assault.[89]

The 20th Connecticut had come up just in time. Featherston's Mississippians were repulsed. Kimball's brigade redeployed its refused line and

---

[88] Underwood, *33rd Massachusetts*, 227.
[89] A. A. Hoehling, *Last Train from Atlanta* (New York: Thomas Yoseloff, Printer, 1958) 115–16.

joined its right with the left of the Connecticut boys, and Maney's Tennesseans, which were forming to finally charge the works, were checked. "After the battle was over General Newton, commanding a division of the IV Corps on our left, sent an officer to know what regiment was on his right," said Fenton, adding that Newton had said "that [the 20th Connecticut] was deserving of all praise, that he never saw a regiment advance with such steadiness and precision in the face of such a terrible fire as this one."[90]

It was not a completely happy day for E. B. Fenton and his 20th Connecticut, however. Fenton was seriously wounded during the battle. "The roar and crash of battle had ceased; the sulphurous smoke had cleared away, but how strange the scenes about us!" he exclaimed. "The plains and hillsides were strewn with corpses of men where they fell. The dead and dying were lying close together, where a few short hours before all was excitement—the excitement of many a brave comrade's last battle—now an oppressive silence prevails." The Yankee soldier explained, "there is the groaning and the crying of the wounded. In quiet tones we speak to each other. The question passes back and forth—'Where are you wounded?' 'Through the body,' 'And you?' 'Arm broken,' 'My knee smashed with a piece of shell,' or 'A minnie bullet through the foot.'" Fenton remembered these somber and quietly given replies. "Words of cheer are spoken, while over the faces of some the strange, pale look is coming that betokens the approach of death."[91]

Fenton lamented, "One lies near who has always been jolly and full of fun in the ranks, but now jesting is forgotten. A few feet away lies an officer—lately promoted—the smile still on his face, so suddenly had the bullet cut the thread of life." A few feet away, "The ambulance corps with their stretchers are kept busy. The hospital tent is full of the wounded. The long and weary night draws to a close. In the early dawn, as we begin to distinguish our comrades here and there, we speak to them. Some of them answer," Fenton remembered, "with feebler voices than before, and some are silent forever, having entered their last sleep in the night."[92]

The next day, Fenton and many of his wounded comrades remained on the blood-soaked Collier Ridge. While the Northern troops celebrated their victory along the Collier Road and the crest of the ridge facing south as they jubilantly waved their captured banners before officers who came by to congratulate them,

---

[90] Fenton, "From the Rapidan to Atlanta," 231.
[91] Ibid., 232.
[92] Ibid., 232–33.

the wounded and dying, Federal and Confederate troops alike lay suffering all across the ridge and ravine just north of the road. "The sun rises, and another day wears on, the living among the dead, wounds are growing sorer and more painful, cries begin to be heard from those whose wounds are in the body and very serious." Fenton meant those who were wounded in the torso, which generally proved to be fatal as gangrene and infection set in and usually killed the victim in up to three to five painful days. "One poor fellow, an Irishman, lay near to me, so badly wounded that the surgeon exclaimed, shaking his head, 'There is no hope whatever of saving this man, he cannot possibly live.'" Fenton saw that "an ugly wound in the head and a shattered hand told the sad story. The surgeons passed him by, giving close attention to those whose chances for recovery seemed reasonably sure."[93]

After suffering a second day in the sweltering Georgia heat, the evening sun finally fell below the western wooded ridges. "Another long and weary night masses, the morning finds us with fewer alive than the day before. Learning that our Irish friend was still alive, and the surgeon ready to attend to him, his wounds were dressed, and with others of the wounded was sent back to the hospital." Fenton was happy to report that the Irishman did ultimately recover, and "Several years later I chanced to meet him, and his gratitude knew no bounds, with tears in his eyes he related to me how I 'had saved his life,' and, drawing me aside, said: 'Let us take a drop for the sake of auld times.'"[94]

The Field and Staff, 31st Mississippi. Sergeant Major Gustave G. T. Hightower of the 31st Mississippi was struck in the arm, which bled severely, putting him out of action. Seeing several of his color guard fall, Ensign James V. Belew of Choctaw County steadied his men. When the fourth color guardsman fell, Belew rallied those around him to follow Major Gillespie down the hill. With bayonets fixed, the regiment followed their regiment's battle flag carried by Belew into the maelstrom. James Belew had just been appointed ensign with the rank of first lieutenant on 15 June. Suddenly two shots rang out above the din of fire striking Belew in the right forearm and head, fracturing his arm and causing him to drop the flag. He was carried to safety, put on the train to Macon, and taken to the Ocmulgee Hospital. Unable to recover from his wounds, the brave young officer died on 24 August and was buried at the Rose Hill Cemetery in Macon.

---

[93] Ibid., 233.
[94] Ibid., 233.

Hood's First Sortie, 20 July 1864

The rear troops of the 31st Mississippi did not escape the casualty list at Peach Tree Creek. Quartermaster Sergeant Finis E. Miller, originally of Company D, the "Dixie Rebels" of Calhoun County, was wounded as well. Born in 1825 in Tennessee, Miller would not return to the Magnolia State where his wife Mary was waiting for him in their home in Pittsboro. He was carried to Columbus, Georgia, where he died and was buried at the Linewood Cemetery.

With Lieutenant Colonel Drane out of action, Sergeant Major Hightower down, and all of the color guard out of action, Adjutant William J. Van de Graff seized the proud regiment's flag. Ahead, Major Gillespie led the advance down the northern slope amid the gathering battle smoke. Van de Graff urged the brave Mississippians on who followed him and the major as they neared Collier Mill. Elements of the 40th Mississippi clung to the left, while they could see the 22nd Mississippi and the remainder of Featherston's Mississippians advancing to their right. Every man sensed that they had the Yankees retreating at a run. Each soldier felt the eyes of the Confederacy that were on them that day, and all were ready to drive the invaders away.

The Chickasaw Guards, Company C, 31st Mississippi. The "Volunteers" of Company C's Chickasaw Guards attacked in a rush. Falling in the charge were Second Lieutenant William Bird Carodine who was killed instantly and left on the field, Third Sergeant Lycurgus Sims who was wounded, and Private John C. Massey who was shot in the left thigh and hip. Massey, who had previously been wounded at Resaca, was eventually moved to the Way Hospital in Meridian, Mississippi, where he spent the rest of the war recovering.

Also injured that day were three members of the Pulliam family from Houston, Mississippi, in Chickasaw County: Quartermaster/Commissary Sergeant James Terrill Pulliam was wounded twice, once in the right arm and once in the calf and hip of the left leg; Private John S. Pulliam was hit in the head with a fragment of a shell; and Captain Thomas Jefferson Pulliam who came up later with the remainder of the Chickasaw Guards from picket duty and was put in command of the regiment before he, too, was wounded. Thus, Old Chickasaw added six more to the bloody rolls of the 31st Mississippi at Peach Tree Creek, and one fatality. Three of them would return to duty, including Captain Thomas J. Pulliam who would become the regiment's major and third in command, and Lycurgus Sims and John Pulliam who would both die from wounds received at Franklin, Tennessee, later that year.

In the center, opposing Featherston's brigade, was Colonel Coburn's 2nd Brigade which was formed east to west: 33rd Indiana and the 85th Indiana, with the 19th Michigan in reserve in a second line. Also, the 22nd Wisconsin's survivors, which had been up on the line just taken by the Mississippians, were mixed in with the rest of the Federal troops readying to form the countercharge. Slugging it out along the center of the gap in the ravine, Coburn's men took fearful losses. The 19th Michigan, which was in the second line, lost four men killed, thirty-three men wounded. During the remaining siege of Atlanta, the regiment suffered only two more men killed, and six men wounded.[95]

According to Lieutenant Colonel Bloodgood of the 22nd Wisconsin, the Wisconsin boys had been compelled to run from their line to avoid certain capture and he had ordered his men to "rally on the reserve" just as the rest of his "brigade came cheering over the...ridge and down into the ravine. Now the [Rebels] came pouring over the ridge we had just abandoned, and rushing down upon our lines in perfect crowds only to meet and fall before our fire. The fight raged in this way for nearly an hour, the [Rebels] coming to the charge time after time and was always repulsed." Coburn's men faced the brave veterans of the 22nd and 31st Mississippi and part of the 3rd Mississippi as they clashed along the Redland Road line.[96] The men of the 22nd Wisconsin had "fairly 'wiped out' all the stain brought upon them by the disaster at Brentwood and Thompson's Station."[97] A veteran of the 22nd Wisconsin proudly wrote home the day after the battle: "Captains Mead and Pugh did their whole duty. Lieutenants Dickinson, Jones and White, were ever at their posts, cool and fearless, Colonel Bloodgood, Adjutant Durgin, and, in fact, most every officer in the regiment," explained the soldier, "have fully proved the falsity of the assertions that they were a set of 'cowardly calves.' And the men of the ranks have shown to the world that the 22nd Wisconsin has some merit left in its columns yet." The veteran bragged, "There is hardly a man to be found in the regiment today but what made a telling shot yesterday."[98]

General John Geary, observing the charge of Featherston's Mississippi Brigade on Collier Ridge, reacted to the 22nd Wisconsin's bravery in defense of the skirmish line. When the Wisconsin men remained atop the ridge until the last minute while the rebels were swarming all around them, Geary exclaimed, "My God! What do these men mean? 'Tis the first time in my life that I ever saw a single skirmish line hold their own against three battle lines of rebels."[99]

---

[95] http://hometown.aol.com/dlharvey/19thinf.htm (1 March 2008).

[96] Priest, ed., *John T. McMahon's Diary*, 104.

[97] Racine Boy to Friend T., 21 July 1864, p. 16, subject file PW-4, Kennesaw Mountain National Battlefield Park, Kennesaw, Georgia.

[98] Ibid., 17.

[99] Ibid., 16.

Hood's First Sortie, 20 July 1864

One veteran of the 22nd Wisconsin recorded the next day, "As we were advancing up the hill the second time, one of the privates of Company C captured a set of rebel colors, but left them on the ground, and afterwards, when the 26th Wisconsin came up, the flag was picked up by some of their men." The soldier continued, "Our officers this forenoon tried to obtain the flag, as it is ours by all the rules of war. While this discussion was going on, Captain Speed, A. A. G. of our division, said to Colonel Bloodgood: 'Colonel, you needn't care for the flag; the 22nd Wisconsin have enough to cover themselves with glory.'"[100]

Major Francis Marion Gillespie of the 31st Mississippi led his men on despite increasingly overwhelming odds. Already wounded when he took command from Lieutenant Colonel Drane, Gillespie, with most of his regiment, had continued over the captured ridge only to be surrounded on three sides. Gillespie did not know that the wound to his arm had severed an artery and blood was fast flowing from his body. He led the Mississippians some 200 to 250 yards past the ridge as many of his comrades fell beside him. They fought with great courage and tenacity and met the Federal counterattack with a hand-to-hand assault. Determined to hang on, the Southerners struck like "bees swarming in the hive" fighting the Yankees in all directions. They held the surging blue wave in check for some twenty plus minutes before the overwhelming number of men in blue forced them back to the ridge.

Major Gillespie, who had so bravely and recklessly rushed his men forward, suddenly went down, mortally wounded in the chest by a minnie ball. He fell at the most advanced position and the decimated and unsupported Mississippians had to fall back to the ridge leaving Gillespie behind on the field. Private J. W. Brewer of the 1st Mississippi Battalion, which had been on the skirmish line in front of Featherston's brigade and fell in with their fellow Mississippians behind them when they neared the Federal works, attempted to rescue Major Gillespie from the field. Brewer had also been wounded and was trying to make his way back to the line. It was said that Major Gillespie was well loved among the Mississippians, not just those in the 31st Mississippi, and Brewer, "prompted by the generous impulses of a noble spirit, could not pass this favorite officer of the Brigade." The brave private gathered the major in his arms and was bearing him away when Brewer was shot through the neck. Unable to carry him any longer, he placed Major Gillespie "in the shade of a tree to die."

---

[100] Ibid., 17.

Thus fell one of the noblest of men, the purest of patriots and bravest of soldiers. Alas, he is dead, and his hunter's horn shall never again reverberate in the hills of Calhoun, his fond friends will never again be welcomed at his hospitable roof, and the social circle of brave spirits around the camp fire shall never hear that cheerful voice, or welcome that benignant smile, but a kind father, mother, brothers and sisters, shall mourn the loss of the brave soldier, and stout hearts of the brave men have shed many, many tears of affection for him, and methinks when the coming Angel shall distribute chaplets to the noble and brave, none will wear a brighter wreath than the chivalric Gillespie.[101]

Major Gillespie did not live to wed the girl waiting for him back home as she became, in the words of S. Newton Berryhill's sad tribute to the Southern dead in his poem, "Tidings from the Battlefield," "a widow ere a bride."

The Dixie Rebels, Company D, 31st Mississippi. Falling with Major Gillespie were twenty-four men from his old Company D, the "Dixie Rebels" from Calhoun County, including Privates Thomas Jesse Edwards of Banner, Mississippi, who was killed, Giles Leroy Cain who was wounded in the leg by a shell, and Robert M. Bailey, a forty-two-year-old who was shot in the left knee and unable to leave the field. Bailey was captured and taken to the US field hospital at Vining Station where his left leg was amputated on 23 July. Bailey's wife Mary waited for him in their home in Banner, Mississippi. He would never return. On 1 August, he was transported by rail to the hospital in Chattanooga, where he died on 26 September.

For Third Sergeant Henry W. Green, it was a heroic but costly day. The young twenty-year-old had risen from private to third sergeant in two years under the watchful eye of Colonel Stephens. His parents, Abraham and Elizabeth Green of Cherry Hill, were certainly proud of their son. Born in Georgia in 1844, the young man had returned to his native state to defend its invasion. The brave lad proved himself that day courageously charging past the ridge and supporting Major Gillespie. Green fell, shot in the right thigh, too crippled to move to safety. Green would not live to see his twenty-first birthday. He was taken by the Federal captors by rail to the Chattanooga hospital where he died on 25 October 1864 after failing to recover from an amputation surgery

---

[101] Surgeon J.N.H. to the *Macon Beacon*, 15 August 1864.

of his leg.[102] With him in the attack were First Lieutenant Thomas J. Lyle and Private Thomas Jefferson Douglas, Sr., who fell mortally wounded.

Fifth Sergeant Thomas A. "Bud" Griffin was wounded severely in the thigh with a gunshot wound to his right lower thigh. He was taken to Macon where he convalesced at the Floyd House. Private Peter May Cobb, whose brother William W. Cobb had died from wounds received at Vicksburg exactly one year before on 20 July 1863, fell wounded and was taken to the Ocmuglee Hospital in Macon to recover. Peter Cobb, born in 1825 in North Carolina, also made it home to his wife, Lucy Ann Parker Cobb, much to the relief of his parents, Gray Cobb and Winifred Wooten Cobb. Corporal Benjamin H. Fuller fell severely wounded in the arm. His wife, Lucinda at home in Ponticola, Pontotoc County, Mississippi, waited anxiously for news of his fate. So, too, did his parents, William F. Fuller and Eliza Lauderdale who prayed for the safe return of their twenty-year-old son. He would recover in time only to be wounded again just three months later at Decatur, Alabama, before he would make it home. A pair of cousins from Sarepta, privates John Ashford Gore and James William Gore, were casualties that day. John Gore was struck in the leg and James Gore was captured.

Another Rebel, thirty-seven-year-old Private James M. Ray of Carroll County fell beyond the works with a severe gunshot wound in the left leg. Believing he would not survive his wound, the Yanks did not treat him until 23 July at their field hospital. Three days later on 26 July, he was taken to their field hospital at Vining Station, where he was treated and on 27 July moved by rail to Nashville. By then it was too late to stop gangrene from setting in and on 4 September he finally succumbed to a "shot wound of leg and effects gangrene; exhaustion from continued irritation of gunshot" and died with "no personal effects." No doubt he thought often of his beloved wife Elizabeth whom he would never see on earth again. He was buried in the City Cemetery in Nashville. Private Benjamin F. Grammar, twenty-eight, was also hit in the leg, but he managed to limp off of the battle field with the help of his younger brother, Private Joseph W. Grammer, twenty-six, and the two continued fighting for the rest of the war.

Private William B. Robertston suffered a "penetrating gun shot wound to his head" and held on to life for two painful days in the hot Georgia sun before he died and was buried in the field by the Northerners. Born in 1837 in

---

[102] Compiled Service Records, *Medical & Surgical History of the War of the Rebellion*, (Washington, DC: US Government Printing Office, 1870) 3: 136.

The Battle of Peach Tree Creek

Alabama, the twenty-seven-year-old Robertson from Banner would never lay eyes on his wife Rachel E. Countiss Robertson again. She would live for sixty more years a Confederate widow. Third Corporal Jasper N. Stewart, another pupil of Colonel Stephens, fell mortally wounded that terrible day on the ridge. He was only twenty. His parents, William Stewart, Jr., and Salina Tedford Stewart, and his brother Anderson A. Stewart, all of Calhoun County, Mississippi, would never be certain of his fate. Private Robert C. Stribbling, too, fell mortally wounded and shared his comrade's fate. The son of Mark Mitchell Stribling and Mary Ann Chapman Stribbling, would never return to Cherry Hill in Calhoun County, Mississippi where his wife, Jemima, awaited him. These three Dixie Rebels were all buried where they fell.

Brothers Isaiah David Stacy, who was twenty, and Miles Henry Stacy, age nineteen, both privates with the Dixie Rebels, fell beyond the works and were separated. Isaiah had been hit in the shoulder and was able to fall back to the works and then back to the Southern lines where he was sent to the disabled camp at Lauderdale, Mississippi, to sit out the rest of the war. Brother Miles was not so lucky. He had joined the Dixie Rebels as a "substitute" for his father, William M. Stacy, on 15 December 1862, when he was only eighteen and had served his country well. He was shot in the right leg and overrun by the blue tide surging back up to the works. Reluctantly, he surrendered to the conquering foe who did not take him from the field until 25 July. On 27 July he was at Chattanooga and by the 29th he was at Nashville where he was finally treated properly.

For First Corporal James F. Ross, the events of the day were just the beginning of his adventures. Just twenty years old, he had been promoted to first corporal of the Dixie Rebels that spring by Colonel Stephens. The young Ross fell behind the Federal lines after receiving gunshot wounds to his shoulder and hip and was unable to move when what was left of his regiment fell back. Thought to be suffering from fatal wounds, he was ignored by the Yankee surgeons for several days until he was moved to the field hospital at Vining Station on 28 July and sent to Chattanooga on 3 August. Ross was sent first to the general hospital and then to the Federal prison camp in Chattanooga. He managed to escape and by 21 August, he had returned to his regiment in the trenches around Atlanta where he resumed his duties.

Private Wilks Adams fell wounded in the action and made it back to his lines the next day. On 22 July, he was taken to St. Mary's Hospital in LaGrange, Georgia, with a number of wounded from Hardee's and Chetham's corps who had attacked Sherman's men at Decatur that day to recover. Wilks

Adams would recover sufficiently to rejoin the Dixie Rebels and serve with them all the way to their surrender at North Carolina the following spring. Nineteen-year-old Private David Henry Alexander was also wounded but was able to continue to serve with the Dixie Rebels all the way to its surrender, as well.

The Dixie Rebels also counted to their casualty list that day Private James Lawson Wilson who was shot in the side. Private James B. Barton, who had earlier seen service with the 4th Mississippi, was wounded in the hand and had his middle and ring fingers amputated at the Ocmulgee Hospital in Macon, Georgia. Barton, from Pine Valley, Mississippi, eventually recovered and returned to the Dixie Rebels to fight the rest of the war. Private Richard M. Bailey was also wounded and taken to the Ocmulgee Hospital, where he was treated, but he never recovered. Finally giving in to his wounds on 14 August 1864, he was buried at the Rose Hill Cemetery in Macon. In all, the Dixie Rebels suffered four killed on the field, nineteen wounded (six mortally), and nine captured of whom eight were among the wounded for a total of twenty-four men. Ten of these men would die from their wounds while only six would return to duty.

Harrison's Brigade. General Harrison's brigade, including from east to west the 129th Illinois led by Colonel Henry Chase, the 79th Ohio under Colonel Henry G. Kennett, and the 102nd Illinois temporarily commanded by Lieutenant Colonel James M. Mannon, Colonel Franklin C. Smith being wounded on 16 June near Gilgal Church, in the first line, and the 70th Indiana led by Lieutenant Colonel Samuel Merrill and the 105th Illinois under Colonel Daniel Dustin in the second line, together with remnants of the displaced 136th New York from the skirmish line, met Featherston's assault from the west side of the far ridge.[103] One Federal soldier in the 136th New York remarked that "the rebels came out of their works and met us like men."[104]

The 40th Mississippi pressed over the Collier Ridge to the left of and in support of the 31st Mississippi, and advanced toward the Collier Mill. To its left, the 57th and 55th Alabama and a portion of the 12th Louisiana in Scott's brigade came up in support of the attack, but were checked by the crossfire in the valley created by Tanyard Branch where it turned to the north toward Peach Tree Creek. By the time that the Alabamians and Louisianans in Scott's brigade crossed the Tanyard Branch and advanced toward the Mill, Harrison's brigade

---

[103] Scaife, *The Campaign for Atlanta*, 156.
[104] Priest, ed., *John T. McMahon's Diary*, 104.

The Battle of Peach Tree Creek

had already begun to organize the Federal's counteroffensive and were in position on the lower ridge near the mill and ready to receive the Rebel parry.[105]

As soon as Featherston's brigade reached the Federal line on Collier Ridge, the 40th Mississippi's veterans found themselves exposed and vulnerable to Federal fire on their left flank and front as Yankees from Harrison's brigade and from the companies of the 136th New York which had been on the skirmish line. The white hats of the New Yorkers from the 136th New York Infantry Regiment, which hailed from the finger lakes region of the Empire State, made them distinctive as they held their ground while waiting for Harrison's brigade to come up in support near the Collier Mill. The onrushing Mississippians had compelled the New Yorkers to fall back, but they had only retreated a couple of hundred yards below the ridge where they rallied on a slight knoll overlooking the mill. From that position the New Yorkers held off the men of the 40th Mississippi from sweeping the ravine through the mill site until Harrison's regiments could arrive. Survivor John T. McMahon of the 136th New York remembered, "at first our men gave way but it was not long before we drove them off the battle ground and we held it with all their dead and wounded and a great many prisoners."[106]

The first reinforcements to join the 136th New York were some hundred men armed with Spencer rifles from the 79th Ohio and the 102nd Illinois under the command of Captain Williamson,[107] specifically Company K of the 79th Ohio and several companies of the 102nd Illinois including companies C, E, G, and K from Mercer County.[108] It is unclear which company was assigned from the 102nd Illinois but possibly it was Company E led by Captain Sedwick.[109] When the fight began, Harrison ordered those armed with Spencer repeating rifles from the 102nd Illinois and the 70th Indiana to join the New Yorkers on the main line, who had been swept up in the retreat to the second ridge. This brigade was somewhat to the left of and overlapped Featherston's brigade, being opposite the 40th Mississippi and part of the 31st Mississippi, and

---

[105] Scrapbook 27, pp. 10–15, MSS 130, Wilbur G. Kurtz Collection, Kenan Research Center, Atlanta History Center.

[106] Priest, ed., *John T. McMahon's Diary*, 104.

[107] Wood, "Report of the Operations of the 3rd Brigade," 44; *OR*, ser. 1, vol. 38, pt. 2, serial 73, p. 345.

[108] Cyrus E. Custis to Wilbur G. Kurtz, 9 March 1932, Maps, Clippings, Notes and Files, MSS 130, box 3, folder 7, Wilbur G. Kurtz Collection, Kenan Research Center, Atlanta History Center.

[109] www.illinoiscivilwar.org/cw102.html (28 September 2008); *OR*, ser. 1, vol. 38, pt. 2, serial 73, p. 354.

Harrison used his position and his Spencer riflemen to full advantage on the left flank of the Mississippians. Here, just to the left of the Collier Mill Harrison's Spencer riflemen began to pour it on the attackers and "punished the enemy severely."[110]

When news of the impending Confederate attack reached Harrison, and, after he and Coburn, commander of the 2nd Brigade in Ward's division, had conferred, the future United States president jumped into action and had his men in motion quickly. While they had to traverse the Tanyard Branch and its steep banks, with a couple of his regiments, the 105th Illinois and 70th Indiana in the rear line, having to cross Tanyard Branch at least twice, Harrison's brigade had a shorter distance to travel to engage the enemy than Coburn and Wood's men. Consequently, "the 1st Brigade got a short distance in advance of the other two brigades, and had crossed the level ground, and was ascending the higher ridge, when it met the Rebels, who had gained the crest of the ridge in advance of our line, and delivered their fire," recalled Newton.[111] Newton's comrades in the 129th Illinois were facing the thrust of the 40th Mississippi and the 31st Mississippi as the left part of Featherston's brigade raced for the ravine on which the Collier Mill rested. When Featherston's Mississippians fired on them, according to Newton, "as they were on higher ground than we were, it did not prove very effective; but now it was our turn, and the slaughter was dreadful."[112]

As the Mississippians were coming down the north slope of Collier Ridge and into the ravine below today's Golfview and Redland Drives, they fired a hurried volley at the approaching blue mass of Ward's division that came over the smaller ridge and into the ravine below them. The Confederates had overshot in their haste, but the Federal counter-volley against the Mississippians, who were silhouetted against the light blue sky over the Collier Ridge above them, found their mark. Over to the left of Featherston's attack, there was a gap between the left of his line and the Tanyard Branch. The 129th Illinois reached this point at about the same time or just after Featherston's men had breached the Collier Ridge line. According to Newton, "we never halted until we reached the crest of the higher ridge, along which was a high rail fence, and which we were climbing over when we met face to face."[113] In those days, Collier Road ran along the crest of the ridge until it neared the Tanyard Branch

---

[110] *OR*, ser. 1, vol. 38, pt. 2, serial 73, 345.
[111] Newton, *129th Illinois*, 400.
[112] Ibid., 400.
[113] Ibid., 400.

and met an old crossroads known as Old Montgomery Ferry Road, which paralleled the Tanyard Branch along the lower part of the southern slope of the Collier Ridge between the Tanyard Branch and the Buckhead Road.[114]

Some have incorrectly referred to the stretch of Collier Road between Peachtree Street and the bridge crossing over Tanyard Branch as Montgomery Ferry Road. Before the Civil War and prior to the settlement and cultivation of this area by pioneers during the 1830s and 1840s, an old Native American trail followed along the southern side of Collier Ridge near its bottom with the plain created by Tanyard Branch running northeast from today's Peachtree Street at or below its intersection with 26th Street to the Collier Mill. By the time of the Civil War, Andrew Jackson Collier and other settlers had carved out several fields between Tanyard Branch and Peach Tree Creek and cultivated them for two or three decades. Moreover, Mr. Collier had built his home along the Buckhead Road (today's Peachtree Street) near the southwest corner of the intersection of today's Peachtree Street and Collier Road, and he had erected a grist mill in the bend of Tanyard Branch half a mile west of his house. His field road, which ran from near his house at the Buckhead Road along the ridge line west to the mill where it intersected with the old Montgomery Ferry Road, had become the predominant path for east-west traffic and the Montgomery Ferry Road had been ignored, so much so, that the Montgomery Ferry Road was no longer suitable for wagon travel in that stretch.[115] Collier Road and old Montgomery Ferry Road converged about a hundred or so yards east of today's bridge over Tanyard Branch and turned sharply north, toward Collier Mill and down into the ravine adjoining it. (This is located near today's Redland Road). "One of my mess-mates," lamented Newton, "marching by my side sprang to the fence in front of me, and the next instant he fell into my arms, pierced by a Rebel bullet; but their was no time to stop, and over we went."[116]

Next, the two lines charged toward one another in a rare race to meet each other in hand-to-hand conflict. With many of the Yankees reaching the ravine first, the Mississippians fought to wrest possession of the ground from them.

---

[114] Scrapbook 26 ½, MSS 130,, Wilbur G. Kurtz Collection, Kenan Research Center, Atlanta History Center, "Collier's Mill" www.buckhead.net/history/colliers-mill/index.html (8 November 2008).

[115] Robert McKee, "Where Trim Homes Stand on Collier Road Fierce Sounds of Battle Rang 91 Years Ago," *Atlanta Journal*, 21 July 1955, 6, MSS 130, Wilbur G. Kurtz Collection, Kenan Research Center, Atlanta History Center; The Buckhead Coalition, "www.buckhead.net/history/colliers-mill/index.html (8 November 2008).

[116] Newton, *129th Illinois*, 400.

Hood's First Sortie, 20 July 1864

"The 2nd Brigade [Coburn's] being a little in our rear, the Rebels began pouring into the temporary break in our lines, when the 129th [Illinois] took a half wheel to the left and checked their advance," explained Newton. The 105th Illinois and the 70th Indiana also wheeled left behind the 129th Illinois and moved to cover the gap. By the time that they had plugged the gap, the left of the 105th Illinois connected to the right of Coburn's 2nd Brigade, and the right of the 70th Indiana connected to the left of the 129th Illinois. "The other brigades now coming up," recorded Newton, "their lines [the Mississippians] were broken and they were thrown into confusion, and in our regimental front it was a hand-to-hand fight."[117] Newton remembered one of his comrades recording that Peach Tree Creek was "one of four or five occasions when the two armies crossed bayonets."[118] Disputing this assertion, Newton explained, "Bayonets were not crossed, as they were not fixed, but in some instances muskets were clubbed."[119] Colonel Henry Chase of the 129th Illinois, "after emptying his revolver, threw it away, caught up a musket, grabbed some of the Rebels by the arms, gave them a kick, and, with language more forcible than polite, ordered them to the rear."[120]

After pushing the Alabamians and Louisianans from Scott's brigade back to the ravine and the skirt of woods across the edge of the field where the Rebels had first appeared, the men of the 79th Ohio and 102nd Illinois turned their attention across the small millpond to their left and the Mississippians of Featherston's brigade that faced the rest of Harrison's brigade along the Collier Road and ridge. "The [79th Ohio and 102nd Illinois] crossed the little bottom in line which the 129th Illinois in strugling through there and crossing the branch fell a little in our rear when they met their foe," explained First Lieutenant Custis of the 79th Ohio who witnessed the action. "The 129th Illinois met the opposing brigade about three rods [50 feet] below the 79th Ohio line on the Collier Road. Co. K of 79th Regt. armed with Spencer rifles and a Co. of 102nd Ill. so armed placed at right angles in rear of 79th [Ohio] battle line poured an enfilading volley in quick succession," continued Custis. "Co. K of the 79th [Ohio] filed left and went into line in our rear and a Co. from the 102nd Ill. went into line with Co. K both armed with Spencer rifles opened fire at close range into [Featherston's Mississippians]. Thier loss was fearful." Custis was able to watch the fighting from the ridge opposite the small millpond where his

---

[117] Ibid.
[118] Ibid.
[119] Ibid.
[120] Ibid.

men had turned back the right half of Scott's brigade. Custis remembered that the Mississippians near the mill were "rushed away in great disorder."[121]

According to Lieutenant Colonel Samuel Merrill of the 70th Indiana, Harrison's old regiment, the men "passed over Peach Tree Creek, a deep and muddy stream, on a bridge of rails and poles, and stacked arms in the bottomland not far from the water. The men soon scattered, some getting dinner, some going to the creek, some picking blackberries." Merrill and his boys did not expect what came next. "About the middle of the afternoon the skirmishers on the hill in front began to fire at a furious rate, and some of our men who had gone up the hill to get a view of the enemy came hurrying down the hill at a breakneck pace." Excited, the men and officers all knew their role and, instead of dreading the challenge, it appeared that Harrison's men were welcoming the opportunity to catch the Rebels out in the open: "Everybody in our command was rushing into line, the officers calling to men, 'Fall in! Fall in!' and the men exclaiming, 'O God, boys, they are out of their works! We've got 'em now!'"[122]

Harrison sent his veteran Midwesterners to meet the onrushing Mississippians. Merrill noted, "Then came the order, 'Forward, double-quick!' and off we rushed. We could see the skirmish line doubling its efforts in loading and shooting from behind the few rails used for protection." The Indianans were moving south beginning from the portion of today's Bobby Jones's golf course located just north of Golf View Road and moving along the right or west side of today's Golf View Road and toward Redland Drive, with the 105th Illinois between it and the Tanyard Branch to the west. "Just as we reached the top of a low ridge, about one-third as high as the big hill and parallel to it, and were about two-thirds of the way from the creek to that hill, we saw the collision between the Confederates and our skirmishers, the later being forced back, loading and firing as they yielded."[123] The large hill was, of course, Collier Ridge on which the Collier Road and Old Montgomery Road met in that sector just above the mill, and the New Yorkers on skirmish fell back near where Redland Road and Golf View Drive meet and begin to bend south and approach today's Collier Road.

---

[121] Cyrus E. Custis to Wilbur G. Kurtz, 3 February 1932, 2, MSS 130, box 3, folder 7, Wilbur G. Kurtz Collection, Kenan Research Center, Atlanta History Center.

[122] Samuel Merrill, *The Seventieth Indiana Volunteer Infantry in the War of the Rebellion* (Indianapolis: Bobbs-Merrill Co., 1900)139.

[123] Ibid., 139.

Hood's First Sortie, 20 July 1864

Merrill continued, "The 129th Illinois was formed in front of the 70th Indiana, but when it had passed over the ridge down into a ravine, we fired a volley over its head and lay down." The Indianans were on the sassafras-laden ridge just northeast of the mill and generally following the path of today's Golf View Drive while by now the charging Mississippians were at Redland Drive and Golf View Drive as they headed for the ravine when they received the first volley from the Indianans. The Indiana leader explained, "As the enemy, attracted by the fact that our division was the only one unprotected by breastworks, came rushing over the hill, the Illinois troops obliqued to the right and gave the Indiana men a chance to move forward."[124] Actually, the men of the 129th Illinois were guided on their right flank by the Tanyard Branch, and as it bent and ran to the southwest from the mill site, the land in front of the 129th Illinois opened up creating a much wider space to defend. As the Illinoisans "obliqued right," or turned southeast in their line to meet the threat posed by the onrushing Mississippians of the 40th Mississippi on Featherston's left flank, the two sides exploded into a brutal struggle for the ravine just east and south of the mill. It was in this area, behind the 129th Illinois and the 70th Indiana that Colonel Benjamin Harrison was posted during the battle. The bushes and trees located around the mill site and the steep bluff over which his two right regiments, the 79th Ohio and the 102nd Illinois crossed to protect Sloan's Battery of General Geary's division, obscured Harrison's view of the fine work of those two regiments during the battle.[125]

Meanwhile, the 70th Indiana found open space in their front in which to maneuver and meet the remainder of the 40th Mississippi and part of the 31st Mississippi, which was next in Featherston's line. "Down the ridge we went, through the sassafras bushes, over a gully some four feet wide and seven feet deep, up the high hill, on the top of which were the piles of rails thrown together by the skirmishers," according to Colonel Merrill. His regiment had followed the 129th Illinois down the first ridge and into the ravine along the path of today's Golf View Drive. Also, to the right of the 70th Indiana, the 105th Illinois, which had also been in the second line, found the space in front of the left half of their regiment open between the right of the 70th Indiana and the left of the 129th Illinois. "The Confederate line broke in our regimental front and fled down the hill, but on the right a few hundred of the enemy made a

---

[124] Ibid., 139–40.
[125] Cyrus E. Custis to Wilbur G. Kurtz, 9 March 1932, p. 1, MSS 130, box 3, folder 7, Wilbur G. Kurtz Collection, Kenan Research Center, Atlanta History Center.

determined fight to stem the tide of the brigade's advance." Merrill described the plight of the 40th Mississippi, which was being flanked by the 129th Illinois to their left. Additionally, there were a number of riflemen from the west side of Collier Mill and the small millpond from the 79th Ohio of Harrison's brigade who were by now advanced far enough to actually be on line and a bit behind the Mississippians, and they began to rain lead down on the left and rear of the now exhausted and outnumbered men of the 40th Mississippi. Describing the action of the 129th Illinois and the 105th Illinois's capture of what is most likely the national flag of the 40th Mississippi, and the capture of the 31st Mississippi's battle flag by one of the skirmishers from the 136th New York, Merrill said, "There is a struggle for and the capture of flags by the regiments of our brigade to the right, and then the hand-to-hand contest is over."[126] One source, however, claims that the 129th Illinois also captured one of Featherston's Mississippi regiments' flags during the struggle.[127]

Veteran J. H. Kelly of the 70th Indiana remembered, "We advanced in two lines, the 129th Illinois in our front. Just as the 70th [Indiana] reached the top of a low ridge and the 129th a small ravine in our front the enemy came pouring over the hill. Both regiments opened fire, the one in front from the ravine," explained Kelly, "and the 70th from its more exposed position on the ridge. The Rebel lines continued to advance in face of our two lines of fire. The lay of the ground enabled the second line to fire over the heads of the first. The Rebels were losing heavily, and," according to the Indianan, "began to halt, waver, kink up, and finally break for the rear. Their front line in going back broke up their two rear lines; so there was a complete rout. In the morning we gathered and buried sixty rebel dead in a space the length of our regiment."[128] The 70th Indiana faced predominately the 31st Mississippi, with portions of the 22nd Mississippi in front of their left, and a part of the 40th Mississippi to the right front of the Indianans.

The 40th Mississippi and her sister regiment the 31st Mississippi to her right could not continue to withstand the withering fire in their front and flank. Moreover, the supporting Alabama and Louisiana regiments of Scott's brigade could not advance far enough up the Tanyard Branch valley to effectively protect the left flank of the Mississippians. The topography of the ground naturally formed a *V* with the Tanyard Branch flowing through it, and with the

---

[126] Merrill, *The Seventieth Indiana*, 140.

[127] T. R. Hartman, "Battle of Peach Tree Creek," *National Tribune*, 20 September 1906, 2 (in which the 129th Illinois claims the capture of one stand of colors).

[128] Merrill, *The Seventieth Indiana*, 143–44.

Hood's First Sortie, 20 July 1864

Collier Ridge on the east, and ridges to the west, each extending 45 degrees out from the Branch and 90 degrees from each other, the Confederates of Loring's division had charged into a death trap. Geary's infantry together with two batteries of artillery were posted along the series of ridges west of the branch, which effectively blocked Scott's men from coming to the aid of the Mississippians.

Lieutenant Colonel Merrill of the 70th Indiana described the flight of the Mississippians. "As our adversaries hastened down the hill and through a wide field in the direction of Atlanta, volley after volley was poured after them, dotting the field with the dead and dying." The ground was littered with fallen Rebels. "Along the slope of the hill inclining toward the city, deep gutters had been washed by the rains, and the foe had hidden in them as a protection from the infantry. Some of these washes were subjected to an enfilading fire from the batteries." This artillery fire came from Sloan's battery on the west side of Collier's Mill. Merrill reported, "The next day these ravines were found to be filled with the mangled remains of Confederate soldiers. A retreating regiment left a flag with the staff stuck in the ground about a quarter of a mile in our front." It is unclear to which regiment the flag belonged. "As night approached as couple of our men added it to the six already captured by the Third Division," Merrill added.[129] According to one veteran of the 40th Mississippi:

> July 20, at Peachtree Creek the regiment suffered heavy loss. Colonel Colbert being absent, sick, Lieutenant-Colonel George P. Wallace commanded the regiment and lost an arm. Major W. McD. Gibbons was mortally wounded and left on the field with the dead, who were buried by the Union troops. This action was an assault upon Sherman's line just after he had crossed the Chattahoochee near Atlanta, the first of Hood's assaults. The regiment behaved nobly and drove the Federal line in its front from the temporary line of rail barricades, but in doing so they crossed an open field in which the brigade was shot to pieces. Nothing remained but to retreat across the field, yielding the toll of sacrifice at every step.[130]

Captain J. A. Cooper, commanding Company C, the "Confederate Rebels" from Attala County, in the 40th Mississippi was wounded severely. He subsequently died on 15 August in an Atlanta hospital.[131] Also wounded from

---

[129] Ibid., 140.

[130] Dunbar Rowland, *Military History of Mississippi, 1803–1898,* ed. H. Grady Howell, Jr. (Spartanburg SC: The Reprint Company, Publishers, 1978) 343.

[131] www.misissippiscv.org (25 February 2008).

the 40th Mississippi was Private William Thomas McDaniel of Company G. By 24 July, he was in a hospital in Griffin, Georgia.[132] Also from Company G, Private John Newton Moore was captured.[133] Chaplin J. F. N. Huddleston was killed, while Company D, the "Attala Guards," lost three men severely wounded while eight men were either killed or captured out of the twenty men that it brought into the fight. In Company H, the "Parrot Rifles," nine men were wounded and thirteen were killed or captured, making it the bloodiest day in the history of the 40th Mississippi. After the battle, it was reported that 10 men were killed, 57 men were wounded, and 27 men were missing or captured for a total loss of 94 men out of the 245 men who participated in the attack, but careful research reveals a total loss of 107 men from the 40th Mississippi at Peach Tree Creek with 12 killed, 58 wounded, and another 37 missing or captured with many of the missing dead on the field.[134]

Some of the scenes of battle experienced by the 70th Indiana that were most memorable included, "The Mexican war veteran, Captain Carson, empties his pistol at the enemy after he had aligned his company, and exclaims as the 129th [Illinois] obliques to the right and gives the left wing of the 70th [Indiana] freedom to move: 'Colonel, can't we go forward?'"[135] Another Mexican War veteran from the 70th Indiana, Captain Endsley, shouts, "The day is ours, but keep back there on the left." A third captain from the Indiana regiment, "Captain Matlock, laughingly answers an anxious inquiry as he is assisted from the field: 'Yes, hit just as I expected.'"[136] Private Matthias Stuck, "faint from the uphill race and from the sight of a dead comrade, asks [Colonel Merrill] to let him shift his position, so that his head may be shaded by a sassafras bush, but is restored to his senses by a bullet through the leg, so as to be able jokingly to ask if he can't find a shade a little farther back."[137] A fourth captain, Meredith, "ought to be in the hospital," according to Colonel Merrill, and "moves at the head of his company with countenance in which pain and triumph mingle." The Indiana colonel described also the heroism of his adjutant: "Acting Adjutant Cox, beautiful as a girl, brave as a lion, rushes through the left

---

[132] www.rootsweb.com/~msattala/40th2.htm (25 February 2008).

[133] John Newton Moore, death notice, *Confederate Veteran* (October 1909): 521.

[134] *OR*, ser. 1, vol. 38, pt. 3, serial 74, 884; *Supplement to the Official Records of the Union and Confederate Armies*, (Wilmington NC: Broadfoot Publishing Company, 1995–2001) pt. 2, vol. 34, ser. 46, 163–74 (hereafter *Supplement to* OR); Rowland, *Military History of Mississippi*, 343.

[135] Merrill, *The Seventieth Indiana*, 141.

[136] Ibid., 141.

[137] Ibid., 141.

of the Illinois regiment to the hilltop, his form as he reaches the crest outlined against the sky, waves his hat exultantly, and beckons a command 'Forward!' for no voice could be heard in the uproar."[138]

As the battle wore on, the Federal troops sent some men to the rear to bring up more ammunition. According to Lieutenant Colonel Merrill, "In the course of the afternoon as the supply of ammunition ran low, men from each company were sent to the ordnance wagons in the rear for boxes of cartridges." The Confederates had no resupply, and many remained pinned down until darkness shielded their withdrawal. "Just after the 70th [Indiana] had won its final position on Peach Tree Heights [Collier Ridge], while the rattle of musketry was almost drowned in the awful roar of the artillery, for it was not only 'cannon to the right of them, cannon to left of them,' but cannon behind them also, firing over their heads." Merrill remembered, "an aide came dashing up to the officer in command of the regiment [Merrill], exclaiming, 'General Sherman sends word, "Hold your ground and he will take Atlanta before sundown."'" Merrill proudly responded, "We'll die right here!" But, Sherman would take another forty days and many more lives before taking the Gate City.[139]

Private J. J. Moore of the 40th Mississippi explained that "Featherston's Brigade was put into the hottest part of the fight at Peachtree Creek. I was, with others," he added, "taken prisoner. After the firing had ceased, and while going to the rear of the Yankee lines, I noticed a young officer with a flag of the 33rd Mississippi. I believe he told me he belonged to the 22nd Michigan [actually the 26th Wisconsin]." Moore explained his journey to a Federal prison camp. "Next day we were taken to Marietta and from there to Chattanooga, crowded in box and stock cars. Our guard through Tennessee were soldiers who had been at the front, and were all right. At Nashville we were put in charge of a lot of hundred day men," who did not give the same courteous treatment.[140]

The Orr Guards, Company A, 31st Mississippi. Company A, nicknamed the "Orr Guards" after its organizer and the first colonel of the regiment, Confederate congressman Jehu A. Orr, had taken the field with one of the largest companies in the regiment with a little over thirty men, but before the day was over, twenty-nine would fall, including its captain, first and third lieutenants, four sergeants, three corporals and nineteen privates. Captain John R. Ketchum was killed while leading his men over the ridge and down into the

---

[138] Ibid., 141–42.

[139] Ibid., 141.

[140] J. J. Moore, Jackson, Mississippi, "Camp Douglas," *Confederate Veteran* (June 1903): 270.

den of oncoming Yankees. Also killed were Third Lieutenant John C. Morrow who left a widow and two small children back home in Saltillo to mourn his loss; Second Sergeant Joel John Morgan Johnson, only twenty-four, who had previously served in General Adams's 14th Mississippi; Private Carol P. Pritchard who was forty-two and who was supposed to be working at the hospital in Lauderdale Springs, Mississippi, but the need for men at the front had compelled his being pressed into service; and two twenty-eight-year-old privates from Red Land, Mississippi, Samuel W. Gillion, and Benjamin F. Black.

First Lieutenant John W. Prude fell in the hand-to-hand fighting and was left on the field where he died, as was Private Francis M. Wood, twenty-seven, who was killed in the fighting. Another Wood, First Sergeant Thomas J. Wood, was wounded in the side and taken to the Ocmulgee Hospital in Macon to recover. The twenty-five-year-old sergeant would later be moved to the hospital in Augusta, Georgia, to convalesce and would not see action again. Third Sergeant H. A. Abernathy was shot in the right side when a bullet grazed him. After being treated in the Macon hospital and receiving a thirty-day furlough, he was as good as new, ready to shoot Yankees again, until hostilities were suspended the following April in North Carolina. Likewise, the thirty-three-year-old Private John M. Aycock was wounded in the arm and bowels, but would return from the Ocmulgee Hospital in Macon to fight with the Orr Guards the rest of the war. So, too, would Private James M. Edington who was wounded in the nose, and First Corporal John R. Hancock who was wounded in the forefinger. For forty-two-year-old George W. Warren, it would be a painful day. The old private was shot in the groin and would spend the rest of the war in hospitals where he had previously served as a nurse.

Finding himself surrounded, 6-foot, 1-inch Private James M. Craigue surrendered. The fair-haired, gray-eyed soldier would spend the rest of the war at Camp Douglas, Illinois. Private George W. Flaherty sustained gunshot wounds to his left leg and shoulder and was left on the field. He was taken on 23 July to the field hospital where his leg was amputated, and on 1 August he was sent to the US hospital in Chattanooga to recover. Private Thomas J. Flaherty would not leave his brother George's side when he fell, and thus he spent the rest of the war in Camp Douglas.

Also captured were the gray-eyed Private Johnson Mathis who joined the Flaherty clan in Camp Douglas, and Private Edward L. McMahan who had fallen with a gunshot wound to his left thigh. The Federal surgeons amputated McMahan's leg at Vining Station on 23 July and then sent him to Chattanooga.

Hood's First Sortie, 20 July 1864

By 10 August he was placed in the general prisoner population and sent to Camp Chase, Ohio, where he suffered and eventually died on 7 December 1864, with "disease of the brain." In other words, the shock of his wounds and the infection to his body from the gangrene to his leg had caused the thirty-eight-year-old McMahan to go into a coma before he died.

Private Martin V. Harman, only twenty-one, was shot in his left arm, which would be amputated at the Ocmulgee Hospital in Macon. Also wounded were fellow Orr Guards Private James R. Manning, hit in the arm; Private Madison Purcell, shot in the hand; and Fourth Corporal William C. Polk, struck in the leg. Privates Charlie C. Reagan and John T. Reagan were both shot: Charlie was hit in the arm and was treated at the hospital in Macon; John, hit in the left arm and back, was left on the field to die. John was a tall, handsome young man, with blonde hair and blue eyes. The 6-foot, 4-inch nineteen-year-old would eventually recover after treatments of "water dressings" by Northern doctors. He spent the rest of the war in Camp Chase.

Three brothers named Skinner had joined the Orr Guards back in Red Land when the company was first mustered into service on 28 February 1862. Only two of them remained. Privates John Beale Skinner and Richard La Fayette Skinner followed their comrades up the ridge. The thirty-three-year-old John fell wounded by a gunshot, but his twenty-six-year-old brother Richard carried him back to safety where he would sit out the rest of the war in hospitals in Macon and Meridian. For two young corporals named Youngblood, it would be their last charge, each falling to crippling wounds to their legs. The twenty-year-old Second Corporal Claiborn J. Youngblood and the twenty-one-year-old Third Corporal Andrew W. Youngblood would be treated in hospitals in Georgia and Mississippi. Of the twenty-nine men in Company A who fell, nine would die, eighteen were wounded, of whom five were captured, and two were captured without wounds. Only seven of those wounded returned to fight with what was left of the Orr Guards.

Captain Sam A. West, from the 79th Ohio in Col. Harrison's brigade, was impressed with the Rebel attack: "This was the first open field fight the enemy had given us from the beginning of the campaign." According to West, the regiment was drawn up by Lieutenant Colonel Azariah Wall Doan, who commanded the Ohioans during the battle, along the foot of a hill. Doan quickly took the regiment up the hill to the summit just as the Rebels were trying to take the height. "The assault of the enemy was an exceedingly vigorous one, but

The Battle of Peach Tree Creek

handsomely repulsed by our forces, with severe loss to him."[141] The 79th Ohio would suffer ten killed and another forty-eight wounded that day.[142] Next to the 79th Ohio, the 129th Illinois came on in support and pressed to retake the lost ridge. They, too, would suffer heavily, losing twelve killed outright and another fifty-two officers and men wounded. To their right, the 102nd Illinois, finding no Rebels in their front, wheeled to the left and began pouring fire on the left and rear of the Mississippians.

> The enemy was discovered advancing in heavy column in a direction toward the left of the brigade and moved directly in front of the 79th Ohio and 129th Illinois and the 70th Indiana, occupying on this occasion the left of the brigade, the 105th Illinois…as a support…, the shock of the charge falling heaviest on the 129th Ill. and 79th Ohio. There being no enemy in our immediate front we changed our position by wheeling slightly toward the left and opened upon the advancing column an enfilading fire, pouring volley after volley in quick succession, such as the Spencer rifle alone can give, until we had the proud satisfaction of seeing the enemy vanquished and seeking safety.[143]

Not being near enough to be in the hand-to-hand fighting, the 102nd Illinois had relatively small losses, but still suffered two killed and ten wounded. Included in the losses sustained by the 102nd Illinois were Private Leyman B. Straw of Company B and Sergeant Harmon C. Shinn of Company H who were killed, and First Lieutenant John C. Reynolds of Company G who was mortally wounded, succumbing to his wounds on 8 August 1864. Behind them the 70th Indiana and the 105th Illinois in the reserve line oblique to the left to fill the gap created between Harrison's and Coburn's brigades. They hit the left front of the 31st Mississippi and the 22nd Mississippi at about the same time as Coburn's brigade. The regiments of Harrison's brigade had come upon the left flank of the Mississippians and found themselves almost to the rear of them when they advanced over the small wooded ridge. They came crashing down on the left flanks of the 40th, 31st, and 22nd Mississippi while Colonel Coburn's brigade hit them from the front.

The Dixie Guards, Company B, 31st Mississippi. The Dixie Guards of Company B were led by the capable Captain Solomon M. Thornton. Enlisting as a private in March 1862, Thornton quickly gained the confidence of his

---

[141] *OR, Supplement*, pt. 1, vol. 7, serial 7, 28–29.
[142] Ibid., 28–29.
[143] *OR*, ser. 1, vol. 38, pt. 2, serial 73, 356.

Hood's First Sortie, 20 July 1864

comrades from Choctaw County and was made captain by April 1863. Captain Thornton led his men up the ridge and after the retreating Yanks. They had gone into the attack with three officers (one captain and two lieutenants), 4 non-commissioned officers (two sergeants and two corporals), and twenty-two privates for a total of twenty-nine men. Twenty-one of the Dixie Guards would fall before the sun went down. After it became obvious that the men had run into a trap, Captain Thornton and his lieutenants rallied the men on the ridge they they held for some twenty-five minutes before having to fall back. During this action the captain fell, shot in the hip and groin. Also wounded were First Lieutenant William A. Womack, shot in the left arm, and Second Lieutenant Alexander W. McLarty (also listed as McCarthy), shot in the left hand. The company, left without an officer, needed no one to lead them or to tell them the difficult work that was at hand. They were tough veterans of three springs of fighting and would have made that charge without an officer to lead them. That was true of all of the 31st Mississippi and, indeed, all of Featherston's Mississippians. They fought on and held their ground begrudgingly until the few Dixie Guards remaining had to fall back with the survivors of the other companies.

Also falling in the attack from Company B were Fourth Sergeant Francis M. Otts, wounded in the left leg and left on the field, and Second Corporal Daniel B. Tharp, wounded severely in the knee. Corporal Tharp would recover to rejoin the regiment. Another Tharp, Private Simeon V. Tharp, fell mortally wounded and was left on the field. He would never be seen again. Sustaining a broken leg from a gunshot fracture of the left tibia, the twenty-three-year-old Sergeant Otts was taken to the Federal field hospital where the next day a Yankee surgeon amputated his leg. The crude procedure, designed to prevent gangrene from occurring, was termed a "circular amputation in middle third, leg." It was successful, and the sergeant was taken to the hospital in Chattanooga on 1 August where he remained for eight months. After recovering sufficiently from his wound, he was released to the provost marshall on 2 April 1865. On 3 April, he was moved to Louisville and then on to Camp Chase on 11 April where he waited out the war.[144]

Private James A. Cooper had seen his last battle. Wounded severely in the "rite" leg which was fractured, the Dixie Guard soldier was taken to the hospital in Macon where on 26 July his leg had "reached pydermia gangrene." He held

---

[144] Jospeh K. Barnes, Surgeon General, US Surgeon General's Office, *Medical & Surgical History of the War of the Rebellion*, 3:136-39.

on to a painful existence for two more months until he died on 25 September. He was buried at the Rose Hill Cemetery.

Privates Tillman Crowell and William J. Crowell were both casualties. Tillman was hit in the "rite" side and disabled for the rest of the war but was able to get away while William was killed and left on the field. Private F. M. James was wounded severely in the left leg by one of the Federal shells that rained down on the Mississippians on Collier's Ridge. Unable to walk, Private James was picked up and carried from the field. After his leg was amputated and he recovered, he was sent home. His service was over.[145] Dixie Guard Private Joel W. Harper fell with a gunshot wound to his right hip and thigh and was taken prisoner.

Another Dixie Guard, Private George D. Hendley, simply vanished and his story is a mystery. He went up the ridge with his comrades and was last seen fighting along with them in the smoke-covered field, but he was lost in the charge and was never heard from again by his mates. Listed among the wounded and captured by the Federal Army on 23 July and sent to the hospital in Chattanooga to recover, he was "lost" by the Federals by 26 July. Perhaps he escaped, as speculated by the Federal reports, but it is more likely that he died along the way and was buried in an unknown and unmarked grave somewhere between Atlanta and Chattanooga or in a cemetery in Chattanooga. There was no mystery in another Hendley's death. Forty-six-year-old Private Osborn W. Hendley fell dangerously wounded in front of the surging blue line, shot in the upper left leg. The captors took him to their field hospital at Vining Station where his leg was amputated. He was put on a train bound for Chattanooga, arriving on 1 August, and was taken to the hospital where he held on to life until 27 August 1864. He is buried there in the Scenic City.[146]

Two Dixie Guards named Lee were also part of the butcher's tally. Privates Thomas W. Lee, wounded in the left hand, and William L. F. Lee, "shocked" (concussed) by a cannonball, would both come back to the Dixie Guards for more action. So too, would Private Bartholomew (Bart) W. Mims who received a slight wound to his left hand. Private William A. McGowen would not see any future action. The veteran from Choctaw County, who had been wounded at Baton Rouge two years before, received a fatal blow and was left on the field to die. Private John Thomas Swindle of Co. B found himself

---

[145] Barnes, *Medical & Surgical History of the War of the Rebellion*, vol. 3, 139-40.

[146] Compiled Service Records, Record Group 269, microfilm rolls 341-46, Mississippi Dept of Archives and History (hereafter CSR, RG-269, R-341-46, MDAH); Barnes, *Medical & Surgical History of the War of the Rebellion*, 3:140.

Hood's First Sortie, 20 July 1864

surrounded and was compelled to surrender. The 5-foot, 5-inch blue-eyed Swindle would sit out the rest of the war at Camp Douglas. Private William G. Skelton of the Dixie Guards was killed that day, his lifeless body resting on the red Georgia soil.

Private James K. Watson, who had written his father just three weeks before predicting victory and exclaiming: "I think we will be shure to whip them at this place.... I think we will have peace soon," had fought his last battle. The brave young Watson had fallen in the fighting and had to be left on the field to die alone. He had been hoping for a furlough for forty days so he could go home to Mississippi. He had been promised a pass in mid-September if he would bring back a couple of lads from his family who would join. The young man's life was ended all too soon, though, as he gave himself as human sacrifice for his friends, his family, and his country.

Thirty-eight-year-old Private Gabriel M. Spruill had been waiting for his medical discharge for months. Stricken with "chronic rheumatism of chest & back" and "at times confined to his bed," the farmer from Choctaw County had been recommended for a discharge due to his disability since the previous October, but the paperwork had gotten stalled somewhere up the line. His captain, Solomon Thornton, had okayed it on 31 October 1863; so had the regiment's physician, James M. Simmons who, in fact, had recommended it. Major James W. Drane, acting as commanding officer of the regiment had approved it on 7 November 1863, followed by Colonel J. A. Orr, temporarily in command of the brigade, and then by Major General W. W. Loring, as division commander, on 10 November 1863. Next, Lieutenant General W. J. Hardee, commanding the Mississipi, Alabama, and East Louisiana Department, approved it that fall. All that remained was for its rubber stamp approval by Richmond and the aging and ailing Gabriel Spruill could go home or to some light duty at a commissary or medical post as had been suggested by Colonel Orr.

Born in Pickens County, Alabama, the fair-haired and fair-complexioned farmer had been absent sick more days than he had been present during his war service, but the South needed him able bodied or not. After seventy days of non-stop fighting in Georgia, Spruill had all but forgotten his discharge application as he looked across the field to the Yankee line of works his regiment had been ordered to take. Rising to the call, Spruill joined his comrades and charged across the hill, only to fall on the other side. When the noise of battle died down that night, Spruill was in Federal hands. The tired, dying man had been wounded in the back and shoulder, blood quickly draining from his torn body.

He was taken to the US field hospital where he died on 22 July. On 1 August the response to his application for a medical discharge arrived in the camp of the 31st Mississippi—approved.

Of the twenty-one Dixie Guards who fell at Peach Tree Creek, five died on the field, fifteen were wounded and one man was captured. Five of the wounded were also captured, three of whom would die in captivity. Another of the wounded men later died, making the tally nine deaths in Company B from the battle. Only eight Dixie Guards escaped injury or capture on the bloody Collier Ridge.

Captain George H. Blakeslee of Company G, 129th Illinois, wrote about his experience at Peach Tree Creek from his vantage point near the Collier Mill. The 129th Illinois of Harrison's brigade had been next to Tanyard Branch just east along its banks and near the mill site. "There was opposed to us that day Featherston's Brigade of Mississippians, composed of the 1st Mississippi Sharpshooters, 22nd, 31st 33rd, and 40th [and the 3rd] Mississippi Regiments. When the charging line of Stewart's braves came surging on," wrote the former soldier, "against a line of veteran bluecoats who had stood on the front line from Perryville in 1862 to that day, a line which all the gallantry of Southern dash could not break, there fell, within twenty paces of our regimental line, a mere boy, having both feet carried away by a shell." The Yankee captain continued, "As soon as the fiercest of the attacks were past, humanity brought him assistance, although we were even yet under fire. We ligatured his limbs to stop the bleeding, which was rapidly sapping his young life." The Federal soldier "picked him up and carried him away from the battle and back to the Federal field hospital." Years after the war, Captain Blakeslee remembered "distinctly how that curly haired boy coyed up to him as he lay in his arms, as though he had reached a safe retreat." Blakeslee explained that "[h]e told the story of his young life between the sobs that shook his slight frame, saying he was not yet fourteen years old, that his father was dead, and his mother did not wish him to enlist, but he had run away, and now he regretted having disobeyed her."[147]

Captain Blakeslee also recalled having captured Captain John C. Evans of Company H, 22nd Mississippi, along with a few of his men who had been

---

[147] Blakeslee, Captain George H., Company G, 129th Illinois *Confederate Veteran* vol. 7 (April 1899): 166.

Hood's First Sortie, 20 July 1864

trapped in the counterattack by Ward's division. Evans turned over his sword, belt, and CSA belt buckle to the Yankee Captain before being sent north to sit out the remainder of the war in a Northern Prison Camp. Evans's company, the Lafayette Farmers from Lafayette County, Mississippi, had been decimated atop Collier Ridge and in the ravine beyond.[148]

After the battle died down, a Yankee soldier from the 22nd Wisconsin discovered an election ticket from the knapsack of one of Featherson's Mississippians. "The heading of the ticket [read], 'Save the Union, No Civil War.'" A number of similar tickets were found among the Confederate prisoners and Rebel dead. Apparently, in a gimmick, many Confederate soldiers held them as an insurance policy if they were captured to show their captors in hopes of more lenient treatment.[149] The next morning when the Michigan soldiers began removing the Rebel wounded and burying the dead, "one detail was shocked to find a badly wounded woman in a Confederate uniform." Private Austin of the 19th Michigan wrote his family: "She was shot in the breast and through the thy & was still alive & as gritty as any reb. I ever saw."[150] Another veteran from the 19th Michigan, Private Joseph W. Ely, recorded in his diary that it was so hot and the field hospitals so overcrowded with wounded and dying, the "[t]he wounded are suffering very much. The flies are very bad."[151]

After the battle, Private Ely helped a captured Confederate doctor treat his wounded Mississippians over the next several days.[152] Perhaps the Rebel surgeon was the one described by a man who visited the battlefield many years later as he retold of his boyhood experience during the charge. On 27 March 2008, on a beautiful spring day in Atlanta the author, together with a handful of witnesses, Frank Chew, Kitty Hodgson, Dr. Linton Hopkins of Emory University, Henry Howell, and Floyd McRae, all convened at the old "Bloody Magnolia Springs" and ravine just south of today's Golfview Drive where a small spring begins at a rock well to hear the story of George Heery and his wife Betty Heery when they were newlyweds. They had just bought a lot where

---

[148] Blakeslee, 166; Rowland, *Military History of Mississippi*, 243.

[149] Boy Racine to Friend T. 21 July 1864, p. 17, subject file PW-4, Kennesaw Mountain National Battlefield Park, Kennesaw, Georgia.

[150] Jones, "'The Flash of Their Guns,'" 1:189.

[151] Ibid., 163; Joseph W. Ely, diary, 21 July 1864, Farnsworth Collection, www.michiganinthewar.org/infantry/19compb.htm (10 November 2008).

[152] Jones, "'The Flash of Their Guns,'" 1:163; Ely, diary, 22 July 1864, Farnsworth Collection, Farnsworth Art Museum, Rockland ME.

they built and moved into the home located where the Bloody Magnolia spring still flows today. The Heerys moved into their newly built house near the end of 1951 and soon had a visit from a most unusual guest, an elderly gentleman who was in Atlanta visiting his daughter and son-in-law who lived in the neighborhood. They had come down to see the spring and ravine. The old man, who was judged to be well into his nineties but still in good health, then related what he had witnessed there in the ravine while serving as a drummer boy for the Confederate Army on 20 July 1864 during the Battle of Peachtree Creek:

> He told us that that ravine which had a stream in it and a stoned-in spring had been used as a hospital station by the Confederate forces, but when they had to retreat he seemed to know that upon their retreat that the same ravine and protected area had been taken over by the Federal forces as a hospital station…and so that's the area that he said and as you can see it's a very sharp ravine and with that fresh water supply down there it would have been an ideal place so that stands to reason….[153]

When asked about the topography of the area Mr. Heery explained that "the only earth [that has been moved] that could amount to anything was…the fill to allow for this road to go though," referring to Golfview Drive. Also, Mr. Heery said that "there's really been almost no change in the topography of the lot that this house was on…" While the Heerys only lived there about 2 1/2 years, they fondly recalled the home and neighborhood because it was their first home and part of Mr. Heery's first houses designed by him as an architect. When asked where the old man was who had visited them was from, the Heerys recalled that he was visiting from someplace fairly far away and that he did not live in Atlanta. Mr. Heery explained that he "was for sure Southern..I would not be surprised if he weren't from Alabama, or Mississippi, something like that…" When asked if he recalled whether the old man was from Mississippi, Mr. Heery responded that "somehow that feels right to me."

Finally, Mr. Heery reiterated that the old gentleman pointed specifically to the spring by explaining that this was the Confederate hospital station and later a Federal hospital station and the battle continued to rage all around, but that they were somewhat sheltered there by the ravine. The wooded ravine can be seen on the left of the photo taken by George Barnard after the battle. Mrs. Betty Heery confirmed her husband's recollections of their encounter with the

---

[153] George and Betty Heery, interview by author, 27 March 2008.

old Confederate. Mr. Heery added that "This stream has a lot less water in it today than it did during the years that we lived here."[154]

---

[154] Ibid.

17

HOLDING ONTO COLLIER RIDGE

The fighting was hand to hand, and step by step.[1]

Featherston's men charged up and over the ridge and unwittingly swarmed down the other slope and into a three-sided Federal counterstroke. Despite the overwhelming odds, the Mississippians fought stubbornly. According to Federal Colonel Benjamin Harrison, "the fighting was hand to hand, and step by step; the [Rebels were] pushed back over the crest in our front and the key-point of the battle-field won." After about twenty minutes, the surviving Mississippians fell back from the ravine and to the Collier Ridge behind them. Ward's men swarmed up the slope pressing the Confederates back to the ridge top and threatened to push them off of the heights. There, however, the Mississippians hung on along the Collier Road bed and fought behind rail ties while their lines thinned by the minute. "Rebel flags waived defiantly in their front line, and were shot down," reported a Federal officer in the 102nd Illinois. After about twenty-five more minutes of desperate fighting on the ridge, the remaining Southerners were compelled to fall back. The massive weight of the blue tide simply could not be turned back. Colonel Harrison, the future president, saw quite a number of the Mississippians "lying down and a few even turning back, while the officers with drawn swords, were trying to steady their lines and push them forward." Most of those Harrison saw lying down would never get up again.[2]

Chickasaw Avengers, Company H, 31st Mississippi. Company H from Chickasaw County mustered thirty men for this day. With three commissioned officers (the captain and two lieutenants), six non-commissioned officers (four sergeants and two corporals), and twenty-one privates, the Chickasaw Avengers had a full complement for duty. Captain George Washington Naron led his men up the old field and over the ridge full of hope and resolve. Naron had been

---

[1] United States War Department, comp., *Official Records of the Union and Confederate Armies in the War of the Rebellion*, 128 vols. (Washington, DC: Government Printing Office, 1880–1901) ser. 1, vol. 38, pt. 2, serial 73, 345 (hereafter *OR*).

[2] Ibid., 345, 356, 364.

Hood's First Sortie, 20 July 1864

given command of the Avengers in November 1863, but he had been the de facto captain of the unit for over a year before then. Its previous captain, George L. Jennings, had been ill for much of 1863 with bronchitis, which finally forced his resignation in November. Naron was a good and capable leader who took care of his men. He was kin to three first cousins serving under him. He had been twice wounded in the war, but never had been put out of action. The captain from Persimmon Springs found himself in the den of battle among the bleeding and broken bodies of his fellow Avengers on top of the ridge when a Yankee bullet struck him in the head, damaging his ear. He turned to his junior second lieutenant (also called third lieutenant), William M. Foster.

For Third Lieutenant Foster, things weren't going any better. He had been shot in the throat and was unable to take over. Down the chain of command, the next in line was First Sergeant Jonathan Graham Blue. Blue had fallen with a painful wound in the leg. Second Sergeant Solomon B. Alford was shot in the breast. Third Sergeant Alexander Henry Pratt boldly carried the attack over the ridge and down after the retreating Yankees until he was caught in the blue counter-stroke, falling mortally wounded beyond the reach of his comrades. Pratt had come home to defend the Peach State where he had been born. The thirty-four-year-old, auburn-haired farmer from Chickasaw County had seen his last sunrise, his blue eyes now transfixed skyward in an eternal gaze. Fifth Sergeant William M. Conner, next in rank, had also charged beyond the help of his friends and fell with a severe wound to his thigh and would share Sergeant Pratt's fate in an unknown grave on the ridge above Collier's Mill.

Fellow Chickasaw Avengers Corporals Newton L. McCollough (McCullough) and William L. McMahan each fell wounded on the bloody ridge. McCullough had been too badly wounded to be removed from the field, and had to be left to the uncertain fate of a wounded and captured soldier. Sent to the field hospital in Vining Station on 25 July by the Federals, the nineteen-year-old McCullough had been shot in the left leg. The bullet had shattered both the tibia and fibula bones requiring the amputation of his limb. McMahan was hit in the head. He would spent the rest of the war absent from duty as a result of the wound.[3]

Six of the Alford clan joined the Chickasaw Avengers, but by 20 July, only three remained. In addition to Sergeant Solomon B. who was wounded in the chest, privates Churchwell ("Church") and Munroe P. Alford crossed the old

---

[3] CSR, RG 269, R-341-46, MDAH; *Medical & Surgical History of the War of the Rebellion*, (Washington, DC: US Government Printing Office, 1870) 3:140.

field into the maelstrom. Like Solomon, Church and Munroe, too, would fall that day, but Munroe would not return. Church had been shot severely in the arm and was one of the lucky few to walk away from the crimson-stained field. Private Abner B. Gilder fell during the charge up the ridge when a Yankee minnie ball passed through part of his left thigh and he was carried off the field.

Also from Company H, privates Charles M. Berry and Reuben P. Faulkner fell mortally wounded and were left on the field. Also wounded was Private Eli Francis (Frank) Naron, first cousin to Captain George W. Naron of the Chickasaw Avengers. Private James A. Burt was wounded in the hand and sent to the Ocmulgee Hospital in Macon, Georgia, and then furloughed. He would eventually recover sufficiently to return to the 31st Mississippi. Private Edward T. Conner, who had joined the Avengers at Resaca, was also hit in the hand. Private Jefferson (James) R. Finley was not so fortunate. He had crossed over the ridge with the 31st Mississippi, but he soon found himself surrounded in a sea of blue. The captured private was sent north to Camp Douglas, Illinois, where Finley suffered from exposure and contracted pneumonia that claimed his life on 6 March 1865. He was buried in the City Cemetery in Chicago. Private Wiley T. McKee, a 5-foot, 9-inch Scotsman, was wounded and captured. Also in the charge was Private Robert J. McMullen until a minnie ball struck his thigh, severely wounding him.

Fellow Chickasaw Avenger, Private James A. Sanders from Persimmon Springs was wounded severely in the hand and was sent to the hospital in Eufaula, Alabama, where he was treated and sent back to Company H in time for the Tennessee campaign that would ultimately claim his life. Thirty-seven year-old Private Thomas B. Slaughter sustained a gunshot wound to his left foot and was captured. He was sent to Camp Chase, Ohio, where the black-haired, black-eyed fellow from Oktibbeha County, Mississippi, sat out the war. Private William Oliver Smith was also wounded and left on the field with a gunshot wound to his left side. Private Nathaniel S. Wofford was hit three times, shot in both thighs, and in an arm. In sum, Company H sent thirty men into the fight, but only seven were unharmed. Of the twenty-three casualties, five died on the field; seventeen were wounded of whom five were captured; and a sixth man, uninjured, was captured. Another three would die from their wounds making the Chickasaw Avengers' death toll eight from the Battle of Peach Tree Creek.

Amid that death, Adjutant William J. Van De Graff, brother-in-law to the former colonel of the 31st Mississippi, Confederate congressman Jehu Orr, was seen waiving the regiment's battle flag, a twelve-star St. Andrew's Cross, at the top of the ridge as he tried to rally those who were still able to carry on the fight. Most of the officers had been shot down, and he was the ranking leader of the regiment realignment on the field, at least for the moment. Presently, a Yankee soldier, Private Dennis Buckley, in Company G of the 136th New York, "knocked the color bearer [Van De Graff] of the 31st Mississippi down with his rifle butt" and reached for the flag.[4]

According to General Featherston, Van De Graff was "a gallant and accomplished officer, a young man of promise and great moral worth." Featherston explained that the adjutant "seized the colors of his regiment and bore them to the front after two or three color bearers had been shot down, and following their example shared their fate. He fell with the colors in his hand." As Van De Graff fell, his comrades began to fall back reluctantly down the ridge. The victorious Yankees did not pursue them. Exhausted but relieved, the Northern troops had prevented disaster from befalling their army in the brutal fighting that day, but they would have more work ahead as the few remaining Mississippians were not yet through.[5]

Private Buckley, a Canadian who had joined the 136th New York, picked up the dropped colors of the 31st Mississippi and began taunting the survivors of the decimated Mississippi Regiment who were reluctantly falling back. It was his last act of gallantry. "While jubilantly waving the captured flag at the Confederate lines, a bullet glanced off the flagstaff and struck Buckley in the forehead, killing him instantly." A Medal of Honor was given to Private Buckley's mother after the war.[6]

The 31st Mississippi's battle flag was thus captured by the 136th New York and taken to Washington, DC. In 1905 it was returned to Mississippi's Department of Archives and History in Jackson, where it remains today. It was the only time that the regiment's flag was captured during the war, although the 31st Mississippi's flag briefly changed hands at the battle of Baton Rouge and the regiment's colors were nearly lost at the battle of Franklin.[7]

136th New York, The Iron Clads. Private John T. McMahon, of Company E in the 136th New York, was impressed with the tenacity of the Confederate assault. "The rebels came out of their works and met us like men, and at first

---

[4] John Michael Priest, ed., *John T. McMahon's Diary of the 136th New York, 1861–1864* (Shippensburg PA: White Mane Publishing Company, 1993) 118–19.

[5] *OR*, ser. 1, vol. 38, pt. 3, serial 74, p. 883.

[6] Priest, ed., *John T. McMahon's Diary*, 118–19; *OR*, ser. 1, vol. 38, pt. 3, serial 74, p. 883; R & P file 503867, RG 94, National Archives, Washington, DC.

[7] Flag Records capture no. 229, acc. no. 68.48, cat. no. 68, flag cabinet, Mississippi Department of Archives and History, Jackson MS.

our men gave way but it was not long before we drove them off the battle ground and we held it with all their dead and wounded and a great many prisoners."[8] According to another veteran of the 136th New York, "the 136th took many prisoners, and the colors of the 31st Mississippi (Rebel) regiment. For the amount of fighting our regiment did, our loss was very slight indeed; two killed and nine or ten wounded will cover our entire casualties for the day." Actually, the 136th New York lost a total of eighteen men along the bloody Collier Ridge, including two killed on the field, one who died of his wounds, one who was captured, and one officer and thirteen enlisted men who were wounded.[9] Captain A. A. Curtiss was shot in the right knee, costing him his leg. Along with Dennis Buckley, Private Samuel Whitmore, both from Company G, were killed, while Privates Hiram Hitchcock and James Mead of Company A were wounded, as were Privates Burr Summers of Company C, Edward Crowel of Company D, and Gaskard Keiper of Company G. Corporal James Fanning of Company G was wounded and never heard from again by his comrades.[10]

Soldiers of the 136th New York from the finger lakes region of the Empire State, lamented the loss of Captain Curtiss. One comrade wrote, "He was one of the bravest of the brave, and in battle or whatever danger be seemed to know no fear.—We all sincerely hope his life may be spared, and although he may never again be able to join his regiment, he will yet do his country service in some capacity."[11] Captain Chapin of Company C remembered his company together with companies A, D, and G, were ordered to take the Collier Ridge with the 22nd Wisconsin and drive out the Rebel skirmishers that were posted there. When this was completed between 1:00 and 2:00 P.M., Chapin's battalion deployed and began improving their line. "On this ridge was an old sunk road, which answered very well for rifle pits. At about the center of my line there was a turn in the road following down the hill and past the old mill. My line on the right was in advance of this road about thirty yards." Chapin recalled that during the afternoon "[s]ome of the men were lying down—others were picking blackberries—but all were on the alert. Word was brought to me by Lieut. Smith of Co. G that the enemy were moving to our left." After confirming Smith's information, Chapin sent word to Colonel Faulkner that the Rebels

---

[8] Priest, ed., *John T. McMahon's Diary*, 104.
[9] Ibid., 119.
[10] LOS to Editor, 7 August 1864, *Wyoming Mirror,* Warsaw NY, 24 August 1864, Warsaw NY; Priest, ed., *John T. McMahon's Diary*, 119.
[11] L.O.S., letter to Wyoming Mirror, supra.

were advancing "and that if we were to hold the position, reinforcements should be sent forward at once."[12]

Chapin looked back at the barren ridge behind him. There was no sign of Harrison's 1st Brigade or of any other friendlies. Meanwhile, in front of his isolated line, "I saw the rebel line of attack advancing by company front—muskets 'right shoulder shift.' My whole thought was to hold that ridge at all hazzards, " explained Chapin. "I ran along the line, told the men we must hold the ridge...—not to waste powder, but to make every shot tell. Every man seemed to realize the situation. They loaded and fired with as much coolness and precision as though they were practicing on parade." "I felt proud of my men," exclaimed Chapin.[13]

Chapin continued to look northward for signs of help. "At this time the 1st Brigade had commenced its movement, but had not yet reached the foot of the ridge. I shouted to them to hurry up if they wanted to save the ridge. About the time they reached the base of the ridge a section of Geary's Battery," began firing into his lines. This battery was Sloan's Pennsylvania, Battery E "which was on a considerable higher elevation than the ridge we occupied, changed the direction of its fire to a left oblique, bringing my men in the range of his guns. I immediately ordered my men to fall back out of range, which they did in good order, meeting the line of the 1st Brigade." Chapin's New Yorkers joined with Harrison's men and, in effect, became a line of skirmishers for the regiments in Harrison's brigade that advanced east of the mill and Tanyard Branch. Chapin recalled, "We charged the rebel line and pushed it back." At this point, Dennis Buckley of Company G on the left of Chapin's line captured the battle flag of the 31st Mississippi. "He was shot while holding the flag aloft," recalled the New York captain. "The rebels made an ineffectual attempt to retake the flag. The rebels came over the brow of the hill and nearly, if not quite, half way down, before they recoiled. Every shot from our line seemed to take effect," explained Chapin. "The rebels being above us, their balls flew over our heads, and when we gained the summit there were more dead and wounded rebels in our rear than in our front."[14]

Sergeant J. B. Benedict of Company G, 136th New York, also remembered the bloody struggle. As left guide of Company G, Benedict was posted on the far left of the New Yorkers' skirmish line and next to the 22nd Wisconsin.

---

[12] W. S. Chapin, statement to Colonel James Wood, 45–46.
[13] Ibid., 46.
[14] Ibid., 46.

When Featherston's Mississippians came across the old field from the Tanyard Branch below, Benedict recalled, "we opened upon then, and maintained a steady fire until they were up to the other side of the fence. At this point one of Geary's Batteries [Sloan's] on our right, opened fire on the rebels." Benedict continued, "Some of their shot coming rather close to us for comfort [In fact, one of the men had his gun knocked out of his hands by a missile from this battery.] our line of skirmishers was compelled to fall back six or eight rods [about 100 to 130 feet] to get out of range." The New York skirmishers fell back to the relative safety of the ravine and Harrison's approaching brigade.[15]

By this point, some of Featherston's Mississippians, particularly in the 31st and 22nd Mississippi in the center of the attack, had breached a gap in the skirmish line of the right part of the 22nd Wisconsin and left of the 136th New York and also reached the ravine while other portions of Featherston's lines scrambled forward to press the broken Federal line. "The rebels had taken advantage of the gap in our line of skirmishers on our left, and under cover of some small brush, was swinging around our left flank. A volley from the advancing brigade line checked them. When the line of battle got up to us," remembered Benedict, "we advanced in front of the line to the top of the hill, where the rebels were, when their line commenced to break." Benedict witnessed the seizing of the Confederate battle flag by Private Dennis Buckley and his death. Benedict then watched as Lieutenant Smith of Company G seized the flag and kept it for the remainder of the contest.[16]

In addition to capturing the flag of the 31st Mississippi, the 105th Illinois in Harrison's brigade also captured a flag, this one a Confederate Second National flag. Harrison's brigade believed they had captured the flag of the 12th Louisiana.[17] The field below that point, on the side near the present day and including the parking lot of Tanyard Creek Park contained the dead, dying, and wounded of men of the 55th Alabama and the 57th Alabama, and a few of the 12th Louisiana from three of her companies that had joined the Alabama units into the maelstrom. Evidently, the 12th Louisiana never lost her colors at Peach Tree Creek, and after the war, many veterans of the 12th Louisiana vehemently objected to reports that the 105th Illinois had captured their flag. Moreover, the position of the 105th Illinois along the Collier Ridge where they claimed to have taken the flag, does not match the location of the 12th Louisiana during the

---

[15] Benedict statement in Woods' report, 47–48.
[16] Ibid., 47.
[17] "Report of the Adjutant General of the State of Illinois," in Adjutant J. N. Reece, *History of One Hundred and Fifth Infantry*, (Springfield IL) 5:686–88.

battle. It does, however, match the location of the left flank of Featherston's Mississippians where the 40th Mississippi was located. The flag of the 33rd Mississippi, on the right of Featherston's line, also lost her colors to units from Wood's brigade, and her flag was a Confederate Second National flag, just like the one captured by the 105th Illinois. It also matches the gold-fringed second national flags that were captured from Featherston's brigade at the Battle of Franklin four months later. The 105th Illinois was located at the point held by men of the left of Featherston's brigade, which included the 40th Mississippi, the 31st Mississippi, and the 22nd Mississippi, with the 22nd and 31st Mississippi's colors accounted for, the most reasonable conclusion identifies the flag as that of the 40th Mississippi.[18]

Over to the right of the 31st and 22nd Mississippi Regiments, the 3rd Mississippi Infantry, which was positioned second from the right of Featherston's brigade, was struggling to hang onto to the recently won Federal line after it had been pushed back to the Collier Ridge Road along with the rest of the Mississippians. Facing men from Coburn's and Wood's brigades, the 3rd Mississippi fought hand to hand against the surging blue hoard. According to Lieutenant Colonel Samuel M. Dyer, the 3rd Mississippi "advanced in its position in line of battle of the brigade through an open field for about 400 yards, exposed to a heavy fire both from artillery and infantry. After driving in his skirmishers easily, I occupied a position on the summit of a slight elevation, partially protected by a rail fence, within about 200 yards of the enemy's line of battle."[19] The biographer of the 3rd Mississippi observed, "The bloodied shock wave of the Third crashed into the first line of blue in a shooting, stabbing, musket-swinging, hand-to-hand melee. The surviving Yanks quickly fell back into the much stronger second line with some of the Third hot on their heels."[20] The men of the 3rd Mississippi joined with the other Mississippians in Featherston's brigade in charging pell-mell into the Federal counterattack that was forming in their front. What resulted was a savage and brutal struggle, thinning the ranks of both sides. But the bitter and close-quarter fighting could

---

[18] For an additional discussion and analysis from historians Howard Michael Madaus and Hugh Simmons, who both also concluded the captured flag is most likely that of the 40th Mississippi, see http://history-sites.com/mb/cw/cwflags/index.cgi?noframes;read'3608 (19 March 2008); and http://rhsresearch.org/Flags.htm (22 August 2007).

[19] *OR*, ser. 1, vol. 38, pt. 3, serial 74, pp. 885–87; H. Grady Howell, Jr., *To Live and Die in Dixie, A History of the Third Mississippi Infantry, C.S.A.* (Jackson MS: Chickasaw Bayou Press, 1991) 327.

[20] Howell, *To Live and Die in Dixie*, 327.

not last. The determination of the Yankees in Ward's division and their advantage in numbers began to tell its toll. After some twenty minutes, the Rebels fell back to the rail-lined road that gave them some protection while the Yankees pursued them. The fighting was so fierce, one Federal veteran described the action as "one of the most horrible fights of the war—in an open field, neither side having breastworks" or protection.[21]

From about 40 yards apart where the surging blue line approached the north face of the Collier Ridge and road, the fighting continued. The Northern fire was hot and found its mark on the exhausted Southerners, further thinning Featherston's ranks while much of the Confederate reply fire was missing its mark as the Mississippians were overshooting the approaching Yankees from the ravine below. For another twenty minutes, the Confederates desperately held on, clinging to the Collier Ridge and rail-lined road, but they continued to take fire from their front and flanks. Additionally, Newton's division had refused its right flank some 90 degrees to protect its lines from the right of Featherston's brigade that had swept past them nearly an hour before. Now, Newton's men poured fire down on the exposed right flank of the Mississippians. Still, Maney's Tennesseans were nowhere in sight. They had stepped into the woods between today's Ardmore Park and Buckhead Road (Peachtree Street) an hour earlier and many of them had laid down there to avoid Federal fire.

Falling in the attack from the 3rd Mississippi Infantry were Colonel Thomas Mellon who was wounded in the head by a shell fragment while he was wildy waving his sword close to the rail fence. Mellon was taken from the field under a hail of bullets, but he would recover. Lieutenant Colonel Dyer then took command of the regiment and tried to hold on to the Federal line they had taken. In Company A, John H. Scott, who was listed as "Color-Corp. from Jan. 1863 to Feb. 1865," was wounded.[22] Also falling were Private John Barfield who had his right arm "shot off," Private Frank Fountain who was shot in the foot, and Captain Abiezar F. Ramsay was killed while leading Company A's Live Oak Rifles.[23]

Another member of the Live Oak Rifles, First Sergeant Oscar Bowen, penned his experience: "While standing out in front of my brigade and...having fired a number of shots into the ranks of the enemy, I received a wound made by a large minnie ball which tore its way into my body and lodged near the

---

[21] Jean M. Cate, ed., *"If I Live to Come Home,": The Civil War Letters of Sergeant John March Cate* (Pittsburgh: Dorrance Publishing Company, 1995) 196.

[22] Research provided by historian Ken Legendre, New Orleans LA.

[23] Howell, *To Live and Die in Dixie*, 327–28.

bladder. I thought I was killed and turned and walked to the rear to die, and while lying on my back I gave to a captain my dying words to my father and mother with their post office address."[24] In all, the Live Oak Rifles lost twenty-three men killed or wounded during the attack. Company C's Downing Rifles saw some thirty men fall in the battle, including privates Jimmy Patterson, William J. Bush, James Matthews, and Thomas N. Rawlings who were all killed. Also mortally wounded from Company C was eighteen-year-old Frank Stone who died the next day, while Color Corporal John T. Tatum was wounded severely.[25] Privates Richard Lanius of Company E's Biloxi Rifles and Corporal John W. Miller of Company G's Gainesville Volunteers were wounded, while Sergeant John James Moore from Company G was captured.[26]

Lieutenant Colonel Dyer, watching his men fall one after another around him and without any support, realized his and other regiments faced annihilation or capture if they remained on the ridge. Lieutenant Colonel Dyer explained, "After holding my position about twenty minutes, and losing many of my best men, and exposed on both flanks, I fell back."[27] Private William McRae of Company B's Sunflower Dispersers was wounded in the leg near the knee and left on the field at the fence along the road. He was never heard from again. In 1900, his family was still trying to locate where their loved one may have been buried. The wounded Corporal John W. Miller was also left on the field to be captured by the enemy. Private Jeremiah King of Company K was shot in the face and left dead on the field, while Lieutenant John P. Grissett of Company D was killed and left on the field as well.[28]

Sergeant Bowen of the Live Oak Rifles wrote of his plight:

> I was carried to the rear where a surgeon examined my wound and said I would live about two hours. Several of my comrades gathered around me and I had them dress me for my burial. After which and as they were not Christians, I exhorted them to prepare to meet God. As I lingered I was taken to the Atlanta depot, and while waiting for a freight train to take the wounded to Macon, I had a spasm and after it was over I was laid out as dead. I rallied and was put in a box car and when on the way to Macon and reaching Barnesville I begged to be taken out of the car to die. I was taken to

---

[24] Oscar du Bose Bowen, *Gospel Ministry of Forty Years* (Handsboro MS: O. D. Brown, 1911) 11; Howell, *To Live and Die in Dixie*, 328.
[25] Research provided by historian Ken Legendre, New Orleans LA.
[26] Howell, *To Live and Die in Dixie*, 328.
[27] *OR*, ser. 1, vol. 38, pt. 3, serial 74, pp. 885–87.
[28] Howell, *To Live and Die in Dixie*, 328–29; Compiled Service Records.

the hospital and examined by a surgeon, who said: "My boy, you will have to die." A number of coffins of different lengths were in the room near me and from which I selected one in my own mind in which my body would take its long sleep. I made inquiry about the cemetery where I would be buried. I have a nurse, a Spaniard, to whom I dictated a farewell letter to my parents and family. I wanted them to know among other things where I died and was buried. I then awaited the coming of the angel of deliverance to take me home.

More than half a dozen surgeons examined my wound and said, in substance, "there is no hope..." Then there followed spasm after spasm, my jaws and teeth were clinched, which I writhed with agony. A poor soldier boy far from home and among strangers, his only earthly companion a Spanish nurse, who looked at him doubtless with pitying eyes.... My farewell letter, written by my Spanish nurse, reached my parents and as soon as he could reach Barnesville my father did so, to be pointed, as he thought, to my grave, but to his astonishment, he found me alive, and looking into my face with dumb silence, the tears ran down his cheeks. As soon as I was able to travel, I received a sixty days furlough and father took me home, where I was embraced in the arms of loved ones who had mourned for me as dead.[29]

In all, the 3rd Mississippi lost 93 men out of the 167 that participated in the attack, with 15 men killed, 73 wounded, and 5 missing. Moreover, a number of the wounded died within a few days, either on the field, or in a Yankee field hospital, prisoner of war camp, or Confederate hospital. According to Captain W. A. Kelly, Company C lost "four killed and twenty-one wounded four of whom have since died others were permanently disabled for military service in the field,"[30] but the captain had failed to include the missing of his company, which made a total loss of some thirty men from the Downing Rifles of Hinds County.

Lieutenant Colonel Philo B. Buckingham, commander of the 20th Connecticut that captured many of the 3rd Mississippi's wounded who had to be left on the field, explained that the 20th Connecticut "had lost more men during this engagement, in killed and wounded, than they had before during the war."[31] Included among their losses was Corporal James White of Company K who was

---

[29] Bowen, *Gospel Ministry of Forty Years*, 11–14; Howell, *To Live and Die in Dixie*, 330–31.

[30] Howell, *To Live and Die in Dixie*, 333.

[31] Ibid., 333; Croffut & Morris, Connecticut During the Rebellion, 1868, 703.

mortally wounded. He died on 7 August 1864 and his body was sent home in either a zinc-coated or metal coffin.[32]

Pontotoc Guards, Company K, 31st Mississippi. The men of Company K crossed the bloody ridge full of resolve to do their duty. Led by Captain George Washington Lewallen, the Pontotoc Guards from in and around the community of Ellistown, Pontotoc County (now located in Union County), Mississippi, represented their little village well. Pressing over the ridge just won, the Pontotoc Guards poured a volley of fire into the blue line and charged down the hill. When more Federal troops appeared in their front, the Pontotoc Guards held their ground with the other Mississippians in the 31st Mississippi and Featherston's brigade. But there were too few to keep pushing the Yankees back, or to stop the blue counter-stroke. Falling in the attack was Captain Lewallen who was wounded and captured.

Privates Thomas Calvin Bell and William C. Duncan of Company K were killed in the desperate assault; Bell served as a wagon-master before the Atlanta Campaign compelled his service in the Georgia trenches. Private Bell never returned to his home and family in Ellistown, Pontotoc County (now in Union County), Mississippi, but his beloved were left to cherish and hold his blood-stained Bible that was returned to his family.[33] Private Hillary C. Cobb never returned to the Southern lines after the charge; he was buried among the unknowns by the Federal victors in the bloody field. Private John M. Ewing fell with a severe wound to his leg. Private James W. Wesson was hit in the side. Both were able to escape capture; so, too, were Corporal William E. Worthy, struck severely in the hip, Private Burnal Henderson Wade, wounded in the ankle, and Private William A. Witt, shot in the arm.

Also from the Pontotoc Guards were brothers Dilmeda M. and Zelabee Beauchamp both of whom were captured in the fighting. Second Lieutenant Pleasant G. McCraw was wounded and presumed taken prisoner, but McCraw was able to avoid capture and eventually made it home to his family. Also casualties at Peach Tree Creek from Company K were Private Levi W. Gentry, who was wounded severely in the left leg and captured, and Private John Andrew Robinson (sometimes listed as "Robertson") who was also captured. Private Robinson was sent to Camp Douglas, Illinois, on 1 August 1864 and he remained there until his release on 18 May 1865. He wrote a letter to the commandant of the prison camp on 10 January 1865 claiming his loyalty to the

---

[32] http://www.chs.org/kcwmp/cwwx.htm (3 April 2008).
[33] Getsinger, Caryn, family reminisces.

The Battle of Peach Tree Creek

United States and asking to be released: "At the time of my enlistment, the greatest excitement prevailed throughout the Country, and I like so many other misguided men of my native state, I drifted into the tide of Rebellion without being aware of the great wrong I was committing."[34] Robinson remained in custody until General Orders 85 brought about his release along with that of many of his comrades after the surrender of Johnston's Army of Tennessee in North Carolina. Private Gentry was mortally wounded in the left leg and captured. He was just twenty-four. The Pontotoc Guards sent about twenty men into the fight and fifteen became casualties. Three died on the field, and one died after seven weeks in a Federal hospital. Eight men of Company K were wounded, and a total of six were captured, including four who were not wounded. Not surprisingly, the folks back home lamented that "[t]he Regiment was almost wiped out in the battle of Peach Tree Creek in Georgia."[35]

When the ridge line became untenable, some of the survivors of the 31st Mississippi carried Lieutenant Colonel Drane to safety as they withdrew from the hill. His near lifeless body had been wounded five times during the charge. It was feared that he would not survive the terrible wounds, but he lived for another thirty-two years.[36]

To the right of Featherston's attack, the 33rd Mississippi found itself facing overwhelming numbers of blue-clad troops who were swarming upon them like bees. These troops were from Wood's brigade which had the longest route to cover in coming over the low sassafras- and scrub-pine-laden ridge. Moreover, to their right, because Maney's division had failed to come up, there was no support on the right of the 33rd Mississippi, save a few skirmishers from the 1st Mississippi Battalion Sharpshooters that had formed upon their right flank during the charge and were trying to lay some covering fire on Newton's lines. One veteran of the 33rd Mississippi noted that his brigade was "badly cut

---

[34] Compiled Service Records, RG 269, microfilm rolls 341–346, National Archives.

[35] Callie B. Young, *From These Hills: A History of Pontotoc County* (Pontotoc MS: Pontotoc County Historical Society, 2010) 133.

[36] Drane Papers, Drane House and Museum, French Camp Library, French Camp MS. After being confined to a bed for over twelve months, he was able to lead a somewhat normal life after the war. He would serve as an attorney in Chester, Choctaw County MS until his death on 8 August 1896. "A braver and truer soldier never entered the Confederate Army. He was always at his post of duty and never flinched in time of danger," was part of the eulogy delivered by one of his comrades at his funeral (Drane Papers, 3).

to pieces by a Brigade on our right not coming up to support our flank—over half of our regiment was killed and wounded."[37]

Colonel Jabez L. Drake led his veterans forward as the refused line of Newton's division steadily poured fire into their lines. With thinning ranks, the 33rd Mississippi continued their advance, protecting the right flank of Featherston's forces as the entire brigade surged up to and over the Collier Ridge. The Mississippians of the 33rd Mississippi continued down the north slope of the ridge like the rest of Featherston's brigade and into a ravine where they were joined from the other side by Wood's brigade of Ward's division. Colonel Drake "charged waiving his sword until he fell. Captain Moses Jackson commanded during the balance of the engagement."[38] The Yankees met Drake's men with a resolve and in such numbers that the Mississippians could not withstand the counterattack. One Mississippian remembered "It was a very bloody affair."[39] Like their sister regiments to their left, the 33rd Mississippi found themselves against overwhelming odds, fighting two or three Federal regiments in their front. Moreover, the blue-clad troops had a second line of regiments behind their first line that was just as strong as the first, while Featherston's Mississippians had no support.

26th Wisconsin. Drake's 33rd Mississippi and most of the 1st Mississippi Battalion Sharpshooters were fighting all of Wood's brigade, with the 26th Wisconsin in their front and the 20th Connecticut in their right front and flank. The 55th Ohio was behind the 20th Connecticut and the 75th Ohio was behind the 26th Wisconsin. Also, parts of the 22nd Wisconsin that had been on picket duty before the assault had rallied with Wood's men when they reached the ravine. According to one veteran of the 26th Wisconsin, "The line was formed on low ground with two parallel ridges in front, separated by a shallow ravine."[40] After the Federal skirmish line had been pushed back off of the farther ridge and to the first ridge where it met the advance of Ward's 3rd Division, the reinforced blue lines fired on the advancing Confederates in earnest as men of the 26th Wisconsin were "exposed to a heavy fire on the front and left flank" because they were in an advanced position in relation to the rest

---

[37] Mathew Andrew Dunn, Letters, *Journal of Mississippi History* 1 (January–October 1939): 123–24.

[38] Ibid., 124.

[39] Ibid.

[40] E. B. Quiner, *The Military History of Wisconsin: A Record of the Civil and Military Patriotism of the State, in the War for the Union* (Chicago: Clark & Co. Publishers, 1866) 756.

of Wood's brigade on the left of the Federal line.[41] "The enemy advanced to within ten paces of our lines…and was met by a terrible fire which he was unable to stand, and finally broke and fled," allowing the 26th Wisconsin to reach and eventually secure a position on top of the hill.[42] In Company C of the Sigel Regiment, the 26th Wisconsin, Private Charles "Stamm's musket misfired. As he threw it down, a bullet cut down Capt. Robert Mueller so Stamm picked up his sword. Soon another soldier fell and the private took his musket to resume firing."[43]

Major Frederick W. Winkler, commanding the 26th Wisconsin, described the fighting in a letter written the next day: "We fought the hardest battle and won the greatest victory yesterday of all the campaign, and my regiment covered itself with glory. We were attacked by superior numbers, the forces on our left failed us; we were outflanked," he exclaimed, as the 20th Connecticut was slow to come up and cover their left flank, "but we whipped the enemy, turned, and pursued him to the position we coveted, got it and held it. We fought the 33rd Mississippi, and virtually annihilated it; we killed the Colonel and thirty-four men, whom we have picked up inside the point we pursued them to," Winkler explained. "And beyond that our fire must have done them severe damage. The ground was covered with wounded; I had no time to count them, but had three stretchers working all night, carrying them to the rear. We took its flags and six officers' swords." The proud Federal Major continued, "Every body is speaking the praise of the 26th today. We had a very critical position and everything depended upon holding it; officers and men did bravely. The regiment we fought had nearly four hundred men; I only two hundred and sixty." Winkler lamented the losses sustained by his regiment, but he celebrated the results of the battle. "I lost severely, two captains killed, one wounded, a lieutenant wounded, seven men killed and thirty-four wounded. Upon the whole, our loss is comparatively light; most of the wounds are light, and our success was great. We took a number of prisoners."[44]

Among the slain was Captain John P. Seeman who was buried together with his comrades along Collier Road on the ridge that his regiment helped recapture. Also among the dead were Captain Robert Mueller, sergeants

---

[41] Quiner, *Military History of Wisconsin*, 756.

[42] Ibid., 756.

[43] James S. Pula, *The Sigel Regiment: A History of the 26th Wisconsin Volunteer Infantry, 1862–1865* (Campbell CA: Savas Publishing Co., 1998) 257.

[44] Russell Scott, "26th Wisconsin," www.russscott.com/~rscott/26thwis/26pgwk64.htm (7 May 2006).

Stephen Feiss and Bernhard Ott, corporals John Held and Franz Reuter, and privates William Arnn, Xavier Braun, Gerhard Niephaus, William Sasse, and Jacob Webber. In addition, thirty-six men were reported wounded from the Sigel Regiment but the losses were even higher.[45] Frank Kuechenmeister of Company K was shot in the right hand, which had to be amputated, while Julius Semich of Company A was shot in the right eye. The wounded Kuechenmeister was able to pick up a souvenir from the battlefield before going to the field hospital for treatment: "a cedar canteen inscribed 'W. E. Ratcliffe, 33d Mississippi Infantry.'"[46] The canteen belonged to Third Lieutenant Warren R. Ratcliffe (or spelled "Ratliff" in the roll of casualties) of Company E known as the "Holmesville Guards" of Pike County, Mississippi, from the 33rd Mississippi, who was listed among the missing.[47]

Adjutant George Traeumer of the Sigel Regiment "seemed to be in hysterics, and for a time I almost feared that he was dying," recalled Colonel Winkler. "The men were so exhausted they could hardly move; some had to be carried back though not wounded." One veteran remembered, "guns were so hot from rapid firing that the men could not touch the barrels." Charles Stamm, who had gotten a late start due the malfunction of his gun, "claimed he fired 113 shots during the fight." The regiment's historian aptly described the incredible heat of battle that canopied that Georgia July day atop Collier Ridge: "The oppressive heat, the unshielded sun, the constant fear and exhilaration of the sharp action, the exhausting charge up the hill, and the dogged defense left many completely exhausted, while others were pushed to the edge of their mental endurance." Colonel Winkler was so tired from the fighting that he "had not strength to speak above a whisper."[48]

During the Federal counterattack, Captain Fuchs of Company G, 26th Wisconsin captured the colors of the 33rd Mississippi, while forty prisoners were captured by his regiment. After the 26th Wisconsin retook the hill for the Yankees, they began receiving fire from the woods to their left (from some of Maney's Tennesseans located on the wooded heights just east of the Ardmore

---

[45] Pula, *The Sigel Regiment*, 263. Two photos showing these graves and the valley briefly taken by Featherston's Mississippians, the only known or surviving pictures of the Battle of Peach Tree Creek, were taken by George Barnard. They were taken from the Collier Road facing north and the marked graves in the foreground are those of Captain Seeman (Seaman) and his fellow deceased comrades from Wood's brigade.

[46] Pula, *The Sigel Regiment*, 261

[47] www.angelfire.com/ms3/davidg33/coE.htm (12 January 2009).

[48] Pula, *The Sigel Regiment*, 263–64.

The Battle of Peach Tree Creek

Park), but this fire was soon checked by the arrival of the 20th Connecticut on the left flank of the 26th Wisconsin, plugging the hole between that regiment and the right of Newton's division. The 26th Wisconsin lost twelve men killed, and forty-three wounded of which six later died, for a total of fifty-five men lost during the fighting.[49] A complete list of the casualties of the 26th Wisconsin can be found as an appendix to this book. Colonel Wood singled out the 26th Wisconsin for its gallant conduct in changing the tide of battle: "The position of this regiment in line was such that the brunt of the enemy's attack fell upon it."[50] Wood added, "The brave, skillful and determined manner in which it met this attack, rolled back the onset, pressed forward in a counter charge and drove back the enemy, could not be excelled by the troops in this or any other army, and is worthy of the highest commendation and praise."[51]

During the battle between Wood's brigade and the right flank of Featherston's brigade, blue- and gray-clad men fought hand to hand or some places within twenty paces of each other firing as fast as they could at one another. According to Colonel Wood, "The men had expended all their ammunition and supplied themselves from the cartridge boxes of the dead and wounded rebels."[52] In the savagery and carnage that ensued, Wood's brigade of some 1,300 men took heavy casualties, 143 men, while Drake's 33rd Mississippi of only 300 men was being annihilated. Before dark 168 men of the 33rd Mississippi would fall. Along with the regiment's Colonel Drake, thirty-four men were killed on the field. Another twenty-two men would die of their wounds, while sixty-one men were wounded, forty-three were captured of which eight later died of wounds, and sixteen were missing in action, of which many were no, doubt, also killed on the field.[53] Research of the sixteen "missing" soldiers reveals that only one was confirmed as having returned to the regiment. The other fifteen "missing" were apparently killed on the field, no record of them being found from either Federal or Confederate sources, yielding a total of dead on the field from the 33rd Mississippi of forty-nine men,

---

[49] Quiner, *Military History of Wisconsin*, 756–57.

[50] Ibid., 757; *OR*, ser. 1, vol. 38, pt. 2, serial 73, pp. 443–44.

[51] Quiner, *Military History of Wisconsin*, 757; *OR*, ser. 1, vol. 38, pt. 2, serial 73, pp. 443–44.

[52] James Wood, "Report of the Operations of the 3rd Brigade, 3rd Division of the XX Army Corps," in *The Atlanta Campaign of 1864*, 30 (Albany: Weed, Parsons & Company, Printers, 1889).

[53] Courtesy, Fred Kimbrell, Historian, 33rd Mississippi; "Compiled Service Records of Confederate Soldiers Who Served in Organizations from the Union and Confederate States of America during the War of the Rebellion," RG 269, National Archives, Washington, DC.

including Colonel Drake. This figure is the same one that Federal accounts place as the number of men that they buried with the colonel. One Northern reporter explained, "It is estimated that every man in Hooker's Corps expended over a hundred rounds of ammunition. At the beginning of the fight the ammunition trains were on the north bank of the creek, but they were rushed over before the troops had generally emptied their boxes."[54]

Historian Phil Noblitt explained the desperation and frustration of Featherston's Mississippians: "Ironically, Featherston's initial success might have turned into a complete rout of the Union forces if Hardee had supported him with Maney's division or if he had committed Maj. Gen. Patrick Cleburne's crack division, which was being held in reserve."[55] Without help from Maney's Tennesseans to their right, the 33rd Mississippi and her sister regiments stood no chance. "Instead," continued Noblitt, "Maney's two lead brigades watched as well as they could from the woods, while his rear brigades took refuge on the back side of a wooded ridge. Although Hardee later sent Maney on a belated and half-hearted assault, it was not until after Featherston's retreat. Loring was justifiably angry."[56]

With no support from Maney's division on the right, continued fire from Newton's division into their ranks, and with the 20th Connecticut's advance along their right flank, Captain Jackson and the remaining men of the 33rd Mississippi found themselves nearly cut off. The color-bearer of the 33rd Mississippi was killed and the flag, a second national flag, was lost to the enemy. According to one veteran, "others attempted to get the colors and were wounded. So we lost our colors. It was a very bloody affair."[57] Sergeant Daniel William Russell from Edinburg, Mississippi, who served in Company A, the "Cumberland Guards" of Neshoba County in neighboring Philadelphia, Mississippi, explained that his mother sent seven sons and a husband to fight for the Magnolia State. The husband "was killed by lighting while drilling in the militia. One brother died in the hospital and one was killed at Peachtree

---

[54] D. Van Nostrand, "How We Fight in Atlanta," in Frank Moore, ed., *Rebellion Record. A Diary of American Events*, vol. 11, comp. G. P. Putnam: New York, 1868) 253.

[55] Phil Noblitt, *Battle of Peachtree Creek,* www.historynet.com/battle-of-peachtree-creek.htm (6 March 2005).

[56] Ibid.

[57] Dunn, Letters, 124.

Creek.... I was badly wounded at Peachtree Creek."[58] In addition to Sergeant D. W. Russell who was wounded atop Collier Ridge, Third Corporal Prince A. Russell and privates Gideon B. Russell, Tate Russell, and W. B. Russell were all killed. Private Augustus E. Russell was simply listed as missing. Augustus had earlier been discharged from further service in the army by having a "substitute" replace him due to his age and health, yet he had chosen to remain to share the fate of his comrades. Their tragic fate would be a mass grave for some forty-nine of them along a dusty Georgia farmroad named Collier.[59]

As the remnants of the 33rd Mississippi fell back, the 20th Connecticut continued to press their right and they advanced into where the 33rd had been, thus placing themselves on the right flank and rear of the 3rd Mississippi, the next regiment in Featherston's line. This move by the 20th Connecticut allowed the Connecticut boys to cut off and capture a number of retreating and wounded Rebels in the 3rd Mississippi who were too badly hurt to fall back. Amazingly, the survivors of Feathertson's brigade continued the fight from a short distance into the night. By the end of the evening, Colonel Drake's 33rd Mississippi would be decimated, with over half of its men dead, dying, and wounded across the bloody field on both sides of Collier Road and the Collier Ridge. The next day, Federal survivors of the fight took on the gruesome job of burying the dead and removing the wounded. Private George Hoenig of the 26th Wisconsin recorded, "This morning the dead rebels were buried, most of them were from the 33rd Mississippi Regiment. We lost about 44 men through deaths and casualties, and captured a rebel flag, white with a red field and a silver star. More than 50 rebels were buried by our regiment alone, among them Colonel Drake from the 33rd, a huge guy with a red beard."[60]

W. H. Conner, a soldier in the 33rd Indiana and a survivor of the assault, had this to say of the 33rd Miss. and Featherston's Mississippians:

[Col. Drake] was almost in front of his men when killed. I can see him yet as he waved his sword cheering his gallant men on the fighting. At this time it was most desperate, almost hand to hand. It was only a question of time as to

---

[58] D. W. Russell, *Confederate Veteran* (February 1909): 54.

[59] Russell, 54; Kimbrell, Fred, Historian 33rd Mississippi; "Compiled Service Records of Confederate Soldiers Who Served in Organizations from the Union and Confederate States of America during the War of the Rebellion," RG 269, National Archives, Washington, DC.

[60] George Hoenig, "The Journal of Pvt. George Hoenig, 26th Wisconsin Regiment," www.angelfire.com/ms3/davidg33/ (10 May 2008); casualty list, courtesy of Fred Kimbrell, http://home.att.net/~captnerdo/33rd.htm (10 May 2008).

which side would gain the day. At this juncture of the fighting the Color Bearer of the 33rd Miss. waved his flag back and forth in front of Co. K 33rd Ind. which was a wonderful daring act.

The 33rd Ind. dashed forward as the Confederates were thrown in confusion. I made a dash for the colors of the 33rd Miss. and caught the flag just as the brave Color Bearer was killed. I did not kill him for which I and very thankful. From the large numbers of the dead and wounded I believe that every one of the Color Bearers were killed.

After[ward] the Confederates had retreated from the hill and were fighting as they retreated...

The next day after the battle we buried the Confederate dead. We dug a circular grave and laid 45 of Col. Drake's men side by side with their feet towards the center and buried Col. Drake in the center. We placed a marker with the following inscription "Col. Drake and 45 of his men."

Comrade Hall of my Company cut the inscription on a board. These brave men were buried the same as our own men in the best possible manner under the circumstances. I will also state that when the Confederates advanced to the attack, the 3rd Div. of the 20th Corps had just crossed Peach Tree Creek and had stacked their guns and were engaged in making our coffee.... My regiment the 33rd Ind. went into the fight with 382 men. The regiment lost 117 killed and wounded, other regiments of the division about the same number.

Featherston's Brigade were wonderful fighters...[61]

Another account of the fighting between Wood's brigade and the 33rd Mississippi was recorded in a diary by Private Charles Buerstatte of the 26th Wisconsin:

20th July—Today we are engaged in a terrible battle with the Rebs at Peach Tree Creek. At 2:00 o'clock PM. our brigade which was at the left Rank of the corps, joined the 4th Corps in battle line. The enemy attacked at which time we advanced. Our regiment was as always in the forward battle line. We advanced over a small hill and into a valley in which a small creek flowed. Then the Rebs came toward us down the hill in front of us. Now the

---

[61] W. H. Conner turned over the captured flag to a division staff officer who told him to give it to him. Credit for its capture was later given to the 26th Wisconsin, which had been to the left of and a little behind the 33rd Indiana during the counterattack. W. H. Conner to Dunbar Rowland (state historian), 20 October 1927, 33rd Mississippi vertical file, Mississippi Department of Archives and History, Jackson, Mississippi.

firing really began. The gunfire exceeded anything I had ever heard before. We loaded and fired as fast as possible. The Rebs came to within 10 paces of us, at which time our musket balls became too thick for them. They turned to the right and retreated up the hill with us behind them. This was a sight which I had never seen before and hope never to see again. The entire field was scattered with dead, wounded and dying. The wounded moaned so much that I could hardly watch. However, we had no time and had to advance up the hill. There stood a fence behind which we petitioned ourselves. The Rebs tried to advance again but did not succeed, because a battery was placed on the hill behind us which greeted the enemy terribly with cannonballs. After 4 hours of firing, we were finally relieved and went to the second battle line. The firing lasted into the night. At night I helped carry more wounded from the field. We also captured a flag from the 33rd Mississippi Regiment.

21st July—This morning our regiment, after a sleepless night, had to bury the dead Rebs which laid before our regiment. They were all from the 33rd Mississippi Regiment. Our regiment lost 9 dead and 36 wounded. We buried over 50 Rebs, among them Colonel Drake and most of the officers of the 33rd Miss. Regiment.[62]

Regimental historian Fred Kimbrell has uncovered an account by a family of Thomas Littleberry Cooper, one of the Mississippians who fought atop Collier Ridge. The Cooper family sought the location of Colonel Drake's grave as well as that of the other Mississippians. They eventually received information from an Atlanta resident:

Col. Drake was buried in the center of the Federal dead [along with his fallen Mississippi comrades], about 50 or 100 in number. There was a plain cracker box board at the head of his grave marked Col. Drake. He was buried a little to the right and rear of the old Collier homestead which is still standing. The Federal dead were exhumed and taken to Marietta. Our dead were taken up and interred in Oakland Cemetery where I suppose the remains of Col. Drake were reentered. I shall show your inquiry to the sexton and see if his grave can be located. I visited the battlefield a few weeks after the battle and noted the destruction that had been done there. I was 15 years old at the time and have lived in this city ever since. I noticed then one grave with 55 Mississippians in it and another with 40 Alabamians besides the kindred of our men who long remembered. A year after the war the battlefield has

---

[62] Casualty list, courtesy of Fred Kimbrell, http://home.att.net/~captnerdo/peachtre.htm (5 January 2009); Pula, *The Sigel Regiment*, 261–63.

changed but little, especially that portion where Loring's Div charged. A few months ago I visited the position of the field of your brigade with a Federal Surgeon of the 55th Ohio Regiment who was in full view when the Confederates came up and jumped an old rail fence and attacked the 3rd Brigade of the 3rd Div of the 20th Army Corps where it connected with the 4th Army Corps. The old Collier Mill Road is still there. The dam of the old mill is there. If any of your command ever visits Atlanta and calls upon me, I will take pleasure in going over the battlefield with you. There is a street rail running within a 1/2 mile of the placed occupied by Loring's Div.[63]

Choctaw Rebels, Company E, 31st Mississippi. In Company E, the Choctaw Rebels held their own for a while at the Collier Ridge until the irresistible blue wave came crashing upon them on three sides. Mustered into service on 8 March 1862 at Pigeon Roost, an old trading post located on the Natchez Trace, the Choctaw Rebels were the last company to join the 31st Mississippi. The Choctaw Rebels, 124 men strong, joined Colonel Orr in April 1862 at Saltillo, Mississippi, near Tupelo. By 20 July, after three springs of fighting, only 20 men were left from the original roll of 124 men when the Choctaw Rebels formed up for the charge.

As was typical of many Civil War units, the Choctaw Rebels had a number of brothers and other relatives serving together. Of the 124 original Choctaw Rebels, at least 80 were related by blood to at least one other in Company E, and most of these family groups were brothers. When adding relations by marriage, virtually all of the Choctaw Rebels were related to each other as quite a number of brothers-in-law also fought together in the unit making the Choctaw Rebels truly a "band of brothers."

Corporal William P. Brooks was shot in the left leg and died on 13 September 1864 at a Federal hospital in Chattanooga. Private Joseph G. B. Brooks, was also wounded, but he managed to get away and was treated at one of the Confederate hospitals in Atlanta. Private Jerry Clark was wounded slightly in the side and was also treated in a hospital in Atlanta. He returned to the Choctaw Rebels on 21 August.

The Dudley family gave five sons to the regiment and three died in service including Third Sergeant James Jacob Dudley who was shot in the leg and foot. He was taken back to the hospital where he later died. The Fondren family sent four loved ones to fight with the Choctaw Rebels and two were wounded in the

---

[63] Casualty list, courtesy of Fred Kimbrell, http://home.att.net/~captnerdo/peachtre.htm (5 January 2009).

The Battle of Peach Tree Creek

fight. Private George H. Fondren was wounded severely in the hip, but managed to escape capture. He eventually recovered after the war, but was crippled for six years. Private Rufus K. Fondren was not able to avoid capture. He was shot in the head and left on the field.

Fourth Corporal Claiborn Preston Gunter received a wound to his hand. His brother, Captain Pleasant Dickson Gunter, had commanded the Choctaw Rebels during fall 1862 until he lost one of his legs from a train accident near Grenada, Mississippi.

Brothers James Monroe Hester, John Franklin Hester, and Joseph R. Hester joined the Choctaw Rebels in spring 1862. Young Joseph was only fourteen. First Sergeant James Hester became sick during the Vicksburg Campaign in summer 1863 and was furloughed home. John and Joseph Hester participated in the charge at Peach Tree Creek where John was wounded severely in the arm and sent to the hospital. Joseph, at sixteen, escaped injury at Peach Tree Creek, helped his brother back to safety, and remained with the Choctaw Rebels until hostilities ended in April 1865.

Third Lieutenant Silas Mercer Dobbs led the veterans of Company E amid the battle smoke. The thirty-four-year-old son of a Baptist minister had led music in the churches of Choctaw and Noxubee Counties in Mississippi in his youth while following his father in the ministry. Mounting pressure from overwhelming Federal troops suddenly compelled Dobbs to rally his men on the ridge as they fell back up the hill from the ravine. With him was Private James E. Bridges who was wounded in the arm, side, and foot but managed to escape capture and fall back to the Rebel trenches. So, too, were privates John C. Manner, Joseph W. D. Ramsey, and John Reynolds, who were each wounded in the arm and sent to the hospital in Atlanta.

Also wounded in the arm was Private James M. Taylor, who enlisted as an underaged volunteer. Young Taylor's arm was broken from the fighting, but he was able to withdraw from the field. The red-haired and 150-pound Lieutenant Dobbs stood nearby. Waiving his sword to rally the survivors, Lieutenant Dobbs was shot in the shoulder. With only a handful of men left, including Private Caradine "Jerry" Jenkins who had returned to his native Georgia to fight for her defense, Dobbs and the Choctaw Rebels withdrew down the field until they reached a point of relative safety about 200 yards away where they, with the rest of Featherston's Mississippians, continued the fight until dark when they were ordered to withdraw.

Twice more the Choctaw Rebels along with the rest of the Mississippi Brigade tried to renew the attack, but it was no use. They were too few, and the

Yankees too many. Further, the men in blue held the high ground and were now prepared to receive them. Also, the Choctaw Rebels were exposed in the old open field and could hardly rise without exposing themselves to deadly fire. The battle for Collier Ridge was over. After three hours, Ward's division held the ridge but at a fearful price. In the space of only a few hundred yards, over 1,200 Federal and Confederate dead and wounded had fallen in that time, reminding many of Hooker's veterans of the carnage at Gettysburg.

Lieutenant Colonel James Drane had led 215 men up the Collier Ridge from the 31st Mississippi, but only 34 returned unhurt. From the Choctaw Rebels just six out of twenty came back unscathed, but they managed to carry off all but two from the field. Brothers Fondren and Brooks were not able to be rescued. Two of the brothers, Dudley and Brooks, would die from their wounds, making 20 July the bloodiest day in the history of the Choctaw Rebels and the 31st Mississippi.

While the Mississippians licked their wounds near Tanyard Branch, up on Collier Road Ward's Federals were caught up in a mixture of celebration and of working to improve their position. First Lieutenant Ralsa C. Rice of the 125th Ohio, which had defended the bridge over Peach Tree Creek at the Buckhead Road, remembered the anxiety caused by Featherston's attack:

> We heard the roar of battle over in the woods to our right and could see the smoke curling up through the treetops. And we could see it farther and farther back. Was Hooker being overpowered? It seemed so. Then came a cheer. That was no rebel yell. Immediately we saw General Hooker riding toward us. With hat in hand he came up and said, "Boys we have whipped them again!" It was now our turn to shout. We wound up with three cheers for General Hooker.[64]

On top of the Collier Ridge, the jubilant, but exhausted Yankees of Ward's division worked to build better defenses and looked among the dead and dying for unused cartridges and caps. "We had seen famishing men crowd for food and water, but now there was a greater rush for powder and ball. As soon as the enemy had been driven from the top of the hill every rail and chink that could be found was used to form a breastwork."[65] Color Sergeant Frank H. Huron of

---

[64] Ralsa C. Rice, *Yankee Tigers, through the Civil War with the 125th Ohio*, ed. Richard A. Baumgartner and Larry M. Strayer (Huntington WV: Blue Acorn Press, 1992) 128.

[65] Samuel Merrill, *The Seventieth Indiana Volunteer Infantry in the War of the Rebellion* (Indianapolis: The Bowen-Merrill Company, 1900) 140–41.

the 70th Indiana, described his bazaar experience across the battle-scarred ridge as darkness cast its shadows over the field. "As soon as the darkness stopped the firing, I took my canteen and those of two dead men lying beside me, and filling them from the little brook in our rear, went to the wounded rebels in our immediate front, who were crying for water." Huron recalled, "After a few trips I found myself perhaps two hundred yards in advance of our line, giving water to one whose feeble cry had drawn me to him. While he was drinking I heard the click of a musket, and turning quickly, saw by the starlight a man not twenty feet away." The surprised Good Samaritan saw him "half hidden in a ditch washed out by the rains, with bayonet fixed and gun leveled at me. To say that I abhorred a man who would shoot another while he was giving water to his wounded comrades is putting it too mildly. I wanted to kill him so bad that I could taste it," remembered Huron, "but just then a faint voice behind him called, 'For God's sake, somebody give me a drink of water,' and my decision was made in a moment." The Indiana soldier planned his escape from the dastardly Rebel. "I would go to that who was ready to shoot me, as if he were the one who was calling, give him a canteen, and while he was drinking, would snatch his gun, whirl it round, and if he didn't surrender, bayonet him before he could dodge."[66]

Huron reached the untrustworthy foe. "He left his bayonet pointing toward me until I was almost against it, then drew it to one side, when I saw there were two others beside him squatted down in the ditch with guns in their hands and bayonets fixed, and I knew they intended to take me in." Sergeant Huron considered his options. "One canteen was empty, so I could not get the three drinking at once, but I handed them the two containing some water, thinking one of them at least would lose his gun while drinking, and if they killed me I would first get one or more of them. Death was better than Andersonville," he reasoned. "But they began drinking, holding their guns on the other side of the ditch, with the third man watching. Just then the weak voice behind them called again, 'Oh, for one drink of water, water, water!' I called to him I would bring him some," explained the sergeant, "and asked them not to drink it all, and I would bring them some more (but I didn't intend to do it). They left a little in one canteen, and I went past them to the other man, thinking to get his gun, but he had none in sight. Then I decided to make a zig-zag run for our line and risk them hitting me," thought Huron, "but as the man drained the last drop and begged for more, I promised to return as soon as I could fill the canteens, and

---

[66] Ibid., 145.

started back past them, thinking it safer to make them believe I was coming back with more water than to run."[67]

Huron began to slowly make his way back in the glimmering darkness as he left the last man who had cried for more water and reached the three armed Rebels in the ditch. "Just as I got to them an impulse seized me to take them in. So I began telling them, if they were not too badly wounded, I could help them in to our surgeons, who would take as much pains with them as with our own soldiers." The fast-thinking Indianan began to embellish. He told them of "our hospital supplies, especially the good eating, and the women nurses, and the splendid barracks and good living they would have after leaving the hospital, or the immediate freedom if they wanted to take the oath and quit fighting;" Huron continued by explaining "that everything was so plenty in the North we could take the best care of them, and as their comrades knew they were wounded they would of course expect them to be captured, and it would be perfectly honorable for them to go where they could be best cared for."[68]

The wily Yankee had played his hand. Now, he began to worry if he had done enough to secure his escape. "I pledged them all this on the honor of a soldier, but was getting uneasy, wondering what to say more, when one of them blurted out, 'What do you say, boys?' and another answered, 'Darned if I care,'" as the relieved, if not surprised, sergeant quickly seized the moment, "and I instantly took hold of their guns, pulling them as though it was understood that I should have them, and they let go. I pitched one gun behind me and took the gun from the other man before he had time to protest, and remarking that I would carry the guns and they could help each other, I took a step toward our lines, and all three of them climbed out of their ditch and walked with me, saying just before we got to where the surgeons were sawing off arms and legs, 'that they didn't need any doctors.'"[69]

---

[67] Ibid., 145–46.
[68] Ibid., 146.
[69] Ibid., 146–47.

18

THICKETS WERE LITERALLY CRADLED BY BULLETS

We took the Yanks in our front entirely by surprise, they were mostly foreigners who couldn't speak English. They threw down their guns and surrendered in droves and that was our undoing. Too many of our fellows were willing to carry prisoners to the rear. There was no reserve line to carry on the victory.[1]

Coming out of the trenches shielding Atlanta from the northwest, Major General Edward Cary Walthall lined up his two available brigades for the attack. The Alabama lawyer and veteran of the Army of Northern Virginia, Colonel Edward Asbury O'Neal, placed his Alabama and Mississippi troops into battle formation on the grounds of and to the east of Mt. Zion Church. His right flank was about 400 yards away from the left of General Scott's Alabama and Louisiana Brigade and they were shielded from each other due to the dense forest and underbrush that separated their forces. The briars and undergrowth was so great in front of Scott's men and between his left and O'Neal's right, that some men found it impossible to penetrate it, but instead some of the men in Scott's left regiments had to zig-zag to the east a bit to get through it before reaching the Federal forces in their front.

On his right, O'Neal's only Mississippi regiment, the 37th Mississippi Infantry, under the command of Colonel Orlando S. Holland, formed the right flank of the brigade. The 17th Alabama, under the leadership of Major T. J. Burnett, was next on the right. O'Neal's own 26th Alabama formed the center led by Major D. F. Bryan. The 1st Corps (Alabama) Sharpshooters was to the left of the 26th Alabama under the command of Captain Sid. B. Smith, while the 29th Alabama led by Colonel John F. Conoley formed on the left of the brigade.[2] Earlier in the year it had been rumored that Holland, who was senior

---

[1] Washington Bryan Crumpton, *A Book of Memories* (Montgomery AL: Baptist Mission Board, 1921) 86; Larry M. Strayer and Richard A. Baumgartner, eds., *Echoes of Battle: The Atlanta Campaign* (Huntington WV: Blue Acorn Press, 1991) 216.

[2] United States War Department, comp., *Official Records of the Union and Confederate Armies in the War of the Rebellion*, 128 vols. (Washington, DC: Government Printing Office,

colonel of the brigade at that time, would be promoted to a brigadier general and given command of the brigade, or a new brigade of Mississippians after General William E. Baldwin died unexpectedly in February 1864 at Mobile. The report that Holland might be given the command worried many Mississippians, including Colonel William S. Barry of the 35th Mississippi and a number of men from Sears's brigade, who feared the promotion or who were jockeying for their own promotions.[3] A number of officers sought the command, but on 1 March 1864, Claudius W. Sears was appointed brigadier, and by the third week of March, Sears was leading the group of Mississippians. Colonel Barry left his command for a brief time to console his discontentment, but the malcontent in Holland could not be mollified. This prompted Major General Dabney H. Maury, commander of the department to write Richmond: "Colonel Holland having been recommended to command the Mississippi Brigade, and another having been appointed its Brigadier, together with the attendant facts, have caused so much feeling amongst the officers that it would be best for the service, I think, that he should not return to the brigade."[4]

Holland joined the Confederate service in fall 1861 as part of Company K, the "Mississippi Boys" from Lauderdale and Clarke Counties, a group of sixty-day volunteers, and was placed with the 5th Mississippi Regiment, part of the Mississippi Infantry Army of 10,000. Elected as first lieutenant while the men were at Corinth on 30 November 1861, he was made captain when William S. Patton became the colonel of the regiment that became known as Patton's 1st Regiment. By February 1862, the sixty days of service was up and the regiment was disbanded. Holland then helped form the 37th Mississippi and became its lieutenant colonel when it organized on 29 April 1862 at Columbus, Mississippi. After its first colonel died, Holland became colonel of the regiment and, in a role reversal, his former boss, William S. Patton, became his lieutenant colonel.[5]

When Holland was not promoted to brigade command, and Colonel E. A. O'Neal with his veteran regiment, the 26th Alabama, fresh off of two year's of

---

1880–1901) ser. 1, vol. 38, pt.3, 941 (hereafter *OR*).

[3] William Pitt Chambers, *Blood and Sacrifice, The Civil War Journal of a Confederate Soldier* ed. Richard Baumgartner (Huntington WV: Blue Acorn Press, 1994) 124–25, 127; Dunbar Rowland, *Military History of Mississippi, 1803–1898,* ed. H. Grady Howell, Jr. (Spartanburg SC: The Reprint Company, Publishers, 1978) 328.

[4] Rowland, *Military History of Mississippi*, 328.

[5] *Supplement to the Official Records of the Union and Confederate Armies.* (Wilmington NC: Broadfoot Publishing Company, 1995–2001) pt. 2 vol. 32, ser. 44, pp. 624, 626, 630; and pt. 2, vol. 34, ser. 46, 139, 144 (hereafter *Supplement to* OR).

fighting with the Army of Northern Virginia returned to Alabama to supplement its numbers and to provide some much needed rest to the group, Holland's regiment was put into a new unit, an all-Alabama brigade under the command of General James Cantey, a native South Carolinian. Holland's 37th Mississippi heralded primarily from east Mississippi and its members had a number of ties with the Alabamians. Holland hoped that this new brigade would give him an opportunity to gain a promotion and a brigadier's star. However, the veteran O'Neal became the acting commander of the brigade during the Georgia Campaign in the absence of General James Cantey who was sick for most of the year while Holland sulked. General Maury had succeeded in "relieving the hitch" concerning the commands in both Sears's and Cantey's brigades. For Holland, however, Peach Tree Creek would mark the highlight of his military career.[6]

O'Neal's brigade marched to the northeast in the woods and along the old Collier Mill Road, a road that followed along a ravine from behind the Mt. Zion Church on Howell Mill Road. The old Collier Mill Road (from Mt. Zion Church to Northside Drive) is no longer present, but it meandered to the northeast as it hugged the left side of the ridge, which banked the ravine until it intersected with the new Collier Road near Northside Drive. The old Collier Mill Road can be somewhat traced today by following a power line diagonally from the rear of the Mt. Zion Church to the northeast toward Northside Drive and its intersection with Collier Road.

O'Neal described the attack: "The line being formed, the command forward was given, and we advanced a short distance quietly, when our pickets becoming hotly engaged, I gave the command to charge the enemy and continued forward and drive every obstacle before them, which order was obeyed with a cheer," explained their commander, "driving a heavy line of skirmishers and one of battle." O'Neal continued, "The ground over which we advanced was very rough and the bushes and undergrowth dense and tangled, yet the line was well formed and advanced in good order..."[7]

As O'Neal's veterans swept through the wooded land to his north and east, they came astride a long ridge that was protruding in their direction. The ridge ran from southwest to northeast, in exactly the same direction that O'Neal's men were traveling. Moreover, about half way along on the ridge, O'Neal's

---

[6] Rowland, *Military History of Mississippi*, 328; Robert Webb Banks, *The Battle of Franklin, November 30, 1864. The Bloodiest Engagement of the War Between the States* (New York: The Neale Publishing Company, 1908) 20–21.

[7] *OR*, ser. 1, vol. 38, pt. 3, serial 74, 742.

Hood's First Sortie, 20 July 1864

men came up on the right of and behind Colonel Charles Candy's 1st Brigade and a part of Colonel Patrick H. Jones's 2nd Brigade of General John W. Geary's division. Colonel Candy's brigade had presently been occupied with watching the action to their front and left as they watched Featherston's Mississippians sweep up the old field to their left, and Scott's Alabamians and Louisianans lapped around the 33rd New Jersey to their front. Now, the woods crashed with a violent roar as O'Neal's Mississippians and Alabamians from the 37th Mississippi and the 17th Alabama came into view on their right and rear. The 28th Pennsylvania, led by Lieutenant Colonel John Flynn, was struck first, and these men fled almost immediately from the surprise assault on their right rear despite repeated efforts by their leaders to rally and refuse their line to the right.

Known as the Goldstream Regiment, the 28th Pennsylvania had been the product of the efforts of General John Geary. Organized on 28 June 1861, the regiment, along with Knap's artillery battery, were mustered in under the direction of John W. Geary, a fellow Pennsylvanian, in Philadelphia for three years. The regiment reenlisted on Christmas Eve 1863, and on 20 July, the veterans of the 28th Pennsylvania found themselves in an untenable position. Veterans of three years of campaigning in the Eastern Theater, the men of the 28th Pennsylvania had fought well at Antietam where they lost 266 men in one day, at Chancellorsville, where they dug in with bayonets, plates, and tin cups and held on when the rest of their division fell back, losing 100 out of 300 men present, and at Gettysburg where they shared in the successes of their division's fighting.[8]

Having watched Featherston's men take the ridge to their left in the distance and then seeing Scott's forces gobble up the 33rd New Jersey in their front, the men of Candy's brigade were preparing to receive the anticipated blows from their front and left. Now, out of nowhere came the frightening and unexpected roar of that familiar Rebel yell from behind them. It was simply too much for the veterans of the 28th Pennsylvania and the others in Candy's brigade to take. Presently, men of the 29th Ohio and 66th Ohio who were also on the line with the Goldstream Regiment, joined the 28th Pennsylvania in the rout. One officer from the 66th Ohio recorded that the Confederates swept through the skirmishers for the 66th Ohio "without taking prisoner or returning a shot, and at double-quick swept on beyond our rear to strike our main line." It

---

[8] "History of the 28th Regiment, Pennsylvania Volunteers, Goldstream Regiment," www.pa-roots.com/~pacw/infantry/28th/28thorg.html (6 March 2005).

appeared to the Ohioan that "the enemy was so bent on larger game," that they disregarded the few Ohioans on the skirmish line and apparently figured that they would surrender to subsequent Southern lines. Just at this time the adjutant for General Geary came "riding up with the order to fall back [as though a formal command were required]," and he "was shot and instantly killed. The position continued to roll up as the 29th Ohio, the regiment next in line to the 66th's [Ohio] left, also broke."[9]

At that time the men of the 134th New York Regiment of Colonel Patrick H. Jones's 2nd Brigade also broke ranks and ran for the rear, its leader, Colonel Allan H. Jackson, having been wounded and put out of the fight.[10] Colonel Jones had been out on the knoll with General Geary supervising the placement of the 33rd New Jersey before the surprise attack, and now he was caught up in the retreat from that position and was not able to direct his brigade. For a few minutes it appeared that all of Geary's division would be swept up in the fleeing mass of men who headed to their left and rear toward Peach Tree Creek and toward the bridges that had been built by Geary's engineers spanning the wide and muddy creek to safety. General Howard recorded in his memoirs that Colonel Jones "changed front as soon as he could, but too late to check the onset [of the Confederate assault], so that nearly the whole right wing was forced back to the bridgehead near Peach Tree Creek."[11] At least three regiments of the 1st Brigade, the 28th Pennsylvania, 29th Ohio, and 66th Ohio, and two of the 2nd Brigade, the 33rd New Jersey, and the 134th New York, had been routed and were effectively out of the fight.

Private Washington Bryan Crumpton from the 37th Mississippi described the breakthrough. "We took the Yanks in our front entirely by surprise, they were mostly foreigners who couldn't speak English. They threw down their guns and surrendered in droves and that was our undoing. Too many of our fellows were willing to carry prisoners to the rear. There was no reserve line to carry on the victory."[12]

Not all of Candy's men fled to the rear, however, as remnants of the 5th Ohio held their position firing into the oncoming Rebels of Scott's brigade to their front while keeping an eye on the approaching threat to their rear. To their

---

[9] David T. Thackery, *A Light and Uncertain Hold, A History of the 66th Ohio Volunteer Infantry*, 201–202.

[10] www.dmna.state.ny.us/historic/reghist/civil/infantry/134thInf/134thInfHistSketch.htm (7 May 2006).

[11] Howard, Autobiography, vol. 1, 617.

[12] Crumpton, *A Book of Memories*, 86.

front, the men of the 27th, 35th, and 49th Alabama Consolidated Regiment formed again and again in repeated attacks. Withdrawing from their right and refusing their line to face in two directions, the 5th Ohio and remnants of the 28th Pennsylvania that had not left the field held off the charging Alabamians and kept them from hauling off a section of Bundy's Battery that had been temporarily abandoned in the withdrawal.

Colonel Ario Pardee of the 147th Pennsylvania was stunned to see his supporting regiments in rear of his line flee the wooded ridge behind him. "So slight was the effort to resist," he explained, "that I was not aware that there was any severe fighting in that direction, but the disorganized masses of men as they rushed by the right of my line told a fearful tale." While Scott's brigade struck their front and right flank, O'Neal's brigade had by this time reached the lower Collier Ridge along today's intersection of Collier Road and Northside Drive, causing the reserve line of Yankees along the ridge behind Pardee's Pennsylvanians to flee. "The men seemed to be panic-stricken, and I regret to say that there was manifested a lack of energy, coolness, and determination on the part of the officers which was truly deplorable. It was impossible to stop any organized body of men."[13]

As Candy's shattered lines fell back, the men of the 134th New York and 119th New York of Jones's Brigade were swept by the sudden presence of O'Neal's brigade on their front, right and rear. The New Yorkers were posted atop the lower Collier Ridge facing southeast near the intersection of today's Collier Road and Northside Drive while O'Neal's onrushing Mississippians and Alabamians struck from the southwest. Quickly, one officer and twenty-five men of the 134th New York who had been on the far right of the lower Collier Ridge behind Candy's brigade were captured by the 37th Mississippi on the far right of O'Neal's attacking column.[14] Another seven men from the 119th New York who were posted just to the left of the surprised men of the 134th New York were unable to avoid capture as the New Yorkers of both regiments stampeded for the rear and safety.[15] In the surprise attack and during the subsequent fighting, the 134th New York lost five men killed, five more men were severely wounded, while one officer and seven men were slightly wounded for a total loss of forty-four men including the missing and captured.[16]

---

[13] *OR*, ser. 1, vol. 38, pt. 2, serial 73, p. 200; Erol Clauss, "The Atlanta Campaign, July 18, 1864" (Ph.D. diss., Emory University, 1965) 88.

[14] *OR*, ser. 1, vol. 38, pt. 2, serial 73, p. 215.

[15] Ibid., 215.

[16] Ibid., 215.

The Battle of Peach Tree Creek

In the 66th Ohio, some twenty-three men were casualties, but miraculously, only two men were killed.[17] It seems that many of the Ohioans were fleet-footed enough to avoid a bullet or capture.

General Candy's brigade lost one of their favorite mascots during the days' fighting as the general's best horse, Bill, was killed. Among the casualties of the 66th Ohio were Lieutenant James P. Conn of Company E, and Lieutenants John R. Organ and William V. Taylor of Company I and G respectively. Lieutenant Conn was struck on the head by a Rebel officer's sword, the blow likely coming from one of Colonel Holland's 37th Mississippians as they rushed over Candy's melting line. While Conn and other officers and non-commissioned officers struggled to rally the Ohioans, several of them paid dearly for their bravery. Conn was able to recover and return to his comrades that evening, but after the war "he continued to complain of the pain caused by his wound. He eventually became mentally unbalanced and ended his days in the Cleveland Hospital for the Insane." Lieutenant Taylor had previously been wounded in both legs at Antietam. He received a head wound at Gettysburg. Now, at Peach Tree Creek, Taylor was "shot in the hand, arm, and shoulder. Once again he survived."[18]

Lieutenant Organ, just twenty-one years old when he received his commission in January 1863, "had been wounded in the initial assault, a minie ball fracturing his thigh bone above the knee, causing profuse bleeding. He had soon found himself behind the Confederate assault line. To their credit, the Southerners improvised from some rags and Organ's tobacco pipe a tourniquet..." As the brutal struggle wore on, the young lieutenant fought for his life as the bloody wound had splintered his thigh. After several hours of fighting, the Yankees were able to retake their original lines and repatriate a number of their fallen comrades who had been captured in the action. "Following the Federal counterattack, Organ was again among friends, but he had lost a great deal of blood." The 66th Ohio's surgeon, Jesse Brock "attempted to amputate the leg. He was on the surgeon's table for about 15 minutes; according to the surgeon, Organ was conscious the entire time, praying constantly. Brock's efforts were in vain; the young lieutenant had lost too much blood. He was buried in a marked grave," and later was reinterred in a cemetery in his home town of Urbana. Surgeon "Brock himself came to harm. In the process of treating a soldier's wounded hand, he pricked his finger on some exposed bone. As it turned out, the wound had been gangrenous, and the doctor

---

[17] Thackery, *A Light and Uncertain Hold*, 204–205.
[18] Ibid., 204–205.

was in danger of losing his own hand; in the end the amputation of his forefinger was sufficient remedy."[19]

In the 119th New York, which had more notice of the surprise attack than their friends in the 134th New York and a jump start on the rout back toward the creek and the bridges over it to safety, only three men were wounded, two of them severely, in addition to the seven men who were missing or captured, for a total loss of just ten men at Peach Tree Creek.[20] Behind them, the men of the 154th New York saw the flight of their sister units, and they, too, broke and ran, leaving only one man to fall victim to capture, while only one man was killed and six men were wounded, five of whom severely, that being some of the New Yorkers who chose to remain and help form a new line across the ravine in the face of the attacking Rebels. When the Confederates first appeared advancing along the lower Collier ridge, the men of the 154th New York were "ordered to lie down with their arms in their hands."[21] In a few moments, the Rebels were on them. "The first line [the 119th New York, the 134th New York, and parts of Candy's 1st Brigade atop the lower ridge] at once gave way before the fire which was hurled against it, and fell back in confusion through our lines, to which their panic was communicated, and the whole right of the line retreated..."[22] Lieutenant Colonel Daniel B. Allen was found to be too exhausted to lead, Major Lewis D. Warner, regrouped the regiment, together with those men who remained to fight in the area near today's Bitsy Grant Tennis Center parking lot, and formed to the left of Williams's 1st Division near the entrance and sign along today's Northside Drive.[23] With one man killed, six men wounded, and one man captured or missing, the 154th New York added eight men to the losses in Jones's 2nd Brigade at Peach Tree Creek.[24]

Over to the left of Jones's lines, Major Charles C. Cresson without any orders from the absent brigade commander, led his 73rd Pennsylvania forward to support the 147th Pennsylvania of Candy's brigade in the front line. After receiving heavy fire on both flanks, Major Cresson moved his regiment back about 80 yards, "changed position to the right [to near today's Evergreen Lane], and moved forward to a small work in my front."[25] From that position,

---

[19] Ibid., 204.
[20] *OR*, ser. 1, vol. 38, pt. 2, serial 73, p. 215.
[21] Ibid., 252.
[22] Ibid., 252.
[23] Ibid., 252.
[24] Ibid., 215.
[25] Ibid., 261.

Cresson's Pennsylvanians continued to "engage the enemy for some two and a half hours" until the Confederates "were compelled to fall back."[26] Cresson's regiment operated during the entire battle independently and apart from any connection with any other unit from its 2nd Brigade, instead working with the 147th Pennsylvania of Candy's 1st Brigade on its left, and later being supported by the 60th New York of Ireland's 3rd Brigade.[27] The 73rd Pennsylvania lost two men killed and one officer and seven men severely wounded for a total loss of ten men during the action.[28]

When the fighting commenced, the 109th Pennsylvania was located in reserve near the position of the 60th New York of Ireland's brigade on the left side of the ridge at the site of today's Bitsy Grant Tennis Center below Overbrook Drive and the ravine between it and the lower Collier Ridge. Attrition in the field and company officers had left Captain Walter G. Dunn in command of the Pennsylvania regiment as they moved forward into the fray in support of the 147th Pennsylvania in their front. As the men of the 109th Pennsylvania moved forward, they began feeling the pressure of the Confederate attack on their right flank, and they hurried their pace. When they reached the ravine, they were met by the 29th Ohio who "were surging to the left in a confused mass, forcing the 109th Pennsylvania along with them."[29] At that same moment the left half of Scott's brigade surged forward and seemed to gain the Federal works and two of Bundy's guns on the far right of Candy's line. As the blue tide streamed back toward the Peach Tree Creek crossings catching with it the supporting units that had been rushed forward, it seemed that a complete rout of Geary's entire lines was eminent. But at that precise moment uncommon courage took a hand.

Sergeant Fergus Elliott of Company G, 109th Pennsylvania, bore the colors of his regiment at Peach Tree Creek. Watching his comrades caught up in the rout of the Federal lines, Elliot tried to stop the color-bearer of the 29th Ohio and asked him to remain with him and stop the retreat that had by this point taken all of the 29th Ohio, most of the 5th Ohio, the 28th Pennsylvania, the 109th Pennsylvania, and the 60th New York with it, leaving only the 147th Pennsylvania and a few artillerists to man the lines in the face of Scott's assault. When the color-bearer of the 29th Ohio refused, Elliott started to follow with the others, but he turned to take one last look at the surging Confederate line

---

[26] Ibid., 261.
[27] Ibid., 261.
[28] Ibid., 215.
[29] *Supplement to OR*, pt. 1, vol. 7, ser. 7, pp. 22–23.

and saw his friend, Sergeant Samuel Gourd of Company F, fall killed, the only man between Elliott and the attacking Rebels. When he saw his friend fall, Elliott said that it "seemed to nerve me to what I first intended doing—make a stand."[30] Just then two more men of the 109th Pennsylvania, Privates Alfred Crossdale of Company A and Michael Moran of Company F, seeing the colors stop, came back to Elliott and exclaimed, "That's right, Ferg, stand where you are, we'll stand with you."[31] The entire right of Geary's lines had collapsed, with one section consisting of two guns left abandoned on the right flank of Candy's front line, and with the withdrawal of the 5th Ohio and the remaining troops behind it, the remaining two sections of four guns in Bundy's battery that had been posted between the left of the 5th Ohio and the right of the 147th Pennsylvania were now exposed and vulnerable to capture. According to Elliott,

> We thus stood for a few seconds, when we were joined by two artillerymen, and I then directed them to get out one of the two guns near us and turn it upon the advancing enemy. Never did two men work more heroically, and in an incredibly short time the gun was loaded with canister and fired and, as the iron missiles sped on their mission of death and destruction, our exultant yells mingled with the groans of the wounded an dying Rebels, and we felt that the tide of battle was turned in our favor.[32]

Next, several other men returned to Elliott's side, including Thomas Why of Company G, when Elliott "ordered the other gun brought out too, and it was the fire from these two guns alone at the ravine," according to Elliott, "with scarcely enough men to handle them, that succeeded in holding the enemy in check until our troops had time to reform and return."[33] During the fighting, Lieutenant Isaiah Robison of the 147th Pennsylvania fell dead while helping Colonel Pardee hold the line. Pardee would later be promoted and given a general's commission for his heroic efforts at Peach Tree Creek as his 147th Pennsylvania stood firm while others ran around them.[34]

According to Captain Henry Bundy, commander of the 13th New York Independent Battery, which was composed of three sections each with two Napoleon 12-pounder guns for a total of six guns in the battery, the right section was commanded by Lieutenant Muller. Bundy placed his battery along the ridge

---

[30] Ibid.
[31] Ibid.
[32] Ibid.
[33] Ibid.
[34] http://standardspeaker.com/History/civwar.htm (7 May 2006).

held by Candy's men in accordance with General Geary's instructions at about 2:00 P.M. that day. When they observed Featherston's Mississippians attacking Ward's 3rd Division to their left, and realizing that they were in position to make an enfilading fire on the Rebels, Bundy gave the order to commence firing on the advancing Confederates. Captain Bundy explained, "Our fire against the enemy at this point was becoming very destructive, when suddenly another portion of their line appeared advancing against our immediate front and on the right flank of the battery."[35] The threat to his front was from Scott's brigade, while the threat to his rear came from the right of O'Neal's brigade. Bundy continued:

> The fire of the battery was immediately directed against them, but the infantry supporting us gave way, and our right being quite exposed, and subject to a most destructive enfilading fire from the enemy's infantry, one section of the battery, under Lieutenant Muller, on the extreme right, had its gunners disabled in a few minutes, and was necessarily temporarily abandoned. I then directed the other two sections of the battery to change front to the right in order to prevent the enemy from removing the section which had been abandoned and to cover the now exposed flank of the division. The fire of our guns in this direction was effective and altogether successful...[36]

Captain Bundy, whose guns had been abandoned on the Federal right, managed to rally some twenty-five infantrymen and artillerists who joined Elliott and his band of defenders. Bundy and his artillerists took charge of the guns, and they continued to pour double rounds of cannister on the Confederate lines, which had now stopped and was beginning to recede. Soon, the 60th New York and the 109th Pennsylvania came back and they took up positions in support of Bundy's battery.

A lieutenant in charge of one of the sections of Bundy's battery that had been lost came up walking with the head 109th Pennsylvania's column crying. He exclaimed to Elliott, "If the 109th had been here I wouldn't have lost those guns, left practically in the hands of the enemy,' pointing at the two guns which still remained in their original position."[37] The 109th Pennsylvania then "took position on the right of the line previously occupied by the 29th Ohio." facing to the right, or at right angles with the original line, and the section of artillery that

---

[35] *OR*, ser. 1, vol. 38, pt. 2, p. 482.
[36] Ibid.
[37] *Supplement to* OR, pt. 1, vol. 7, ser. 7, pp. 22–23.

had been abandoned was recovered by volunteers and brought into the new line.[38] The 109th Pennsylvania lost three men killed, nine officers and men wounded, and four officers and men missing for a total loss of sixteen men. With the losses sustained in her sister regiments, Jones's 2nd Brigade lost 27 men killed, 58 men wounded, and 83 men missing, for a total loss of 168 men.[39]

While Bundy and Elliott struggled to save the Federal guns, Lieutenant Colonel Flynn worked feverishly to rally his Goldstream Regiment, the 28th Pennsylvania. During this time, a comical episode occurred as Flynn dueled with a Confederate colonel commanding a Mississippi regiment that was surging through his lines. "Lieut. Col. Flynn and a rebel Colonel, each with a gun in his hands, fought each other for a considerable time, each dodging around a bush repeatedly, so as to give or avoid a shot." Flynn managed to avoid injury, but his counterpart, apparently Lieutenant Colonel William W. Weir of the 37th Mississippi, was wounded.[40]

Private Crumpton of the 37th Mississippi continued his description of O'Neal's attack on the right of the lower Collier Ridge:

> Stone's [Scott's] Brigade on our right had to come up through an old field, facing a battery of four guns [the remaining two sections of bundy's battery] and were unsuccessful. Lieutenant Pierce English, gun in hand, with three of us, found ourselves on a hill, rather behind the battery on our right, which was firing on Stone's [Scott's] Brigade. We had used up all our ammunition; we picked up Yankee cartridge boxes, which strewed the ground. Their guns carried a ball about two calibers smaller than ours. We abandoned the slow method of drawing the rammer to load. We tore the cartridge, placed it in the muzzle, stamped the breech on the ground; the weight of the bullet carried the cartridge home, and we had only to cap and fire. It was almost like a repeating rifle.
>
> For an hour we went "squirrel hunting." There seemed to be no danger in our front. The Yanks had continued their flight we thought, to the river. We fired on the battery to our right so fast, they almost ceased firing. They turned a gun on us, but fired only one time. Probably they were short of ammunition,

---

[38] Ibid.
[39] *OR*, ser. 1, vol. 38, pt. 2, serial 73, p. 215.
[40] The Battle of Peach Tree Creek, *Chicago Tribune*, 27 July 1864, Special Collections, Middle Tennessee State University Library, Nashville TN; Rowland, *Military History of Mississippi*, 329.

for the caissons were being rushed forward as fast as the horses could carry them, but we shot the horses down.[41]

During this struggle, the 60th New York Regiment, from Colonel Ireland's 3rd Brigade, came up and formed to the right and flank of the 5th Ohio, and helped to stave off Crumpton and his fellow Mississippians. Some of the men of the 5th Ohio managed to get two of the abandoned guns of Bundy's battery, and turn them on the flanking Rebels. The veterans of the 5th Ohio continued to fight for two hours in their refused position, much of the time without ammunition. The top of their flagstaff was shot away, and they had one officer severely wounded, nine men wounded, but only two men were killed. Apparently, the Rebels had been overshooting their targets on the ridge. Also, the attackers had concentrated their fire on the artillerists and their horses, wounding or killing all of the men and horses that were working or supporting the right section of Bundy's battery.

Bundy's battery lost three men killed, and eight wounded, six of whom were from the right section. Two of the men killed were officers, one had been shot nine times, while the other had received seven bullets. Three of the wounded were also officers.[42] In addition to Bundy's battery, one section of Battery I, of the 1st New York Light Battery [Winegar's], which was composed of three sections, each with two 3-inch ordnance rifles, was in line along the ridge held by Candy's brigade. This section lost one man killed, three men wounded, and six horses wounded during the fighting. Battery I would eventually fire eighty-four rounds at the Rebels during the battle.[43]

One of the veterans of the 37th Mississippi Infantry, the well-respected and older soldier Bill Nicholson, had been a Texas Ranger before returning to his native state to defend Mississippi in the war. The old man had rheumatism in his leg, but he continued to serve with the regiment throughout the war carrying an old six shooter pistol on a holster around his waist that he had from his Texas Ranger days. According to one of his fellow soldiers, "it was the joke of the company when Nick, every few weeks, went out into the bushes, tried his pistol at a tree, then for a couple of hours cleaned and reloaded it. There were no pistol cartridges in those days, and loading was a slow process." Being the only man in his company to carry a revolver, he had never found the opportunity or need

---

[41] Crumpton, *A Book of Memories*, 86–87.
[42] *OR*, ser. 1, vol. 38, pt. 2, p. 482.
[43] *OR*, ser. 1, vol. 38, pt. 2, p. 479.

to use it in battle, but he insisted on carrying it saying that the time would come when he would need it.[44]

Now, on the wooded ridge below the Collier Mill the time appeared to have come. Nicholson saw a Federal soldier approaching through the woods in front of them. Turning to the lieutenant, Nicholson said, "Pierce, kill that Yankee." At that moment not a singe gun was loaded and the old Texas Ranger "had forgotten [about] his pistol [around his waist]. Perhaps the Yank's gun was empty, too, for we saw him twenty steps away dodge into the bushes."[45]

To the left of the 37th Mississippi, the 17th Alabama found itself tangled with half of Ireland's brigade that had come into the ravine to plug the gap. According to Colonel O'Neal, the brigade advanced in good order, despite the heavy undergrowth, "except on the left, where from some misapprehension, some one gave the command 'guide left,' which," despite the efforts of the brigade commander to keep the line together, "threw the 29th Alabama Regiment too far to the left, and left too much ground for the [1st Corps Alabama Sharpshooters] and the 26th Alabama Regiment to cover, attenuating their line almost to a skirmish line."[46]

Describing the pocket that his brigade had advanced into, O'Neal reported that Federal troops reformed on three sides to counter his assault. To his left along the ridge overlooking the ravine that his men had entered was Williams's 1st Division, posted along today's Norfleet Road and McKinley Road. To his right were the remains of Geary's 2nd Division that had been routed from the lower Collier Ridge, along today's Collier Road at and near its intersection with today's Northside Drive. Some of Geary's men had not fled, but instead fell back to the heights along today's Cottage Lane and Overbrook Drive turned right and rear, and steadied themselves to receive O'Neal's assault. In the valley between Overbrook Drive and Williams's division on the next ridge, units of Ireland's brigade rushed to plug the gap and stop O'Neal's surge. Thus, the shape of the reformed Federal line appeared in the form of a crescent with O'Neal's men forced to bend on both sides to face up to and return fire from the Federal foe.

O'Neal explained, "We continued to push forward driving the enemy before us, and advanced to within a short distance of some works the enemy had thrown up [at the lines of Williams's men held by Robinson's 3rd Brigade near

---

[44] Crumpton, *A Book of Memories*, 87.
[45] Ibid., 87.
[46] *OR*, ser. 1, vol. 38, pt. 3, serial 74, p. 742.

today's Northside Drive], having passed a line to our right some hundred yards."[47] The line that they had passed on the right was the end of Geary's 2nd Division held by portions of Candy's 1st and Jones's 2nd brigades along the lower Collier Ridge (at today's intersection of Collier Road and Northside Drive) that had fled the field.[48] The Alabama commander was describing the area just north of today's Overbrook Drive along today's Northside Drive where his men had come from the southwest, across today's Collier Road where the woods were dense, and, angling northeast, downhill through the thickets and undergrowth across today's Northside Drive and approaching the entrance to today's Bisty Grant Tennis Center. Just below the entrance to the Center, and just east of the present Northside Drive in the low-lying area immediately north of Overbrook Drive, the woods opened up into a field, providing O'Neal and his men with a full view of the Federal lines and the danger that faced his lines on both flanks.

O'Neal described the action on the right of his brigade. "The 37th Mississippi and the three right companies of the 17th Alabama Regiment had swung around by a right wheel to face this line in the field, and had commenced a heavy and telling fire on it, when it was discovered we were not supported by the troops on our right."[49] According to one veteran of the 37th Mississippi, "The 37th wheeled to meet the necessities of the movement and delivered a telling fire, but the lack of support compelled the brigade to retire. A second advance was made with like results," he added.[50] This fight occurred just north of today's Overbrook Drive and east of today's Northside Drive as Ireland's 3rd Brigade and portions of the routed units of Geary's remaining two brigades fought stubbornly to fend off O'Neal's attack. If Ireland's men and the others could not stop them, Geary's entire line would be swept from the ridges overlooking Peach Tree Creek, and nothing would prevent O'Neal's forces from reaching the fields along the creek and the fords and bridges in Geary's rear (located at today's Bobby Jones' Golf Course).

O'Neal subsequently complained that his assault was not properly supported on his right and that he did not have sufficient reinforcements to exploit the gains initially made by his men. Concerning the first claim, he asserted "we were not supported by the troops or our right, who had failed for some cause to come up, and that we were being flanked and enfiladed by a

---

[47] Ibid.
[48] Ibid.
[49] Ibid.
[50] Rowland, *Military History of Mississippi*, 328–29.

battery."⁵¹ To his right were the men of Scott's brigade, which had assaulted the enemy's lines boldly, but, like O'Neal's lines, Scott's men were unsupported, were separated by ridges between the attacking forces, lacked sufficient numbers to exploit their gains, and could not go further after Federal troops rallied.

As for the second assertion by O'Neal, his and the other three Confederate brigades of Stewart's Army of Mississippi that made assaults (Featherston, Scott, O'Neal, and Reynolds), could all make the same claim. All four Southern brigades were separated by dense undergrowth and wooded ridges and ravines from each other. All four brigades enjoyed initial success in surprising and breaking Federal skirmish or advance lines. All four brigades were stopped by rallied Federal forces. All four brigades lacked reinforcements to exploit their initial successes. In fact, O'Neal's brigade was the only one that received any reinforcements at all.

Private W. I. Mothershead of Company F, from the 17th Alabama, wrote, "The battle is still raging, our company has lost most all killed and wounded, our regiment behaved well, swept all before it."⁵² Company F was known as the Winter Greys and they hailed from Montgomery County, Alabama. Mothershead subsequently died on 2 September 1864 at a Macon, Georgia hospital.⁵³ In the 17th Alabama Infantry Regiment, seventy-six men fell victim in the bloody onslaught during O'Neal's attack. Major Thomas J. Burnett was severely wounded. In total, the 17th Alabama lost eighteen men killed, fifty wounded, and ten captured, with two of the wounded being captured, for a total of seventy-six confirmed casualties at Peach Tree Creek. Two of those wounded later died bringing the number of deaths to twenty.⁵⁴

---

⁵¹ *OR*, ser. 1, vol. 38, pt. 3, serial 74, p. 742.

⁵² W. I. Mothershead to Cousin, 23 July 1864, folder 5, SG024896, Alabama Archives, Montgomery, Alabama; Thompson, 89.

⁵³ Thompson, 89.

⁵⁴ In Brewer's monograph on the 17th Alabama *Alabama, Her History, Resources, and Public Men, from 1540 to 1872*, he reports that the 17th Alabama lost 130 men at the Battle of Peach Tree Creek. The discrepancy could be due to the lack of documentation on the slightly wounded or those whose service records are incomplete or the fading memories over the years of veterans who contributed to Brewer's work. The seventy-six confirmed casualties comes from a meticulous review of the compiled service records of the regiment by the regiment's modern-day historians Illene D. and Wilbur E. Thompson (*The Seventeenth Alabama Infantry: A Regimental History and Roster* [Bowie MD: Heritage Books, Inc., 2001]).

The Battle of Peach Tree Creek

Over on the center and far left of O'Neal's brigade, the 26th, 1st Corps Sharpshooters, and 29th Alabama found that they had struck a gap in the Federal lines that had formed along two ridges that ran northeast, the same direction as their charge. Upon reaching the gap, the Alabamians could see the valley leading up to Peach Tree Creek in the distance. It seemed that one more push, and total victory would be realized. While the center and right of O'Neal's brigade swept the first ridge that held Candy's brigade, and rolled up the right flanks of the 5th Ohio and 28th Pennsylvania Regiments, the left of O'Neal's brigade faced a gap between the ridge and another parallel ridge a couple of hundred yards north.[55]

To General Geary it appeared that all was lost as he was being struck by the Confederates from front, right flank, and rear, as about half of his men moved to counter the Rebel onslaught while the other half struggled to find safety in the rear. Later, Geary would report that while the Southern attack would "surge in immense masses," his brigades "stood as firm as a rock and mowed down column after column of that vast, struggling mass that charged them from three sides."[56] O'Neal's men poured out from the wood southwest of the intersection of today's Collier Road and Northside Drive. One historian aptly wrote, "Surging up [from the direction of today's] Northside Drive, troops from Alabama and Mississippi crumpled up the Yankee line on [today's] Collier, joined shoulders with the Arkansans [Reynolds's men to the left] and poured down the ravine towards [today's] Bitsy Grant Tennis Center 'with a hideous rebel yell.'"[57]

At this pivotal point on the battlefield, Major General Joseph Hooker could plainly see Featherston's Mississippians streaming over the Collier Ridge to his left, fleeing remnants of Candy's and Jones's brigades were being hotly pursued by Scott's Alabamians and Louisianans to his front, and an unchecked surging line of Alabamians was coming up the valley between the two ridges to his right. He also saw General Geary, who had just come in ahead of his fleeing men from the front. Hooker and Geary quickly realized the need to plug the gap to their right that had split the 1st and 2nd brigades on the front and rear ridges respectively. Hooker ordered Ireland's 3rd Brigade to fill the void. After dispatching Ireland, the two generals rallied the retreating men and directed the

---

[55] *OR*, ser. 1, vol. 38, pt. 2, serial 73, pp. 136–42, 213–15, 273, 285.

[56] *OR*, ser. 1, vol. 38, pt. 2, serial 73, p. 140; Clauss, "The Atlanta Campaign, July 18, 1864," 89.

[57] Diane C. Thomas, "City-Scape," *Atlanta: The Magazine of the Urban South* 22 (October 1982): 16.

fire against Scott and Featherston, which helped to check their advance. While Hooker and Geary busied themselves with stopping Scott's assault, Colonel Ireland set out to meet O'Neal's unchecked Alabamians, which had by this point wrecked half of Candy's brigade, put fear into Jones's brigade, and threatened to reach Peach Tree Creek's banks.[58]

As the 26th Alabama in the center pressed down the back of the first ridge, they were met by the surge of the 111th Pennsylvania of Ireland's brigade that had rushed from near the Collier Mill to plug the gap (located in the ravine just north of Overbrook Drive and the Bitsy Grant Tennis Center). Among the members of the 111th Pennsylvania was Private James T. Miller. He had written his brother on 15 July that during the "whole campaign so far [the soldiers] have not had what might properly be termed a general battle."[59] Private Miller believed that "we could flog Johnston's army all to pieces at any time if we could only get them in an open field fight."[60] He was about to get his wish.

Quickly, Colonel Ireland pushed his regiments into the fight. The 111th Pennsylvania "advanced across the ravine [just south of the tennis courts at the Bitsy Grant Tennis Center] and up the opposite slope, and, arriving at the top [along Evergreen Lane just south of Overbrook Drive], the right of the regiment was immediately enveloped—front, flank, and rear—by the line of the enemy, who were advancing from our right."[61] Cobham had been awarded with the rank of brevet general just the day before for his conduct in commanding the 2nd Brigade in Geary's division in fall 1863.[62] The Pennsylvanians fought portions of O'Neal's brigade for some time in their exposed position along the ridge, but were "eventually compelled to retire."[63] Colonel Cobham and his 111th Pennsylvania had helped to stave off disaster for Geary's division and managed to stop the 26th Alabama's forward progress. But it came at a dear price. "The Battle of Peach Tree Creek lasted, for the 111th Pennsylvania, only thirty minutes: 'The most fatal half hour in its history.'" The Pennsylvania regiment lost 80 out of the 200 men in the fight. Of that number, seventeen men were killed, including Colonel Cobham and Private Miller. "Not since Antietam had

---

[58] *OR*, ser. 1, vol. 38, pt. 2, serial 73, pp. 136–42, 213–15, 273, 285; *OR*, ser. 1, vol. 38, pt. 2, serial 74, pp. 941–42.

[59] Jedediah Mannis and Galen R. Wilson, eds., *Bound to Be a Soldier: The Letters of Private James T. Miller, 111th Pennsylvania Infantry, 1861–1864* (Knoxville: University of Tennessee Press, 2001) 149.

[60] Mannis and Wilson, eds., *Bound to Be a Soldier*, 150.

[61] *OR*, ser. 1, vol. 38, pt. 2, serial 73, p. 318.

[62] Mannis and Wilson, eds., *Bound to Be a Soldier*, 165.

[63] *OR*, ser. 1, vol. 38, pt. 2, serial 73, p. 318.

the regiment suffered so severely."[64] According to the after-action report filed by Lieutenant Colonel Thomas M. Walker who took over command after Colonel Cobham fell, the 111th Pennsylvania lost the colonel and ten enlisted men killed, five officers and twenty-seven men wounded, and three officers and twenty-nine men missing, for a total of seventy-five casualties.[65] Among the captured were Captain Ham Sturdevant of Company D.[66] Opposing them on the Southern side, the 26th Alabama suffered severely, losing about seventy-five men.[67]

Following the 111th Pennsylvania, the 149th New York formed to its right and met the 1st Corps Alabama Sharpshooters head on. Trailing a bit behind these two regiments in the tangled undergrowth as they struggled to advance into position along the right flank of the 149th New York, the 102nd New York Regiment plugged the last of the space between the 149th New York and the second ridge on which the 2nd Brigade, commanded by Colonel Patrick H. Jones, was realigning their lines to meet the unexpected assault. In front of the second ridge, the 149th New York ran into the 29th Alabama and the two regiments began to slug it out at close range.

The left of O'Neal's brigade had managed to gain a position deep into the Federal lines, and they were somewhat sheltered by the dense undergrowth and forest, but they soon realized that they were too few to press their advantage, and worse, they had to contend with gunfire on both flanks. At the outset of the charge, the 60th New York and 29th Pennsylvania had been ordered to the front ridge to support Candy's beleaguered brigade and to help save Bundy's artillery battery from capture. Now, as the left half of O'Neal's brigade swept along the back of the ridge, portions of the 60th New York and 29th Pennsylvania were able to direct fire from their position on the front ridge into the right flank of the advancing Alabamians, particularly the 26th Alabama and the 1st Corps Alabama Sharpshooters. Further to the north, on the second ridge, units from Jones's brigade showered bullets onto the 29th Alabama. The 78th New York, led by Lieutenant Colonel Harvey Chatfield, was pressed into service. Chatfield

---

[64] John Richards Boyle, *Soldiers True: The Story of the One Hundred and Eleventh Regiment Pennsylvania Veteran Volunteers and of Its Campaigns in the War for the Union, 1861–1885* (New York: Eaton & Mains; Cincinnati: Jennings & Pye, 1903) 237–38; Samuel Penniman Bates, *History of Pennsylvania Volunteers, 1861–1865*, 5 vols. (Philadelphia: T.H. Davis & Company, 1875) 3:1021; Mannis and Wilson, eds., *Bound to Be a Soldier*, 151.

[65] *OR*, ser. 1, vol. 38, pt. 2, serial 73, p. 318.

[66] Mannis and Wilson, eds., *Bound to Be a Soldier*, 175.

[67] "26th Alabama," www.rootsweb.ancestry.com/~alcw26/26thala.htm (20 March 2008).

explained, "The regiment moved forward, but owing to the dense undergrowth and rough nature of the ground, the advance was rendered very difficult and the line irregular, besides an almost utter inability to keep in view the other regiments of the brigade."[68] Additionally, the 137th New York, Colonel David Ireland's last available regiment, had been ordered to come up and support the three regiments which had plugged the gap, and this regiment helped to bolster the line to ensure that there were no breakthroughs.[69]

29th Alabama. During this assault, Corporal Richard H. Smith, of Company C (the Avalance Company) from the 29th Alabama, carried the regiment's flag leading the way up the valley. There, the "staff that the flag was attached to was shot out of Richard's left hand [wounding him] and before the flag could hit the ground another soldier picked it up and carried it on!" For Corporal Smith, the war was over. He was sent to the Macon hospital were his left arm became infected and was amputated above the elbow.

By now the battle had been raging all through the hills and hollows below Peach Tree Creek for more than an hour, and O'Neal's veterans had portions of Geary's division on the run. "The movement was so adroitly executed that most of those in Geary's outer line were captured," explained a Federal officer.[70] The Alabamians and Mississippians had broken through the first line and had routed about half the regiments in Candy's and Jones's brigades as they had struck the unprotected right flank and rear of these units. Peach Tree Creek and the plain south of it where Geary's and Ward's division had formed and set up camps earlier in the day were in plain sight. But on the last ridge overlooking the broad ravine where the Bitsy Grant Tennis Center sits today, the veterans of Williams's division formed up, determined to hold the position and stave off disaster.

Included in O'Neal's brigade was a detachment of sharpshooters who carried the famous and deadly Whitworth rifles. This group was commanded by Captain William H. Lindsey of Company I from the 26th Alabama who had previously fought with distinction at Fredericksburg and had been captured at Chancellorsville 3 May 1863 and paroled on 18 May 1863. His second in command, First Lieutenant E. Samuel Stuckey had been wounded at

---

[68] James Lee McDonough and James Pickett Jones, *War So Terrible, Sherman and Atlanta*, (New York: W. W. Norton & Company, 1987) 213.

[69] *OR*, ser. 1, vol. 38, pt. 2, serial 73, pp. 136–42, 213–15, 273, 285; *OR*, ser. 1, vol. 38, pt. 2, serial 74, pp. 941–42.

[70] Howard, Autobiography, 617.

The Battle of Peach Tree Creek

Chancellorsville on 3 May 1863 but returned to the regiment in June 1864; he was killed during the exchange of fire with Williams's division.[71]

In the 29th Alabama on the far left of O'Neal's line, Private John E. Johnson and his brigade "charged into a thickly wooded ravine. Federal troops overlooking the ravine soon caught the Southerners below in a terrible crossfire. A bullet tore through John Johnson's neck." As relayed by his descendants, "Johnson's wife and infant son, whom he had never seen, had just arrived in Atlanta to visit him. John Johnson died on August 9th. His wife saved his bloodstained coat as a reminder of her slain husband."[72]

In New York, the *Ithaca Journal* and *Binghamton Standard* published two letters taken from the lifeless body of Private M. D. McQueen who died in the attack with his 29th Alabama. The letters were captured by a Yankee soldier with the 137th New York that, together with Ireland's brigade, had plugged the hole in the Federal line between Geary's and Williams's division and then driven O'Neal's Alabamians back out of the bulge. The first letter, dated 18 July, to his wife Axis, explained "we are expecting hard fighting today." The second, also to his wife, would be his last.

> As I did not get to send you my letter day before yesterday, I try again to send. We are fighting now, all we can. I hear sad news. The Yanks have burnt Talledega and captured Opelaca, and cut the railroad above here. We got the best of the fight yesterday, where I was. I think now they will capture the most of this army. If I get captured you may rest easy—I will return to you if ever permitted. I want you to keep John and Hugh with you, and do the best you can. I could write a heap to you if I had time and paper. I never did not want to see you all so bad in my life.[73]

Three brothers named Dobbins charged down the wooded ravine toward the Federal lines near where Johnson fell. All three were shot down. Only one of them, Private J. T. Dobbins of Company A, 29th Alabama, got up. According to his family, J. T. fell within 50 yards of where his two brothers were killed. "Shot in the neck by a mini ball," the nineteen-year-old struggled for life as Federal troops moved around the battlefield that evening. Left for dead by the Federal surgeons and stretcher bearers, a group of "Southern ladies came out on the battlefield after the union troops passed through." Risking arrest and

---

[71] "26th Alabama," www.rootsweb.ancestry.com/~alcw26/26thala.htm (20 March 2008).

[72] The coat is on display at the Atlanta History Center.

[73] *Ithaca Journal*, 24 August 1864.

deportation or imprisonment, these ladies "picked up the wounded, took them home, hid them, and nursed as best they could." Young J. T. Dobbins was one of these "picked up by such a lady and hidden in her attic, being shot in the neck he could not swallow food, so she fed him thin broth and cool milk in the mornings, after he gained sufficient strenth to look out a dormer window, he found that he was on a goat farm!" After a few days, he was able to be transported and moved back into Atlanta where Dobbins was sent to Hospital F, at the Floyd House and Ocmulgee Hospital, in Macon, Georgia, to recover.[74]

A Northern newspaperman who walked over the battlefield the next day recorded, "I have seen most of the battle-fields in the South-west, but nowhere have I seen traces of more deadly work than is visible in the dense woods in which Geary's right was formed. Thickets were literally cradled by bullets [The sage brush and saplings were cut down by gunfire.], and on the large trees, for twenty feet on the trunk," he added, "hardly a square inch of bark remained. Many were torn and splintered with shell and round-shot, the enemy in their attack on Geary and Williams using artillery, which they did not bring into action on other portions of the line." The correspondent noted, "Until nightfall the unequal contest was waged, but Geary held his hill inflexibly. The enemy sullenly left his front during the evening, firing spitefully as he retired."[75]

While most of Candy's and Jones's brigades were crushed and fled in the confusion from the lower Collier Ridge, General Geary praised the work of five regiments, the 147th Pennsylvania, 119th New York, the 73rd Pennsylvania, the 109th Pennsylvania, and the 60th New York of Ireland's 3rd Brigade, that remained on the lower Collier Ridge to hold on to the left of his line and prevent the loss of his artillery.[76] Private Frederick N. Kollock of Philadelphia, who served in Company B of the 29th Pennsylvania, reported on the work of his division. "This morning we advanced intending to throw our works onto another hill, but the Rebs came out of their works, and met us in the open field, neither party having any works, but they were driven back with a very heavy loss on their side and very light one on ours leaving, all their dead and wounded."[77]

---

[74] www.geocities.com/Heartland/Estates/3071/enlisted/dobbins.html (8 January 2009).

[75] D. Van Nostrand, "How We Fight in Atlanta," in Frank Moore, ed., *Rebellion Record. A Diary of American Events*, vol. 11, comp. G. P. Putnam, 252.

[76] *OR*, ser. 1, vol. 38, pt. 2, serial 73, p. 138.

[77] Kollock, Frederick N., Diary during the War 1864, Company B, 29th Pennsylvania, Ireland's 3rd Brigade, Geary's 2nd (White Star) Division, transcribed by Charles S. Harris, p. 8, subject files, Chickamauga National Military Park Library, Chickamauga, Georgia.

The Battle of Peach Tree Creek

One Federal officer described the action along Geary's front where Scott's brigade and O'Neal's brigade had attacked. "The limbs of trees and the underbrush were as badly broken and cut up as those had been on Geary's front the last day at Gettysburg."[78] John Geary and his division were surprised in the woods south of Peach Tree Creek. They had deployed incorrectly, facing southeast rather than south or even southwest where the Rebel assault would derive. They had advanced too far in front of their supporting units and their right flank was exposed and unprotected in the wooded jungle between the Collier Road and Mt. Zion Church. Geary and his division very nearly suffered another Chancellorsville defeat.

Geary and his division would be saved from another Chancellorsville at Peach Tree Creek, however, for several other reasons in addition to the heroism of the few men and the artillerists who remained on the lower Collier Ridge. First, Colonel Ireland and his 3rd Brigade were quickly rushed into the fight to plug the hole created by Geary's shattered lines as the fast-thinking General Hooker and Colonel Ireland correctly assessed the danger and sprang into action. Second, Williams's 1st Division was in position along the ridge behind and to the right of Geary to receive and parry the assault of O'Neal's brigade after it swept the right of Geary's first two brigades off the lower Collier Ridge. Third, and perhaps most importantly, the attacking Confederates were not in sufficient numbers to follow up on their success.

With only 1,450 or so men, Scott's brigade ran out of steam after sweeping through the 33rd New Jersey's position and after running into Geary's artillery. During the battle, O'Neal may have been in charge of as many as 2,000 Confederates, but his line became engaged with two Federal divisions in a crescent-shaped line as he faced the enemy on his left, front, and right. Moreover, O'Neal's brigade, like the other three attacking brigades in Stewart's corps, Featherston's, Scott's, and Reynolds's, did not have any support on either flank. Finally, as Scott's and O'Neal's men advanced and began to take prisoners, many of the Southerners began to fall out of line and participate in taking the captured Yankees to the rear. This opportune circumstance significantly diminished the effectiveness of the 12th Louisiana of Scott's brigade, which seized the position of the 33rd New Jersey and accounts for the comparatively light casualty rates suffered by portions of that unit.

---

[78] Howard, Autobiography, vol. 1, 618.

19

A SQUARE STAND-UP FIGHT FOR THREE HOURS

General [Alpheus Starkey] Williams, with that sudden inspiration which characterizes true military genius, saw at a glance the arrangement of his troops which, according to the nature of the ground and the unexpected exigencies of the moment, was best adapted to meet this unlooked-for demonstration of the enemy. He hurried his brigades into position on the double-quick, and though they moved with all possible celerity, was unable to get them in their proper places ere they received a terrific fire from the enemy.[1]

Responding to the Confederate onslaught, Williams's 1st Division prepared to give the Confederates a warm reception. Williams's veterans rushed up to the ridge where the Bitsy Grant Tennis Center lies today and filed to the west along the ridge overlooking Norfleet Road and between it and McKinley Road. The troops had crossed the Peach Tree Creek that morning, stacked arms, and were preparing their "noon day" meal when the Rebel attack began. It was just after 4:30. Colonel Packer of the 5th Connecticut, expected "to have a warm time to-day," as he described the stiffening resistance of the Confederates as they drew closer to Atlanta. His men each carried sixty rounds of ammunition in their cartridge boxes, but the ensuing attack would be even hotter than they had expected. One soldier from Packer's 5th Connecticut explained that "Peach Tree Creek came near being a very unfortunate surprise." A Federal officer explained, "The blow [of Walthall's attack] came while Robinson was in motion by the left flank endeavoring to get into the ravine and connect with Geary.... Troops could not be worse situated to resist an attack," he added. "Sheridan's Division at Chickamauga was broken to pieces under such circumstances," explained the Federal commander. "But," added Captain Edwin E. Marvin of the 5th Connecticut, "the 20th Corps or 1st Brigade [Williams commanded the 1st Division.] were not caught napping like the 11th Corps at Chancellorsville."[2]

---

[1] Nostrand, "How We Fight in Atlanta," in Moore, ed., *Rebellion Record*, 11:253–54.
[2] Edwin E. Marvin, *The Fifth Regiment Connecticut Volunteers, A History* 1889) 324–

The Battle of Peach Tree Creek

Williams's men and those of Geary's units that had remained stiffened as they parried the repeated thrusts of O'Neal's veteran Southerners along the slight ridge overlooking today's entrance to the Bitsy Grant Tennis Center at Northside Drive. "At the bottom of the ravine [now the intersection of Overbrook Drive and Northside Drive] some of the fiercest fighting in all the war took place. The opposing lines mingled and soldiers fought with bayonets, clubbed muskets and bare hands." O'Neal's men had pushed back twice their number, but Geary's and Williams's reserves rushed to stop the Alabamians and Mississippians from penetrating any further. "The ravine flooded with smoke, flashing guns and the hoarse shouting of thousands of men. At this point, the Confederates were squarely behind the whole Yankee line and barely a third of a mile from the all-important bridges over Peachtree Creek."[3]

Perhaps the most unheralded, but successful general in all of the entire Federal armies, General A. S. Williams was tenacious, competent, and proved quite adept at responding to unexpected challenges throughout the war. Alpheus Starkey Williams was born on 20 September 1810 at Deep River, Connecticut, to a wealthy family. His father died when he as only eight and his mother died when he was seventeen, but they left him an estate of $75,000. With this money, Williams attended Yale University and graduated in 1831, and then he embarked for Europe for eighteen months where he studied European military history extensively. Williams was particularly interested in French military history and the Napoleonic Wars, and he toured many battlefields, arsenals, and museums and learned much about weaponry. Williams returned to America and settled in Detroit, Michigan, in 1836 where he began a law practice, married, and started a family. He also served as probate judge of Wayne County, president of a bank, owner of the Detroit *Advertiser* newspaper, postmaster of Detroit, and member of the board of education before the war. While he never attended West Point, Williams was active in the local militia, known as the "Brady Guards," beginning in 1838, including service in the Patriot War (an unsuccessful attempt to annex part of Canada to the United States by Michigan "Patriots") and the Mexican War, and continuing for twenty-three years until the start of the Civil War.[4]

27; Howard, Autobiography, 618.

[3] Diane C. Thomas, "City-Scape," *Atlanta: The Magazine of the Urban South* 22 (October 1982): 16.

[4] www.michigan.gov/dmva/0,1607,7-126-2360_3003_3009-16956--,00.html (30 November 2008), "The Alpheus Williams Website," http://bhere.com/plugugly/williams/index.html (30 November 2008); Alpheus Starkey Williams, *From the Cannon's Mouth, The*

Hood's First Sortie, 20 July 1864

Williams's Civil War career began with the training of Michigan troops and appointment as a brigadier general on 17 May 1861. It would be his first and last appointment. By October 1861, he was in command of 5,000 men under General Banks in Washington, DC. During the Civil War, there were two ways an officer could be promoted: political appointment and promotion from generals higher up the ladder. With the shift in power in the North to the Republican Party following Lincoln's election as president, many politicians from this party managed to get appointments and promotions to positions of command far beyond their abilities. These were known as "political generals,"[5] and while the South had her share of them, the newly empowered Republican Party had riddled the US army with them. The Federal army would spend most of the war ridding itself of most of these ill-considered appointments. The other way to climb the ladder in the Federal army was by promotion. This was usually within the discretion of the commander of the Army in which an officer was serving, and, almost always, professional soldiers promoted fellow graduates from West Point.

Unfortunately for Williams, he was neither a Republican nor a West Pointer. What A. S. Williams was, however, was a capable and effective field commander who never appeared to complain about his lack of promotion and who never curried favor with the press. At the Battle of Cedar Mountain, Williams's force met and battered Stonewall Jackson's famed "Stonewall Brigade," where Williams broke the Virginia brigade's lines and drove them until Williams's men ran into the main Confederate body, "outnumbered, out of ammunition, and left unreinforced," and lost a third of his command and all of his officers. Williams's command discovered the famous "Lost Orders" of Robert E. Lee during the Antietam campaign. During the Battle of Antietam, when General Mansfield was killed early in the fighting, Williams led a corps and drove Hood's Texans out of the East Woods and Miller cornfield until, again, his men ran out of ammunition and were left unsupported. During the disaster at Chancellorsville, he hastily entrenched his men and stopped Jackson's flank attack after it had driven elements of the Federal army for 2 miles. There, Williams's efforts helped to save General Hooker and the Army of the Potomac from annihilation. At Gettysburg, Williams fortified and

---

Civil War Letters of General Apheus S. Williams, ed. Milo M. Quaife (Detroit: Wayne State University Press, 1959) 3-10; Jeffrey Charnley, "Neglected Honor: The Life of General A. S. Williams of Michigan (1810–1878)" (Ph.D. diss., Michigan State University, 1983) 17-23.

[5] www.historycooperative.org/journals/jala/21.1/simpson.html (30 November 2008).

entrenched the Federal line at Culp's Hill where his men thwarted Rebel efforts to gain these heights for three days.

During the Georgia Campaign, Williams's Red Star Division had fought well at Resaca, New Hope, and Kolb's Farm. At Peach Tree Creek, his men would be called on again to help stave off disaster. As glaring as the empty spot on history bookshelves is concerning this brave warrior, the failure of either the Lincoln administration or his generals to promote Williams to at least major general is equally embarassing.[6]

Early on 20 July, General Williams led his 1st Division across Peach Tree Creek over the bridges that had been constructed by Geary's 2nd Division. Nicknamed "Pop," Williams rode his favorite horse Plug Ugly, a fitting description for both rider and horse. Wounded in three or four places by the explosion of a shell during the Battle of Chancellorsville and thought to be dead, Plug Ugly survived the injury in time to carry Williams through Maryland and Pennsylvania the next month during the Gettysburg Campaign. There, while riding along a road in Maryland's Pleasant Valley, Williams tried to jump a rail fence that had been partially torn down when Plug Ugly slipped on the side of a narrow ledge on the side of a road, sending the horse down the side to the road below, a fall of about 8 to 10 feet. Williams was able to leap off the animal to the side of the ledge and safety. When his men went to the aid of Plug Ugly and removed Williams's saddle, the poor animal was thought to be dead again, but "with a big grunt he got to his feet" and was "as sound as ever." During the Georgia Campaign, Plug Ugly would succumb to fatigue and Rebel bullets, and Peach Tree Creek would be the last time Plug Ugly would carry old Pap Williams into battle.[7]

Williams advanced his division to the right of Geary's lines and along a farmroad that ran along a wooded ridge until his men reached a group of deserted houses about 600 yards northeast of the Hiram H. Embry's house located on the Howell Mill just to the west. There, he was ordered to halt by General Hooker when it was discovered that there were Rebels posted at the Embry plantation. These Confederates were elements of the 24th South Carolina and perhaps some Georgia troops from Gist's brigade of Hardee's corps that had been posted here during the forenoon, and the 24th South Carolina had remained on skirmish line, shielding the eastward movement of Hardee's and Stewart's men between 1:00 P.M. and 4:00 P.M. Williams's 1st

---

[6] http://bhere.com/plugugly/williams/index.html (20 November 2008).
[7] Ibid.

Hood's First Sortie, 20 July 1864

Brigade led by General Joseph F. Knipe was massed to the right of the road and the deserted houses (or near today's Norfleet and McKinley roads), while the 3rd Brigade commanded by Colonel James S. Robinson was massed to the south of the road near the houses (along the ravine just south and east of Norfleet Road where it connects with Northside Drive). Williams's 2nd Brigade was under the direction of General Thomas H. Ruger and posted in the ravine behind his first two brigades (in the area of Wilson Road between Howell Mill Road and Northside Drive.)[8]

When sounds of the battle first resounded from the ridges to the east in front of the IV Corps and the rest of the XX Corps, the truculent Williams lined his division up along the ridge facing southeast with Knipe's 1st Brigade on the right, Robinson's 3rd Brigade on the left, and Ruger's 2nd Brigade in reserve. Knipe's brigade was posted along the southern edge of the wooded ridge between McKinley Road and Norfleet Road just to the east of Howell Mill Road, which was hidden from view of Walthall's advancing Rebels. An old country road ran from Peach Tree Creek (behind, or just north of, today's Bitsy Grant Tennis Center and just east of today's crossing at Northside Drive), first southward until the location of the entrance of the tennis center, and then to the southwest along the lower part of the ridge and roughly following the course of Norfleet Road. A few deserted farmhouses were located along this road about 600 yards from its intersection with Howell Mill Road and the Hiram H. Embry house.

When it became clear that the Confederates were attacking, Williams deployed Knipe's brigade southwest of the deserted houses and further down the country road toward the Embry house so that when fully deployed, Knipe's brigade stretched from to where today's Belvedere Road meets McKinley Road on its right, and near the deserted houses above Norfleet Road about halfway between Howell Mill Road and Northside Drive. Robinson's brigade formed on the wooded ridge above the deserted houses by connecting with the left of Knipe's brigade, and continued the line to the northeast to Northside Drive in front of today's Bitsy Grant Tennis Center where it connected with portions of Jones's 2nd Brigade of Geary's division. Ruger's brigade was posted to the west and rear of the ridge to connect with the XIV Corps to Williams's right,

---

[8] United States War Department, comp., *Official Records of the Union and Confederate Armies in the War of the Rebellion*, 128 vols. (Washington, DC: Government Printing Office, 1880–1901) ser. 1, vol. 38, pt. 2, serial 73, pp. 33–34 (hereafter *OR*).

which placed Ruger's brigade in the area of Wilson Road and Longwood Drive between Howell Mill Road and Northside Drive.[9]

In the rear of Williams's division, the men of Ruger's 2nd Brigade waited nervously for orders as they heard the commotion of battle getting closer in the wooded ridges in the distance. "The firing in front was more rapid, indicating an advance of the skirmish line," said one veteran. Next, the division's artillery raced up the wooded lane to the front and out of sight. Williams had been ordered by Hooker to send his skirmishers forward to flush out the Rebels around the Embry house and Williams had sent his artillery up to support the movement when the unexpected Confederate attack struck his skirmishers. In front of Robinson's brigade, one of Williams's staff officers, Captain E. H. Newcomb from the 61st Ohio, led a line of skirmishers forward. "Suddenly the musketry, off to our left, broke out into heavy and rapid volleys. The cheers and yells, which also reached us from that direction, plainly indicated that another battle was on." Until that point, Williams's three brigades had not been deployed into battle formation. "We had only compacted our lines on the hillside [along the ridge between today's Norfleet Road and McKinley Road], as if to make room in the rear for others." "But," recalled Corporal Brown of the 27th Indiana, "we at once formed in order for defense, double-quick." The Indiana corporal also remembered that his comrades in Ruger's brigade that had just arrived at some partially constructed earthworks; after the firing broke out in earnest, "we worked like beavers to strengthen" it. According to Corporal Brown, "almost immediately our 1st and 3rd Brigades were furiously assaulted."[10]

One of Williams's officers recorded the day's events. "A heavy picket was thrown out, and was considered a sufficient precaution against any hostile demonstration of the enemy, since nothing was thought of but an advance against his position. The troops were permitted to rest quietly in the shade, and were not troubled," the veteran officer explained, "with building the usual breastworks deemed necessary at each change of the line of battle. Temporary barricades of rails were thought a sufficient strengthening of the line for all necessary purposes." After being lulled into a mid-summer afternoon's dream, the men were quickly and rudely awakened to the nearing danger by "a fierce, rapid fire [that] broke out along our picket lines, which quickly grew into a

---

[9] Ibid.

[10] Edmund R. Brown, *A History of the 27th Indiana* (Monticello IN: Edmund R. Brown, 1899) 518; Robert M. Bunker, interview with author, July 2009.

volleying roll of musketry in front of Ward's and Geary's divisions. The storm soon extended along the line," said the officer, "toward the right where Williams' division lay grouped along the crest of a rather high and densely-wooded hill." According to the Yankee officer, "Between Williams and Geary's Divisions lay a deep hollow, down which, masked by the timber, the enemy was now advancing in heavy masses."[11]

O'Neal's veterans swept through Geary's right and headed unchecked down the wooded ravine toward the flats next to Peach Tree Creek and the bridges that provided the only means of escape for Geary's men. At this critical moment, Alpheus Seth Williams took over. "General Williams, with that sudden inspiration which characterizes true military genius, saw at a glance the arrangement of his troops which, according to the nature of the ground and the unexpected exigencies of the moment, was best adapted to meet this unlooked-for demonstration of the enemy." His lieutenants marveled at their commander's quick grasp and prompt audacity. "He hurried his brigades into position on the double-quick, and though they moved with all possible celerity, was unable to get them in their proper places ere they received a terrific fire from the enemy."[12]

Williams described the surprise attack. "I was in the act of advancing a section of artillery and a strong reserve to the skirmish line for the purpose of dislodging the enemy from his breast-works at Embry's house," explained the veteran General, "when heavy volleys of musketry…rolling in an increased volume toward my position, warned me that the enemy were attacking in force." Williams immediately ordered Knipe to double-quick his brigade to the right along the ridge, and Robinson to extend the line to the left to connect with Geary's lines. Williams also deployed one section of Winegar's artillery, the 1st New York Light Battery I, which consisted of six 3-inch ordnance rifles, in line with Knipe's brigade "to sweep the ridge." He placed a section of Woodbury's battery, the 1st New York Light Battery M, which contained four Napoleon 12-pounders, between Knipe and Robinson "to command the ravine on our left front," and he placed another section of Woodbury's battery "to observe the broad ravine on the right."[13]

---

[11] D. Van Nostrand, "How We Fight in Atlanta," in Frank Moore, ed., *Rebellion Record. A Diary of American Events*, vol. 11, comp. (G. P. Putnam: New York, 1868) 253.

[12] Nostrand, "How We Fight in Atlanta," in Moore, ed., *Rebellion Record*, 11:253–54.

[13] *OR*, ser. 1, vol. 38, pt. 2, serial 73, p. 34; William R. Scaife, *The Campaign for Atlanta* (Atlanta: self-published, 1993) 154.

The Battle of Peach Tree Creek

The section placed between Knipe's and Robinson's brigades was commanded by Lieutenant Ide while the section that covered the ravine with Ruger's 2nd Brigade was led by Lieutenant Smith. According to historian Erol Clauss, Woodbury's battery "poured canister into the gray mass," which was the left flank of O'Neal's brigade as it continued northeastward after shattering the right half of Geary's division. According to Captain John D. Woodbury, commander of the battery, Lieutenant Ide's artillery "assisted materially in repulsing three distinct charges of the enemy upon these [1st & 3rd] brigades," while Lieutenant Smith's section effected "good execution in throwing solid shot into the enemy's ranks" trying to advance in the ravine behind Williams's division. According to Woodbury, the battery lost only one man wounded and one horse killed during the fighting.[14]

In Knipe's brigade, one veteran of the 5th Connecticut described the sudden Confederate assault: "[We] were lying in the woods awaiting the hour...to attack the rebel lines, when Hood, with all his available force, charged out upon the Union line as a surprise. Hearing the old 'yell,' the boys flew into position in a moment, and the effect of the rebels' first volley was lost, as they were charging up hill and fired too high. It settled down now into a square stand-up fight for three hours, the enemy charging again and again, and being as often repulsed."[15] Knipe's 1st Brigade and Robinson's 3rd Brigade of Williams's 1st Division were posted on the ridge behind Geary's 2nd Division of Hooker's XX Corps, which was posted on two ridges in front of Williams's division. Ruger's 2nd Brigade of Williams's division was posted in reserve behind the other two brigades. "The rebels swept in the skirmish line with their line of battle," recorded one veteran. "Both musketry and artillery opened in heavy volleys from the start. Very soon the wounded began to come back," said one veteran in the reserve line, "and it was not long before we were expecting orders to advance to the assistance of the first line, or to see them withdraw to the rear of our position."[16] Due to the length of the wooded ridge on which Williams's division was located, part of Knipe's brigade was exposed to a potential Confederate attack while Robinson's brigade was entirely covered in its front by Geary's men on the ridge in front of Williams's division.

---

[14] Erol Clauss, "The Atlanta Campaign, July 18, 1864" (Ph.D. diss., Emory University, 1965) 93; *OR*, ser. 1, vol. 38, pt. 2, serial 73, p. 34; *Supplement to the Official Records of the Union and Confederate Armies* (Wilmington NC: Broadfoot Publishing Company, 1995–2001) pt. 1, vol. 7, ser. 7, pp. 35–36 (hereafter *Supplement to* OR).

[15] Marvin, *The Fifth Regiment Connecticut*, 327–28.

[16] Brown, *History of the 27th Indiana*, 518.

Hood's First Sortie, 20 July 1864

Knipe's brigade consisted of the 5th Connecticut under Colonel Warren W. Packer, the 3rd Maryland Detachment led by Lieutenant Colonel David Gove, the 123rd New York known as the "Washington County Regiment" commanded by Colonel Archibald L. McDougall, the 141st New York with Colonel William K. Logie, and the 46th Pennsylvania under Colonel James L. Selfridge. Sergeant Bull of the 123rd New York recalled that the topic of conversation had been the likelihood that Hood and his army was evacuating Atlanta and that the Federal Army would march into the Gate City as victorious conquerors the next day. "We were congratulating ourselves on this unexpected good luck when suddenly…there was a rifle shot on our front. It was as unexpected as would be thunder from out of a clear sky. A look of surprise and almost consternation came to every face," remembered Bull; "we knew the critical position our mass formation put us in; but the feeling was only for the moment. The first shot was followed by others in quick succession, then came the rattle of musketry, and with it the familiar 'Rebel Yell.' We knew then for a certainty that serious work was ahead of us."[17]

The New Yorker quickly helped his regiment fall into line, while the remaining regiments of Williams's division also formed up almost instantly. "On the sound of the first shot every man jumped to his feet and into line. There was no waiting for orders, the men knew what was required to get where they could make a defense. It was but the work of a moment to sling knapsacks and take guns from the stacks," remembered Sergeant Bull, "in far less time than it takes to tell it we were ready to march. Meanwhile the musketry firing was coming closer and closer, the yells of the enemy louder and louder, and the bullets began to sing and whistle around us and through the trees over our heads."[18]

Knipe's brigade was lined up east to west: 123rd New York on the left and next to Robinson's 3rd Brigade; next came the 3rd Maryland Detachment; in the center was the 141st New York; to the west, or second from the right was the 5th Connecticut; finally, on the far right, or western most point as Williams's men faced south and southeast, came the 46th Pennsylvania. With the right of Geary's lines in front of Robinson's brigade on the left, Knipe's brigade was vulnerable to an attack from their right front, right flank, and right rear.

---

[17] "Union Regimental Histories," www.civilwararchive.com/Unreghst/unnyinf9.htm (7 May 2006); Scaife, *The Campaign for Atlanta*, 154; Rice C. Bull, Diary, in Henry Woodhead, ed., *Voices of the Civil War—Atlanta* (Richmond: Time-Life Books, 1997) 147.

[18] Bull, *Atlanta*, 147.

Moreover, dense woods covered the ridges and ravines in all three directions, masking the advance of the Rebels on Knipe's men.

Captain Henry W. Daboll of Company G, 5th Connecticut, commanded the skirmishers of Knipe's 1st Brigade on 20 July. Fellow Captain Edwin Marvin described the action:

> The dense masses of the enemies parallel lines of battle were advancing close upon him through the thick underbrush when first discovered. There was no time to send timely notice to the main line in the rear by messenger, so the brigade which was closed in mass could be deployed and put in line of battle and readiness for action before the enemy would have been right among them, although of course he attempted it, but he did the very best thing which was possible for him to do under the circumstances. He rallied his skirmishers into a mass, and by firing volleys from so considerable a number of pieces deceived the rebels into believing that they had fallen upon the main line of Union troops, and consequently drew the fire of the whole rebels line of battle, which served notice at once on the Union line that there was real business ahead of such magnitude that they must be prepared for it at once, and they were consequently well in line when the rebel columns struck them.[19]

According to Colonel Warren W. Packer of the 5th Connecticut, the Rebel attack made his men hold their portion of the line "tight for the space of three hours, but did not make us yield one inch of ground." According to Captain Marvin, "When the assaulting line first struck the 1st Brigade it very considerably outflanked it on the right and consequently enfiladed it, but the right of [the 5th Connecticut] regiment was flung back, and the 27th Indiana of [the] 2nd Brigade [was] brought up in support," stabilizing the Federal line. Marvin described it as a "'square stand-up fight of give and take' without cover or defense on either side, until the Confederates were entirely satisfied and hauled off for safety." Colonel Packer described the battle along Peach Tree Creek as "very hot for a three hours' fight."[20]

Captain Harlan P. Rugg, also of the 5th Connecticut, explained that the men had stacked arms and were making coffee when the enemy attacked "very

---

[19] Marvin, *The Fifth Regiment Connecticut*, 327.

[20] Marvin, *The Fifth Regiment Connecticut*, 327–28. With fourteen killed, nine mortally wounded, thirty-nine wounded, and one captured, it was the largest loss sustained in the war for the 5th Connecticut except for the Battle of Cedar Mountain in which they lost thirty-eight killed, ten mortally wounded, sixty-seven wounded, and sixty-four captured.

suddenly and violently. The line of battle was quickly formed, and only just in time to save ourselves. But our regiment held the line bravely, under a terrible cross fire, the Forty-sixth Pennsylvania on our right and the One Hundred and Forty-First New York on our left, and the terrible battle of Peach Tree Creek was fought till after dark." The next day, Captain Rugg recorded, "Details from our army are engaged in burying the dead of both Northern and Southern men. Losses in regiment: 40 wounded, 20 killed; others in hospital dying. At night attack made on the enemy by 14th Corps." Actually, the 5th Connecticut lost either sixty-three or sixty-four men as they struggled to hold on to the ridge. Colonel Packer reported that his regiment lost four officers and forty-six men wounded, and fourteen men killed for a total of sixty-four men, while Captain Marvin recorded the names of sixty-three casualties in his regimental history.[21]

While the rage of the battle appeared to be its heaviest on the left in front of Ward's and Geary's divisions, the 1st and 3rd Brigades of Williams's division was "also firing volley after volley, without hesitation." Falling during the action was Adjutant Seth C. Carey of the 123rd New York who was wounded. "Among other riderless horses that we observed at length, running at large, was one that we all recognized as being General Knipe's, the commander of the 1st Brigade. The report naturally passed along the line that General Knipe had been killed." Presently, the general appeared on foot as he hurried back to the rear line, almost in a trance. "His horse had been so badly wounded that he considered it unsafe to ride it," so he had turned the animal loose.[22]

Knipe had come to the reserve line in search of General Williams to ask for assistance on his exposed right flank. The Confederates were pouring into the ravine on the right and rear of his brigade and the gap between it and the XIV Corps, threatening to turn Knipe's brigade and rout the 46th Pennsylvania, the regiment on his right flank. The wounding of his horse on which the general was riding coupled with the threat on his right flank seemed to unnerve the veteran officer who had been wounded twice at Winchester, Virginia, two more times at Cedar Mountain, and again at Resaca, Georgia.

What happened next would have been comical were it not for the danger that faced the Yankee division. Knipe came looking for General Williams to ask for a regiment, but Williams was on the front line at the time with his other brigade, Robinson's 3rd Brigade. Knipe "was a mercurial, demonstrative little

---

[21] Marvin, *The Fifth Regiment Connecticut*, 325, 328–29; *OR*, ser. I vol. 38, pt. 2, serial 73, 46.

[22] Brown, *History of the 27th Indiana*, 518–19.

man always; but now he was wrought up more than common. He was frantic," according to Corporal Brown of the 27th Indiana, not even responding to General Hooker, who overheard Knipe's request for support.[23]

> When [Hooker] found what Knipe wanted he turned and pointed to a regiment near by and said, "There, General Knipe, take that one." "No-o, no-o, I don't want that one," Knipe fairly screamed, with long drawn emphasis on the noes. In the meantime he had not stopped, but had hurried by, still calling for General Williams. Hooker called, "Here General Knipe, General Knipe! Come here!" Knipe did not hear, or affect to hear, at first, and one of Hooker's staff started after him, calling him to come back. Knipe finally turned and came back a few steps. Hooker this time pointed to the 27th [Indiana] and said laconically, "Take that one." "All right!" said Knipe, "I'll take that one," still speaking in high tones and drawing out his words. Then, coming up to the regiment, as the men had fallen in ranks, he shrieked, "Twenty-seventh Indiana, I want you. This old brigade never has been whipped, and it never will be whipped."[24]

The 27th Indiana quickly followed the Pennsylvania general into position. "To reach the desired position it was necessary for us to cross an open space of sixty or seventy-five yards, where the regiment would be exposed to a cross-fire at close range." According to Bruce Elmore of the 143rd New York of Robinson's brigade, General Williams was well-liked, "but Knipe (who was rumored to be taking over command of the division should Williams be promoted) is not liked at all." Colonel Silas Colgrove, commander of the 27th Indiana, conferred with General Knipe and the two quickly agreed on the place to form the regiment "along the remnant of an old fence bordering a ravine. They were instructed to make a dash for the point indicated, without regard to order, and, once there, to open fire and hold the position at all hazzards." Soon, the veterans of the 27th Indiana "were speedily taking part in the fray." One veteran of the Hoosier Regiment described the scene: "there was not space enough assigned to the 27th for all the men to get into line. They did, therefore, as men sometimes do in forts, but what we never did at any other time: Those not able to get position in the front line loaded their muskets and handed them to those before them to fire."[25]

---

[23] Ibid., 521.
[24] Ibid., 521–22.
[25] Ibid., 519; Bruce Elmore to wife, 29 July 1864, MSS 673 F, Manuscript Collection, Kenan Research Center, Atlanta History Center.

Hood's First Sortie, 20 July 1864

Corporal Brown remembered that the Rebels were very persistent. While the ground to their left was open, the view of the Indianans to their front and right was obscured by a "jungle of trees and bushes." According to Brown, through the jungle "the enemy could approach very near without being observed.... When compelled to fall back, the rebels would immediately reform and return to the attack, or others would return in their stead. It appeared to us that they would only retire into the thicket a short distance and then return again." During the fighting, the 27th Indiana sustained a number of casualties from unknown positions in the woods when they could not see their foe. "For this reason, orders were eventually given to continue firing into the dense woods, even after the enemy had retired and were not in sight."[26] The men continued firing until hostilities ended with darkness, many firing over 100 rounds during the action.

General Knipe was the subject of another humorous event during the battle. The General "passed in rear of the 27th [Indiana] while we were hotly engaged. He was still afoot and carrying his sword in his hand, unsheathed, as it had been before. He was also in his high state of excitement and was urging and encouraging the men, with all his former demonstratives and energy," remembered some of the veterans at a reunion after the war. According to one Hoosier veteran:

> A sergeant of the 27th said in very bland tones, "General, have you any chewing tobacco?" "Yes, I have some tobacco," the general replied, in the same high-keyed, long-drawn tone. And, jabbing his sword in the ground, with great energy, he produced from his breeches pocket a small piece of "plug," and handed it to the sergeant. The latter began turning it over and "sizing it up," as the boys now say, trying to decide whether or not there was too much of it for one good chew. When the general saw what the sergeant was about he said in a perfectly natural, though, plaintive, tone—all of his strained, keyed-up condition entirely gone,—"*That's all I've got.*" All the boys in hearing laughed heartily, the sergeant took out his knife, cut the tobacco in two parts, put one in his mouth and handed the other back to the general, who thereupon pulled his sword out of the ground and went on his way.[27]

Robinson's 2nd Brigade lined up east to west between the right of the reserve line of Geary's division and the left of Knipe's 1st Brigade, with the

---

[26] Brown, *History of the 27th Indiana*, 519.
[27] Ibid., 522.

143rd New York commanded by Colonel Horace Boughton on the left, the 82nd Ohio led by Colonel David Thomson to its right, then the 61st Ohio under Colonel Stephen J. McGroarty to the right center, and the 101st Illinois directed by Lieutenant Colonel John B. Le Sage on the far right. Behind this line, the 82nd Illinois under the direction of Lieutenant Colonel Edward S. Salomon was posted in reserve. As O'Neal's brigade surged over the lower portion of Collier Ridge sweeping Geary's division before it, the left of Robinson's line buckled. According to Lieutenant Colonel Salomon, "At 4 P.M. the assembly was sounded, the men fell in, and before the forward signal could be given we heard the clattering sound of heavy musketry in our front. We were hurried forward in double-quick into position."[28] The pressure of O'Neal's attackers forced back and routed the right half of Geary's division past Robinson's line (just east of today's Northside Drive proceeding north along Northside Drive). As O'Neal's Alabamian and Mississippi troops rolled down the valley north of the Collier Ridge (at the intersection of today's Collier Road and Northside Drive and proceeding northeast toward the Bitsy Grant Tennis Center), they ran straight into Robinson's fresh line that was ready to meet the Rebels (along the ridge at the entrance to the Bitsy Grant Tennis Center and west across Northside Drive between Norfleet Road and McKinley Road).

"Robinson's brigade hastened along the crest of the hill, then facing by the left flank, marched down the slope to receive the swarming masses of the overconfident and defiant foe," explained one of Williams's officers. "The fire of the enemy was so murderous, and his advance so impetuous, that it seemed for a time as if Robinson's line must surely yield. It was an awful moment. The combatants were mingled with each other, and fighting hand to hand. The safety of the corps, and indeed the entire army," recorded the Yankee officer, "seemed to depend upon the courage and determination of those devoted men. Should they give way, the enemy would get possession of the hill, command the rear, break the centre, capture hundreds of prisoners, all our artillery, and drive the remnant of our troops back to the creek," he continued, "and perhaps to the Chattahoochee."[29]

First Lieutenant George Young of the 143rd New York Infantry Regiment, at about 4:30 P.M., "was riding with urgent orders to regimental commanders from the brigade commander, Col. James Robinson. Confederate forces had

---

[28] *OR*, ser. I, vol. 38, pt. 2, serial 73, pp. 91–100; Scaife, *The Campaign for Atlanta*, 154.

[29] Nostrand, "How We Fight in Atlanta," in Moore, ed., *Rebellion Record*, 11:254.

launched an unexpected attack, and Robinson's brigade was under heavy fire." As a staff officer to Robinson's headquarters, Young was responsible for communicating the brigade commander's orders to each of the regiments up and down the line, and in the process Lieutenant Young was exposed to fire from the advancing Confederates. "As the 23 year old Lt. rode toward the front lines, a Confederate bullet hit Young's right leg below his knee. A surgeon removed the bullet but an infection remained. After the war, Young endured repeated operations to heal his leg, but the wound became infected each time," according to a display at the Atlanta History Center's award-winning exhibit, *Turning Point: The American Civil War*. "The chronic infection finally claimed his life in 1909, 45 years after the Battle of Peach Tree Creek." Lieutenant Young's coat, hat, and trousers worn during the battle are on display at the Atlanta History Center.[30]

The men of the 143rd New York had to guard against being rolled up on their left flank from the surging Rebel attack. Consequently, they fell back from their exposed position in the sway between the Collier Ridge and the ridge immediately to their rear on which the remainder of Williams's division had formed. According to Colonel Boughton, "We were immediately ordered into position, and my regiment, being in the advance of the brigade, moved in the direction of the firing on the double-quick." Boughton led his men toward the end of Geary's front line, which extended along the lower Collier Ridge near the intersection of today's Collier Road and Northside Drive. "The line was formed by each regiment going on the right by double file into line, which threw my regiment on the extreme left of the division."[31]

The rest of Robinson's brigade stopped along the southern crest of a ridge (from just west of today's Northside Drive at the entrance of the Bitsy Grant Tennis Center to the southwest toward Howell Mill Road between McKinley Road and Norfleet Road). Boughton's 143rd New York continued to advance in the wooded ravine toward Geary's lines, unaware that his comrades had stopped behind him and formed on the ridge. "While forming the enemy opened upon us heavily, but the movement was not in the least checked." Boughton continued to move his men forward. "In pursuance of orders, I immediately moved my regiment forward with a view to connect with the 2nd Division [atop the lower Collier Ridge at today's intersection of Collier Road and Northside Drive], which was on my left and in advance." Boughton explained, "Before this

---

[30] Atlanta History Center, exhibit, *Turning Point: The American Civil War*.
[31] *OR*, ser. I. vol. 38, pt. 2, serial 73, p. 106.

connection was formed the enemy had succeeded in forcing the right of Colonel Irelands's brigade, of the 2nd Division, from its position, and it fell back to the rear of my line, leaving my left flank exposed."[32]

In front of Robinson's lines, one Union war correspondent from the *Cincinnati Commercial* reported seeing Confederates raise their hands as if to surrender only to then fire a volley at Robinson's line once the Northern troops exposed themselves, although no Federal officer recorded this violation of the rules of war in any post-action report. The newspaper writer added: "These wretched and cowardly tactics were practiced on other portions of the line."[33]

One Federal soldier wrote of his experience in the dense wooded ravine just north of the intersection of today's Collier Road and Northside Drive. He explained that the "noonday air became dark and heavy with the powder smoke, which hung like a canopy over the pale, bloody corpses of the slain. Wounded men were borne to the rear by the scores, the blood streaming from their lacerated flesh, presenting a sight which at any other time would sicken the heart with horror." The Yankee could hardly see more than 20 feet in the thickening smoke that filled the wooded valley. "The rattling roll of the musketry sounded like the continuous roar of a cataract, and was joined by the thunderous chime of the deep throated cannon, which spouted unceasing volumes of flame and iron into the faces of the foe."[34] Another veteran of Robinson's brigade described the fight as "one of the bloodiest battles of the war" and "some of the most desperate fighting of the campaign." The soldier explained, "Rapidly forming under fire, the division received the enemy's charge, made with an impetuosity that brought him right into the Federal lines, and resulted in much hand to hand fighting, of which Robinson's Brigade did its full share."[35]

Looking to his right for support, Boughton and the 143rd New Yorkers realized that the rest of Robinson's brigade had stopped short. According to the New York commander, "The 82nd Ohio Veteran Volunteers, which was on my right, did not advance so far as I had done, and I discovered that my right was also unprotected." Boughton continued: "At this time the enemy's fire was very heavy, and in his pursuit of Colonel Ireland's brigade, he came on confidently,

---

[32] Ibid., 106–107.

[33] J.W.M, "Attack on Gen. Williams," *New York Tribune*, 28 July 1864; Clauss, "The Atlanta Campaign, July 18, 1864," 93–94.

[34] J.W.M., "Attack on Gen Williams," *New York Herald*, 29 July 1889.

[35] Robert G. Carroon, *From Freeman's Ford to Bentonville, The 61st Ohio Volunteer Infantry* (Shippensburg PA: Burd Street Press, 1998) 31.

approaching to within twenty yards of my line, which was in dense woods" in the sway between the two ridges, "when I gave orders to open fire, which was done with such precision and effect as to temporarily check his advance." The lieutenant colonel added, "Deeming it impossible to hold the position I occupied, isolated as it was, I decided to retire to a ridge thirty or forty yards to the rear, on which the brigade line had already been established."[36]

As they were falling back to join the remainder of Robinson's line, Adjutant Ratcliff was killed and Lieutenant Waterbury of Company A was mortally wounded. A number of enlisted men had already fallen in the fight at the ravine. When they reached the ridge and tied into the left of the 82nd Ohio, Boughton "ordered a barricade to be hastily constructed, which was being done when the enemy made another charge upon us and was handsomely repulsed, leaving some of his dead within thirty yards of our works. His attacks were made with great desperation," said Boughton, "but finding them of no avail he sought shelter behind his works." The 143rd New York lost 7 men killed, and 41 wounded for a total of 48 men lost in the day's fighting. According to Bruce Elmore of the 143rd New York, Lieutenant Waterbury and Gilbert D. Lawrence were among the 14 or 15 who died as a result of wounds received during the battle. He also lamented the wounding of Sergeant R. W. Porter in a letter to the sergeant's wife.[37]

Defending to the right of the New Yorkers, the 82nd Ohio lost twelve killed, including Lieutenant Asa H. Gary and eleven enlisted men, forty-five wounded and five missing and assumed captured, for a total of sixty-two casualties in the action.[38] To the right of the 82nd Ohio, the 61st Ohio lost twenty men killed, five officers and fifty-two men wounded, and two men missing, for a total loss of seventy-nine men. Among the wounded was Colonel McGroarty who lost his left arm and Lieutenant Colonel Brown who lost a leg. Brown's wound would prove fatal; he died a few weeks later in Chattanooga. One veteran reported that the 61st Ohio lost 74 out of 174 in action, but the loss sustained by the Confederates in their front was even greater. According to Captain John Garrett of the 61st Ohio, "the enemy advanced until some of his men fell within ten feet of our line." Another Ohioan remembered that "In front of the regiment's position were counted 78 dead Confederates and 188 of their rifles were picked up there. In the final charge, the 61st Ohio captured the colors

---

[36] *OR*, ser. I, vol. 38, pt. 2, serial 73, p. 107.

[37] Ibid., 104–108; Bruce Elmore to wife, 29 July 1864, MSS 673 F, Manuscript Collection, Kenan Research Center, Atlanta History Center.

[38] *OR*, ser. I, vol. 38, pt. 2, serial 73, pp. 110–11.

of the 61st [24th] South Carolina, and took as prisoners its Colonel, two Captains, three Lieutenants, the color bearer, and 29 privates." The captured soldiers were likely from both O'Neal's Alabamians and the South Carolinians.[39]

The Ohio captain who found himself in command of the 61st Ohio by the end of the day's fighting, added, "Having maintained our position against vastly superior numbers, until every field officer and more than half of the men were either killed or wounded, we were ordered to retire, which we did in good order, to the second line, where we remained for a short time," explained Garrett, "and then retook our former position and maintained it to the close of the fight...."[40] Garrett's Ohioans were facing the blows delivered originally by the men of O'Neal's hard-hitting Alabamians, while a second wave soon struck another blow from Jones's 24th South Carolina. The South Carolinians would lose sixty-three casualties while trying to wrest the ridge away from the Ohioans.[41] On the far right of Robinson's brigade, the 101st Illinois found no enemy in its immediate front. Consequently, they were soon ordered to support the 46th Pennsylvania on the right Knipe's brigade, which was being flanked by Reynolds's Arkansans. Fighting with the Pennsylvanians and men from the 27th Indiana that had also been sent to protect the flank of the 46th Pennsylvania, the 101st Illinois lost five killed and thirty wounded.[42]

The 82nd Illinois had been in reserve when O'Neal's first parry into Robinson's front was blunted. According to Lieutenant Colonel Salomon, "My regiment had been about thirty minutes in the second line when several men were wounded by stray shots, when I received orders to relieve the 46th Pennsylvania Volunteers, of the 1st Brigade." After Reynolds's Arkansas

---

[39] Ibid., 108–109; Carroon, *From Freeman's Ford*, 13–14, 31. See F. S. Wallace, "At Peach Tree Creek: The Magnificent Fighting Done by Williams' Division," *National Tribune*, 10 June 1909, where the 61st Ohio claims the capture of the colors of a South Carolina regiment at the Battle of Peach Tree Creek. Compare, however, to research of noted flag historian Greg Biggs who concludes that no flag was lost by the 24th South Carolina at Peach Tree Creek, the unit's colors being a Charleston Depot flag that was never captured. Thus, the flag captured by the 61st Ohio could have either been another one used by the 24th South Carolina or a flag from one of O'Neal's Alabama regiments that first struck that part of the Federal line.

[40] *OR*, ser. I, vol. 38, pt. 2, serial 73, p. 109.

[41] Eugene W. Jones, Jr., *Enlisted for the War: The Struggles of the Gallant 24th Regiment, South Carolina Volunteers, Infantry, 1861–1865* (Highstown NJ: Longstreet House, 1997) 179; T. A. Stevenson to unknown, 28 August 1885, Special Collections, Duke University.

[42] *OR*, ser. I, vol. 38, pt. 2, serial 73, p. 103.

Brigade found the exposed right flank of Knipe's 1st Brigade, General Williams rushed several units to plug the hole including the 82nd Illinois. "I marched the regiment in double-quick forward, arrived at Colonel Selfridge's regiment, and relieved him under a heavy fire, losing several men on the road," explained Salomon. "I brought the regiment into position and gave the enemy, who was only from thirty to thirty-five yards from us, a full volley, which did considerable execution. I kept up a brisk and rapid fire for over three hours, the rebels replying with great obstinacy," remembered the Illinois commander. "I had to draw fresh supplies of ammunition twice during the fight, and every man fired from 135 to 140 rounds." The 82nd Illinois lost Lieutenant Bechstein and nine other men killed and thirty-seven men wounded, for a total of forty-seven men in casualties for the day.[43] The 45th New York left Robinson's brigade for Nashville on 6 July, and the 31st Wisconsin joined the brigade on 21 July and did not participate in the action. So, the losses in Robinson's brigade were 54 killed, 210 wounded, and 5 captured or missing, for a total of 271 men.

In Ruger's brigade, Colonel Silas Colgrove, commanding the 27th Indiana, was struck in the side, which "turned black and blue by a cannon shot that grazed him," and he was believed to be mortally wounded.[44] The offending artillery round was "an unexploded shell, which otherwise would have passed harmlessly over, struck the limb of a tree and glanced downward. The colonel was at the time reclining on his side, in rear of the regiment. The shell struck under him, passing between his arm and body." The force of the shell was such that "it lifted him up several feet and whirled him over and over." The colonel sustained a large contusion in his side that took him out of the war. His sword, which he was wearing at his side at the time, bore "the marks of the tremendous force of the blow, being bent and twisted like a piece of tin or scrap-iron that has passed through a hot fire."[45] Colgrove and his Indianans remembered that the Battle of Peach Tree Creek was their fiercest fight during the Atlanta Campaign, and it reminded many of the battles in the East such as Gettysburg and Chancellorsville where they had fought the year before. One Hoosier veteran recalled, "The 27th Indiana fired 100 rounds per man in the battle [at Peach Tree Creek]."[46]

---

[43] *OR*, ser. I, vol. 38, pt. 2, serial 73, p. 100.

[44] Scaife, *The Campaign for Atlanta*, 154; Bryant, Edwin E., Third Wisconsin Veterans, 1861–1865, 256; George H. Cutter, diary, 20 July 1864, 90, Special Collections, Hargrett Library, University of Georgia, Athens, Georgia.

[45] Brown, *History of the 27th Indiana*, 520.

[46] Edwin E. Bryant, *Third Wisconsin Veterans, 1861–1865* (Madison WI: Democrat

The Battle of Peach Tree Creek

Some twenty years after the battle of September 1895, a party of the veterans of the 27th Indiana visited the battlefield. "After some difficulty, they found the exact spot where the regiment was engaged. The entrenchments, dug the night after the battle, substantially where the line had been during its progress, served as the best guide to identification. The ground had not been improved," remembered veteran Edmund Brown, "and the old parapet remained very clearly marked. The graves where we buried our dead comrades at the close of battle were also distinctly visible, though apparently empty. The slabs of sandstone which we set up for headstones were still in place."[47] The bodies had been reinterred at the national cemetery in Marietta.

"Our location during the battle," according to Brown, "was about a fourth of a mile east of the old Atlanta and [today's Howell Mill Road], and immediately east of the first deep ravine in that direction." The ravine between today's Gladstone Road and Monterey Drive marks the 27th Indiana's location during the battle, somewhat recessed and behind Belvedere Drive, which marked the approximate location of the refused right of the 46th Pennsylvania. The line of the remainder of the 46th Pennsylvania and Knipe's 1st Brigade ran generally along and to the immediate south of McKinley Road. Brown explained, "It was this ravine [between Gladstone Road and Monterey Drive] that was on our right while we were engaged. A branch of it also curved eastward and partially covered our front. The ground between this ravine and the above road was occupied by men from the XIV Corps."[48]

As the veterans walked the ground they had defended three decades before, they recalled how thickly the Rebel dead laid, especially in the ravine near their line, and on the slopes beyond: "In front of both the 46th [Pennsylvania] and 27th [Indiana], dead bodies frequently lay across each other. Neither could the piteous moans and complaints of the wounded, continuing all through the night, fail to come to mind," remembered one veteran. "The vacant cabins…which were now on our left, were used as field hospitals. One or two of the rebel wounded which had been carried there were loud and instant in their outcries."[49]

While the 27th Indiana of Ruger's reserve brigade was busy, several "of the right companies of the Third [Wisconsin] opened a fire on the enemy, which assisted a regiment of the Fourteenth Corps."[50] That regiment was the 104th

---

Printing Company, 1891) 256.
[47] Brown, *History of the 27th Indiana*, 521.
[48] Ibid., 521.
[49] Ibid., 521.
[50] Bryant, *Third Wisconsin Veterans*, 256.

Illinois of McCook's brigade, which was busy fending off Reynolds's Arkansans. Private George H. Cutter of Company H, 3rd Wisconsin, described the Confederate assault as "a sour one."[51] A considerable number of Ruger's brigade did not engage in the fight, as they were posted on the ridge behind the other two brigades of Williams's division. The 3rd Wisconsin was posted on the western edge of that ridge, near Howell Mill Road, and was within rifle range of the action in front of the 104th Illinois to its west. A fair number of Ruger's veterans were casualties of "stray balls."[52] The 3rd Wisconsin saw two of its men killed while five more were wounded.[53]

---

[51] Cutter, diary, 20 July 1864, 90, Special Collections, Hargrett Library, University of Georgia, Athens, Georgia.

[52] Ibid., 90.

[53] Bryant, *Third Wisconsin Veterans,* 256; Cutter, diary, 20 July 1864, 90, Special Collections, Hargrett Library, University of Georgia, Athens, Georgia.

THAT IS WHERE BUT LITTLE FUN CAME

> Everything was still as death for a few seconds when the enemy fired into us at very short range. Our line soon gave way and we retreated to the road that we marched up to reach the position.[1]

After the initial shock wave of O'Neal's charge subsided, and the shattered portions of Williams's and Geary's divisions regrouped, O'Neal realized that he did not have enough men to carry the attack further or to capitalize on his initial success. In addition, the Yankees in the wooded ridges ahead were no longer running, but were stiffening their resistance. His men might be vastly outnumbered by the Federals. Further, Reynolds Arkansas Brigade, which was to be his support on the left, was not coming into view. O'Neal couldn't know that Reynolds's boys were about to have their hands full over in the next wooded hollow with parts of Williams's and Palmer's divisions. And, while heavy firing could be heard over the ridge to the right, Scott's brigade was apparently too far away to help O'Neal. Besides, from the sound of things, Scott's men were busy with their own fight.

Meanwhile, Bill Nicholson, the Texas Ranger, Lieutenant Pierce English, Wash Crumpton, and the rest of the squad in the 37th Mississippi saw the Federal troops begin to reform around them on three sides. "A hasty counsel was held and we decided they were returning and we'd better get out. What had become of the balance of our forces we did not know."[2] Crumpton continued:

> With our guns all loaded, we started out the way we came in. On rising a very steep hill in the woods we saw, fifty yards away, the woods black with Yankees. They had dropped in behind us, but with no idea there was danger from that direction, they were looking to their front. We all fired into the

---

[1] Eugene W. Jones, Jr., *Enlisted for the War: The Struggles of the Gallant 24th Regiment, South Carolina Volunteers, Infantry, 1861–1865* (Highstown NJ: Longstreet House, 1997) 179; T. A. Stevenson to unknown, 28 August 1885, Special Collections, Duke University, Durham NC.

[2] Washington Bryan Crumpton, *A Book of Memories* (Montgomery AL: Baptist Mission Board, 1921) 87.

thickest bunch of them, then fairly rolled down the steep hillside. Three of us rushed down a ravine and after passing a spur went up another ravine. Poor old Bill Nick, went across the spur and we gave him up as lost.[3]

24th South Carolina. Colonel O'Neal sent word back to General Walthall requesting additional men to support his attack and continue to press the advantage gained. Colonel Ellison Capers and his 24th South Carolina Infantry Regiment from Gist's brigade of Walker's division had been detached from its brigade that morning during the eastward shift before the charge. Gist's men were covering the ground between Howell Mill Road and today's Northside Drive, shielding the shifting grey columns making for the assault. When the repositioning of the Confederate lines concluded, Capers found General Walthall's division in the rear of the South Carolinians. Now, after the charging Rebels had advanced from the trenches and beyond the picket lines, Capers's men were left without a job. When O'Neal came back requesting support, 385 South Carolinians suddenly found themselves useful. Walthall sent Capers's men to support O'Neal. Early in their advance, Capers was wounded in the arm and side. While the wound was not serious, it required immediate medical attention and Capers had to retire to the hospital. Thus, twenty-nine-year-old Lieutenant Colonel Jesse Stancel Jones led the veteran South Carolinians forward. Earlier in the day, the 24th South Carolina "lost one man in picket near the [Embry] house before the attack was made soon after the battle commenced" as elements of Williams's division began probing up the nearby road.[4]

Lieutenant Colonel Jones and his South Carolinians marched down the Collier Road toward the sound of firing until coming up to a wooded ridge just east of the Embry plantation. Jones and his men waited at the Olyinska house on the old Collier Road for orders from O'Neal on where they were to deploy in the woods ahead.[5] While they waited, they could hear the sounds of battle raging nearby, "creat[ing] considerable consternation among the men. While waiting, the Yankees shot down one of the 24th's soldiers as he performed a

---

[3] Ibid., 87–88.

[4] Scrapbook 28 and 29 ½, MSS 130, Wilbur G. Kurtz Papers, Kenan Research Center, Atlanta History Center; Jones, Jr., *Enlisted for the War*, 177. Supplement to *OR*, pt. 1, vol. 7, serial 7, pp. 153–54.

[5] This old road and house were located in rear of the Mt. Zion Church behind the parking lot and down to the northeast past a power line cut. The power line easement, while straight, points the direction—northeast—of O'Neal's attack, but the old Collier Road meandered along the side of the slope of the ridge east of the power line until it met the valley behind which Geary's division was posted.

work detail." During this time, fellow South Carolinian "Major Preston...galloped down the road with a battery of artillery and was killed below the house, they carried him back by our line," lamented T. A. Stevenson of the 24th South Carolina after the war. "As the artillerymen sadly removed Preston's body, the ambulance passed along the 24th's line again. After these two instances, the men hunkered down utilizing all available protection."[6]

Shortly thereafter, Colonel O'Neal came up and led the regiment up a country road through the woods toward the Federal lines. "While on this march we had one man killed," remembered Stevenson.[7] Lieutenant Colonel (Bushrod) Jones placed one of his companies in front as a skirmish line and the 24th South Carolina disappeared in the deep woods that masked Williams's men who were covering the old road along a ridge just above it to the north and northwest. According to Stevenson, when the skirmish line advanced out of sight into the Georgia wilderness in their front, "they saw them no more." As the South Carolinians got into position, one of the men was struck dead by a stray minnie ball. Then, out of nowhere, the earth seemed to erupt into an explosion of fire and as the Yankees poured lead into the unsuspecting Rebels: "Everything was still as death for a few seconds when the enemy fired into us at very short range. Our line soon gave way and we retreated to the road that we marched up to reach the position."[8]

Soon, the veteran regiment rallied on the road and order was quickly restored. Colonel Jones then led the men forward to a point in the woods where the Carolinians could return fire on the Yankees. They remained in that position, taking and receiving punishment, for the rest of the afternoon. There was no support for the South Carolinians or the rest of O'Neal's brigade; the Confederate lines being stretched thin in a single line as they advanced on Williams's 1st "Red Star" Division.[9]

The 24th South Carolina suffered terribly in the struggle for they were slugging it out with a brigade of Williams's division in the wooded fight, and Williams's men had the advantage of being up the hill from the Carolinians. During the contest, Private R. J. Rivers, of Company D in the 24th South Carolina, who had a bad arm and was known as the "one handed man" because

---

[6] Jones, Jr., *Enlisted for the War*, 177–79; Supplement to *OR*, pt. 1, vol. 7, serial 7, pp. 153–54.

[7] Supplement to *OR*, pt. 1, vol. 7, serial 7, pp. 153–54.

[8] Supplement to *OR*, pt. 1, vol. 7, serial 7, pp. 153–54; Jones, Jr., *Enlisted for the War*, 179; T. A. Stevenson to unknown, 28 August 1885, Special Collections, Duke University.

[9] Supplement to *OR*, pt. 1, vol. 7, serial 7, pp. 153–54.

of it, was shot in the same arm, ending his war service. One of the veterans felt that the Carolinians had been badly used by Colonel O'Neal, as it appeared to them that they had no support on either flank in the wooded fire fight. This sentiment could have been shared by all of the units fighting with Stewart's forces at Peach Tree Creek. The land occupied in their attack, replete with wooded ridges and ravines, simply swallowed up each of Stewart's brigades in succession, despite their individual and initial successes against their blue foe. During this brutal fighting just west of today's Northside Drive, the 24th South Carolina apparently lost her flag to the men of the 61st Ohio.[10]

The casualties in the 24th South Carolina were high, with fifteen men killed, forty-four wounded, and four men missing or captured, making the total losses in the regiment sixty-three men, one of the worst days of the war for this unit, which had been severely depleted at Chickamauga and would soon be decimated at Franklin. According to Captain F. S. Wallace of the 61st Ohio, "The Colors of a South Carolina Regiment were captured and the prisoners were the Colonel, 2 Captains, 3 Lieutenants, the Color Bearer and 29 privates of that Regiment."[11]

O'Neal was also given the 2nd Corps Alabama Sharpshooters to support his attack. The 2nd Corps Sharpshooters was led that day by Captain W. H. Lindsey of the 26th Alabama. The 24th South Carolina and the sharpshooters joined the remainder of O'Neal's brigade in making a second charge, "but being unsupported we were compelled again to fall back and take another position," according to O'Neal. "We drove the enemy nearly a mile, captured some of his works, and had punished him severely," explained the veteran commander. Nevertheless, O'Neal's veterans captured 293 men, mostly from Geary's surprised division, inflicted a number of battle casualties among Geary's and Williams's divisions, and lost only 279 in killed, wounded, and missing.[12]

---

[10] See F. S. Wallace, "At Peach Tree Creek," *National Tribune*, 10 June 1909, 2, in which the 61st Ohio claims the capture of the colors of a South Carolina regiment at the Battle of Peach Tree Creek.

[11] Jones, Jr., *Enlisted for the War*, 179; T. A. Stevenson to unknown, 28 August 1885. Special Collections, Duke University; F. S. Wallace, "At Peach Tree Creek," *National Tribune*, 10 June 1909. No Confederate unit in this area claims to have lost their colors. While the 24th South Carolina supported O'Neal's Alabamians in their attack on Williams's division, their colors were allegedly never captured during the war, and the remnant of one of their flags is on display at the South Carolina Confederate Relic Room and Museum in Columbia. There were no other South Carolina units in action in this part of the battlefield.

[12] United States War Department, comp., *Official Records of the Union and Confederate Armies in the War of the Rebellion*, 128 vols. (Washington, DC: Government

The Battle of Peach Tree Creek

37th Mississippi. According to Sergeant Robert Webb Banks, O' Neal's brigade lost 287 men, and his regiment, the 37th Mississippi, captured 152 prisoners. Colonel Orlando S. Holland quickly wrapped up the Yankee prisoners and sent them to the rear under a heavy detail while he pressed his regiment forward over today's Northside Drive and across Collier Road. Holland's Mississippians continued to roll up Jones's and Candy's brigades of Geary's division as a number of Federal regiments broke and ran for the flats next to Peach Tree Creek and the bridges leading to safety beyond. Suddenly, and about as quickly as they had crushed the exposed Federal flank, Holland's men were stopped.[13]

When sounds of the fighting first reached the Federal rear, Ireland's brigade formed and rushed to plug the hole in Geary's lines and repel the attacking Confederates. As Holland's Mississippians and three companies of the 17th Alabama to their left clipped the Collier Ridge, they were halted around today's Cottage Lane. From there, a portion of Ireland's Federals together with a number of men from various units in Candy's and Jones's brigades wrested control of the ridge away from the Mississippians and Alabamians. Without support, Holland's men could not advance any further and they could not hold very long. Meanwhile, O' Neal and the remainder of the brigade were being thwarted by Williams's division and the remainder of Geary's men in a crescent-shaped line created by Ireland's counterattack. Writing his father on 25 July, Sergeant Banks explained, "Colonel Holland and his regiment distinguished themselves, driving the enemy from the trenches and planting the colors of the 37th Mississippi on his works in advance of the brigade. In addition to this, they captured 152 prisoners. Out of 210 men, he lost only 48, so rapid was his charge."[14]

J. B. Lightsey, a private from Company K remembered, "we turned back to meet General Sherman at Peach Tree Creek, where he had constructed some temporary breastworks. There was a sanguinary battle fought there, with a heavy loss on each side and Hood drove the enemy away from their position." Lightsey lamented losing one of his best friends. "We lost many brave, good, and noble men in this conflict, amongst whom was Wyatt Jones, our color bearer, from Co. K, 37th Miss. Regiment. He was in advance of our Company

---

Printing Office, 1880–1901) ser. 1, vol. 38, pt. 3, serial 74, p. 742 (hereafter *OR*).

[13] Robert Webb Banks, *The Battle of Franklin, November 30, 1864. The Bloodiest Engagement of the War Between the States* (New York: The Neale Publishing Company, 1908) 20.

[14] Banks, *The Battle of Franklin*, 21.

and was shot as he mounted the enemy's works." The comrade continued, "There was not a better soldier, nor a braver man in the Company than Wyatt Jones, and his death was much regretted by the entire command."[15]

Falling in the attack from the 37th Mississippi on the right of O'Neal's brigade, were three men killed, including Ensign S. W. Jones, forty wounded, including Lieutenant Colonel William W. Wier, Second Lieutenant W. H. Craft of Company B, Second Lieutenant John West of Company C, and Captain C. C. Ferrell, Lieutenant D. F. Lott, and Private Hudson of Company F. Additionally, the 37th Mississippi lost two men missing making their casualties listed at three killed, forty wounded, and two missing for a total of forty-five men. Sergeant Orange McCarty, Jr., of Company E of the 37th Mississippi lost a leg but survived.[16]

According to one 37th Mississippi historian, "In the battle of Peachtree Creek, the brigades advanced until they found themselves flanked by the irregular Federal line. The Thirty-seventh wheeled to meet the necessities of the movement and delivered a telling fire, but the lack of support compelled the brigade to retire." The Mississippi veteran continued, "A second advance was made with like results. 'We drove the enemy nearly a mile, captured some of his works and had punished him severely when compelled to fall back.'"[17]

As some the men of the 37th Mississippi including Wash Crumpton came walking back from the battle front through the woods, they came across General Walthall and his staff.

> We saw General Walthall, our Division Commander, and staff riding leisurely down the road. I shouted to him, telling of his danger. One of his party came galloping saying, "Go back to the front you stragglers." With that our Lieutenant [Pierce English] walked away. Demanding that we should go back, I remarked, I'd speak to the General. When he came up, in a few words I told him Stone's [Scott's] Brigade hadn't come up, that the Yankees were only a little way down the road. On his expressing great doubt saying, "We

---

[15] www.rootsweb.ancestry.com/~msjasper/jbl2.htm (10 January 2009).

[16] Dunbar Rowland, *Military History of Mississippi, 1803–1898*, ed. H. Grady Howell, Jr. (Spartanburg SC: The Reprint Company, Publishers, 1978) 328–29. After the war, he returned home to Mississippi to his wife Catherine Frances Walker and his daughter Sarah Rosetta McCarty who was born on 2 August 1860. In 1865, Orange took his wife and daughter across the Mississippi to settle in Burke, Texas, where they kept cattle and hogs along the Neches River.

[17] "37th Mississippi Infantry," www.reynolds-genealogy.com/research/37th_mississippi_regiment.htm (15 October 2008).

certainly carried everything," the smart Alex of an aide shouted out, as he galloped off, "I'll see." A short distance away he wheeled his horse and a hundred bullets flew through the woods in his direction. In the middle of the road there was a brass cannon left by some one. The General said, "You two men remain right here by this gun and when I send you a force, pilot them to that hill you were on."[18]

Crumpton and his buddy "Chunky" Thompson, who was called that because he was not chunky, obeyed the general's orders and waited for help to arrive. The two soldiers looked at the Napoleon 12-pounder cannon and tried to figure out how they would fire it. "We looked at the gun and found it loaded, but how to shoot it, we did not know. Finally, however, we thought we knew and were determined we'd fire it, if the Yanks came." Crumpton, and the squad from the 37th Mississippi continued to wait for reinforcements, anxiously looking into the distant woods for signs of approaching Yankees. "After a time the Forty-fifth Arkansas came, a very small number of men. Later another bunch—probably 500 gathered at last." This was probably either the 9th Arkansas returning from picket duty and some Tennessee troops in General Quarles's Brigade that came up late in the attack to try and support O'Neal.[19]

After the battle, Private J. B. Lightsey joined a burial detail that returned to the woods along Collier ridge to find their comrades who had fallen. "I was on this battlefield about two weeks after this battle and of all the sickening sights that I ever beheld it was there. In burying the hundreds of slain soldiers they were piled into heaps of 15 or 20 like heaps of logs and not enough dirt placed upon the heaps to cover them." The horrified veteran explained, "When I saw them, there were many arms, legs and even skulls perfectly bare, and I saw one poor fellow that they did not pretend to bury at all, as he lay with his face to the enemy, just as he fell, resembling a shriveled mummy. There were no scavengers of nature there, and it seemed all nature abhorred such a sickening scene. That is where but little fun came."[20]

Quarles's Brigade. Quarles's brigade consisted of the 1st Alabama under Major Samuel E. Knox, the 42nd Tennessee under Colonel Isaac N. Hulme, the 46th and 55th Tennessee under the command of Colonel Robert A. Owens, the 48th Tennessee led by Lieutenant Colonel Aaron S. Godwin, the 49th

---

[18] Crumpton, *A Book of Memories*, 88.
[19] Crumpton, *A Book of Memories*, 88–89.
[20] www.rootsweb.ancestry.com/~msjasper/jbl2.htm (10 January 2009).

Hood's First Sortie, 20 July 1864

Tennessee commanded by Colonel William F. Young, and the 53rd Tennessee led by Colonel John R. White.[21]

Private Washington Crumpton, who would later become a Baptist minister and leader in the Alabama Baptist Convention, described the scene as the Confederates prepared for a second attack:

> Then came a Senior Colonel, drunk as a fool. I'll not mention his name, because of subsequent history. He called for the men General Walthall left there. He wanted to know the direction to the hill, from which we had been driven. I pointed the direction and suggested modestly, that my companion and I, with a few others, should act as skirmishers, for there was no telling what changes had occurred. He cursed me and told me he was capable of running that business. After a time, in the wildest confusion, we were at the bottom of the hill.
>
> I said, "There's the hill, Colonel, I can't tell you what's on top." He ordered the charge. When within twenty or thirty steps of the top, a solid blue line of Yankees rose up. At the first fire, half of our men fell. I fired my gun, then attempted to load it, lying down. It had been fired so much [earlier in the initial charge], it had gotten cold and clogged; the bullet hung half way down. Standing half bent, trying to ram the bullet home, the gun was shot out of my hand, the stock literally torn to splinters. Fortunately, some of us escaped, the Yanks firing down hill, as is most generally the case, over shot us.[22]

It is unclear who the "drunk" colonel for whom the soldier was referring, but it is believed that it may have been Colonel John R. White of the 53rd Tennessee who was killed just eight days later during the battle of Ezra Church. The 49th Tennessee lost two men killed and three wounded, while the 46th Tennessee saw five men killed during the day's fighting.[23] Quarles's brigade would lose twenty-four men before the day was over, mostly during the futile second attack.

---

[21] Crumpton, *A Book of Memories*, 88–89; William R. Scaife, *The Campaign for Atlanta* (Atlanta: self-published, 1993) 183–84.

[22] Crumpton, *A Book of Memories*, 88–89.

[23] Scaife, *The Campaign for Atlanta*, 184; Thomas A. Head, *Sumner County, Tennessee in the Civil War*, ed. Diane Payne (Hendersonville TN: self-published, 1972) 343, 349, 351; Edwin H. Rennolds, *A History of the Henry County Commands which Served in the Confederate States Army* (Jacksonville FL: Sun Publishing Company, 1904) 205–206, 208–209.

Chaplain James H. McNeilly of Quarles's brigade remembered, "After our repulse I had with me one of our litter bearers, and we found some of our men not seriously hurt who went on to their command. We found the body of one of our regiment lying in a little country road near a deserted cabin," explained McNeilly. "I did not know the location of any of the troops and felt that if we tried to carry the body to our own lines we were just as likely to run into the lines of the enemy, so we determined to bury him where he was killed. We found an old ax at the cabin," continued the Chaplain, "and with that and a board for a shovel we scooped out a grave two or three feet deep, rolled him in his blanket, and laid him in the grave. We placed some limbs with thick leaves on his body and covered him over with earth." The Tennessee preacher led a brief funeral for the fallen comrade. "Then I read the burial service and offered a prayer, and I carved his name on the trunk of a tree at the head of the grave. We left him there, hoping to come back and remove him; but in the pressure of daily battles I never could go again to the place, which was between the lines."[24]

---

[24] James H. McNeilly, "A Day in the Life of a Confederate Chaplain," *Confederate Veteran*, vol. 26 (1918): 471.

IT WAS CHICKAMAUGA AGAIN

One volley we gave them allmost [sic] in their teeth and then for about five minutes it was Chickamauga again; a mixture of clubbing and stabbing, of damning, cursing and swearing, for about 5 minutes more or less, on such occasions one forgetts to consult the watch, when the Johnnies concluded to go home.[1]

Reynolds's Arkansas Brigade. Supporting O'Neal's attack was General Daniel H. Reynolds and his Arkansas brigade. They lined up just west of and along the Howell Mill Road below the Hiram Embry plantation. Numbering just 540 men, the Arkansas brigade was without the 9th Arkansas, which had been deployed on the skirmish line to cover the division's front before the charge. As the Arkansans marched forward, they passed the Mt. Zion Church on their right as they angled to the northeast crossing the Howell Mill Road and moving into the woods northeast of the Embry plantation grounds. They quickly found trouble as the men on the left flank reached and rushed the Federal skirmish line, taking it and firing into the retreating Yankees. These men were part of Williams's division, which had fired in one rank before falling back in an effort to make a loud enough noise to alert the remainder of the division of the impending threat. On the right of Reynolds's attackers, the Federal concentration was much deeper in the woods and up on the ridge above.

Reynolds's brigade soon met heavy resistance as the right flank continued to try to connect with the left of O'Neal's brigade, which was disappearing fast over the wooded ridge to the right of it and in the heavily forested distance in front. This occurred in the area near today's intersection of Springlake and Collier roads. There, "a brigade of Arkansas troops [Reynolds's brigade] plunged into the ravine paralleling Norfleet Road and started for the Yankees on the other side."[2] While their orders were to be guided by the units to their right

---

[1] John Henry Otto, *Memoirs of a Dutch Mudsill*, ed. David Gould and James B. Kennedy (Kent OH: Kent State University Press, 2004) 270.

[2] Diane C. Thomas, "City-Scape," *Atlanta: The Magazine of the Urban South* 22 (October 1982): 16.

The Battle of Peach Tree Creek

while swinging to their left as they advanced, the men of both O'Neal's and Reynolds's brigades found it difficult to swing left during their assault. The topography replete with wooded ridges and ravines, coupled with the enemy's positions that faced southeast instead of south or southwest, and the futile efforts to connect with and support the attack of the brigade somewhere in the distant woods to their right, precluded any leftward oblique. Reynolds's brigades engaged and fought the enemy along Howell Mill Road, which they reported as the Pace's Ferry Road.[3] Then, with Federal fire raining down on them from the ridge on the other side of the ravine, the Arkansans peeled back to the road turned north to try and flank the Federal line. Over to the left, Reynolds's men were routing the Yankees up the road when they began receiving enfilade fire from artillery and rifles on their right flank[4] from the 46th Pennsylvania where Colonel James L. Selfridge refused his right flank.[5]

Sarah Huff, a mere child at the time of the battle, witnessed the carnage along the Howell Mill Road theater: "Within one mile of where mother and members of her family stood, trees as big as a man's body were mowed down. Mount Zion Baptist Church, school houses and numerous dwellings, slave quarters, and farms were demolished." Eight-year-old Huff remembered, "The reports of the cannon sounded like thunder claps and the musketry was like hail on the roof in the time of a summer flurry squall. I recall hearing brother say, 'If they turn their guns this way we will be torn all to pieces!'"[6]

Selden's Alabama Battery. When General Dan Reynolds saw that his left flank was exposed to Federal fire, which rained on them from the 104th Illinois (posted west of Howell Mill Road on a knoll just below today's Glenbrook Drive) and from the 3rd Wisconsin (posted along a second ridge behind Knipe's brigade along today's Monterey Drive), he sought out and got artillery support for his Arkansans. According to Reynolds, "I at once directed Major Preston, Chief of Artillery of [Walthall's] Division, to move a battery to a position on the left of the road and drive the enemy from my left flank."[7] Major Preston directed Selden's Alabama battery with its four Napoleon 12-pounder guns up

---

[3] Scrapbook 28, pp. 30–33, MSS 130, Wilbur G. Kurtz Papers, Kenan Research Center, Atlanta History Center.

[4] United States War Department, comp., *Official Records of the Union and Confederate Armies in the War of the Rebellion*, 128 vols. (Washington, DC: Government Printing Office, 1880–1901) ser. I, vol. 38, pt. 3, serial 74, p. 938 (hereafter *OR*); Willis, *Arkansas Confederates in the Western Theater* (Dayton OH, 1998) 512–14.

[5] *OR*, ser. I, vol. 38, pt. 2, serial 73, pp. 56–57.

[6] Sarah Huff, "My 80 Years in Atlanta," 11, subject files, Atlanta History Center.

[7] *OR*, ser. I, vol. 38, pt. 3, serial 74, p. 938; Willis, *Arkansas Confederates,* 512–14.

the Howell Mill Road to the Embry plantation. There, on the slope of a hill in front of the Hiram Embry place, the battery got into position (just west of the Howell Mill Road, and northwest of its intersection today with the present course of Collier Road). Selden's Alabama battery, under the command of Lieutenant Charles W. Lovelace, then went into action. Major Preston, brother of Sally "Buck" Preston who was the love interest of General Hood, remained with Seldon's battery and began to direct their fire when he was struck down and killed. The battery was exposed to both sharpshooter and artillery fire. One Federal battery opened up on them from the northeast in their front, and another battery began firing on them from their left, up the Howell Mill Road. At this point, Cockrell's Missouri Brigade was called to come up to support the battery and Reynolds's exposed left flank.

Seldon's battery continued to fire at the Federal guns in front of them, and changed front to fire at the Federal guns to their left and silenced them for a time, but the rifle fire from the sharpshooters continued to keep a severe fire on them on the open hill. Lieutenant Lovelace was wounded, but he continued to lead the battery until they had expended all of their ammunition, which only took about twenty minutes of rapid firing. When Lovelace reported that he was out of ammunition, he was ordered to limber up and withdraw, and Lieutenant Watkins was ordered to bring up the Lookout Tennessee Battery to replace it.

Barry's Tennessee Battery. Supporting Walthall's advance and replacing Selden's battery were the four Napoleon 12-pounder guns and their crews from the Lookout Tennessee Battery, which was normally commanded by Captain Robert L. Barry. However, on this day the Lookout battery was under the command of Lieutenant Richard L. Watkins. The battery hotly contested a Federal battery opposing it in the woods to the east of the Embry plantation, and after a sharp fight, silenced the Yankee battery and compelled it to retire. Barry's battery expended another 260 rounds of ammunition, or 65 rounds to each gun, before it, too, had exhausted its ammunition and withdrew after sunset.[8] But the action cost the Tennessee artillerists fifteen casualties in men killed, wounded, and captured.[9] Captured from Barry's battery was Private John C. Roberts, a twenty-nine-year-old farmer from near Chattanooga, Tennessee.[10]

---

[8] *OR*, ser. I, vol. 38, pt. 3, serial 74, pp. 967–69.
[9] Civil War Centennial Commission, *Tennesseans in the Civil War, A Military History of Confederate and Union Units with Available Rosters of Personnel*, 2 vols. (Nashville: 1964–1965) 1:124.
[10] Clement Anselm Evans, ed., *Tennessee*, vol. 10 of *Confederate Military History*, 19 vols. (1899; repr., Wilmington NC: Broadfoot Publishing Company, 1987) 688. Roberts

The Battle of Peach Tree Creek

Prior to the attack, the Federals had probed as far south as the outskirts of the Embry plantation. According to Second Lieutenant Henry F. Perry of the 38th Indiana in Palmer's XIV Corps, earlier in the day "our skirmishers were hotly engaged with the skirmishers of the enemy." Perry described his unit's success: "Pushing the enemy before us for half a mile we captured a line of rifle pits on the crest of a high ridge, and then moving into the woods to the left of a public highway halted, and began the erection of fortifications." After working on the earthworks for a little while, Williams's division of the XX Corps came up and took up positions along the ridge relieving men of the XIV Corps who moved further to the right.[11]

The 1st Division, commanded by Brigadier General Richard W. Johnson who had just returned to command from being wounded at Picket's Mill and then again at Pine Mountain, had come down the Marietta Road, or Howell Mill Road, below Peach Tree Creek, and moved out astride the road, connecting with the right of the XX Corps. When Williams's division arrived, Johnson moved his 3rd Brigade, which had been left of Howell Mill Road, to the right or west of Howell Mill Road and west of McCook's 1st Brigade. Johnson's 1st Brigade under the command of Colonel Anson G. McCook, remained on the left connecting with the right of Williams's division of the XX Corps.[12]

The ridge that Johnson's division had previously occupied east of the Howell Mill Road was now held by Williams's division. There, a ravine crossed the road, cutting in behind the ridge and splitting McCook's position. To cover the line, McCook placed the 104th Illinois on the knoll at the exposed end of the ridge (located on Glenbrook Drive west of Howell Mill Road), and the rest of his force was placed about 150 yards behind and (along a lesser ridge that protruded below the ravine) parallel to Peach Tree Creek. The remainder of McCook's brigade was deployed as follows: in the first line to the west or right

---

subsequently took an oath not to take up arms against the United States in Nashville and was paroled. He later served as a justice of the peace and on the school board in Chattanooga and was a well-respected and prominent citizen.

[11] Henry F. Perry, *History of the 38th Indiana Volunteer Infantry* (Palo Alto CA: F.A. Stuart, Printer, 1906) 144.; *OR,* ser. 1, vol. 38, pt. 1, serial 72, pp. 507, 524, 742; *OR,* ser. 1, vol. 38, pt. 1, serial 73, p. 33.

[12] *OR,* ser. 1, vol. 38, pt. 1, serial 72, p. 531; William R. Scaife, *The Campaign for Atlanta* (Atlanta: self-published, 1993) 150. McCook had only recently replaced General William P. Carlin on 2 July, on a temporary basis, while Carlin went on leave for thirty days, a curious time to leave his command. After the futile and bloody repulses sustained at Kennesaw Mountain just days before, however, it is likely that many of Sherman's officers and men would have taken a thirty-day leave if it had been available to them.

and rear of the 104th Illinois by some 150 yards, the 15th Kentucky commanded by Colonel Marion C. Taylor (who commanded the first line), next, the 42nd Indiana led by Captain Masters, and on the far right, the 88th Indiana under Lieutenant Colonel Cyrus E. Briant (located along the southern side of today's Northcliffe Drive west of Howell Mill Road). In the second line from left to right, or east to west, were posted the 10th Wisconsin led by Captain Jacob W. Roby (located east of Howell Mill Road along the western half of Wilson Road), next the 21st Wisconsin under Lieutenant Colonel Harrison C. Hobart (who commanded the second line), then the 94th Ohio of Colonel Rue P. Hutchins, and on the far right the 33rd Ohio commanded by Lieutenant Colonel James H. M. Montgomery (located at site of the northern houses on Northcliffe Drive west of Howell Mill Road).[13]

McCook's brigade immediately began erecting breastworks at about 10:00 A.M., but were soon halted by General Johnson who relayed that they expected that the division would be advancing again soon. "Orders circulated about ten to entrench. But only a few moments later, the orders were countermanded. The men waited, unable to clearly see what was up ahead." According to one veteran of the 21st Wisconsin, "their was no open field in front of our Division; neither had we time to mack [sic] any works." Soon thereafter, the crash of musketry and artillery fire to the left in front of the IV and XX corps could be heard as it rolled nearer to McCook's men. Only about half of McCook's regiments "had formed in line when Hood sallied forth in colums without any preliminary Artilillerie firing." Then, a line of enemy infantry was seen sweeping down upon the exposed flank of the 104th Illinois. It was Reynolds's Arkansans. "Passing into the woods in front of the Federal position, the rebels emerged suddenly from the brush in front of the Federal lines, and the lines erupted in musket fire."[14]

104th Illinois, The La Salle County Regiment. The 104th Illinois Infantry Regiment was formed during the late summer 1862 when Louisville became threatened due to General Bragg's offensive into the Bluegrass State. "Recruited entirely from LaSalle County," the inexperienced regiment was "captured following a severe fight with a combined-arms force commanded by

---

[13] *OR*, ser. 1, vol. 38, pt. 1, serial 72, p. 539; Steven J. Adolphson, "An Incident of Valor in the Battle of Peach Tree Creek, 1864, (The 104th Illinois)," *Georgia Historical Quarterly* 57 (1973): 406–20; Scaife, *The Campaign for Atlanta*, 150.

[14] Kirk C. Jenkins, *The Battle Rages Higher: The Union's Fifteenth Kentucky Infantry* (Lexington: University Press of Kentucky, 2003) 230–31; Otto, *Memoirs of a Dutch Mudsill*, 269.

the Confederate raider, Colonel John Hunt Morgan," according to the regiment's historian, Steven J. Adolphson. After receiving their parole, the regiment was relegated to guard duty at Camp Douglas in Chicago where it appeared that they would spend the rest of the war and not be able to join the ranks of the "fighting 300," a post-war term often referred to by Federal army veterans when describing the some 300 regiments that did the majority of the North's fighting during the war.[15] But a young officer, a rising star in the ranks of the Army of the Cumberland, twenty-four-year-old Lieutenant Colonel Douglas Hapeman, saved the regiment from obscurity. In April 1863, the regiment received its notice of exchange, meaning it was properly exchanged for a like number of captured, but paroled, Confederates.[16]

A native of Euphratah, New York, Douglas Hapeman migrated as a child with his family to Aurora, Illinois, in 1844. Soon, they moved to Earlville, Illinois, in northern LaSalle County, where Hapeman was a student in a log schoolhouse until his mother died. This tragedy was followed soon by the loss of his father. Hapeman was thus orphaned by the age of ten. At the age of thirteen, Hapeman began an apprenticeship at a newspaper office in Ottawa. By the time that hostilities began in 1861, Hapeman had mastered the trade of printing and was a member of the Prairie State's historically predominant political party, the Democrats. In fact, Hapeman had to that point in his young life associated himself with the "loyal Democrats" wing of the party, or what would later be referred to as "peace Democrats," but after the firing on Fort Sumter by Southerners in April 1861, Hapeman became a "war Democrat," meaning someone who supported fighting to preserve the Union, but not necessarily someone who supported the abolition of slavery as advanced by the new Republican Party. After Hapeman bravely led a company of the 11th Illinois as a second lieutenant during the battles of Fort Donelson and Shiloh, his former employer, newspaper editor William Osman, who had served during the Mexican War, wrote prophetically of the young officer, "There is no truer soldier in the service. He takes to the business *con amore* [with love].... We expect before the war is over, to hear of him at head of a regiment."[17]

Twenty-five by the start of the Georgia Campaign, Hapeman made an unusual regimental leader. His hazel eyes stood out between his reddish blonde hair and "a closely trimmed beard running along his cheek and jaw line."

---

[15] Adolphson, "An Incident of Valor," 406.
[16] Ibid., 406–407.
[17] Ibid., 407.

Described by a fellow officer as "strictly business-like, careful and sure without ostentation," Hapeman was not a "martinet, but maintained discipline with a firm, though kindly hand. Hapeman would not allow his men to play baseball on Sunday," but the spiritual Methodist-Episcopalian, was not pretentious. Choosing to lead during battle on foot, he was still "easily recognized by the men in his dress coat, officer's hat, high leather boots with spurs, gauntlets, patent leather haversack, and field glasses, and he favored a 36-caliber Manhattan army revolver as a side arm." When encountering enemy fire, Hapeman would command his regiment to "lie down," thus preventing the needless exposure of his men. From the prone position, his men would continue to load, fire and fight until ordered to advance or charge. In combat, Hapeman seemed "perfectly cool" as he commanded his men.[18]

On the morning of 20 July, the 104th Illinois carried 244 men and 13 officers to the southern bank of Peach Tree Creek in the pre-dawn hours. The men of McCook's brigade had been roused at 3:00 A.M., and by daylight they were across Peach Tree Creek at Howell's Mill to join the remainder of Johnson's 1st Division.[19] With his vastly depleted force, Hapeman had been frustrated at the "replacement policy followed by Illinois and a great many other states in the North. Being one of the higher numbered regiments in terms of date of entry into the service, they were not eligible to receive replacement recruits as some of the older regiments." But his regiment's size was typical of most regiments, both North and South. Few regiments mustered 300 men or more by this point of the war, while many were less than 200 men.[20]

The 104th Illinois Regiment was placed on a knoll in advance of the remainder of McCook's brigade, west of Howell Mill Road, to link up with the second line of Williams's division to their left. "Because of the rough terrain and poor visual contact owing to the dense underbrush, their echelon formation became broken so that the 104th was actually in advance of the other regiments by at least 125 yards and separated from them by a deep ravine that ran along its right flank and to the rear." Soon, the men of the regiment "stacked arms on the northern face of a low ridge and began throwing up earthworks but stopped when Hapeman was ordered to prepare to advance. It was an extremely hot day and the men sought the shade of the trees and bushes awaiting the order to fall in."[21]

---

[18] Ibid., 407–10.
[19] Ibid., 410–11; *OR*, ser. 1, vol. 38, pt. 1, serial 72, pp. 532, 537–38.
[20] Adolphson, "An Incident of Valor," 410–11.
[21] Adolphson, "An Incident of Valor," 413.

According to one observer, "the afternoon was rapidly passing with no sign of an advance. Sometime between 3:30 and 4:00 P.M. the Confederates began their furious attack against the Federal troops to the left..." The sound of the firing moved from left to right in the distant woods, but seemed to get closer and closer when suddenly the right front and flank of Hapeman's line exploded into life. "Men who had been forward of the 104th's position as a picket force, came rushing headlong over the slight earthworks that had been thrown up. Corporal John Shapland of Company D was in the ravine with another comrade cooking their dinner when the firing began." The corporal recalled, "Leaving my meat I ran for the hilltop, and saw...Colonel [Hapeman] swinging his sword and saying, 'Fall in, men; Fall in!' It was the last call for many."[22]

Hapeman had just gotten his line into position when Reynolds's Arkansans came "pouring through the woods yelling like demons." Hapemen's men fired a volley that sent the Arkansans down into the shelter of a ravine where Reynolds's men began to probe to their left looking for the flank of the Illinois regiment's line. "The Confederates then went into a column formation and moved in a flanking movement up the ravine which ran perpendicular to the right of Hapeman's line of battle. This strategem was momentarily hidden from the regiment's view, owing to the defilade afforded by the terrain to Hapeman's front." Hapemen and his men peered forward into the dense brush and woods, looking for signs of hostile activity when, "Suddenly the Confederate column reappeared, and deploying into a line, smashed into the regiment's right flank, pouring a murderous enfilading fire along the right of Hapeman's entire line." Some of Reynolds's men had moved so far to the right and rear of the Illinoisans that "One of the Confederate regiments...[was] actually shooting into the regiment's rear."[23]

"Notwithstanding the suddenness of the attack and fierceness of the struggle, there was no panic in our ranks," wrote Captain William F. Strawn of Company F. Complimenting the leadership of Lieutenant Colonel Hapeman, Strawn explained that the regiment "had become so accustomed to the coolness of our regimental officers that one and all took it for granted that to simply obey orders was the surest way to come out all right." One of the first victims of the Rebel fire was Private William M. Wilson from Company E. Wounded in his shoulder, Wilson began "making his way for the rear—a dangerous move at the time," when he found Hapeman: "He stood up straight with his sword drawn

---

[22] Ibid., 413.
[23] Ibid., 413.

and revolver in hand, urging the men to stand firm, every inch the soldier he was." Wilson reflected, "I think yet it was a wonder he escaped alive; he seemed to be alone on top of a knoll some thirty feet in rear of Company E where bullets were flying lively."[24]

The 104th Illinois then came under a massive attack as a portion of Reynolds's Arkansas Brigade found their right flank and rear on the exposed knoll. "One-half of the companies in the regiment's right wing had been killed, wounded, or captured in the Confederate's second assault. This had the effect of doubling them back on the regiment's left wing." At that point, "Hapeman then ordered what was left of the Companies A, B, and C to fall back."[25]

When it appeared that the La Salle regiment would crumble beneath the weight of the Confederate onslaught, a sudden volley from the crest behind them on the right rang out among the hardwoods. It was the 15th Kentucky coming to the aid of the Illinois soldiers and causing "a short pause in the attack." Reynolds's Arkansans recoiled as they were struck from an unexpected direction. About this time an order came from the rear to Hapeman and his isolated regiment: "the General commands that not another step backward be taken from here."[26]

Hapeman had already sent word that he needed reinforcements on his right at the commencement of the attack lest his regiment be swept from the knoll. McCook sent the 10th Wisconsin, but they arrived and deployed on his left, where no threat was posed. "Hapeman again sent for aid on his right. The action had now reached its most critical stage." Color Company E, amidst a "storm of lead" was "taking a terrible punishment in its role as support to the regimental color guard" at the center of the line. Captain John S. H. Doty, Company E commander, after being struck with five bullets, lay mortally wounded. Doty cried out, "Drive back those rebels first, then take care of me!" Then, a few minutes before he expired, Doty murmured, "Tell my father that I die for the flag. Good bye boys." After Doty died, Lieutenant Ransom P. Dewey took charge. Describing his commander as "iron nerved," the young lieutenant

---

[24] William Wirt Calkins, *The History of the One Hundred and Fourth Regiment of Illinois Volunteer Infantry, War of the Great Rebellion, 1862–1865* (Chicago: Donohue & Henneberry, 1895) 224–25; William M. Wilson to William Wirt Calkins, n.d., Phoebe H. MacLean personal papers, quoted in Adolphson, "An Incident of Valor," 414.

[25] Adolphson, "An Incident of Valor," 414.

[26] *OR*, ser. 1, vol. 38, pt. 1, serial 72, p. 547; Adolphson, "An Incident of Valor," 414–15.

explained that Hapeman's courage had "turned what seemed utter destruction into victory."[27]

Captain J. W. Ford, brigade assistant adjutant general for McCook's brigade, described the attack in the briefest of terms: "At 4:30 P.M. the rebels made a furious attack on our position, entering a portion of our partially constructed works, but after an hour of very hard fighting the enemy was driven back...." Lieutenant Colonel William G. Halpin of the 15th Kentucky regiment witnessed the fight as well: "The 15th [Kentucky] seeing the rebel colors planted on the works of the 104th [Illinois], opened fire in conjunction with that regiment and soon caused a hasty retreat."[28]

According to a historian for the 15th Kentucky, "The first Federal volley caused the [Rebel] lines to shudder, and the men fell back, moving by the flank and passing west into the ravine, out of sight of the Federal line." One veteran recalled that the Rebel color-bearer who planted the flag on the Federal works "was shot and bayoneted where he stood, and his flag captured." The Confederates reformed and charged again. McCook's brigade took a moment to catch their breath and reform. Ford continued, "But as soon as the lines were properly formed again the enemy made another attack, but more feebly than before. After the exchange of a few volleys the rebels fell back and a line of skirmishers was sent after them."[29]

Some evidence suggests that Cockrell's brigade supported the left of Reynolds's assault that drove into the gap behind Hapeman's right and rear. The left of Cockrell's brigade stopped its advance due to a "broad and deep mill pond," but the right portion of the brigade continued to charge in the deep woods. With Reynolds's small Arkansas brigade, consisting of 540 during the assault, Cockrell's Missourians probably participated in the flank attack on the 104th Illinois. There is conflicting evidence concerning the casualties sustained by Cockrell's brigade during the action. Its brigade commander, F. M. Cockrell,

---

[27] Calkins, *History of the One Hundred and Fourth*, 432; Wilson quoted in Adolphson, "An Incident of Valor," 415; Ransom P.Dewey,, Deposition to R.A. Alger, 2 September 1897, Phoebe H. MacLean personal papers, quoted in Adolphson, "An Incident of Valor," 416.

[28] *OR*, ser. 1, vol. 38, pt. 1, serial 72, pp. 532, 547; Adolphson, "An Incident of Valor," 416.

[29] Jenkins, *The Battle Rages Higher,* 232; Douglas Hapeman, war diary, 20 July 1864, Special Collections, (SC 647), Abraham Lincoln Presidential Library; Calkins, *History of the One Hundred and Fourth,* 221; Thomas Mears Eddy, *The Patriotism of Illinois*, 2 vols. (Chicago: 1865–1866) 2:190; Adolphson, "An Incident of Valor," 416; *OR* ser. 1, vol. 38, pt. 1, serial 72, p. 532. The identity or disposition of the lost Rebel flag is unknown.

who was absent at the time of the conflict, subsequently completed his report on 20 September 1864 after two months of fighting around Atlanta. He lists the casualties at only one killed and fourteen wounded. Cockrell's report identifies from the 1st and 3rd Missouri cavalry (dismounted) Sergeart Craighead as killed, and Captain H. Wilkerson and Lieutenant J. T Mahan wounded. Cockrell also reports that many of the casualties were due to exposure to the right regiment in the attack (presumably the 1st and 3rd Missouri cavalry) from Federal artillery. Another account based on witnesses to the battle from the brigade was published in 1879 and put the losses at sixty-one killed and wounded, a figure comparable to Reynolds's brigade losses of sixty-seven killed, wounded, and missing. A third account, a diary entry by Lieutenant George Warren who participated in the assault, recorded, "Somewhere between 40 and 60 of the brigade are killed and wounded, some of them terribly mangled by shells."[30]

The millpond that blunted the advance of the Missourians was located in the area just east of today's I-75 and west of Brookview Drive, between the present Glenbrook Drive and reaching north to near Tennyson Drive. The right of the Missouri Brigade, which was led during the charge by Colonel Gates, proceeded up the slope across today's Wadsworth and Glenbrook drives and into the sway between Glenbrook and Beaverbrook drives, which led to the rear of the 104th Illinois. There, the right of Cockrell's Missourians and the left of Reynolds's Arkansans were stopped by the balance of McCook's brigade (atop the ridge where today's Northcliffe Drive runs), fire from Dilger's battery on Cockrell's left flank, and by the heroic efforts of Colonel Hapeman and his Illinoisans. Ector's Texas Brigade supported the left of the Missouri brigade during its advance, but found a large open field where the Texans became exposed to rifle and artillery fire, which prevented their further advance. This field was located between today's Bohler Road and Noble Creek Drive just west of I-75.[31]

In the midst of the crisis, Lieutenant James M. Wright of Company I, watched Colonel Hapeman respond. "With the rebels upon us in flank and charging with the bayonet, Colonel Hapeman, the mark of a hundred bullets,

---

[30] *OR*, ser. 1, vol. 38, pt. 3, serial 74, pp. 916–20; R. S. Bevier, *History of the First and Second Missouri Confederate Brigades, 1861–1865, and from Wakarusa to Appomattox, a Military Anagraph* (St. Louis: Bryan, Brand & Company, 1879) 240; Phil Gottschalk, *In Deadly Earnest* (Columbia MO: Missouri River Press, 1991) 382. Dilger's Federal Battery was in position to rake Cockrell's line as it came into range in support of Reynolds.

[31] http://wms.co.fulton.ga.us/ms/sitemap/top.php (3 January 2009).

quickly restored confidence, reformed the broken fragments of the right wing, and with these and the left wing of five companies, charged on the exultant enemy who were them among us. It then became a hand to hand and bayonet fight, led by Colonel Hapeman." Hapeman pulled back the remnants of his crumbling right wing, and refused his line in the middle at a 90-degree angle so that his men faced both south and west. Pulling men from the untried left of his line, he quickly reinforced and restored order to his battered right. The young lieutenant colonel of the La Salle men again sent word to McCook that his right needed support. This time, the 21st Wisconsin came forward and formed on the refused right flank of the 104th Illinois, but Major Fitch of the 21st Wisconsin explained that when his men reached the knoll, Hapeman's Illinoisans already stopped Reynolds's Arkansas troops. Fitch said that the Confederate line "melted away...like mist before the morning sun."[32]

One veteran in McCook's brigade remembered, "The battle was going on furiously, while [the 21st Wisconsin], the 33rd Ohio, 42nd Indiana and the 86th [88th] Ill. were tearing through the brush in order to extend the line to the right. The 104th Ill. was the last Regt. which had come into line on the right previous to the assault." The 104th Illinois, located on the knoll along today's Glenbrook Drive, was vulnerable to an attack on his right flank. Major Fitch rushed the 21st Wisconsin to support. "The rebs overreaching our line, swung round to take the 104th [Illinois] in flank and rear, when luckily we came near and immediately charged the wheeling rebels." Captain John Henry Otto of Company D, 21st Wisconsin remembered, "One volley we gave them allmost [sic] in their teeth and then for about five minutes it was Chickamauga again; a mixture of clubbing and stabbing, of damning, cursing and swearing, for about 5 minutes more or less, on such occasions one forgetts [sic] to consult the watch, when the Johnnies concluded to go home."[33]

Reynolds pulled back his battered and tiny brigade, and failing to find any support on either flank, established vedettes on both sides "to keep from being surprised or surrounded and cut off." Reynolds reported that his brigade had "inflicted considerable punishment on the enemy, killing and wounding a number of them and capturing a few prisoners. Opposing his left the battered

---

[32] James M. Wright, deposition to R. A. Alger, 15 November 1897, Phoebe H. MacLean personal papers, Madison CT, quoted in Adolphson, "An Incident of Valor," 415–16; *OR*, ser. 1, vol. 38, pt. 1, serial 72, pp. 537–38; Adolphson, "An Incident of Valor," 415–18. Michael H. Fitch, *Echoes of the Civil War as I Hear Them* (New York: RF Fenno and Company, 1905) 215; Adolphson, "An Incident of Valor," 416.

[33] Otto, *Memoirs of a Dutch Mudsill*, 270.

Hood's First Sortie, 20 July 1864

veterans of the 104th Illinois had held. Again, the Yankees held the high ground, and again the right flank was threatened as the right five companies of the Illinois troops were assaulted when the Arkansans attempted to sweep around their right and rear. But the Illinois men held firm, as the left of the line that was not tested supported their right. The right half recoiled and fell back ninety degrees so that they faced the west instead of the south. "The three companies on the right of the 104th [Illinois] fell back in a few moments, and one of...[the Rebels] planted a Confederate flag on the line of the 104th Illinois." There, the 104th met and repelled the left half of the Arkansas brigade's attack. Hapeman reported that two officers and fourteen men were killed, while one officer and twenty-four men were wounded, and four men were captured and one man was missing for a total loss of forty-six men, all from the right wing. According to regimental historian Steven J. Adolphson, the 104th Illinois lost at Peach Tree Creek 15 men killed, including 2 of Hapeman's best company commanders, 26 wounded, including 2 mortally, 4 captured, and 1 missing, for a total loss of 46 men as well, while only 194 officers and men were present for duty at day's end.[34]

McCook's reports reflect that his brigade sustained a total of seventy-one casualties, with forty-six of the losses coming from the 104th Illinois alone. In the 15th Kentucky of McCook's defending brigade, six men were casualties with one man killed and five wounded. Major Fitch who had rushed his 21st Wisconsin to support the exposed right flank of the 104th Illinois, lost three men wounded. For his part in the battle, young Douglas Hapeman was justly promoted to a full colonel by the Governor of Illinois and, after the war, he received the Medal of Honor.[35]

The same rewards did not fall to his superior, Colonel McCook, however. While Northern reporters swooped in and wrote high accolades of Colonel Anson G. McCook and his alleged bravery, with much of the newspaper fodder being provided by the colonel himself, there was much criticism of his performance among the men. One Captain William Strawn wrote, "Bah!"

---

[34] *OR*, ser. I, vol. 38, pt. 3, ser. 74, p. 938; Willis, *Arkansas Confederate*, 512–14; Jenkins, *The Battle Rages Higher*, 232; *OR*, ser. 1, vol. 38, pt. 1, serial 72, p. 538. Adolphson, "An Incident of Valor," 416–17.

[35] *OR*, ser. I, vol. 38, pt. 3, serial 74, pp. 524, 536. Jenkins, *The Battle Rages Higher*, 289–406; *OR*, ser. 1, vol. 38, pt. 1, serial 72, p. 557; E. B. Quiner, *The Military History of Wisconsin: A Record of the Civil and Military Patriotism of the State, in the War for the Union* (Chicago: Clark & Co. Publishers, 1866) 137-39; Calkins, *History of the One Hundred and Fourth*, 368; Adolphson, "An Incident of Valor," 418.

Strawn elaborated, "The brigade having been placed in an awkward position and made to believe there was no enemy within striking distance, when the time came, handled itself!" While McCook was not censured for failing to entrench his troops and for exposing the 104th Illinois, his service as a brigade commander was over as his superiors quietly removed him. McCook received orders to report to Chattanooga, over his objection, to be mustered out with his old command, the 2nd Ohio. On 26 July, just six days after the battle, Colonel Marion C. Taylor of the 15th Kentucky would take over temporary command of the brigade until General Carlin returned on 2 August from his mid-summer vacation.[36]

Corporal John H. Forbes of the 74th Ohio watched Reynolds's Arkansans hit McCook's lines from his position in Moore's brigade, which was posted on a ridge to the right and rear: "The rebels charged on the first line of the 1st Brigade, and succeeded in placing their colors on their works, but they were repulsed and the colors captured, together with a number of prisoners." The Federal veteran added that "the battle raged until nearly dark," with "wild yells of the charge" that came nearer and nearer to his lines during the hot afternoon, but reached no further than McCook's brigade lines.[37]

On the Confederate side in Reynolds's Arkansas Brigade, the assault cost the undersized brigade 6 killed, 52 wounded, and 9 missing, for a total loss of 67 men out of 540 present for the attack. In the 1st Arkansas Mounted Rifles, Private Morris Lewis was killed while 1st Lieutenant Alfred Page was wounded. The 2nd Arkansas Mounted Rifles reported ten casualties on 20 July coupled with the thirteen men lost the day before. Thus, the 2nd Arkansas Mounted Rifles lost nine men wounded and one captured, with two of the wounded also being captured, and four of the wounds proving to be mortal. With one man killed and another one wounded during the 19 July fight at Moore's Mill, the 4th Arkansas lost another eight men at the Battle of Peach Tree Creek, with three men killed, four wounded, one mortally, and one captured.[38]

---

[36] *OR*, ser. 1, vol. 38, pt. 1, serial 72, pp. 531–34; Adolphson, "An Incident of Valor," 417, 420; Scaife, *The Campaign for Atlanta*, 150.

[37] Theodore W. Blackburn, *Letters from the Front: A Union "Preacher" Regiment (74th Ohio) in the Civil War* (Dayton OH: Press of Morningside House, 1981) 215.

[38] *OR*, ser. I, vol. 38, pt. 3, serial 74, p. 938; www.couchgenweb.com/civil war/4mcnair (27 May 2007).

Hood's First Sortie, 20 July 1864

In the 9th Arkansas, which arrived to the conflict late, casualties were also high: eleven men who were wounded, including one mortally, and two men were captured. In the 31st Arkansas, which had been merged with the 4th Arkansas, three men were killed. With 59 casualties on the day before fighting above Moore's Mill, Reynolds's Arkansas Brigade lost 126 men during the two days. Reynolds reported that only 473 men were left in his brigade after the battles of Moore's Mill and Peach Tree Creek.[39]

Captain Otto of the 21st Wisconsin wrote that "Most of the 44th Georgia Regt. we took prisoner." He probably meant one or more of the Arkansas regiments of Reynolds's brigade that opposed him, but it is possible that one of the Georgia regiments of Walker's division that had earlier been on skirmish in the area had a detachment that had been captured that morning or that, like the 24th South Carolina, had joined in the assault with other units. "By the time we had our and the rebel wounded away it was dark and rain had set in which lasted nearly all night," remembered one Wisconsin soldier. Captain Otto recorded one touching story from those captured: "One smart looking, perhaps 16 years old boy, wept bitterly and asked me: 'Will we be killed sir?' —'No my boy. We do not kill prisoners if they behave. You will be taken care of.' —'You see' he said, 'father has been killed and I am his only boy.' —'Where was your father killed?' I inquired. 'Right here' he replied pointing to the front and sobbing again. Such is war."[40]

In Quarles's brigade, Lieutenant James A. M. Nesbitt of Company D, 49th Tennessee Infantry Regiment, was wounded, but he recovered in time to be promoted to captain and lead his company back to the Volunteer State during Hood's Tennessee campaign that fall. When the regiment learned that General Johnston had been replaced by General John Bell Hood, Quartermaster Sergeant John W. Sparkman of the 48th Tennessee in Quarles's brigade responded with, "I do not know the cause and I am afraid it will have a bad effect for the army had the utmost confidence in Gen. Johnston." Quarles's brigade was earlier on skirmish duty, but as the battle wore on during the hot July evening, his men were recalled and were put in reserve behind O'Neal's and Reynolds's brigades. Some of them, including the 53rd Tennessee, saw considerable action as General Walthall ordered them to support the right of O'Neal's line after the

---

[39] James Willis, *Arkansas Confederates in the Western Theater* (Dayton OH: Morningside House, 1998) 727–822; Ronald R. Bass, *History of the 31st Arkansas Confederate Infantry* (Conway: Arkansas Research Press, 1996) 75; *OR*, ser. I, vol. 38, pt. 3, serial 74, p. 938.

[40] Otto, *Memoirs of a Dutch Mudsill*, 270.

The Battle of Peach Tree Creek

37th Mississippi had been repulsed. The brigade continued to sustain casualties in the late afternoon fire in the woods behind O'Neal's lines along today's Collier Road west of Northside Drive that must have been terrific. Quarles reported his losses as seven killed and seventeen wounded for the day.[41]

O'Neal's assault had, like the attacks of Featherston and Scott to his right, initially met with success, but, also like Featherston and Scott, had been unsupported in sufficient numbers to continue the offensive and rout of the enemy. The veteran Alabama officer who would later become Alabama's governor lamented, "We drove the enemy nearly a mile, captured some of his works, and had punished him severely, and were executing the order of the major-general [Walthall] to kill or capture everything in our front, when…we were compelled to fall back."[42]

O'Neal's brigade captured a remarkable 293 prisoners, while they sustained just 279 casualties in killed, wounded, and captured or missing, a remarkable feat for an attacking unit to inflict greater casualties than it received. By striking the unprotected right flanks of Geary's division in the thickly wooded ridges and ravines west of Collier Mill, O'Neal's brigade was able to quickly overrun large portions of Candy's and Jones's brigades, capturing many, and turning entire regiments into flight. The path of O'Neal's brigade through the rough Georgia forest resembled that of a tornado. Two days after the battle, the 73rd Ohio passed through the woods where O'Neal's veterans slammed into Geary's and Williams's divisions. Private William Cline recorded in his diary, "this day [we passed] a parte of the Batel grounde foughte By the 20 corpse on the 20 Day of the month the timber is literley [mowed] off By grape and Shell ande the timber is cute to peaces Buy Hour mineyes Bute the rebels [were] Repulst."[43] Had it not been for the timely arrival of Ireland's brigade, coupled with the individuals and units of Candy's and Jones's brigades that remained to fight, O'Neal's brigade may have routed Geary's entire division.

Geary's division was also fortunate to have two brigades of Williams's division posted along the ridge immediately to the north of Geary's broken line, and as Geary's men poured northward along the ravine toward Peach Tree Creek to the rear, the pursuing Alabamians and Mississippians of O'Neal's brigade suddenly found themselves exposed to a flanking fire from their left

---

[41] Evans, ed., *Tennessee*, 455; *Tennesseans in the Civil War*, 2:302; *OR*, ser. 1, vol. 38, pt. 3, serial 74, pp. 930–31.

[42] *OR*, ser. 1, vol. 38, pt. 3, serial 74, p. 941.

[43] Cline, Diary, 160–61, 164–67.

side by Williams's division. Finally, O'Neal's brigade did not have sufficient numbers to sustain the momentum gained by their successful charge and they had to fall back and reform and try again. O'Neal was given Colonel Ellison Caper's 24th South Carolina with some 300 men to bolster his brigade as they mounted a second assault. By this time, however, Federal resistance had strengthened and the Yankees were ready for O'Neal's men. O'Neal rallied his battered brigade plus Caper's men for a third try. This time, he had the assistance of parts of Quarles's brigade. Again, O'Neal was stopped. After several unsuccessful attempts to break Williams's line along today's Bitsy Grant Tennis Center and ridge, and Geary's refused line in the ravine below it, O'Neal's men drew off with their ambulatory casualties and disappeared in the fading light in the woods to the south and west as darkness settled upon the battlefield. Included in O'Neal's losses were the very capable and experienced Lieutenants Samuel H. Moore, acting assistant adjutant-general, and Thomas S. O'Brien, assistant inspector-general, of O'Neal's brigade staff, who were both captured.[44]

On the Federal side, Williams's 1st (Red Star) Division, did much to repel O'Neal's assault and saved Geary's division from another Chancellorsville. According to General Alpheus Seth Williams, "I had a severe fight on the 20th, was attacked in the woods and lost nearly 700 men and six good officers, killed and wounded." According to his official report, Williams recorded 119 men killed, 458 men wounded, and 3 men missing for a total loss of 580 men. However, research confirms 126 men killed, 471 wounded, and 10 missing, plus 2 men from Williams's staff: Captain Bennett, an assistant topographical engineer, was severely wounded in the head, and Captain Newcomb, an aide who was killed, for a total loss of 609 men in Williams's division. Williams lamented after the battle, "My veteran division has been sadly cut up, so that I am reduced in numbers to a brigade." In a private letter to one of his daughters, Williams confided that his division "saved one of the other divisions [Geary's] from a great repulse and flight."[45]

Private Crumpton and the men of the 37th Mississippi who had begun the attack with so much success and pluck found themselves in a somber mood as they reflected that night in camp about their failed assault and lost comrades:

---

[44] *OR*, ser. I, vol. 38, pt. 3, serial 74, pp. 942–43.

[45] Alpheus Starkey Williams, *From the Cannon's Mouth, The Civil War Letters of General Apheus S. Williams*, ed. Milo M. Quaife (Detroit: Wayne State University Press, 1959) 335; *OR*, ser. I, vol. 38, pt. 3, ser. 73, p. 34; *OR*, ser. I, vol. 38, pt. 3, ser. 73, 34–112; Williams, *From the Cannon's Mouth*, 336, 338.

Drunkeness and foolhardiness had lost half our men. Getting back to camp that night we talked of the doings of the day. How we talked of poor old Bill Nick! We mourned him as dead, when about ten o'clock, he limped into camp with his empty pistol strapped about him. When asked about it, he said: "They tried to kill me by shooting at me, and I don't see how they missed me. Then they undertook to run me down and I shot five of them with my revolver." Think of the weary marches for two years, loaded down, as he was, he clung to the old Texas weapon saying, "Some day I'll need it," and that day had come![46]

Private Crumpton, and many others in the Army of Mississippi, were dissatisfied that they had made a gallant charge and had fought well, but that someone had let them down. Each of the brigades in Loring's and Walthall's divisions had attacked more or less independently without support from any other brigade or unit. Thus, the ragged survivors of each attacking brigade, from Featherston to Scott to O'Neal to Reynolds, all felt betrayed by their comrades in other brigades. But, by the same token, they each felt that their own regiment or brigade had done their full measure.

In the weeks that followed, the men of the Army of Mississippi came to realize and believe that they had each done their jobs, but Hardee's men had for some unknown and unexplained reason failed to carry out the attack to the fullest. They also blamed Hood for needlessly sending them into the headlong attack without proper support. Crumpton summed it up by explaining, "Of course the common soldier didn't know, but certain we were, with a fresh column to have followed up the drive, the results would have been a complete victory, for there was little fight in the enemy. I am certain many of them did not stop until the Chattahoochee was reached." Whether it was wishful thinking or not, Crumpton spoke for many a man from the gulf states who continued to regret Johnston's departure. "Our men were cast down because of the removal of Joe Johnston, the loved commander."[47]

---

[46] Washington Bryan Crumpton, *A Book of Memories* (Montgomery AL: Baptist Mission Board, 1921) 89.

[47] Ibid., 89–90.

NO, NO, GENERAL, I DID NOT LOSE ANY MEN

In the battle of the 20th, regardless of my orders, [Captain Hubert Dilger] moved forward to the front line and had several of his cannoneers killed by the enemy's sharpshooters. After the battle I said to him that he had violated my orders in going too far to the front, and in doing so had lost several men. "No, no, general, I did not lose any men." I told him that it had been reported to me that several of his men had been picked off by the enemy's sharpshooters. "Oh, yes, with dem leetle balls; none by artillery." Belonging to the artillery, he did not count a man killed unless he was killed by a cannon ball or shell. He was a fearless fellow and had a splendid battery, and was never so happy as when engaged with the enemy.[1]

General French recorded in his journal entry for 20 July:

This morning it was resolved to attack the three corps of the enemy that were on the Peach Tree creek and separated from the corps that were near Decatur. Sears's Brigade being on duty on the river and creek, I moved with the brigades of Cockrell and Ector to the right and formed line of battle in front of the Ragdale House. This position was the extreme left of the army.

The plan of battle was a good one. Hardee was to gain the enemy's rear, swing to the left, taking their line in flank, while we attacked the line in front in echelon of brigades as the battle swept down the creek. Walthall was on my right, and I was to keep within about three hundred yards of him. In advancing I came to an open field in front of the enemy. Their line was fortified, with two field batteries in position that kept up a continuous fire on my line. Gen. Loring's troops broke through the enemy's line of works. Reynolds and Featherston had to abandon the captured line by reason of the

---

[1] R. W. Johnson, *A Soldier's Reminiscences in Peace and War* (Philadelphia: J. B. Lippincott Company, 1886) 281.

flank fire on them. The failure of Hardee deranged the plan of battle. After dark we withdrew.[2]

French issued orders for his two available brigades, Ector's Texans and Cockrell's Missourians, to form up and prepare to advance at around 4:00 P..M. His instructions to the two brigades were to advance in support of Walthall's division while keeping 300 to 400 yards apart. French was without Sears's Mississippi brigade, which together with Adams's Mississippi Brigade of Loring's division, was still guarding the Confederate lines that clung onto to the Chattahoochee River and its fords below Peach Tree Creek. At the time, Sears's brigade led by Colonel Barry was withdrawing from its position opposite Moore's Mill where it had checked portions of Palmer's XIV Corps for the past three days, while Adams's brigade, which was covering Sears's withdrawal, could not participate in the assault until about dusk. While Ector's and Cockrell's brigades were forming, the veterans of the Confederate frontier began to take Federal artillery fire, sustaining some casualties. As Ector's brigade, being led by Brigadier General William H. Young, moved forward, the ground was so covered with dense undergrowth and felled abatis from Confederate defensive efforts that French had to lead the men to the right, around the obstruction, one company at a time. According to Mitchell McCuistion of the 9th Texas in Ector's brigade, there was "heavy fighting in our Front and on the Right. We have not been engaged yet think we will soon." Rumor along French's lines was that their comrades were doing well to the east. McCuistion said they were "reported to be driving the Enemy on the right."[3]

As soon as French was able to establish the lines of his two brigades along the edge of a field, he studied the situation. Across the field to his front, some 600 yards in the wooded distance, lay the enemy. The bluecoats were strongly entrenched, along a ridge on the far side of the field, and they were supported by two batteries of artillery. Gates led the Missouri brigade forward across the right end of the field and toward the woods north and east of the field in support

---

[2] Samuel G. French, *Two Wars* (1901; repr., Huntington WV: Blue Acorn Press, 1999) 218–19.

[3] William R. Scaife, *The Campaign for Atlanta* (Atlanta: self-published, 1993) 182–83; David V. Stroud, *Ector's Texas Brigade and the Army of Tennessee, 1862–1865* (Longview TX: Ranger Publishing, 2004) 167; United States War Department, comp., *Official Records of the Union and Confederate Armies in the War of the Rebellion*, 128 vols. (Washington, DC: Government Printing Office, 1880–1901) ser. I, vol. 38, pt. 3, serial 74, p. 902 (hereafter *OR*). French, *Two Wars*, 218; Mitchell Henderson McCuistion, diary, 20 July 1864, Special Collections, University of Texas at Austin Library.

Hood's First Sortie, 20 July 1864

of Walthall's men who could be heard fighting ahead and to the right. Meanwhile, French looked to the far side of the field and to his left, where a wooded ridge screened his view from what lay to the west. If he sent Ector's Texans forward, there would be no Rebel forces to his left to support the brigade, and they would risk being flanked, or cut off, inviting disaster to the Confederates. Moreover, the prospects of a frontal assault against the Federal fortifications looked bleak. French could see the futility of sending Ector's men across the 600 yard field in the face of at least equal if not greater strength in enemy infantry plus at least eight artillery pieces. Thus, French ordered Ector to slide to the right, into the forest that screened his advance, and behind Gates's Missourians that had already advanced by the same route. Soon, French and Ector came upon Gates's Missourians, who had halted "under the brow of a hill about 300 yards from the line of the enemy's entrenchments." Throughout this time, Gates's and Ector's men continued to take on casualties, primarily from the Federal artillery.[4]

General Stewart then rode up and joined French. The two generals surveyed the new position, and Stewart ordered French to place a battery on the high ground. He also directed Sears's brigade, which was just arriving, to support the artillery and cover French's exposed left flank. While French issued orders for Sears's brigade and the artillery to come up, darkness began to obscure the view of positions, and soon the attack would be called off. During the late afternoon, however, the Texans, North Carolinians, and Missourians were subjected to severe artillery and some rifle fire. The two brigades began the attack from along a trench line located near today's Davis Circle just west of DeFoor Avenue on the east, to Casey's Hill, located about a mile and a half to the west. Gates formed the Missouri brigade on a line facing north roughly along today's Collier Road at its juncture with Interstate 75. Ector's Texans lined up west of Gates roughly along Collier Road west of Interstate 75.[5]

In Ector's brigade, the 32nd Texas Cavalry had one man killed, while the 29th North Carolina claimed twenty-eight killed (or thought to be wounded and left on the field) and three men missing. The 39th North Carolina had fifteen men killed and four missing. According to Mitchell Henderson McCuistion of the 9th Texas, there was "nobody hurt today from our Regt." While the 10th Texas Cavalry (Dismounted) lost only two men wounded and two men captured

---

[4] Stroud, *Ector's Texas Brigade*, 167; *OR,* ser. I, vol. 38, pt. 3, serial 74, p. 902.
[5] *OR,* ser. I, vol. 38, pt. 3, serial 74, p. 902; Stroud, *Ector's Texas Brigade*, 168; Georgia Historical Marker, "French's Division Hood's Left Flank," MSS 130, file 15, Wilbur G. Kurtz Papers, Kenan Research Center, Atlanta History Center.

at the Battle of Peach Tree Creek, they lost one man killed, nine men wounded, and two men missing or captured during the several days of fighting while defending the Chattahoochee River-Peach Tree Creek line prior to the battle, for a total of sixteen casualties during the second and third weeks of July. Ector's brigade, which had moved on Peach Tree Creek in front of the Ragdale house, withdrew during the night with the rest of French's division. Fittingly, it is likely that there were more men who were slightly wounded who were not included in the casualty reports of Ector's "wild" Texans and North Carolinians where it seems that one had to be severely wounded, killed, or missing to be listed as a casualty. Ector's brigade reported six killed, thirty-two wounded, and six missing for a total of forty-four casualties during fighting along the Chattahoochee River and Peach Tree Creek up through July 19, and two killed, nine wounded, and twenty-eight missing (all twenty-eight coming from the 29th North Carolina) for a total of thirty-nine casualties during the Battle of Peach Tree Creek and eighty-three casualties overall.[6]

The Huff family watched as the battle proceeded above their farm. "We were on the edge of the battlefield, which extended several miles around the northeastern line of the city. For mother and her children that was a fateful day," remembered child Sarah Huff. "[Mother] refused to entertain the slightest idea of leaving her home. All the neighbors except George Edwards, the button factory proprietor, ...had been gone for weeks." Young Sarah explained, "He was the loyal friend who later saved mother's house from burning by doing the same as he did for his own—running up the British flag over it."[7]

When General French ordered Gates to support Walthall's attack, the Missourians were soon stopped by a deep millpond that was in their front near Peach Tree Creek. The brigade moved back under the cover of some nearby woods, but they were in an exposed position.[8] In the Missouri Brigade, Lieutenant George Warren recorded the day's events in his diary.

> July 20—This morning there was every indication of an early engagement. Troops were being hurried from left to right. About noon we were put in

---

[6] http://history-sites.com/mb/cw/txcwmb/index.cgi?noframes;read'8412 (10 February 2008); McCuistion, diary, dated 20 July 1864; Chuck Carlock, *History of The Tenth Texas Cavalry (Dismounted) Regiment, 1861–1865* (North Richland Hills TX: Bibal Press, 2001) 156, 161; *OR,* ser. I, vol. 38, pt. 2, serial 74, p. 908.

[7] Sarah Huff, "My 80 Years in Atlanta," 12, subject files, Atlanta History Center.

[8] R. S. Bevier, *History of the First and Second Missouri Confederate Brigades, 1861–1865, and from Wakarusa to Appomattox, a Military Anagraph* (St. Louis: Bryan, Brand & Company, 1879) 240.

motion, marched about three miles to the right, halted, closed up ranks and loaded. Gen. French gave the command, forward march. Advancing in line of battle about a quarter of a mile we joined on to the line on our right. When this was done the whole line advanced at a charge. The enemy opened on us heavily with artillery. After charging several hundred yards through a dense woods, our advance was checked by a broad and deep [millpond]. We halted on the bank for a short time, then fell back to the woods for protection. The line to the right of us continued to charge.... We laid down under the fire of their batteries and remained there some five hours until night.... They gave it to us hot and heavy until dark. A shell struck the ground a few feet from me and buried me under a half cart load of dirt. Grape came over continuously, in installments of a half peck each. Just before night I was struck in the head by a stray minie, the ball furrowing up a ridge across the top so I can thank a merciful providence for a narrow escape. Somewhere between 40 and 60 of the brigade are killed and wounded, some of them terribly mangled by shells.[9]

Cockrell's brigade suffered: "The Missourians did not fire a shot, but were kept under fire and lost 61 killed and wounded, among the killed being Lt.-Colonel [D. Todd] Samuels of Gates' regiment." The veteran Missouri Brigade was frustrated at being exposed to Federal artillery fire and unable to "strike a blow in retaliation."[10]

In response to French's probes by Ectors's Texans and Cockrell's Missourians, Federal troops under Major General John W. Palmer's XIV Corps set forth a fiery reply. After crossing Peach Tree Creek and repulsing the surprise attack made on it by Brigadier General Daniel H. Reynolds's Arkansans and Colonel Michael Farrell's Mississippians on the afternoon of 19 July, Palmer's 2nd Division under the command of Brigadier General Jefferson C. Davis moved forward and dug in along a ridge below Peach Tree Creek. Joining Davis's division, the 1st and 3rd divisions crossed the creek on the

---

[9] Phil Gottschalk, *In Deadly Earnest* (Columbia MO: Missouri River Press, 1991) 382; George Warren, diary, 20 July 1864.

[10] Bevier, *History of the First and Second Missouri*, 240; Clement Anselm Evans, ed., Kentucky, vol. 1 of *Confederate Military History*, 19 vols. (1899; repr., Wilmington NC Broadfoot Publishing Company, 1987) 153. Lt. Col. D. Todd Samuels who led the 3rd Missouri Dismounted Cavalry before its consolidation with the 1st Missouri Dismounted Cavalry during a reorganization on 29 August 1863 at Demopolis AL. Colonel Elijah Gates was given command of the 1st and 3rd Missouri Dismounted Cavalry, while Lt. Col. Samuels was made second in command. William C. Parker was made its major and the unit fought dismounted as infantry for the remainder of the war.

evening of 19 July and the following morning. Throughout the day Palmer's corps advanced their lines, capturing a series of high ridges south of the creek, improving their position and digging in. During the morning, Captain John A. Norris of Company C, 98th Ohio in Mitchell's brigade, "while going out to visit the left of the skirmish line, was wounded through the right knee joint so severely as to render immediate amputation necessary to save his life, according to his regimental commander." The firing was so hot during the afternoon that one regiment in Mitchell's Second Brigade of Davis' Division, the 78th Illinois, expended 17,000 rounds of ammunition, or about 80 rounds to each man.[11]

Opposite French's Southerners across the field were units from Colonel Marshall F. Moore's 3rd Brigade of Johnson's 1st Division. The brigade was dug in along the crest of a ridge about 100 yards in advance of the rest of the Federal lines. To protect his left flank, Colonel Moore placed a strong entrenched line commanding the Howell Mill Road, a bit in rear of the knoll on which the 104th Illinois was formed. According to Colonel Moore, "My position was an excellent one, having an open range in front for artillery and musketry of at least half a mile. A battery was placed in position there a little after noon."[12]

This battery was the 1st Ohio Battery commanded by Captain Hubert Dilger and consisting of four 10-pounder Parrott rifles. Dilger was a Prussian officer who had come to the United States with another officer from the Prussian army to "witness the war." When he and his friend arrived in New York, however, the two men determined to each join a side and fight. "It fell to Dilger's lot to join the Federal Army."[13]

The Prussian officer enjoyed the American frontier. Wearing buckskin clothing, Dilger was "known throughout the army as 'Leather Breeches.' He was a gallant fellow, and when an engagement took place generally rushed his battery out to the skirmish line," according to his commander. General Johnson explained, "I was always fearful that the enemy would charge upon him suddenly and capture his entire outfit, and so I had him instructed not to leave the main line unless ordered forward." Now, as the Confederates appeared in line of battle below Peach Tree Creek, the stubborn Prussian disobeyed his commander again:

---

[11] *OR*, ser. 1, vol. 38, pt. 2, serial 72, pp. 507, 524, 694, 689, 742.

[12] *OR*, ser. 1, vol. 38, pt. 2, serial 72, p. 602.

[13] Scaife, *The Campaign for Atlanta*, 151; Johnson, *A Soldier's Reminiscences*, 281.

Hood's First Sortie, 20 July 1864

In the battle of the 20th, regardless of my orders, he moved forward to the front line and had several of his cannoneers killed by the enemy's sharpshooters. After the battle I said to him that he had violated my orders in going too far to the front, and in doing so had lost several men. "No, no, general, I did not lose any men." I told him that it had been reported to me that several of his men had been picked off by the enemy's sharpshooters. "Oh, yes, with dem leetle balls; none by artillery." Belonging to the artillery, he did not count a man killed unless he was killed by a cannon ball or shell. He was a fearless fellow and had a splendid battery, and was never so happy as when engaged with the enemy.[14]

According to Captain Henry F. Perry of the 38th Indiana, "The third brigade, accompanied by Dilger's battery, was massed in a deep depression of an open field some 200 yards in rear of the rifle pits which we had captured two hours before." Perry explained that "Details were made from the regiments and sent forward with picks and shovels to reverse and strengthen the captured works." Colonel Moore described the approach of the Missourians and Texans toward his lines. They "opened a terrific fire of canister and shell upon my line, from which, together with the skirmishing, I lost in killed and wounded 3 officers and 34 men. The enemy twice advanced a line of battle into the edge of the field in our front, but did not attempt to cross it."[15]

Moore's brigade covered the ridge that was to the right and somewhat recessed from McCook's position. There, Dilger advanced his battery into the edge of a field where he could rake approaching Rebel lines. "There was an open field in front of us, and the guns of the Buckskin Battery would have mowed them down if they had attempted to come across." The 21st Ohio and 37th Indiana supported Dilger's battery. Corporal John H. Forbes, of the 74th Ohio in Moore's 2nd line, continued, "There was heavy skirmishing and artillery firing in our front." Three men from the 74th Ohio were wounded, including John Hennesey. Corporal Forbes would not live long to celebrate his army's victory at Peach Tree Creek, however. He was cut down along with three of his comrades just two days later in skirmishing with the Rebel lines.[16]

According to Captain Perry of the 38th Indiana, "Heavy columns of infantry could be seen hurriedly marching toward our left, and...a full battery

---

[14] Johnson, *A Soldier's Reminiscences*, 281.

[15] Henry F. Perry, *History of the 38th Indiana Volunteer Infantry* (Palo Alto CA: F.A. Stuart, Printer, 1906) 144–45; *OR*, ser. 1, vol. 38, pt. 2, serial 72, p. 602.

[16] Theodore W. Blackburn, *Letters from the Front: A Union "Preacher" Regiment (74th Ohio) in the Civil War* (Dayton OH: Press of Morningside House, 1981) 215, 220.

The Battle of Peach Tree Creek

opened upon our position while crashing volleys of musketry to our left plainly told that the fight was on." Perry continued, "Our works, which had just been completed, were quickly manned by the brigade, Captain Dilger's battery occupying a position immediately to the right of the road, and the Captain soon had his guns in full play, although a curtain of woods shut out from view the lines of the enemy. The same woods hid us from view of the rebel artillery."[17]

Captain Perry described it as a "fine artillery duel and for half an hour the air was filled with bursting shells. The most of these exploded at a distance of from 50 to 100 yards in our rear." Losing one officer and four men wounded, the 38th Indiana held its ground while inflicting a severe fire on French's veterans on the other edge of the field. "The fighting continued until near night, and consisted of fierce assaults of the enemy, which were repulsed in every instance with heavy loss to the assailants." Also falling in the battle from the 38th Indiana was Private James S. Jenkins of Company K, who was killed. In the 21st Ohio, also of Moore's brigade, Sergeant Major Earl W. Merry was wounded in the foot, which had to be amputated, but the Ohioans captured one Confederate near Nancy Creek the evening before and they would catch two more Rebels on 22 July. Sergeant Major Merry was the lone casualty in the Ohio regiment on 20 July, but Captain Daniel Lewis, while telling his men that they had dug their trenches deep enough the next day, raised his head out above the trench line to prove it. At that moment, the imprudent captain was struck in the head and killed by a Rebel sharpshooter. His men kept digging.[18]

The 19th Indiana Battery, which contained four Napoleons and two 3-inch ordnance rifles under the command of 1st Lieutenant William P. Stackhouse, joined Johnson's 1st Division after crossing the newly constructed bridge over Peach Tree Creek about 4:00 P.M. Also from the 1st Division, the veteran 2nd Brigade commanded by General John H. King, with the 69th Ohio, 11th Michigan, 15th US, 16th US, 18th US, and 19th US, also helped to shore up the blue lines as they repelled the Confederate thrusts north of the Embry plantation. Later in the afternoon, King's brigade was sent to the left, back across Peach Tree Creek and over to the left flank of Newton's exposed division on the Buckhead Road to cover the gap. Captain James Biddle of the 16th US Regulars remembered the Confederate batteries opening up a "terrific fire, shell grape & cannister (the worst fire I was ever exposed to) the very air seemed to

---

[17] Perry, *History of the 38th Indiana*, 145.
[18] Ibid., 145, 367, 378; Bradley J. Quinlin, historian, 21st Ohio Infantry ; *OR*, ser. 1, vol. 38, pt. 1, serial 72, p. 614.

be alive with pieces of shell & bullets, the ground was torn up with unexploded shells, big trees were cut half off & the line of breastworks in our rear was knocked to pieces." During the day's fighting, the 11th Michigan lost 2 men killed and 9 wounded. The total losses in King's command were: one killed, twenty-four wounded, and one missing, for a total loss of twenty-six men. In all, Johnson's division lost 189 men during the battle, including Johnson's adjutant, Captain E. T. Wells who was severely wounded. According to Dr. Charles W. Jones, chief surgeon for the XIV Corps, Johnson's 1st Division had about 125 men treated at the field hospital at Vining's Station.[19]

The 3rd Division commanded by Brigadier General Absalom Baird connected with the right of Johnson's 1st Division and the left of the 2nd Division under General Davis. Baird deployed his 3rd Brigade on the left and the 1st Brigade on the right. The 2nd Brigade under Colonel Newell Gleason was held in reserve, having been involved in skirmishing earlier in the day while securing some Rebel works in their front. During the action, Gleason's brigade lost Captain L. F. Daugherty who was killed instantly and several other men were wounded. Daugherty was only days away from completing his three years of service and was scheduled to be mustered out soon. Four men in the 87th Indiana of Gleason's brigade also fell wounded during the fighting. Major James A. Connally described the action on the far right of the Federal lines: "[W]e disposed of [the attack] in about ten minutes, and didn't have more than twenty men hurt, but we had worked all night before building strong breastworks, and so were better prepared for the attack than many other Divisions, where the men had slept the night before, and were consequently, caught without fortifications, or but incomplete ones."[20]

Major Preston, brother to Sally "Buck" Preston, the woman of Hood's affection, was killed. He had led Selden's battery into position near the Embry

---

[19] *OR*, ser. 1, vol. 38, pt. 2, serial 72, pp. 560–93, 834; Scaife, *The Campaign for Atlanta*, 153; Mark W. Johnson, *That Body of Brave Men, The US Regular Infantry and the Civil War in the West* (Cambridge: Da Capo Press, 2003) 517; James Biddle, diary, 20 July 1864, Burton Historical Collection, Detroit Public Library; John Robertson, *Michigan in the War* (Lansing MI: W. S. George & Company, 1882) 321; Thomas Livermore, *The Atlanta Campaign*, in vol. 8 of *Papers of the Military History Society of Massachusetts*, edited by The Military Historical Society of Massachusetts (Wilmington NC: Broadfoot Publishing Co. 1989) 442; *OR*, Supplement, pt. 1, vol. 7, serial 7, p. 12.

[20] *OR*, ser. 1, vol. 38, pt. 2, pp. 742, 790; Jack K. Overmyer, *A Stupendous Effort: The 87th Indiana in the War of the Rebellion* (Bloomington: Indiana University Press, 1997) 147; James A. Connolly, *Three Years in the Army of the Cumberland* (Bloomington: Indiana University Press, 1959) 239.

plantation and directed its fire until he fell. Hood had courted Miss Preston, a South Carolina belle, while recovering from his wounding at Gettysburg. Hood had proposed marriage to Miss Preston, who was residing in Richmond, before Hood left for Georgia, but Miss Preston refused. When Hood pressed, she became evasive. Hood then told her as he left that he considered himself engaged to her. Sally Buck replied, "Well, I don't consider myself engaged to you." The two continued to write during Hood's time in Georgia, but by the time that Hood took command of the Southern forces at Atlanta, the relationship had cooled. After her brother's death, it was over. With a strange kind of premonition, Sally Buck Preston had said that there was a feeling of death hanging around John Bell Hood.

23

WE WILL HAVE TO FIGHT TO GET ATLANTA

> To remain was utter destruction, sheer desperation. Sadly, reluctantly, these gallant men abandoned the point purchased at so priceless a cost, and again shot, and shell, and ball diminished fearfully the ranks already more than decimated by the murderous fire through which they had advanced.... Returning from that field of blood crowded with their slain, they met their right making its first advance upon the foe. Falling back beyond a sheltering hill, and forming under cover of its crest, they maintained their ground till night, in mercy, veiled from view the dark discolored earth where lay so many warriors, brave and true, weltering in their gore.[1]

For what seemed like forever to the survivors in Featherston's brigade, they clung on to the dearly won ridge against all odds. They did not want to give it up, but after nearly an hour of gruesome fighting, there simply were not enough to stop the blue counterattack. When the few remaining men were counted on the ridge it was discovered that every field officer and every captain on the field in the 31st Mississippi had either been killed or wounded and the regiment was left wholly without a commander until twenty-nine-year-old First Lieutenant William D. Shaw of Company G assumed command. Thus, all six field and staff officers and all seven of the company captains who participated in the attack had been put out of action in just over an hour. Those who could move then fell back with Lieutenant Shaw a couple hundred yards to a slight undulation down the old field which afforded some protection. There they kept up the fight. Continuing to contest the field, the Mississippians rallied three more times to try and retake the lost ridge, but were repulsed each time.

Earlier in the contest, when it became clear that Featherston's and Scott's forces could not sustain the breach they had created, their division commander, the demonstrative General Loring, called for General Stewart to send him reinforcements and asked for his third brigade, Adams's Mississippi Brigade, to come if it could be spared from its duties guarding the Chattahoochee River. Stewart consented and when word reached Adams's men that their sister

---

[1] J. L. Power scrapbook, Mississippi Department of Archives and History, Jackson, Mississippi.

brigades had been in a severe fight and may now be in trouble, the men came racing to the rescue. Unfortunately, by the time that Adams's men arrived, the fighting had played out. According to Lieutenant Berryhill, "Adams marched up to the scene of action but got in about the close of the fight and did not get to fire a gun."[2]

Earlier in afternoon, when Featherston's Mississippians overran the Collier Ridge, General George Thomas, the "Rock of Chickamauga," crossed Peach Tree Creek behind Newton's division and was on Buck Head Road directing the placement of some artillery to protect Newton's left flank. As Featherston's attack threatened Newton's right, and drove elements of Hooker's XX Corps toward Peach Tree Creek, Thomas anxiously watched Ward's 3rd Division mount its counterattack from the creek's base. An officer of the 70th Indiana watched Old Slow Trot as he followed Ward's progress.

> He is always working at his short, thick whiskers. When satisfied he smooths them down, when troubled, he works them all out of shape…and it was at that moment, when our right and left, fighting in the woods, seemed ready to give way, he had his whiskers all out of shape…. But when he saw the rebels running, with us after them, he took off his hat and flung it on the ground and shouted, "Hurrah! Look at the Third Division! They're driving them!" His whiskers were soon in good shape again.[3]

During the afternoon, Sherman, had been following the sounds of the fighting all along the front. Hearing the loud cannon fire in front of McPherson's forces while only hearing the muffled sounds of rifle fire to his right, along Peach Tree Creek and General Thomas's front, Sherman wrongly assessed the situation before him. The Federal leader believed that his "pets," the Army of the Tennessee under General "Birdseye"McPherson were facing two corps of the Confederate army, while General Dick Schofield and his Army of the Ohio confronted the remaining third of Hood's force, with only token resistance in the form of the Georgia State Militia and some cavalry facing Thomas's Army of the Cumberland.[4] Sherman had it exactly backwards from the actual situation.

---

[2] Mary Miles Jones and Leslie Jones Martin, ed., *The Gentle Rebel: The Civil War Letters of William Harvey Berryhill* (Yazoo City MS: The Sassafras Press, 1982). Letter to his wife 25 July 1864.

[3] Lloyd Lewis, *Sherman, Fighting Prophet* (Lincoln: University of Nebraska Press, 1993) 384.

[4] Thomas B. Buell, *The Warrior Generals, Combat Leadership in the Civil War* (Pittsburgh: Three Rivers Press 1997) 372–73.

Hood's First Sortie, 20 July 1864

Sherman believed that Thomas and his army was living up to his moniker, "Old Slow Trot," by failing to walk into Atlanta while Schofield and McPherson fought off and pressed in the remainder of Hood's Army. During the mid-afternoon, Sherman received a note from McPherson informing him that "the enemy was in such strength on the eastern [Decatur] road to the city that he could not advance." At the time, Sherman was with Schofield on the Cross Keys Road (Briarcliff Road) and, from prisoners taken from Cheatham's (formerly Hood's) corps during the day while fighting along the eastern reaches of Peach Tree Creek along the North and South Forks of the creek, it was evident that Schofield's force was facing fully one of the three Southern corps. Thus, the Federal leader sent a note to Thomas at 3:25 P.M. urging him to "push hard for Atlanta, sweeping everything before him."[5]

When Sherman received word from Thomas that he had become "generally engaged" with the Confederate forces, meaning that a full scale battle was in progress, the Federal commander was naturally skeptical. Even as dusk fell on the Georgia sky, Sherman still believed that Thomas had failed to seize the advantage afforded him to "walk into Atlanta," and he fired off another note to his commander of the Army of the Cumberland:

> I have been with Howard and Schofield today, and one of my staff is just back from General McPherson. All report the enemy in their front so strong that I was in hopes none were left for you, but I see it is the same old game; but we must not allow the enemy to build a new system of fortifications.... I wish you to press forward all the time, and thereby contract the lines.... Schofield made a dash...capturing about 100 prisoners.... All...are of Hood's Corps, though each division commander insists that he has to fight two corps...[6]

Sherman added that he would "push Schofield and McPherson all I know how," at the end of his letter, perhaps realizing that maybe Thomas wasn't wrong about being hit by two corps. Again, however, at 8:00 P.M., Sherman prodded Thomas with a third note urging him to advance, but it was not until about midnight when the days' final reports came in from his left and right wings when Sherman realized that it was McPherson, and not Thomas, who had

---

[5] Ibid., 372; United States War Department, comp., *Official Records of the Union and Confederate Armies in the War of the Rebellion*, 128 vols. (Washington, DC: Government Printing Office, 1880–1901) ser. 1, vol. 38, pt. 2, serial 72, p. 834 (hereafter *OR*); *OR*, ser. 1, vol. 38, pt. 5, serial 76, p. 196.

[6] *OR*, ser. 1, vol. 38, pt. 5, serial 76, pp. 196–97.

been fooled. At the same time Sherman wrote to Thomas, he also sent a note to McPherson informing him of Thomas's claim of being attacked by two Confederate corps and dismissing it by merely claiming that Thomas's claims "are in error."[7]

Sherman had assumed that Thomas's army could have merely walked into Atlanta while McPherson tangled with the entire Southern army and that Thomas had lost "our only chance of entering Atlanta by a quick move." When he received Sherman's note, McPherson dispatched a response at 8:45 P.M., reluctantly explaining that all that he had faced that day was Confederate cavalry and four guns. Wheeler and his force had done a remarkable job of holding back McPherson's three Federal corps, and had staved off disaster for the Gate City, at least for a while. To justify his slow advance, McPherson's note explained that the "four pieces of artillery...are armed with short Enfield rifles, making it difficult at times to dislodge them." Historian and critic B. H. Liddell Hart believed that "Sherman's left wing missed a chance of gaining Atlanta while Hood's attention was occupied with Thomas."[8]

In his last note to McPherson before his death on 22 July, Sherman wrote a lengthy description of the days' events once he realized he was wrong to assume Hood would attack McPherson, leaving Thomas's approach to Atlanta open. At 1:00 A.M. on the morning of 21 July, Sherman sent to McPherson: "I was in hopes you could have made a closer approach to Atlanta yesterday, as I was satisfied you had a less force and more inferior works than will be revealed by daylight, if, as I suppose, Hood proposes to hold Atlanta to the death. All afternoon heavy and desperate sallies were made against Thomas, all along his lines from left to right, particularly heavy against Newton and Geary, but in every instance he was roughly handled."[9] Therefore, 20 July would, be another missed opportunity for Sherman to cut off the Confederate line of retreat and shorten or end the bloody Georgia Campaign.

After Sherman visited the Peach Tree Creek battlefield on the morning of 21 July, it was clear that Thomas had won a major victory and that the Confederate army had begun a new, much more aggressive, policy. Sherman

---

[7] Ibid., 197–98, 208.

[8] Ibid., 208; B. H. Liddell Hart, *Sherman* (New York: Frederick A. Praeger, Inc., 1958) 279–80; Erol Clauss, "The Atlanta Campaign, July 18, 1864" (Ph.D. diss., Emory University, 1965) 101. His criticism was widespread as McPherson had failed for a second time to gain the Confederate rear during a flank march; McPherson failed to take Resaca at the start of the campaign.

[9] *OR*, ser. 1, vol. 38, pt. 5, serial 76, p. 218.

Hood's First Sortie, 20 July 1864

sent a dispatch to General Halleck at the War Department in Washington, DC, relating the events of the battle and estimating Confederate losses at 200 dead and 1,200 wounded in front of Newton's division, and 400 dead and 4,000 wounded in front of Hooker's corps, for a total estimated loss of 5,800 Rebels killed and wounded. Moreover, Sherman estimated his own losses at 100 in Newton's division and 1,500 in Hooker's corps. General Howard also reported 200 Rebels buried in front of Newton's division. The next day, when asked where the Rebels had gone, General Hooker of the XX Corps replied, "some of them are in hell, the rest back in Atlanta."[10]

Major General Loring, lamenting on the failure of many of Hardee's men to come up and be a factor that day said, "At this time, when engaged in a desperate, though successful, struggle against overwhelming odds in our front, it was with pain that we discovered that the co-operating forces had not yet engaged the enemy..., thus enabling him to pour into our ranks an enfilading fire from both directions, which gradually thinned my brave officers and men and enabled the enemy in our front to rally, finally compelling Featherston and Scott to fall back" 250 and 150 yards respectively. One Federal veteran described the turning of the tide of battle: "Our folks drove them, and kept up a fire upon them until they had gained the cover of the woods."[11]

For the next three or four hours until dark, the survivors would keep up the fight, continuing to rally for more counterattacks. There was a desperate sense of urgency within each of the Mississippians. They couldn't just leave the hill to the Yankees after paying such a high price. Many of their number littered both sides of the battle-scared ridge. Some of their comrades who had been on picket duty presently returned. One of them was Captain Thomas J. Pulliam of Company C who suddenly was the ranking officer on the field. Captain Pulliam learned of the slaughter from Lieutenant Shaw of Company G who had been in command since the fall back from the top of the ridge. But Pulliam needed no report. He could see the death and destruction that had been dealt the brave Mississippians whose blood now soaked the Georgia red clay for as far as his eyes could see in every direction. He would later write the official report of the battle for the regiment and stated, "All the officers and men acted with great gallantry. I regret that I am unable to give a full account of this sanguinary conflict, as it was not my fortune to be with the regiment in the charge upon the

---

[10] Ibid., 211; Newton, *129th Illinois*, 400.
[11] *OR*, ser. 1, vol. 38, pt. 3, serial 74, pp. 876–78; Jean M. Cate, ed., *"If I Live to Come Home,": The Civil War Letters of Sergeant John March Cate* (Pittsburgh: Dorrance Publishing Company, 1995) 196.

enemy's works." The captain would share in the bloody fate with his fellow Mississippians, however, receiving a painful wound in one of the counterattacks.

The survivors of the 31st Mississippi and Featherston's brigade kept up the fire from a skirt of woods that they hung on to on the far side of the field. It was no use. They simply were too few and had sacrificed too much to gain the works and hold them against an entire division. In front of Harrison's brigade, according to one Federal on the burial detail, "more than 150 of the enemy's [Confederate] dead were buried in its immediate front the next morning." Harrison's men, which constituted one-third of the Federals opposing Featherston's Mississippians, lost 32 killed and 149 wounded for a total of 181 casualties.[12] One Federal solider from Ward's 3rd Division would later remark of the Mississippians that "they met us like men." Another one said that they had never seen such tenacity and fierce fighting in the entire war than what they saw that day in the fields and hills above Peach Tree Creek. "Our steps were marked with blood," wrote one of Loring's men of the battle. One of Featherston's veterans described the withdrawal to a Mississippi newspaper:

> To remain was utter destruction, sheer desperation. Sadly, reluctantly, these gallant men abandoned the point purchased at so priceless a cost, and again shot, and shell, and ball diminished fearfully the ranks already more than decimated by the murderous fire through which they had advanced.... Returning from that field of blood crowded with their slain, they met their right making its first advance upon the foe. Falling back beyond a sheltering hill, and forming under cover of its crest, they maintained their ground till night, in mercy, veiled from view the dark discolored earth where lay so many warriors, brave and true, weltering in their gore.[13]

After the battle, one Federal veteran of General Harrison's brigade, in the 105th Illinois, which helped turn back the Rebel charge wrote jubilantly to his mother the next day:

> We have had a great battle and routed the rebels most thoroughly. Yesterday morning we left camp and formed on the left of the 4th Corps [Actually, they were on the right of the IV Corps.] The day was intensely hot and the forenoon was spent getting up to the line as we were obligated to

---

[12] Henry Stone, *The Siege and Capture of Atlanta,* 113.
[13] J. L. Power scrapbook, Mississippi Department of Archives and History, Jackson, MIssissippi.

Hood's First Sortie, 20 July 1864

working slow. About one o'clock we halted a little in the rear of what was to be our position and waited for the skirmishers to clear the way. We remained scouting here in the area about two hours.

At 3 o'clock firing suddenly began heavy on our left and non combattants and stragglers were seen running to the rear. Another minute and the great storm of musketry rolled around to our front and thence far as we could hear to the right. Our brigade was ordered quickly into line. We were lying right under a hill and Loring's rebel divisions charged over the hill upon us, but they caught a "tartar." Our line was ordered forward and forward we went right up the hill at them. They waved their colors and charged madly at us and for a minute it seemed as if they would overpower us, but our line dashed on, met them midway on the hill and hurled back their charging columns.

Now commenced an awful scene, the rebels ran in confused masses from us and the very heavens seemed to tremble at the terrific fire we poured into them. Their dead and wounded covered the ground, and in perfect terror many of them threw down their guns and ran into our lines to escape destruction.

We reached the top of the hill and held our position there, a position of us keeping off the enemy while others carried rails to throw up in front of us. The battle raged meanwhile awfully all around us and at one time we were nearly flanked by the giving way of a brigade somewhere on our right [Geary's division]; but we held our ground and fought till night put an end to the conflict. In the dusk the rebels drew off their forces and the "red field was won."

I walked over the ground in front of us when the moon rose and helped take off the rebel wounded. It was nearly morning before they were all brought in. Today [21 July] we have been carrying the dead, and waiting for another battle but it has not come yet.

Our regt. lost only 14 men killed and wounded. Our boys are very careful, always laying down to load and fire except when advancing and at the command halt and drop flat to the ground. This is the first fair fight we have had and it must have been desperate on the part of the rebels. Our boys would not give back an inch and I believe they would have gone in with the bayonets before they would have retreated a step.

The heat was so awful that many of our men went sun struck, but all worked nobly enveloped in a dense cloud of smoke with faces begrimed with powder.[14]

---

[14] George F. Cram to mother, 21 July 1864, in George F. Cram, *Soldiering with Sherman: The Civil War Letters of George F. Cram*, ed. Jennifer Cain Bornstedt, 125–26; see also 191 (DeKalb: Northern Illinois University Press, 2000). This soldier was John Bachelder who later died from his wounds.

The Battle of Peach Tree Creek

The Illinoisan soldier, George F. Cram, followed up this letter with another on 24 July to his mother:

> The rebels have removed their best General and Hood now has command. So far his movements bid fair to completely ruin his army. The morning after we had the great fight General Hooker rode around to see us. Oh, it would have done you good to see the boys cheer him. His face looked just like a sunbeam. When he came along to our regt. we brought out a battle flag which we captured, he stopped and coming up to us said, "Boys what regt. is this?" The 105 Ill., we replied. Then said he, "You did splendidly, splendidly but they did just as well on the right, the corps is all right." We gave him cheer after cheer and it was carried from regt. to regt. all along the line as he rode on.
>
> When we went into the fight, wounded, worthless, but [doubting] general [Ward] was commanding the division in absence of Butterfield, and when our brigade dashes up the hill and turned the rebel line, he sat on his horse clapping his hands and shouting, See my brigade! See my brigade![15]

After the battle, the non-combatants on the Northern side, the cooks, clerks, and shirkers, began to return from their paths of escape across Peach Tree Creek. Colonel Merrill of the 70th Indiana mused with a freed black man named Juniper who had become employed as a cook for a company in the 70th Indiana during the Georgia Campaign. Merrill described the chaotic scene in the rear of the Federal lines when the threat posed by the Rebel assault was realized: "The hillside and valley behind the advancing lines were alive with non-combatants, cowards, cooks, and mules laden with frying pans, rushing wildly from the impending storm." Merrill met up with Juniper shortly after the fighting subsided: "Juniper, the cook for Company B, was a powerful Negro. He could take a barrel of whisky by the chines and drink from the bung," remembered Merrill. "It was amusing to hear him tell how his long legs helped him to beat the IV Corps down 'dat ar hill.' 'No, sir! Didn't see no 70th [Indiana] Rigement boys runnin.' When I struck de crick I runned out on a long log and jumped, but went chock in de mud way 'bove my knees.'" Juniper continued to explain his flight to the colonel. "Didn't have no time to lif' one foot till a soger, and den a nigga, lit wif bof feet on my back, and went a flyen to

---

[15] Cram to mother, 24 July 1864, in Cram, *Soldiering with Sherman*, 126.

de shore. Dar dis chile war stuck in de mud, playen leap-frog wid dar ar whole coah.'"[16]

Back in Atlanta, Confederate Captain J. B. Austin of Bate's division rode into town along Buckhead Road (today's Peachtree Street) as it turned into Ivy Street (today's Peachtree Center Avenue) with the wagons laden with wounded men. Austin recorded, "We found the city in a wild state of excitement. Citizens were running in every direction. Terror-stricken women and children went screaming about the streets seeking some avenue of escape from hissing, bursting shells, as they sped on their mission of death and destruction." Austin continued, "Perfect pandemonium reigned near the Union Depot. Trunks, bed clothing and apparel were scattered in every direction. People were stirring in every conceivable way to get out of town with their effects."[17]

Thirteen-year-old D. N. Johnson remembered that when the war broke out he was only ten, but his two older brothers, Arch, and Alex who was only fifteen, both joined the Confederate army. Arch served with Cobb's Legion and was wounded in the arm while Alex died of measles within three months of joining. But young Johnson remained with his father, who was too old to serve, and his sisters. The Johnsons had a home on the north side of Atlanta, but they also had a place in Madison where D. N.'s father had moved his slaves and much of his property when war came to Georgia. When it appeared that a fight for Atlanta was imminent, Mr. Johnson and his son returned to Atlanta to retrieve his daughters who had been cared for by relatives. The young boy remembered, "When we reached home Confederate soldiers were camped all around the house. The battle of Peach Tree Creek was being fought that day. We got a Confederate wagon to bring a large box that contained food, trinkets, deeds and the family Bible to the Decatur Depot." Johnson explained,

> We started on the train for Madison and met a courier telling the engineer that the railroad had been cut into between Stone Mountain and Madison. He backed to Atlanta and we spent the night at the old Markham House. I thought I had never seen so many soldiers," added the boy. "Wheeler's Cavalry passed through Atlanta and went on to Decatur where they fought some Yankee raiders that night. The Decatur depot was burned and we lost

---

[16] Samuel Merrill, *The Seventieth Indiana Volunteer Infantry in the War of the Rebellion* (Indianapolis: Bowen-Merrill Co., 1900) 143.

[17] Samuel Carter III, *The Siege of Atlanta, 1864* (New York: St. Martin's Press, 1973) 207; *Tennesseans in the Civil War, A Military History of Confederate and Union Units with Available Rosters of Personnel*, 2 vols. (Nashville: Civil War Centennial Commission, 1964–1965) 2:22.

our box of prized possessions. We had to take the train going around by Macon to get back to Madison.[18]

Back along the Collier Ridge, a number of Featherston's survivors found themselves the prisoners of Ward's victorious Yankees. Out of 1,230 in the Mississippi brigade that had taken Collier Ridge, 246 of them had been captured, of which 132 were wounded, leaving just 114 men who were immediately shipped north to prison camps. The wounded Mississippians who had been injured too severely or who had advanced too far into the broken Federal lines to fall back were eventually taken to Federal hospitals, and those that survived the ordeal were taken to Federal prison camps after they had recovered sufficiently to be transferred.[19] One Federal veteran of the 22nd Wisconsin reported, "The prisoners say we will have to fight to get Atlanta. We expect to fight to get it," he continued, and soon "Atlanta, the great magnet of this campaign will be ours."[20]

---

[18] J. N. Johnson, reminiscences, in vol. 15 of *Confederate Reminiscences and Letters, 1861–1865*, ed. United Daughter of the Confederacy, Atlanta Chapter, 83–85 (Atlanta: United Daughters of the Confederacy, 2000).

[19] *OR*, ser. 1, vol. 38, pt. 2, serial 73, p. 329.

[20] Racine Boy to Friend T. 21 July 1864, 17, subject file PW-4, Kennesaw Mountain National Battlefield Park, Kennesaw, Georgia.

BE ON THE LOOKOUT FOR BREASTWORKS

Cheatham's Division...advanced through the woods until we found the Yanks, behind breastworks.[1]

The same emergency which had necessitated the shifting of Cheatham's Corps to the right, a few hours earlier in the day, and occasioned the delay in the first attack, had now, in the opinion of General Hood, required the withdrawal of a division from Hardee at this critical moment, and prevented the renewal of the attack.[2]

Cleburne's Division. After receiving a request from General Stewart to support Featherston's breakthrough, Hardee called upon Cleburne to replace Walker's division and renew the assault. The plan would be for Cleburne's division to strike Newton's position east of Buckhead Road (today's Peachtree Street) while Maney's division would hit west of the road. Hardee also learned from a staff officer that Bate's division had been located in the cane thicket and was being redirected toward the Federal flank. Hardee sent orders to Maney's Tennessee Division to renew the attack with Cleburne's advance. Thus, by 6:15, Hardee finally had three divisions moving in the direction of Newton's sole division, over two hours after Walker's men had first been repulsed in their lone assault, and over five hours from the time of Hood's intended attack. Yet there might still be time to deliver a devastating blow to the isolated Yankee division.

With any element of surprise clearly lost, the Confederates would be attacking Federals who were now prepared to receive them. Nevertheless, Hardee's renewed attack had potential due to the large force at his disposal. Should Bate's, Cleburne's, and Maney's divisions all strike Newton's lines at

---

[1] Samuel T. Foster, *One of Cleburne's Command, The Civil War Reminiscences and Diary of Captain Samuel T. Foster, Granbury's Texas Brigade, C.S.A.,* ed. Norman D. Brown (Austin: University of Texas Press, 1980) 107.

[2] S. L. Black to Thomas Benton Roy, 31 May 1880, in Roy's "General Hardee and the Military Operations around Atlanta," *Southern Historical Society Papers* 8 (August/September 1880): 347–50.

the same or nearly the same time, Hardee's corps would have massed some 12,700 men against only 2,700 defenders: Bate's division mustering some 3,000 men, Cleburne's division some 4,900 strong, and Maney's division of another 4,800. But Hardee did not press the attack vigorously or promptly enough to take advantage of his overwhelming numerical advantage.

While making arrangements, Hardee and Cleburne were perilously close to the Federal lines. Adjutant Buck described the scene: "Genls. Hardee and Cleburne, with staffs and escorts, met upon a road running through our lines, and rode forward towards a slight rise of ground. Soon a puff of smoke arose and a shell passed over the group," continued Buck. "Hardee was of the opinion that one of our batteries was in front, and drawing the fire from the Federals, and [he] continued to ride onward; and it was not until the second discharge that he discovered that the fire was point blank at our party," explained the Confederate adjutant, "[and not] until the third shot, killing Sergeant Marshall of Cleburne's couriers, solved all doubt." According to Atlanta historian Wilbur G. Kurtz and veteran Cyrus E. Custis of the 79th Ohio, Cleburne "came near getting killed on Peachtree Road as he and staff were riding on said road."[3]

"We could distinctly hear the sound of axes felling trees to strengthen the works in our front, and Cleburne had but to rise to the crest of a wooded ridge, not 200 yards away [near the intersection of today's Palisades Road with Peachtree Street] to encounter the enemy," wrote Adjutant Buck. "Preliminary orders for the assault were given, and Cleburne had selected messengers to send to each of his three [actually four] brigade commanders with instructions to advance, when a staff officer galloped up," explained Buck, "announcing that McPherson was approaching the city from the east, pressing back the cavalry, and that General Hood directed a division to be sent at once to check this movement, and ours being in reserve, was the one to go."[4] According to Buck, "this withdrawal and the approach of night, prevented any further advance by Hardee."[5]

Major Samuel L. Black remembered:

Bate's Division, finding no enemy in its immediate front, on account of the circular formation of the enemy's lines, had been sent forward through dense

---

[3] I. A. Buck, "Cleburne's Division at Atlanta," p. 3, subject file PW-5, vertical files, Kennesaw National Battlefield Park, Kennesaw, Georgia; Cyrus E. Custis to Wilbur G. Kurtz, 29 October 1932, MSS 130, box 3, folder 4, Wilbur G. Kurtz Papers, Maps, Clippings, Notes and files, Kenan Research Center, Atlanta History Center.

[4] Buck, "Cleburne's Division at Atlanta," 3.

[5] Ibid., 3.

Hood's First Sortie, 20 July 1864

timber to find and turn his flank; Walker's Division, temporarily disabled in the first assault, was shifted and ordered forward to co-operate with Bate's flanking movement; Cleburne's Division, hitherto in reserve, was brought up, and with his two available divisions, Cleburne's and Maney's, Hardee prepared to renew the attack in front; and the final orders had been given to the division commanders to move to assaults, when the order, above referred to, was received from General Hood, directing that a division be withdrawn and sent to the extreme right of the army. This necessitated a countermand of the assault as it was on the point of execution, and Cleburne's Division was withdrawn and dispatched as directed. Against such forces and works as were in Hardee's front it would have been folly to throw troops in detail and without concert; and before the new disposition thus made necessary could be perfected, General [Hardee] countermanded the movement and ordered the troops to be withdrawn to their former position. The same emergency which had necessitated the shifting of Cheatham's Corps to the right, a few hours earlier in the day, and occasioned the delay in the first attack, had now, in the opinion of General Hood, required the withdrawal of a division from Hardee at this critical moment, and prevented the renewal of the attack.[6]

Colonel Thomas Benton Roy, Hardee's assistant adjutant general, recalled that by the time Cleburne's division was deployed and ready to advance, a courier from Hood came up in a big hurry with urgent orders to send a division to the Decatur Road to save Atlanta from capture.

Our division, which had been in reserve, was, on the evening of that day, ordered up to replace troops beaten in the first assault, and was formed in a depression facing the wooded ridge occupied by the enemy. The preliminary order for the assault had been given, and Cleburne had selected an officer to send to each brigade commander with the order to advance, when a staff officer galloped up, and announced that General Hood had directed that a division be sent at once to Atlanta, and ours was the one to go. Five minutes more would have been too late. The division was accordingly withdrawn, and marched back through Atlanta, Cleburne and staff riding ahead to ascertain the position assigned us. It was on the extreme right of the army, with the left of our division resting on the Augusta railroad.[7]

---

[6] Black to Thomas Benton Roy, 31 May 1880, in Roy, "General Hardee and the Military Operations around Atlanta," 347–50.
[7] Ibid.

The Battle of Peach Tree Creek

Key's Arkansas Battery. Preceding the attack by Cleburne's division was Captain Thomas J. Key's Arkansas Battery consisting of four Napoleons that had followed Walker's division. Key's battery had arrived together with the rest of Hotchkiss's battalion "on Peachtree Road about where Spring Street joins it. Cleburne's troops had finally assembled there and were being held in reserve… about 4 or 4:30 P.M." From his position just a few yards behind Walker's Georgians, Key could see that the Yankees were in a good position. "The two lines were very close—so near that I walked to within 150 yards of their batteries, which were throwing canister—and I proposed to Major Hotchkiss to run up one gun at a time and load them with canister so as to mow down the Yankee lines when our troops charged [referring to Cleburne's division]." Major Thomas R. Hotchkiss commanded the artillery battalion that was attached to Cleburne's command. By now, it was after 6:30. "He consented, but while I was in the act of executing this dangerous and difficult movement, Hardee revoked the order for the charge because it was too late in the evening."[8]

Actually, Hardee had just received the urgent dispatch from General Hood requesting that he send a division to the Decatur Road on the extreme right of the Confederate line to stop a Federal advance. Throughout the afternoon, General Joseph Wheeler's Confederate cavalry had been fighting off parries by the Federal Army of the Tennessee under General James B. McPherson. When it became apparent that Wheeler's weary cavalrymen could not continue to hold against the 25,000 Yankees, Wheeler sent a desperate request to Hood for help. Hardee immediately called off the attack, sending Cleburne's division to Wheeler's aid.[9] According to Captain Mumford H. Dixon, who recorded in his diary, Cleburne's withdrawal from the Peach Tree Creek line occurred at 5:00. Dixon's entry for 20 July was, "Left our works and moved on the enemy. General Walker's Division attacks the enemy and we in reserve. At 5 o'clock ordered to Atlanta, distance four miles. Slept on the edge of town."[10]

Dixon must have been mistaken, for at 6:30, Hood's chief of staff, General W. W. Mackall, had just sent a dispatch to Wheeler on the far right, informing

---

[8] Wilbur G. Kurtz to members of Atlanta Civil War Roundtable, 16 June 1955, MSS 130, Box 29, folder 7, 2, Wilbur G. Kurtz Papers, Maps, Clippings, Notes and files, Kenan Research Center, Atlanta History Center; Wirt Armistead Cate, ed., *Two Soldiers: The Campaign Diaries of Thomas J. Key, C.S.A. and Robert J. Campbell, U.S.A.* (Chapel Hill: University of North Carolina Press, 1938) 92.

[9] United States War Department, comp., *Official Records of the Union and Confederate Armies in the War of the Rebellion*, 128 vols. (Washington, DC: Government Printing Office, 1880–1901) ser. 1, vol. 38, pt. 1, serial 74, pp. 698–99 (hereafter *OR*).

[10] Supplement to *OR*, pt. 1, vol. 7, serial 7, p. 68–72.

him that Hood had ordered Cheatham to send a brigade to his aid. It was only after Hood realized that Cheatham was stretched too thin to adequately support Wheeler and that a larger Confederate presence on his weak right flank was needed, that he sent for a division to assist Wheeler. Hood sent a dispatch to Wheeler at 7:15 P.M. informing him that Hardee was sending Cleburne's division to him. "Five minutes more would have been too late, as it would have found us heavily engaged," wrote Captain Buck.[11]

Lowrey's Brigade. Private John Kern of the 45th Mississippi in Lowrey's brigade recorded in his diary the marching and countermarching that his regiment had endured. "Wednesday, July 20, 1864. Cloudy & warm. Moved to the right & moved back, then moved out to the front under fire part of the way, halted just in rear of the picket line. Remained there till dark & ret'd to our works & moved through Atlanta & out on the Augusta R.R. Drew rations & slept a little." Kern added that an assistant surgeon, Dr. Shurtleff, and "Frank Martin were captured." Even though Lowrey's brigade and the rest of Cleburne's division had withdrawn as the evening sun drew long shadows across the battlefield, Lowrey's Mississippians and Alabamians still suffered two killed, thirty-nine wounded, and four captured for a total loss of forty-five men. Lowrey's brigade had occupied the ground along the Buckhead Road where Stevens's brigade had been slaughtered three hours earlier and found it to still be a dangerous place.[12]

When it was apparent that Stevens's assault had failed, Colonel Nisbet and his comrades from the 66th Georgia fell back to the safety of a wooded ridge a couple of hundred yards from the Yankee works (near today's Palisades Road). "We met M. P. Lowrey's Mississippi Brigade of Cleburne's Division, going in. If they had come up sooner, we could have held our captured works," explained Nisbet. "General Lowrey said, 'Colonel, you must be mistaken about the enemy being fortified. General Hood informed me that they had just crossed the creek.'" The Georgia colonel continued, "I told Lowrey that was a mistake, and offered to deploy my regiment and uncover the enemy's position, which was accepted. I deployed, and drove back their skirmishers who had advanced as we fell back." Nisbet described the futile effort: "I halted my line in full view of their breastworks, and waited for Lowrey to come up. After viewing the

---

[11] *OR*, ser. 1, vol. 38, pt. 5, serial 76, pp. 893–94; Buck, "Cleburne's Division at Atlanta," 3–4.

[12] John Kern, diary, 20 July 1864, Old Courthouse Museum, Vicksburg, Mississippi; David Williamson, *The Third Battalion and the 45th Mississippi Regiment* (Jefferson NC: McFarland & Company, Inc., 2004) 215–19; *OR*, ser. 1, vol. 38, pt. 3, serial 74, p. 733.

situation he agreed with me that it would be a useless waste of lives to assault their works again, with what force we had. We returned to our original line."[13]

Captain Key continued to trade fire with the Federal artillery until dusk, when he "withdrew my battery to [a] spring near the fine Gothic house...."[14] Cleburne's men withdrew to help fend off General Frank Blair's XVII Corps, which was advancing on Atlanta from the east, but not before his men were exposed to the Federal fire along the Buckhead Road as they waited to assault Newton's works.

Another Confederate battery, the Marion Light Artillery of Hoxton's battalion, was sent forward to support Cleburne's assault, but it did not engage as the attack was called off before the guns could deploy. Lieutenant A. J. Neal of the battery wrote after the battle to his father, "We have had some sharp fighting on the lines today resulting I fear in no good to us. I had heard of some successes but most places we failed to accomplish anything. Cheatham [Maney] and Cleburne's Divisions moved out and attacked the enemy in force." Neal, whose battery followed Cleburne's late afternoon aborted assault, mistook the earlier fighting by Walker's division. "They succeeded in driving them handsomely for over half a mile till they came to the main lines strongly entrenched. Our troops advanced within fifteen paces of the Yankee works and could have taken them but the order was countermanded and we remained there for three hours." Neal, whose horse was wounded as he led his battery into position along Buckhead Road explained, "Our Battery was carried out but did not become engaged."[15]

Granbury's Texas Brigade. On the left of Cleburne's line, Granbury's Texas Brigade advanced into position to assault Newton's line, and it began receiving fire from the works while waiting for the order to attack. Captain Samuel T. Foster described the action: "We opened a tremendous fire with artillery and small arms, which is kept up until it is dark—very dark." Captain B. R. Tyrus, commanding the 6th and 15th Texas Cavalry Consolidated

---

[13] James Cooper Nisbet, *4 Years on the Firing Line*, ed. Bell Irvin Wiley (Jackson TN: McCowat-Mercer Press, 1963) 210.

[14] Cate, *Two Soldiers*, 92. Kurtz to members of Atlanta Civil War Roundtable, 1941, 2, Wilbur G. Kurtz Papers. The house was known as White Columns. The old mansion served for decades as home to WSB TV channel 2 and Radio AM 750 (1940s to 1980s); the columns are still present, but the mansion has since been torn down and replaced by a massive white complex replete with studios and offices. The spring described by Key was located "somewhere near the Christian Church at Spring and Peachtree Streets."

[15] A. J. Neal to father, 20 July 1864, 29, vertical files, Kennesaw Mountain National Battlefield Park Library, Kennesaw, Georgia.

Hood's First Sortie, 20 July 1864

(Dismounted),was wounded in the action leaving Lieutenant T. L. Flynt in command. First Lieutenant Robert Marvin Collins of Company B in the 15th Texas Cavalry (Dismounted) was wounded. Falling with Captain Tyrus and Lieutenant Collins were two men killed and fourteen others wounded, for a total loss of eighteen men in the regiment. According to Collins, "On the morning of the 20th we were moved still further to the right in the direction of Decatur. We remained here in line of battle until about 3 o'clock in the afternoon, when we were moved in double-quick time back to the Peachtree Creek road, and," the Texas lieutenant added, "our Division [Cleburne's] manned a line of works at right angles to this road just in front of a big church house." This was in the area of White Columns. "The right center of Granbury's Texas Brigade, being near the road [Buckhead Road], with Govan's Arkansas Brigade, or Joshes, as we boys called them, to our right." Collins explained that "I was detailed and put in command of Company C, Lieut. John W. Stewart of Grayon County, Texas being too indisposed to go into battle with his company. Every movement pointed with the unerring finger of certainty to the fact that somebody was going to get badly hurt, and that in short order."[16]

"In front of our brigade was an open field about 400 yards across. About 4:50 the command was given, 'Forward, march!,'" exclaimed Collins. "We quit the works and moved out into the field. The Federals greeted us with terrific fire of shot and shells, but as we were moving down the hill they passed over our heads, doing no damage except that of making a fellow feel like he was very small game to be shot at with such guns." The young Texan led his new command across the farm of Andrew Jackson Collier as Granbury's men climbed towards Newton's lines. "On we go, now the lines come to the fence of a farm, the line halts and the men take hold of it and just bodily lift it up and throw it down. Just at this moment a blinding flash right in our front and a shell explodes." Granbury's Texans were being shelled by Goodspeed's battery. "It seemed to be filled with powder and ounce balls. It laid a good many of the boys out, and among the number was Capt. Ben Tyrus and myself." Collins was referring to Captain Benjamin R. Tyrus who led the 6th Texas Cavalry into the fight.[17]

---

[16] Foster, *One of Cleburne's Command*, 107; James A. Mundie, Jr., *Texas Burial Sites of Civil War Notables*, 341; Collins, *Echoes of Battle*, 212; TX CSA pension application 27277. Collins would recover and go on to serve as the editor of the Decatur "Post" and the Denton "Monitor" after the war.

[17] Collins, *Echoes of Battle*, 212.

The Battle of Peach Tree Creek

Collins joined the long list of Rebels wounded along the southern slope of the hill crossed by Buckhead Road. "As I fell I noticed that about two inches square of my gray Georgia jeans pants had gone in with the shot; this was conclusive that a piece of the shell had passed through my thigh and had necessarily cut the femoral artery, and that therefore," the young Lieutenant lamented, "I would be a dead Confederate in just three minutes, as my understanding was that the femoral artery cut would let all the blood in a man out in that time." Collins considered his options. "However, I made a grip on the wound with my right hand, intending to stop the blood as much as possible, and thereby hold on to life long enough to give my past history a hasty going over and to repeat all the prayers I knew." Collins began to reflect, when just then "Four big stout fellows picked me up on a litter and started back to the line of breastworks." He continued to consider his mortal deeds. "We had to pass through a galling fire of minies, shot and shell; I was not alarmed at all at this, because my mind was made up to quit the earth and I was now only waiting, as the saying goes, for death to strike me square in the face."[18]

After reciting his prayers, Collins considered why he was not yet dead. After a little while, "I finally ventured to inquire of one of the men carrying me if I were bleeding much. He was a witty Irishman, and replied, 'Not a drap of the rudy current to be seen, Lieutenant.'" Collins began to realize that he might yet live. "These words brought back my hope that had already gone over the hills out of sight, and made me remark than an improvement in gait would soon land us out of reach of these Yankee bullets." Now the moral man began think ahead. "Then I chuckled in my sleeve when the thought occurred that maybe this would well win a good furlough, and if it does won't I have fun with those Georgia girls. This may all sound like a strange line of thoughts to run through one's mind in so short a time and under such circumstances," explained Collins, "but all this is sound common sense compared to some things we are guilty of doing during our natural lives."[19]

The young Texan described his plight. "Pretty soon I was dumped over on the safe side of our earthworks, the field surgeon examined my wound and pronounced it an ugly one, but not necessarily fatal. I thanked him from the bottom of my heart for these words." His journey away from the battlefield was an uncomfortable one. "About 10 of us were piled into an old ambulance and the driver pulled out for Atlanta. We were landed at the City Hall, the commons

---

[18] Ibid.
[19] Ibid.

around this building having been turned into a carving pen, and the doctors had more subjects than they had table room," said Collins. "I was laid on a big broad pine table and four stout men put to hold me, one to each arm and leg, while Doctors D. F. Stuart of Houston [Texas] and C. Lipscomb of Denton [Texas], went into the ugly wound with probes and fingers in search of the missing piece of my Georgia jeans." The Texas lad explained, "Chloroform was too scarce and costly to be used on me, and besides there were so many needing attention that the doctors could not spare time to administer it except in very bad cases; therefore, I had to endure the pain." Collins added that "The ball that struck me was mashed flat on one side to about the size of a quarter, and went in the flat way turning on the femoral artery."[20]

"I was then stored away on a nice clean cot in a new tent in a little park just across the street from the Trout House," explained Collins, "and remained there overnight and was shipped early next morning along with many others down to a little city on the Macon road called Forsythe." While there, Collins became addicted to the morphine that was given to him for eighteen straight days to relieve the pain, but he would eventually recover and return to duty.[21]

Captain J. William Brown commanded the 7th Texas Infantry, some 110 men strong, and saw only 1 man fall wounded. The 17th and 18th Texas Cavalry (Dismounted) had 182 present for duty, and had 2 men wounded from the long-range fire. Captain Foster recorded the change in plans as Cleburne's division was withdrawn to stop McPherson's advance on the Decatur Road. "As soon as it gets dark our Brigade is withdrawn very quietly and marched to the city. Thence down the Augusta RR until we reach our line of breastworks running south." Foster described the march along the Confederate line. "We take along the breastwork to the south for about 1 1/2 miles when we find the end of them. We then turn more to the west and stop and commence to build works—connecting with the main line."[22]

Polk's Brigade. In Polk's brigade, the 1st Arkansas, which had been consolidated with the 15th Arkansas, was commanded by Lieutenant Colonel William H. Martin. According to one private in the 1st Arkansas, the shell and rifle fire that these reserves were exposed to was quite severe. Private William E. Bevens recorded that on "July 20 there was hard fighting at Peach Tree

---

[20] Ibid.
[21] Ibid.
[22] Clement Anselm Evans, ed., *Texas*, vol. 15 of *Confederate Military History*, 19 vols. (1899; repr., Wilmington NC: Broadfoot Publishing Company, 1987) 184–85; Foster, *One of Cleburne's Command*, 108.

Creek in which we lost heavily. Our noble Captain Shoup was wounded and the command devolved upon Second Lieutenant Clay Lowe. He and John R. Loftin were the only commissioned officers we had left." Also in Polk's brigade, the 2nd Tennessee saw its second in command, Lieutenant Colonel Edwin L. Drake of Winchester, Tennessee, fall severely wounded. Two men were captured from the 2nd Tennessee during the evening while two others had been captured from the regiment the day before.[23]

Washington Artillery. Supporting Hardee's assault was the 5th Company of the famous Washington Artillery of New Orleans, which followed Bate's division in the line of attack. This remarkable group of some of the Queen City's finest men was organized in 1838 as a state militia unit to defend the city and the Louisiana coast from would be invaders.

> Young men wishing to advance in New Orleans commerce and society saw membership in the Washington Artillery as prestigious and as a stepping stone to a better life through better connections within the commercial world. The Washington Artillery was often referred to as a "blue-stocking outfit" because of the great number of men of means and social standing within its ranks. Membership in the Washington Artillery was not by open invitation to the public, either. You had to be more than willing and able in order to be accepted into the Washington Artillery.[24]

When war broke out in 1861, the first four of the group's five companies went to Virginia to fight, and they made quite a record of valor during the war. So, too, did the fifth company which remained in the Deep South and was attached to the Army of Tennessee under Hardee's corps and assigned to Cobb's artillery battalion. During the Georgia Campaign, the battalion usually

---

[23] Clement Anselm Evans, ed., *Tennessee*, vol. 10 of *Confederate Military History*, 19 vols. (1899; repr., Wilmington NC: Broadfoot Publishing Company, 1987) 455; William E. Bevens, *Reminiscences of a Private: William E. Bevens of the First Arkansas Infantry, C.S.A.*, ed. Daniel E. Sutherland (Fayetteville: University of Arkansas Press, 1992) 182–83; Evans, ed., *Tennessee*, 499, 712; *Tennesseans in the Civil War, A Military History of Confederate and Union Units with Available Rosters of Personnel*, 2 vols. (Nashville: Civil War Centennial Commission, 1964–1965) 2:168.

"The 44 year old Lt. Colonel [Drake] who could claim three great-grandfathers as veterans of the Continental Army during the Revolutionary War, lay for two months in a hospital bed in Barnesville, Georgia, before recovering in time to join his command as it fell back from the Tennessee Campaign in December" (Edwin L. Ferguson, *Sumner County, Tennessee in the Civil War*, ed. Diane Payne [Tompkinsville KY: self-published, 1972 www.rootsweb.com/~tnsumner/sumnfg15.htm [1 March 2008]).

[24] http://www.geocities.com/heartland/woods/3501/aproud.htm (24 May 2008).

fought alongside Bate's division. On 20 July, at Peachtree Creek, the Washington Artillery was again supporting Bate's division as it made its way forward for the assault.[25]

Commanded by Captain Cuthbert H. Slocumb, the Washington Artillery Battery moved up and to the right to support Bate's attack. The battery had four 12-pounder Napoleons, and the men were having difficulty in following their command unit that day. As explained earlier, General Bate's division got lost in a cane thicket along Clear Creek. In the meantime, the Washington Artillery "swung far to the right and rear with Bate's infantry, but soon became separated." General Bate then ordered First Lieutenant Joseph Adolphe Chalaron to take a section of artillery, pieces 3 and 4, to "go forward to the skirmish line 'to harass the enemy with artillery shots as they crossed the bridge.'" Chalaron found that the bridge that he was to fire upon was at a point on the creek where there was a very "pronounced curve (in the shape of a shoe), the bridge being at the point of the shoe. Our position was at the heel." According to Private Philip Daingerfield Stephenson, the two guns were put into battery near a road "in a wood to the left side of a tobacco barn with an opening in front of us reaching to the water's edge." Lieutenant Chalaron put Sergeant Thomas C. Allen and piece 4 next to the barn, and piece 3 to the left and rear of piece 4 where they could see the flags of the "enemy infantry in close order. For a while after opening my guns," Chalaron continued, "I had some sport" with the Yankee column, and, as Corporal Oscar A. Legare, a gunner on piece 3 rejoiced, they "shot with telling effect and was highly elated."[26]

Before Chalaron's guns could do any more damage, a shell came crashing in nearby from across Peachtree Creek. "The enemy were on the opposite bank which was high, a naked red clay bank.... We did not know they were there until a shot from a masked battery revealed it.... We could see nothing but their smoke when they fired." Stephenson thought that the Federal battery was less than a quarter of a mile away, while Chalaron believed that they were at least three times that distance. While the Confederate artillerists debated the distance, in the meantime, "within two discharges, the enemy had determined our range...it was an unequal fight.... They could see every man of us." Moreover,

---

[25] Nathaniel Chearis Hughes, Jr., *The Pride of the Confederate Artillery, The Washington Artillery in the Army of Tennessee* (Baton Rouge: Louisiana State Press, 1997) 1–6, 13, 196.

[26] Hughes, *The Washington Artillery*, 196–97; Philip Daingerfield Stephenson, *Civil War Memoir*, 214–15.

the Yankees had some infantry posted as skirmishers who had also begun peppering away at the artillerists. Private Stephenson remembered, Private William F. Tutt, "who rammed and sponged, and I, who loaded, found it certain death to stand up. So we crouched by the muzzle of our gun on either side, loading it in that position."[27]

It was futile to remain. Lieutenant Chalaron gave the order to withdraw, and piece 4 limbered up, and, under Sergeant Tom Allen's direction, prepared to withdraw. Meanwhile, Corporal Oscar Legare shouted to Chalaron "that he had a load in his gun…and he had dead range and begged to be allowed to fire. I yielded." Lamented Chalaron, "Oscar Legare hurried and sighted the piece and gave the command to fire. The friction pin, however, failed. Number Four [the person assigned to bring the pin] rushed to insert another and was about to jerk the lanyard when Oscar 'stopped him.'" Oscar "wanted to make absolutely sure of the shot, so he leaned forward, carefully 'resighted the piece.'"[28] Just then "bright discharges" could be seen from across the creek. "An instant later a round of spherical case struck Piece Three about a foot from Oscar's head, 'dug a deep groove in the gun and exploded immediately.'" Corporal Oscar Lagare was killed instantly while Private Charles R. Percy was mortally wounded. "Charlie Percy [had been] crouching close behind Oscar, manning the trail of the piece…. Alas, the two boys were torn to pieces, from the waist up. We found long strips of flesh high up on the trees behind them."[29]

Lieutenant Chalaron decried, "Never again did I yield to requests for any delay in executing orders & I had many such demands for last. After gently placing the remains of the dead and dying on their limbers, the section then withdrew, "humiliated at the thought of withdrawing under fire and saddened at the great loss we had sustained." Stephenson recalled the sad departure as the section

> …threw down a fence skirting the road on our right (as we retreated) and faced to the front again. Tearing at great speed through the forest, we made for sounds of battle to our left front. Evidences of strife were all about us, dead and wounded men and horses, upturned limber chests, etc.… We seemed to be by ourselves ["strangely isolated"]—no infantry support whatever, just out in the woods in the hottest kind of contest. We were of

---

[27] Stephenson, *Civil War Memoir*, 214–15; Hughes, *The Washington Artillery*, 197.
[28] Hughes, *The Washington Artillery*, 198; Stephenson, *Civil War Memoir*, 214–15.
[29] Hughes, *The Washington Artillery*, 198; Stephenson, *Civil War Memoir*, 214–15.

little use at this new position. The day was almost gone, and the fighting about us over when we got there. Night soon brought cessation.[30]

Unable to help Bate's division in the cane thicket, Captain Slocumb's battery had to wait until Bate redirected his line toward the west and northwest, instead of to the north. By the time Bate's division got into position, his men were already under attack from the now waiting Yankees. Moreover, Walker's division had already been beaten back. Eager to provide covering fire for Bate's men, Slocumb and his men pushed their four guns into the woods southeast of the Federal line. Not able to get into a good firing position, the battery was exposed to a raking fire from the guns and small arms fire from the ridge above them. Thus, the Washington Artillery lost one killed and four wounded, two mortally, in the day's futile action.[31]

After the battle, Hardee's men withdrew to the defenses encircling Atlanta from the northeast side. Lumsden's Alabama Battery, which was not engaged at Peach Tree Creek, covered the defenses at what is now Piedmont Park, but soon withdrew further south to a line along North Avenue just east of Piedmont Avenue. According to two of its veterans, George Little and James R. Maxwell, "after the battle of Peachtree Creek, with his [Howard's and Schofield's] entrenchments forming quite an angle in our front, some 800 yards away, but his lines stretched from that angle almost perpendicularly away from us toward the left." In other words, Lumsden's battery covered Atlanta from the northeast corner of her defenses and there faced Schofield's Army of the Ohio, or XXIII Corps to their right, or east; and to their left, or north, they faced Howard's IV Corps, which had closed the ring on the city from the north.[32]

General Howard, using reports from his subordinates, described Hardee's final attempt to renew the assault as the late afternoon sun began to set. "The last strong effort made by the Confederates in this engagement took place on Hardee's right. It was evidently Bate's Division, supported by Walker, which was making the final effort to turn the flank of the Army of the Cumberland." The assault Howard witnessed was the late flanking move by Bate's division as

---

[30] C. G. Johnsen to J. Cecil Legare, 20 July 1864, Chalaron Papers; Hughes, *The Washington Artillery*, 198; Stephenson, *Civil War Memoir*, 214–15.
[31] Hughes, *The Washington Artillery*, 198; Stephenson, *Civil War Memoir*, 214–15; http://www.geocities.com/heartland/woods/3501/aproud.htm.
[32] George Little and James R. Maxwell, *A History of Lumsden's Battery, C.S.A.* (Tuscaloosa AL: R. E. Rhodes Chapter, United Daughters of the Confederacy, 2002) 47; William R. Scaife, *The Campaign for Atlanta* (Atlanta: self-published, 1993) 127–28, 130a, 185.

previously explained. "It was an effort to take Newton in reverse through the gap between my Divisions. Thomas…hastened Ward's artillery to the proper spot near Newton's bridge where it could be most effective to sweep the Clear Creek bottom and the entangled woods that bordered it."[33]

Howard continued, "Not only artillery but all the cannon that belonged to Newton's Division was ranged in order, and began and followed up with terrible discharges, using solid shot, shells, and canister, their brisk fire, beginning just as the Confederate brigades emerged from the shelter of the woods and were aiming to cross the Peach Tree Creek itself. This artillery fire," explained Howard, "combined with all the oblique fire that Newton could bring to bear, broke up the assaulting columns and rendered all attempts to turn Thomas' position futile."

Bate's men were finally moving in the right direction and, coming out of the cane thicket, sought to cross the creek and sweep the Federal flank and rear, a move that should have been made three hours earlier. To support Bate's and Cleburne's planned attack, Hardee and Stewart had ordered another attack along the rest of the line. According to Howard, "While this was going on [Bate's flank attack], there was again a renewed supporting effort put forth by all the Confederate Divisions, from Walker's right [actually Cleburne's men along today's Palisades Road] to French [west of Howell Mill Road], to sustain their attack, but," the Federal commander retorted, "Thomas' men from Newton to Palmer's center were still watching, and easily stopped and drove back the advancing lines."[34]

After the battle, a number of dead and maimed horses were found laying along the Buckhead Road and in and around the outer trenches on Atlanta's northern defensive works. Hardee's corps withdrew into these works on the evening of 20 July after recovering their dead and wounded men. Cleburne's division had already been detached and sent through Atlanta to defend an important hill east of the city. A. J. Neal of Hoxton's Florida Battery called the "Marion Light Artillery," wrote to his mother on 23 July, "My horse received a wound in the fight of the 20th, as I was riding at the head of the battery, which came near disabling him, I intend in future to ride a battery horse in battle, for it is more trouble to get good horses than ever."[35] The number of dead animals

---

[33] Howard, *Autobiography*, 619.

[34] Ibid., 619.

[35] A. J. Neal to mother 23 July 1864; Mills Lane, ed., *"Dear Mother: Don't Grieve about Me. If I Get Killed, I'll Only Be Dead": Letters from Georgia Soldiers in the Civil War* (Savannah GA: Beehive Press, 1977) 321.

was so great around the Buck Head Road area that Quartermaster Sergeant James Freeman Brown of the 66th Georgia was recommended for detail collecting horse and mule hides.

While the defeated Confederates were salvaging dead animal skins, the Federals were celebrating. For John Newton and his undersized division, it had been a glorious victory. Colonel Opdycke wrote his wife on 23 July, three days after the battle, that "we are all feeling much elated with our success. Our Division and Hooker's Corps had a splendid victory on the 20th. I never have seen the dead rebels lie so thickly strewn upon the ground, since the battle of Shiloh." As for the Federal officers' opinion of the new Southern commander's performance in his first battle at the helm, Opdycke wrote, "General Howard and the regular officers say that Hood will soon be in a 'muddle.' It is fortunate for us that Johnston was relieved by Hood." Opdycke added, "Hood's maiden voyage is unfortunate for his government, but I hope he will never do better." Much credit for the success of his division was due to General Newton. However, Opdycke offered a view held by many in Newton's ranks. "General Newton drinks hard, I have seen him very tipsy when trying to direct his troops in the face of the enemy; his division succeeds in spite of him, not from any merit of his." Newton's tiny division was only at a strength of some 3,200 men at the time of the battle, but only some 2,700 effectives were present on the field or south of the creek during the action, according to its commander. Newton's division had "lost more heavily than any other in the army" earlier during the campaign.[36]

According to a Northern correspondent, "In twenty minutes—no more—the rebel columns were routed and flying back to the forests from which they came forth, with an almost complete loss of organization. It was the last seen of them in that portion of the field," he added, "and the stirring cheers that went up from Newton's men were the charmed peroration of the history made by the unfaltering lads in blue upon that field. 'Wasn't it dusty?' exclaimed General Newton, as he came riding back, his face aglow with triumph and his horse laboring for breath." Toward the end of the day and just before dusk covered the field that would mercifully end the bloodshed, a Rebel surgeon drove up Buckhead Road "into Kimball's lines with an ambulance and a brace of

---

[36] Emerson Opdycke to to wife Lucy, 21 July 1864 in Glenn V. Longacre and John E. Haas, eds., *"To Battle for God & the Right": The Civil War Letters of Emerson Opdycke* (Champaign: University of Illinois Press, 2007) 202–203; G. P. Putnam, "How We Fight in Atlanta," in Frank Moore, ed., *Rebellion Record. A Diary of American Events*, vol. 11(New York: D. Van Nostrand Co., 1868) 249.

splendid mules." The unsuspecting physician inquired of a Federal soldier where had he been captured when he was rudely informed that he was the one who was now "captured." The Southern doctor "could hardly credit his senses when he found the brogan on the other foot."[37]

Most of the casualties in Hardee's corps had been sustained in Walker's division along the Buck Head Road and in the woods east of the road below today's Brighton Road, and also in Maney's division west of Buck Head Road along Collier Road and Old Montgomery Ferry Road near today's Piedmont Hospital. Walker had lost 284 men while Maney lost 277 men. Maney's division suffered only 30 fatalities while losing 247 men wounded. There were no men lost to capture among Maney's Tennesseans, indicating that his division failed to reach the Federal works. Moreover, the unusually low percentage of fatal casualties, about 10 percent, instead of the customary 16–20 percent, reflects that Maney's division fought the Federals at some distance.

In Walker's division, 75 men were killed out of the 282 men lost, with 59 men killed out of 213 lost in Stevens's brigade. Walker's division sustained 26.6 percent in fatal casualties while another 176 men were wounded. Also, Walker's division lost thirty-nine men to capture of which six were included among the wounded with thirty-three captured in Stevens's brigade alone. While Walker's men suffered an unusually high percentage of fatal casualties, they had failed to dislodge or penetrate the Federal position except briefly near Buck Head Road, where portions of Stevens's and brigade struck the Federal works.[38]

In Gist's brigade, sixty-three additional losses were sustained in the 24th South Carolina, which was detached and fought with O'Neal's brigade in Walthall's division during the Peach Tree Creek assault. Also, some fifteen men were lost from the 46th Georgia on 19 July 1864. Therefore, while only 25 men became casualties during Gist's portion of the attack at Peach Tree Creek, his brigade lost some 103 men in two days' fighting. In Stevens's brigade, 1 man was killed and 1 was captured on 19 July, making his total losses for the Peach Tree Creek fighting 215.

Hardee's infantry suffered for his unsuccessful assault along Buck Head Road: Walker's division, 284 men; Maney's division, 277 men; Bate's division,

---

[37] Nostrand, "How We Fight in Atlanta," in Moore, ed., *Rebellion Record*, 11:251.

[38] Compiled Service Records Micro film rolls-341-46, Mississippi Department of Archives and History, Jackson MS; Lillian Henderson, ed., *Georgia Confederate Pension and Record Office. Roster of the Confederate Soldiers of Georgia, 1861–1865*, 7 vols. (Hapeville GA: Longino & Porter, 1955–1958) vols. 1–6.

19 men lost, including 3 killed; and Cleburne's division, 69 men lost, including 16 killed. In the artillery units deployed in Hardee's corps, ten men were lost with three killed. Altogether, Hardee lost some 659 men, of which 127 were killed, or 19 percent, roughly one in five. One biographer of those Tennessee troops who served under Hardee has suggested that Hardee lost a thousand men at Peach Tree Creek, a figure that has been widely regarded as accurate, although there have never been any calculations to support the claim. The casualties demonstrate that only a portion of Hardee's forces, about half of Stevens's brigade, engaged the Federal lines in any meaningful manner, and only Stevens's brigade and two of Maney's brigades sustained significant losses. Thus, a much more accurate figure for Hardee's total losses sustained during his assault are 659 with 127 men killed and 44 captured.[39]

Part of the story of Peach Tree Creek is what happened to Hardee and his men and why they failed despite having a golden opportunity. Proving the number of casualties, their nature, and the units that sustained them helps to answer these questions and solve some mysteries about the battle. Moreover, analysis of casualty figures and units engaged helps to prove or disprove allegations that have been made about Hardee and his subordinates at Peach Tree Creek for failing to follow Hood's orders to risk an all-out offensive. The evidence tends to support the conclusion that while Old Reliable did give orders to advance, he failed to deliver a decisive attack against the enemy, and he apparently failed to relay the intent of Hood's order to make a determined advance. Any suggestion that he did relay the importance of the attack belies the facts. Hardee's entire corps lost less men than Featherston's lone Mississippi brigade despite having nearly twenty times more men for the assault.

Sometime after the battle during the siege of Atlanta, Hood had a conversation with General Cleburne about the failures at Peach Tree Creek and the Battle of Atlanta that occurred on 22 July. During their visit, Cleburne explained that Hardee had instructed him prior to launching his attack at Peach Tree Creek to "be on the lookout for [enemy] breastworks." Hood added that Cleburne looked surprised when learning of Hood's actual plans for the battle. It seemed to Hood that Cleburne had not received the intent of his orders for a strong offensive that day by Hardee.[40]

---

[39] John Berrien Lindsley, ed., *Military Annals of Tennessee, Confederate*, 2 vols. (Wilmington NC: Broadfoot Publishing Company, 1995) 1:100.

[40] John Bell Hood, *Advance & Retreat* (1880; repr., New York: Da Capo Press, 1993) 186. Hood unfairly adds that it is likely that Hardee gave the same instructions for caution to each of his four division commanders.

The Battle of Peach Tree Creek

Hardee had some 17,973 infantry, plus another 1,201 men in the artillery, and 287 men in his staff and escort, for a total of 19,461 men available for the assault in 14 brigades. In contrast, Stewart had only some 4,620 men in 4 assaulting and 3 supporting brigades during the battle. With 659 men lost out of the some 19,500 present, Hardee's corps sustained about 3 percent casualties at Peach Tree Creek, as compared to Stewart's corps, which would lose 1,529 out of the 4,620 men who participated in the attack, or 35 percent total casualties.[41]

Startingly, the 1st Georgia Confederate Infantry Regiment (which lost 90 men) and the 66th Georgia Infantry Regiment (which lost 81 men) of Stevens's brigade suffered 171 casualties out of the 284 men lost in Walker's division, or 60 percent of the division's losses despite being only 2 out of the 17 regiments in the division's attack. These two Georgia regiments, the first and the last numbered units, made the assault from the left of Stevens's brigade along Buckhead Road.

Captain I. A. Buck, adjutant general for General Cleburne, explained that the delay of the attack from 1:00 P.M. until 4:00 P.M. was fatal to the Confederate plans at Peach Tree Creek: "So much time had been lost between the intended and actual hour of advance, that the Armies of the Cumberland and Ohio had meanwhile crossed and fortified," explained the Rebel captain, "so that the attack proposed upon unprotected troops while crossing, was converted into an assault upon a strongly entrenched position—and failed." Buck observed that Walker's division had been "badly cut up and forced to retire before powerful artillery, massed by Thomas upon the north side of the creek."[42]

While Buck inaccurately adds the Army of the Ohio in his description of the failures at Peach Tree Creek by Hardee's corps, his general summation was accurate enough. The failure to attack at 1:00 P.M. when Newton's division had not yet secured the heights at the Collier house, and when the bridge over Peach Tree Creek had not yet been completed that allowed the Federal artillery to cross to the south bank and deploy, coupled with the failure to perform a reconnaissance of the ground before the charge and the subsequent failure to coordinate the assault by his division and brigade commanders, resulted in a complete failure by Hardee and his corps to achieve the task assigned to them at Peach Tree Creek.

Historian Albert Castel adroitly explains that the reason Hardee failed is because his attack "was made blindly, was uncoordinated, employed only a

---

[41] *OR*, ser. 1, vol. 38, serial 74, pp. 661, 679–80.

[42] Buck, "Cleburne's Division at Atlanta," 2.

third of his available force, and in the case of the Tennesseans [Maney's division] was delivered in a half-hearted fashion that wasted any chance of turning Newton's right or Ward's left." Castel points out that because there was no reconnaissance performed prior to the attack, Bate's division was "virtually eliminat[ed]" from the battle; the failure to properly coordinate the attack, he reasons, caused Stevens and Gist to attack independently, resulting in such losses that chilled any further strong efforts by other units. "These failures," argues Castel, "far more than the rudimentary breastworks of Kimball's and Blake's troops, explain why Newton was able to repulse so easily Hardee's much stronger force while losing a mere 102 men [actually 107]."[43]

Hardee's piecemeal attack had failed to reconnoiter or to consider the terrain. In contrast, Newton's division had taken and fortified the all-important high ground prior to the surprise Confederate charge. With portions of Hardee's uncoordinated and un-reconnoitered attack blunted against the walls of Newton's lines, wrecking the two Georgia Regiments of Stevens's brigade and thinning the ranks in other supporting units, one soldier who witnessed the scene wrote:

> Hood thought that he would strike while the iron was hot, and while it could be hammered into shape, and make the Yankees believe that it was the powerful arm of old Joe that was wielding the sledge.
>
> But he was like the fellow who took a piece of iron to the shop, intending to make him an ax. After working for some time and failing, he concluded he would make him a wedge, and, failing in this, said "I'll make a skeow." So he heats the iron red-hot and drops it into the slack-tub, and it went s-k-e-o-w, bubble, bubble, s-k-e-o-w, bust.[44]

---

[43] Scaife, *The Campaign for Atlanta*, 382.

[44] Sam R. Watkins, *Co. Aytch* (Columbia TN: Times Printing Company, 1882) 173. Hardee's Corps was withdrawn at dusk and returned to their trenches that they had occupied prior to the assault. Bate's division withdrew to today's northern limits of Piedmont Park where a marker identifies a portion of this division's trench line that remains. To Bate's left, Walker's division stretched across the White Columns Plantation. A portion of these works is also identified by a marker in front of the property. Maney's division occupied the line to the left of Walker's men that ran across the ground where Interstate I-75 and Interstate I-85 intersect and form the Downtown Connector. To Maney's left, Loring's division held the line along the heights just west of the interstate, from today's Atlantic Station and over a hill that Atlanta City Planner and Historian Wilbur G. Kurtz aptly named Loring Heights.

IT WAS THE SADDEST DAY I EVER SAW

> I have just ridden along our division front, also Hooker's. The slaughter was severe: dead rebels lie thickly strewn upon the ground. Our casualties were light. Hooker thinks his losses are heavy, but I saw only seven dead of his men, along a front where I counted 150 rebels.[1]

One Northern newspaper correspondent who had covered the war for four years would write that he had never seen the dead strewn more thickly than what he saw on the ridge above and around the Collier Mill. A Federal soldier from the 5th Connecticut in Knipe's brigade said that 20 July was "the saddest day I ever saw," and that it was "sickening" to see the "suffereing & dying conditions of the poor fellows that lay there wounded in every part of the body, some crazy & raving.... Doctors were busy cutting off limbs and piling them in heaps to be carried off and buried, while the stench was horrible."[2]

Physicians were not immune to the *hors de combat*, however. One such surgeon who continued to care for the wounded and dying of his regiment while remaining in harm's way was A. J. Gilson, assistant surgeon of the 5th Connecticut in Knipe's brigade. Gilson "was under fire all through the fight and was seen to carry off wounded men from the field under the most galling fire we had yet seen upon the bare field." Gilson was the only surgeon from Knipe's brigade on the field and he dressed every wounded soldier from his regiment before being carried off the field after suffering from his own wounding.[3]

Among the legends that grew out of the Peach Tree Creek fighting, "it was said that after this battle an Irishman who had come to this country to search for a brother and had years before given up the unavailing search, being here sent out to bury the dead, found his brother among them." In another instance, "a German, serving as a nurse in a hospital, had placed in his charge his own

---

[1] Opdycke to wife Lucy, 21 July 1864.

[2] Cited in Albert Castel, *Decision in the West: The Atlanta Campaign of 1864* (Lawrence: University Press of Kansas, 1992) 380.

[3] Edwin E. Marvin, *The Fifth Regiment Connecticut Volunteers, A History* (Hartford CT: Press of Wiley, Waterman & Eaton, 1889) 330.

brother whom he had left a babe in the fatherland." Another tragic story comes from a father serving in Thomas's Army of the Cumberland: "A Union soldier shot down the leading Confederate in a charge, and found that it was his own son who fell dead at his feet."[4]

There were at least two recorded instances of women who served with the Confederate army during the battle. According to a Federal orderly who was captured during the battle, "A female major rode up and saluted the general. She was… wearing a cap with feathers and gold lace, flowing pants, a long velvet coat that reached just below her hips, fastened with a crimson sash and partly open at the bosom." Private Frederick N. Kollock of Company B, 29th Pennsylvania from Philadelphia, recorded in his diary, "Everything is quiet except an occasional shot from the pickets, weather very warm, among the prisoners of yesterday were two females in uniform."[5]

Details of the battle reached Macon on 22 July, as a "special correspondence from the Memphis Appeal" wrote "From the Front," on the day of the battle: "the men swept forward with a yell such as only a rebel can give, and the enemy's skirmishers were soon encountered and driven back upon the main line, where temporary works had been erected. Our men never faltered," explained the reporter, "but dashed forward through the leaden rain and drove the enemy in disorder from the works, capturing a number of prisoners." The correspondent related "that up to this hour the enemy are steadily and surely being driven back, as with the exception of Walker's front, where no trouble seems to have occurred, they have been driven across the creek fully one mile on an average of the whole line." The journalist was exaggerating, of course, for except for stragglers, "shirkers" and "deadheads," those who always shirked their responsibilities or broke for the rear at the first sign of trouble, and the non-combatants, cooks, teamsters, and quartermasters, and a few men in Newton's division who were trapped by the approach of Bate's division and Mercer's brigade, no one ran to the north side of Peach Tree Creek during the conflict. It is revealing, however, that the writer pointed to Walker's front as being the lone exception to the alleged flight by the Yankees "fully one mile on an average."[6]

The correspondent continued, "Prisoners are coming in in large squads and as I write a party of about two hundred has just arrived, and I understand that

---

[4] Ibid., 330.

[5] Richard Hall, *Patriots in Disguise* (New York: Marlowe & Company, 1994) 162; http://us.geocities.com/womansoldier/21st.cent.htm (3 April 2008); Kollock, 8.

[6] "From the Front," *Macon* [GA] *Daily Telegraph*, 22 July 1864, 1.

The Battle of Peach Tree Creek

others are on the way. The whole number brought in up to the present writing is, I suppose, about 800, although it is difficult to form an estimate at a point where they are hastily collected and being rapidly sent to the rear." Actually, Northern losses to capture at Peach Tree Creek did not exceed 300, with virtually all of them coming from the exposed right flank of Geary's division to elements of Scott's and O'Neal's brigades. There, Geary admitted to losing 165 men as portions of Candy's and Jones's brigades were routed in the woods south of today's Collier Road near Northside Drive. Of this number, some thirty-eight men from the 33rd New Jersey were lost to Scott's brigade. General O'Neal reported that his brigade captured 293 of the enemy, while to his left front Williams's division counted only 13 men lost to capture to O'Neal's and Reynolds's men.[7]

The Macon readers were interested to learn that, according to the special correspondent, "Our loss, so far as I can ascertain, has been comparatively small, as I have not seen more than twenty ambulances laden with wounded passing to the rear." Assuming that 6 to 10 wounded were carried per ambulance, then only some 120 to 200 Confederates were wounded. The writer had neglected to count the number of killed, seriously wounded and left on the field, and captured men at Peach Tree Creek, which accounted for a great number of the Confederate losses.[8]

One unexpected result after the Battle of Peach Tree Creek was the resignation of General Hooker. On the morning of 21 July, Sherman and Thomas visited the battlefield together in front of the XX Corps and met with "Fighting Joe" Hooker at his headquarters. Hooker spoke with pardonable pride of what his men had done, mentioning his heavy losses. To this Sherman flippantly snapped: 'Oh, most of 'em will be back in a day or two,'" implying that many of Hooker's men had run away during the fighting. "Hooker's reaction to this unwarranted implication of desertion is not recorded, but it so infuriated Lieutenant Colonel C. H. Asmussen, the Assistant Inspector General of the Corps, that he begged a fellow officer for a pistol that he might shoot the 'God-damned son of a bitch.'"[9] Despite Sherman's popinjay attitude, Hooker had his dignity and reputation to defend.

---

[7] "From the Front," *Macon* [GA] *Daily Telegraph*, 22 July 1864; United States War Department, comp., *Official Records of the Union and Confederate Armies in the War of the Rebellion*, 128 vols. (Washington, DC: Government Printing Office, 1880–1901) ser. 1, vol. 38, pt. 2, serial 73, pp. 141, 215 (hereafter *OR*); *OR*, ser. 1, vol. 38, pt. 3, serial 74, p. 942.

[8] "From the Front," *Macon* [GA] *Daily Telegraph*, 22 July 1864.

[9] Walter H. Hebert, *Fighting Joe Hooker* (Lincoln: University of Nebraska Press, 1999)

Hood's First Sortie, 20 July 1864

It was in this climate after the battle of Peach Tree Creek that, when the beloved commander of the Army of the Tennessee, James B. McPherson, was killed on 22 July during the Battle of Atlanta and Sherman passed up Hooker and appointed Major General Oliver Otis Howard to command on 27 July. When Hooker discovered that he had been superseded, it was too much for him to take. He wrote his superior, Major General Thomas, tendering his resignation, adding "I have just learned that Major General Howard, my junior, has been assigned to the command of the Army of the Tennessee. If this is the case I request that I may be relieved from duty with this army. Justice and self-respect alike," he added, "require my removal from an army in which rank and service are ignored."[10]

Apparently, Hooker had counted on his high favor with President Lincoln to override Sherman's appointment of Howard and to place Hooker in command of the Army of the Tennessee, but Sherman would not back down and Lincoln would not risk losing Sherman over Hooker. While the *Official Records* are ominously silent on the strained correspondence between Sherman and the president on this issue, one dispatch from Sherman to General Henry Halleck at the War Department in Washington sent the same day as Hooker tendered his letter of resignation reveals Sherman's unwillingness to yield: "All are well pleased with General Howard's appointment but General Logan and Hooker.... General Hooker is offended because he thinks he is entitled to the command. I must be honest and say he is not qualified or suited to it. He talks of quitting.... I shall not object. He is not indispensable to our success. He is welcome to my place if the President awards it, but I cannot name him to so important a command as the Army of the Tennessee."[11]

In his memoirs, Grant wrote poignantly about old "Fighting Joe" Hooker: "I...regarded him as a dangerous man. He was not subordinate to his superiors. He was ambitious to the extent of caring nothing for the rights of others. His disposition was, when engaged in battle, to get detached from the main body of the army and exercise," according to Grant, "a separate command, gathering to his standard all he could of his juniors." If the pompous Hooker had shown restraint, he could have enjoyed the credit of capturing Atlanta, for just forty days later, his XX Corps would receive that honor. Sherman subsequently wrote Halleck on 4 September, just three days after the Gate City had fallen, "Hooker

---

283.

[10] Ibid., p. 285; *OR*, ser. 1, vol. 38, pt. 5, serial 76, p. 272.

[11] *OR*, ser. 1, vol. 38, pt. 5, serial 76, p. 286; *OR*, ser. 1, vol. 38, pt. 5, serial 76, p. 272.

was a fool. Had he staid a couple of weeks he could have marched into Atlanta and claimed all the honors."[12]

On 29 July, Hooker bade his farewell to the men of the XX Corps by riding around the lines of his command. One of the soldiers, Harvey Reid of Shannon, Illinois, and a student at the University of Wisconsin in Madison before the war, a clerk for the 22nd Wisconsin, noted, "He seemed much affected by the parting. As he passed the line of the 33rd Massachusetts he stopped and shook hands with the Colonel and several of the Captains with that clinging, convulsive grasp that so forcibly expresses sorrow at parting." Reid had a keen eye and sharp pen. He revealed one of Fighting Joe's problems in his next lines: "But it was really sad to see the ravages the demon, *alcohol*, has made in his noble countenance. For now that he has gone, it will do no harm to tell you, what has been a common subject of conversation in his Corps, that the gifted, world famed, General Hooker is almost a drunkard and I believe that herein lies the secret of the hesitancy to intrust him with a High Command. His old soldiers say that he lost the battle of Chancellorsville by being grossly intoxicated." The Wisconsin clerk added, "But still, he is unquestionably a superior Corps commander, his troops have the utmost unbounded confidence in him and all are sorry to part with him."[13] Hooker had fought well at Peach Tree Creek, and, as it turned out, the battle was his swan song.

After the battle, the tired, but jubilant Yankees, worked well into the night creating earthworks and strengthening their lines in the event that the Rebels renewed their attack. When they had finished and settled down it was near midnight. Then, the men took time to thoroughly clean their guns and get them into working order. "After midnight we lay down on our arms, within hearing distance of the groans of the wounded and dying on the field." Thomas's Army of the Cumberland spent 21 July burying the dead and tending to the wounded of both sides. "It was a big job, requiring a heavy detail during the forenoon to complete it." In McCook's brigade, of Palmer's XIV Corps, which had defended the western-most point of the Confederate assault, "The following morning the burrying began which took all day, there were so many of them [Rebel dead]."[14]

---

[12] Hebert, *Fighting Joe Hooker*, 286; Grant, Ulysses S., Personal Memoirs of U. S. Grant, 2:539; *OR,* ser. 1, vol. 38, pt. 5, serial 76, p. 793.

[13] Harvey Reid, *Uncommon Soldiers: Harvey Reid and the 22nd Wisconsin March with Sherman*, ed. Frank L. Byrne (Knoxville: University of Tennessee Press, 2001) 175–76.

[14] W. H. Newlin, *The Preacher Regiment, 1862–65, History of the 73rd Illinois Volunteer Infantry* (Springfield: Regimental Reunion Association of Survivors of the 73rd

Hood's First Sortie, 20 July 1864

Colonel Opdycke of Bradley's 3rd Brigade in Newton division who had led the defense of the Federal left flank and pushed back Mercer's Georgia Brigade from reaching the Buckhead Road and cutting off the Yankees, took time out the next day to ride over to view the carnage that resulted along Hooker's XX Corps line. "I have just ridden along our division front, also Hooker's. The slaughter was severe: dead rebels lie thickly strewn upon the ground. Our casualties were light. Hooker thinks his losses are heavy, but I saw only seven dead of his men, along a front where I counted 150 rebels." Opdycke was apparently unaware that many of Hooker's men had already been either buried or removed from the front by midday on 21 July, and most of the Rebels were not buried until that evening or over the next several days. Also left in the wake of the battle was an artillery caisson that had become mired in the mud along the banks of Clear Creek where Mercer's and Gist's brigades had attacked Newton. Eighty years after the battle, Atlanta attorney Frank Bird recalled playing on the old caisson in the 1940s with his childhood friends before it was "discovered" and removed in the 1950s.[15]

On Friday, 22 July, as portions of Thomas's army advanced down Buckhead Road toward Atlanta, one Federal soldier recorded that they "passed a nice, large, bay horse, lying dead in the road, which was said to have been the rebel General Stephenson's [Stevens]. It was conceded by the enemy that [Stevens] was killed. The Atlanta papers contained this admission." Federal reports included the rumors that generals Featherstone, Long, Pettis, and Stevens had been killed. Featherston was very much alive, while Long and "Pettis" had not participated in the attack, there being no General Long present, and General Edmund W. Pettus was occupied with commanding a brigade in Hood's old corps east of Atlanta at the time.[16]

After Sherman's army left Atlanta to begin its March to the Sea in November, James Bell, a fifteen-year-old boy from Dalton, Georgia, whose family had moved to Atlanta, visited the Peach Tree Creek Battlefield where he had "hunted and fished in Peachtree Creek valley prior to that summer." It was the first time since July that Bell had been able to return to the war-torn battlefield. There, Bell "saw the graves of the soldiers—huge banks of earth

---

Illinois Infantry Volunteers, 1890) 326; John Henry Otto, *Memoirs of a Dutch Mudsill*, ed. David Gould and James B. Kennedy (Kent OH: Kent State University Press, 2004) 270.

[15] Opdycke to wife Lucy, 21 July 1864, *To Battle for God and the Right*, 202–203; Bird, Frank, interview with author by phone, 15 May 2008.

[16] Newlin, *The Preacher Regiment*, 326; Otto, *Memoirs of a Dutch Mudsill*, 270; William R. Scaife, *The Campaign for Atlanta* (Atlanta: self-published, 1993) 180.

enclosed in rail pens—along Collier Road." Some of these graves were visible in the photograph taken months after the battle by George Barnard.[17]

Federal General John Geary, a veteran of Gettysburg and many other terrible battlefields of the war would state in his report that his men faced that day some five times their number and that he estimated the Confederate losses in his division's front was at least 2,500 men. General William T. Ward, also a veteran of the Army of Potomac and many Eastern Theater battles, estimated that there were 500 Rebels killed in front of his division, 2,500 wounded and 246 taken prisoner. If these claims were true, then every man in Featherston's brigade (1,230 Mississippians) that opposed Ward's division (some 5,091 strong), would have had to have been counted over twice each just to add up to Ward's estimate, let alone the number who Ward believed attacked him, and the Confederates opposing Geary (who had about 5,600 men) would have had to have been multiplied by at least ten times to make up the "five times" the number of Geary's own division that he claims opposed him. While overestimating the enemy's strength as well as the casualties that were inflicted against them was commonplace during the war, it is yet remarkable that these generals would be so impressed with their attackers given the relative sparsity in the attacking columns. One Federal veteran in Ward's division even described the battle as "pluck and numbers. The rebs had the most men and we the pluck, we had only two lines of battle." As it turned out, the Confederates in this part of the field had only one line of battle in Stewart's corps.[18]

It was unheard of for an attacking unit to inflict greater casualties on the defenders, particularly late in the war. Featherston's initial assault was met on Collier Ridge by only a skirmish line consisting of Colonel Edward Bloodgood's 22nd Wisconsin and four companies of the 136th New York, about 300 men. The 1,230 attackers enjoyed at least a three-to-one superiority in the initial charge, which attributed to its success. Had Hardee's corps found and then assaulted the left flank of the Federal line, Hardee's great strength in numbers should have had a huge impact. This is what General Johnston, and later General Hood, had planned and desired. The exposed left flank of the

---

[17] Wilbur G. Kurtz, "What James Bell Told me About the Siege of Atlanta," 15 July 1935, pp. 1–5, Wilbur G. Kurtz Papers, MSS 130, Kenan Research Center, Atlanta History Center; George N. Barnard, *Photographic Views of Sherman's Campaign* (New York: Dover Publications, Inc., 1977) 34.

[18] *OR*, vol. 1, ser. 38, serial 73, pp. 138–41, 334–39; Jean M. Cate, ed., *"If I Live to Come Home,": The Civil War Letters of Sergeant John March Cate* (Pittsburgh: Dorrance Publishing Company, 1995) 196.

Federal line created just the kind of opportunity for General Hardee with his corps of nearly 20,000 men to attack it and roll it up and into Peach Tree Creek. Defending the left flank was just one Federal division, General Newton, with his undersized 2,700 man division of Howard's IV Corps.[19]

It is little wonder why Lieutenant General Stewart, major Generals French, Walthall, and Loring, and brigadier generals Featherston, Scott, O'Neal, and Reynolds all would subsequently lament that if General Hardee and his corps had vigorously assaulted the Federal works that day the way that they each had done, that the Battle of Peach Tree Creek would have had a much different history and the fate of Atlanta and the war could have been different. One survivor of the charge wrote, "Over rough ground, across a tortuous creek, through an open field, the enemy's artillery and small arms making fearful slaughter, these devoted men, undismayed, pressed on, and gained the goal. The works were taken, the enemy dislodged. But the triumph proved an empty shedding of blood, a vain sacrifice of human life."[20]

In the fight, Ward's division lost some 561 men while Geary's division lost another 476 men. In all, Sherman's armies would suffer about 2,167 casualties, over 10 percent of the almost 20,000 men who participated in the battle. Over half of Sherman's casualties at Peach Tree Creek, some 55 percent, were inflicted by just two Confederate brigades, Featherston and Scott, both of Loring's division. Featherston's brigade which confronted Ward, lost 679 out of the 1,230 men who made the assault, 55 percent of his force, making it the eighth highest loss by a Confederate brigade in the war by percentage. Scott's brigade, which opposed Geary's division, lost 446 out of the some 1,450 men in the attack. Loring's veterans, some 2,680 strong, had lost 1,099 men. Thus, Loring's division suffered a whopping 40.6 percent casualty rate in the bloody battle, one of the highest divisional casualty rates in the war.[21]

Walthall's division, which like Loring, had only two brigades (O'Neal and Reynolds) on the field of attack, lost an additional 429 men as it attacked Williams's division. Incredibly, his men inflicted 580 casualties in Williams's division. General Williams reported 119 killed, 458 wounded, and 3 missing in his division from the assault. Williams explained that "a little over two-thirds of

---

[19] *OR*, vol. 1, ser. 38, pt. 1, serial 72, p. 290.

[20] J. L. Power, 1864 scrapbook, Mississippi Department of Archives and History, Jackson, Mississippi.

[21] *Fox Regimental Losses in the American Civil War, 1861-1865* (Albany: Albany Publishing Co., 1889) 286–94; Burke Davis, "The Civil War, Strange and Fascinating Facts," www.civilwarhome.com/casualties.htm (15 May 2008).

my command received and rolled back the repeated assaults of a numerically superior and confident force of the enemy."[22]

In reality, Williams's division of 5,300 men had beaten back a force of only about 3,000 determined Rebels under Walthall after being bloodied in the process. While Williams celebrated the hard-fought victory, he lamented the loss of so many of his braves who had met Walthall's Rebels and had stood firm. Seth Williams was particularly saddened to learn of the mortal wounding, capture, and death of one of his staff officers, Captain E. H. Newcomb of the 61st Ohio the following day. On 21 July, "while on picket line—he fell into the hands of the enemy & died as we subsequently learned the same day. We discovered his grave beneath an ash tree a few yards from the Atlanta & Paces Ferry [Howell Mill] Road on the southeast side."[23]

Remarkably, four Confederate brigades, Featherston's, Scott's, O'Neal's, and Reynolds's, totaling only about 4,420 men, had taken on and, for a while, pushed back much of the Federal's XX Corps, a force of some 15,991 veteran troops, and inflicted 1,617 casualties upon them, or 10 percent, while losing 1,443 of its own, a staggering 33-percent loss among the four combined brigades. In fairness to Hooker's XX Corps, they were posted, in large part, without entrenchments at the time they were hit, and, due both to the terrain and to their deployment, were struck in the right flank in two of their divisions (Geary's and Williams's), and they were hit at a thin "skirmish line" that was in front of in one division (Ward's). The XX Corps was able to meet the initial surprise and setback with a counter-stroke that pushed back a determined foe and reestablished their lines. Nevertheless, the comparative fighting strengths of the opposing forces along Collier Ridge Road and the relative casualties suffered by them demonstrate the fierceness of the Army of Mississippi's attack on the XX Corps and tend to prove General Hood's long-argued position that aggressive and decisive action can rout a surprised foe (even one three or four times larger than it), particularly if made on the flank of the enemy.

General French, also of Stewart's corps, lost some 260 men in action that day in which his division had been ordered to "demonstrate" (or skirmish heavily) against the Yankees in their front to prevent them from reinforcing the Federal lines being assaulted by Loring and Walthall. French's men opposed portions of Palmer's XIV Corps. French had only two of his brigades involved

---

[22] *OR*, ser. 1, vol. 38, serial 73, p. 34.
[23] Robert M. Bunker, interview with author, 20 July 2009.

Hood's First Sortie, 20 July 1864

(Cockrell and Ector) in skirmishing to keep Palmer's corps occupied and prevent it from reinforcing Williams's division.[24]

Stewart's losses were approximately 1,657 men. There were also about twenty-eight men lost in the supporting Southern artillery units. In Hardee's corps, Captain Cuthbert H. Slocumb lost four men, with two men wounded and two men killed in the Washington Artillery, and Captain Evan P. Howell lost one man missing in the Georgia Light Artillery. Additionally, four more losses in Hardee's artillery were reported. In Stewart's corps, Captain Robert L. Barry's Lookout Battery from Chattanooga, Tennessee lost fifteen men, and Lieutenant Charles W. Lovelace commanding Selden's Alabama Battery saw one man killed and one wounded. Also, Major William C. Preston was killed while leading Selden's Battery into place on the Embry plantation on a knoll in front of the house. A present-day state historical marker is located near the site where Preston lost his life, the northwest corner of the intersection of Collier Road and Howell Mill Road.[25]

Adding Hardee's and Stewart's losses, the Confederates sustained some 2,598 men in 3 days of fighting below Peach Tree Creek, including 2,316 during the charge. Thus, General Hood's first assault cost the Southern Army about 2,316 men out of the some 20,000–24,000 who participated in the battle, or about 10 percent of the forces engaged. The next morning the Federal troops were engaged in carrying off the wounded and burying the dead. The Mississippians had been compelled to abandon the field and leave many of their comrades who had fallen to the Yankees to bear an uncertain fate. "For some time after the fighting was over I carried water to the wounded Confederate soldiers," explained W. H. Conner of the 33rd Indiana. "The loss on both sides was very great. I was in many fights but never saw more dead and wounded than I saw at Peach Tree Creek."[26] The countryside bore the scars of battle for years after the war. "Although the fight lasted less than one day," remembered Sarah Huff who had witnessed the fight from her mother's farm near Howell Mill Road, "the havoc wrought by its fury continued to show for more than a

---

[24] *OR*, vol. 1, ser. 38, serial 73, pp. 34, 138–41, 334–39, 369.

[25] Scaife, *The Campaign for Atlanta*, 88–91, 93; Nathaniel Cheairs Hughes, Jr., *The Pride of the Confederate Artillery, The Washington Artillery in the Army of Tennessee* (Baton Rouge: Louisiana State Press, 1997) 197–99; *Tennesseans in the Civil War, A Military History of Confederate and Union Units with Available Rosters of Personnel*, 2 vols. (Nashville: Civil War Centennial Commission, 1964–1965) 1:124.

[26] W. H. Conner to Dunbar Rowland (state historian), 20 October 1927, 33rd Mississippi vertical file, Mississippi Department of Archives and History, Jackson, Mississippi.

quarter of a century." One Federal officer from the 104th Illinois remarked, "fully half of Cos. A, B, C, D, & E...were killed, wounded, or dragged off to the rebel hells called prisons." The total Federal losses were approximately 2,167 men.[27]

One unusual casualty from the Battle of Peach Tree Creek came from a Federal soldier in Blake's brigade of Newton's division. Peter Sparks of the 40th Indiana sustained a double hernia during the action. According to Sparks, "I was detailed to carry ammunition a cross a branch, water waist deep, and it was hard to keep from slipping, and the severe strain caused my rupture on both sides. I was not relieved from duty, just worried it through till I got home at Lafayette, Indiana," when he had it repaired twenty years after the war.[28]

In a Federal hospital bed, Colonel Thomas Reynolds lay, his leg shattered from a painful wound from the battle. Considering amputation, the Northern doctors discussed the wound. The Federal colonel lay helpless as he awaited his fate. The native Irishman interrupted the council of surgeons, explaining that they could not amputate as it was not just any old leg, but that his was his "imported leg." It is not clear whether his exhortations influenced the Federal medical staff, but the surgery was called off and the Irishman kept his foreign limb.[29]

Some twenty years after the war, Federal general Richard W. Johnson, who commanded a division in Palmer's XIV Corps, visited Atlanta. While there, he had dinner with Captain Evan P. Howell who had commanded a Confederate artillery battery on Buckhead Road. During the course of the evening's conversation it was discovered that a shell purportedly fired from Howell's battery had wounded Johnson during the Georgia Campaign. "I am glad it did not kill you," said Howell. When the Federal general asked if the Southern captain, who had become the editor of the *Atlanta Constitution*, if he would like to have the shell back. Johnson had kept the shell as a memento of the fighting. "No indeed," replied the venerable Southerner. "I hope I shall never see another twelve-pound shell as long as I live."[30]

Commissary Sergeant Rufus Mead, of the 5th Connecticut in Knipe's brigade of General Williams's 1st Division of the XX Corps, said that 20 July

---

[27] Sarah Huff, "My 80 Years in Atlanta," 12, subject files, Atlanta History Center.

[28] http://sparksfamilytree.net/familytree/wga94.html (9 November 2008).

[29] Alfred J. Bollet, "The Truth About Civil War Surgery," *Civil War Times* 43/4 (October 2004): 27.

[30] R. W. Johnson, *A Soldier's Reminiscences in Peace and War* (Philadelphia: J. B. Lippincott Company, 1886) 279–80.

was "the saddest day I ever saw." The sergeant had seen the battlefield all along the front of the attack of Loring and Walthall's divisions and he saw the wounded of both sides being treated by Federal doctors. Rufus explained that it was "sickening" to look at "the suffereing [sic] and dying conditions of the poor fellows that lay there wounded in every part of the body, some crazy and ravins.... Doctors were busy cutting off limbs which were piled up in heaps to be carried off and buried, while the stench was horrible."[1]

With over 1,099 casualties out of just 2,680 engaged from the two brigades of Featherston and Scott, Loring's division had been decimated. Many of the casualties had been fatalities, while a high number of those wounded had also been captured, leaving Loring's division severely depleted for the remainder of the war. According to surgeon William Grinstead, surgeon in chief of Ward' 3rd Division, "There were 110 rebel wounded brought into [the] hospital." Grinstead added that "Six [Rebels] died the same night they came in, and some 30 subsequently prior to their transportation." Colonel James Wood recalled that his brigade buried 138 of the enemy's dead from behind and near their advanced line of battle.[2]

---

[1] Castel, *Decision in the West*, 380; Marvin, *The Fifth Regiment Connecticut*, 330.
[2] Castel, *Decision in the West*, 381; *OR*, vol. 1, ser. 38, pt. 2, serial 73, p. 337.

26

A NEGATIVE VICTORY PLAINLY WON

The plan of battle was a good one. Hardee was to gain the enemy's rear, swing to the left, taking their line in flank, while we attacked the line in front in echelon of brigades as the battle swept down the creek (from right to left). ...Gen. Loring's troops broke through the enemy's line of works. [Loring's men]... had to abandon the captured line by reason of the flank fire on them. The failure of Hardee deranged the plan of battle.[1]

Peach Tree Creek was a negative victory plainly won.[2]

Hood is a tragic figure. He is as pitiful as the desperate South during her death throws. He has become the face of butchery. After his deplorable decision to attack Federal works at Franklin, he has been castigated by many. After the war, when the survivors wrote their memoirs, Hood found himself hopelessly unable to defend his generalship during the Atlanta and Tennessee campaigns, and he vented with a painful, but heartfelt, response that became known as his *Advance and Retreat*. Hood should be condemned for his dismal mistake at Franklin. But, that day, 30 November 1864, would be four months away. He should not be condemned in the same fashion for his performance at Atlanta. Franklin was the only battle where Hood ordered a direct assault against prepared Federal works that included an awaiting enemy during his direction of the Army of Tennessee.

Peach Tree Creek was a surprise assault on a portion of an unsuspecting enemy who was in motion and vulnerable to attack as they attempted to cross a wide stream. The battles near Atlanta and Ezra Church that soon followed were attempts by Hood to launch surprise assaults against one flank and then the other. The Battle of Peach Tree Creek delivered some success for the

---

[1] Samuel G. French, *Two Wars* (1901; repr., Huntington WV: Blue Acorn Press, 1999) 218–19.

[2] "Atlanta July 20, 1864," *Savannah Republican*, 25 July 1864; Sam Davis Elliott, *Soldier of Tennessee, General Alexander P. Stewart and the Civil War in the West* (Baton Rouge: Louisiana State Press, 1999) 208.

Hood's First Sortie, 20 July 1864

Confederates, at least in Stewart's lines, and had Stewart's men attacked at full strength, the results could have been far more devastating to the Federals. As it was, the attacks created severe losses to Hooker's XX Corps. The Battle of Atlanta also delivered some success and promised even greater yields for the Rebel army, but again, uneven performance by Hood's subordinate officers and uncoordinated assaults coupled with a determined and timely response by McPherson's Army of the Tennessee staved off disaster for the blue coats.

Both attacks completely surprised Sherman and his generals but they should not have been surprises given the news that Hood's had been appointed as the new commander and the capture of elements from the two Rebel corps in front of General Thomas's army on the eve of the battle. Both attacks could have succeeded in driving one of Sherman's corps from the field. Both attacks did drive portions of two of Sherman's armies from the field. Both attacks forced Sherman to become more cautious. Both attacks reduced Sherman's combat strength and ability to wage offensive war, pushing Sherman to lay siege to the Gate City. Both attacks bought time for the doomed city and a chance for a reversal of her fortunes.

These are the only two examples that demonstrated Hood's offensive capabilities during the defense of the Gate City. Hood additionally conceived of a third assault on a part of Sherman's forces that resulted in the Confederate disaster at the Battle of Ezra Church where one of Hood's subordinates, General Stephen D. Lee, misread the Federal strength and misapplied Hood's instructions for the battle plan.[3] After the fall of Atlanta, Hood demonstrated considerable skill in eluding Sherman and causing great destruction in North Georgia, and, for a season, forced Sherman to chase him through the Northwest Georgia mountains. This maneuver was an imaginative attempt to shift the momentum of the war to the Confederates. Sherman and his legions which had long since held the momentum had lost it. Morale among many of Sherman's men sank as it appeared to many of them that the war was an endless cycle of conflict. Hood's decision to carry the war into Tennessee as winter approached,

---

[3] Hood desired to send Lee's corps out of the Atlanta defenses to block the Federal forces marching around the city to the west while screening Stewart's corps from view as Stewart's men prepared to make an assault on the unsuspecting Federal column from the west the next morning, 29 July 1864. Lee derailed Hood's plan by attacking the Federal column in front, causing the Federal troops to quickly file into defensive positions along the high ground that Lee was expected to reach on 28 July. Then Lee compounded it by continuing to send in additional units in piecemeal assaults against the Federal position. The result was the most lopsided Federal victory during the Atlanta Campaign.

was considered foolish by many, and genius by others. But desperate times call for desperate measures, and that is precisely what Hood was called upon by his president to do. Except for the grand mistake at Franklin and the disaster at Nashville that followed, any failures made by Hood during his six months of generalship over the Army of Tennessee can be laid at the feet of Jefferson Davis. After all, it was Davis who decided which strategy to implement: Johnston's Fabian Policy, or the Hood Offensives in what Hood described as the Lee-Jackson School of War.

It will never be known whether Johnston would have fared any better than Hood, or whether, if Johnston had successfully delayed Sherman's capture of Atlanta longer than Hood did, whether it would have changed the November presidential election in the North or the outcome of the war. But John Bell Hood was given the task of repelling Sherman's forces from the Gate City and he did not accomplish this task. So, Hood's defense of Atlanta must be judged as a failure, although it is probable that no one, not even the magnificent General Robert E. Lee, could have reversed the tide of fortune for the South at Atlanta. The loss of the Army of Tennessee as an effective fighting unit after summer and fall 1864, the fall of Atlanta, and the collapse of the Confederacy is the responsibility of President Davis. His decision to risk the loss of an army to save the Gate City forced drastic measures such as the elevation of Hood to command and a mandate for him to pursue offensive tactics when circumstances may not have warranted it. Ultimately, Davis lost both the army and the city and with them the war.

Hood's audaciousness and his attempt to put Sherman on the defensive should be commended. When judged purely for his skill in planning a battle, Hood's performance at Peach Tree Creek was competent. Historian Stanley Horn notes that Hood "was resourceful as well as aggressive" at Peach Tree Creek, and while Hood was disappointed at his failure to smash General Thomas's Army of the Cumberland, he lost no time planning his next maneuver. "He at once began to lay other stratagems for the enemy's discomfiture."[4] Horn goes on to praise Hood's plan of attack at Peach Tree Creek: "Regardless of its outcome, the plan was brilliant in its conception. The conventional movement against the enemy's flank was supplemented and

---

[4] Stanley F. Horn, *The Army of Tennessee* (Norman: University of Oklahoma Press, 1953) 354.

covered by the apparent retreat of the whole army from its line in front of the city. There seems no doubt that the maneuver completely befuddled Sherman."[5]

Hood's orders that General Stewart had relayed to his men were to "drive the Yankees to the creek and then down it. That if they encountered any breastworks, they were to fix bayonets and storm them. They [were] to stop for no obstacles. The assault [was to] be desperate."[6] All of the subordinate reports from Stewart's officers included references to the character of the attack. There are no such accounts in the reports of Hardee's men or officers, and, considering the veteran quality of the men in his corps, the absence of such an order is telling. Surely, to consider that the men of this corps would fail to make a determined effort when ordered to do so is unimaginable, particularly so when they were asked to make a desperate assault two days later, which they did with much vigor in the Battle of Atlanta. Thus, for whatever reason, Hardee simply either lacked the desire to put his full effort into the assault, or he failed to appreciate its possibilities or consequences upon the other Southern units making the assault with him. One historian recorded that Hardee "simply 'lay down.'"[7] In summarizing Hardee's actions from the conflicting reports, historian Samuel Carter in his work *The Siege of Atlanta* (1973) explained "the facts appeared to be that Hardee, reconnoitering the Federal line, had encountered heavy firing, concluded that the Union troops were well entrenched, and hesitated openly to charge a strongly fortified position."[8]

Whether he liked it or not, Hardee was responsible for starting the attack that day on the Federal flank and the success or failure of the assault depended mostly on him and his men. By holding back, he was exposing the rest of the Confederate troops who attacked down the line to greater risk. Hardee's restraint may have avoided greater casualties among his veterans, but his caution also clearly prevented any chance that the Confederates had for a decisive victory at Peach Tree Creek. His men were the hammer, the strongest,

---

[5] Ibid.

[6] Stewart's Report, in United States War Department, comp., *Official Records of the Union and Confederate Armies in the War of the Rebellion*, 128 vols. (Washington, DC: Government Printing Office, 1880–1901) ser. 1, vol. 38, serial 74, pp. 870–73 (hereafter *OR*).

[7] Samuel Carter III, *The Siege of Atlanta, 1864* (New York: St. Martin's Press, 1973) 205.

[8] Ibid., 205. While Hardee failed to perform adequate reconnaissance prior to the attack as suggested by Carter, the timid attack made by his corps can be construed, in large part, to have been merely a reconnaissance in force at Peach Tree Creek.

Battle of Peachtree Creek

and arguably the best corps in the Army of Tennessee. They certainly were the largest.[9]

At Peach Tree Creek, Hardee had the opportunity to place his men in a gap of the Federal line, between two of Sherman's three armies, and strike one of them in the flank. By attacking General Thomas's Army of the Cumberland in the side, Hardee could then roll up the rest of Thomas's line, pressing the fleeing Yankees to Peach Tree Creek, and perhaps across it, and all the way to the Chattahoochee River. The potential results could have been as dramatic as Stonewall's charge at Chancellorsville, or Albert Sidney Johnston's attack on the first day at Shiloh where, in both cases, the Federal army fled in disorder, losing substantial numbers of men and arms, and, with their backs to a large river, facing disaster.

Rarely in the campaign for Atlanta did the Southern army have an entire corps that was available for offensive action without having to commit a portion of its strength for defense. Because the Southerners were outnumbered almost two to one throughout the campaign, they were almost always fully committed to defensive positions, and they were stretched to the limit to accomplish that role. At Peach Tree Creek, while Sherman's armies approached Atlanta in a wide clockwise arc and became separated, Hood's men had a chance to take on one of Sherman's armies alone.

Here was an opportunity for Hardee to demonstrate his ability to command an army in the field, or a part of the army, by having tactical command of the attack. Old Reliable had shied away from field command the year before. Here, it was forced upon him. With generals Polk dead and Bragg and Johnston gone, Hardee had no other peers remaining in the Army of Tennessee. This was his chance to shine—his chance to make his mark in the war—to do what he had trained all of his life for—to make a difference in a major battle or campaign of a great war—a chance to win a decisive victory on the field of battle. The fate of Atlanta, and with it the war, hung in the balance.

---

[9] Many historians over the years have followed Hood's opinion that Hardee commanded the "Ablest Corps in the army." Hardee's force had fought in most or all of the major battles in the Western Theater, contained some crack outfits, including the famous Kentucky Orphan Brigade, and it was nearly double the size of the other two corps at the beginning of Hood's tenure as commander. However, there were a number of excellent regiments and brigades among Stewart's Army of Mississippi, later called the Third Corps of the Army of Tennessee, which had also fought in a number of battles in the West, including the Missouri Brigade of French's division which was considered by many of their peers as the best brigade in the army.

Hood's First Sortie, 20 July 1864

But Old Reliable would not rise to the occasion, instead choosing to question both the soundness of Hood's appointment to command of the army, as well as his decision to attack. In his temerity, Hardee would fail to exploit the opportunity presented to him. General Manigault recorded in his journal, "Had Hardee done as it was said he should have done, continued to move forward, he would not only have divided the Federal Army, cutting them in two, but he would also have captured a large number of guns, in rear of which the enemy had been driven back in confusion."[10] Had Hardee done a proper reconnaissance of the Federal positions before him, he would have discovered that a serious gap had arisen between the left of General Newton's division on the heights immediately south of Peach Tree Creek along Buck Head Road, and the remaining two divisions of General Howard's IV Corps that had moved to the east, nearer to General Schofield's Army of the Ohio and its XXIII Corps. This gap was, by midday of 20 July, nearly 2 miles wide, according to General Howard who had accompanied his two divisions, Stanley's and Wood's, to the left to hookup with Schofield's men.[11]

After the Battle of Jonesboro, some six weeks later, General Sherman confided to Confederate General Govan of Arkansas who had just been captured, that "nothing saved him on that occasion but the unaccountable remissness or deficiency of our commanding officers, who, after having broken his lines, and with a large number of pieces within his grasp, failed to take advantage of the favorable opportunity." The Northern leader explained that the Rebels "halted their column, and remaining stationary, gave him time to rally his men, bring up help, and finally to recover his ground, his artillery, and a complete restoration of his line." Sherman added that "he had been wholly unprepared for an attack, but one division was entrenched, the others were uncovered, and the horses of his artillery were at some distance from the guns. Had the attack been a determined one," said the Union commander, "and well led, the consequence to him would have been disastrous in the extreme."[12]

Hardee's biographer criticizes his performance at Peach Tree Creek as well. In his well-researched and delivered work, Nathaniel Cheairs Hughes, Jr., explains, "Generally considered, however, Peachtree Creek does stand as one of Hardee's poorest performances. Meticulous regard for details rather than

---

[10] Lockwood Tower, ed., *A Carolinian Goes to War: The Civil War Narrative of Arthur Middleton Manigault, Brigadier General* (Columbia: University of South Carolina Press, 1964) 224.

[11] *OR*, ser. 1, vol. 38, serial 72, p. 202.

[12] Tower, ed., *A Carolinian Goes to War*, 224.

concentration on essentials characterized the action." Hughes added that "Hardee's judgment concerning the shifting of troops to the right was poor. He failed to make a personal reconnaissance initially. The attack was delivered piecemeal, and subordinate units were not closely controlled." Hughes aptly points out that "Contact between Bate's and Walker's Divisions appears to have been lost, and the attack of Maney followed that of Walker at too long an interval, permitting the enemy to defeat first one and then the other. Perhaps Cleburne should have been committed earlier." Hughes concluded that allowing "Bate's Division to thrash about ineffectually on the enemy flank represents a serious error on Hardee's part."[13]

One might argue that it would not have mattered when or where Hardee attacked that day, or how hard his men may have tried, that he simply would have added to the list of Southern losses. In support of this conclusion, Newton was well entrenched and on good ground with raking artillery fire that covered his left flank. Moreover, the Army of the Cumberland, except for Ward's division, was on high ground south of the creek by the time of the assault. But Thomas's men were hardly prepared to receive a general assault.

In his official report, written in April 1865, General Hardee made no mention of being ordered to "take the works at all hazzards" or that the fight was to be a "general one." To the contrary, he defended his actions by trying to blame Hood for failing to supervise the assault. In his official report, written after Hood had published his report on the Atlanta Campaign, Hardee explained:

> I was ordered, as above stated, to move half a division length to the right; but was directed, at the same time, to connect with the left of Chetham's Corps. The delay referred to by General Hood was not caused by my failure to post a staff officer to prevent my command from moving more than half a division length to the right, for Major Black, of my staff, was sent to the proper point for that purpose; but it arose from the fact that Cheatham's Corps, with which I was to connect, was nearly two miles to my right, instead of a division length.

Additionally, Hardee recalled that he was ordered late in the day to send one of his divisions (Cleburne's) to support Cheatham, which prevented him from renewing the assault, and owing to this and to the lateness of the hour, he

---

[13] Nathaniel Cheairs Hughes, Jr., *General William J. Hardee: Old Reliable* (Baton Rouge: LSU Press, 1965) 225.

called off the attack. But by the time that Hardee decided to send Cleburne forward at Peach Tree Creek, it was too late.[14]

Only a couple of official reports from units under Cleburne that record the day's events survive. Polk's, Lowery's and Granbury's brigades all report that they were not engaged in the action of 20 July, but that they received some casualties due to being exposed to enemy shell and grape fire during that afternoon. Total loses in Cleburne's division during the 20 July assault were as follows: Polk, four; Lowery, forty-five; Granbury, twenty; Govan unknown, but estimated at five to ten; total losses for Cleburne's division were thus at about seventy-five. Hardee lost about 659 men to Newton's loss of just 102 men while engaging for the most part in long-range skirmishing with the Yankees and uselessly exposing his men to Federal artillery fire without trying to advance.

General Samuel French, kept a diary during the war. His entry for 20 July contained:

> The plan of battle was a good one. Hardee was to gain the enemy's rear, swing to the left, taking their line in flank, while we attacked the line in front in echelon of brigades as the battle swept down the creek [from right to left].... Gen. Loring's troops broke through the enemy's line of works. Reynolds and Featherston had to abandon the captured line by reason of the flank fire on them. The failure of Hardee deranged the plan of battle.[15]

On 13 September 1864, General Hood, who was seeking Hardee's removal and in response to Hardee's denials of responsibility for the failure at Peach Tree Creek, retorted, "In the battle of July 20, we failed on account of General Hardee." Hood explained that despite commanding "the best troops of this Army," Hardee continuously failed throughout the defense of Atlanta.[16] While this statement overreaches and comes from a bitter and defeated general, it is fair to lay the loss at Peach Tree Creek at the feet of Hardee and two of his subordinates, Bate and Maney. Biographer Nathaniel Hughes pointed out that Hardee had faced the dilemma of two conflicting orders: (1) to bring on a general engagement, and (2) to shift to the right before delivering it. He had chosen the more cautious course when he needed to be aggressive and that his

---

[14] William J. Hardee, *Hardee's Rifle and Light Infantry Tactics: For the Instruction, Exercises, and Maneuvers of Riflemen and Light Infantry* (New York: J. D. Kane Publishing, 1862) 339–40.

[15] French, *Two Wars*, 218–19.

[16] Hood to President Davis, 13 September 1864, OR ser. I, vol. 39, Part II, Serial 78, 832.

actions had "seriously embarrassed his commander's plans." Hughes added, "Since his action delayed the attack, resulted in a major and unexpected troop movement, and produced confusion, Hardee should be held sharply responsible for his independent decision."[17]

While it is certainly debatable as to who were the best troops in the Southern army, the majority of Hardee's corps were tested veterans and were highly regarded by all. They would certainly have obeyed an order for an all out assault. As there is a complete absence of any record that such an order was ever given to any of Hardee's divisions, brigades, or regiments, Hood's order for such a charge must have stopped with Hardee. One writer for the *Augusta Daily Chronicle and Sentinel* explained that Hardee's troops were disappointed that they had not made a more aggressive assault due to their "overly prudent" leaders.[18]

Looking more closely at Hood's writings, yields some additional evidence that points to Hardee's failure to relay the full intent of Hood's orders to attack at Peach Tree Creek to his subordinates. Hood explained that during a conversation between him and Cleburne at Hood's headquarters a few days after the battles of 20 July and 22 July, that the two shared freely about the "condition of the Army and the causes of failure in the [two] engagements." Hood explained that "I then unfolded to him the plans of action, together with the peremptory orders to halt at nothing on our side of Peach Tree Creek." The young Confederate commander continued, "Cleburne seemed surprised, and thereupon informed me that as his Division was about to move forward to the attack on the 20th, General Hardee rode along the line, and in the presence of those around him, cautioned him to be on the lookout for breastworks."[19] Hood

---

[17] Hughes, *General William J. Hardee*, 225–27. It is possible that, upon seeing Stevens's brigade being repulsed along Buckhead Road, Hardee ordered Maney to halt his division and not to press an attack, but to merely remain in a supporting position and exchange skirmish fire from a distance while Hardee investigated the situation further and sent a staff officer to locate Bate, which is what resulted. This conclusion is logical given the results of the day. Unfortunately, no record exists of Hardee's conversations with or orders to Maney during the battle. Hardee certainly was close enough to Maney's position to issue any order that he desired, including whether to halt or to advance. It is thus reasonable to assume that Maney was acting under orders from Hardee to stop, but again, the record is silent. If this assumption that Hardee ordered Maney to halt is correct, then no blame for failing to press an attack should be placed on Maney or his men.

[18] *Augusta Daily Chronicle and Sentinel*, 26 July 1864; Elliott, *Soldier of Tennessee*, 208.

[19] John Bell Hood, *Advance & Retreat* (1880; repr., New York: Da Capo Press, 1993) 185–86.

subsequently guessed that Hardee had given similar precautions to each of his other division commanders and their men before they began their assaults, although there is no evidence to support it. As Hardee's orders to Cleburne to renew the assault were given two hours or more after his other divisions had launched their attacks and found the enemy in works, Hood's assumption that Hardee warned his initial attacking troops about breastworks is unfounded.

However, Hood's report of Cleburne's apparent surprise that Hood had instructed Hardee and Stewart to stop at nothing to take the enemy's works and to not halt until Peach Tree Creek was reached and the enemy was driven before them, rings true. When told the specifics of Hood's orders for the assault, Hood recalled that Cleburne "seemed surprised," as if he had never heard these instructions before. This piece of evidence, coupled with the complete absence of any report, letter, or diary account from any officer or soldier in Hardee's corps recording the specific instructions given by Hood when virtually every report from Stewart's regiments included and even emphasized these instructions about the nature and vigor of the attack point to Hardee's failure to relay the full import of Hood's orders to his subordinates. It demonstrates that either Hardee questioned the wisdom of Hood's orders, or, as Hood asserted, was found "wanting in that boldness requisite for offensive warfare."[20] As for Old Reliable, both statements were true at Peach Tree Creek.

Perhaps Stewart and his men would not have invested so much of their blood in taking the real estate in their front had they been aware of the cautiousness with which Hardee's men had approached the assignment. The limited success enjoyed by Stewart's Army of Mississippi at Peach Tree Creek came at a high price. The failure of Hardee to properly execute the order caused Stewart's men, particularly Featherston's Mississippi Brigade, to become exposed and enveloped. With well over half of Featherston's veterans killed, wounded, or captured by Ward's counterattack, Featherston's brigade had to fall back when they could not hold onto the ridge any longer. The failure of Maney's Tennessee Division to assault the Federal lines at the time that Featherston's brigade attacked caused considerable resentment and distrust among the soldiers of both units. Watching the futility of Stewart's initially successful attack, one writer commented that the Battle of Peach Tree Creek was "a negative victory plainly won."[21]

---

[20] Ibid., 186.
[21] "Atlanta, July 20, 1864," *Savannah Republican*, 25 July 1864; Elliott, *Soldier of Tennessee*, 208.

FRESH TIDINGS FROM THE BATTLEFIELD

Death did his work well that day, unutterable, filled all our hearts and enshrouded our command with gloom. God help the homes and comfort the hearts that dark day made desolate and bereaved.... This memorable day will mark an era of grief in many a desolate Mississippi home.[1]

In surveying the blood soaked field, Brigadier General Featherston lamented:

My orders were to fix bayonets and charge their works when we reached them, to stop for no obstacle, however formidable, but to make the attack a desperate one. I was informed that the same orders had been delivered by the Commander-in-Chief, General Hood, to each and every army corps. I thought the battle had been well planned, and heard it spoken of by my associates in arms in terms of commendation. The whole corps, so far as I heard an expression of their opinions, anticipated a brilliant victory.

I was struck with surprise, at the time we moved to the front, that no guns, either artillery or small arms, were heard on our right, save a feeble skirmish. I supposed from hearing no firing on our right, and knowing that many divisions had time to reach the creek, that they had found no enemy in their front. Had the attack been vigorously made by all the troops on our right, and the plan of battle been strictly carried out, I then believed, and still believe, the victory would have been a brilliant one, and the Federal forces on the south side of Peach Tree Creek would have all been either killed, wounded or captured. The orders seem to have been misunderstood by the troops on our right, or for some cause not fully carried out.[2]

An observer in Featherston's brigade said that immediately after the battle Featherston was deeply grieved and when he tried to give a report of the results

---

[1] J. L. Power 1864 scrapbook, Special collections, Mississippi Department of Archives and History, Jackson, Mississippi.

[2] Featherston Report, in United States War Department, comp., *Official Records of the Union and Confederate Armies in the War of the Rebellion*, 128 vols. (Washington, DC: Government Printing Office, 1880–1901) ser. 1, vol. 38, serial 74, pp. 880–84 (hereafter *OR*).

to his division commander, General Loring, and began to read off the massive list of casualties in his brigade, he wept bitterly and was unable to continue. Every regimental commander, save one, cried Featherston, was either killed or wounded. It was the only time during the war that the general, known for his composure and stoicism, was seen to be overcome with emotion. One of the staff officers in Featherston's brigade wrote after the battle:

> The gallantry, rapidity and coolness, with which these noble men moved through that storm of fire, are above all praise. Heroes, patriots, martyrs, their wounds and death attest their spirit, and set the seal to their devotion. They and theirs deserve well of their country. Privates and officers (line and field and staff) all acted well their parts.... Death did his work well that day, unutterable, filled all our hearts and enshrouded our command with gloom. God help the homes and comfort the hearts that dark day made desolate and bereaved.
>
> Overwhelmed by a sense of the dread slaughter, Gen. Featherston wept, when reporting the carnage to his Division commander, an undemonstrative man, unaccustomed to emotional display, and inured to war's death dealing work, upon Virginia's blood dyed fields, such destruction overcame even him, a veteran, hardened by many arduous campaigns....[3]

For the 31st Mississippi, 215 men carried guns and swords up the old sloping field and took the ridge. Only 34 returned unhurt. Some sixty-seven souls were sacrificed for their country. Many were buried in unmarked graves on the bloody ridge overlooking Peach Tree Creek. Still more men who were mortally wounded were buried in remote cemeteries such as in Macon, Chattanooga, Nashville, Louisville, and Camp Chase, Ohio, and Camp Douglas, Illinois.[4]

There were a total of 181 casualties out of the 215 men who made the charge and 67 of them died from wounds received in the Battle of Peach Tree Creek. An incredible 84.18 percent of the 31st Mississippi were casualties in the three hours of battle. One in three were fatal casualties, making the 31st Mississippi's roll call of sorrow among the highest, if not the highest, in all of the Civil War for one battle, particularly so because it all occurred during one afternoon's charge. Thus, the 31st Mississippi's losses at Peach Tree Creek

---

[3] Power, 1864 scrapbook, Special Collections, Mississippi Department of Archives and History, Jackson, Mississippi.

[4] Compiled Service Records for the 31st Mississippi Vol. Infantry, microfilm rolls 341–46, Mississippi Department of Archives and History, Jackson, Mississippi.

rank, in terms of percentage of men engaged, among the highest at 84.13 percent in the war except for units which were surrendered en masse. Moreover, the number of fatal casualties sustained by the "Bloody Magnolias" number among the highest by any Confederate unit during the war, as well.[5]

The void of Mississippi's husbands, fathers, sons, and brothers that was created that afternoon in the hot summer sun in Georgia would never be filled. Thomas Markam, chaplain of Featherston's brigade recalled the fighting "at Peach Tree Creek, above Atlanta, where, of our 1,230 that went in, but 650 [actually only 551] came out. Ah! How often, as we entered those fields of slaughter, looking at our devoted ranks, the pathos and power of those lines" decimated beyond belief that day reminded him of the carnage at Waterloo. Featherston's brigade suffered more casualties, both in percentage and in actual loses, that day than any other brigade that fought at Peach Tree Creek, and rank among the highest brigade losses by percent in all of the war.[6]

---

[5] In Lt. Col. William F. Fox's statistical analysis of regimental losses during the Civil War, the 1st Texas Regiment of Hood's Division at the Battle of Antietam saw 45 killed and 141 wounded out of a total of 226 men present for a loss of 82.3 percent, which has historically been accepted as the highest casualty for a battle by percentage among any Confederate unit during the war. Among Federal regimental losses during the war, the 154th New York lost 200 out of 239 engaged at Gettysburg for a loss of 83.682 percent, according to John W. Busey and David G. Martin in their *Regimental Strengths and Losses at Gettysburg* (1982), making the 154th New York conspicuous for the highest Federal regimental loss in a single battle by percent. Prior to this work, the losses sustained by the 1st Minnesota at Gettysburg had been widely accepted as being the highest by percentage in a single battle during the war by any unit, North or South, based upon William Fox's *Regimental Losses in the American Civil War* (1889). According to Fox, the 1st Minnesota lost 50 killed and 174 wounded for a total loss of 227 out of a total of 262 men engaged for a loss of 85.496 percent. But Busey and Martin revealed that the 1st Minnesota had 330 men present at Gettysburg. In Irene B. Warming's *Minnesota in the Civil and Indian Wars, 1861–1865, A Narrative of the First Regiment,* based upon the report of Captain H. C. Coates, Warming showed that out of 330 men engaged, the 1st Minnesota suffered 232 casualties (4 officers and 47 men killed, 13 officers and 162 men wounded, and 6 men missing) or 70 percent of the men engaged. According to Robert W. Meinhard's "The First Minnesota at Gettysburg," the 1st Minnesota suffered at least 80 fatalities and another 149 wounded for a total of 229 casualties out of 330. Finally, in Richard Moe's history of the 1st Minnesota, *The Last Full Measure,* he points out that the count should have included the missing men and places the regiment's losses at Gettysburg at 70 percent. Thus, with the additional 6 missing troops making the total casualties 235 men for the battle, the1st Minnesota's losses by percentage was 71.21percent, not 85.5percent as claimed by Fox, still remarkably high, but not the highest by a regiment in the war.

[6] Thomas Markam, "Tribute to the Confederate Dead," *Southern Historical Society Papers* 10 (April 1882): 177; Rev. Thomas Markam, address delivered to Veterans at New

Battle of Peachtree Creek

Featherston's brigade lost 679 men out of the 1,230 men engaged, an incredible loss of 55.2 percent. Only 551 of his men returned unhurt. Featherston's brigade losses at Peach Tree Creek rank, when compared in *Fox's Record of Brigade Losses by Confederate Brigades*, as the eighth highest.[7] The high number of both the casualties and the fatal casualties attests to the closeness and toughness of the fighting as well as the length of time that the Mississippians kept up the fight. The carnage left many Federal veterans of both battles comparing the field to Gettysburg.

There were five flags confirmed captured by Ward's division with three battle flags and two second national patterned flags. One battle flag was the 31st Mississippi's twelve-star battle flag (captured by the 136th New York), while one second national flag was identified as that of the 33rd Mississippi. A sketch depicting the captured flags that Ward's men proudly waved as General Hooker inspected their lines the following day reveal two second national patterned Confederate flags and three battle flags containing the St. Andrews Cross Western Theater (rectangular) style were in their possession.[8]

After the Battle of Peach Tree Creek wrecked the Army of Mississippi, Stewart felt compelled to write an address to try to quell the unrest and disharmony:

> Soldiers: Somewhere, and sometime we must make a final stand in this great struggle. If we are brave men, entitled to Independence, and resolved to win it or perish, any time and place our commanding General may choose will suit us. Can we find a better position than we now occupy? And is not

---

Orleans, 6 April, 1882, in Clement Anselm Evans, ed., Mississippi, vol. IX of *Confederate Military History*, 19 vols. (1899; repr., Wilmington NC: Broadfoot Publishing Company, 1987) 214–15.

[7] Fox, *Regimental Losses*, chap. 15. Fox claims that Richard Garnett's brigade at Gettysburg lost 65.9 percent of its force during Pickett's famous charge. In comparison, Busey and Martin found Iverson's brigade at Gettysburg with a loss of 903 out of a total strength of 1,384 for a percentage loss of 65.2 percent as the highest Confederate brigade loss by percentage, while Garnett's Brigade sustained a loss of 948 out of some 1,459 engaged for a percentage loss of 65.0 percent, making it the second worst at Gettysburg.

[8] Hugh Simmons, correspondence with author, 20, 22 August 2007; Greg Biggs, correspondence with author, 2,7,8, and 29 December 2008, author's personal papers, Dalton, Georgia; Howard Michael Madaus and Robert D. Needham, *The Battle Flags of the Confederate Army of Tennessee* (Milwaukee Public Museum, 1976) 77, 97, 100; "57th Alabama," www.managementaides.com/my_interests/hispanic_america.htm (22 November, 2008); "57th Alabama," www.archives.state.al.us/referenc/flags/072.html (22 November, 2008).

one day in the year as good as another? If he so decide, let us resolve that henceforth we tread no step backward—that here and now we stand or fall.

To succeed we must work hard and fight hard; and many of us must die. You, at least, who have faced him an hundred times, do not fear death. I believe, and so do you, in an overruling, special Providence, that in some mysterious way guides the course of events and shapes the destinies of nations. Our cause is just. Heaven favors it, and will give us success if we do our duty. Let us put our trust in God, using the means He has given us, and we cannot fail.

I appeal to every officer and man to labor day and night to make our positions strong and impregnable; so that if need be, it can be held by a small force while our main body operates in some other way. Let us learn a lesson from our busy, persevering foe, and employ all the skill and industry we possess, as well as a high and noble courage, in defense of our glorious cause. Let us leave nothing undone that we can do, and this hated, cowardly enemy, who makes war upon women and children, shall be delivered into our hands, that we may execute upon him the vengeance of Heaven for his crimes.[9]

The Battle of Peach Tree Creek was a fruitless assault in which, as in all bloody battles, only the grim reaper won. For the Army of Mississippi and the four brigades that made the initial assault, Peach Tree Creek was particularly sad. For Featherston's Mississippians who lost over half of their brigade, the battle was devastating with over five out of eight men lost. Perhaps the best explanation for the effect of 20 July 1864 on the Magnolia State was that the Battle of Peach Tree Creek produced the largest loss of life in the history of that state up to that point. This tragedy would be repeated and this bloody record broken on 30 November 1864 at Franklin, Tennessee. S. Newton Berryhill relayed the impact of the loss sustained by loved ones back home in the Magnolia State in his poem "Tidings from the Battle Field," which made a fitting epitaph for the Bloody Magnolias:

"Fresh tidings from the battle field!"

A widowed mother stands,
And lifts the glasses from her eyes
With trembling withered hands.
"Fresh tidings from the battle field!

---

[9] Alex. P. Stewart, address to his corps, quoted in , "From Atlanta," *Macon* [GA] *Daily Telegraph*, 2 August 1864.

Battle of Peachtree Creek

Your only son is slain;
He fell with 'victory' on his lips,
And a bullet in his brain."
The stricken mother staggers back,
And falls upon the floor;
And the wailing shriek of a broken heart
Comes from the cottage door.

"Fresh tidings from the battle field!"
The wife her needle plies,
While in the cradle at her feet
Her sleeping infant lies.
"Fresh tidings from the battle field!
Your husband is no more,
But he died as soldiers love to die—
His wounds were all before."
Her work was dropped—"O God!" she moans,
And lifts her aching eyes;
The orphaned babe in the cradle wakes,
And joins its mother's cries.

"Fresh tidings from the battle field!"
A maid with pensive eye
Sits musing near the sacred spot
Where she heard his last good-bye.
"Fresh tidings from the battle field!
Your lover's cold in death;
But he breathed the name of her he loved
With his expiring breath."
With hands pressed to her snowy brow,
She strives her grief to hide;
She shrinks from friendly sympathy—

A widow ere a bride.[10]

---

[10] S. Newton Berryhill, "Fresh Tidings from the Battlefield," in Ernestine Clayton Deavors, ed., *The Mississippi Poets*, 81 (Memphis: E. H. Clarke & Brother, 1922).

28

EPILOGUE: PEACH TREE CREEK NATIONAL MILITARY PARK?

> A few years afterwards, I revisited this battlefield, with a party of Southern gentlemen.... The ground located, I mentioned the fact of a Rebel battery, which seemed to have our range perfectly.... As I was talking, one of the party...turned to me, and said:... "Well, it was my battery;"... "I took off my hat to him and gave him my hand."[1]

After the war, the Battle of Peach Tree Creek became synonymous with the starting point of the Battles for Atlanta, and the blood-stained fields of the A. J. Collier farm became a natural meeting place for veterans who returned after the war to reminisce and reflect. During one of those visits, Major Stephen Pierson of the 33rd New Jersey had an opportunity to discuss the events of the battle along the Collier Ridge with a Rebel officer whose battery opposed him. It was Captain Evan P. Howell whose's Georgia battery had been posted just west of Buck Head Road (Peachtree Street) along the hill around today's 28th Street and that deployed facing northwest. Howell's battery commanded the valley below it along today's Ardmore Park and Tanyard Creek Park in front of the attack by Featherston's and Scott's brigades.

Pierson and many of his comrades were swept from the field along the western portions of today's Tanyard Branch Park as the advance position of his 33rd New Jersey was overrun by Scott's Southerners. As he dashed for the rear and protection by the Federal reinforcements, Pierson looked across the long field to the other side of Taynard Branch where he saw Howell's battery in action. The battery appeared to him to have measured the Federal position atop Collier Ridge and the corresponding lower Collier Ridge west of Tanyard Branch along today's Collier Road near the Tanyard Creek Park.

"A few years afterwards, I revisited this battlefield, with a party of Southern gentlemen, some of whom had been in the Confederate service. The

---

[1] Stephen Pierson, "From Chattanooga to Atlanta in 1864–A Personal Reminiscence (1907)," *Proceedings New Jersey Historical Society*, vol. 16 (1931): 291–92.

ground located, I mentioned the fact of a Rebel battery, which seemed to have our range perfectly," Pierson explained, "as the shells came quick and fast and exploded in just the right place almost every time. As I was talking, one of the party, Capt. Evan Howell, of the *Atlanta Constitution*, turned to me, and said: 'Doctor, do you know whose battery that was?' 'No.' 'Well, it was my battery;'" The old Confederate continued: "furthermore, this battle was fought on my grandfather's plantation, where I was born and raised, and you may believe I made my guns talk for all they were worth that day." The New Jersey major then said, "I took off my hat to him and gave him my hand." The two former enemies became friends that day along the Tanyard Creek Park as they shared each other's stories of the war and the reasons they had each fought. Pierson continued, "It is not always easy, but it is always helpful, to put oneself into the other man's place. It gives a broader, juster view of the situation. I believed that afternoon, just as firmly as I did that July day in '64, and do now, that he was wrong and we were right." "But," added the Yankee veteran, "as I listened to him and tried to put myself in his place, I gained a clearer conception of why it was that he believed he was right and I wrong. I gave to him then, as I give to him now, my honor and respect."[2]

Pierson noted that the old battlefields from Dalton to Atlanta "were ploughed with shot and shell, and they were harrowed by minnie bullets. Those forests were pruned, perhaps not with skill, but certainly with an energy that was terribly effective. And the hillsides and plains were dotted with many little burial mounds not made by the Indians." The former Yankee officer remembered, "On my visit to these fields in '81, I was assured by a farmer that for several years one of the valuable crops he gathered from his old fields was lead. After each rain storm he and his hands would go out and gather up the leaden bullets that had been uncovered. Then," explained Pierson, "he would scratch it over with a harrow, and wait until another rain made the bullet: 'sprout' again. The lead he sold, and it brought a good price. I judged that the crop was still growing, for I saw several kegs full of bullets on his stoop!"[3]

In 1900, an Atlanta battlefield reunion was planned for 20 July at the old Peach Tree Creek battlefield along Collier Road atop the Collier Ridge. Over 5000 veterans from both the Federal and Confederate armies were present. "Long tables will be spread in the old trenches, and this multitude of men, who fought so valiantly thirty-six years ago, will be seated at the most elaborate

---

[2] Ibid.
[3] Ibid., 287.

barbecue ever given," wrote R. F. Maddox, chairman of the Committee of Invitation for the event who sent out announcements in papers and magazines throughout the country. "The old trenches and earthworks constructed for battle defense have changed but little during the lapse of years," explained Maddox. The advertisement appeared in the *Confederate Veteran*, the *New York Times*, and across the United States, and it attracted veterans from all parts of the country. Many purchased round-trip train tickets through the Southeastern Passenger Association that offered a single fare regardless of distance.[4]

Generals O. O. Howard, commander of the Federal IV Corps, was present, as was General A. P. Stewart, commander of the Confederacy's Army of Mississippi. These two men were the ranking officers at the reunion, but they were joined by a host of other leaders including General Albert D. Shaw, commander in chief of the Grand Army of the Republic, General John B. Gordon, commander in chief of the United Confederate Veterans, General Joseph Wheeler, General Stephen D. Lee, and former president Benjamin Harrison. Fittingly, the reunion occurred atop the Collier Ridge where Featherston's brigade had reached and passed in a vain effort to defeat the Federal forces encircling Atlanta, and the long tables that had been laid out for the occasion stretched for fully a half mile, roughly the width of Featherston's breakthrough, with the Federal veterans seated on the north side of the table and the Confederate Veterans seated on the south side of the table.[5]

During this time, battlefields preservation had grown to a national question. Several national battlefield parks were commissioned including Chickamauga, Antietam, and Gettysburg. By 1900, Shiloh and Vicksburg had also been established as national military parks as a "wave of nationalism and preservation" swept the country. In the 1910s, the nation's interest was diverted to World War I, and in the 1920s the country was too busy industrializing to commemorate battlefields of the previous century. By the 1930s interest in preservation returned as many veterans had been lost to the ages, and only a few octogenarians remained to tell their stories.[6]

Thus, focus turned to how to commemorate the battles around Atlanta, and the discussion centered on two locations: Peach Tree Creek and Kennesaw

---

[4] R. F. Maddox, "Atlanta Reunion: To All Veterans," *Confederate Veteran*, vol. 8 (June 1900): 257.

[5] Ibid., 257.

[6] Timothy B. Smith, *This Great Battlefield of Shiloh, History, Memory, and the Establishment of a Civil War National Military Park* (Knoxville: University of Tennessee Press, 2004) xvi–xvii.

Mountain. While Kennesaw Mountain was not one of the battles that was fought around Atlanta or for possession of the Gate City, it was an important action that led Sherman's forces to change tactics in the Atlanta encirclement, and, moreover, it was a Confederate victory that stroked local egos. Additionally, some of the land at Kennesaw Mountain had already been donated and at least one monument had been erected. On 13 August 1904, "60 acres of land in Cobb County west of Marietta [was] transferred to the Dan McCook Brigade Association." This became the start of what is today's Kennesaw Mountain National Battlefield Park.[7]

Today, Kennesaw Mountain National Battlefield Park contains 2,923 acres of preserved and interpreted property. The Peach Tree Creek Battlefield contains approximately 3,000 houses, and relatively little green space, but the Tanyard Creek Park, Ardmore Park, Ellsworth Park, Springlake and Norfleet Park, Spring Valley Road Conservation Park, Brookwood Hills Park (private), and the Bobby Jones Golf Course protect and preserve at least some of the portions of the battlefield near the areas that saw some of the heaviest fighting. The Tanyard Creek Park contains a granite monument with several plaques that include a description of the Atlanta Campaign, the Battle of Peach Tree Creek, and several maps. Unfortunately over the years, neglect, theft, and vandalism have reduced the park to a piecemeal effort to tell the battle's story.[8]

Peach Tree Creek Park (now known as Tanyard Creek Park) was one of five Atlanta Campaign "Pocket Parks" constructed by FDR's Works Progress Administration (WPA). These five parks were located at Ringgold Gap, Rocky Face, Resaca, Cassville, and Peach Tree Creek. Today, each of the five parks remain but they are each in need of upgrading and improving with updated markers and signs. Pocket parks have been created over the years for a variety of reasons: to provide green space in an urban or residential area, to tell a local story of importance, to give a place to sit on a bench or on the ground, to preserve a bit of history, or to utilize and turn into park space land that is otherwise unusable or unsuitable for development.[9]

---

[7] Official Website Kennesaw Mountain Battlefield Park, "Kennesaw Mtn.," www.nps.gov/kemo/index.htm (15 June 2008); "Kennesaw Mtn.," http://ourgeorgiahistory.com/ogh/ Kennesaw_Mountain_National_Battlefield_Park.

[8] In the event that the Bobby Jones Golf Course ever ceases to operate, the property would provide an ideal venue to preserve and tell the battlefield's story. The park could even be expanded to include Tanyard Branch Park and the old Collier Mill site.

[9] "Indiana Regiments in the Civil War," http://www.indiana.edu/~liblilly/wpa/wpa_info.html (16 June 2008).

Hood's First Sortie, 20 July 1864

In the late 1930s, while interest in the Civil War had begun to wane in much of the country, in Atlanta, a Civil War bug struck the city thanks in large part to Margaret Mitchell's novel *Gone With the Wind*. During this time, too, one man, Wilbur G. Kurtz, Sr., an artist, historian, engineer, mapmaker, writer, and city planner and administrator for Atlanta, tirelessly worked to record and preserve the Gate City's history and the Civil War era in Georgia. We are all indebted to the work of Kurtz in identifying, recording, preserving, writing, and seeing to the placement and dedication of numerous historical markers across Atlanta and Georgia, most of which were erected, written, located, and placed by the lone hands of this remarkable man. Beginning in the 1930s and continuing until the centennial events of the Civil War in the 1960s and his death, Kurtz devoted his life to protect and preserve Atlanta's and Georgia's history through the placement and dedication of historical markers and monuments.[10]

On 11 April 1960, Chester Bainbury had the fortune to tour the Atlanta battlefield sites with Wilbur G. Kurtz as his guide. Also joining them was Bell I. Wiley, a professor of history at Emory University whose knowledge of the Atlanta battles was perhaps equal to or greater than Kurtz. According to Bainbury, "At 423 Collier Road we came upon a marker concerning a gap in the Federal line. This marker is on the lawn of the residence at that address, and Kurtz said the owner, D. Glenn Sudderth, had demanded that the marker be placed there." Kurtz explained: "'Usually we had to ask permission, and had no very enthusiastic response. This was a novel demand.' I went to the door," said Bainbury, "and when Sudderth answered my ring and I told him our mission, he broke into smiles, reached in the hall closet, and brought out a rusted old rifle-musket barrel which had been exploded at its muzzle end." Bainbury could see the pride in Sudderth. "'I dug this out of my back yard,' he said. 'I was digging around for minnie balls, and this turned up. It's a muzzle-loader.'" This spot atop Collier Ridge was the apex of the Confederate breakthrough by Featherston's Mississippians.[11]

Bainbury and his learned guides then proceeded westward until they came to a house "in whose front yard a Civil War entrenchment has been allowed to remain," and they next visited the Collier Mill site and a little monument placed along Collier Road a little south of the old site, where "two old millstones from

---

[10] Wilbur G. Kurtz Papers, MSS 130, Kenan Research Center, Atlanta History Center.

[11] Bainbury, Chester, Bainbury's Civil War Diary, edited by Charles Wesley Lawrence, Cleveland Plain Dealer; 1960, Kurtz Papers, MSS–130, Kenan Research Center, Atlanta History Center.

Collier's Mill have been set up." The tour next traveled to the Bobby Jones Municipal Golf Course. There, Kurtz described the heavy fighting that had taken place where O'Neal's brigade had nearly routed Geary's and Williams's divisions as portions of Hooker's XX Corps had been backed up to the bridgeheads over Peachtree Creek at today's golf course site. "'When the trees were being cut for the golf course,' Kurtz told us, 'a good many saw blades were ruined by cutting into hardware shot into the trees in this battle. A great deal of the fighting took place right here.'"[12]

Unfortunately, Kurtz failed to write the history of the many stories that he helped to uncover and preserve for Georgia's Civil War history, instead choosing to spend his efforts to collect information and to place historical markers for future generations. Also, unfortunately for present-day history seekers, many of the markers have been moved for non-history related reasons. Issues such as traffic flow and placement of markers to more pleasant locations such as parks and easements have all reduced the usefulness of markers.

The possibility of a Battle of Peach Tree Creek National Military Park reached its zenith in 1931 as the War Department studied the subject and surveyed the land on which the battles of Peach Tree Creek, Atlanta, and Ezra Church were fought. On 27 December 1931, the *Atlanta Journal* reported, "It is estimated that 48 acres of land will be required and that the total cost of the park system will be $315,000, including three $50,000 monuments marking the sites of the battles of Atlanta, Peachtree Creek, and Ezra Church." In 2013 US dollars, 4.8 acres would cost $4.5 million—if one could find land available on the historic site—and the monuments would cost an additional $713,000. It was the vision of the committee that proposed the Atlanta battlefield parks to erect a visitor's center on or near Peachtree Street and Collier Road for all three Atlanta battles along with a driving park linking the Battle of Peach Tree Creek site to the battles of Atlanta and Ezra Church sites, one similar to the driving parks of Vicksburg and Richmond.[13]

As the Great Depression was in its height, this proposal was never funded. The Peachtree Road corridor was already being developed into subdivisions as wealthy Atlantans began building homes north of the city soon after the turn of the century. For instance, "In 1912, developers B.F. Burdett and E.F. Chambless began the subdivision that is now Brookwood Hills. Development was

---

[12] Chester Bainbury, Diary, 11 April 1960. Charles Wesley Lawrence ed. *Cleveland Plain Dealer*, 8.

[13] "Proposed Military Park" *Atlanta Journal*, 27 December, 1931, courtesy Steve Davis, RDJ file no. 346.

interrupted by World War I, but took off in the post-war boom." In the Peach Tree Creek battlefield sector, the majority of the property available for purchase and preservation remained in the estates of the old Andrew Jackson Collier and G. W. Collier farms.[14]

By the late 1930s, the Collier properties were sold off and developed into neighborhoods including expansion of the Brookwood Hills Subdivision. In 1939, the Brookwood Hills Community Club was formed, which signified a new era for the lands on which the bloody struggle for control of the Gate City occurred. After the veterans died out and the reunion picnics ceased, the Cyclorama's proximity to Grant Park and the Atlanta Zoo would eventually replace Peach Tree Creek as the focal point of the Atlanta battles by the 1940s and 50s. Soon, upscale neighborhoods would supplant the countryside that marked the battlefield that had scarred Andrew Jackson Collier's farm. By the end of the 1930s, the dream of a Peach Tree Creek National Military Park became, as with the old Southern Confederacy, gone with the wind.

---

[14] "Brookwood Hills Subdivision," www.buckhead.net/brookwood-hills/ (31 December 2008).

Roster Confederate Casualties at Peach Tree Creek

Alabama:
1st Alabama: (partial list)

1. Co. K:	Privates:	John Gorman	Missing
2.		J. Hamilton	Missing
3.		John P. Tharp	Missing

Total: Killed-0   Wounded-0   Captured or Missing-3   Total-3

*According to Dr. Edward Young Mc Morries, Private, Co C, 1st Ala., the regiment was not engaged at Peach Tree Creek. Mc Morries, Edward Young, History of the First Regiment, Alabama Volunteer Infantry, C.S.A., State of Alabama Dept. of Archives and History, Bulletin No. 2, The Brown Printing Co., Montgomery, AL (1904).

17th Alabama:
Company A: The Bartow Avengers from Lowndes County
1:	Corporal	Samuel B. Taylor	Wounded & Captured-died 10-20-64
2:	Privates:	Richard Leach	Killed
3:		William McShores	Wounded
4:		John Taylor	Wounded

Company B: Deen's Company from Butler County
5:	Privates:	Willis D. Kirksy	Wounded-died 8-5-64
6:		George H. McClure	Killed
7:		J. W. Mc Pherson	Killed
8:		Felix G. Walker	Captured-sent to Camp Douglas, Ill.

Company C: The Butler Rifles from Butler County
9:	1st Lieutenant:	Buford Dendy	Wounded
10:	Privates:	George Cornathan	Wounded
11:		William A. Grayden	Wounded
12:		J. E. Johnson	Killed
13:		John L. Powell	Wounded
14:		Henry O. Seale	Captured-sent to Camp Douglas, Ill.
15:		Manning C. Spradley	Wounded
16:		H. Thornton	Wounded

Company D: Bragg's Company from Coosa County
17:	Privates:	Rufus G. Adkins	Wounded
18:		Z. T. Bryant	Wounded
19:		Samuel H. Clisby	Killed
20:		William H. Macon	Wounded
21:		James W. Prickett	Wounded
22:		W. C. Richardson	Killed
23:		James A. I. Smallwood	Killed

Company E: The Dowdell Rangers from Randolph County
24:	Privates:	Newton Daniel	Wounded
25:		Richard Head	Wounded
26:		William Hodges	Wounded
27:		Theophilas Holder	Killed
28:		Francis M. Miller	Captured-sent to Camp Douglas, Ill.
29:		William F. Owen	Killed

The Battle of Peach Tree Creek

30:	J. T. Smith	Wounded
31:	Elisha Suggs	Wounded
32:	Elijah N. Taylor	Wounded

Company F: The Winter Greys from Montgomery County

33:	Sergeants: Henry B. Bray	Wounded
34:	Thomas S. O'Brian	Captured-sent to Johnson Island, Ohio
35:	Privates: Abijah Minto Addison	Wounded
36:	James Baker	Wounded
37:	W. H. Broadway	Killed
38:	O. F. Brown	Killed
39:	O. H. P. Cook	Wounded
40:	Patrick Griffin	Wounded
41:	H. P. Hall	Wounded
42:	Stephen Halso	Wounded
43:	Joseph Lovett	Wounded
44:	Charles B. McMillin	Killed
45:	David B. Mothershead	Wounded
46:	Thomas F. Owen	Wounded
47:	James Welch	Wounded

Company G: Ragland's Company from Ragland County

48:	Sergeant: L. S. Johnson	Wounded & Captured
49:	Privates: John J. Phillips	Wounded
50:	Robert Roberts	Wounded
51:	Lemuel Wynne	Wounded

Company H: McMillan's Company from Monroe County

52:	Lieutenant: R. M. Andress	Killed
53:	Privates: Neal H. Chisholm	Killed
54:	C. T. Dees	Killed
55:	W. W. Odione	Wounded
56:	N. J. Robinson	Wounded
57:	Henry Templin	Killed
58:	M. Lafayette Wiggins	Killed

Company I: The Pike Rangers from Pike County

59:	Captain: John Samuel Bones	Wounded
60:	Sergeant: William T. Harris	Wounded
61:	Privates: Early Adams	Wounded
62:	Wylie H. Hammonds	Captured-sent to Camp Douglas, Ill.
63:	Aldolphus M. Head	Wounded
64:	Alfred Johnson	Wounded
65:	Morgan McVay	Wounded
66:	Adoniram J. Pitts	Wounded
67:	Sampson M. Ward	Wounded
68:	James R. Weaver	Killed
69:	John R. Weaver	Wounded

Company K: The Butler True Blues from Butler County

70.	Captain: Thomas J. Burnett	Wounded
71.	Privates: Hillery Cunningham	Wounded
72.	John Henry Fife	Wounded
73.	Wylie H. Hammonds	Captured-sent to Camp Douglas, Ill.
74.	Thomas P. Hodge	Captured-sent to Camp Douglas, Ill.

Roster

75.	William J. Moore	Wounded
76.	George Wallace	Captured-sent to Camp Douglas, Ill.
Also:		
77. Co. D:	W. J. Robbins	Wounded, died at Ocmulgee Hosptial, Macon

Total: Killed-18 Wounded-51*   Captured-10**   Total- 77 (losses claimed: 130)
*Note-three of those wounded later died bringing the number of deaths sustained to 21.
**Note-two of those Captured were also Wounded.
Source-Thompson, Illene D. & Wilbur E., The Seventeenth Alabama History, a Regimental History and Roster, Heritage Books, Inc. (2001); Compiled Service Records, National Archives; Brewer, p. 617.

26th Alabama Infantry: (partial list & includes some from the 1st Corps (Ala.) Sharpshooters)
Field & Staff:
70:         (Adjt.)Lieutenant: Samuel H. Moore   Captured
Company A: "Dixie Boys" from Fayette County
71:         3rd Sergeant: Wiley S. Enis   Wounded
72:         Privates: Henry A. Brasher   Wounded
73:                      John L. Harbin   Captured
74:                      John F. Kelley   Wounded (lost leg)
75:                      Joseph Henry Stewart   Wounded
Company B:
76:         1st Lieutenant: E. Samuel Stuckey Killed
Detailed to Whitworth Rifle Sharpshooters upon his return to the Regiment in June, 1864.
Company C:
77:         Privates: George W. Kincannon   Wounded- (flesh wound to left thigh)
Company D:
78:         Captain: Isaac Henry Sanders   Wounded
79:         Private: Wilson J. Moore   Wounded (lower back)
Company E: (Fayette County) none known
Company F:
80:         Sergeant: James Hamilton Dowdle   Wounded
Company G.
81:         2nd Lieutenant: James Henry McFerrin Wounded
Company H:
82:         Private: James M. Byron   Wounded (right leg)
Company I:
83:         Private: Benjamin F. Wright   Wounded
Total regimental casualties were around 75.
Source-Compiled Service Records;
http://www.rootsweb.ancestry.com/~alcw26/26thala.htm. (March 20, 2008).

27th Alabama Infantry:
1. Co. B: Privates: H.C. Davis   Wounded, right arm amputated, Ocmulgee Hospital Macon, Ga. on 7-26-64
2.   William Molt   Wounded
3.   William W. Williams   Wounded, shoulder, Captured

The Battle of Peach Tree Creek

4. Co. D: Private: John A. Sapp — Wounded
5. Co. F: 2nd Lt.: John H. Jacks — Wounded
6. Co. I: 2nd Lt.: M. V. Vaden — Wounded
7.   Privates: John J. Herron — Wounded, in Ocmulgee Hosp. 7-22-64
8.   John P. Smith — Wounded
9. Co. K: Private: J. B. Randolph — Wounded, left forearm

Total: Killed-0, Wounded-9, Captured or Missing-1, Total-9
Source-Tennessee State Library & Archives (MF 1045, Roll 2).

29th Alabama: (partial list)

Company A:
1. Privates: Joel B. Childress — Wounded, jaw by a "stray shot"
2. J. T. Dobbins (age 19) — Wounded, shot in neck (& 2 brothers killed)
3. ___ Dobbins — Killed (left onfield)
4. ___ Dobbins — Killed (left on field)

Company B: Blount County Hornets
5. Privates: John Blackburn Campbell — Killed (left on field)
6. Robert Duncan — Wounded, left shoulder & Neck "badly" by Artillery fire, & Captured-sent to Camp Chase, Ill. Paroled June 11, 1865.

Company C:
7. Privates: Jasper Yielding — Killed
8. J. R. Yielding — Captured, (deserted ?-July 22, 1864 and was sent to Camp Chase, Ill.)

Company F (Blount County Tiger Boys):
9. Corporal: James S. Armstrong — Wounded, left foot
10. Privates: J.T. Armstrong — Wounded
11. William J. Armstrong — Wounded, nose, deserted, joined Roddy's Cav.
12. K.L. Holt — Wounded

Company G: Seal's Guards
13. Private: Moses Smith — Wounded-head

Company H:
14. Private: David Crumpton (age 18) — Wounded thigh, Ocmulgee Hospital, Macon, Ga. bullet removed on July 27, 1864
15. M. D. McQueen — Killed

Company I:
16. 2nd Sgt. William M. Welch — Wounded, died 7-26-64
17. Corporal Joseph Gibbens (Givens?) — Captured
18. Privates: James. A. Dawkins (Dockins?) — Captured
19. Walter Terry Eason — Killed
20. William Garrett — Captured, died 3-25-65
21. Elder Gomillion — Wounded, Captured, died 9-1-64
22. William Holland — Captured
23. William Holmes — Captured

Roster

24.		Alfred P. Martin	Captured, died 1-14-65
25.		Jonathan G. W. Miller	Captured
26.		James Wells	Captured
27.		William Wells	Captured, died 8-3-64

Company K:
28.	Captain:	John C. Hailey	Killed
29.	Privates:	Nicholas Carter	Killed
30.		James David Zorn	Killed
31.		John H. Walker (37)	Wounded-left hand, sent to Marshall Hosp., Columbus, GA

Co. Unknown
32.	Private:	John E. Johnson	Killed

Total: Killed-10, Wounded-12, Captured-11 (1 also wounded), Total-32*
*Note-this is only a partial list. Company I's roll is indicative of what the other Companies' casualty lists probably looked like. Total regimental casualties were around 75.
Source-http://www.geocities.com/Heartland/Estates/3071/Untitled/Page_1x.html (January 8, 2009).

30th Alabama:
1. Privates:Co. E:		Frank Roundtree	Wounded, leg
2.		Munday Spraggins	Wounded, mortally
3.	Co. F:	Ed Lackey	Wounded, severe right leg, discharged
4.	Co. H:	Henry Robinson	Wounded, severe, arm, discharged
5.		William Weeks	Wounded, severe, discharged
6.	Co. I:	Clinton Summers	Killed
7.		E. H. Trainer	Wounded, severe, discharged
8.	Co. K:	Alexander Brasher	Wounded, severe, discharged
9.		James H. Durrett	Wounded, captured, sent to Camp Chase

Total: Killed-1, Wounded-8 (1 mortally), Captured-1 (also wounded), Total-9
Source-Stephens, Larry D., Bound for Glory, A History of the 30th Alabama Infantry Regiment, Confederate States of America, p. 259.

35th Alabama: Col. Samuel Ives

Company B:
1. Corporal:	Joseph Nicholas Thompson	Wounded
2. Privates:	Marcus D. L. Green	Wounded lost a leg; was color bearer

-Wheeler, Robert, Co. B, became color bearer afterward
3.	George Goodwin	Wounded
4.	Charles Hardy	Wounded
5.	Scott Harrington	Killed

Company C:
6. 2nd Lt.	John A. Stewart	Wounded
7. Sgt.	William T. Craig	Wounded, amputated left ring finger.

Company G:
8. 1st Lt.	Evans, Augustus Franklin	Wounded
9. Sgt.	William G. Whitfield	Wounded
10. Privates:	Charles Howard	Captured

The Battle of Peach Tree Creek

11.   John Williams   Captured
Company H:
12. 2nd Lt.Thomas W. Carlock (born @1841)   Wounded, 5'10" tall, florid complexion, light hair, gray eyes
Total: Killed-1   Wounded-9   Captured or Missing-2   Total-12
Source-Tennessee State Library & Archives (MF 1045, Roll 2; Banning, pp. 52, & 71-152.)

39th Alabama:
1. Captain: C. H. Mathews   Killed
Source-Brewer, p. 649; Confederate Military History, Vol. VIII, Alabama, p. 179.

49th Alabama:
The 49th Alabama added no officers and sixteen more men to the casualty list with 15 men wounded and one man killed. With the casualties in the 29th and 35th Alabama, the Consolidated 27th- 35th - 49th Alabama thus lost 33 men wounded, 2 captured, and 2 killed for a total of 37 casualties.
Source-Tennessee State Library & Archives (MF 1045, Roll 2).

50th Alabama:
1. Wesley Harless   Killed

55th Alabama Infantry: Colonel John Snodgrass
1:     Lt. Colonel: John Henry Norwood   Wounded
2:     Major: John H. Gibson   Killed
3:     Major: Joseph Henry Jones   Killed
4:     1st Lt. & Acting Adjt.   Benjamin Moore   Killed
5:     Lt., Asst. Adjt.   John C. Howell   Wounded & Captured; left leg amputated, died 7-30-64
6:     Sgt. Major: Julyius Frazier   Captured, released Pt. Lookout, MD, 3-4-65
7:     Ensign: William M. Cowan   Wounded, in hospital, Macon, GA 3 gunshot wounds, rt. leg and lt. shoulder; carried flag
Company A:
8:     Privates: H. M. Mobley   Wounded & Captured, left leg amputated 7-24 Vining Station, died Chattanooga 7-30-64
9:     William Turner   Captured, released 6-13-65
Company B:
* 2nd Lt. John Clay Howell   Wounded & Captured, died 7-30-64, U.S.A. General Hospital, Kingston, Ga. gunshot wound and

Roster

    leg amputation (see #5. above)

Company C: (Calhoun County)
10: Captain: Peter Nunnelly — Wounded
11: 2nd Lt. John W. Easley — Wounded & Captured, 35 year old, left arm amputated 10-17-64, died 11-7-64 Nashville
12: Corporal: Michael D. Forbes — Captured, sent to Camp Douglas, Ill., released 7-17-65, 5',5" tall, dark eyes, dark hair, dark complexion, home-Oxford, Ala.
13: Privates: James M. Henderson — Captured, sent to Camp Douglas, Ill, died 3-13-65
14: Henry Murphy — Captured, sent to Camp Douglas, Ill, discharged 6-13-65
15: John W. Oliver — Captured, sent to Camp Douglas, Ill, discharged 6-15-65, dark complexion, dark hair, hazel eyes, 5' 8" tall
16: Lewis Oliver — Captured, sent to Camp Douglas, Ill, died 12-7-65

Company D: (Jackson County)
17: Captain J. W. Thompson — Wounded
18: Sergeant: John F. Isbell — Captured, sent to Camp Douglas; exchanged at Lookout, MD; reported at Gen'l Hospital, Richmond, VA, 1 March 65
19: Sergeant: Thomas H. Wright — Captured, sent to Camp Douglas
20: Private: John A. Haigwood — Wounded, sent Ocmulgee Hospital, Macon

Company E: (Jackson & Marshall Counties)
21: Captain: John W. Evans — Killed
22: Captain: Newton Mc Cullough — Wounded, died 7-26-64, USA field hospital
23: 2nd Lt.: S. W. Kelley — Wounded
24: 1st Sgt.: William T. Venable — Wounded & Captured, died, Camp Chase
25: 2nd Sgt.: R. P. Doss — Wounded, died 7-22-64, USA field hospital
26: Sgt.: Andrew M. Findly (Findley?) — Wounded & Captured, leg amputated Vining Station 7-25-64, died Chattanooga 8-16-64
27: Corporals: Nathaniel F. Pendergrass — Wounded left thigh, Captured, died 8-5-64, Chattanooga, age 22
28: James Perry — Wounded, left thigh, left knee, right hand, Captured, died 7-23-64, Chattanooga
29: Privates: D. Ealson — Wounded & Captured, arm
30: David Nelson (30) Captured, released 5-19-65 Camp Chase
31: William W. Swafford — Wounded & Captured, leg amputated, died 8-12-64 USA Hospital, Kingston, Ga.
32: William M. Waffer — Wounded & Captured, left leg amputated, 7-24-64 Vining Station. (Died ?)
33: William Williams — Wounded & Captured, shoulder, 7-26-64, Vining Station hospital (died?)

Company F:

The Battle of Peach Tree Creek

34:	1st Lt.:	John A. Mc Vay	Wounded
35:	2nd Lt.	W. H. Ramsey	Killed
36:	Sergeants:	William F. (S?) Burch	Wounded & Captured, left arm amputated 7-23-64 Vining, died 8-17-64 Chattanooga
37:		William G. Cloud	Wounded, died 8-4-64
38:	Corporal:	Silas C. Swaim	Captured, sent to Camp Chase
39:	Privates:	Baltimore Cooper	Wounded, calf of right leg, Floyd House, Macon, Ga.
40:		Alexander F. Jackson	Wounded & Captured
41:		Thomas C. Jenkins	Wounded, sent Ocmulgee Hospital, Macon
42:		Evonder F. McCampbell	Wounded & Captured, severe flesh wound of left thigh by cannon ball
43:		John Priest	Wounded & Captured, left leg flesh
44:		Henry H. Wells	Wounded, sent Floyd House, Macon
45:		Lorenzo D. Williams	Captured, died 12-22-64, Camp Douglas

Company G: (Marshall County)

46:	Captain	C. (Arthur) B. Carter	Killed
47:	1st Lt.:	D. R. Fletcher	Wounded
48:	2nd Lt.:	A. S. Mitchell	Wounded
49:	2nd Lt.:	John O. Robbins	Wounded
50:	Sgt.:	William A. Johnson	Wounded; admitted to Ocmulgee Hosp.
51:	Privates:	Charles Byles (Boyles?)	Wounded & Captured left leg amputated; died Camp Chase, 12-9-64
52:		Nathaniel Craig (age 21)	Wounded
53:		Andrew J Fletcher	Captured, sent Camp Douglas; died 1-2-65
54:		Noel C. Grammar	Wounded, admitted to Ocmulgee Hosp.
55:		William A. Haynie	Captured, sent Camp Douglas, out 6-13-65
56:		Daniel Hartrum	Captured sent Camp Douglas, out 3-24-65
57:		James Jones	Wounded & Captured-died Nashville, 1-28-65
58:		William King	Wounded & Captured
59:		R. G. Nixon	Captured, sent Camp Douglas, out 4-6-65
60:		Francis M. Reagan	Captured, sent Camp Douglas, died 12-7-64
61:		Thomas L. Lewis	Captured, sent Camp Douglas, out 5-1-65
62:		William Lewis	Captured, sent Camp Douglas, out 5-1-65
63:		Alexander J. Mc Campbell	Wounded & Captured, sent to Camp Chase; age 21, fair complexion, dark hair, gray eyes, 5' 6"; released 7-13-65
64:		William R. Martin	Captured, sent Camp Douglas, died 1-65
65:		William M. D. Wildman	Wounded & Captured, sent to Camp Chase; died 4-2-65, age 38; hit by cannonball in the right leg
66:		Joseph A. Woodall	Missing

Company H: (Jackson County)

67:	Captain	J. H. Cowan	Wounded

Roster

68: 1st Lt. Thomas F. Foster (age 24) Wounded & Captured, leg amputated, sent to Johnson's Island, exchanged 3-22-65
69: Sergeant: Columbus Cicero Henderson Captured, sent Camp Douglas, out 6-12-65, lt. complex, lt. hair, 5' 7" tall, blue eyes
70: Corporals: John Gross Wounded & Captured, arm amputated, died 8-15-64 Nashville
71: John B. Keys Wounded, sent Ocmulgee Hospital, Macon
72: Privates: Alexander Duncan (age 21) Captured 7-19-64, died 10-29-64 Nashville, light complex, sandy hair, blue eyes, 5' 7" tall
73: Charles Hampton Captured, sent Camp Douglas, died 9-5-64
74: Lafayette Howard Wounded, sent to Ocmulgee Hospital, Macon
75: Rufus J. Lawless Captured, sent Camp Douglas, out 5-11-65, 5' 1" tall, gray eyes, lt. complex, brown hair
76: Jesse G. Maxwell Wounded, sent Ocmulgee Hospital, light complex, dark hair, hazel eyes, 6' 0"
77: Daniel J. Sratt Wounded, head, sent Floyd House, Macon
78: Elias P. Wilbanks Captured, sent Camp Douglas, 5-11-65; light complex, brown hair, blue eyes, 5' 10" tall
79: C. L. Wilson Wounded & Captured, probably died at Field Hospital

Company I:
80: 2nd Lt.: John B., Starkey Wounded, fair complex, light hair, blue eyes, 5' 7" tall
81: Sgt.: S. H. Green Captured, sent Camp Douglas, out 6-17-65, light complex, dark hair, blue eyes, 5' 9 tall
82: Privates: James Caine Wounded & Captured, flesh wound, right arm severe, sent Camp Chase; died 6-4-65
83: W. D. Darwin Captured, fair complex, light hair, blue eyes, 5' 10" tall
84: J. W. C. Hood Wounded & Captured, sent Camp Douglas, out 6-17-65, fair complex, light hair, blue eyes, 5' 9" tall
85: James Hood Wounded & Captured, died Field Hospital
86: John W. Hood (age 21) Wounded & Captured, died 8-10-64 Chattanooga
87: William Jenkins Captured, sent Camp Chase, died 2-5-65
88: Thomas N. Robertson (age 25) Wounded & Captured, cannon ball shot in left thigh, died 7-25-64
89: Miles C. Taylor Captured, sent Camp Douglas out 3-26-65

Company K:
90: Sergeants: James H. Foster Captured, sent Camp Douglas, out 6-17-65, dark complex, brown hair, brown eyes, 5' 4"
91: William D. Sharp Wounded thigh St. Mary's Hosp. La Grange
92: Corporal: Jacob Weaver Wounded, 2 fingers amputated St. Mary's Hospital, La

The Battle of Peach Tree Creek

93:	Privates:	Henry H. Bridges (age 25)	Grange Captured, sent Camp Chase, died 8-6-64
94:		Darling Canada [Kennedy?]	Wounded left hand, loss of 4 fingers
95:		Robert R. Kirby	Captured sent Camp Douglas, out 6-17-65 dark complex, black hair, gray eyes, 5' 8" tall
96:		H. M Paty (Patty?)	Wounded & Captured, right shoulder, Vining Station Field Hospital, died 7-26-64
97:		H.N. Perry	Mortally Wounded (Killed)
98:		Anderson C. Tracey (age 38)	Wounded & Captured, left thigh, shoulder, & side, died 7-27-64, Vining Station
99:		Francis M. James	Wounded & Captured, leg amputated, Vining Station Field Hospital, died 7-29-64

Total: Killed-7   Wounded-59   Captured or Missing-62   Total-99
Sources-Tennessee State Library & Archives (MF 1045, Roll 2); Rex Miller, The Forgotten Regiment, a day-by-day account of the 55th AL Infantry Regiment, CSA (Dayton, OH: Morningside Bookstore, 1984); Brewer pp. 667-8.

57th Alabama: (330 present)

1:	Lt. Colonel:	W. C. Bethune	Wounded
2.	Major:	W. R. Arnold	Killed
3.	Adjutant:	John C. Judkins	Wounded
4.	2nd Lt. & (AAQM)	F. T. Dickinson	Wounded, died 7-23-64

Company A:

5.	Captain:	James P. Wood	Wounded
6.	1st Lt.:	John W. Mc Crary	Wounded, died 7-30-64
7.	2nd Lt.:	J. M. Hamill	Wounded
8.	3rd Lt. (Jr 2nd Lt.)	F. G. Colbert	Wounded & Captured, paroled 5-28-65
9.	Privates:	Benjamin F. Darby	Captured, died 10-30-64 Camp Chase
10.		William Mott (age 38)	Wounded & Captured, died 9-8-64 in hospital at Chattanooga
11.		Harmon G. Parks	Captured, died 7-24-64 Field Hospital
12.		Wilks Quattlebaum	Captured, died 2-2-65 Camp Douglas
13.		W. B. Swan	Captured, sent Camp Douglas, out 5-11-65

Company B:

14.	Captain:	Daniel Martin	Wounded
15.	Corporal:	John Thorn	Captured, paroled Camp Douglas 6-17-65
16.	Privates:	Edward Baker	Captured, died 9-12-1864 buried Chicago
17.		Jeptha W. Ferrer	Killed
18.		Arthur M. Redding	Captured
19.		James F Taylor	Captured, paroled Camp Douglas 6-5-65

Company C:

20.	Jr. 2nd Lt.	William D. Dennis	Wounded

Roster

21.	Corporal:	Harry A. Johnson	Captured, died Camp Chase 1-11-1865
22.	Privates:	James T. Dawson	Captured
23.		S. T. Dickinson	Captured
24.		Bryant H. Smith	Captured, died 3-5-65 Camp Chase
25.		Stephen Smith (age 25)	Captured, paroled Camp Chase 6-12-65

Company D:

26.	Captain:	J. S. Bruner	Wounded
27.	Privates:	William H Faulk (age 19)	Wounded
28.		Eldred Powell	Wounded & Capt., died 8-4-64 Chattanooga

Company E:

29.	1st Lt.:	J. Thomas Culver	Wounded
30.	Jr. 2nd Lt.:	Alexander D. Wood (age 22)	Wounded
31.	Corporals:	Albert H. Hogan	Wounded, Captured, died 8-20-64 Chattanooga
32.		Lewis Q. Phillips	Wounded, died 7-22-64 buried Field Hospital
33.	Privates:	John A. Boney	Wounded
34.		Shadrack D. Dees	Wounded, Captured, died 7-23-64
35.		Isaac R. Etheridge	Wounded, died 7-25-64
36.		Jacob Haymans (age 37)	Wounded
37.		J. T. Jackson	Captured
38.		Thaddeus A. Kelley	Captured, released 8-21-1865
39.		William R Pybus (Pylens?)	Captured, paroled Camp Douglas 6-17-65
40.		Asa M. Rhodes	Killed
41.		James Wood	Wounded, died 7-22-64 buried Field Hospital

Company F:

42.	Captain:	Rueben H. Lane	Wounded
43.	1st Lt.:	J. C. Baskins	Wounded
44.	2nd Lt.:	Richard A. Ramsey (age 27)	Captured paroled 6-16-65
45.	Privates:	Joseph Jones	Killed
46.		J. N. Register	Wounded, died 7-31-64

Company G:

47.	2nd Lt.:	Benjamin G. Byrd, Jr.	Wounded, died 8-29-64 Macon
48.	Privates:	John Clements	Captured, paroled 6-8-65
49.		James Powell	Wounded, died 9-13-64 Macon
50.		Charles W. Tindall	Captured, sent to Lookout Mt. Md
51.		Malikiah William Walker	Captured, died 11-22-64 Camp Douglas

Company H:

52.	Captain:	Bailey M. Talbot	Wounded, died 8-7-64 Chattanooga
53.	1st Lt.:	Alexander M. Faison (age 36)	Wounded
54.	Jr. 2nd Lt.:	John W. Conner	Wounded
55.	Privates:	John Bolland	Captured
56.		D. Carliles	Captured, paroled 6-10-65
57.		Needham Carlisle	Wounded, died 7-22-1864
58.		Mack/Mike Mathews	Captured, sent to Camp Douglas

The Battle of Peach Tree Creek

59.	William Mc Matthews (age 40)	Captured
60.	John Pipkin	Wounded, died 7-31-64

Company I:
61. Captain:	Augustus L. Milligan (age 37)	Wounded
62. Privates:	James M. Bass	Captured
63.	J. W. Bolling	Captured

Company K:
64. 2nd Lt.:	T. Walter Wiley (age 24)	Wounded, Captured, paroled 6-16-65
65. 4th Sgt.:	Levi Garrison	Captured, died 12-2-65 Camp Chase
66. Corporal:	John Hudson	Captured, paroled 6-7-1865
67. Privates:	Lacy Bailey	Wounded, died 8-27-1864 Macon
68.	Noah Cook	Captured, 5'6", Light hair, blue eyes, light complex, paroled 6-13-65
69.	W. B. Cowin	Captured
70.	Milton G. Hudson	Captured, paroled 6-16-65
71.	Thomas King	Captured, paroled 6-10-65
72.	Gilbert Mathews (age 44)	Wounded, Captured, died 12-15-64 Nashville
73.	Thomas Mc Cullock	Captured
74.	Frank Ming	Captured, paroled 6-12-65
75.	J. T. Randolph	Killed
76.	William P. Redmon	Captured, paroled 6-5-65
77.	Levi Roberts	Captured, paroled 6-16-65
78.	William J. Spence (Spencer)	Captured, paroled 6-10-65

Total: Killed-5 Wounded-36 Captured or Missing-44 Total-78 (lost 157 men)
Sources-Tennessee State Library & Archives (MF 1045, Roll 2); Brewer, pp. 668-9; http://history-sites.com/~kjones/ALofficers.html (June 13, 2009).

Arkansas:
1st Arkansas Mounted Rifles:
Company B (The Des Arc Rangers from Prarie County):
1.	1st Lt.:	Wiley Dyer	Captured-July 19th at Moore's Mill

Company D:
2.	Private:	Morris Lewis	Killed-July 20th

Company E (The Lawrence County Rifles):
3.	Private:	William Taylor	Wounded-July 19th at Moore's Mill

Company F:
4.	Private:	James Johnson	Wounded-July 19th at Moore's Mill

Company K:
5.	1st Lt.:	Alfred Page	Wounded-July 20th

Total: Killed-1, Wounded-3, Missing or Captured-1, Total-5 (2 wounded and 1 captured at Moore's Mill).

2nd Arkansas Mounted Rifles:
1.	Major:	James P. Eagle	Wounded-July 19th at Moore's Mill

Company B:

Roster

2.   1st Sgt.:   William W. Easley   Wounded-July 20th (died 8-5-64)
3.   Private: John M. Bell   Wounded, mortally-July 19th at Moore's Mill
4.   J. P. Talkington   Wounded & Captured-July 20th

Company C:
5.   Corporals: Leonidas Davis   Killed-July 19th at Moore's Mill
6.   Hynson M. Hicks   Wounded-July 20th (died 7-21-64)
7.   Privates: John R. Birmingham   Wounded-July 20th
8.   John E. Callahan   Wounded-July 20th (died 8-10-64)

Company D:
9.   Private: James H. Selvidge   Wounded-July 19th at Moore's Mill

Company G:
10.   Private: Samuel King   Wounded-July 19th at Moore's Mill

Company H:
11.   2nd Lt.:   John A. Kirkpatrick   Wounded-July 19th at Moore's Mill
12.   Sergeant: J. E. Johnson   Wounded-July 20th
13.   Corporal: John Aston   Wounded-July 19th at Moore's Mill (died 7-20-64)
14.   Privates: Mutt Beale   Wounded-July 19th at Moore's Mill
15.   S.S. Brooks   Wounded-July 19th at Moore's Mill
16.   Alfred C. Conway   Wounded-July 20th
17.   Robert N. Crank   Wounded-July 19th at Moore's Mill
18.   J. Victor Green   Wounded-July 19th at Moore's Mill
19.   L. R. Muldrow   Wounded-July 19th at Moore's Mill
20.   C. C. Robinson   Killed-July 19th at Moore's Mill
21.   A. D. Sullivan   Wounded-July 20th

Company I:
22.   Sergeant Denis Boultinghouse   Wounded and Captured-July 20th (died 9-13-64)
23.   Privates: John B. Graves   Captured-July 20th
24.   Alexander Womack   Missing/Captured-July 19th at Moore's Mill (died of small pox at Camp Douglas 12-6-64)

Total: Killed-2, Wounded-20 (7 of which died), Missing or Captured-4 (2 also wounded), Total-24 (2 killed, 11 wounded and 1 captured at Moore's Mill).

4th Arkansas:

Company A:
1.   Private: Joseph L. Bankston   Captured-July 20th

Company B:
2.   1st Lt.:   William L. Cobb   Wounded-July 20th (died 8-11-64)
3.   Hospital Steward Private John P. Clark Wounded-July 19th at Moore's Mill

Company E:
4.   1st Sgt.:   William M. Arnett   Killed-July 20th
5.   Privates: Joseph R. Parker   Killed-July 20th
6.   James J. Tucker   Killed-July 20th

Company F:
7.   Private: Rufus W. May   Killed-July 19th at Moore's Mill

Company G:
8.   1st Sgt.:   Columbus K. Garner   Wounded-July 20th

Company I:

The Battle of Peach Tree Creek

9.	Private:	Robert Joslin	Wounded-July 20th
Company K:			
10.	Private:	F. D. W. Watson	Wounded-July 20th

Total: Killed-4, Wounded-5 (1 of which died), Missing or Captured-1, Total-10 (1 killed, and 1 wounded at Moore's Mill).

9th Arkansas:

Company A:
1. Privates: William Lamb — Captured-July 19th at Moore's Mill
2. Joseph Lights — Wounded-foot-July 19th at Moore's Mill
3. William M. Mc Fall — Captured-July 19th at Moore's Mill
4. James M. Sterling — Captured-July 20th

Company B:
5. Sergeant: Marcus Lafayette White — Wounded-July 20th
6. Private: William E. Henderson — Killed-July 19th at Moore's Mill

Company D:
7. Corporal: Alexander D. Black — Wounded-foot-July 19th at Moore's Mill
8. Privates: David E. Stinson — Wounded-July 20th
9. James M. Sterling — Wounded-July 20th

Company F:
10. Privates: German L. Bass — Wounded-July 20th
11. Alphonse Brewster — Wounded-July 20th
12. Elbert F. Cook — Wounded-July 20th (died 7-24-64)
13. A. N. Hopkins — Wounded-July 20th
14. Albert G. Lessel — Wounded-right thigh-July 20th
15. James M. McGuffy — Wounded-July 20th
16. Zebulon T. Morris — Wounded-July 19th at Moore's Mill
17. Benjamin F. Pritchard — Wounded-July 19th at Moore's Mill
18. Benjamin C. Rice — Wounded-July 20th

Company G:
19. Privates: James M. Baskin — Wounded-arm-July 20th (arm amputated at Macon, and sent home on 11-10-64)
20. John Thomas Berry — Wounded-July 19th at Moore's Mill (died in Hospital at Forsyth, Ga.)
21. Rolling Jasper Sanders — Wounded-July 20th

Company H:
22. Private: John D. Summers — Wounded-July 18th above Moore's Mill

Company I:
23. Captain: Samuel Lindsey — Wounded-right arm-July 19th at Moore's Mill (arm amputated at Macon hospital)
24. Sergeant: Duncan B. McKenzie — Killed-July 19th at Moore's Mill
25. Private: Eugene G. Fudge — Wounded-July 19th at Moore's Mill

Total: Killed-2, Wounded-20 (2 of which died), Missing or Captured-3, Total-25 (2 killed, 8 wounded, and 2 captured at Moore's Mill).

Roster

31st Arkansas Regiment:
1. Sergeants: J. W. Carter — Killed-July 19th at Moore's Mill
2. Andrew Lin — Killed-July 20th
3. Privates: W.W. Babb — Killed-July 19th at Moore's Mill
4. W. W. Daugherty — Wounded-July 19th at Moore's Mill
5. Stephen M. Mathews — Killed-July 20th
6. Edmond S. Stafford — Wounded-July 19th at Moore's Mill
7. Iven Thomas — Killed-July 20th

Total: Killed-5, Wounded-2, Missing or Captured-0, Total-7 (2 wd. & 2 killed at Moore's Mill)

Source-Bass, Ronald R., History of the 31st Arkansas Confederate Infantry, p. 75.

Florida:
3rd Florida Infantry Regiment:
1. Private: Asher E. Stevens — Wounded

7th Florida Infantry Regiment:
1. Privates: Co. C Henry D. Sapp — Wounded
2. Co. D Charles J. McKinney — Wounded
3. Co. F Charles M. Prevatt — Wounded (July 19, 1864)
4. Co. G Ervin Eunis — Killed
5. Co. K Payne Perry — Killed

Total: Killed-2, Wounded-3, Total-5

Georgia:
1st Confederate Georgia Regiment:
1. Colonel: George A. Smith — Killed
2. Sgt. Major: William L. Braswell — Killed
3. 1st Lieutenant: Charles E. Ross — Captured (released: Johnson's Island, Oh, 6-15-65)

Company A: Independent Volunteers from Bibb County
4. Jr. 2nd Lt.: John R. Field — Wounded
5. Privates: E. Augling — Killed
6. Henry Y. Ferrell — Wounded (also wounded at Chickamauga)-in hospital at Macon-parole Macon, 1865
7. Samuel Fields — Killed (while carrying the colors after the bearer was shot down)
8. Thomas Ford — Wounded (present by 8-31-64)
9. J. C. George — Killed
10. William G. George — Killed
11. Soloman M. Groce — Wounded (sick in hospital, Macon 8-31-64
12. Thomas L. Hill — Wounded (captured Macon 4-20 & 21-65)
13. William A. Jackson — Wounded (captured Macon 4-20 & 21-65)
14. George H. Johnston — Wounded (right arm-hospital Macon)
15. J. C. Keel — Wounded (surrendered N. Carolina 4-26-65)
16. J. Ryan — Killed

The Battle of Peach Tree Creek

17. Monroe E. White   Wounded (ambulance driver by 8-31-65)
Company B: Ringgold Volunteers from Catoosa County
18. 2nd Lt.: Henry L. Ray   Captured (sent to Johnson's Island, Oh.; released 6-15-65)
19. Corporal: Charles W. Gaines   Wounded (in hospital 8-31-65)
20. Privates: Samuel Crawford   Wounded
21. Robert Crowder   Wounded (surrendered N. Carolina 4-26-65)
22. John L. Ford   Killed
23. Jesse French   Wounded (in hospital 8-31-64)
24. Samual E. Gilliland   Captured (sent to Camp Douglas; took Oath on 3-25-65 and joined U.S. Infantry; deserted 8-18-65)
25. ___ Roberson   Wounded
26. Van Buren Trammell   Captured (sent to Camp Douglas, Ill.; joined U.S. Infantry on 4-6-65; deserted from Ft. Riley, Kansas 8-2-65)
27. C. Tyler   Wounded
28. T. Williams   Wounded
Company C: The "Brown Infantry" from Bibb County (second Co. E)
29. 2nd Lt.: Wyatt E. Saunders   Wounded (through right wrist, resulting in permanent disability; born 10-12-1838; in hospital in Macon 8-31-64)
30. 5th Sgt.: Wiley H. Wagnon   Wounded (in hospital in Macon 10-27-64)
31. 4th Cpl.: William S. Sullivan   Killed (born 1840)
32. Privates: N. T. Bugh   Wounded
33. William T. Easley   Killed
34. Joseph W. (James?) Owens   Wounded (with supply train duty 8-31-64)
35. J. B. Ross   Wounded

2nd Company C: Fulton County
36. Private: M. Newton Bankston   Captured (sent to Camp Douglas, Ill.; released 6-16-65)
Company D: Fulton County
37. Qtr-Mst. Sgt. Benjamin W. Jones   Wounded (born 3-22-1831; died 5-11-1904)
2nd Company D: Catoosa and Walker County
38. Captain: Russell J. Jones   Wounded (also wounded at Chickamauga; absent wounded 8-31-64)
39. 1st Sgt. Morris Quinn Workman   Wounded (absent wounded 8-31-64)
40. Privates: J. H. Bartlett   Captured (7-19-64)
41. Ruben S. Hairn (or Hain)   Wounded (absent wounded 8-31-64)
42. James K. Ward   Wounded (born 4-11-1842)
Company E: The "Etowah Infantry" Bartow County
43. 4th Sgt.: William M. Goodwin   Killed
2nd Company E: Bartow County
44. Lieutenants: ___ Cass   Wounded
45. ___ Sanders   Wounded
46. Sgt.: ___ Hambright   Wounded
47. Cpl.: ___ Gray   Wounded
48. Privates: F. L. Bell   Wounded (in hospital Griffin, Ga., 8-

Roster

31-64)
49.	James M. Bell	Killed
50.	Samuel W. Braswell	Killed
51.	Alexander Cox	Captured (sent to Camp Douglas, Ill., took Oath and released 1-18-65)
52.	Henry Day	Wounded (in hospital Macon, Ga. 8-31-64)
53.	John J. Dedmon	Wounded (in hospital Macon, Ga. 8-31-64)
54.	Thomas Eatly	Killed
55.	John D. Goodwin	Wounded (in hospital Macon, Ga. 9-16-64)
56.	Thomas C. Haddock	Wounded (in hospital Macon, Ga. 9-16-64)
57.	Aaron W. Hambright	Wounded (in hospital Macon, Ga. 8-31-64)
58.	___ Jenkins	Wounded
59.	W. J. King	Wounded (in hospital Macon, Ga. 8-31-64)
60.	J. W. L. Mercer	Killed
61.	Peter Mercer	Killed
62.	T. M. Mercer	Killed
63.	___ Sullivan	Wounded

2nd Company F:
64.	Sgt.: ___ Anderson	Wounded
65.	Privates: ___ Hollis	Killed
66.	William T. Lenox	Wounded (in both thighs)
67.	___ Lindy	Killed

2nd Company G: Floyd County
68.	1st Lt.: Charles P. Deane	Wounded & Captured (in Nashville 12-16-64, released from Johnson's Island, Oh. 5-22-65)
69.	3rd Cpl. Joseph E. Moore	Captured (sent to Camp Douglas, released 6-16-65)
70.	Privates: Nathaniel Atkins	Wounded (and permanently disabled, in hospital 8-31-64)
71.	Henry C. Pierce	Wounded & Captured (joined U.S. Army 4-4-65)
72.	Lewis D. Pollard	Killed
73.	John M. Wood	Captured (released Camp Douglas 6-16-65)

The Battle of Peach Tree Creek

Company H:
74.	Private:	Charles H. Boyd	Killed
2nd Company H:
75.	4th Sgt:	John H. Reynolds	Killed
76.	Privates:	Green Fields	Wounded
77.		William Riley Fields	Killed
78.		W. R. Johnson	Captured (Camp Douglas, took oath 1-1-65; exchanged Pt. Lookout, Md. 2-21-65)
79.		John H. Lee	Captured (Camp Douglas, died of pleurisy 1-24-65)
80.		John Long	Wounded
81.		Duncan Lucas	Wounded (died of wounds 8-15-64)
82.		John B. Rogers	Killed
83.		James W. Taylor	Captured (Camp Douglas, died of fever 12-11-64)
Company I:
84.	Privates:	Franklin Acre	Killed
85.		Peyton F. Childress	Captured (Camp Douglas, joined 6th U.S. Infantry 3-25-65)
86.		___ Glass	Wounded
2nd Company I: Catoosa County
87.	1st Sgt.:	T. N. Glass	Wounded (absent wounded 8-31-65)
88.	Private:	Myrick L. Ansley	Captured (Camp Douglas, joined 6th U.S. Infantry 3-25-65)
2nd Company K:
89.	Sgt.:	___ Thompson	Killed
90.	Private:	William H. Foster	Captured(Camp Douglas took oath 4-22-65)

7-19	Killed-0 Wounded-0	Captured-1	Total-1
7-20	Killed-26 Wounded-49*	Captured-16 (18)	Total-91
Total:	Killed-26 Wounded-49**	Captured-17 (19)***	Total- 92

*Note-two of those Wounded were also Captured
**Note-one of those wounded later died.
***Note-two of those Captured later died, bringing the number of deaths sustained to 19.
(Sources-Henderson, Lillian, Roster of the Confederate Soldiers of Georgia, Vol. I; Macon Daily Telegraph, Aug. 22 & Aug. 25, 1864.)

1st Georgia Battalion Sharpshooters:
Company D:
1.	3rd Cpl.:	John F. Hall	Wounded
Total:	Killed-0 Wounded-1	Captured-0	Total-1

1st Georgia Regulars Infantry:
Company I:
1.	Private:	Thomas A. Murphey	Wounded (sent to hospital Augusta)
Total:	Killed-0 Wounded-1	Captured-0	Total- 1

2nd Georgia Battalion Sharpshooters:
Company D:

1.   Private: C. P. Huffman   Wounded (sent to hospital)
Total: Killed-0 Wounded-1   Captured-0   Total- 1
Source-Roster of the 2nd Ga. Battl., S.S., G.G.M./Vol. 35, No. 1-2 (Issue 136-6, Winter/Spring, 1995), courtesy, Chickamauga National Battlefield Park Library, vertical files.

25th Georgia Infantry:
Company D:
2.   Private: Virgil Waters   Killed
Company E: Liberty Volunteers from Liberty County
3.   Privates: Seaborn E. Jones   Wounded (abdomen & 2 fingers amputated, hosp. Macon; 7-29-64 given 60 day furlough)
4.   John Osgood Parker   Captured (fell into ravine and was captured; born 10-10-1848; discharged 2/65)
Company I:
5.   Private: James H. Blitch   Captured
Company L: Calhoun Repeaters from Calhoun County
6.   1st Lt.   W. A. Brown   Killed
7.   Privates: William H. Bailey   Killed (7-19-64)
8.   John Christy (or Christie) Killed
9.   W. G. Daniels   Wounded
10.   Lewis Gardner   Killed
11.   David Mimms   Killed
12.   Green Murkerson   Wounded (in thigh, in hospital, Macon)
13.   William E. Neal   Captured

7-19:   Killed-1 Wounded-0   Captured-0   Total-1
7-20:   Killed-5 Wounded-3   Captured-3   Total-11
Total: Killed-6 Wounded-3   Captured-3   Total-12

29th Georgia Infantry:
Company A:
1.   3rd Cpl.: John F.(Franklin?) Hall Wounded
2.   Private: William E. Harper   Wounded (through left breast, born Morgan Co., Ga., 12-23-1840, died Confederate Soldiers Home, Atlanta, 7-29-1904)
Company B: Ochlock Light Infantry from Thomas County
3.   Privates: Richard Thomas Hicks   Wounded (discharged 1864)
4.   W. A. Roberts   Wounded
Company C:
5.   1st Lt.:   Jasper Marion Roberts   Killed (may have been in Co. G).*
6.   Privates: James C. Braswell   Wounded (right shoulder)
7.   Burrell H. Howell   Killed
8.   John W. McClellan   Wounded (died)
Company D: Berrien Minutemen from Berrien, Clinch, and Lowndes Counties

The Battle of Peach Tree Creek

9.   Private: Elias Lastinger   Killed (he was from Bulloch Co., Ga.)
Company H: Thomas County Volunteers from Thomas County
10.   Private: Thomas M. Wilbanks   Wounded (in leg amputated
                                                         below the knee)

Company I: Berry Infantry from Floyd County
11.   Sgt.:   James W. Phillips   Wounded (at PC, leg amputated, &
                                                         then in train collision between Macon
                                                         & Atlanta)
12.   Private: Kerr W. Berryhill   Wounded (resulting in loss of right eye and
                                                         Captured; Camp Douglas, released 6-
                                                         18-65, born 8-31-1841)
Total (all on 7-20): Killed-3 Wounded-9   Captured-1
                                                   Total-12**

* http://www.southernmessenger.org/flag_poles.htm. (March 1, 2008).
**Note one of the wounded was also captured.

30th Georgia Infantry:
Company A: Butts Invincibles from Butts County
1.   1st Cpl.: John H. McCallum   Wounded & Captured (also wounded at
                                                         Chickamauga; rel. Camp Douglas 6-16-
                                                         65)
2.   Privates: James B. Cook   Killed
3.   Frederick Herring   Killed
Company B: Bailey Volunteers from Butts County
4.   Privates: Barney Amerson   Killed
5.   William H. Bryant   Wounded (died of wounds 1864; also
                                                         wounded at Chickamauga)
Company C: Hunter Guards from Butts and Spalding Counties
6.   2nd Cpl.: James W. Willis   Wounded (in right arm in hospital; on
                                                         home furlough at war's end; also
                                                         wounded at Chickamauga; born 10-24-
                                                         1840)
Company D: Huguenin Rifles from Bibb County
7.   Privates: Marion Heard   Captured
8.   John R. Miller   Wounded (also wounded at
                                                         Chickamauga)
Company F: Campbell Sharpshooters from Campbell County
9.   Privates: John G. Maxwell   Captured (7-19-64)
10.   Andrew J. White   Captured (took oath at Louisville, Ky.
                                                         9-19-64; died of small pox in Indiana
                                                         1865)
Company H: Fayette Volunteers from Fayette County
11.   Privates: Taverner H. Flowers   Wounded (through right thigh, unable
                                                         to return; b. 4-9-1838, likely died on
                                                         field)
12.   Daniel M. Franklin   Wounded and Captured (parole from
                                                         Camp Douglas 3-4-1866; James River,
                                                         Va 3-18-1866)
Company I: Clayton Invincibles from Clayton County
13.   Private: Ira Allen Estes   Wounded (and overcome by heat and

Roster

Company K: Chattahoochee Volunteers from Campbell County
14. Privates: Marion R.(or Warren E.) Barefield Wounded
15. Z. T. Estep Wounded (left knee)
16. David Hattaway Wounded (in leg necessitating amputation)

sent home; born 4-22-1833)

7-19:	Killed-0 Wounded-0	Captured-1	Total-1
7-20:	Killed-3 Wounded-10	Captured-4	Total-15
Total:	Killed-3 Wounded-10	Captured-5	Total-16*

*Note two of the wounded were also captured.

36th Georgia Infantry:
Company I: Whitfield County
1. Private: Starling Cochran   Captured(enlisted 3-19-1862, deserted 7-20-64, took oath of allegiance to U. S. Govt. at Louisville, Kty., & released to remain North of Ohio River during war on 7-31-1864)

Total: Killed-0 Wounded-0   Captured-1   Total- 1

37th Georgia Infantry:
Company A: Spring Place Volunteers from Murray County
1. Private: Thomas B. Stacey   Captured (7-19-06)
Company F: Franklin Rangers from Franklin County
2. Cpl.: Thomas W. Crowe   Wounded (in right hand necessitating amputation of 3rd finger; surrendered at North Carolina on 4-26-1865, born 6-10-1844, died 3-8-1925)
Company K: Lulu Guards from Muscogee County
3. Privates: James Boyett   Killed
4. Aaron Long   Killed (7-19-1864 on skirmish line while guarding crossing at Peach Tree Creek)

Total: Killed-2 Wounded-1(4)* Captured-1   Total- 4 (7)*
*Note-3 unknown wounded in Company H.

39th Georgia Infantry:
Company A: Cohutta Rangers from Murray County
1. Private: William M. Jay   Captured (7-20-64 at Dalton; released Camp Douglas 5-11-65)

Total: Killed-0 Wounded-0   Captured-1   Total- 1

40th Georgia Infantry:
Company F: Paulding Washington Guards from Paulding County
1. Private: R. P. Driskoll   Captured (7-20-64; died Camp Douglas of small pox 12-4-64)

Total: Killed-0 Wounded-0   Captured-1   Total- 1

41st Georgia Infantry:

The Battle of Peach Tree Creek

Company E: Troup Light Guards from Troup County
1.   Private: Thomas J. Gilbert   Wounded (left arm amputated above elbow, born 12-1-36, died 1913 in Troup Co.)
Total: Killed-0   Wounded-1   Captured-0   Total- 1

42nd Georgia Infantry:
Company H: Walton Tigers from Walton County
1.   Private: George W. Cauley   Killed (on picket near Atlanta, 7-20-64)
2.   J. S. Eason   Wounded (7-22-64 at Peach Tree Creek)
3.   William W. Turnbull   Killed (near Atlanta 7-20-64)
Total: Killed-2   Wounded-1   Captured-0   Total-3

46th Georgia Infantry:
Company C: Muscogee Volunteers from Muscogee County
1.   3rd Cpl.: J. M. Fletcher   Wounded
2.   Privates: J. D. Moye   Wounded (thumb of left hand shot off)
3.   G. E. Parker   Wounded (also wounded at Franklin)
4.   Robert Wiseman   Wounded (sent to hospital at Columbus, Ga.)
Company D: Chattahoochee Sentinels from Chattahoochee County
5.   Private: James D. Bishop   Wounded (surrendered NC 4-28-65)
Company E: Harris Blues from Harris County
6.   1st Sgt.: F. A. Worrell   Killed (7-19-64)
7.   2nd Sgt.: Lorenzo D. Hutchinson   Captured (7-19-64, was appt. 2nd Sgt 7-18)
8.   3rd Cpl.: Leander P. Hopkins   Wounded (7-19-64, also wounded in left hip at Franklin, Tn., & captured 12-17-64, released Rock Isl., Ill., 5-17-65, died 1921)
9.   Privates: W. A. Bailey   Wounded (& permanently disabled)
10.   William J. Bass   Captured (7-19-64)
11.   Henry S. Cash   Captured (7-19-64)
12.   Thomas Jefferson Daniel   Captured (7-19-64)
13.   Joseph D. Hart   Captured (7-19-64)
14.   Robert M. Moss (or Morris)   Captured (7-19-64, released Camp Douglas 6-18-65)
15.   Allen E. Richardson   Captured (7-19-64)
16.   Alfred A. Smith   Captured (7-19-64, released Camp Douglas 6-20-65)
17.   Thomas B. Smith   Captured (7-19-64)
18.   James Eugene C. Speer (or Spears)   Captured (7-19-64, released Camp Douglas 6-16-65)
Company F: Webster County Invincibles
19.   Privates: William P. Davis   Killed (accidentally killed)
20.   Theophilus P. Everett   Wounded
21.   James D. (or Joseph D.) Shepherd   Wounded (captured on Taylor's Ridge, Ga. 10-16-64; released Camp Douglas 6-16-65)
22.   Jacob Young   Wounded

Roster

Company H: Marion Volunteers from Marion County
23. 2nd Cpl.: George J. Barker   Wounded (7-19-64, left leg permanently disabled)
24. Privates: James M. Adams   Killed (7-20-64)
25. Jesse Benson   Killed (7-19-64)
26. P. T. Ingram   Captured (7-20-64, released 6/65 Camp Chase, Ohio)

Company I: Talbot Grenadiers or Volunteers from Talbot County
27. Private: Ludy Pyles Jones   Wounded (through right leg, partial fracture of tibia; b. 3-17-24, furloughed for 60 days from Macon hospital)

Company K: Price Volunteers from Muscogee County
28. Privates: A. D. Dunnagan   Killed (7-19-64)
29. George H. Phillips   Wounded (in leg, on light duty as shoemaker in Quartermaster Dept. at Columbus, Ga. 5-1-65, born at Indian Springs, Ga. 8-30-44)

7-19:	Killed-3 Wounded-2	Captured-10	Total-15
7-20:	Killed-2 Wounded-11	Captured-1	Total-14
Total:	Killed-4 Wounded-13	Captured-11	Total-29

52nd Georgia Infantry:

Company A: Habersham Guards from Habersham County
1. Private: Barron D. Kinsey   Wounded (necessitating amputation of third finger, born in Georgia 5-9-40, died from bronchitis contracted in service 1903)

Company C: Lumpkin County
2. Private: John W. Smith   Captured (released Camp Douglas, 6-16-65, born Buncombe Co., N.C., 1826)

Company D: Boyd Guards from Lumpkin County
3. 4th Sgt.: John C. Head   Captured

Company F: Beauregard Braves from Rabun County
4. Privates: Elisha M. Johnson   Captured (released Camp Douglas, 6-16-65, born White Co., 1841)
5. William M. Young   Captured (released Camp Douglas 6-12-65, born McDowell, NC, 11-28-34, died of paralysis, Rabun Co., Ga. 12-1-1900)
6. John Shook   Captured (Camp Douglas, enlisted in Co. K, 5th U.S., 4-18-65)
7. William T. Smith   Captured (died of intermittent fever at Camp Douglas, 9-7-64)
8. Andrew Jackson Worley   Captured (released Camp Douglas, 6-16-65, born Rabun Co., Ga. 6-11-33)
9. James Worley   Captured (released Camp Douglas, 6-16-65)

The Battle of Peach Tree Creek

Company G: Alleghany Rangers from Union County
10.   Captain: Julius H. Barclay   Killed

Total: Killed-1   Wounded-1   Captured-8   Total-10

54th Georgia Infantry:
Company A: Lamar Infantry from Bibb County
1.   Privates: Joseph J. Churchill   Captured (released Camp Douglas, 6-16-65, also wounded in head, loss of sight in right eye at Kennesaw Mountain 6-27-64)
2.   William Dunlap   Captured (released Camp Douglas, 6-13-65)
3.   Miles W. Kitchens   Wounded (thigh, in hospital, born 11-28-44)
4.   F. M. Ryle   Wounded (sent home on sick furlough, born 2-2-1833 in Williamson Co., Ga.)
5.   James A. Tidwell   Wounded (right hand, unfit for further duty)

Company C: Bartow Infantry from Emanuel County
6.   5th Sgt.   E. H. Bryant   Wounded (died at Oliver Hospital 8-3-64)
7.   Privates: John K. Hall   Captured (released Camp Douglas, 7-30-65)
8.   Privates: J. C. Johnson   Wounded (right wrist & permanently disabled, born 2-2-36 in Ga.)
9.   H. T. Scott   Wounded (sent home for rest of war, born 1845 in Ga.)
10.   John F. Simpson   Wounded (left hand, necessitating amputation of four fingers, & wounded through left breast, surrendered in N.C., born 7-22-44 in Ga.)

Company D: Screvin County
11.   Privates: Edward W. Miller   Wounded (right leg & left shoulder, hospital, paroled from hospital 5-26-65)
12.   J. B. Newton   Wounded (hospital, sick with measles in Augusta, Aug., 1864, born in Ga. 11-23-44)
13.   E. Peel   Killed

Company E: Berrien County
14.   Private: William H. Griffin   Wounded (Ocmulgee Hospital, Macon, Ga.)

Company K: Appling County
15.   Privates: John Westberry   Wounded (left thigh, born Liberty Co, Ga 1830)
16.   G. W. Williams   Wounded (right side)
Total: Killed-1   Wounded-12   Captured-3   Total-16

56th Georgia Infantry:

Roster

Company H: Carrol Invincibles from Carrol County
1.	Lt.:	Sim K. Goolsby	Wounded (right arm, necessitating amputation)
2.	Lt.:	S. L. Hilton	Wounded (right arm, necessitating amputation)

Company K: Heard County
3.	1st Lt.:	Isaac J. Stephens	Wounded (7-21-64)

Total: Killed-0   Wounded-3   Captured-0   Total-0

57th Georgia Infantry:

Company A: The Dixie Boys from Thomas County
1.	1st Cpl.:	James Fleming Cone	Wounded (in Way Hospital, Meridian, Ms., on account of wounds 1-26-65)
2.	Privates:	Benjamin J. Worrell	Killed
3.		Robert Worrell	Killed

Company B: Laurens County
4.	Private:	Augustus G. Fountain	Killed (aka Anderson Augustus Fountain)

Company C: Laurens County
5.	Privates:	Everett H. Blackshear	Wounded (through left breast & lungs, born 4-21-46, surrendered N.C.)
6.		Enoch Hall Linder	Wounded (right arm, necessitating amputation near shoulder, died 1891)*
7.		John F. Simpson	Wounded (in breast & left hand, index finger amputated, born 7-26-44 Ga., Surr. NC)

Company D: Smith Guards from Wilkerson County
8.	Private:	Solomon Horton	Wounded (died from wounds)

Company H: Independent Volunteers from Baldwin County
9.	3rd Sgt.:	James M. Fouche	Killed (previously captured at Vicksburg)
10.	Privates:	Greenberry Dunn	Wounded (previously captured at Vicksburg, died Baldwin Co., Ga. 1-28-1892)
11.		John Jenkins Hemphill	Wounded (previously captured at Vicksburg)
12.		John Owens	Wounded (died, Washington Co., Ga.)
13.		James M. Reynolds	Wounded
14.		James T. Robinson	Wounded (right leg, born 9-10-1822 Ga., died from effects of wound on 1-17-1894)

Company K: Oconee Grays from Wilkinson County
15.	5th Sgt.:	John M. Davis	Wounded (born 1839 Ga.)
16.	Privates:	Willis Stapleton	Killed
17.		Peter Youngblood	Captured

Total: Killed-5   Wounded-11   Captured-1   Total-17

* A flag memorial honoring Private Linder is located on Luther Ward Road in Powder Springs, Ga. http://www.southernmessenger.org/flag_poles.htm. (March 1, 2008).

The Battle of Peach Tree Creek

63rd Georgia Infantry:
Company A: Richmond County
1.   Privates: Henry Booth   Wounded
2.   Eugene F. Verdery   Wounded (in head, hospital in Macon, died 12-21-1921 Richmond Co., Ga.)

Company B:
3.   Private: John Boswell   Captured (died U.S.A. Hospital Nashville, 7-21-64 from exhaustion)

Company C:
4.   Private: Joseph Churchill   Wounded (eyes injured by bursting of a bomb in Atlanta, surrendered Atlanta 5/65, died 3-7-1899 Newton Co., Ga.)

Company F: Chatham County
5.   Private: F. J. Watson   Wounded (Ocmulgee Hospital 7-22-64)

Company I: Bartow County (& others)
6.   1st Sgt.: W. N. Carter   Wounded (born 8-28-1829)
7.   Privates: John Francis Cook   Wounded (hospital Vineville, suburb of Macon, Ga, born 7-14-1845 Talbot Co, Ga)
8.   Johnathan Harris Goodwin   Wounded (left shoulder, hospital Macon)

Total: Killed-0   Wounded-7   Captured-1   Total-8

65th Georgia Infantry:
Company A: (Gilmer Light Guards from Gilmer and Pickens Counties)
9.   Private: Riley Evans   Wounded
Company D: ("Freemen of Floyd County")
10.   Frank M. Watters   Killed
Company E: (Fannin County)
11.   Private: Robert Laughter   Deserted (7-20-64, missing)
Company K: (Habersham County)
12.   Private: Elijah Kinsey   Wounded (right shoulder, born 7/1935 Ga.)

Total: Killed-1   Wounded-2   Captured-1   Total-4

66th Georgia Infantry:
Field & Staff:
1.   Lt. Col.   Algemon S. Hamilton   Wounded
2.   Major: Robert Newton Hull   Wounded
Company A: Bibb County (& others)
3.   Captain: Briggs Hopson Napier   Wounded (left knee, gun shot wound, amputated leg in hospital, Macon)
4.   1st Lt.:   James Conner   Wounded (left leg & left arm-gun shot wound, in hospital Macon, Ga., died 1865)
5.   1st Cpl.: Sugar J. Partin   Wounded (in breast)
6.   4th Cpl.: Iverson Sanders   Wounded (died Foard Hospital,

Roster

			Forsyth, Ga. 8-22-64)
7.	Privates:	R. Griffin	Wounded
8.		J. G. M. Harrington	Wounded (hospital Macon, Ga)
9.		Thomas J. Whitley	Wounded (left shoulder & right arm, born Walton Co, Ga 11-25-1830, in Cobb Co. at close of war)

Company B: DeKalb County (& others)

10.	Captain:	J. A. Wright	Wounded (hospital)
11.	Jr. 2nd Lt.:	James L. Saulsburry	Wounded (shot in leg, died)
12.	Privates:	Isaac Araner	Killed (missing)
13.		James Atcherson	Killed (by wound in head)
14.		John H. Harris	Wounded (died 10-9-64, Macon hospital)
15.		William Harrison	Wounded (left shoulder)
16.		John A. J. Little	Killed
17.		R. G. Moore	Wounded
18.		William C. Williams	Wounded

Company C: Newton County (& others)

19.	Captain:	Henry F. Parks	Killed
20.	2nd Lt.:	John Neil Smythe	Wounded (elected Captain after Peachtree)
21.	Privates:	William Rabun Hurst	Killed
22.		A. W. Kitchens	Wounded

Company D: Manhan Infantry from Bibb & Jones Counties

23.	Captain:	Charles J. Williamson	Wounded (amputated left arm above elbow, in hospital Macon, died Macon 1891)
24.	Privates:	George W. Davis	Wounded(severely in left hand causing loss of thumb, hospital Macon, born Randolph Co, Ga 12-14-37, died Bibb Co, 3-7-1921)
25.		Thomas J. Massengale	Wounded (left thigh, resulting in partial paralysis, born Ga. 9-28-1845)
26.		Reuben A. Vann	Wounded

Company E: DeKalb County (& others)

27.	2nd Lt.:	John F. Smith	Wounded
28.	4th Cpl.:	Bennett S. Tuggle	Killed
29.	Private:	William P. Hudgins	Wounded (rt. leg, amputated, born Ga 1819)
30.		S. R. Jackson	Wounded

Company F: Putnam County (& others)

31.	2nd Lt.:	Josiah Fourney Adams	Wounded (born Putnam Co., Ga. 4-9-1844, died Putnam Co., Ga. 1-17-1910)
32.	Ord. Sgt.:	A. James Meriwether	Wounded
33.	1st Sgt.	Thomas M. Leverett	Captured (Camp Chase, paroled 3-4-1865)
34.	2nd Sgt.:	William T. Farrar	Wounded
35.	5th Sgt.:	Lewis Clark	Wounded
36.	2nd Cpl.:	J. K. Bearden	Wounded (died of wounds by 8-31-64)

The Battle of Peach Tree Creek

37.	2nd Cpl.:	William H. Harley	Wounded
38.	Privates:	Joseph Cochran	Wounded & Captured (guns shot in both hips, died Vining Station Hospital)
39.		Harvey A. Honeycutt	Killed
40.		H. Taylor Honeycutt	Wounded
41.		Hiram Inlow	Wounded (gun shot left clavicle)
42.		____ (Litter Bearer)	Captured (died, Camp Chase 2-13-65)
43.		David Pinkerton	Killed (missing)
44.		Thomas Spain	Captured (Camp Chase, died pneumonia 2-13-65)
45.		Francis Whelchel	Killed

Company G:

46.	4th Sgt.:	John M. Davis	Wounded
47.	Sgt.:	A. H. Winfrey	Killed
48.	Privates:	George C. Clements	Wounded (right leg, permanently disabled, gun shot wound, born Ga., 10-5-1845)
49.		James Merritt	Wounded (developed palsy in left arm & cancer of face from wounds, born Greene Co., Ga. 11-30-1823, died in Receiving & Distributing Hospital, Atlanta, 7-25-64)
50.		Archie Nicholson	Killed
51.		W. M. Pierce	Wounded (surrendered N. C.)

Company H: DeKalb County (& others)

52.	Captain:	Lorenzo D. Belisle	Wounded (left shoulder & hip, permanently disabled, detail duty Macon rest of war, born Ga. 1-4-1847, died Milledgeville 9-26-1913)
53.	4th Sgt.:	John H. Belisle	Captured (Camp Chase, released 4-21-65, enlisted Co. E, U.S. Volunteers 4-22-65, born Stewart Co., Ga. 1-16-1842)
54.	Privates:	Daniel King	Wounded
55.		J. H. Meade	Killed
56.		G. W. Muaick (Musick)	Killed
57.		W. T. Stidham	Killed
58.		Elihu Stidham	Killed
59.		Joel Williams	Wounded

Company I:

60.	1st Lt.:	A. C. Patman	Wounded (in head, hospital, Macon)
61.	2nd Lt.:	Thomas J. Kernaghan	Wounded
62.	1st Sgt.:	Charles D. McCoy	Wounded
63.	2nd Sgt.:	T. H. Chandler	Wounded
64.	2nd Sgt.:	S. C. Hibler	Wounded (died hospital by 8-31-64)
65.	Privates:	George W. Clark	Wounded
66.		W. P. Nichols	Killed (missing)
67.		A. J. Nowland	Killed (missing)
68.		J. H. Pool	Killed (missing)

Roster

69.		C. Pyran	Wounded	

Company K:
70.	Captain:	Thomas L. Langston	Wounded (hospital Macon)	
71.	Jr. 2nd Lt.:	Isham J. Davis	Wounded	
72.	1st Sgt.:	Phillip Howard Thomas	Wounded (ankle, amputated)	
73.	2nd Sgt.:	Thomas A. Kennaday	Killed (missing)	
74.	Privates:	John M. Brantley	Wounded	
75.		Jacob Burger	Killed (by wound in head)	
76.		Andrew McDuffie	Killed	
77.		John W. Nowell	Wounded (in back, leg & right eye-lost)	
78.		John Peacock	Wounded	
79.		M. J. Peacock	Wounded	
80.		G. M. Teal	Killed	
81.		Thomas J. Whitley	Wounded	
Total:	Killed-22 Wounded-55		Captured-5*	Total- 81

Note-one of the Captured was also wounded.

Georgia Light Artillery:

From Hardee's Corps Artillery, Johnston's Battalion
Captain John B. Rowan's Ga. Light Artillery Battery(4 Napoleons)

1.	Private:	Thomas J. Pergerson	Captured (deserted 7-20-64)	
Total:	Killed-0 Wounded-0		Captured-1	Total- 1

Kentucky:
5th Kentucky Infantry:

1.	Sgt.:	Fernando W. Campbell	Wounded, disabled	
2.	Corporal:	G. W. Arnold (Co. A)	Wounded	
3.	Private:	R. C. Bowman (Co. F)	Wounded, foot	
Total:	Killed-0 Wounded-3		Captured-0	Total-3

6th Kentucky Infantry:

1.	Private:	A. Jeff Henderson (Co. E)	Wounded, lost finger	
Total:	Killed-0 Wounded-1		Captured-0	Total-1

9th Kentucky Infantry:

Company A:
1.	1st Corporal:	E.E. Dunn	Wounded	
2.	Private:	R. Boone Chastain	Wounded	
3.	Private:	Moses H. Hester	Wounded (also was a teamster)	
4.	Drummer:	Benjamin White	Wounded	
Total:	Killed-0 Wounded-4		Captured-0	Total-4

Louisiana:
12th Louisiana Infantry: (partial list)

1.	Major	H. V. McCain	Wounded
2.	1st Lt. & Acting Adjt. M. S. Mc Leroy		Killed
3.	Co. B, Captain J. A. Bivin		Killed
4.	1st Lt.	J. W. McGuire	Wounded

The Battle of Peach Tree Creek

5. Co. D, 1st Lt.   J. F. Kelly   Wounded
6. Co. H, 1st Lt.   J. L. Reno   Wounded
Total-57 killed & wounded; 9 missing   Total-66
Source-Tennessee State Library & Archives (MF 1045, Roll 2).

Pointe Coupee' Battery:
no casualties reported.

The Washington Artillery:
1. Corporal: Oscar A Legare'   Killed
2. Privates: Cordelius Johnson "Tony" Barrow   Wounded
3.   Ben Bridge, Jr.   Wounded
4.   Charles (Charlie) R. Percy   Wounded, mortally
5.   Evans Ricketts   Wounded, mortally
Total: Killed-1 Wounded-4 (2 mortally)   Captured-0   Total-5

Mississippi:
1st Mississippi Battalion Sharpshooters: (about 110 present) Major James M. Stigler
1.   Adjutant: Robert M. Brown (?)   Killed
Company A: Captain W. W. Mobly Commanding
2.   Captain: W. W. Mobly   Wounded, severe
3.   Sergeants: W. H. Blankenship   Wounded, severe
4.   D. F Breckinridge   Wounded, severe
5.   T. C. Dodson   Wounded, slight
6.   Corporal: W. H. Blackwood   Wounded, severe
7.   Privates: J. W. Brewer   Wounded, severe
8.   J. L. Butler   Missing
9.   R. A. Coleman   Wounded, slight
10.   J. H. Johnson   Missing
11.   J. M. Light   Wounded, severe
12.   H. L. Smith   Missing
13   W.H. Strayham   Killed
14.   J. R. Walker   Wounded, severe
K-1, W-9, M-3, Total-13
Company B: Lieutenant E. C. Blackwood (Co. A) Commanding
15.   Sergeant: R. H. Horton   Killed
16.   Privates: W. H. Cannon   Killed
17.   J. H. Fourville   Wounded, severe
18.   I. R. Ifroks   Wounded, severe
19.   John Johnson   Missing
20.   J. M. Porter   Wounded, slight
21.   A. W. Rhyne   Wounded, slight
22.   H. H. Williams   Missing
23.   W. W. Wilson   Wounded, slight
24.   W. H. Womack   Missing
K-2, W-5, M-3, Total-10
Company C: Captain R. W. Jones Commanding
25.   Sergeants: F. W. Robertson   Killed
26.   C. White   Missing
27.   Privates: R. W. Boydsboro   Wounded, slight

Roster

28.	C. Moon	Wounded

K-1, W-2, M-1, Total-4
Company D: Lt. John Wright Commanding

29.	Privates:	A. M. Clarke	Wounded, severe
30.		G. B. Melton	Wounded, severe
31.		J. T. Tolbert	Wounded, slight
32.		J. M. Taylor	Wounded, severe

K-0, W-4, M-0, Total-4

Total: Killed-5, Wounded-20, Missing or Captured-7, Total-32

3rd Mississippi: (167 present) Colonel Thomas A. Mellon

1.	Colonel:	Thomas A. Mellon	Wounded in the head by a shell
Company A:		The Live Oak Rifles (Jackson County), Captain Abiezar F. Ramsay Commanding	
2.	Captain:	Abiezar F. Ramsay	Killed
3.	1st Sgt.:	Oscar de Bose Bowen	Wounded, dangerous tore bladder
4.	Sergeant:	Taylor M. Mc Rae	Wounded, severe
5.	Corporal:	Hiram L. Flemming	Wounded, severe
6.	Color Cpl.:	John H. Scott	Wounded, slight
7.	Privates:	John Barfield	Wounded, right arm "shot off"
8.		A. S. Barnes	Wounded, dangerously
9.		Solomon Cates	Wounded, severe
10.		Eli Collins	Wounded, dangerously
11.		A. Danaly	Wounded, severe
12.		Francis Fountain ("Frank")	Wounded, severe, shot in the foot
13.		Benjamin F. Johnson	Wounded, severe
14.		Josiah Mobbs	Wounded, severe
15.		R. F. Morris	Wounded, slight
16.		William Panila (Perriller?)	Killed
17.		R. Pennington	Killed
18.		H. J. Ramsey	Wounded, slight
19.		John Reeves	Killed
20.		Martin Ryan	Wounded, slight
21.		Levi Scarborough	Wounded, slight
22.		William Webb	Wounded, slight
23.		A. J. Woodcock	Wounded, severe
24.		Unknown	Killed

K-5, W-18, Total-23

Company B: The Sunflower Dispersers (Sunflower County), Lt. P. H. Westbrook Commanding

25.	Sergeant:	Elbert F. Kinsey	Wounded, dangerously
26.	Corporals:	John E. Scott	Wounded, dangerously
27.		James F. Scroggins	Wounded, severe
28.	Privates:	M. Ellett	Missing
29.		D. F. Green	Wounded, severe
30.		F. Lum	Wounded, severe
31.		William Mc Rae	Killed-Wounded leg(died on field)
32.		Francis M. Miller	Wounded, severe

The Battle of Peach Tree Creek

33.		Newton J. Scroggins	Killed
34.		N. J. Smith	Wounded, severe
35.		W. Dorsey Stewart (Stuart?)	Wounded, slight

K-1, W-9 (1 died on field), M-1, Total-11

Company C: The Downing Rifles (Hinds County), Lt. Andrew J. Willis Commanding

36.	Lieutenants:	Andrew J. Willis	Wounded, slight
37.		Charles Edward Sharkey	Wounded, severe
38.	Sergeants:	Arthur D. Arrington	Wounded, severe
39.		William J. Bush	Killed
40.	Corporals:	John B. Lowery	Wounded, severe
41.		John Mc G. Slater	Wounded, severe
42.		John T. Tatum	Wounded, severe
43.	Privates:	George W. Briscoe	Wounded, severe
44.		B. F. Calvert	Missing
45.		Robert W. Carlisle	Wounded, severe
46.		John W. Cook	Wounded, severe
47.		Andrew Ewing	Wounded, severe
48.		Thomas Graves	Wounded, severe
49.		Jo Hand	Missing
50.		D. G. Hardy	Wounded, slight
51.		George W. Hardy	Wounded, severe
52.		John C. Hardy	Wounded, severe
53.		William Kelly	Wounded, severe
54.		Alfred D. Lowery	Wounded, severe
55.		Marcelus A. Mc Gehee	Wounded, severe
56.		Hamilton Marshall	Wounded, severe
57.		Henry C. Marshall	Wounded, severe
58.		James M. Mathews	Killed
59.		Simon J. Matthews	Wounded, severe
60.		Robert H. Murphy	Wounded, severe
61.		J. W. Patterson ("Jimmy")	Killed
62.		T. H. Rawlings (Thomas N.?)	Killed
63.		William G. Rizer (Riser?)	Missing
64.		Charles Russell	Wounded, severe
65.		Benjamin F. Stone ("Frank")	Wounded, severe (18 yr. old, died 7-21-64)

K-4, W-23 (died-1+), M-3, Total-30

Company D: The Chunkey Heroes (Newton County), Captain William E. Thomas Commanding

66.	Lieutenant:	John P. Grissett	Killed
67.	Sergeant:	Ebenezer S. Edwards	Wounded, severe
68.	Privates:	William W. Clearman	Wounded, severe
69.		Samuel J. Cooksey	Wounded, severe
70.		R. L. Giles	Wounded, severe
71.		Richard O. Harris	Wounded, slight
72.		George F. Reynolds	Wounded, severe

K-1, W-6, Total-7

Company E: The Biloxi Rifles (Harrison County), Captain John P. Elmer Commanding

Roster

73.   Private: Richard Lanius   Wounded
K-0, W-1, Total-1

Company F: The Shieldsboro Rifles (Hancock County)
none, may have been on picket duty and not on field.

Company G: The Gainesville Volunteers (Hancock County), Lt. John W. Miller Commanding

74.   Lieutenant: John W. Miller   Wounded & captured
75.   Sergeant: John James Moore   Missing (captured)
K-0, W-1, M-2 (1 wounded), Total-2

Company H: The Dahlgren Guards (Harrison County)
none, may have been on picket duty and not on field.

Company I: The John M. Sharps (Yazoo County), Lt. Robert James McCormack Commanding

76.   Lieutenant: Robert Newton Pearce   Wounded, severe
77.   Corporals: J. P. Carson   Wounded, slight
78.   James Robert Shurley   Wounded, severe
79.   Joseph H. Thomas   Wounded, dangerously
80.   Privates: John Barfield   Wounded, severe
81.   Riley M. Everett   Wounded, severe
82.   John W. Holt   Wounded, severe
83.   James N. Marshall   Wounded, slight
84.   William H. Moorman   Wounded, severe
85.   J. A. Pittman (James A.?)   Wounded, severe
86.   J. L. Thomason (Judge L. ?)   Wounded, severe
87.   John D. Weed   Killed-Wounded, mortally
88.   William A. Whitfield   Killed
K-1, W-12 (died-1+), Total-13

Company K: The McWille Blues (Copiah County), Lt. Murray M. Peyton Commanding

89.   Lieutenant: C. C. Temple   Wounded, severe
90.   Privates: Jeremiah King   Killed-shot in the face and
                                                    left on the field
91.   Jacob Mayou   Wounded, severe
92.   John Watts   Wounded, severe
93.   Ben W. White   Wounded, severe
K-1, W-4, Total-5

Total: Killed-15   Wounded-73   Missing-5   Total-93*

*Note-According to the Official Report, the 3rd Mississippi lost 11 men killed, 71 wounded, and 6 missing for a total of 88 men. A review of the Regiment's Compiled Service Records reveals the names and figures provided above. Additionally, many of the wounded died within a few days. According to Captain W. A. Kelly, Company C saw 4 of its 21 men wounded within a week of the battle.

Sources-Compiled Service Records, Microfilm Rolls 130-45; Howell, To Live and Die in Dixie, pp. 328 & 338.

22nd Mississippi Infantry: (190 present)   Major W. A. Oates

The Battle of Peach Tree Creek

1.	Major:	W. A. Oates	Wounded
2.	Adjutant:	C. ("Claudie") V. H. Davis	Killed

Company A: The Mississippi Grays, Captain Gavin Commanding

3.	Captain:	Gavin	Wounded, slight
4.	Sergeants:	F. M. Hartzoff	Killed
5.		Wiley	Wounded, severe
6.	Corporals:	Ed Buckley	Killed
7.		Roper	Wounded, severe
8.	Privates:	William Armstrong	Wounded, severe
9.		Thomas Burnette (or J. T. Bennett)	Killed
10.		J. H. Blackman	Wounded, severe
11.		C. L. Harper	Wounded, severe
12.		A. A. Hartzoff	Wounded, slight
13.		T. J. Hooker	Wounded, severe
14.		W. S. Ingram	Wounded, severe
15.		J. T. Ingram	Wounded, severe
16.		B. H. Lewis	Wounded, slight
17.		B. F. Mobley	Wounded, severe
18.		W. Maggin	Wounded, severe
19.		S. Sanders	Wounded, slight
20.		J. A. Scarborough	Wounded, severe
21.		T. A. Weathersby	Wounded, slight
22.		J. N. Warner	Wounded, slight

K-3, W-17, Total-20

Company B: The Hinds Light Guards, Lieutenant G. W. Huntley, Commanding

23.	Lieutenants:	G. W. Huntley	Wounded, severe
24.		Sam Watson	Wounded, severe
25.	Sergeant:	W. H. Boley	Wounded, slight
26.		M. Goode	Killed
27.	Corporals:	E. W. Jacobs	Missing
28.		M. S. Miles	Wounded, severe
29.	Privates:	J. M. Bloodsoe	Missing
30.		E. A. Errenbach	Wounded, slight
31.		L. H. Johnson	Wounded, severe
32.		E. Marsh	Killed
33.		J. M. Meacham	Wounded, slight
34.		W. A. Mc Lellan	Wounded, slight
35.		B. H. Oberman	Wounded, slight
36.		T. J. Selman	Wounded, slight
37.		E. A. Wells	Killed

K-3, W-10, M-2, Total: 15

Company C : The Sarsfield Southrons, Captain Hughes Commanding

38.	Captain	Hughes	Wounded, slight
39.	Sergeants:	Creswell	Wounded, slight
40.		Mc Clancy	Killed
41.	Privates:	A. J. Matthews	Killed
42.		E. Mc Leroy	Wounded, slight

K-3, W-2, Total-5

Company D: The Rodney Guards, D. R. Mackey Commanding

43.	Sergeant: J. W. Coleman	Wounded, slight

Roster

44.	Corporal: W. H. Gardner		Wounded, slight

K-0, W-2, Total-3

Company E: The Liberty Guards, Lieutenant A. W. Underwood Commanding

45.	Lieutenant:	A. William Underwood	Killed (Missing-possibly captured)
46.	Sergeant: N. B. Tate		Wounded, slight
47.	Corporals:	H. L. Hawks	Wounded, slight
48.		M. Neyland	Wounded, slight
49.	Privates: M. Forman		Wounded, slight
50.		F. B. Gillis	Wounded, slight
51.		W. R. Greer	Killed
52.		William H. Griffin	Wounded, severe
53.		R. L. Anders	Wounded, slight
54.		J. T. Longino	Wounded, slight
55.		Monroe Morgan	Killed
56.		William Mc Neal	Killed
57.		L. G. Neyland	Killed
58.		C. W. Mc Gehee	Wounded, died 8-13-64
59.		A. Teal	Wounded, mortally

K-5, W-10, Total-15

Company F: The De Soto Rebels, Lieutenant N. G. Usher Commanding

60.	Sergeants:	J. Crawford	Missing
61.		A. Davidson	Wounded, slight
62.		Thomas Davidson	Wounded, severe
63.	Privates: W. R. Cox		Killed
64.		W. M. Duckett	Wounded, slight
65.		J. D. Henderson	Missing
66.		M. C. Lum	Killed
67.		J. W. Morris	Wounded, slight
68.		F. M. Veach	Wounded, slight

K-2, W-5, M-2, Total-9

Company G: The Black Hawk Rifles, Captain G. W. Sharkey Commanding

69.	Lieutenant:	J. D. Usher	Wounded, slight
70.	Private: D. M. Newell		Wounded, slight

K-0, W-2, Total-2

Company H: The Lafayette Rifles, Captain W. L. Gay Commanding

71.	Captain: J. T. Formsby		Wounded, slight
72.	Lieutenant:	J. B. Blaylock	Killed
73.	Sergeant: W. J. Wilson		Wounded, slight
74.	Corporals:	A. Barlow	Killed
75.		W. H. Morris	Killed
76.	Privates: A. F. Craig		Killed
77.		J. Fletchall	Wounded, severe
78.		B. Goldner	Killed
79.		A. M. Graham	Wounded, severe
80.		J. T. Jordon	Wounded, severe
81.		A. B. Owens	Wounded, severe
82.		W. B. Parks	Wounded, slight
83.		James Wilson	Wounded, slight

The Battle of Peach Tree Creek

K-5, W-8, Total-13
Company I: The Swamp Rangers, Captain William L. Gay Commanding
84. Captain: William L. Gay — Wounded, severe
85. Lieutenant: Charles Roth — Killed
86. 2nd Sergeant: Richard Brown — Killed
87. Privates: Andrew Braswell — Killed
88. Edward Petz — Wounded, severe

K-3, W-2, Total-5
Company K: The Pegues Defenders, Lieutenant Glover, Commanding
89. Sergeants: J. A. Hardin — Killed
90. C. Quillion — Wounded, slight
91. J. W. Robertson — Killed
92. Corporals: J. A. Johnson — Wounded, severe
93. E. Jones — Wounded, severe
94. Privates: B. F. Douglas — Wounded, severe
95. G. W. Forrest — Wounded, severe
96. J. B. Franklin — Wounded, severe
97. C. F. Pinion (Tinson?) — Missing

K-2, W-6, M-1, Total-9

Total: Killed-26 Wounded-66 Captured or Missing-5 Total-97*
*Note-According to the Official Records and Regimental Report, the 22nd Mississippi had 190 present for duty, and lost 21 killed, 64 wounded, and 5 captured.
Sources-Tennessee State Library & Archives, Micro Film 1045, Roll 2; Author's file no. 385; http://members.aol.com/missregt/Miss22G.html#Twenty-Second (January 10, 2009); O.R. Vol. 38, Part II, Serial No. 74, p. 884.

31st Mississippi Infantry: (215 Present)   Lt. Colonel James L. Drane
Field & Staff:
1. Lt. Col. James L. Drane — Wounded severely
2. Major Francis Marion Gillespie — Killed
3. Adjutant William J. Van de Graff — Killed
4. 1st Lt. (Ensign) James V. Belew — Wounded (rt. fore arm & head) died 8-24-64
5. Sgt. Major Gustave G.T. Hightower — Wounded (arm)
6. Quartermaster Sgt. Finis E. Miller — Wounded & died

K-2, W-2 (mortally-2), C-0, Total-6
Company A: (The Orr Guards):
7. Captain John R. Ketchum — Killed
8. 1st Lt. John W. Prude — Killed
9. 3rd Lt. John C. Morrow — Killed
10. 1st Sgt. Thomas J. Wood — Wounded (side)
11. 2nd Sgt. Joel John Morgan Johnson — Killed
12. 3rd Sgt. H. A. Abernathy — Wounded (right side)
13. 1st Corporal John R. Hancock — Wounded (fore finger)
14. 2nd Corporal Claiborn J. Youngblood — Wounded (leg)
15. 3rd Corporal Andrew W. Youngblood — Wounded (legs)
16. 4th Corporal William C. Polk — Wounded (leg)
Privates:
17. John M. Aycock — Wounded (arm & bowels)

Roster

18. Benjamin F. Black — Killed
19. James M. Craigue — Captured
20. James M. Edington — Wounded (nose)
21. George W. Flaherty — Wounded (left leg & shoulder) & captured
22. Thomas J. Flaherty — Captured
23. Samuel W. Gillion — Killed
24. Martin V. Harman — Wounded (left arm)
25. James R. Manning — Wounded (arm)
26. Johnson Mathis — Captured
27. Edward L. Mc Mahan — Wounded (left thigh), captured, died 12-7-64
28. Carol P. Pritchard — Killed
29. Madison Purcell — Wounded (hand)
30. Charlie C. Reagan — Wounded (arm)
31. John T. Reagan — Wounded (left arm & back), captured
32. John Beale Skinner — Wounded
33. Richard La Fayette Skinner — Wounded
34. George W. Warren — Wounded (groin)
35. Francis M. Wood — Killed

K-8, W-18 (mortally-1), C-7, Total-29

Company B (The Dixie Guards):

36. Captain Solomon M. Thornton — Wounded (hip & groin)
37. 1st Lt. William A. Womack — Wounded (left arm)
38. 2nd Lt. Alexander W. Mc Larty — Wounded (left hand)
39. 4th Sgt. Francis M. Otts — Wounded (left leg), captured
40. 2nd Corporal Daniel B. Tharp — Wounded (knee)

Privates:

41. James A. Cooper — Wounded (leg), died 9-25-64
42. Simeon V. Tharp — Mortally Wounded (died)
43. Tillman Crowell — Wounded (rt. side)
44. William J. Crowell — Killed
45. Joel W. Harper — Wounded (rt. hip), captured
46. George D. Hendley — Missing, captured, lost, presumed dead
47. Osborn W. Hendley — Wounded (upper lt. leg), captured, died 8-27-64
48. F. M. James — Wounded (left leg)
49. Thomas W. Lee — Wounded (left hand)
50. William L. F. Lee — Wounded (concussion)
51. William A. Mc Gowen — Killed
52. Bartholomew (Bart) W. Mims — Wounded (left hand)
53. William G. Skelton — Killed
54. Gabriel M. Spruill — Wounded, captured, died 7-22-64
55. John Thomas Swindle — Captured
56. James K. Watson — Killed

K-4, W-15 (mortally-5), C-5, Total-21

Company C (The Chickasaw Guards):

57. Captain Thomas Jefferson Pulliam — Wounded
58. 2nd Lt. William Bird Carodine — Killed
59. Qtr./Commissary Sgt. James Terrill Pulliam — Wounded (right arm & calf & hip of

The Battle of Peach Tree Creek

	left leg)
60. 3rd Sgt. Lycurgus Sims	Wounded
61. Private John C. Massey	Wounded (left thigh & hip)
62. Private John S. Pulliam	Wounded (head)

K-1, W-5, C-0, Total-6
Company D (The Dixie Rebels):

63. 1st Lt.Thomas J. Lyle	Killed
64. 3rd Sergeant Henry W. Green	Wounded (rt thigh), captured, died 10-25-64
65. 5th Sergeant Thomas A. "Bud" Griffin	Wounded (rt lower thigh)
66. 1st Corporal James F. Ross	Wounded (shoulder & hip), captured
67. 3rd Corporal Jasper N. Stewart	Mortally wounded, missing, died
68. Corporal Benjamin H. Fuller	Wounded (arm)

Privates:

69. Wilks Adams	Wounded
70. David Henry Alexander	Wounded
71. Richard M. Bailey	Mortally Wounded, died
72. Robert M. Bailey	Wounded (left knee), captured, died 8-26-64
73. James B. Barton	Wounded (lost middle & ring fingers)
74. Giles Leroy Cain	Wounded (leg)
75. Peter May Cobb	Wounded
76. Thomas Jefferson Douglas, Sr.	Killed
77. Thomas Jesse Edwards	Killed
78. James William Gore	Captured
79. John Ashford Gore	Wounded (leg)
80. Benjamin F. Grammar	Wounded (leg)
81. James M. Ray	Wounded (left leg), captured, died 9-4-64
82. William B. Robertston	Mortally Wounded (head) died 7-22-64
83. Isaiah David Stacy	Wounded (shoulder)
84. Miles Henry Stacy	Wounded (rt. leg), captured
85. Robert C. Stribling	Mortally wounded, died
86. James Lawson Wilson	Wounded (side)

K-3, W-19 (mortally-7), C-9, Total-24
Company E (The Choctaw Rebels)

87. 3rd Lieutenant Silas Mercer Dobbs	Wounded (shoulder)
88. 3rd Sergeant James Jacob Dudley	Wounded (leg & foot), died
89. Corporal William P. Brooks	Wounded (left leg), captured, died 9-13-64
90. 4th Corporal Claiborn Preston Gunter	Wounded (hand)

Privates:

91. James E. Bridges	Wounded (arm, side & foot)
92. Joseph G. B. Brooks	Wounded
93. Jerry Clark	Wounded (side)
94. George H. Fondren	Wounded (hip)
95. Rufus K. Fondren	Wounded (head), captured
96. John Franklin Hester	Wounded (arm)
97. John C. Manner	Wounded (arm)
98. Joseph W. D. Ramsey	Wounded (arm)

Roster

99. John Reynolds	Wounded (arm)
100. James M. Taylor	Wounded (arm)

K-0, W-14 (mortally-2), C-2, Total-14
Company F (Calhoun Tigers):

101. Sgt. James Nelson	Killed
102. 4th Sgt. James Wilson, Sr.	Wounded, captured & died 9-17-64
103. 3rd Corporal William J. Wilson	Wounded & Captured (hip and back)

K-1, W-2 (mortally-1), C-2, Total-3
Company G (The Palmetto Guards):

104. Captain John Franklin Manahan	Wounded (thigh)
105. 1st Sgt. Samuel H. Robinson	Wounded
106. Sgt. Joseph C. Rasberry	Wounded (back) captured, died 3-27-65
107. 4th Sgt. William H. Biggers	Killed
108. 1st Corporal Benjamin Franklin Rasberry	Wounded (face)
109. Corporal Francis M. Prather	Wounded

Privates:

110. Thomas R. Atkins	Wounded
111. Henry J. Easterwood	Wounded (left hand)
112. William Jefferson Evans	Wounded (leg)
113. Reuben T. Gray	Wounded & captured
114. Ezekiel Mc Marks	Wounded (thigh)
115. John T. Mc Cully	Wounded (foot)
116. John C. Mc Cullough	Captured
117. William A. Morris	Killed
118. Cullen Lark Pitts	Wounded (foot & toe)
119. Rufus C. Suggs	Mortally Wounded (shot in head by a bullet that penetrated his brain) died 7-22-64

K-2, W-12 (mortally-2), C-3, Total-16
Company H (The Chickasaw Avengers):

120. Captain George Washington Naron	Wounded (head, damaging his ear)
121. 3rd Lt. William M. Foster	Wounded (throat)
122. 1st Sgt. Jonathan Graham Blue	Wounded (leg)
123. 2nd Sgt. Solomon B. Alford	Wounded (breast)
124. 3rd Sgt. Alexander Henry Pratt	Killed
125. 5th Sgt. William M. Conner	Killed

Corporals:

126. Newton L. Mc Collough (Mc Cullough)	Wounded (left leg), captured, died 2-24-65
127. William L. Mc Mahan	Wounded (head)

Privates:

128. Churchwell ("Church") Alford	Wounded (arm)
129. Munroe P. Alford	Killed
130. Charles M. Berry	Killed
131. James A. Burt	Wounded (hand)
132. Edward T. Conner	Wounded (hand)
133. Reuben P. Faulkner	Killed
134. Jefferson (James) R. Finley	Captured, died 3-6-65
135. Abner B. Gilder	Wounded (left thigh)

The Battle of Peach Tree Creek

136. Wiley T. Mc Kee	Wounded, Captured
137. Robert J. Mc Mullen	Wounded (thigh)
138. Eli Francis (Frank) Naron	Wounded.
139. James A. Sanders	Wounded (hand)
140. Thomas B. Slaughter	Wounded (left foot), captured
141. William Oliver Smith	Wounded (left side), captured
142. Nathaniel S. Wofford	Wounded (both thighs, and an arm)

K-5, W-17 (mortally-1), C-5 (died in captivity-1), Total 23

Company I (The Jackson Rifles)

143. Captain Cyrus Seymour White Richards	Wounded & captured.
144. 3rd Lt. John C. Hallum	Wounded (bowels & legs), died 7-31-64.
145. 1st Sgt. John C. Gregory	Captured & died 1-1-65.
146. 4th Sgt. Charles C. Cameron	Wounded (hip)

Corporals:

147. James M. Franks	Wounded (abdomen)
148. George B. Gray	Killed

Privates:

149. Myres W. Broomhall	Killed
150. Sylvester P. Broomhall	Wounded (hand and finger)
151. George W. Butler	Wounded (rt leg), captured & died 12-17-64.
152. Wiley Carpenter	Killed
153. Thomas J. Cockerham	Wounded (leg) & captured.
154. Robert E. Conn	Captured
155. James Henry Cooper	Wounded (hand).
156. James R. Daves	Wounded (leg, hand), captured, died 9-1-64
157. John J. Lever	Killed
158. Leroy Minter	Captured
159. Jonathan Montgomery	Wounded (thigh)
160. Hyrum Marion Nail	Killed
161. Pinkney Raspberry	Wounded (hip)
162. James W. Ray	Killed
163. George T. Smith	Mortally wounded, died 8-1-64.
164. Elizah D. Stewart	Killed
165. James R. Trussell	Captured
166. Charles S. Wiltshire	Killed

K-8, W-11 (mortally-4), C-8 (died in captivity-1), Total-24

Company K (The Pontotoc Guards)

167. Captain George Washington Lewallen	Wounded and captured
168. 2nd Lt. Pleasant G. McCraw	Wounded
169. Sgt. Dilmeda M. Beauchamp	Captured
170. Corporal Zelabee Beauchamp	Captured
171. Corporal William E. Worthy	Wounded (hip)

Privates:

172. Thomas Calvin. Bell	Killed
173. Hillary C. Cobb	Killed
174. William C. Duncan	Killed
175. John M. Ewing	Wounded (leg)

Roster

176. Levi W. Gentry — Wounded (leg), captured, died 9-8-64
177. William A. McDowell — Captured
178. John Andrew Robinson (or Robertson) — Captured
179. Burnal Henderson Wade — Wounded (ankle)
180. James W. Wesson — Wounded (side)
181. William A. Witt — Wounded (arm)

K-3, W-8 (mortally-1), C-6, Total-15

Totals for 31st Miss.:
Killed-37, Wounded-123 (mortally-28), Captured-47 (died-2), Total-181 (total died-67)

33rd Mississippi Infantry: (about 300 present)   Colonel Jabez L. Drake
(Courtesy Fred Kimbrell, researcher and historian, 33rd Miss.)

Field and Staff:
1. Col. Jabez L. Drake — Killed

Company A:
2. Capt. James E. Simmons — Wounded
3. 2nd Lt. David F. Cadenhead — Wounded
4. 3rd Lt. Simon J. Kennedy — Mortally Wounded
5. 1st Sgt. Daniel William Russell — Wounded
6. 4th Sgt. William D. Deskin — Killed
7. 1st Corp. Theodore C. Mixon — Killed
8. 3rd Corp. Prince A. Russell — Killed
9. Corp. Andrew Jackson Hudson — Wounded
10. Privates: L.W. Allen — Wounded
11. James Monroe Deskin — Killed
12. William P. Edwards — Wounded
13. David A.J. Kennedy — Captured & Wounded
14. William L. Lee — Killed
15. William W. Livingston — Wounded
16. John Hamil McDonald — Captured & Wounded
17. John Martin Oxford — Captured & Mortally Wounded
18. Benjamin G. Powell — Wounded
19. Augustus E. Russell — Missing (he was discharged by substitute, yet he remained)
20. Gideon B. Russell — Killed
21. Tate Russell — Killed
22. W.B. Russell — Killed
23. McCager C. Sanders — Wounded
24. Jasper Savell — Wounded

K-8   W-13 (2 mortally)   C-3   M-1   Total-23

Company B:
25. 1st Lt. Hampton Wall — Wounded (commanding Co.)
26. 3rd Lt. William B. Raiford — Missing & Wounded (later returned)
27. 1st Sgt. James L. Varnado — Mortally Wounded
28. 5th Sgt. Francis E. Downey — Wounded
29. Corp. James Ellison Cockerham — Wounded
30. Corp. Kincheon R. Webb, Jr. — Wounded
31. Privates: Calvin — Wounded
32. Richard T. Carter — Wounded

The Battle of Peach Tree Creek

33.		Ephram A. Hughey	Wounded
34.		Howell McDaniel	Wounded
35.		Meredith McDaniel	Captured & Wounded
36.		Winsor H. Spinks	Killed
37.		James M. Stewart	Wounded
38.		Thomas P. Tarver	Mortally Wounded
K-1	W-13 (2 mortally) C-1	M-1	Total-14

Company C:

39.	Capt.	Lewis Clark Maxwell	Wounded
40.	2nd Lt.	John Madison May	Wounded
41.	1st Sgt.	Elihu May	Wounded
42.	4th Sgt.	James S. Gwin	Mortally Wounded
43.	1st Corp.	Lawson H. Hill	Wounded
44.	2nd Corp.	Alonzos M. Flippin	Captured & Mortally Wounded
45.	3rd Corp.	Joseph Sandifer Burns	Wounded
46.	Privates:	Louis Dunn	Wounded
47.		Emanuel Hickman	Killed
48.		John P. Poe	Wounded
49.		Elijah Hickerson Smith	Mortally Wounded
50.		R.G. Spurling	Wounded
51.		Zephaniah J. Summers	Wounded
52.		Zachariah Williams	Killed
K-2	W-12	(3 mortally) C-1	Total-14

Company D:

53.	1st Lt.	David A Herring	Killed (commanding Co. at time)
54.	3rd Sgt.	William D. Coleman	Wounded
55.	3rd Sgt.	Joel L. East	Missing
56.	3rd Corp.	Isaac S. Burt	Missing
57.	Privates:	Benjamin Henry Buckley	Captured & Wounded
58.		Edward Alexander Buckley	Killed
59.		John Witey Buckley	Killed
60.		James S. Cain	Wounded
61.		Seaborn L. Cupit	Wounded
62.		George W. Gill	Missing
63.		Isaac Hall	Missing
64.		James F. Hall	Killed
65.		Joseph B. Mitchell	Killed
66.		William Columbus Sermons	Missing
67.		Pleasant M. Smith	Wounded
68.		William Green Smith	Captured & Wounded
69.		Edward F. Speikes (Speaks)	Wounded
70.		James Tarver	Killed
71.		James J. Wallace	Captured
72.		George W. Ward	Captured
K-6	W-7	C-4 M-5	Total-20

Company E:

73.	Capt.	John S. Lamkin	Captured
74.	2nd Lt.	Richard Autin Miskell	Killed
75.	3rd Lt.	Warren R. Ratliff (Ratcliffe?)	Missing
76.	1st Sgt.	David Holmes	Captured

77.	1st Sgt.	Thomas Dilla Richmond	Wounded
78.	3rd Sgt.	William J. Lamkin	Killed
79.	2nd Corp.	Lucius M. Quinn	Wounded
80.	3rd Corp.	Raiford Holmes	Captured & Mortally Wounded
81.	4th Corp.	William G. Holmes	Captured & Wounded
82.	Privates:	George W. Briley	Wounded
83.		Lewis (Levi) Ellzey	Captured & Mortally Wounded
84.		Martin P. Foil	Killed
85.		John T. Harvey	Killed
86.		Abner L. Lamkin	Killed
87.		Francis Marion Lee	Wounded
88.		Samuel R. Lewis	Mortally Wounded
89.		Green W. Morgan	Killed
90.		William N. Morgan	Killed
91.		Lawrence Osburn	Killed
92.		Silas C. Rushing	Captured & Wounded
93.		Benjamin Franklin Ware	Captured
K-8	W-9	(2 mortally) C-7	M-1 Total-21

Company F:

94.	Captain	John W. Sharkey	Killed
95.	1st Sgt.	David Treadwell	Wounded
96.	2nd Sgt.	Andrew J. Allen	Wounded
97.	4th Corp.	John A. Dorsey	Wounded
98.	Corp.	Allen S. Tucker	Wounded
99.	Privates:	David H. Bailey	Wounded
100.		E. Judson Cockcroft	Wounded
101.		Hiram P. Dabbs	Mortally Wounded
102.		William M. Edwards	Wounded
103.		William W. Horne	Captured
104.		Hardy P. Mayo	Captured
105.		Isaac Anderson Riddle (Riddell)	Wounded
K-1	W-9	(1 mortally) C-2	M-0 Total-12

Company G:

106.	2nd Lt.	Andrew G. West	Captured & Mortally Wounded
107.	1st Sgt.	Mather E. Pittman	Killed
108.	2nd Sgt.	George W. Hill	Captured
109.	3rd Sgt.	Hardin E. Dixon (Dickson)	Mortally Wounded
110.	4th Sgt.	Joseph P. West	Killed
111.	5th Sgt.	Paschal McGuire (McGiven)	Captured
112.	4th Corp.	John M. High	Wounded
113.	Privates:	James Terrell Bailey	Captured
114.		Thomas M. Bingham	Captured
115.		James A. Bowen	Captured
116.		Robert C. Cannon	Captured
117.		Mason Carver (or Marian Carder)	Captured & Wounded
118.		Alfred T. Childress	Wounded
119.		William B. Dowdy	Wounded
120.		Jasper Elliott	Mortally Wounded
121.		Joseph Ellcott	Mortally Wounded

The Battle of Peach Tree Creek

122.		James A. Fields	Mortally Wounded
123.		Jonathan G. Haney	Wounded
124.		William J. Helms	Captured & Wounded
125.		Golding P. Hill	Mortally Wounded
126.		James G. Hill	Captured
127.		Thomas S. Lewis	Missing
128.		Benjamin F. Martin	Missing
129.		James C. Morman (Marmon)	Wounded
130.		William B. Middleton	Mortally Wounded
131.		George P. Oliver	Captured
132.		Francis M. Patterson	Missing
133.		John W. Phillips	Missing
134.		Benjamin S. Poe	Captured
135.		William H. Ringer	Captured
136.		John H. Tharp	Captured
137.		William R. Towls	Missing
138.		John Elijah Wiggins	Wounded

K-2 W-15 (7 mortally) C-14 M-5 Total-33

Company H:

139.	2nd Lt.	Milton J. M. Dobbins	Mortally Wounded
140.	3rd Lt.	Robert M. Barnes	Wounded
141.	2nd Sgt.(Ensign)	Edwin F. Leavell	Captured & Mortally Wounded
142.	Sgt.?	Marion (Monroe) L. Spencer	Captured
143.	4th Sgt.	Caswell N. Newsom	Wounded
144.	5th Sgt.	Hugh R. Sharp	Killed
145.	2nd Corp.	James L. Dunn	Wounded
146.	Privates:	Edwin A. Bullock	Wounded
147.		James H. Ford	Killed
148.		George W. Hickman	Captured & Wounded
149.		Granville B. Kimball	Missing
150.		Levi (Leonidas) Lard (Laird)	Wounded
151.		Richard E. Legg	Wounded
152.		James Barton Miller	Missing
153.		Patrick Murphy	Wounded
154.		William S. Owens	Missing
155.		Thomas S. Shuford	Captured

K-2 W-10 (2 mortally) C-4 M-3 Total-17

Company I:

156.	Ensign	William M. Cope	Captured & Mortally Wounded
157.	5th Sgt.	Samuel A. Carter	Captured
158.	2nd Corp.	John S. Burgess	Mortally Wounded
159.	1st Corp.	Alva W. Middleton	Wounded
160.	Musician	Mitchell P. Derden	Wounded
161.	Privates:	Henry Clay Baker	Wounded
162.		Newton J. Bonner	Captured & Wounded
163.		Newton M. Felder	Captured & Wounded
164.		Caswell Finch	Captured & Mortally Wounded
165.		James Flowers	Captured
166.		John C. Humphries	Mortally Wounded
167.		James H. Pollard	Captured & Wounded

Roster

168.	Robert A. Shields		Wounded		
169.	Edward J. Wrenn		Mortally Wounded		
K-0	W-12	(5 mortally)	C-7	M-0	Total-14

Company K: none; on picket on another part of the line and not engaged.

Total: Killed-31 Wounded-100(mortally-24) Captured-43 Missing-6*total-169
*Note- with only 1 man confirmed as having returned, and the Federal records reflecting 43 captured, it is most likely that the remaining 15 men listed as missing were killed on the field. This would yield a total of killed on the field of 46 men which is consistent with Federal reports of burying Colonel Drake and 45 of his men in a large circle around him in a mass grave.

37th Mississippi:

1.	Lt. Colonel:	Wier	Wounded
2.	Ensign:	S. W. Jones	Killed

Company A: 2nd Lt. G. W. Raemer commanding
3-7.   1 killed, 4 wounded;
Company B: 2nd Lt. E. P. Harris commanding
8-12.   2nd Lt. W. H. Craft and 4 others wounded
Company C: Capt. M. L. Moody commanding
13-16.   2nd Lt. John West and 3 others wounded;
Company D: 1st Lt. J. L. Peters commanding
17-23.   7 wounded;
Company E: 2nd Lt. C. C. McEachern commanding
24-26.   3 wounded;
Company F: Capt. C. C. Ferrell commanding

27.	Captain	C. C. Ferrell	Wounded
28.	Lieutenant:	D. F. Lott	Wounded
29.	Privates:	Hudson	Wounded
30.		Name not given (1 missing);	Missing

Company G: Lieutenant T. J. McCaugns commanding
31-35.   1 killed, 4 wounded;
Company H: Lieutenant D. P. English commanding
36-38.   3 wounded;
Company I: Capt. C. H. McLemore commanding
39-41.   3 wounded:
Company K: Lieutenant William McCurdy commanding
42-45.   3 wounded, 1 missing.

Total: Killed-3, Wounded-40, Missing-2, Total-45.
Source-Rowland, Dunbar, Military History of Mississippi 1803-1898, pp. 328-9.

40th Mississippi: (245 present)   Lt. Colonel G. P. Wallace Commanding

1.	Lt. Colonel:	G. P. Wallace	Wounded, lost arm
2.	Major:	W. Mc D. Gibbons	Killed
3.	Chaplin	J. F. N. Huddleston	Killed

Company A: Oak Bowery Invincibles (Jasper County), Captain C. A. Huddleston
              Commanding

4.	2nd Lt.:	R. R. Wiley	Wounded, severe
5.	Privates:	Bradley	Wounded, severe

The Battle of Peach Tree Creek

6.		J. Bryant	Wounded, slight
7.		R. M. Sanders	Wounded, slight

K-0, W-4, Total-4

Company B: Standing Pine Guards (Leake County), J. W. Johnson Commanding

8.	Privates:	J. B. Langston	Wounded, slight
9.		A. Johnson	Wounded, slight

K-0, W-2, Total-2

Company C: Confederate Rebels (Attala County), Lt. J. H. Williams Commanding

10.	Private:	W. D. Ellington	Wounded, slight

K-0, W-1 Total-1

Company D: (20 present) Attala Guards (Attala County), Captain James W. Boyd Commanding

11.	Captain:	James W. Boyd	Wounded
12.	1st Sgt.:	E. C. Brister	Missing
13.	Corporals:	J. W. Greer	Wounded, severe
14.		F. W. Richbury	Wounded, severe
15.	Privates:	I. Brister	Missing
16.		F. G. Cook	Missing
17.		W. P. Cudd	Missing
18.		W. P. Gordon (Galvin?)	Missing
19.		G. A. Gunn	Missing
20.		R. Holland	Wounded, severe
21.		B. J. Thomas	Missing
22.		W. F. Vick	Missing

K-0, W-4, M-8, Total-12

Company E: Steam Mill Rangers (Neshoba County), Captain W. R. Pierce Commanding

23.	Captain:	W. R. Pierce	Wounded, severe
24.	Sergeant:	I. G. Fox	Missing
25.	Corporal:	J. W. Skinner	Missing
26.	Privates:	I. P. Mc Kinney	Wounded, slight
27.		B. A. Smith	Wounded, severe
28.		B. F. Trussell	Wounded, severe
29.		B. M. Smith	Wounded, slight

K-0, W-5, M-2, Total-7

Company F: Mississippi Tigers aka Neshoba Tigers (Neshoba County), Captain W. L. Bassett

30.	Lieutenant:	W. H. Williamson	Wounded, severe
31.	Sergeant:	J. Fincher	Missing
32.	Corporals:	J. R. Mc Ruth	Killed
33.		B. Williamson	Wounded, slight
34.	Privates:	W. Barnett	Wounded, slight
35.		D. Barnes	Wounded, slight
36.		F. M. Ellis	Missing
37.		T. L. Hanna	Wounded, slight
38.		S. R. Hobson	Missing
39.		J. A. Johnson	Wounded, severe
40.		P. Nelson	Killed
41.		G. G. Seale	Wounded, severe
42.		Tod Sistrunk	Wounded, severe

Roster

43.	B. F. Stewart	Wounded, severe
44.	W. Willis	Missing

K-2, W-9, M-4, Total-15

Company G: Dixie Rangers (Leake & Winston Counties), Captain J. A. Cooper Commanding*

*Note-normally commanded Company C.

45.	Captain: J. A. Cooper	Wounded, died 7-20-64
46.	Lieutenant: P. Webb	Wounded, severe
47.	1st Sgt.: F. P. Clark	Killed
48.	Sergeant: H. Minchew	Wounded, severe
49.	Privates: N. R. Dionne	Missing
50.	L. A. Hill	Wounded, slight
51.	W. H. Hill	Missing
52.	W. Kelly	Wounded, severe
53.	William Thomas McDaniel	Wounded, hospital Griffin, Ga.
54.	John Newton Moore	Captured (reported as Missing)
55.	D. B. Musgrove	Missing
56.	John G. Moore	Missing
57.	J. W. Moore	Missing
58.	William A. Ware	Missing
59.	J. K. Williams	Missing

K-1, W-6, C or M-8, Total-15

Company H: Parrott Rifles (Leake County), Lt. E. N. Chambers Commanding

60.	Lieutenant: E. Chambers	Wounded, slight
61.	Sergeants: G. M. Houston	Wounded, severe
62.	G. Johnson	Missing
63.	P. B. Langford	Wounded, slight
64.	Corporals: J. D. Mays	Missing
65.	J. T. West (Watts?)	Wounded, severe
66.	Privates: M. Dew	Wounded
67.	J. R. Johnston	Wounded, slight
68.	G. W. Pigg	Missing
69.	H. H. Rhinewall	Wounded
70.	M. H. Sharp	Missing
71.	W. T. Young	Wounded, severe
72.	Unknown	Wounded
73.	Unknown (2nd Lt. William P. Love?) Missing	
74.	Unknown (Private Oatty Nelson?) Missing	
75.	Unknown	Missing
76.	Unknown	Missing
77.	Unknown	Missing
78.	Unknown	Missing
79.	Unknown	Missing
80.	Unknown	Missing
81.	Unknown	Missing

K-0, W-9, M-13, Total-22*

*Note-Company H's Bi-Monthly Report for July-August 1864, dated July 20, 1864 states that 9 men were wounded and 13 were captured (or missing). (Source, Supplement to OR, Part II Record of Events Vol. 34, Serial 46, pp. 163-174.)

Company I: Capt. Culbertson's Company (Kemper County), Lt. J. W. Terry

The Battle of Peach Tree Creek

Commanding
82.	Lieutenant:	J. W. Terry	Wounded, severe
83.	Sergeants:	J. W. Germany	Wounded, severe
84.		Z. Johnson	Killed
85.		J. S. Perkins	Killed
86.		J. W. Pilgrim	Wounded, severe
87.		R. T. Rea	Killed
88.	Corporals:	N. Phillips	Wounded, severe
89.		William Ruthben	Killed
90.	Privates:	W. Franklin	Wounded
91.		I. Palmer	Wounded, severe
92.		James Phillips	Wounded, slight
93.		W. W. Pilgrim	Killed
94.		A. B. Smithhand	Wounded, severe

K-5, W-8, Total-13

Company K: Campbell Guards (Attala County), Lt. L. H. Hollingsworth Commanding

95.	Lieutenant: W. P. Lum		Wounded, severe
96.	Sergeants: John Carter		Wounded, severe
97.		Hollingsworth	Wounded, severe
98.		W. Linte	Wounded, slight
99.		John Nash (John C. Nash?)	Killed
100.	Corporals: J. D. Patterson		Missing
101.		W. Robertson	Wounded, severe
102.	Privates: J. Asburn		Wounded, dangerously
103.		George Ball	Killed
104.		R. B. Henning	Missing
105.		James G. Ingle	Wounded, severe
106.		J. M. Ingle	Wounded, slight
107.		J. A. Massey	Wounded, severe

K-2, W-9, M-2, Total-13

Total: Killed-12 Wounded-58   Missing or Captured-37   Total-107*

*Note-The report filed in the Official Records states that 10 men were killed, 57 wounded, and 27 missing or captured for a total of 94. A review of the Compiled Service Records, a list of casualties from the battle and the Supplement to the Official Records reveal 107 casualties.

Sources-OR, Series I, Vol. 38, Part II, Serial 74, p. 884; Supplement to OR, Part II Record of Events Vol. 34, Serial 46, pp. 163-174; Howell, H. Grady, Jr., For Dixie Land I'll Take My Stand, pp. 368-75; Rowland, pp. 339-44 at 343.

Missouri: (partial list)
1st & 3rd Missouri Cavalry:
1.	Captain	Harris Wilkerson	Wounded
2.	Lieutenant	J.T. Mahan	Wounded
3.	Co. A: Private	G. W. Goens	Wounded
4.	Co. B: Sgt:	S. I. Craighead	Killed
5.	Privates:	James Stevenson	Wounded
6.	Co. E: Privates:	Jacob Cravens	Wounded
7.		John Kersey	Wounded

Roster

8. Co. G: Private: James Goen   Wounded
9. Co. K: Private: G.W. Lewis   Wounded

1st & 4th Missouri Infantry:
1. Co. E: Private: Thomas A. Wilson   Wounded
2. Co. F: Private: Edward Hudson   Wounded
3.   Musician: Charles E. Barrett Wounded

2nd & 6th Missouri Infantry:
1. Co. I: Privates: I. B. Ayden   Wounded
2.   George Wallington   Wounded

3rd & 5th Missouri Infantry:
1. Co. E: Private: Thomas Ingram   Wounded

Sourcres-O.R. Vol. 38, Part III, Ser. 74, p. 917; Cockrell's Brigade Casualties at Peach Tree Creek, Tennessee State Library and Archives, (National Archives, microfilm box 1045, roll 1 (old microfilm roll 22, Box 15)).

North Carolina:
29th North Carolina Infantry: 1 killed, 6 wounded, 28 missing, total 35
39th North Carolina Infantry: 3 killed, 10 wounded, 2 missing, total 15

South Carolina:
16th South Carolina Infantry:
Company A:
1.   Sergeant: Horace G. Martin   Wounded
2. Co. D: 1st Lt.:   William M. Goodlet   Captured
1.   2nd Lt.:   James Josiah David   Killed
2.   Corporals: Jesse Fowler   Killed
3.   Richard Fowler   Killed
4.   James W. Harvey   Killed
5.   Enoch Howell   Killed
6.   D. J. Loftis   Wounded
7.   W. M. Smith   Killed
8.   Private: W. L. Howard   Killed
9. Co. I: Private: W. S. Linder   Killed
Total: Killed-8   Wounded-2   Captured-1   Total-11

24th South Carolina Infantry:
1.   Colonel Ellison Capers   Wounded, slightly.
2. Co. A: Cpl.:   John W. Clayton   Killed, 24 yr. old.
3.   Privates: Theodore Hamilton   Wounded & Captd, 29, died at Camp Chase
4.   John Hazzard   Missing, returned.
5.   William Locklear   Wounded, hip, 23 yr old.
6.   William Rowlinski   Wounded & Captured
7. Co. B: 2 Lt.:   William J. Green   Killed, 27 yr. old.
8.   3rd Lt.: F. P. Tatum   Wounded, 29 yrs. old.
9.   Sgts.:   W. H. Crawford   Wounded
10.   William B. Easterling   Wounded, thigh, 21 year old, brown eyes, dark hair, dk complex., 5'8".

473

The Battle of Peach Tree Creek

11.	Corporals: G. W. Bennett	Wounded, arm, 28 years old.
12.	Isaac Johnson	Killed, 28 yr. old.
13.	Privates: Goodwin Barrentine	Wounded, hand.
14.	W. L. Easterling	Wounded, hand, 40 year old.
15.	James Goodwin Odom	Wounded, died in hospital.
16.	Samuel Parham	Killed
17.	William Parker	Killed
18.	Freeman Peel	Wounded, shoulder.
19.	Sam Sweat	Wounded, died of wounds.
20.	Edward Woodle	Wounded & Captured, thigh broken, Camp Douglas, exchanged City Point, Va. 3-22-65.
21.	Co. C: 1st Sgt.:John W. Connerly	Wounded, 26 yr old.
22.	Privates: Peter R. Appleby	Wounded, 20, Marshall Hosp, Columbus, Ga.
23.	John W. Barrs	Wounded
24.	B. M. Johnson	Wounded, shoulder, 31 yr old.
25.	Co. D: Sgt.: Charles E. Bowers	Wounded, ear.
26.	2nd Sgt.: Philip Thomas	Wounded, finger, 34 yrs. old.
27.	Cpl.: William Thomas	Killed
28.	Privates: Jacob Brown	Wounded, foot; 18 year old.
29.	Charles DeLoach	Wounded, 35 yr. old.
30.	Ruben Jordan Rivers	Wounded in crippled arm
31.	George E. Snider	Wounded, hospital, Macon, 32 yr old.
32.	John Strickling	Killed, 49 yr. old.
33.	Wells, Eldred	Wounded, shoulder, 26 yr old.
34.	Co. E: Capt.: Joseph K. Risher	Wounded, slightly, 28 yr. old.
35.	1st Lt.: R. G. W. Bryan	Wounded, head, 31 year old.
36.	Privates: Andrew Johnson	Wounded, breast, 29 yr old, 5'9", dark eyes, dark complexion, black hair.
37.	John S. Lyons	Absent without leave, Captured.
38.	Emanuel Padgett	Wounded, left hip & side, comp. fracture, left tibia, hospital, Macon, 32 yrs. old.
39.	W. E. Preacher	Wounded, breast, slightly; promoted to Corporal July 24, 1864.
40.	Reddin Ritter	Wounded, hospital, 20 yrs. old.
41.	Henry Smith	Wounded, thigh, born 3-9-1839.
42.	L. B. Stewart	Wounded, leg, 17 yr old.
43.	Co. F: Capt.:Samuel W. Sherard	Wounded, breast, 32 yr. old
44.	5th Sgt.: F. J. Stacks	Wounded, shoulder.
45.	4th Cpl.: Jas. L. Clinkscales	Killed, red hair, blue eyes, fair skinned, farmer, 5'10", 21 year old.
46.	Privates: William M. Heaton	Killed; wife-Mary Ann Heaton, 22 year old.
47.	William T. McFadden	Wounded, 27 yr. old.
48.	James A. Simpson	Killed
49.	William Alexander Stewart	Wounded, hand, born 1843.
50.	Co. G: Privates: Thomas R. Bailey	Wounded, right arm amputated, Ocmulgee Hospital, Macon, Ga.

Roster

51.	Andrew Locklear	Wounded, face & hip, 32 year old.
52.	Co H: Sgt.: Green S. Simpson	Wounded, side & arm, 24 yr. old.
53.	Corporal: Joseph Campbell McClintock	Wounded, shoulder, 36 yr old, 6'1", blue eyes, black hair, fair complexion.
54.	Privates: James W. Bingham	Wounded, hand & ankle, 30 years old; blue eyes, dark hair, dark complexion.
55.	George Glover	Killed
56.	John M. Lemon	Missing, returned.
57.	James McGarity	Missing, returned.
58.	Co. I: Sgt.: Memphis W. Prescott	Killed, 20 yrs. old.
59.	Private: J. Ezra Moore	Killed, 24 yrs old.
60.	Co. K: 2nd Lt.: Robert M. Winn	Killled
61.	1st Sgt.: G. Mc Weaver	Wounded, lost leg
62.	Privates: Whitfield Martin	Killed
63.	John S. Williams	Wounded, leg.

Total: Killed-15 Wounded-44   Captured or Missing-4   Total-63
Sources: Compiled Service Records, National Archives.

Tennessee: (partial list)*
*Note-the majority of the Tennessee troops engaged at Peach Tree Creek came from Maney's (Cheatham's) all-Tennessee Division while several Tennessee Regiments served in Tyler's (Smith's) Brigade and Quarles' Brigade in the battle. While the identity of many of the casualties from these units are unknown, Maney's Division casualties are known by number if not by name and total 277, with 30 killed and 247 wounded during the July 20th battle. Additionally, Polk's Brigade, in Cleburne's Division, lost 1 man wounded and 41 captured during the action on July 18th and 19th.

2nd Tennessee:
1. Lt. Colonel: William J. Hale
2. Co. C, 4th Sgt.: Timothy L. Cunningham   Captured, 7-19-64, sent to Camp Douglas, then to Point Lookout, Md. Paroled June 10, 1865.

http://www.rootsweb.com/~tnsumner/sumnfg15.htm (March 1, 2008).

5th Tennessee:

1. Lieutenants:	G. C. Camp	Wounded
2.	G. W. Crawford	Wounded
3.	J. W. Howard	Wounded
4.	D. Kirkpatrick	Wounded
5.	H. R. Linderman	Wounded
6. 1st Sgt.:	Newton J. Fields	Mortally wounded
7. Sergeant:	W. J. Edgar	Wounded
8. Corporal:	D. C. Bancum	Wounded
9. Privates:	S. A. Allen	Mortally wounded
10.	G. R. Alley	Wounded
11.	T. J. Brouch	Mortally wounded
12.	E. M. Doughty	Wounded
13.	Aaron M. Pinson	Killed

The Battle of Peach Tree Creek

14.	J. B. Ray	Wounded
15.	John R. Rumley (or Rumbly)	Wounded
16.	Ed Wallace	Wounded

Total: Killed-1 Wounded-15 (3 mortally) Captured-0 Total-16
Lindsley, John Berrien, Military Annals of Tennessee, Confederate, Vol. I, p. 203; Rennolds, Lieutenant Edwin H., A History of the Henry County Commands which Served in the Confederate States Army, 1904, p. 89.

8th Tennessee:

1. Co. A, Private:	John Y. Blackwell	Wounded, minie ball above lt. ankle shattered both bones; hosp. at Cuthburt, Ga., on crutches 15 years after the war.
2. Co. C, Private:	William A. Craig	Captd., Atlanta, 7-19-64, sent Camp Douglas, Ill., then Pt. Lookout, Md. paroled 6-4-65.
3. Co. F, Captain:	James J. Cullom	Killed
4. Co. H, Privates:	M. M. Dean	Wounded
5.	Frank Hendall	Wounded, left leg. Partial loss of leg
6.	Stephen Johnson	Wounded
7.	William Martin	Wounded
8.	P. Logan	Wounded

http://www.rootsweb.com/~tnsumner/sumnfg15.htm (March 1, 2008); Head, Thomas A., Campaigns and Battles of the Sixteenth Regiment, Tennessee Volunteers, p. 224.

9th Tennessee: -no casualties found. Fleming, James R., The Confederate Ninth Tennessee Infantry, pp. 188-197; Lindsley, John Berrien, Military Annals of Tennessee, Confederate, Vol. I, pp. 280-2.

10th Tennessee Cavalry:
1. Lieutenant: Co. A, J. W. Townsend   Killed (July 15, 1864)
Source-Lindsley, Vol. II, p. 684 & 686.

11th Tennessee:

1. Co. C, Private:	J. R. McClellan	Killed
2. Co. F, Privates:	T. J. Elllis	wounded, died
3.	I. Morgan	Killed
4.	W. J. Newton	Killed
5. Co. H, Private:	A. W. Martin	Killed

Lindsley, John Berrien, Military Annals of Tennessee, Confederate, Vol. I, p. 303-6.

12th Tennessee: (Consolidated with the 22nd Tenn. Battalion and 47th Tenn. Infantry)
1. Colonel William M. Watkins (formerly of the 47th Tenn.) Wounded, left thigh
2. Co. A, Lieutenant: Richard Rogers   Killed
3.   Privates: J. D. Crain ("Jeff Crane")   Killed
4.   John Gambrell (formerly 22nd Tenn. Battl.) Killed
5.   Abe B. Gurgames   Wounded, mortally
6.   Allworth Kennedy   Killed

Lindsley, John Berrien, Military Annals of Tennessee, Confederate, Vol. I, p. 303-6.

Roster

13th Tennessee: (merged with the 154th Tennessee)
1. Co. A: Private: W. W. Claxton — Killed
2. Co. B: 1st Sgt. W. H. Cogbill — Wounded
3.   Private: R. V. Folwell — Killed
4. Co. C: Private Joe Tuggle — Killed
5. Co. H: Private: W. M. Aiken — Captured, sent to CampChase
6.   Private: W. S. Coulter — Captured, sent to Camp Chase
7.   Private T. J. Chambers — Wounded

Vaughan, A. J., Personal Record of the Thirteenth Regiment, Tennessee Infantry, pp. 40-67.

15th - 37th Tennessee: none reported.

16th Tennessee:
1. Lieutenant: J. D. Brown — Wounded, severe groin
2. Co. C, Lt: John Akeman — Wounded 4 times, killed
3. Private: R. M. Safley — Wounded, severe, shot through the lungs
4. Co. I, Private: A. J. Agent — Killed
5. Co. K, Private: Rufus Owen — Killed
6. Private: R. I. West — Killed

Head, Thomas A., Campaigns and Battles of the Sixteenth Regiment, Tennessee Volunteers, pp. 137, & 166-90; Lindsley, John Berrien, Military Annals of Tennessee, Confederate, Vol. I, p. 341.

18th Tennessee:
1. Co. C: Private: Morgan Leatherwood — Killed
2. Co. G: Private: William H. Marshall — Captured, sent to Camp Douglass, Ill. Guard stuck bayonet into left hip in attempt to escape on way to prison. Paroled at end of war. Had chronic diarrhea.

McDonough, James Lee & James Pickett Jones, War so Terrible, Sherman and Atlanta, pp. 211-2; Tennesseans in the Civil War, Part 2, p. 246; http://www.rootsweb.com/~tnsumner/sumnfg15.htm (March 1, 2008).

19th Tennessee:
1. Co. B, Captain: James G. Deadrick — Wounded
2. Co. K, Private: Andy G. Johnson — Wounded

Sources-Worsham, Dr. W. J., The Old Nineteenth Tennessee Regiment, C.S.A., p. 128; compare Cheatham, B. F., Papers, Tennessee State Library and Archives, which relates that the 19th Tennessee suffered 11 wounded, with none killed or captured.

20th Tennessee:
1. Company H: Private: Nathan E. Morris — Wounded

Mc Murray, W. J., History of the 20th Tennessee Regiment Volunteer Infantry, C.S.A., p. 168.

23rd Tennessee:
1. Private: George Whited — Killed

The Battle of Peach Tree Creek

Lindsley, John Berrien, Military Annals of Tennessee, Confederate, Vol. I, p. 399.

25th Tennessee:
1. Private   George Whited   Wounded, died
-was detached from his regiment which was with the Army of Northern Virginia.

28th Tennessee:
1. Colonel: D. C. Crook   Wounded, chest
2. Captain: W. C. Bryant   Wounded, mortally; died in Griffin, Ga. Hospital

Lindsley, John Berrien, Military Annals of Tennessee, Confederate, Vol. I, p. 431.

30th Tennessee:
1. Company H: 3rd Sergeant F. M. Browning Wounded, leg above ankle

38th Tennessee: (Lt. Colonel Andrew D. Gwynne)
1. Co. G: Privates: Isaac H. Sturdivant   Wounded
2.   J. W. Sudduth   Killed
3.   John D Thomas   Wounded
4.   J. W . Winter (or Winder) Killed
5. Co. H: Private: R. L. Mc Ray   Killed

Lindsley, John Berrien, Military Annals of Tennessee, Confederate, Vol. I, p. 508; Thomas, J. D. and L. F. Burks, Chairman His. Comm. Camp Rodes, Feb. 22nd 1897, Roll of The Tuscaloosa Plow Boys, Company G, 38th Tennessee Infantry Regiment.

46th-55th Tennessee:
Company D:
1.   Corporal Wiley L. Brake   Killed
2.   3rd Sgt.: Thomas Lankford   Killed
2.   Private   Louis Smothermon   Killed
2 others killed
Total: Killed-5 Wounded-0   Captured-0   Total-5
http://www.geocities.com/csa1sniper/46thD.html (January 8, 2009); Rennolds, pp. 205-8.

49th Tennessee:
Company C:
1.   Privates: W. H. Banks   Killed
2.   J. W. Grimes   Killed
3.   J. H. Balthrop   Wounded
4. Co. D: Lt.   James A. M. Nesbitt Wounded
Company G:
5.   Private: William Prewitt   Wounded
Total: Killed-2 Wounded-3   Captured-0   Total-5
http://www.tngenweb.org/civilwar/crosters/inf/inf49/cog.html (January 8, 2009).

52nd Tennessee:
1.   2nd Lt.   John Jenkins(transferred from 154th Tenn.) Wounded, disabled arm

Roster

154th Tennessee:
1. Co. L: Private: Thomas B. Turley Wounded

Texas: (partial list)
10th Texas:
1. Co. A: Privates: M. V. Goode Captured
2. Co. D: Privates: Henry Smith Wounded (chest)
3.   S. S. Tillman Wounded (severe)
4. Co. I: Private: Ferdinand Williams Captured
Source-Carlock, Chuck, History of The Tenth Texas Cavalry (Dismounted) Regiment 1861-1865, pp. 3 & 156.

Roster of Federal Casualties at Peach Tree Creek

Connecticut:
5th Connecticut Infantry:
Field & Staff:
1. Adjutant: William A. Daniels Wounded
2. Asst. Surgeon: A. J. Gilson Wounded
Company: B
3. Sergeant: L. M. Snow Wounded
4. Privates: George M. Clark Mortally Wounded
5. E. B. Coolidge Wounded
6. George May Wounded
7. Edward S. Mott Mortally Wounded
8. Robert Renmin Wounded
9. Michael Riley Wounded

Company: C
10. Lieutenant: Isaac N. Welden Wounded
11. Privates: Robert Bell Wounded
12. Eugene H. Duffey Killed
13. Jacob Miller Wounded
14. Lewis Thilo Captured

Company: D
15. Privates: George Barnes Wounded
16. Thomas Evans Wounded
17. Charles A. Farren Wounded
18. William Hasselbacker Wounded
19. John H. McCormick Killed
20. John McKenney Wounded
21. August Meyer Killed
22. Henry L. Mitchell Wounded
23. Hugo Oberempt Wounded
24. Patrick Smith Killed
25. Peter Welch Wounded
26. John N. Williams Wounded

Company: E

27.	Privates:	Myron G. Bishop	Mortally Wounded
28.		John Davis	Mortally Wounded
29.		George Gillbert	Mortally Wounded
30.		Gilbert Saunders	Wounded
31.		Peter Thornley	Wounded
32.		William H. Vanvoorst	Wounded

Company: F
33.	Corporal:	William A. Taylor	Killed
34.	Privates:	George Campbell	Mortally Wounded
35.		Christopher Sailor	Wounded

Company: G
36.	Lieutenant:	Albert L. Gavitt	Wounded
37.	Corporal:	Charles H. Corey	Wounded
38.	Privates:	George Bedford	Killed
39.		George W. Briggs	Wounded
40.		John Carr	Killed
41.		John Clay	Killed
42.		Richard Condon	Wounded
43.		Minott C. Hale	Mortally Wounded
44.		Burton Hodges	Wounded
45.		James P. Howard	Wounded
46.		William Murray	Wounded
47.		James Neval	Wounded
48.		Sylvester Partritt	Killed
49.		Eben E. Scribner	Wounded
50.	Sergeant:	George M. Wilcox	Killed, buried Marietta, Plot G 6854

Company: H
51.	Privates:	George F. Cheeney	Wounded
52.		Napolean J. Stone	Wounded
53.		John Young	Mortally Wounded

Company: I
54.	Privates:	Charles Cunningham	Killed
55.		Henry McCabe	Wounded
56.		William Meighan	Wounded
57.		Harris Shaver	Wounded
58.		Edward Teator	Wounded
59.		James Tuttle	Wounded

Company: K
60.	Privates:	Mortimer W. Brown	Killed
61.		William H. Cordner	Wounded
62.		Philip Devricks	Killed
63.		Philip Fisher	Mortally Wounded

Killed: 14   Wounded: 48 (Mortally Wounded 9)   Captured: 1
            Total: 63

Roster

Sources: Compiled Service Records, National Archives; Marvin, Edwin E., The Fifth Regiment Connecticut Volunteers, 1889, pp. 328-9. According to Colonel Packer's Official Report, however, there were 4 officers and 46 men wounded, and 14 men killed for a total loss of 64; OR, Series I, Vol. 38, Part II, Serial 73, p. 46.

20th Connecticut Infantry:
Company B:
1.   Private: W. J. Brown   Killed
Company C:
2.   Private: U. T. Wells   Wounded, died 7-23-64
Company I:
3.   Corporal: James Faucett   Killed
4.   Private: William Darwin   Killed

http://www.interment.net/data/us/ga/cobb/marienat/index.htm (June 13, 2009).

Kentucky:
15th Kentucky Infantry:
Company A:
1.   Privates: Edward Green   Wounded
2.   Conrad Ritter   Wounded
Company E:
3.   Sergeant: William J. Shake   Wounded
4.   Corporal: James H. Fields   Wounded
Company G:
5.   Private: Hugh O'Rourk   Wounded
Company I:
6.   Private: Jacob Durst   Killed.
Killed-1   Wounded-5   Missing-0   Total-6

Sources: Compiled Service Records, National Archives; Jenkins, Kirk C., The Battle Rages Higher, The Union's Fifteenth Kentucky Infantry, pp. 289-406.

16th Kentucky Infantry:
Company F:
1.   Private: T. Whieher   Killed 7-17-64

17th Kentucky Infantry:
Company H:
1.   Private: Melvin Shultz   Wounded, died 8-1-64

28th Kentucky Infantry:
Company B:
1.   Privates: Michael Hogan   Killed
2.   Barney Oprien   Killed
Company E:
3.   Private: J. T. Davis   Wounded, died 7-26-64

Illinois:
*Colonel Anson Mc Cook Earned the Medal of Honor in the battle

The Battle of Peach Tree Creek

16th Illinois Infantry:
Company D:
1. Private: John McGoverns — Killed 7-17-64
Company F:
2. Private: David Montgomery — Killed 7-17-64

36th Illinois Infantry:
1. Co. E, Private: Edward R. Zellar — Wounded, discharged 7-28-64
2. Co. G, Private: Benjamin Stephens — Wounded, died
3. Co. I, Sgt.: Wormley — Wounded
4. Co. K, Private: Adam Mitchell — Wounded, died 7-27-64
Total- Killed-0   Wounded-7 (2 mortally)   Captured-0   Total-7

38th Illinois Infantry:
1. Private: Thomas Doner — Wounded, died 8-8-64

42nd Illinois Infantry:
Company H:
1. Private: E. H. Wilcox — Wounded, died 7-23-64
Company I:
2. Corporal: W. J. Hewitt — Wounded, died 7-26-64

44th Illinois Infantry:
Company C:
1. Private: William T. Boyd — Wounded, died 7-28-64
Company D:
2. Privates: George Hewitt — Wounded, died 7-24-64
3. Drummer: Henry H. Hollister — Wounded, died 8-16-64, Nashville

Company G:
4. Privates: John Sumner — Wounded, died 7-24-64, Chattanooga
5. William G. Young — Wounded, died

60th Illinois Infantry:
Company I:
1. Private: John Jackson — Killed

73rd Illinois Infantry (The Preacher Regiment):
1. Co. C, 1st Lt: William H. Newlin — Wounded
2. Private: William Martin — Wounded
3. Co. D, Corporal: John Gay — Wounded, died 8-2-64, Kingston
4. Co. G. Privates: George C. Daerfler — Killed
5. Orland Meacham — Wounded, died 8-12-64, Chattanooga
6. Co. H, Private: Marion Fuller — Wounded, died 8-18-64 at home
7. Co. K, Private: Martin Moody — Wounded, died 7-28-64 at Chattanooga
* Private: Joseph Jarvis — Died at Andersonville Prison 7-20-64
Total: Killed-1   Wounded-8 (4 mortally)   Captured-0   Total-9

Roster

Sources: Compiled Service Records, National Archives; Newlin, William H., The Preacher Regiment, pp. 35, 38, 52, 64 & 66.

79th Illinois Infantry:
Company E:
1.   Private: William Wilson   Wounded, died 7-27-64
Company H:
2. Private: Thomas W. Blevins   Wounded, died 8-6-64

82nd Illinois Infantry:
Company A:
1.   Private: George Schurge   Killed
Company D:
2.   Private: Ludwig Winthe   Killed

85th Illinois Infantry: (Casualties sustained on July 19, 1864 at Battle of Moore's Mill)
Company: A
1.   1st Lieutenant: Daniel Havens   Captured
2.   1st Sergeant: John K. Milner   Wounded
3.   Sergeants: Newton King   Captured
4.   William McLaughlin   Captured
5.   Josiah Stout   Captured
6.   Corporal: Alonzo McCain   Captured
7.   Privates: John F. Anno   Wounded, died 7-25-64
8.   John Bortzfield, Jr.   Wounded
9.   William Bortzfield   Wounded
10.   Benjamin E. Jordan   Captured
11.   Charles W. Reagan   Killed
12.   Philip Sanit   Killed
13.   Dallas A. Trent   Captured
14.   David Wood   Captured
Company B:
15.   1st Lieutenant: Albert D. Cadwallader   Wounded (right arm amputated)
16.   1st Sergeant: George D. Prior   Killed
17.   Sergeants: John H. Cleveland   Wounded (right arm amputated)
18.   Thomas Cluney   Wounded
19.   Charles T. Kisler   Wounded
20.   Corporals: John Johnston   Killed
21.   David Sigley   Wounded & Captured
22.   Warren Tippy   Killed
23.   Privates: Jesse Bailor   Captured
24.   Oliver P. Behymer   Wounded
25.   William Buffalow   Wounded & Captured
26.   David Cornman   Killed
27.   Bazil Cozad   Killed
28.   Charles D. Dair   Captured
29.   Amos Eveland   Killed

The Battle of Peach Tree Creek

30.		Daniel Gorin	Killed
31.		William D. Holmes	Wounded
32.		Stephen D. Nott	Captured
33.		John H. O'Leary	Captured
34.		Joshua T. Singleton	Wounded & Captured
35.		Charles Spink	Killed
36.		W. W. Tye	Killed
37.		George Winchell	Captured
38.		William B. Winchell	Captured

Company C:
39.	Captain:	George A. Blanchard	Captured
40.	1st Lieutenant:	James M. Hamilton	Captured
41.	1st Sergeant:	John Houseworth	Captured
42.	Sergeant:	George Black	Captured
43.	Corporals:	William D. Alkire	Captured
44.		Jeremiah Holley	Captured
45.		Andrew McClarin	Wounded & Captured
46.		Thomas Stagg	Wounded & Captured
47.	Privates:	Michael Atchinson	Captured
48.		David Bradford	Captured
49.		James M. Gardner	Captured
50.		Edwin M. Hadsall	Wounded
51.		Louis Ishmael	Captured
52.		John W. Mosier	Captured
53.		George W. Moslander	Captured
54.		Sterling Pelham	Captured
55.		Aaron Ritter	Wounded & Captured
56.		Benjamin F. Scovil	Captured
57.		John Stubblefield	Captured
58.		William A. Tyrrell	Captured
59.		Jeremiah Wagoner	Wounded
60.		Thomas M. Young	Wounded & Captured

Company D:
61.	Sergeant:	Miles McCabe	Wounded
62.	Corporal:	Joseph B. Conover	Wounded & Captured (lost right arm)
63.	Privates:	Noah Davis	Wounded
64.		Cadmus Floro (Cadmas Flow)	Killed
65.		Joseph Larance	Captured
66.		John Sizelove	Captured
67.		James H. Welch	Killed

Company E:
68.	1st Lieutenant:	Hugh A. Trent	Wounded
69.	1st Sergeant:	A. J. Taylor	Wounded
70.	Color Sergeant:	William F. Hohamer	Wounded & Captured
71.	Corporals:	Bowling Green	Wounded
72.		Ezekiel Sample	Wounded
73.		James H. Sheets	Wounded & Captured
74.	Privates:	John H. Arnold	Wounded

Roster

75.		William Clarey	Captured
76.		Richard Griffin	Wounded
77.		Franklin F. Scott	Wounded
78.		James T. Senter	Wounded
79.		James E. Thomas	Wounded
Company F:			
80.	Captain:	John Kennedy	Killed
81.	Color Corporal:	Edward Scattergood	Wounded & Captured
82.	Corporals:	Philip Beck	Killed
83.		Nathan Kellogg	Wounded & Captured
84.	Privates:	John J. Clark	Captured
85.		William Dean	Wounded
86.		Reuben Hamilton	Wounded
87.		Americus Hinsey	Wounded
88.		Maurice Landerer	Killed
89.		Joel F. Terry	Captured
90.		B. F. Varnum	Wounded
91.		Jacob Whittaker	Wounded
Company G:			
92.	Private:	Francis M. Plank	Wounded
Company H:			
93.	Private:	Eli Severns	Wounded

Killed-16   Wounded-42   Captured or Missing-47 (12 also wounded)   Total-93

Sources: Aten, Henry J., 85th Illinois Volunteers, 1862-1865, pp. 203-4; http://www.interment.net/data/us/ga/cobb/marienat/index.htm (June 13, 2009).

88th Illinois Infantry:

1. Co. A, Private:	Henry Kitchen		Killed
2.	David P. Peterman		Wounded, died 7-28-64
3. Co. D, Musician	L. G. Frank		Killed 7-19-64
4. Co. E, Corporal	Patrick Reynolds		Killed
5. Co. G, Sergeants:	Perry A. Wattles		Wounded, discharged 9-14-64
6.	David G. White		Wounded, discharged 8-21-64
7. Private:	Eli Washburn		Wounded, died 8-14-64
8. Co. I, Private	Joseph Mickee		Wounded, died Nashville 7-24-64

Total: Killed-3   Wounded-5 (3 mortally)   Captured-0   Total-8

89th Illinois Infantry:

1. Co. B, Sergeant: Isham William — Wounded, died 8-12-64
2. Co. G, Private: David Woolsey — Wounded, died 8-3-64

96th Illinois Infantry:

1. Co. G, 1st Sgt: Aaron Scott — Wounded, died 8-2-64

100th Illinois Infantry:

Company D:
1. Corporal: Nelson Platts — Wounded, died Chattanooga 9-16-64
2. Private: William E. Dundore — Wounded, died 7-22-64

Company E:

The Battle of Peach Tree Creek

3.	Privates:	Henry Boyd	Wounded, died Chattanooga 8-2-64
4.		James McCune	Wounded, died Chattanooga

Company G:
5.	Private:	Joseph Fishburn	Wounded, discharged 7-21-64

Company H:
6.	Private:	Peter H. Dosse	Wounded, died Chattanooga 8-13-64

Company I:
7.	Corporal:	John Hays	Wounded, died Vining Station 7-24-64
8.	Private:	Thomas Robsom	Wounded, died 8-23-64

101st Illinois Infantry:

Company B:
1.	Captain:	T. B. Wooff	Killed

Company C:
2.	Private:	A. E. Walker	Wounded, died 7-25-64

102nd Illinois Infantry:

Company: B
1.	Sergeant:	Alonzo Beswick	Wounded
2.	Privates:	Daniel R. Boyd	Wounded
3.		Manuel Trout Henderson	Wounded
4.		Lyman B. Straw	Killed

Company: G
5.	1st Sgt..	John C. Reynolds	Died 8-8-64 of wounds at Peach Tree Creek
6.	Sgt.:	John McHard	Died 7-25-64 of wounds at Peach Tree Creek

Company: H
7.	Sergeant:	Harmon C. Shinn	Killed
8.	Private:	Samuel Knight	Killed near Peach Tree Creek by falling tree while building breastworks on 7-19-64.

Company: K
9.	Corporal:	I. N. Stevenson	Wounded, died
	Private:	Albert Kiddoo	Died 11-10-64 of wounds at Peach Tree Creek

K-3   W-7 (4 mortally)   C-0   T-10

*Source-Fleharty, S. F., A History of the 102nd Illinois Infantry Volunteers, pp. 205-14.

104th Illinois Infantry:

Company A:
1.	Sergeant:	Oliver P. Harding	Killed
2.	Private:	Alonzo H. Larkins	Killed

Company B:
3.	Corporal:	Edward Woolsoncroft	Killed
4.	Private:	Nelson F. Noxon	Wounded, died at Vining Station 7-30-64

Company C:
5.	Captain:	David C. Rynearson	Killed

6.	Privates:	Edward Munson	Killed
7.		Washington G. Parker	Killed
8.		James W. Pomeroy	Captured

Company D:
9.	Sergeant:	Henry E. Price	Killed
10.	Corporals:	Thomas Burnham	Killed
11.		Thomas G. Stevens	Killed
12.	Musician:	Otho Hobart	Killed
13.	Privates:	Hiram Anderson	Wounded, died 8-2-64 Vining's Station
14.		William R. Coyle	Killed
15.		Norman Grant	Killed
16.		John S. Powers	Killed

Company E:
17.	Captain:	John S. Doty	Killed
18.	Privates:	John W. Abbott	Killed
19.		Peter Dunn	Killed
20.		John McCullough	Killed
21.		William Pilkington	Wounded, died
22.		Charles Ruger	Wounded, died 7-29-64

Company F:
23.	Private:	Samuel McCashland	Wounded, died 7-29-64

Company G:
24.	Sergeant:	John Thorson	(Thorsen)Killed

Killed- 18   Wounded-5   (Mortally Wounded-5)   Captured or Missing-1
                                        Total-24

(*Note-104th Ill. Reported Casualties were: Killed-15, Wounded-26 (2 mortally), Captured-4, missing-1, Total-46).

Sources: Compiled Service Records, National Archives; Adolphson, Steven J., An Incident of Valor in the Battle of Peach Tree Creek, 1864, The Georgia Historical Quarterly, Vol. LVII (1973), pp. 406-420.

105th Illinois Infantry:
Company C:
1.	Private:	J. Strawn	Killed

Company H:
2.	Private:	A. L. Grear	Killed

125th Illinois Infantry:
Company D
1.	2nd Lt:	John L. Jones	Killed July 19, 1864
2.	Corporal:	Carroll Moore	Killed July 19, 1864

OR reports: Killed-   Wounded-   Captured or Missing-   Total-
http://civilwar.ilgenweb.net/reg_html/125_reg.html (January 2, 2009).

129th Illinois Infantry:
Company C:
1.	Private:	G. R. Sarvis	Killed

Company G:
2.	Private:	Francis Penfield	Killed

The Battle of Peach Tree Creek

Company K:
3.   Sergeant: George Kay   Killed
4.   Private: Valentine Mack   Killed

Battery "C" 1st Illinois Light Artillery:
1.   Corporal: Thomas A. Fitzsimmons   Wounded, died 7-26-64, Vining Station
2.   Private: Bordman Hall   Wounded, died 7-30-64, Chattanooga

Indiana:
9th Indiana Infantry:
Company B:
1.   Private: Charles Murswick   Killed

22nd Indiana Infantry:
Company B:
1.   Privates: Joshus Allen   Killed 7-19-64
2.   William Rose   Killed 7-19-64
3.   Abram Snyder   Killed 7-19-64
Company E:
4.   Private: Albert Morrison   Killed 7-19-64

27th Indiana Infantry:
1.   Colonel: Silas Colgrove   Wounded
Company A:
2.   Corporal: Marion J. Allee   Wounded
3.   Privates: William Dodson   Wounded
4.   Noah J. Palmer   Wounded
5.   Henry Squire   Wounded-gunshot right hand, lost index finger.

Company B:
6.   Privates: Alonzo C. Bugher   Wounded
7.   Alexander Callahan   Wounded
8.   George W. Herrondon   Mortally Wounded (died Sept. 19, 1864)
9.   George W. Stout   Killed (may have been killed in rifle pits during siege)
10.   Richard Trueblood   Wounded
Company D:
11.   Private William A. Smith   Missing
Company E:
12.   Corporal: William Wagoner   Wounded
13.   Privates: Joseph T. Barbour   Wounded
14.   David Everheart   Wounded
15.   Jackson Hopper   Wounded
16.   James Lashley   Killed (but may have been killed at New Hope Church, compare: Brown, E.R., History of the 27th Indiana, p. 594 & 628.

17.		John Murat	Wounded
18.		Berry Street	Wounded
19.		John Weber	Killed

Company F:
20.	Orderly Sgt.	Calvin Arthur	Wounded
21.	Privates:	Daniel Burk	Wounded
22.		Thomas F. Pratt	Killed (may have been killed in rifle pits during siege)

Company G:
23.	Privates:	George W. Prosser	Wounded (lost leg)
24.		John K. Whetstine	Killed (may have been killed in rifle pits during siege)

Company H:
25.	Privates:	James M. Richards	Wounded
26.		William Statten	Killed

Company I:
27.	Sgt.:	Stewart (Stuart), Aaron S	Wounded, severe-gunshot to left foot
28.	Privates:	James B. Bradshaw	Killed
29.		Howard, John	Wounded, severe-gunshot left forearm & hand.

Company K:
30.	Corporal	August Donnermann	Wounded
31.	Privates:	Celestine Eckert	Wounded
32.		Bernard Knust	Wounded
33.		Lawrence Offer	Wounded (may have been mortal because no further record of him with regiment)

Killed-7* Wounded-25   Captured or Missing-1   Total-33*
*Note-the Regiment's Biographer reported 4 killed and 36 wounded at Peach Tree Creek, for a total loss of 40 men. It appears that 3 of the killed, were killed during the Atlanta Campaign, but maybe not at Peach Tree Creek).

Sources: Brown, E.R., History of the 27th Indiana, pp. 561-640; Scaife, p. 154; Bryant, Edwin E., Third Wisconsin Veterans, 1861-1865, p. 256; Cutter, Geo. H, Diary, 3rd Wisconsin, p. 90, University of Georgia Hargrett Library Special Collections. http://www.geocities.com/pentagon/barracks/3627/companya.html. (July 30, 2008).

33rd Indiana Infantry:
Company A:
1.	Privates:	William L. Champion	Wounded
2.		Francis Dane	Killed
3.		Clark Freet	Wounded, died
4.		W.F. McCoy	Wounded
5.		John C. McDonald	Wounded
6.		James P. Seaton	Wounded
7.		Andrew J. Sink	Wounded, died
8.		Aaron J. Williams	Wounded, died

Company B:
9.	Sergeant:	Winfield S. Reed	Killed

The Battle of Peach Tree Creek

10.	Privates:	David Fisher	Wounded
11.		J. S. Gillis	Wounded
12.		G. A. Linkas	Wounded

Company C:

13.	Color-bearer:	Albert H. Law	Wounded
14.	Corporals:	J. F. Bromwell	Wounded
15.		Benjamin Pointer	Wounded
16.	Privates:	Peter Allen	Wounded
17.		Jesse Blana	Wounded
18.		James M. Carpenter	Wounded, died
19.		Henry Crafton	Wounded
20.		James W. Marley	Wounded
21.		James A. Medaris	Wounded
22.		John Paul	Wounded

Company D:

23.	Sergeants:	Jacob Moore	Wounded
24.		A. C. Winterrowd	Killed
25.	Corporals:	James B. Husted	Killed
26.		Alexander McClure	Wounded
27.	Privates:	A.P. Bone	Wounded
28.		Ewing Bone	Wounded
29.		William Bumgarner	Wounded
30.		James Campbell	Killed
31.		Joseph C. Campbell	Wounded
32.		Calvin Col(e)man	Killed
33.		William Coleman	Wounded
34.		Oscar Crank	Wounded
35.		Clinton Garrison	Wounded
36.		Joseph N. Kelley	Wounded
37.		Samuel B. Law	Wounded
38.		Benjamin Maple	Wounded
39.		William Story	Wounded
40.		George Thompson	Wounded

Company E:

41.	Lieutenant:	Floyd T. Duncan	Wounded (arm amputated)
42.	Privates:	Geore F. Bain	Killed
43.		David A. Baker	Killed

Company F:

44.	Captain:	Joseph T. Fleming	Wounded
45.	Lieutenants:	J.C. McClurkin	Wounded
46.		W.S. McCullough	Wounded
47.	Sergeants:	Henry Logan	Killed
48.		William McKeesick	Wounded, died
49.		Robert F. McConnell	Wounded
50.	Privates:	Daniel Heminger	Wounded
51.		John S. Heslie	Wounded
52.		Peter Hibble	Wounded
53.		Andrew J. Hill	Killed
54.		W. M. Hughes	Wounded
55.		Robert McMorton	Wounded

Roster

56.		Francis Ritchie	Killed
57.		Samuel Shoemaker	Wounded
58.		James C. Spellman	Wounded
59.		James W. Taylor	Wounded

Company G:
60.	Privates:	John Brickerton	Wounded
61.		Benjamin F. Bryant	Killed
62.		Napolean B. Thayer	Killed

Company H:
63.	Privates:	S. F. Bosell	Wounded
64.		James H. Brewer	Killed
65.		Caleb Filer	Wounded
66.		William Hacker	Wounded
67.		Henry Jones	Wounded
68.		Jacob Newbern	Wounded
69.		Reuben Spires	Wounded

Company I:
70.	Sergeant:	C. C. Painter	Killed
71.	Corporals:	Matthew W. Eastman	Killed
72.		W. H. Owens	Wounded
73.		Thomas H. Simmons	Killed
74.	Privates:	William Chandler	Wounded
75.		James Cheever	Wounded
76.		Henry H. Crist	Wounded (He alerted Colonel Coburn of Featherston's advance while picking blackberries.)
77.		Thomas Hawkins	Wounded
78.		George W. Holder	Wounded, died
79.		Bennett Miller	Wounded
80.		Walter F. Miller	Killed
81.		W. B. Reed	Wounded
82.		Samuel Thayer	Wounded
83.		Shubal C. White	Wounded, died

Company K:
84.	Sergeant:	William Nodurft	Wounded
85.	Privates:	Samuel Frankenberger	Wounded
86.		Alfred Goodrich	Wounded
87.		Thomas Goodwine	Killed
88.		Marcus L. Hatton	Killed
89.		Rinsey Hendricks	Wounded
90.		William Lester	Wounded
91.		G. K. Sheffer	Wounded
92.		Samuel J. Williams	Killed

Killed-21 Wounded-71 (mortally-7)   Captured or Missing-0   Total-92
Sources: McBride, John R., History of the 33rd Indiana Veteran Volunteer Infantry, pp. 131-2.
http://www.interment.net/data/us/ga/cobb/marienat/index.htm (June 13, 2009).

38th Indiana Infantry:
1. Co. K: Private   John S. Jenkins   Wounded, died 7-21-64

The Battle of Peach Tree Creek

40th Indiana Infantry:
1. Co. F: Private: G. T. Williams   Killed

42nd Indiana Infantry:
1. Co. H: Private: J. P. Sleyer (John Peter Selzner)   Killed

53rd Indiana Infantry:
1. Co. D: Captain: P. Mothis   Wounded, died 7-22-64

57th Indiana Infantry:
1. Co. I: Private: Nathan Clements   Killed

Source: http://freepages.genealogy.rootsweb.ancestry.com/~acorntree/places/ind/del_co/war/hlmcwded.html (June 13, 2009).

70th Indiana Infantry:
1. Co. A: Privates: Clark Converse   Wounded, died 8-18-64
2.   John Custer   Wounded, died 8-16-64, Vinings Station, Ga.
3. Co. B: Corporal: Achilles Rodgers   Wounded, died July, 1864
4. Privates: Robert H. Million   Wounded, died 7-22-64, Chattanooga
5.   John H. Newton   Wounded, died 8-12-64, near Atlanta
6.   George A. Price   Wounded, died 7-29-64, Chattanooga
7.   Louis Goodrich   Killed
8. Co. C: Private: Tilghman S. Harlin   Wounded, died 7-23-64
9. Co. D: Privates: Robert Johnson   Wounded
10.   John H. Poe   Wounded, died 8-21-64
11. Co. E: Private: Matthias Stuck   Wounded, leg
12. Co. F: Corporal: Samuel Bassett   Killed
13. Private: Wat. C. Howard   Killed
14. Co. G: 1st Sgt.: Josiah Lowes   Wounded
15. Sgt.:   Samuel J. Smock   Wounded
16. Corporal: William H. Mc Laughlin   Wounded
17. Private: David Grube   Wounded
18. Co. H: Privates: Levi Baker   Wounded
19.   John T. Hammons   Wounded
20.   James Singleton   Killed
21.   Mason Warner   Wounded, died 8-27-64
22. Co. I: 1st Lt.:   George W. Grubbs   Wounded, slightly
23. Corporal: Andrew J. Johnson   Wounded, slightly
24. Co. K: Captain: James T. Matlock   Wounded
25. Private: James C. Spaulding   Killed

Killed-5   Wounded-20 (mortally-9)   Captured or Missing-0   Total-25

Source-Merrill, Samuel, The Seventieth Indiana Volunteer Infantry In the War of the Rebellion, pp. 291-372.

Roster

85th Indiana Infantry: *Colonel John P. Baird, Resigned, July 20, 1864. Reason not known.
1. Field & Staff: Scout: Abner Howard   Wounded, severe in hip by minnie ball
2. Co. C: Sergeant: Mitchell C. Purcell   Killed
3. Co. D: Privates: John J. Burson   Wounded, died Chattanooga, 8-20-64.
4. Charles E. Young   Wounded, died Chattanooga, 8-12-64
5. Co. F: Private: Thomas Loftus   Wounded, died Chattanooga, 9-29-64
6. Co. G: Privates: Issac Montgomery   Wounded, died Chattanooga, 1-17-65
7. William W. Whitley   Wounded, discharged 9-28-64, died
8. Co. H: Privates: Hiram Case   Wounded, died Chattanooga, 12-2-64
9. Jonathan W. Rehmel   Wounded, died Chattanooga, 9-14-64
10. Co. I: Private: Tillman Shupe   Wounded, died 7-21-64
11. Co. K: Sergeant: Charles Ault   Killed

Killed-3   Wounded-35   Captured or Missing-3   Total-41

Sources-Official Records reveal a total of 41 casualties, with 3 killed, 35 wounded, and 3 captured or missing; see: O.R., Series I, Vol. 38, Part II, Serial No. 73, p. 414, and Welcher, Frank J., & Liggett, Larry, Coburn's Brigade: 85th Indiana, 33rd Indiana, 19th Michigan & 22nd Wisconsin in the Western Civil War, Carmel Press (1999) For the source of the roster of casualties listed, see: Brant, Rev. J.E., History of the Eighty-Fifth Indiana Volunteer Infantry, Its Organization, Campaigns and Battles, Bloomington, Indiana, 1902.

86th Indiana Infantry:
1. Co. B: Private: Orson Morgan   Killed
2. Co. H: Sergeant: J. J. Alger   Killed

http://www.interment.net/data/us/ga/cobb/marienat/index_a.htm (June 13, 2009).

87th Indiana Infantry:
1. Lieutenant: Jacob Leiter   Wounded
2. Privates: David Fisher   Wounded
3. Alfred Hizer   Wounded
4. Unknown   Wounded

Source-Overmyer, Jack K., A Stupendous Effort, The 87th Indiana in the War of the Rebellion, p. 147.

Massachusetts:
33rd Massachusetts Infantry:
1. Co. A: Private: W. F. Smith   Wounded, died 7-25-64

Michigan:
10th Michigan Infantry:
1. Co. A: Private: E. R. Scolley   Killed, died 7-20-64
2. Co. D: Lieutenant: Richard Teak   Killed, died 7-20-64

19th Michigan Infantry:
1. Co. B: Lt.: A. A. Gressete   Killed
2. Lt.: P. A. Pullman   Killed

The Battle of Peach Tree Creek

3. Co. C: Privates: E. W. Page — Killed
4. G. W. Worden — Killed
5. Co. E: Private: Harris Gorham — Wounded, died 7-23-64
6. Co. F: Private: W. H. Allen — Killed
7. Co. H: Private: Peter Moore — Killed

22nd Michigan Infantry:
1. Co. B: Private: A. B. Abernathy — Wounded, died 8-7-64
http://www.interment.net/data/us/ga/cobb/marienat/index_a.htm (June 13, 2009).

New Jersey:
33rd New Jersey Infantry:
1. Co. A: Privates: Isaac Knight (age 19, born England) — Killed, by a cannon shell
2. David Wolf — Captured, sent Andersonville, exchanged in Atlanta Sept. 19, 1864
3. Leroy Wright — Killed, buried Marietta Plot G, 6761
4. Co. B: Corporal: Robert Harrison (age 38) — Killed
5. Privates: Bartholowmew Cunningham — Killed
6. James Losey — Killed
7. James McCombs (age 34) — Killed
8. Co. C: Private: Mathias Weiler — Captured, sent Andersonville, exchanged Sept. 19, 1864, Atlanta
9. Co. D: Corporals: Martin Braan (age 17) — Killed
10. Alex McGill (age 33) — Killed - Marietta National Cemetery, Section G, Grave 6814
11. Privates: Edward (Edwin) B. Arnold — Captured, sent Andersonville-survived
12. Patrick Carroll — Captured, sent Andersonville, exchanged April 5, 1865
13. Alexander McGill — Killed
14. George Pershaw — Captured, Andersonville, exchanged April 1, 1865
15. Martin Van Buren — Captured, Andersonville, exchanged Nov. 14, 1864. Died of Disease Dec. 18, 1864, U.S. Transport Baltic
16. John Vorhees (Vorhies)(age 35) — Killed, buried Marietta, Plot G 6759
17. Peter Wenckler — Captured, Andersonville – Died from wounds Dec. 15, 1864, Savannah, Ga.
18. Charles H. Williamson — Captured, Andersonville, exchanged Savannah, Nov. 14, 1864.
19. Co. E: Privates: Frederick Ernest (age 24) — Killed
20. James Fortune age 33, b. Ireland — Killed, died at Vining Station, Ga. 7-29-64, Marietta National Cemetery, Section I, Grave 361
21. James Lathrop — Killed

Roster

22.	Benjamin Wilson (age 24)	Killed
23. Co. F: Private:	Ezra Conklin (age 18)	Killed
24. Co. G: 1st Sgt.:	Oscar F. Bucken	Missing
25. Corporal:	Patrick Burns	Captured, Andersonville, exchanged Sept. 19, 1864, Atlanta
26. Private:	John Higgins	Captured, Andersonville, Died of disease Sept. 28, 1864
27. Co. H: Corporal:	Thomas H. Eaton	Missing
28. Privates:	Hugh Shields (age 26) b. Ireland	Killed-Marietta National Cemetery, Section G, Grave 7155
29.	Newton C. Dealing	Missing
30. Co. I: Privates:	Charles Anys	Killed
31.	Martin Braan	Killed
32.	Frederick Ehrnest	Killed
33.	Thomas Williams (age 45)	Killed
34. Co. K: Privates:	William Green (age 22)	Killed
35.	Philip Hilgar	Misssing
36.	John Long (age 28)	Killed
37.	William Thompson (age 39)	Killed
38.	Patrick Travers (age 39)	Killed

Total: Killed-22 Wounded-20 Missing or Captured-42 Total-84

Sources-Compiled Service Records, New Jersey State Archives, research courtesy Gary Abrams; Zinn, John G., The Mutinous Regiment, The 33rd New Jersey in the Civil War, p. 131 ;
http://www.njstatelib.org/NJ_Information/Searchable_Publications/civil%20war/NJCWn959.html

New York:
Unknown Regiment:
1. Co. C: 1st Sgt.:   E. C. Beldon   Killed

28th New York Infantry:
1. Co. D: Private: John Barett   Wounded, died 7-29-64

102nd New York Infantry:
1. Co. H: Private: M. H. Bartlett   Killed
2. Co. K: Corporal: D.W. Gould   Killed

107th New York Infantry (partial list):
1. Major   Lathrod Baldwin   Wounded, left eye, since died
2. Co. K: Private John N. Bonney   Wounded, left arm, slight

123rd New York Infantry:
1. Field & Staff: Adj. Seth C. Cary   Wounded
2. Co. A: Cpl   Joseph C. LaPoint   Wounded
3.   Pvt.   Leroy Wright   Killed
4. Co. B: Sgt.   Joseph H. Middleton   Wounded
5.   Cpl.   James B. Taylor   Wounded
6.   Pvt.   William O. Akins   Wounded, died 7-22-64
7.   Pvt.   George W. Harrington   Wounded

The Battle of Peach Tree Creek

8. Co. C: Sgt.		William Hutton, Jr.	Wounded, died 7-23-64
9.	Pvt.	William H. Allen	Killed
10.		Henry Welch	Killed
11. Co. D: Cpl.		D. Ray Williamson	Wounded
12.	Pvt.	Joel Harvey	Wounded
13.	Pvt.	Barney Shandley	Killed
14. Co. E: 1st Lt.		John H. Daley	Killed
15.	Cpl.	Robert McEachron	Wounded
16.	Pvt.	Darius J. Brown	Wounded
17.	Pvt.	George Donley	Killed
18.	Pvt.	Alvah Gray	Wounded
19.	Pvt.	Samuel Stiles	Wounded
20. Co. F: Pvt.		Ebenezer Kinney	Wounded
21.	Pvt.	John M. McMurray	Wounded
22.	Pvt.	George H. Robinson	Wounded
23.	Pvt.	James Stowe	Wounded
24.	Pvt.	Taylor A. Hopkins	Killed
25.	Pvt.	John Byrne	Wounded
26. Co. G: Pvt.		Henry Colter	Wounded
27.	Pvt.	Peter Cowan	Wounded
28.	Pvt.	Clark H. Lawton	Wounded
29.	Pvt.	Henry Welch	Killed
30. Co. H: Pvt.		Henry Danforth	Killed
31.	Pvt.	Chester Orcutt	Wounded
32.	Pvt.	Michael Hileg	Wounded, died 7-25-64
33. Co. I: Cpl.		Frederick A. Slocum	Wounded
34.	Pvt.	Thomas Hennelly	Wounded & captured
35.	Pvt.	George Higby	Wounded
36.	Pvt.	Jacob Hermon	Wounded
37.	Pvt.	Henry Chapman	Killed
38. Co. K: Capt.		Henry O. Wiley	Killed
39.	Cpl.	Chauncy S. Gillford	Wounded
40	Cpl.	Henry Welch	Wounded
41.	Pvt.	Thomas Donohoe	Wounded

Total: Killed-11 Wounded-30 (3 died)   Missing or Captured-1   Total-41
Sources- http://www.interment.net/data/us/ga/cobb/marienat/index_a.htm (June 13, 2009).
http://www.28thga.org/123ny_main.html (July 21, 2009).

134th New York Infantry:
1. Co. B: Private: Richard Rosa   Killed
2. Co. D: Private: David C. Allen   Killed
http://www.interment.net/data/us/ga/cobb/marienat/index_a.htm (June 13, 2009).

136th New York Infantry: (partial list)
1. Co. A: Privates: Hiram Hitchcock   Wounded
2.   James Mead   Wounded
3. Co. C: Burr Summers   Wounded
4. Co. D: Edward Crowel   Wounded
5. Co. G: Corporal: James Fanning   Wounded, missing

Roster

6.	Privates:	Dennis Buckley	Killed, captured flag of 31st Miss., shot in head by ricochet bullet off flagstaff
7.		Gaskard Keiper	Wounded
8.		Samuel Whitmore	Killed

Total: Killed-2   Wounded-15 wounded (1 mortally)   Captured-1   Total-18

Source- Priest, John Michael, John T. McMahon's Diary of the 136th New York 1861-1864, p.119.

137th New York Infantry:
1. Co. B: Sergeant: Charles Williams   Wounded, died 7-21-64
2. Co. H: Private: Charles Coney   Killed

Source- http://www.nytompki.org/tmilt137.htm. (November 29, 2008).

138th New York Infantry:
1. Co. G: Private: Samuel Whitmore   Killed

141st New York Infantry:
1. Field & Staff: Colonel: William K. Logie   Killed
2.   Lt. Col.: A. J. McNett   Wounded, lost his right arm
3.   Maj.:   Clauharty   Wounded, severe
4.   Adj.:   Hazard   Wounded, severe
5.   Lt.   Shapper   Wounded, severe
6.   Captain: Townsend   Wounded, slight
7.   Lt.:   Willor   Wounded, slight
8. Co. A. Lt.   Charles F. Babbit   Wounded, died 7-21-64
9.   Privates: James C. Burtt   Wounded, died 7-26-64
10.   William W. Koons   Wounded, died 8-4-64
11.   Asa Bullard   Killed
12.   Stephen Mead   Wounded, died 7-30-64
13. Co. C: Benjamin G. Thompson Killed
14.   Judd Albertson   Wounded, died 7-21-64
15.   William C. Carnrike   Killed
16.   William H. Decker   Wounded, died 7-21-64
17.   Horace G. Edwards   Killed
18.   Charles A. Swarthout Killed
19. Co. D: John Q. Adams   Wounded, died 7-27-64
20.   Henry Coburn   Wounded, died 9-18-64
21.   Israel Elliot   Wounded, died 9-30-64
22.   Henry Thorp   Killed
23. Co. E: Andrew Benneway   Killed
24.   William C. Youmans   Wounded, died, date unk.
25. Co. F: Russell B. Carrington Wounded, died, date unk.
26.   John Gray   Wounded, died, date unk.
27.   George Owston   Wounded, died 9-1-64
28.   Leander Partridge   Wounded, died 8-7-64
29. Co. G: Sgt.:   Andrew T. Grant   Wounded, died 7-21-64
30.   Privates: Henry W. Gernon   Killed
31.   Oscar R. Leonger   Wounded, died 8-12-64

The Battle of Peach Tree Creek

32.	Thomas Schoonoyer	Killed
33.	Hiram J. Whitehead	Wounded, died 7-20-64
34. Co. H: 1st Lt.	Theodore M. Warren	Killed
35.	Albert E. Butler	Wounded, died 8-6-64
36.	Palmer G. Linsay	Wounded, died 8-21-64
37.	Jacob Norton	Killed
38.	Albert Pierce	Wounded, died 7-24-64
39. Co. I:	George Brees	Killed
40.	George Haxton	Wounded, died 9-27-64
41.	Daniel Luther	Wounded, died 8-19-64
42. Co. K:	Frank Bloss	Killed
43.	Richard Gay	Killed
44.	Andrew J. McCann	Wounded, died date unknown

Half the regiment was disabled, and this is a list of the killed, and those who died of wounds; information from the muster-out rolls in the office of the Adjutant-General at Albany, NY.
Clayton, W. W., History of Steuben County New York, 1879. Pages 127-131.
http://freepages.genealogy.rootsweb.ancestry.com/~familyskeletons/Civil%20War/141st%20Regiment.htm (July 21, 2009).

143rd New York Infantry: (40 total)

1. Adjutant:	William Ratcliff (Age 29)	Killed
2. Co. A: Segts.	Amos P. Akins (19)	Killed
3.	Philo Buckley (21)	Wounded
4.	Frederick W. Burns (23)	Wounded
5. Privates:	Thomas Bates (19)	Wounded
6.	Joseph J. Beebe (18)	Wounded, died 10-5-64
		Hosp. No. 1, Chattanooga, Tenn.
7.	Edward R. Cantrell (22)	Wounded
8.	Edwin J. Everden (22)	Killed
9.	Lewis J. Kanise (18)	Wounded
10.	Nathaniel V. Lent (30)	Wounded
11.	Adam Lohmann (27)	Wounded
12.	John M. Lounsbury (22)	Wounded, died 11-12-64
13.	John McWilliams (21)	Wounded, died 7-21-64
14.	Peter Van Orden (21)	Wounded, died 7-22-64
15.	Theodore C. Van Siclen (19)	Killed
16.	Gilbert J. Young (27)	Wounded, died 8-5-64, Kingston, Ga.
17. Co. B: Corporals:	John H. Jacocks (28)	Wounded
18.	Gustus Rose (27)	Wounded, died 8-1-64, hosp., Lookout Mountain, Tn
19. Private:	Charles H. T. Decker (18)	Wounded
20. Co. C: Sgt.	McKendree N. Dodge (18)	Wounded
21. Private:	Gilbert Laurence (19)	Wounded, died 7-26-64, Field Hosp.
22. Co. E: 1st Lt.:	Peter L. Waterbury (24)	Wounded, died 7-24-64
23. Co. F: 1st Sgt.:	Aaron Hoagland (28)	Wounded, died 7-21-64
24. Corporal:	George Murray (27)	Wounded
25. Privates:	Andrew Hanchen (29)	Killed

Roster

26.		Robert E. Jacoby (25)	Wounded
27.		John Wingert (25)	Wounded
28. Co. G: Corporal:		William Roe 28)	Wounded
29.	Private:	Charles H. Baker (22)	Wounded
30. Co. H: 1st Sgt.:		Rufus W. Porter (22)	Wounded
31.	Corporals:	Jonathan French (28)	Wounded
32.		Charles G. Reese (18)	Wounded, died 2-19-65, hosp. 11, Nashville
33.		Andrew Stickels (23)	Wounded
34.	Privates:	Selah Atwell (18)	Wounded, died 7-22-64
35.		Amos M. Chapman (21)	Wounded died, 7-22-64, Vining's Station, Ga.
36.		Seymour J. Falkerson (18)	Wounded, died 7-21-64
37. Co. I: Privates:		Albert A. Kizer (20)	Wounded, died 9-1-64, hosp. Chattanooga
38.		George W. Purvis (18)	Wounded
39. Co. K: Corporal:		David N. Dibble (20)	Killed
40.	Private:	Elias B. Hill (44)	Wounded

Total: Killed-6 Wounded-34 (14 died) Missing-0 Total-40
http://skaneateles.org/143_inf/143_inf.html#roster (July 21, 2009).

149th New York Infantry:
1. Co. A: Private: Thomas Devans   Killed
2. Co. B: Private: Jacob Grub   Killed
3. Co. C: Private: James Foley   Wounded, died 7-28-64
4. Co. D: Private: Alvin Haynes   Killed
5. Co. E: Privates: John Hart   Killed
6.   William D. Orr   Killed
7. Co. F: Corporal: S. R. Lewis   Killed
8.   Private: John Unbranch   Killed
9. Co. G: Private: J. M. Ward   Killed
10. Co. I: Privates: Robert Goodfellow   Killed
11.   Michael Murray   Killed

154th New York Infantry:
1.   Corporal: Nathius Thisen   Killed
2.   Private: John Wood   Wounded, died 7-22-64

1st New York Light, Battery I, (Lieut. Charles E. Winegar)
1.   Private: Simon Schiok   Killed

Ohio:
McLaughlin's Squadron:
1. Co. A: Private: William J. Yeager   Killed 7-18-64
Source-Hinman, Wilbur F., The Story of The Sherman Brigade, p. 1089.

1st Ohio Infantry:
1. Co. K: Sergeant: John Spencer   Killed

5th Ohio Infantry:

The Battle of Peach Tree Creek

1. Co. A: Corporal: Jacob Direling (Dierling) 18   Killed
2.   1st Sergeant: George Heinzenberg, 24   Wounded, discharged 7-26-64
3. Co. D: Private: James Roberts, 31   Killed
4.   Private: Hugh Liddy   Wounded, died 8-2-64
5. Co. E: Private: John Anderson, 18   Captured
6. Co. G:1st Sergeant: Alexander C. Carr, 24   Wounded, discharged 12-1-64

Killed-2   Wounded-3 (10)   Captured or Missing-1   Total-6 (12)
Source-Official Report shows 2 killed and 10 wounded for a total of 12 casualties for the 5th Ohio.
http://freepages.history.rootsweb.ancestry.com/~cemeteryproject/5th/5thOhio.html (8-3-08).

6th Ohio Battery:
1.   Private: Abraham Weary   Wounded (died 9-24-64 Vining Station)
Source-Hinman, Wilbur F., The Story of The Sherman Brigade, p. 1080.

15th Ohio Infantry:
1. Co. B: Sergeant   J. S. Penrose   Killed
2.   Private: James H. Warden   Killed

21st Ohio Infantry:
1.   Captain: Daniel Lewis   Killed (7-21-64)
2.   Segt. Major: Earl W. Merry   Wounded (lost foot)
Source-Bradley J. Quinlin, Historian, 21st Ohio Infantry; O.R., Ser. I, Vol. 38, Part I, Serial 72, p. 614.

29th Ohio Infantry:
1. Co. A: Corporal: Henry D. Rood   Captured
2. Co. C: Private: John C. Shaw   Missing
3. Co. H: Private: Benjamin Lee   Wounded, died 7-22-64
http://freepages.genealogy.rootsweb.ancestry.com/~rebeccafalin/military/29th/

31st Ohio Infantry:
1. Co. G: Private: John W. Freeman   Killed

35th Ohio Infantry: (Butler Co., Ohio)
1. Co. A: Captain: Lewis F. Daugherty   Killed
2. Co. G: Private: John Foster   Killed

40th Ohio Infantry:
1. Co. A: Private: S. Dyer   Killed
2. Co. G: Private: Simon Hartle   Killed

41st Ohio Infantry:
1. Co. G: Private: Theodore Hawley   Wounded, fingers shot off one hand
Kimberly, Robert L., and Ephraim S. Holloway, The 41st Ohio Veteran Volunteer Infantry in the War of the Rebellion, 1861-1865, pp. 92, & 113.

Roster

49th Ohio Infantry:
1. Co. B: Sergeant: Phillip Miller   Wounded, died 07-23-64
2. Co. D: Corporal: R. V. Tindell   Wounded, died 8-19-64
3. Co. H: Private: M. W. Staller   Wounded, died 8-6-64

51st Ohio Infantry:
1. Co. E: Privates: Joel Frank   Wounded, died 7-21-64
2.   T. West   Killed
3. Co. H: Private: G. K. Luke   Wounded, died 8-10-64

52nd Ohio Infantry:
1.   Lt. Colonel: Charles W. Clancy   Captured
Company A: (Van Wert & Paulding Counties)
2.   1st Lt.:   W. H. Lane   Wounded
3.   Privates: J. W. Harper   Killed
4.   Jesse Roberts   Killed
Company B: (Jefferson County)
5.   Privates: L. D. Mercer   Killed
6.   Henry Bargar   Killed
7.   James C. Haynes   Killed
Company C: (Belmont County)
8.   Privates: Fenton C. Carter   Killed
9.   W. F. Beatty   Killed
10.   F. H. Scott   Killed 7-18-64
Company D: (Tuscarawas County)
11.   George Neighbor   Captured
Company E: (Jefferson County)
12.   Lt.:   James H. Donaldson   Killed
13.   George W. Chalfant   Wounded (lost leg)
14.   Elias Dimmit   Killed
15.   Eli W. Gordon   Killed
16.   Samuel M. Hamlon   Killed
17.   David Henry   Killed
18.   James C. Lease   Killed
Company F: (Belmont County)
Company G: (Jefferson County)
19.   Jonathan Carman   Killed
20.   James W. Donaldson   Killed
21.   Benjamin F. Miser   Killed
22.   Francis Scott   Killed
Company H: (Cincinnati)
23.   William J. Campbell   Killed
24.   John Klank   Killed
25.   Charles Lespie   Killed
26.   Charles W. Smelzer   Killed
Company I: (Cleveland, Painesville & the Western Reserve)
27.   Captain: P. C. Schneider   Killed
Company K: (Cincinnati)
28.   John Bitner   Killed
29.   Thomas Duke   Killed

The Battle of Peach Tree Creek

30.	Horace B. Jewell	Killed
31.	Elijah Mc Neal	Killed
32.	Samuel Smith	Killed

Killed-27 Wounded-47   Captured-14   Total-88
Source-Stewart, Nixon B., Dan McCook's Regiment, 52nd Ohio Volunteer Infantry.

55th Ohio Infantry:
1. Co. C: Corporal   Albert G. Barnett   Killed
2.   Private   Wilbert L. Green (Gunn) 21   Wounded
3. Co. E: 1st Sergeant   John Cowpe, 30   Killed
4.   Private   Edwin T Hood , 22   Wounded
5. Co. F: Private   Taylor Filson, 19   Wounded
6. Co. G: Private   Patrick Burmingham, 32   Killed
7.   Private   Amos Metzgar, 18   Wounded
8. Co. H: Private   Benjamin Dunlap, 23   Wounded
9.   Corporal   Addison Golden, 30   Wounded
10.   Private   Seth Golden, 18   Wounded
11.   Private   Joseph McConahy, 18   Wounded
12.   Private   Frank Ray, 20   Wounded
13.   Private   Isaac Reed, 19   Wounded
14.   Corporal   Charles L Wilson, 21   Wounded
15. Co. K: Private   Jacob Yager , 21   Wounded

Killed-3 Wounded-12   Captured of Missing-0   Total-15* (22)

*Sources: OR says lost between 20-30 men killed and wounded; by deducting the other regimental losses given from the brigade losses reported by Wood, the 55th Ohio appears to have lost 22 men killed and wounded. The losses listed by name above are confirmed by a review of the rosters provided at:
http://freepages.history.rootsweb.ancestry.com/~cemeteryproject/55th/55thOhio.html (8-3-08). The discrepancy in the figures may be accounted for by having 7 slightly wounded men who were not picked up by name on Federal muster rolls.

61st Ohio Infantry: (partial list)
1.   Colonel   Stephen J. McGroarty   Wounded, lost left arm
2.   Lt. Colonel: William H. Brown   Wounded, mortally
3. Co. A Private   Samuel E Zeboldt, 19   Killed
4. Co. B Private   John Cavanaugh, 19   Wounded
5.   Private   George W Kirtz, 18   Wounded, died Louisville, Ky
6.   Corporal   Dennis McDonald, 34   Wounded, died 7-22-64
7.   Private   Henry Reese, 33   Killed
8.   Corporal   Cornelius Spellman, 43   Killed
9. Co. C Private   William E Justus, 37   Killed
10. Co. E Private   Joel Frank, 18   Killed
11.   Sergeant   Marcus T Leiter (Leifer), 18   Killed
12. Co. F Private   Patrick Horn, 32   Killed
13.   Private   William Ross   Killed
14. Co. G Private   James Beaver, 19   Wounded
15.   Private   Edward McShane, 23   Wounded
16. Co. H Sgt./Cpl.   James W Grafton, 18   Killed
17.   Private   John Jones, 26,   Killed

Roster

18.	Corporal	David B Long, 33	Wounded, discharged
19.	Private	James D Richards, 27	Killed
20. Co. I	Private	Herman Bales, 41	Killed
21.	Private	Conrad Buchler (Buckler), 18	Killed
22.	Private	Andrew Strayler (Strauer), 19	Wounded, died 7-25-64
23. Co. K	Private	Paris A Brewer, 19	Killed
24.	Private	Jeremiah Ginley, 18	Killed
25. Company not known:		Samuel Christy	Wounded
26.	Captain	E. H. Newcomb	Mortally wounded (7-21-64)

Killed-15 (20)   Wounded-10 (57)   Captured or Missing-0 (2)   Total-25 (79)

Source- http://freepages.history.rootsweb.ancestry.com/~cemeteryproject/61st/61stOhio.html (August 3, 2008); Carroon, Robert G., From Freeman's Ford to Bentonville, The 61st Ohio Volunteer Infantry.

64th Ohio Infantry:
1. Co. A: Corporal: William N. Dilley — Wounded
2. Co. B: Sergeant: Henry Partridge — Captured
3. Private: William F. Fields — Wounded, died 7-24-64 Chattanooga Hosp.
4. Co. D: Private: Thomason Mount — Wounded
5. Co. F: Privates: George Bolenbaugh — Wounded (died 8-30-64)
6. Alexander Fisher — Wounded
7. Co. G: 2nd Lt.: Robert Fisher — Wounded
8. Co. H: Sergeant: Francis M. Trago — Killed
9. Co. I: Private: George W. Stock — Wounded (died Sept. 1864 at home in Ohio)

Total: Killed-1   Wounded-7 (3 mortally)   Captured-1   Total-9

Source-Hinman, Wilbur F., The Story of The Sherman Brigade, pp. 939-985.

65th Ohio Infantry:
1. Co. A: Private: Amos Smith — Killed 7-18-64 near Buckhead
2. Co. B: Private: Samuel R. Moore — Captured
3. Co. C: Private: Levi Seavolt — Wounded, died 7-22-64
4. Co. F: 1st Lt.: Joseph S. Covert — Wounded
5. Co. H: Sergeant: William H. Thompson — Wounded
6. Corporal: Henry Huffman — Wounded (died 8-1-64 at Chattanooga)
7. Co. I: Corporal: David Crowner — Wounded

Total: Killed-1   Wounded-5 (2 mortally)   Captured-1   Total-7

Source-Hinman, Wilbur F., The Story of The Sherman Brigade, pp. 1012-1057.

66th Ohio Infantry: (partial list)
1. Co. D: Private: William T. Boggs (28) — Killed
2. Co. E: Lt.: James P. Conn — Wounded, struck on head by sword
3. Private: William D. Rowland (19) — Wounded, died Chattanooga 9-8-64
4. Co. G: Lt.: William V. Taylor — Wounded, hand, arm, and shoulder
5. Co. I: Lt.: John R. Organ — Wounded, mortally; died 7-20-64
6. Private: Samuel Brinin (Brannon) — Killed

Total: Killed-2   Wounded-2 (2 died)   Captured-1   Total-23 (Regt reports claim 2 killed and 21 wounded).

The Battle of Peach Tree Creek

Source-Thackery, David T., A Light & Uncertain Hold, A History of the 66th Ohio Volunteer Infantry; pp. 204-5; & 257-85.

69th Ohio Infantry:
1. Co. F: Private: Henry Steckel   Wounded, died 7-23-64

73rd Ohio Infantry:
1. Co. B: Private: William May   Killed

74th Ohio Infantry:
1. Private: John Hennesey   Wounded (Killed 7-22-64)
2. Corporal: John H. Forbes   Killed (7–22-64)
3. Sgt.: Edward Wright   Wounded (7-22-64)
4. Private: Addison Tolbert   Killed (7-22-64)

2 others wounded Total-3 wounded 7-20-64.
Source-Blackburn, Theodore W., Letters From the Front, A Union "Preacher" Regiment (74th Ohio) in the Civil War, pp. 214-5.

79th Ohio Infantry:
1. Co. A Corporal   William Huston Bone   Wounded
2. Privates: William T. Baner   Killed
3.   David S. Perrine   Wounded; died 8-14-64, Chattanooga
4. Co. C: Privates: William Elster   Killed
5.   Morris McMillan   Killed
6. Co. E Private   Jonathan Ireland   Killed
7. Co. G: Private: Lewis Johnson   Killed
8. Co. H Private   Joseph H. Wolfe   Wounded, died 7-30-64

Sources-National Tribune. "A Western Man's Account of Peach Tree Creek" W.H. Wells. Co. C. 79th O.V.I. Seymour, Indiana. June 7, 1883; and http://www.rootsweb.ancestry.com/~ohwarren/Bogan/bogan112.htm#A (August 3, 2008).

82nd Ohio Infantry:
1. Co. B: Private: A. H. Gary   Killed
2. Co. D: Privates: Peter McCarvin   Killed
3.   William Paine   Killed
4. Co. I: Sergeant: Nicholas Rader   Killed
5. Co. K: Private: Samuel Brown   Wounded, died 7-23-64

97th Ohio Infantry:
1. Co. B: Private: Robert Haney   Wounded, died 7-28-64

113th Ohio Infantry:
1. Private: John Weber   Killed 7-19-64

125th Ohio Infantry:
1. Co. B: Private: Edwin C. Woodworth   Wounded, 7-20-64
2. Co. C: Private: Jesse B. Luse   Wounded, lost arm 7-18-64 at Nancy Creek
3. Co. E: Private: Samuel Rogers   Killed 7-18-64 at Nancy Creek

Roster

4. Co. F: Sergeant: Jacob Jewell — Wounded, in side 7-18-64 at Nancy Creek
5. Private: Samuel Sailor — Wounded, died 7-28-64
6. Company Unknown:Unknown — Wounded, 7-18-64 at Nancy Creek
7. Unknown — Wounded, 7-18-64 at Nancy Creek
8. Private Charles Allabaugh — Wounded 7-20-64, died 8-8-64
Total- Killed-1   Wounded-7   Total-8
Source-Clark, Charles T., Opdyke Tigers, p. 287.

Ohio Soldiers Regiment Unknown:
1. Co. E: Private: Elias Dimit — Killed
2. Co. G: Private William Burton — Killed

Pennsylvania:
28th Pennsylvania Infantry: "Goldstream Regiment"
1. Captain: Thomas H. Elliott, (Adjt. General on Geary's staff) — Killed
2. Co. A: 2nd Lt. Isaiah B. Robinson — Killed
3. Co. C: Privates: Samuel Knox — Wounded, died 8-22-64, buried Chattanooga, grave 479
4. Charles B. Macaully — Killed
5. Co. D: Corporal: John N. Moyer — Wounded, died 9-19-64 Nashville
6. Co. E: Private: John Sauer — Wounded, died 8-22-64
7. Co. H: Captain: Frank B. M. Bonsal — Wounded
8. Corporal: Oliver P. Adams — Killed
9. Private: Peter Reichender — Wounded
10. Co. I: Privates: John C. Atkinson — Wounded, died 9-27-64
11. James Mullin — Killed
12. Co. K: Privates: James A. Brady — Wounded, died 7-27-64
13. James Ray — Killed
Total: Killed-6 Wounded-7   Total-13
Source: http://www.pa-roots.com/pacw/infantry/28th/28thorg.html (February 21, 2009).

29th Pennsylvania Infantry:
1. Co. A: Private: John P. Feitig — Killed
2. Co. B: Private John Cavanaugh — Wounded, died 8-3-64
3. Co. F: 1st Sergeant: Charles H. Martin — Wounded, died 7-23-64
3. Co. H: Private: Dominick Mallon — Wounded, died December 1, 1864
4. Co. K: Private: James Ray — Killed
Total: Killed-2 Wounded-3   Total-5
Source: http://www.pa-roots.com/pacw/infantry/paregimentsnew1.html (February 21, 2009); http://www.interment.net/data/us/ga/cobb/marienat/index_cacl.htm (June 13, 2009).

43rd Pennsylvania Infantry:
1. Co. K: Private: Samuel Baker — Killed

46th Pennsylvania Infantry:
1. Adjutant: Luther R. Whitman — Wounded, died 8-6-64
2. Co. A: 1st Lt. D. C. Selheliner — Wounded, died 9-21-64
3. Co. B: Privates: John Holshower — Killed

The Battle of Peach Tree Creek

4.		Samuel Wilmet	Killed
5. Co. C:	Sergeant:	C. C. Cavanaugh	Killed
6. Co. D:	2nd Lt.:	Samuel Wolf	Killed
7.	Sergeant:	Henry Weidensaul (17)	Wounded, was 14 when enlisted
8.	Corporals:	John Houser	Wounded
9.		Frederick Sarber	Killed
10.	Privates:	Alexander Barr	Killed
11.		John W. Chisholm	Wounded
12.		John C. Ebersole	Killed
13.		Joseph Geiger	Wounded, died 7-31-64; buried Chattanooga, grave, 247
14.		Dan'l. Koppenhafer	Wounded, died 8-26-64, buried Chattanooga, grave, 503
15.		William Luce	Wounded, died 9-2-64, buried Chattanooga, grave, 638
16.		Christopher Mease (Mearse)	Killed
17.		John McDevitt	Killed
18.		Levi Ney	Wounded, died July 1864
19.		John Shelly	Wounded, with loss of leg
20.		G. E Stoutseberger	Wounded, died 2-27-65
21.		William Vanscoter	Wounded & missing
22. Co. E:	Captain:	Sefra T. Ketrer	Wounded, died 7-21-64
23.	1st Sgt.:	Daniel D. Baker	Wounded; died Vining's Station, Ga., 7-31-64
24.	Corporal	Henry Connor	Killed
25.	Privates:	Henry Durstine	Wounded, discharged
26.		Jno. L Espenshade	Wounded, died 9-22-64
27.		Henry Fricker	Wounded, died 7-26-64
28.		Hiram Raymond	Wounded, discharged
29. Co. F:	Private:	John Vodrey	Wounded, died 7-25-64
30. Co. G:	Privates:	N. Nelson	Killed
31.		J. H. Snath	Killed
32. Co. H:	Corporal:	George A. Post	Wounded, died 7-29-64
33.	Privates:	John D. M'Cahan	Wounded, died 7-25-64
34.		Hezek'h J. Wright	Killed
35. Co. I:	Privates:	Jacob Bowman	Wounded, died 8-17-64, Chattanooga, grave 18657
36.	Lt.:	Henry J. Davis	Killed
37.		Joseph Gloegle	Wounded, in hospital
38. Co. K:	Sergeant:	Joseph Long	Killed
39.	Privates:	John Medlicott	Wounded, died 10-27-64

Total: Killed-15 Wounded-24 Captured or Missing-1 Total-39

Source: http://www.pa-roots.com/pacw/infantry/46th/46thorg.htm (February 21, 2009); http://www.interment.net/data/us/ga/cobb/marienat/index_cacl.htm (June 13, 2009). According to Fox's Regimental Losses, Chapter 2, the 46th Pennsylvania lost 51 men killed at Peach Tree Creek. However, according to the Official Records, they sustained: 26 officers and men killed or mortally wounded, 86 wounded, and 1 missing. O.R., Series I, Vol. 38, Part II, pp. 56-57

73rd Pennsylvania Infantry:
1. Co. D: Private: William Grahams   Captured, died

Roster

2.Co. E: Private: Joseph Procter   Wounded
Total: Killed-0   Wounded-1   Captured-1   Total-2
Source: http://www.pa-roots.com/pacw/infantry/73rd/73dorg.html (February 21, 2009).

77th Pennsylvania Infantry:
1.Co. A: Private: John W. Fraker   Wounded
Total: Killed-0   Wounded-1   Total-1
Source: http://www.pa-roots.com/pacw/infantry/77th/77thorg.html (February 21, 2009).

79th Pennsylvania Infantry:
1. Co. C: Private: Peter Hahn   Wounded, died 7-22-64
2. Co. F: Private: George Stein   Wounded, died 7-23-64

109th Pennsylvania Infantry:
1. Co. C: Privates: Charles O' Rourke   Captured; died Andersonville 8-26-64, grave, 6,908
2.   Oliver Price   Captured; died Andersonville 10-19-64, grave, 11,168
3. Co. E: Private: Felix Pilf   Wounded
4. Co. F: Private: James Purcell   Captured
5. Co. I: Private: William Dixon   Wounded
Total: Killed-0   Wounded-2   Captured-3   Total-5
Source: http://www.pa-roots.com/pacw/infantry/109th/109thorg.html (February 21, 2009); Veale, Moses. The 109th Regiment Penn. Veteran Volunteers, Philadelphia: J. Beale, Printer, 1890.

111th Pennsylvania Infantry:
1.   General: Geo. A. Cobham, Jr.   Killed, promoted to Brevet Brig. Genl., 7-19-64
2.   Sgt. Major: Logan J. Dyke   Wounded, with loss of arm
3. Co. A: 2nd Lt.:   Cyrus A. Hayes   Captured
4.   1st Sgt.   James R. Raymond   Wounded, discharged
5.   Corporals: Conrad B. Evans   Captured
6.   Albert M. Walton   Missing
7.   Privates: Benjamin Babcock   Captured
8.   Volney R Gleason   Killed; bur. Marietta Natl Cemetery, sec. G, grave 168
9.   William H. Joslin   Captured
10.   Monroe Miller   Wounded
11.   Anthony Malvin   Wounded, July 19, 1864
12.   Felix Pilf   Wounded
13. Co. C: 1st Lt.:   William C. Hay   Wounded
14.   Sergeants: John D. Evans   Wounded
15.   Wyley L. Mackey   Wounded & Captured
16.   Corporal: Robert Donnell   Wounded & Captured
17.   Privates: Charles Meschler   Wounded, died 8-3-64; Chattanooga, grave, 284
18.   Charles P. Scott   Wounded & Captured
19.   Samuel S. Weidler   Wounded & Captured
20.   Landsley Wood   Killed, bur. Marietta Natl Cemetery, sec. G,

The Battle of Peach Tree Creek

			grave 167
21.	Co. D: Captain:	H. R. Sturdevant	Captured
22.	Sergeant:	Chris'r. G. Herrick	Wounded
23.	Corporal:	George C. Oliver	Captured
24.	Privates:	Milo M. Adams	Wounded
25.		Nathan J. Branch	Captured
26.		Stephen Baker	Wounded
27.		Andrew Hultberg	Captured
28.		Charles Hultberg	Killed
29.		David L. Hodges	Captured
30.		Morris Lee	Captured
31.		James T. Miller	Killed; bur. Marietta Cemetery, sec. G, grave 173
32.		Alexander Morton	Captured
33.		Philip Schirk	Wounded
34.		Franklin Stilson	Wounded, discharged
35.		D. Porter Siggins	Killed
36.		John Smith	Killed
37.	Co. E: 1st Lt.:	Jesse Moore	Wounded
38.	2nd Lt.:	Hiram Bissell	Captured
39.	Corporals:	Frederick White	Wounded
40.		S. W. Butterfield	Wounded, died Chattanooga, 9-5-64; bur. grave 537
41.		William N. Dehass	Wounded, July 19, 1864
42.		Thomas Gehr	Wounded, July 19, 1864
43.	Co. F: 2d Lt.:	John L. Wells	Captured
44.	Sergeant:	Michael Gorma	Killed
45.	Corporal:	Charles Deislang	Wounded
46.	Privates:	William H. Austin	Wounded
47.		Howard Burk	Captured
48.		Horatio G. Cooley	Wounded
49.		Peter Franz	Captured
50.		George Helireigle (Hellsiegel)	Wd., died 7-23-64; bur. Marietta, sec. C, grave, 674
51.		Ira B. Munsel	Captured
52.		Masters Rowland	Captured; died 8-6-64; Andersonville; grave, 11,868
53.		John Thompson	Wounded
54.		Theodore Wenike	Wounded
55.	Co. G: 1st Lt.:	Christian Sexauer	Wounded
56.	Privates:	Jacob B. Haffer	Wounded
57.		John Mason	Wounded
58.	Co. H: 1st Lt.:	William P. Gould	Wounded
59.	Sergeant:	John H. Henry	Captured
60.	Corporal:	Isaac S. Baldwin, Jr.	Wounded
61.	Privates:	George Houk	Wounded
62.		John Palmer	Killed
63.	Co. I: Captain:	Henry Dieffenbach	Wounded
64.	Sergeants:	Charles Long	Captured
65.		Peter Fraley	Killed, bur. Marietta Natl Cemetery, sec. G, grave, 175

66.	Privates:	William Foust	Wounded
67.		William A. Hites	Captured
68.		Charles M. Irvin	Captd, died 7-28-64; bur. in Marietta, sec. B, grave, 116
69.		Nicholas Kimmel	Captured
70.		William Kissell	Captured
71.		John Smith	Wd, died 7-21-64; bur. in Marietta, sec. C, grave, 671
72.		John Thompson	Captured
73.		Christo'r Wingert	Captured; died Andersonville 9-23-64, grave, 9,573
74. Co. K:	Privates:	George B. Byer	Killed, bur. Marietta, sec. G, grave 169 or 171
75.		John G. Cain	Killed, burMarietta, sec. G, grave 170
76.		Asa O. Douglass	Wounded, died Chattanooga, 8-25-64; bur. grave 366
77.		David Kauffman	Wounded
78.		Edward Lewby	Killed, 7-19-64; bur. Marietta, sec. G, grave 302
Total:	Killed-13 (1 on 7/19)	Wounded-39 (3 on 7/19)	Captured-30 Total-78

Source: http://www.pa-roots.com/pacw/infantry/111th/111thorg.html (February 21, 2009); Bates, Samuel P. History of the Pennsylvania Volunteers, 1861-1865, Harrisburg, 1868-1871.

147th Pennsylvania Infantry:
1. Co. E:	Private:	James Mooney	Wounded, died 8-11-64
2. Co. F:	Private:	John G. Kraff	Killed; bur. Marietta Natl Cemetery, sec. G, grave 293
3.		Gust. Wunderlich	Killed
4. Co. I:	Private:	John M'Calillnoo	Wounded, discharged
5. Co. K:	Private:	William H. Harrison	Wounded
Total:	Killed-2	Wounded-3	Total-5

Source: http://www.pa-roots.com/pacw/infantry/147th/147thorg.html (February 21, 2009).

Pennsylvania Light Artillery, Battery E (Knap's):
At the battle of Peach Tree Creek, on the 20th of July, Captain M'Gill was severely wounded, and soon after resigned, the command devolving on Lieutenant James A. Dunlevy. Two men were killed and a number of others were severely wounded.
1.	Captain:	James D. M'Gill	Wounded
2.	Sergeant:	James B. Hazlett	Killed, bur. Marietta, section G, grave, 585
3.	Privates:	Frederick Hoffman	Wounded, died 8-11-64
4.		Henry G Morris	Wounded
Total:	Killed-1	Wounded-3	Total-4

Source: http://www.pa-roots.com/pacw/artillery/indbatteorg.html (February 21, 2009).

Wisconsin:
3rd Wisconsin Infantry:
1. Co. D:	1st Sergeant:	George W. Norton	Wounded
2.	Privates:	William H. Biedelman	Wounded, died 8-22-64 at Vining

The Battle of Peach Tree Creek

			Station
3.		Lorenzo Clintsman	Wounded
4.		Cornelius Cornell	Killed
5.		Andrew Oliver	Killed
6. Co. F: Privates:	George R. Sinnett	Wounded, died 8-1-64 Atlanta
7.		Daniel Snider	Wounded
Total:	Killed-2 Wounded-5	Captured or Missing-0	Total-7

10th Wisconsin Infantry:
1. Co. G: Private: William P. Hoffman   Wounded, mustered out 11-3-64
http://www.wisconsinhistory.org/roster/results.asp#regiment (December 21, 2007).

21st Wisconsin Infantry:
1. Co. B: Corporal: Thomas Rohan   Wounded, mustered out 6-8-65
2. Co. F: Corporal: Andrew C. Barr   Wounded, mustered out 6-8-65
3. Co. I: Private: George A. Dubois   Wounded, transferred to 3rd Wisc. 6-8-65

Total: Killed-0 Wounded-3   Captured or Missing-0   Total-3

22nd Wisconsin Infantry:
1. Co. A: Privates: Clement A. Northway   Wounded, died 8-1-64 Atlanta
2.   Frederick Tessin   Wounded, died 8-12-64 Atlanta
3. Co. B: Sergeant: Weaver F. Schoening   Wounded
4.   Privates: Thomas Court   Wounded
5.   John Jacobson   Killed
6.   Sumner Nelson   Wounded, leg amputated
7.   William C. Orr   Wounded
8.   Nelson Salisbury   Wounded
9. Co. C: Corporal: Rollin R. Read   Wounded
10.   Privates: William H. Bright   Wounded, right arm amputated
11.   James Owens   Wounded
12. Co. D: Privates: Wendel Fuhr   Killed
13.   James Griffin   Wounded, died 7-30-64, Chattanooga
14.   Henry C. Hunt   Wounded
15.   Thomas Morrison   Killed
16.   Peter Weiskoff   Killed
17. Co. E: Sergeant: Albert D. Warner   Wounded, died 8-20-64, Atlanta
18.   Corporal: Albert Walker   Killed
19. Co. F: Privates: Anderson   Wounded
20.   William R. Edwards   Wounded
21.   Theodore Hanson   Wounded, died 8-8-64
22.   Charles Lapp   Wounded, died 8-20-64 Chattanooga
23. Co. G: Private: Gullick (Galac) Anderson   Killed
24. Co. H: Privates: James Holland   Wounded
25.   James N. Ingersoll   Killed
26.   Iverson   Wounded
27.   William Madama(Mattinore)   Killed
28.   Schultz   Wounded
29. Co. I: Privates: Norwood Bowers   Wounded
30.   Bennett Hanson   Wounded, died 8-3-64 Chattanooga

Roster

31.	Henry Hunt	Wounded
32. Co. K: Corporals:	Josiah D. Hall	Wounded
33.	Sylvester McMannes	Wounded
34.	Wilford E. Parriott	Wounded
35. Privates:	Harlow T. Bouton	Wounded
36.	Richard Shanahan	Wounded

Total: Killed-8   Wounded-28 (Mortally Wounded-7)   Captured or Missing-0   Total-36

*Note Racine Boy letter of July 21, 1864, shows 7 killed and 36 wounded for a total of 43 losses; Kennesaw Mountain National Park, Subject Files, No. PW-4, p. 17.

24th Wisconsin:

1. Co. C: Private:	John Hadeler	Wounded
2. Co. D: Private:	Martin Unzer	Wounded
3. Co. E: Private:	John D. Barrett	Killed

Total: Killed-1   Wounded-2   Captured or Missing-0   Total-3

26th Wisconsin:

1. Co. A: Corporal:	Henry Van Eweyke	Wounded
2. Privates:	Stephan Fiess	Killed
3.	Andreas Gathmann	Wounded, died 7-25-64
4.	Julius Semisch	Wounded
5.	Fred. Sholtz	Wounded
6. Co. B: Sergeants:	William Braunschweig (Branneschwig?)	Wounded
7.	Charles Weinreich	Wounded
8. Privates:	William Ewald	Wounded
9.	William Lauer	Killed
10.	Wilhelm Sasse	Killed
11.	August Wendorff	Wounded
12.	Fred. Winter	Wounded
13. Co. C: Captain:	Robert Mueller	Killed
14. Corporals:	August Truemper	Wounded
15.	Ferdinand Krueger	Wounded
16. Private:	Peter Weber	Wounded
17. Co. D: Sergeant:	Michael Huntz	Wounded
18. Corporals:	John Held	Killed
19.	Bartholomaeus Peissue	Wounded
20. Privates:	William Kraemer	Wounded
21.	Wilhelm Milke	Wounded, died 8-7-64 Nashville
22.	F. K. Warner	Wounded
23.	Jacob Weber	Killed
24. Co. E: Captain:	William Steinmeyer	Wounded
25. Sergeant:	Phillip Zipp	Wounded
26. Musician:	Xaver Braun	Killed
27. Privates:	Ed Dreblob	Wounded
28.	John Urban	Wounded
29. Co. F: Sgt.:	Henry Lippman	Wounded, died 10-23-64 Chattahoochee
30. Corporal:	John Voight	Wounded
31. Privates:	William Arm	Killed
32.	Gerhard Niephaus	Killed

The Battle of Peach Tree Creek

33.	Louis Busch	Wounded
34.	P. Newman	Wounded
35.	Jacob Schmidt	Wounded
36.	Joachim Schultz	Wounded
37.	Friedrich Winter	Wounded, died 8-16-64, Nashville
38. Co. G: 1st Lt.:	Nicholas Vollmar	Wounded, died 8-21-64
39. Privates:	William Hughes	Wounded
40.	Peter Phillipsen	Wounded
41. Co. H: Sergeant:	Randolph Seibelist	Wounded
42. Corporals:	Peter Mauer	Wounded
43.	Franz Reuter (Ruter)	Killed
44. Privates:	Valentine Mueller	Wounded, died 8-17-64 Kingston
45.	Franz (Franklin Zager) Zeiger	Wounded
46. Co. I: Captain:	John P. Seeman	Killed
47. Sergeant:	Christian Crusius	Wounded
48. Privates:	J. Bulda	Wounded
49.	Ed Johnson	Wounded
50. Co. K: Sergeant:	Henry Lorch	Wounded
51. Privates:	Conrad Hartsman	Wounded
52.	J. Karr	Wounded
53.	Friedrich Kemmle	Wounded
54.	Charles Orth	Wounded
55. Sergeant:	Bernhardt Ott	Killed

Total: Killed-12 Wounded-43 (mortally wounded-6)   Captured or Missing-0 Total-55

Total Wisconsin Casualties at Peach Tree Creek:
Killed-23 Wounded-79   (Mortally Wounded-15) Captured or Missing-0   Total-102
Sources: Compiled Service Records, National Archives; Quinner, E. M., The Military History of Wisconsin in the War for the Union.

United States (Regular Army):
Captain E. T. Wells, Adjutant to General Richard Johnson   Wounded severely
15th U.S. Infantry:
1. Co. A: (3rd Batl) Private: George Townsend   Wounded, died 7-30/1864

Federal Soldiers Unit Unknown:
1.	Sergeant: David Corning	Killed
2.	J. Boyett	Killed
3.	Private: E. M. Croxton	Killed
4.	A. Turner	Killed

http://www.interment.net/data/us/ga/cobb/marienat/index.htm (June 13, 2009).

BIBLIOGRAPHY

Primary Sources
Treatises and Official Records
Atlas to Accompany the Official Records of the Union and Confederate Armies in the War of the Rebellion. Washington, DC: Government Printing Office, 1891.
"Capture of Colors of 31st Miss. at Peachtree Creek, The Army of The Cumberland," National Archives, Washington, DC.
"Cockrell's Brigade Casualties at Peach Tree Creek," National Archives, microfilm 1045, roll 1 (old microfilm roll 22, box 15), Tennessee State Library and Archives, Nashville.
"Compiled Service Records of Confederate Soldiers Who Served in Organizations from the Union and Confederate States of America during the War of the Rebellion," record group 269, National Archives, Washington, DC.
Congress of the Confederate States of America. *Journal of the Congress of the Confederate States of America.* 1861–1865. 7 volumes. Washington, DC: US Government Printing Office, 1904–1905.
Featherston, Winfield Scott. "Official Report of the Tennessee Campaign," subject file, Manuscript Division, Tennessee State Library and Archives, Nashville.
"Featherson's Brigade Casualties at Peach Tree Creek," microfilm 1045, roll 2, Tennessee State Library and Archives, Nashville.
"Inspection Reports and Related Records Received by the Inspection Branch in the Confederate Adjutant and Inspector General's Office, Featherston's Brigade, Loring's Division, Stewart's Corps, Army of Tennessee." 20 August 1864 and 22 September 1864, microfilm M935, roll 1, National Archives, Washington, DC. Courtesy of James Odgen, Historian, Chickamauga and Chattanooga National Military Park, US Department of the Interior.
John Bell Hood Letters. Record group 9, volume 33, record 151, box 15–16, Mississippi Department of Archives and History, Jackson, Mississippi.
Johnston, Henry Phelps, compiler. *Record of Service of Connecticut Men in the Army and Navy of the United States during the War of the Rebellion.* Hartford CT: Case, Lockwood & Brainard, 1889.
Medical & Surgical History of the War of the Rebellion, Part 3, Surgical Volume 2. Washington, DC: US Government Printing Office, 1870.
Power, J. L., compiler. Army of Mississippi recently organized regiments and battalions under requisition of 7,000, 8 May 1862, record group 9, volume 33, record 151, box 15–16, Mississippi Department of Archives and History, Jackson, Mississippi.
———, compiler. J. L. Power 1864 Scrapbook, file z 742v, record group 9, volume 33, record 151, box 8, Mississippi Department of Archives and History, Jackson, Mississippi.
———, compiler. J. L. Power and Family Papers, file z 0100.000s, record group 9, volume 33, record 151, box 8, Mississippi Department of Archives and History, Jackson, Mississippi.
———, compiler. List of engagements in Mississippi, record group 9, volume 33, record 151, box 15–16, Mississippi Department of Archives and History, Jackson, Mississippi.
———, compiler. Mississippi Casualties at Gettysburg, & letter dated March 9, 1907 presumably by Power; record group 9, volume 33, record 151, box 15–16, Mississippi Department of Archives and History, Jackson, Mississippi.
———, compiler. Return of Breckinridge's division, 21 July 1862, record group 9, volume 33, record 151, box 15–16, Mississippi Department of Archives and History, Jackson, Mississippi.
"Quarterly Report of Deceased Soldiers of 31st Regt. Miss. Volume for the 3rd Quarter of the year 1862," Compiled Service Records, RG 269, roll 341, Mississippi Department of Archives and History, Jackson, Mississippi.

"Record of Union Battlefield Burials, Atlanta Campaign," Marietta National Cemetery, Marietta, Georgia.

Rice, F. "Grand Summary of Casualties in Cheatham's Division," Benjamin F. Cheatham Papers, Tennessee State Library and Archives, Nashville.

Roster of Confederate cemetery in Chattanooga, Tennessee, National Park Service, Chattanooga.

"Scott's Brigade Casualties at Peach Tree Creek," microfilm 1045, roll 2, Tennessee State Library and Archives, Nashville.

Supplement to the Official Records of the Union and Confederate Armies. Wilmington NC: Broadfoot Publishing Company, 1995–2001.

Thackery, David T. *A Light and Uncertain Hold, A History of the 66th Ohio Volunteer Infantry.*

Thomas, J. D. and L. F. Burks, *Chairman His. Comm. Camp Rodes*, 22 February 1897, Roll of the Tuscaloosa Plow Boys, Company G, 38th Tennessee Infantry Regiment.

United States Department of the Interior. "Atlanta Campaign." Kennesaw Mountain National Battlefield Park, Kennesaw, Georgia.

United States National Archives and Records Administration. "Sixth Census of the United States, 1840." Microfilm M704.

———. "Seventh Census of the United States, 1850." Microfilm M432.

———. "Eighth Census of the United States, 1860." Microfilm M653.

United States Naval observatory records and vertical files, US Naval Academy, Nimitz Library, Annapolis, Maryland.

United States War Department, compiler. *The Official Military Atlas of the Civil War.* Washington, DC: Government Printing Office, 1891.

———, compiler. *Official Records of the Union and Confederate Armies in the War of the Rebellion.* 128 volumes. Washington, DC: Government Printing Office, 1880–1901.

Diaries, Journals, Personal Accounts, and Letters

"Appomattox." Untitled article, *Richmond Dispatch*, quoted in the *Macon Daily Telegraph*, 4 August 1864, Washington Library, Macon, Georgia.

Bainbury, Chester. *Bainbury's Civil War Diary.* Edited by Charles Wesley Lawrence. Cleveland OH: Cleveland Plain Dealer, 1960.

T. Otis Baker Papers, Company B, 10th Mississippi Infantry, Subject files, Mississippi Department of Archives and History, Jackson, Mississippi.

Robert W. Banks Letters. Carter House Library and Museum, Franklin, Tennessee.

Banks, Robert Webb. *The Battle of Franklin, November 30, 1864. The Bloodiest Engagement of the War Between the States.* New York: The Neale Publishing Company, 1908.

Bell, Rachael. Letter to Mrs. Mollie J. Bell, 8 July 1862. Thornton Collection, Special Collections, Mitchell Memorial Library, Mississippi State University, Starkville, Mississippi.

Berryhill, S. Newton. "Fresh Tidings from the Battlefield." In Ernestine Clayton Deavors, editor, *The Mississippi Poets.* Memphis: E. H. Clarke & Brother, 1922.

Berryhill, William Harvey. *The Gentle Rebel: The Civil War Letters of William Harvey Berryhill, 1st Lt., Co. D, 43rd Regt., Miss. Vols.* Edited by Mary Miles Jones and Leslie Jones Martin. Yazoo City MS: The Sassafras Press, 1982.

Bevens, William E. *Reminiscences of a Private: William E. Bevens of the First Arkansas Infantry, C.S.A.* Edited by Daniel E. Sutherland. Fayetteville: University of Arkansas Press, 1992.

Biddle, James. Diary. Burton Historical Collection, Detroit Public Library.

Biggers, J. A. Diary. 2nd Mississippi Cavalry, Subject Files, Mississippi Department of Archives and History, Jackson, Mississippi.

Binford, James R. Recollections of the 15th Regiment of Mississippi Infantry, CSA, Chickamauga and Chattanooga National Military Park Library, Subject Files.

Bibliography

Black, S. L. Letter to Thomas Benton Roy, 31 May 1880. In Thomas Benton Roy, "General Hardee and the Military Operations around Atlanta," *Southern Historical Society Papers* 8/[ISSUE #] (August/September 1880): 347–50.

Brown, W. C. Diary. Special Collections, Chattanooga-Hamilton County Bicentenial Library, Tennessee.

Bryan, Marquis L. Letter to wife, 16 April 1864, Coffee County Historical Society, vertical file box 13, Coffee County, Tennessee.

Captain I. A. Buck Subject File, PW-5, Cleburne's Division at Atlanta, Kennesaw National Battlefield Park, Kennesaw, Georgia.

Burnett, Major Thomas J. Letter to wife, 18 June 1864, *Georgia Journal*, 13 November 1924, Pearce Civil War Collection, Navarro College, Corsicana, Texas.

Caldwell, Frank Hollis. Reminiscences, Special Collections, Chattanooga-Hamilton County Bicentenial Library, Tennessee.

Campbell, Henry. "Three Years in the Saddle" (diary), Special Collections, Wabash College, Crawfordsville, Indiana.

Cannon, J. P. *A History of the 27th Regiment Alabama Infantry. "Bloody Banners and Barefoot Boys."* Edited by Noel Crowson and John V. Brogden. Shippensburg PA: Burd Street Press, 1997.

———. *Inside of Rebeldom: The Daily Life of a Private in the Confederate Army*. Washington, DC: National Tribune, 1900.

Chambers, William Pitt. *Blood and Sacrifice, The Civil War Journal of a Confederate Soldier*. Edited by Richard Baumgartner Huntington WV: Blue Acorn Press, 1994.

Cline, William. Diary. Special Collections, University of Notre Dame Library.

Conner, W. H. Letter to Dunbar Rowland (state historian), 20 October 1927, 33rd Mississippi vertical files, record group 9, box 8, Mississippi Department of Archives and History, Jackson, Mississippi.

Cooper, R. C. Letters, Confederate file 37, Carter House, Franklin, Tennessee.

Sylvester, Lorna Lutes, editor. "'Gone for a Soldier': The Civil War Letters of Charles Harding Cox," *Indiana Magazine of History* 68/3 (September 1972): 181–239.

Craig, R. A. B. Letters, Confederate file 35, Carter House, Franklin, Tennessee.

Crenshaw, R. F. Letter to Ella Austin, 13 December 1860, Archives and Special Collections, J. D. Williams Library, University of Mississippi, Oxford, Mississippi.

Crittenden, John. Letters, Center for American History, box 2, file 2 Q 491, University of Texas, (copy also available at Auburn University Library).

Crumpton, Washington Bryan. *A Book of Memories*. Montgomery AL: Baptist Mission Board, 1921.

Cutter, George H. Diary, in author's personal papers, Dalton, Georgia.

Davis, Jefferson. The Rise and Fall of the Confederate Government. 2 volumes. New York: D. Appleton & Company, 1881.

Day, D. L. *My Diary of Rambles with the 25th Massachusetts Volunteer Infantry*. Milford MA: King and Billings, 1884.

Dickinson, Charles H. Diary, Wisconsin State Historical Society, call number RSI, N 168-volume I; F 587.C48, Madison, Wisconsin.

Dillworth, Colonel W. S. Letter to editor, *Macon Daily Telegraph*, 20 June 1864, Geneological and History Department, section 100-104 N, Washington Memorial Library, Macon, Georgia.

Dixon, Mumford H. Diary. David M. Rubenstein Library, Duke University, Durham, North Carolina.

Dobbs, Josephine Manning Austin. Civil War stories as told to her by her father, Joseph Manning Austin (1853–1931). In *Confederate Reminiscences and Letters, 1861–1865*, 3–5. Volume 3. Atlanta: United Daughters of the Confederacy, 1996.

Drake, Edwin L. *The Annals of the Army of Tennessee and Early Western History*. Volume 1. Jackson TN: The Guild Bindery Press, 1878.

Dunn, Matthew A. Letters, Special Collections, section Z-1792.00f, Mississippi Department of Archives and History, Jackson, Mississippi (also available at Kennesaw Mountain National Battlefield Park, vertical files Mississippi-11, Kennesaw, Georgia).

Early, Jubal A. and Ruth H. Early. *Lieutenant General Jubal Anderson Early, C.S.A.: Autobiographical Sketch and Narrative of the War Between the States.* Philadelphia: J.B. Lippincott Company, 1912.

Elmore, Bruce. Letter to wife, 29 July 1864, MSS 673 F, Manuscript Collection, Kenan Research Center, Atlanta History Center.

Faulkinbury, Henry Newton. Diary. Mississippi Department of Archives and History, Jackson, Mississippi. Special permission by Bob Lurate.

Featherston Collection, Archives and Special Collections, J. D. Williams Library, University of Mississippi, Oxford.

Fitch, Michael H. *Echoes of the Civil War as I Hear Them.* New York: RF Fenno and Company, 1905.

French, Samuel G. *Two Wars.* 1901; reprinted, Huntington WV: Blue Acorn Press, 1999.

Gates, Arnold, editor. *The Rough Side of War: The Civil War Journal of Chesley A. Mosman.* Garden City NY: Basin Publishing Company, 1987.

Gill, Maynard. Letters to President Davis and General Bragg, June 1864, Compiled Service Records of Confederate Soldiers Who Served in Organizations from the Union and Confederate States of America during the War of the Rebellion, record groups 269, R 342, Mississippi Department of Archives and History, Jackson, Mississippi.

Gleeson, Ed. "New York Irish-Catholic Bricklayer in Gray. Colonel Mike Farrell Falls at Franklin," Carter House, Franklin, Tennessee.

Grant, Ulysses S. *The Civil War Memoirs of Ulysses S. Grant.* New York: C.L. Webster & Company, 1885.

Hampton, Thomas B. Letters, file 2R30, Center for American History, University of Texas at Austin.

Hapeman, Douglas, war diary.

Hazen, William B. *A Narrative of Military Service.* Boston: Ticknor and Sons, 1885.

Howard, O. O. *Autobiography of Oliver Otis Howard.* Volumes 1 and 2. New York: The Baker & Taylor Company, 1907.

Hudson, Weldon I., editor. *The Civil War Diary of William Spencer Hudson.* St. Louis: Micro-Records Publishing Co., 1973. Mississippi Department of Archives and History, Jackson, Mississippi.

Huff, Sarah, "My 80 Years in Atlanta," subject files, Atlanta History Center, Atlanta, Georgia.

Hurst, Samuel H. *Journal-History of the Seventy-Third Ohio Volunteer Infantry.*

Ives, Washington. *Civil War Journal and Letters of Serg. Washington Ives, 4th Florida C.S.A.* Transcribed and edited by Jim R. Cabaniss. Tallahassee: self-pubished, 1987. Unpublished copy of journal at vertical files, Chickamauga National Battlefield Park Library, Chickamauga, Georgia.

J. B. Sanders Subject File (Company H, 37th Mississippi), Mississippi Department of Archives and History, Jackson, Mississippi.

James W. Drane, Jr. personal papers. Crossville, Tennessee.

James M. Wilcox subject file. Folder 7, Mississippi Collection, Kennesaw Mountain National Battlefield Park, Kennesaw, Georgia.

Jennings, James Madison. Letters to Martha Kimbriel Jennings, in *The History of Webster Co., Miss.* Dallas TX: Curtis Media Corp., 1985.

Johnson____. Letter to General Johnson, 13 August 1863, Special Collections, Thornton Collection, Mitchell Memorial Library, Mississippi State University, Starkville, Mississippi.

Johnson, J. N. Reminscences. *Confederate Reminiscences and Letters, 1861–1865,* 83–85. Volume 15. Atlanta: United Daughters of the Confederacy, 2000.

Bibliography

Johnson, R. W. *A Soldier's Reminiscences in Peace and War*. Philadelphia: J. B. Lippincott Company, 1886.

Johnson, Willa Davis. "Reminiscences of the Sixties." *Confederate Reminiscences and Letters, 1861–1865*: Georgia Division, United Daughters of the Confederacy, 1996–2000.

Johnston, Joseph E. *Narrative of Military Operations during the Late War Between the States*. New York: D. Appleton & Company, 1874.

Kennerly, James A. Letter to sister, 8 August 1864, vertical files, James Kennerly Papers, Wilson's Creek National Park Library, Republic, Missouri.

Kern, John, diary, Old Courthouse Museum, Vicksburg, Mississippi.

King, Green. Letters. Confederate file 102, Carter House, Franklin, Tennessee.

King, Jack. Letter to wife, 19 July 1864. In Mills Lane, editor, *"Dear Mother: Don't Grieve about Me. If I Get Killed, I'll Only Be Dead": Letters from Georgia Soldiers in the Civil War*. Savannah GA: Beehive Press, 1977.

Kirwan, A. D., editor. *Johnny Green of the Orphan Brigade*. Lexington: University of Kentucky Press, 1956.

Kollock, Frederick N. Diary during the war, 1864, Company B, 29th Pennsylvania, Ireland's 3rd Brigade, Geary's 2nd (White Star) Division, transcribed by Charles S. Harris, subject files, Chickamauga National Military Park Library, Chickamauga, Georgia.

Landingham, Irenus Watson. Letter to mother, 14 July 1864, folder 5, Special Collections, Auburn University Library, Auburn, Alabama.

Longacre, Glenn V., and John E. Haas, editors. *"To Battle for God & the Right": The Civil War Letters of Emerson Opdycke*. Champaign: University of Illinois Press, 2007.

Maddox, R. F. Letter, *Confederate Veteran* 8 (June 1900): 257.

Markam, Rev. Dr. Thomas R. "Tribute to the Confederate Dead," *Southern Historical Society Papers*, volume 10 (April 1882): 175.

McCall, Phil, editor. "Private Isaiah Crook Diary, 37th Ga., Smith's Brigade, Bate's Division, Hardee's Corps," vertical files, Kennesaw Mountain Battlefield Park Library, Kennesaw, Georgia.

McCuistion, Mitchell Henderson. Diary, Special Collections, University of Texas at Austin Library.

McDermid, Angus. "Letters from a Confederate Soldier," edited by Benjamin Rountree, *Georgia Review* (1964).

McElroy, Cyrus Decatur. *The Diary of a Confederate Volunteer*. San Antonio: Southern Literary Institute, 1935.

McNeilly, James H. "A Day in the Life of a Confederate Chaplain," *Confederate Veteran*, volume 26 (1918): 471.

Mannis, Jedediah and Galen R. Wilson, editors. *Bound to Be a Soldier: The Letters of Private James T. Miller, 111th Pennsylvania Infantry, 1861–1864*. Knoxville: University of Tennessee Press, 2001.

Miller, J. M. *Recollections of "A Pine Knot" in the Lost Cause*. Greenwood MS: Greenwood Publishing Company, n.d.

Montgomery, Frank Alexander. *Reminiscences of a Mississippian in Peace and War*. The Robert Clarke Company Press, 1901. Available online at docsouth.unc.edu/fpn/montgomery/montgom.html.

Mothershead, W. I. Letter, folder 5, location SG024896, Alabama Archives, Montgomery, Alabama.

Murphy, Virgil S. Letter to cousin, 21 June 1864, vertical files, Kennesaw Mountain National Battlefield Park Library, Kennesaw, Georgia.

Neal, A. J. Letter to father, 20 July 1864, pp. 28–29, vertical files, Kennesaw Mountain National Battlefield Park Library, Kennesaw, Georgia.

Nisbet, James Cooper. *4 Years on the Firing Line*. Edited by Bell Irvin Wiley. Jackson TN: McCowat-Mercer Press, 1963.

Norton, Reuben S. Journal 1861, Special Collections, Rome/Floyd County Library, Rome, Georgia.

Oldham, Martin Van Buren. *Civil War Diaries of Van Buren Oldham, Company G, 9th Tennessee, 1863–1864*. Edited and introduction by Dieter C. Ullrich. Martin: University of Tennessee at Martin Library, 1998.

Otto, John Henry. *Memoirs of a Dutch Mudsill*. Edited by David Gould and James B. Kennedy. Kent OH: Kent State University Press, 2004.

P. C. Key Family Letters. Hargrett Rare Book and Manuscript Library, University of Georgia.

Palmer, Solomon. Diary, subject file PW-51, Kennesaw National Battlefield Park, Kennesaw, Georgia.

Park, Horace. Letters, file Ms 2386, Hargrett Rare Book and Manuscript Library, University of Georgia, Athens, Georiga.

Pierson, Stephen. "From Chattanooga to Atlanta in 1864–A Personal Reminiscence (1907)," *Proceedings New Jersey Historical Society*, volume 16 (1931): 506–43.

Pressnall, James S. Memoirs, subject files, Carter House, Franklin, Tennessee.

Power, J. L. 1864 scrapbook, Mississippi Department of Archives and History, Jackson, Mississippi.

Priest, John Michael editor. *John T. McMahon's Diary of the 136th New York, 1861–1864*. Shippensburg PA: White Mane Publishing Company, 1993.

Rice, Ralsa C. *Yankee Tigers, through the Civil War with the 125th Ohio*. Edited by Richard A. Baumgartner and Larry M. Strayer. Huntington WV: Blue Acorn Press, 1992.

Rorer, Walter A. Letters. Transcribed by T. Glover Roberts. Carter House, Franklin, Tennessee.

Roundtree, Benjamin, editor. "Letters from a Confederate Soldier," *Georgia Review*, volume 28 (Fall 1964): 267.

Roy, T. B. "General Hardee and the Military Operations Around Atlanta," *Southern Historical Society Papers*, volume 8 (January 1880): 382.

Sherman, William T. *Marching through Georgia, William T. Sherman's Personal Narrative of His March through Georgia*. Edited by Mills Lane. New York: Behive Press/Arno Press, 1978.

Shoup, F. A. "Works at the Chattahoochee River," *Confederate Veteran*, volume 3 (January 1895): 262–65.

Smith, Benjamin L., Jr. Autobiography, Confederate vertical files, Carnton Archives, Franklin, Tennessee (copy also available in author's personal papers, Dalton, Georgia).

Smith, Elias. Letter to Sydney Howard Gay, 31 May 1864, MS 0475, Sydney Howard Gay Papers, Columbia University, Butlery Library, New York, New York.

Smith, Robert Davis. Diary. Special Collections, Chattanooga-Hamilton County Bicentenial Library, Tennessee.

Stephens, M. D. L. "Recollections of 31st Mississippi," Special Collections, record group 9, volume 136, record group 151, box 20, section 3-289, Mississippi Department of Archives and History, Jackson, Mississippi.

———. A Brief History of the Stephens Family, 14 February 1911, copy in author's personal papers, Dalton, Georgia.

———. *A History of Calhoun County*. Transcribed by Ken Nail. Pittsboro MS: Calhoun County School District, 1975.

Stevenson, Carter L., to T. A. Stevenson, 28 August 1885, Special Collections, David M. Rubenstein Rare Books and Manuscript Library, Duke University, Durham, North Carolina.

Stewart, Alexander P. "Address to his Corps," *Macon Daily Telegraph*, 2 August 1864, Washington Memorial Library, Macon, Georgia.

Sykes, Columbus. Letters to wife, Columbus Sykes subject file Ml-4, p. 30A, Kennesaw National Battlefield Park Library, Kennesaw, Georgia.

Thomas, Jim. "Soldiers of Florida," vertical files, Chickamauga National Military Park Library, Chickamauga, Georgia.

Thompson, J. C. Letter to A. P. Stewart, 8 December 1867, box 1, folder 5, Joseph E. Johnston Collection, Earl Gregg Swem Library, College of William & Mary, Williamsburg, Virginia.

Thompson, W. C. "From the Defenses of Atlanta to a Federal Prison Camp," *Civil War Times Illustrated* 3/10 (February 1965): 40–44.
Thornton, Solomon M. Letters, Special Collections, Thornton Collection, Mitchell Memorial Library, Mississippi State University, Starkville, Mississippi.
Tower, Lockwood, editor. *A Carolinian Goes to War: The Civil War Narrative of Arthur Middleton Manigault, Brigadier General.* Columbia: University of South Carolina Press, 1964.
Tuttle, Miletus. Letters, Hargrett Rare Book and Manuscript Library, University of Georgia, Athens, Georgia.
Walthall Collection, Archives and Special Collections, J. D. Williams Library, University of Mississippi, Oxford, Mississippi.
Warren, George. Diary.
Watkins, Sam R. *Co. Aytch.* Chattanooga TN: Times Printing Company, 1900.
Watson, James. "Private Watson Writes Home," *The Webster Progress* (Bellfontane MS), 15 July 1937, James Watson subject file (private, Company B, 31st Mississippi Infantry), Kennesaw Mountain National Military Park Library, Kennesaw, Georgia.
Watson, Joel Calvin. Diary. Special Collections, Grenada Public Library, Grenada, Mississippi.
Wiggins, Sarah Woolfolk, editor. *The Journals of Josiah Gorgas, 1857–1878.* Tuscaloosa and London: University of Alabama Press, 1995.
Wilkes, Abner James. "A Short History of My Life in the Late War between the North and the South, 46th Mississippi, Sears' Brigade," Wilson's Creek National Battlefield Park Library, Republic, Missouri.
William A. Drennan Papers. File Z-131, Special Collections, Mississippi Department of Archives and History, Jackson, Mississippi.
Winkler, Frederick C. Civil War letters, American Civil War Collection, Dakota State University, Madison, South Dakota.
Womack, William A. Diary. Author's personal papers, Dalton, Georgia.
Wood, James. "Report of the Operations of the 3rd Brigade, 3rd Division of the XX Army Corps," in *The Atlanta Campaign of 1864.* Albany NY: Weed, Parsons & Company, Printers, 1889.
Wood, J. B. Letters to Sarah Wood. Author's personal papers, Dalton, Georgia.
Worsham, J. W. Reminiscences of the battle around Atlanta. In *Confederate Reminiscences and Letters, 1861–1865.* Volume 3. Atlanta: United Daughters of the Confederacy, 1996. Courtesy of Chickamauga National Battlefield Park Library.
Wyatt, J. N. Letter to J. B. Cunningham, 10 August 1864. *Confederate Veteran,* volume 5 (1897): 521.
Younger, Edward, editor. *The Diary of Robert Garlick Hill Kean.* New York: Oxford University Press, 1957.
Racine Boy Letter to Friend T., 21 July 1864, subject file PW-4, Kennesaw Mountain National Battlefield Park, Georgia.
A. J. Neal Papers, Emory University Archives, Atlanta, Georgia.

Secondary Sources
Newspapers and Periodicals
The Atlanta Journal
Atlanta Appeal
Augusta Daily Chronicle and Sentinel
Binghamton Standard
The Chattanooga Daily Rebel
Tribune
Daily Commercial
Cincinnati Daily Gazette
Clarion-Ledger Jackson Daily News

Columbus Crisis
Columbus Sentential
Confederate Veteran Magazine
Daily Southern Crisis
Georgia Journal & Messenger
Harper's Weekly
Ithaca Journal
National Tribune
New York Herald
New York Times
New York Tribune
New York Weekly Tribune
Daily Intelligencer
Macon Daily Telegraph
Meridian Star
The Ottawa Illinois Republican
Savannah Republican
Southern Historical Society Papers
The Pantagraph
Tri-Weekly Citizen
Walker County Messenger
Wyoming Mirror
Yalobusha Pioneer

Published Books and Articles

Adamson, A. P. *Brief History of the 30th Georgia Regiment*. Jonesboro GA: Freedom Hill Press, 1987.

Adolphson, Steven J. "An Incident of Valor in the Battle of Peach Tree Creek, 1864, (The 104th Illinois)," *Georgia Historical Quarterly*, volume 57 (1973): 406–20.

Allendorf, Donald. *Long Road to Liberty, The Odyssey of a German Regiment in the Yankee Army: The 15th Missouri Volunteer Infantry*. Kent OH: Kent State University Press, 2006.

Anders, Leslie. *The Eighteenth Missouri*. Indianapolis, Bobbs-Merrill, 1968.

Andrews, J. Cutler. *The North Reports the Civil War*. Pittsburgh: University of Pittsburgh Press, 1955.

Aten, Henry J. *History of the Eighty-Fifth Regiment, Illinois Volunteer Infantry*. Hiawatha KS: Regimental Association, 1901.

Bailey, Ronald H. *The Civil War: Battles for Atlanta, Sherman Moves East*. Alexandria VA: Time-Life Books, 1985.

Banning, Leroy F. *Regimental History of the 35th Alabama Infantry, 1862–1865*. Bowie MD: Heritage Books, 1999.

Barnard, George N. *Photographic Views of Sherman's Campaign*. New York: Dover Press, 1977.

Barnard, Harry V. *Tattered Volunteers: The Twenty-Seventh Alabama Regiment, C.S.A.* Northport AL: Hermitage Press, 1965.

Bass, Ronald R. *History of the 31st Arkansas Confederate Infantry*. Conway: Arkansas Research Press, 1996.

Bates, Samuel Penniman. *History of Pennsylvania Volunteers, 1861–1865*. 5 volumes. Philadelphia: T.H. Davis & Company, 1875.

Bearss, Edwin C. *The Campaign for Vicksburg*. 3 volumes. Dayton OH: Morningside Press, 1985.

Bearss, Margie Riddle. *Sherman's Forgotten Campaign: The Meridian Expedition*. Baltimore: Gateway Press, 1987.

Bibliography

Beaudot, William J. K. *The 24th Wisconsin Infantry in the Civil War: The Biography of a Regiment.* Mechanicsburg PA: Stackpole Books, 2003.

Bennett, Lyman G., and William M. Haigh. *History of the 36th Regiment Illinois Volunteers during the War of the Rebellion.* Aurora IL: Knickerbocker & Hodder, 1876.

Bergeron, Arthur W., Jr., and Clement Hoffman Stevens, "The Confederate General." In William C. Davis, editor, *The End of an Era.* Six volumes. (Garden City NY: Doubleday, 1984)Bettersworth, John K., editor. *Mississippi in the Confederacy as They Saw It.* 2 volumes. Baton Rouge: Brepolis Publishers, 1961

Bevier, R. S. *History of the First and Second Missouri Confederate Brigades, 1861–1865, and from Wakarusa to Appomattox, a Military Anagraph.* St. Louis: Bryan, Brand & Company, 1879.

Blackburn, Theodore W. *Letters from the Front: A Union "Preacher" Regiment (74th Ohio) in the Civil War.* Dayton OH: Press of Morningside House, 1981.

Bollet, Alfred J. "The Truth About Civil War Surgery," *Civil War Times* 43/4 (October 2004): 34–41.

Bonds, Russell S. *War Like the Thunderbolt.* Yardley PA: Westholme Publishing, 2009.

Bowen, Oscar du Bose. *Gospel Ministry of Forty Years.* Handsboro MS.

Bowers, John. *Chickamauga and Chattanooga: The Battles that Doomed the Confederacy.* New York: Harper Collins, 1994.

Bowman, John S. editor. *The Civil War Day by Day.* New York: Dorset Press, 1989.

Boyle, John Richards. *Soldiers True: The Story of the One Hundred and Eleventh Regiment Pennsylvania Veteran Volunteers and of Its Campaigns in the War for the Union, 1861–1885.* New York: Eaton & Mains; Cincinnati: Jennings & Pye, 1903.

Bradford, Ned, editor. *Battles and Leaders of the Civil War.* New York: The Fairfax Press, 1979.

Bradley, G. S. *The Star Corps, 22nd Wisconsin.*

Bradley, James. *The Confederate Mail Carrier.* Mexico MO: James Bradley, 1894.

Bradley, Mark L., editor. "The Battle of Bentonville. As Described by Another Eye-Witness–A Native of North Carolina–Now a Distinguished Citizen of Arkansas." *Civil War Regiments: A Journal of the American Civil War* 6/1 (1998): 93–106.

Brant, J. E. *History of the Eighty-Fifth Indiana Volunteer Infantry, Its Organization, Campaigns and Battles.* Bloomington IN: Indiana University Press, 1902.

Brewer, Willis. *Alabama: Her History, Resources, War Record, and Public Men, from 1540 to 1872.* Montgomery AL: Barrett & Brown, 1872.

Brown, Edmund R. *A History of the 27th Indiana.* Monticello IN: Edmund R. Brown, 1899.

Brown, Thaddeus C. S., Samuel J. Murphy, and William G. Putney. *Behind the Guns: The History of Battery I, 2nd Regiment, Illinois Light Artillery.* Carbondale: Southern Illinois University Press, 1965.

Bryant, Edwin E. *Third Wisconsin Veterans, 1861–1865.* Madison WI: Democrat Printing Company, 1891.

Buell, Thomas B. *The Warrior Generals, Combat Leadership in the Civil War.* Pittsburgh: Three Rivers Press 1997.

Busey, John W., and Martin, David G. *Regimental Strengths and Losses at Gettysburg.* 4th edition. Hightstown NJ: Longstreet House, 2005.

Calkins, William Wirt. *The History of the One Hundred and Fourth Regiment of Illinois Volunteer Infantry, War of the Great Rebellion, 1862–1865.* Chicago: Donohue & Henneberry, 1895.

Cannan, John. *The Atlanta Campaign, May–November, 1864.* Conshohocken PA: Combined Publishing, 1991.

Carlock, Chuck. *History of The Tenth Texas Cavalry (Dismounted) Regiment, 1861–1865.* North Richland Hills TX: Bibal Press, 2001.

Carroon, Robert G., editor. *From Freeman's Ford to Bentonville, The 61st Ohio Volunteer Infantry.* Shippensburg PA: Burd Street Press, 1998.

Carter, Samuel, III. *The Siege of Atlanta, 1864.* New York: St. Martin's Press, 1973.

Carter, W. R. *History of the First Regiment of Tennessee Volunteer Cavalry in the Great War of the Rebellion, With the Armies of the Ohio and Cumberland, under Generals Morgan, Rosecrans, Thomas, Stanley and Wilson, 1862–1865*. Knoxville: Gaut-Ogden Company Printers, 1902.

Castel, Albert. *Decision in the West: The Atlanta Campaign of 1864*. Lawrence: University Press of Kansas, 1992.

Cate, Jean M., editor. *"If I Live to Come Home": The Civil War Letters of Sergeant John March Cate*. Pittsburgh: Dorrance Publishing Company, 1995.

Cate, Wirt Armistead, editor. *Two Soldiers: The Campaign Diaries of Thomas J. Key, C.S.A. and Robert J. Campbell, U.S.A.* Chapel Hill: University of North Carolina Press, 1938.

Catton, Bruce. *The American Heritage New History of the Civil War*. Edited by James M. McPherson. New York: Penguin, 1996.

———. *A Stillness at Appomattox*. Garden City NY: Doubleday, 1954.

Charnley, Jeffrey. "Neglected Honor: The Life of General A. S. Williams of Michigan (1810–1878)." Ph.D. dissertation, Michigan State University, 1983.

Cisco, Walter Brian. *States Rights Gist: A South Carolina General of the Civil War*. Shippensburg PA: White Mane Publishing Company, 1991.

Clark, Charles T. *Opdycke Tigers, 125th O. V. I.: A History of the Regiment and of the Campaigns and Battles of the Army of the Cumberland.*

von Clausewitz, Karl. *On War*. Translated by James John Graham. London: N. Trübner, 1873.

Clemmer, Gregg S. *Valor in Gray: Confederates who Received the Medal of Honor*.

Coffey, David. *John Bell Hood and the Struggle for Atlanta*. Abilene TX: McWhiney Foundation Press and McMurry University, 1998.

Coggins, Jack. *Arms & Equipment of the Civil War*. Garden City NY: Doubleday, 1962.

Coleman, Kenneth. *A History of Georgia*. Athens: University of Georgia Press, 1977.

Collins, John L. "Gallant Mike Farrell," *Confederate Veteran* 34/10 (1926): 372.

Commager, Henry Steele, editor. *The Blue & the Gray*. New York: The Fairfax Press, 1982.

Connecticut Adjutant General's Office. *Record of Service of Connecticut Men in the Army and Navy of the United States during the War of the Rebellion*. Hartford CT: Press of the Case, Lockwood & Braintwood Co., 1889.

Connelly, Thomas L. *Army of the Heartland, The Army of Tennessee, 1861–1862*. Baton Rouge: Louisiana State Press, 1967.

———. *Autumn of Glory, The Army of Tennessee, 1862–1865*. Baton Rouge: Louisiana State Press, 1971.

———. *The Marble Man: Robert E. Lee and his Image in American Society*. Baton Rouge: Louisiana State Press, 1977.

Connolly, James A. *Three Years in the Army of the Cumberland*. Bloomington: Indiana University Press, 1959.

Cope, Alexis. *The 15th Ohio and Its Campaigns, War of 1861–5*. Columbus OH: Alexis Cope, 1916.

Cox, Jacob D. *Atlanta*. 1903; reprinted, Dayton OH: Morningside Press, 1987.

Cozzens, Peter. *The Battle of Chickamauga: This Terrible Sound*. Champaign: University of Illinois Press, 1996.

———. *The Battles for Chattanooga, The Shipwreck of Their Hopes*. Champaign: University of Illinois Press, 1994.

Crabb, Martha L. *All Afire to Fight: The Untold Tale of the Civil War's Ninth Texas Cavalry*. New York: First Post Road Press, 2000.

Cram, George F. *Soldiering with Sherman, The Civil War Letters of George F. Cram*. Edited by Jennifer Cain Bornstedt. DeKalb: Northern Illinois University Press, 2000.

Crute, Joseph H. Jr. *Units of the Confederate States Army*. Midlothian VA: Derwent Books, 1987.

Cubbison, Douglas R. "'A Hard Nut To Crack': The Siege of Decatur, Alabama, October 26–29, 1864," *Columbiad: A Quarterly Review of the War Between the States* 2/1 (Spring 1998): 97–115.

Cunningham, H. H. *Doctors in Gray: The Confederate Medical Service.* Baton Rouge: Louisiana State Press, 1958.
Cunningham, O. Edward. *Shiloh and the Western Campaign of 1862.* New York: Savas Beatie, 2007.
Daniel, Larry J. *Shiloh, The Battle that Changed the War.* New York: Simon & Schuster, 1997.
Davis, Burke. *The Civil War, Strange and Fascinating Facts.* New York: Fairfax Press, 1982.
Davis, Stephen. *Atlanta Will Fall: Sherman, Joe Johnston, and the Yankee Heavy Battalions.* Wilmington DE: Rowman &Littlefield, 2001.
———. "A Reappraisal of the Generalship of John Bell Hood in the Battles for Atlanta." In Theodore P. Savas and David A. Woodbury, editors, The Campaign for Atlanta & Sherman's March to the Sea, Volumes I & II, Essays of the American Civil War. Campbell CA: Savas Woobury Publishers, 1994.
———. "How Many Civilians Died in Sherman's Bombardment of Atlanta?," *Atlanta History: A Journal of Georgia and the South* 45/4 (2003): 4–23.
———. "So Much for Historical Accuracy: The Misplacement of the Howell Battery Marker," 27 July 1997, author's personal papers, Dalton, Georgia.
Davis, William C. *The Commanders of the Civil War.* New York: Smithmark, 1991.
———. *The Orphan Brigade: The Kentucky Confederates Who Couldn't Go Home.*
———, and Bell I. Wiley. *The Image of War, 1861–65.* 6 volumes. New York: Doubleday, 1981–1983. (Reprint in 2 vols: New York: Black Dog and Leventhal, 1994.)
Dodge, Grenville. *The Battle of Atlanta and Other Campaigns.* Council Bluffs IA: The Monarch Printing Company, 1911.
Dodge, Grenville M. "The Late Gen. J. M. Schofield," *Confederate Veteran,* volume 14 (October 1907).
Dodson, William Carey. *Campaigns of Wheeler and His Cavalry, 1862–1865.* 1899; reprint, Jackson TN: The Guild Bindery Press, 1980.
DuBose, John Witherspoon. *General Joseph Wheeler and the Army of Tennessee.* New York: The Neale Publishing Company, 1912.
Dwight, Captain Henry. "How We Fight at Atlanta," *Harper's New Monthly Magazine,* volume 29 (October 1864): 939–43.
Dyer, John P. *The Gallant Hood.* Indianapolis: Bobbs-Merrill Company, Inc., 1950.
Eddy, Thomas Mears. *The Patriotism of Illinois.* 2 volumes. Chicago: Clark & Co., 1865–1866.
Elliott, Sam Davis. *Soldier of Tennessee, General Alexander P. Stewart and the Civil War in the West.* Baton Rouge: Louisiana State Press, 1999.
Evans, Clement Anselm, editor. *Confederate Military History.* 19 volumes. 1899; reprint, Wilmington NC: Broadfoot Publishing Company, 1987.
Fellman, Michael. *The Making of Robert E. Lee.* New York: Random House, 2000.
Fenton, E. B. "From the Rapidan to Atlanta. Leaves from the Diary of Commpanion E. B. Fenton, Late Twentieth Connecticut Volunteer Infantry. Read before the Commandery of the State of Michigan MOLLUS, Detroit, April 6th, 1893." In Sydney C. Kerksis, editor, *The Atlanta Papers,* 213–34. Dayton OH: Morningside Books, 1980.
Ferguson, Edwin L. *Sumner County, Tennessee in the Civil War.* Edited by Diane Payne. Tompkinsville KY: Monroe County Press, 1972.
Ferguson, John Hill. *On to Atlanta, The Civil War Diaries of John Hill Ferguson, 10th Illinois Regiment of Volunteers.* Lincoln: University of Nebraska Press, 2001.
Fitch, John. *Annals of the Army of the Cumberland.* Philadelphia: J. B. Lippincott & Company, 1864.
Fleharty, S. F. *A History of the 102nd Illinois Infantry Volunteers.* Chicago: 1865.
Fleming, James R. *Band of Brothers: A History of Company C, 9th Tennessee Regiment.*
———. *The Confederate Ninth Tennessee Infantry.* Gretna LA: Pelican Publishing Company, 2006.

Foner, Eric. *Free Soil, Free Labor, Free Men: The Ideology of the Republican Party before the Civil War*. New York: Oxford University Press, 1995.
Foote, Shelby. *Fort Sumter to Perryville*. Volume 1 of *The Civil War: A Narrative*. New York: Vintage Books. 1958.
Foster, John Y. *New Jersey and the Rebellion*. Newark NJ: 1868.
Foster, Samuel T. *One of Cleburne's Command, The Civil War Reminiscences and Diary of Captain Samuel T. Foster, Granbury's Texas Brigade, C.S.A.* Edited by Norman D. Brown. Austin: University of Texas Press, 1980.
Fowler, John D. *Mountaineers in Gray: The Nineteenth Tennessee Volunteer Infantry Regiment, C.S.A.* Knoxville: University of Tennessee Press, 2004.
Fox, William F. *Regimental Losses in the American Civil War, 1861–1865*. Albany NY: Albany Publishing Company, 1889.
Fryman, Robert J. "Fortifying the Landscape, An Archaeological Study of Military Engineering and the Atlanta Campaign." In Clarence R. Geier and Stephen R. Potter, editors, *Archaeological Perspectives on the American Civil War*, 43–55. Gainesville: University Press of Florida, 2002.
Garrett, Franklin. *Atlanta and Its Environs*. 2 volumes. Athens: University of Georgia Press, 1954.
Garrison, Web. *Atlanta and the War*. Nashville: Rutledge Hill Press, 1995.
Gillum, Jamie. *An Eyewitness History of the 16th Regiment Tennessee Volunteers, May 1861–May 1865*. Self-published, 2005.
Glass, F. M. "Long Creek Rifles: A Brief History." Sallis MS: Long Creek Rifles Chapter, United Daughters of the Confederacy, 1909.
Govan, Gilbert Eaton, and James W. Livingood. *A Different Valor: The Story of General Joseph E. Johnston, C.S.A.* New York: Bobbs-Merrill, 1956.
Goodson, Gary Ray, Sr. *Georgia Confederate 7,000, Army of Tennessee, Part II: Letters and Diaries*. Shawnee CO: Goodson Enterprises, 2000.
Goodspeed, Wilbur. *Biographical and Historical Memoirs of Mississippi*. Chicago: Goodspeed Publishing Co., 1891.
Gottschalk, Phil. *In Deadly Earnest*. Columbia MO: Missouri River Press, 1991.
Gresham, Matilda McGrain. *Life of Walter Quintin Gresham, 1832–1895*. 2 volumes. Chicago: Rand, McNally & Company, 1919.
Groom, Winston. *Shrouds of Glory: From Atlanta to Nashville: The Last Great Campaign of the Civil War*. New York: Atlantic Monthly, 1995.
Haas, Garland A. *To the Mountain of Fired and Beyond, The Fifty-Third Indiana Regiment from Corinth to Glory*. Carmel IN: Guild Press of Indiana, 1997.
Hafendorfer, Kenneth A. *Mill Springs, Campaign and Battle of Mill Springs, Kentucky*. Louisville KY: KH Press, 2001.
Hall, Richard. *Patriots in Disguise*. New York: Marlowe & Company, 1994.
Hart, B. H. Liddell. *Sherman*. New York: Frederick A. Praeger, Inc., 1958.
Head, Thomas A. *Campaigns and Battles of the Sixteenth Regiment, Tennessee Volunteers, 1861–1865*. Nashville: Cumberland Presbyterian Publishing House, 1885.
———. *Sumner County, Tennessee in the Civil War*. Edited by Diane Payne (self-published, 1972).
Hebert, Walter H. *Fighting Joe Hooker*. Lincoln: University of Nebraska Press, 1999.
Henderson, Lillian, editor. *Georgia Confederate Pension and Record Office. Roster of the Confederate Soldiers of Georgia, 1861–1865*. 7 volumes. Hapeville GA: Longino & Porter, 1955–1958.
Henry, Robert Selph. *"First with the Most": Forrest*. Indianapolis: Bobbs-Merrill Company, 1944.
Hewett, Janet B., editor. *The Roster of Confederate Soldiers, 1861–1865*. 16 volumes. Wilmington NC: Broadfoot Publishing Company, 1995.
Hinde, Paul. "Benj. Harrison, 23rd President, in Battle of Peachtree Creek," *Inn Dixie Magazine* (January 1937).
Hinman, Wilbur F. *The Story of the Sherman Brigade*. Alliance OH: Press of Daily Review, 1897.

Bibliography

Hoehling, A. A. *Last Train from Atlanta*. New York: Thomas Yoseloff, Printer, 1958.
Hood, John Bell. *Advance & Retreat*. 1880; reprinted, New York: Da Capo Press, 1993.
Horn, Stanley F. *The Army of Tennessee*. Norman: University of Oklahoma Press, 1953.
Hornady, John R. *Atlanta: Yesterday, Today and Tomorrow*. Atlanta: American Cities Book Company, 1922.
Howell, H. Grady, Jr. *For Dixie Land I'll Take My Stand: A Muster Listing of All Known Mississippi Confederate Soldiers, Sailors and Marines*. 5 volumes. Madison MS: Chickasaw Bayou Press, 1998.
———. *Going to Meet the Yankees, A History of the "Bloody Sixth" Mississippi, C.S.A.* Jackson MS: Chickasaw Bayou Press, 1981.
———. *To Live and Die in Dixie, A History of the Third Mississippi Infantry, C.S.A.* Jackson MS: Chickasaw Bayou Press, 1991.
Hoyt, Bessie Willis, *Come When the Timber Turns*. Banner Elk NC: Pudding Stone Press, Lees-McRae College, 1983.
Hughes, Nathaniel Cheairs, Jr. *General William J. Hardee: Old Reliable*.
———. *The Pride of the Confederate Artillery, The Washington Artillery in the Army of Tennessee*. Baton Rouge: Louisiana State Press, 1997.
Hughes, Robert M. *General Johnston*. Great Commanders series. New York: D. Appleton and Company, 1893.
Jenkins, Kirk C. *The Battle Rages Higher: The Union's Fifteenth Kentucky Infantry*. Lexington: University Press of Kentucky, 2003.
Johnson, Mark W. *That Body of Brave Men, The US Regular Infantry and the Civil War in the West*. Cambridge: Da Capo Press, 2003.
Johnson, Robert Underwood, and Clarence Clough Buell, editors. *Battles and Leaders of the Civil War*. 4 volumes. New York: The Century Company, 1887–1888.
Jones, Terry L. "'The Flash of Their Guns Was a Sure Guide': The 19th Michigan Infantry in the Atlanta Campaign." In Theodore P. Savas and David A. Woodbury, editors, *The Campaign for Atlanta & Sherman's March to the Sea*, 157–95. 2 volumes. Savas Campbell CA: Woodbury Publishers, 1994.
Jordan, Weymouth T., Jr., editor. *North Carolina Troops, 1861–1865: A Roster*. 15 volumes. Raleigh NC: University Graphics, 1966–1999.
Kellogg, Mary E., editor. *Army Life of an Illinois Soldier, Including a Day by Day Record of Sherman's March to the Sea: Letters and Diary of the Late Charles W. Willis*. Washington, DC: Globe Printing Company, 1906.
Kennett, Lee. *Marching through Georgia: The Story of Soldiers & Civilians during Sherman's Campaign*. New York: Harper-Collins Publishers, 1995.
Key, William. *The Battle of Atlanta and the Georgia Campaign*. New York: Twayne Publishers, 1958.
Kimberly, Robert L., and Ephraim S. Holloway. *The 41st Ohio Veteran Volunteer Infantry in the War of the Rebellion, 1861–1865*. Huntington WV: Blue Acorn Press, 1999.
Krick, Robert K. *The Gettysburg Death Roster, The Confederate Dead at Gettysburg*. 3rd edition. Dayton OH: Morningside Press, 1981.
Lanman, Charles. *The Red Book of Michigan: A Civil, Military, and Biographical History*. Detroit: E.B. Smith & Company, 1871.
Lewis, Lloyd. *Sherman, Fighting Prophet*. Lincoln: University of Nebraska Press, 1993.
Lindsley, John Berrien, editor. *Military Annals of Tennessee, Confederate*. 2 volumes. Wilmington NC: Broadfoot Publishing Company, 1995.
Little, George, and James R. Maxwell. *A History of Lumsden's Battery, C.S.A.* Tuscaloosa AL: R. E. Rhodes Chapter, United Daughters of the Confederacy, 2002.
Livermore, Thomas L. *Numbers and Losses in the Civil War in America, 1861–65*, Boston: Houghton, Mifflim and Company, 1900.

Madaus, Howard Michael, and Robert D. Needham. *The Battle Flags of the Confederate Army of Tennessee*. Milwaukee Public Museum, 1976.

Marcoot, Maurice. *Five Years in the Sunny South*. St. Louis: Missouri Historical Society, 1890.

Marvin, Edwin E. *The Fifth Regiment Connecticut Volunteers, A History*. Hartford CT: Press of Wiley, Waterman & Eaton, 1889.

Mauck, Elaine C. *The Mountain Campaigns in Georgia, or War Scenes on the Western & Atlantic Railroad*. Camden SC: North Mountain Press, 1995.

McBride, John R. *History of the 33rd Indiana Veteran Volunteer Infantry*. Indianapolis: Wm. B. Burford, Printer, 1900.

McCarley, J. Britt. *The Atlanta Campaign: A Civil War Driving Tour of Atlanta-Area Battlefields*. Atlanta: Cherokee Publishing Compan, ND.

McDonough, James Lee. *Shiloh, in Hell before Night*. Knoxville: University of Tennessee Press.

———, and Thomas Connelly. *Five Tragic Hours, The Battle of Franklin*. Knoxville: University of Tennessee Press, 1983.

———, and James Pickett Jones. *War So Terrible, Sherman and Atlanta*, New York: W. W. Norton & Company, 1987.

McGee, Benjamin F. *History of the 72nd Indiana Volunteer Infantry of the Mounted Lightning Brigade*. Lafayette: S. Vater & Co., 1882.

McMorries, Edward Young. *History of the First Regiment Alabama Volunteer Infantry, C.S.A.* Montgomery: Brown Printing Company, 1904.

McMurray, W. J. *History of the Twentieth Tennessee Regiment Volunteer Infantry, C.S.A.* Nashville: Elder's Bookstore, 1976.

McMurry, Richard. *Atlanta 1864: Last Chance for the Confederacy*. Lincoln: University of Nebraska, 2000.

McMurry, Richard M. *John Bell Hood and the War for Southern Independence*. Lexington: University Press of Kentucky, 1982.

McPherson, James M. *Battle Cry of Freedom: The Civil War Era*. New York: Ballantine, 1988.

McWhiney, Grady, and Perry D. Jamieson. *Attack and Die: Civil War Military Tactics and the Southern Heritage*. Chicago: University of Alabama Press, 1982.

Meinhard, Robert W. "The First Minnesota at Gettysburg," *Gettysburg Historical Articles of Lasting Interest*, 1 July 1991, 83.

Merrill, Catharine. *The Soldier of Indiana in the War for the Union*. Indianapolis: Merrill & Company, 1869.

Merrill, C. E. "Fearful Franklin," *Nashville World*, [ca. December 1884]. Reprinted in "Save the Franklin Battlefield" (newsletter), April 2002, pp. 3–4.

Merrill, Samuel. *The Seventieth Indiana Volunteer Infantry in the War of the Rebellion*. Indianapolis: The Bowen-Merrill Company, 1900.

Miles, Jim. *Fields of Glory*. Nashville: Rutledge Hill Press, 1995.

Miller, John A. "A Memoir of the Days of '61," H. B. Simpson History Complex, Hillsboro, Texas.

Miller, Rex. *The Forgotten Regiment: A Day-by-day Account of the 55th Alabama Infantry Regiment, C.S.A., 1861–1865*. Williamsville NY: Patrex Press, 1984.

Mitchell, Joseph B. *The Badge of Gallantry*. New York: 1968.

Moe, Richard. "Narrative of the First Regiment." In *Minnesota in the Civil and Indian Wars, 1861–1865*, 1–66. Volume 1. St. Paul: Pioneer Press Company, 1891.

———. *The Last Full Measure, The Life and Death of the First Minnesota Volunteers*. New York: Henry Holt & Company Inc., 1993.

Moore, J. J. "Jackson, Mississippi, Camp Douglas," *Confederate Veteran* (June 1903).

Morris, Roy, Jr. *Sheridan: The Life and Wars of General Phil Sheridan*. New York: Crown Publishing, 1992.

Newlin, William H. *The Preacher Regiment, 1862–65, History of the 73rd Illinois Volunteer Infantry*. Springfield: Regimental Reunion Association of Survivors of the 73rd Illinois Infantry Volunteers, 1890.
O'Connor, Richard. *Thomas: Rock of Chickamauga*. New York: Prentice-Hall, 1948.
Obreiter, John. *The Seventy-Seventh Pennsylvania at Shiloh, History of the Regiment*. Harrison PA: Harrisburg Publishing Company, 1908.
Overmyer, Jack K. *A Stupendous Effort: The 87th Indiana in the War of the Rebellion*. Bloomington: Indiana University Press, 1997.
Owen, Thomas McAdory. *History of Alabama and Dictionary of Alabama Biography*. Volume 3. Chicago: S. J. Clarke Publishing Company, 1921.
Parks, Joseph H. *General Leonidas Polk, C.S.A.: The Fighting Bishop*. Baton Rouge: Louisiana State University Press, 1962.
Perry, Henry F. *History of the 38th Indiana Volunteer Infantry*. Palo Alto CA: F.A. Stuart, Printer, 1906.
Poole, John Randolph. *Cracker Cavaliers: The 2nd Georgia Cavalry under Wheeler and Forrest*. Macon GA: Mercer University Press, 2000.
Pula, James S. *The Sigel Regiment: A History of the 26th Wisconsin Volunteer Infantry, 1862–1865*.
Purdue, Howell and Elizabeth. *Patrick Cleburne Confederate General*. Hillsboro TX: Hill Junior College Press,1973.
Quiner, E. B. *The Military History of Wisconsin: A Record of the Civil and Military Patriotism of the State, in the War for the Union*. Chicago: Clark & Co. Publishers, 1866.
Rabb, James. *W. W. Loring. Florida's Forgotten General*. Manhattan KS: Sunflower University Press, 1996.
Reed, Wallace Putnam. *History of Atlanta*. Syracuse NY: D. Mason & Company, 1889.
Reid, Harvey. *Uncommon Soldiers: Harvey Reid and the 22nd Wisconsin March with Sherman*. Edited by Frank L. Byrne. Knoxville: University of Tennessee Press, 2001.
Rennolds, Edwin H. *A History of the Henry County Commands which Served in the Confederate States Army*. Jacksonville FL: Sun Publishing Company, 1904.
Ridley, Bromfield L. *Battles and Sketches of the Army of the Tennessee*. Mexico MO: Missouri Printing & Publishing Company, 1906.
Rietti, J. C. *Military Annals of Mississippi*. 1893; reprint, Spartanburg SC: The Reprint Company, 1976.
Robertson, John. *Michigan in the War*. Lansing MI: W. S. George & Company, 1882.
Roddy, Ray. *The Georgia Volunteer Infantry, 1861–1865*. Kearney NE: Morris Publishing, 1998.
Rollins, Richard, editor. *The Returned Battle Flags*. Redondo Beach CA: Rank & File Publications, 1995.
Rowland, Dunbar. *Military History of Mississippi, 1803–1898*. Edited by H. Grady Howell, Jr. Spartanburg SC: The Reprint Company, Publishers, 1978.
Roy, Thomas Benton,"General Hardee and the Military Operations Around Atlanta," *Southern Historical Society Papers*, volume 8 (August and September 1880): 347–50.
Russell, D. W. *Confederate Veteran* (February 1899).
Russell, James Michael. *Atlanta 1847–1890: City Building in the Old South and the New*. Baton Rouge: Louisiana State Press, 1988.
Sandburg, Carl. *Abraham Lincoln, The Prairie Years & The War Years*. New York: Harcourt Brace & Company, 1954.
Scaife, William R. *The Campaign for Atlanta*. Atlanta: self-published, 1993.
Schuyler, Hartley and Graham. *Illustrated Catalog of Civil War Military Goods*. New York: Dover Publications, 1985.
Secrest, Philip. "Resaca: For Sherman a Moment of Truth," Atlanta Historical Journal 22/1 (Spring 1978): 9–41.

Secrist, Philip L. *Sherman's 1864 Trail of Battle to Atlanta*. Macon GA: Mercer University Press, 2006.

Siegel, Alan A. *Beneath the Starry Flag, New Jersey's Civil War Experience*. New Brunswick NJ: Rutgers University Press, 2001.

Sifakis, Stewart. *Compendium of the Confederate Armies*. 10 volumes. New York: Facts on File, Inc., 1992–1995.

Smith, Timothy B. *Champion Hill, Decisive Battle for Vicksburg*. New York: Savas Beatie LLC, 2004.

———. *This Great Battlefield of Shiloh, History, Memory, and the Establishment of a Civil War National Military Park*. Knoxville: University of Tennessee Press, 2004.

Stephens, Larry D. *Bound for Glory, A History of the 30th Alabama Infantry Regiment, Confederate States of America*. Ann Arbor MI: Sheridan Books, 2005.

Stewart, Bruce H., Jr. *Invisible Hero: Patrick R. Cleburne*. Macon GA: Mercer University Press, 2009.

Stewart, Nixon B. *Dan McCook's Regiment, 52nd Ohio Volunteer Infantry, a History of the Regiment, Its Campaigns and Battles from 1862–1865*. 1900; reprint, Huntington WV: Blue Acorn Press, 1999.

Stone, Henry. "1st Wisconsin Volume Inf." In Sydney C. Kerksis, editor, *The Atlanta Papers*. Dayton OH: Morningside Press, 1980.

———. "From the Oostanaula to the Chattahoochee." In *The Mississippi Valley, Tennessee, Georgia, Alabama, 1861–1864*, edited by Military Historical Society of Massachusetts, 419. Volume 8 of *Military Historical Society of Massachusetts Papers*. Wilmington NC: Broadfoot Press, 1990.

Strayer, Larry M., and Richard A. Baumgartner, eds. *Echoes of Battle: The Atlanta Campaign*. Huntington WV: Blue Acorn Press, 1991.

Stroud, David V. *Ector's Texas Brigade and the Army of Tennessee, 1862–1865*. Longview TX: Ranger Publishing, 2004.

Sullivan, James R. *Chickamauga and Chattanooga Battlefields*. National Park Service Historical Handbook, series 25, Washington, DC: National Park Service, 1956. Chickamauga and Chattanooga National Military Park, Chickamauga, Georgia.

Sunderland, Glenn. *Five Days to Glory*. South Brunswick NJ: A. S. Barnes, 1970.

Sword, Wiley. *The Confederacy's Last Hurrah*. Lawrence: University Press of Kansas, 1992.

Symonds, Craig L. *Joseph E. Johnston, a Civil War Biography*. New York: W. W. Norton & Company, 1992.

———. *Stonewall of the West, Patrick Cleburne and the Civil War*. Lawrence: University of Kansas Press, 1997.

Tennesseans in the Civil War, A Military History of Confederate and Union Units with Available Rosters of Personnel. 2 volumes. Nashville: Civil War Centennial Commission, 1964–1965.

Thatcher, M. P. *A Hundred Battles in the West*. Detroit: L. F. Kilroy, Printer, 1884.

Thomas, Emory M. *The Confederate Nation: 1861–1865*. New York: Harper Collins Publishers, 1979.

Thomas, Wilbur D. *General George H. Thomas, The Indomitable Warrior*. New York: Exposition Press, 1964.

Thompson, Ed Porter. *History of the Orphan Brigade 1861–65*. Cincinnati: Caxton Publishing House, 1868.

Thompson, Illene D. and Wilbur E. *The Seventeenth Alabama Infantry: A Regimental History and Roster*. Bowie MD: Heritage Books, Inc., 2001.

Tucker, Glenn. *Chickamauga, Bloody Battle in the West*. Dayton OH: Bobbs-Merrill Company, 1961.

Tucker, Phillip Thomas. "The First Missouri Brigade at the Battle of Franklin," vertical files, Wilson's Creek National Park Library, Republic, Missouri.

Underwood, Adin B. *33rd Massachusetts*.
Upson, Theodore F. *With Sherman to the Sea, The Civil War Letters, Diaries and Reminisces of Theordore F. Upson*. Bloomington: Indiana University Press, 1958. Copy at Zack Henderson Library, Georgia Southern University, Statesboro, Georgia.
Van Horne, Thomas B. *History of the Army of the Cumberland*. 2 volumes. Cincinnati: Robert Clarke & Company, 1876.
Vaughan, Alfred J. *Personal Record of the Thirteenth Regiment, Tennessee Infantry, C.S.A*. Memphis: S. C. Toof & Company, 1897.
Walker, Cornelius Irvine. *Rolls and Historical Sketch of the Tenth Regiment So. Ca. Volunteers in the Army of the Confederate States*. Charleston SC: Walker, Evans, & Cogswell, 1881.
Walker, Scott. *Hell's Broke Loose in Georgia, A History of the 57th Georgia*. Athens: University of Georgia Press, 2005.
Wallace, Frederick Stephen. ["At Peachtree Creek"], *National Tribune*, 10 June 1909, Library of Congress, Washington, DC.
Warner, Ezra J. *Generals in Gray*. Baton Rouge: LSU Press, 1959–1988.
Welcher, Frank J., and Larry Liggett. *Coburn's Brigade: 85th Indiana, 33rd Indiana, 19th Michigan & 22nd Wisconsin in the Western Civil War*. Carmel IN: Carmel Press, 1999.
Wert, Jeffry D. *General James Longstreet, The Confederacy's Most Controversial Soldier*. New York: Simon & Schuster, 1993.
Wiley, Bell Irvin. *Embattled Confederates, An illustrated History of Southerners at War*. Illustrated and compiled by Hirst D. Milhollen. New York: Harper & Row, 1964.
———. *The Life of Johnny Reb, The Common Soldier of the Confederacy*. Baton Rouge: Louisiana State University Press, 1943.
Willett, Elbert Decatur. *History of Company B (originally Pickens Planters), 40th Alabama Regiment, Confederate States Army, 1862 to 1865*. Anniston AL: Norwood, 1902.
Williamson, David. *The Third Battalion and the 45th Mississippi Regiment*. Jefferson NC: McFarland & Company, Inc., 2004.
Williams, Alpheus Starkey. *From the Cannon's Mouth, The Civil War Letters of General Apheus S. Williams*. Edited by Milo M. Quaife. Detroit: Wayne State University Press, 1959.
Williams, T. Harry. *Lincoln and His Generals*. New York: Alfred A. Knoff, 1952.
Willis, James. *Arkansas Confederates in the Western Theater*. Dayton OH: Morningside House, 1998.
Wills, Charles Wright. *Army Life of an Illinois Soldier: One Hundred and Third Illinois*. Washington, DC: Globe Printing Company, 1906.
Wood, Edwin Orin. *History of Genesee County, Michigan, Her People, Industries and Institutions*. Indianapolis: Federal Pub. Company, 1916.
Woodhead, Henry, editor. *Voices of the Civil War—Atlanta*. Richmond: Time Life Books, 1997.
Woodworth, Steven. "A Reassessment of Confederate Command Options during the Winter of 1863–1864." In Theodore P. Savas and David A. Woodbury, *The Campaign for Atlanta & Sherman's March to the Sea, Volumes I & II, Essays of the American Civil War*. Campbell CA: Savas Woobury Publishers, 1994.
Woodworth, Steven E. *Nothing but Victory, The Army of the Tennessee*. New York: Alfred A. Knopf, 2005
Wright, George W. "Sgt. James E. Wright," *Confederate Veteran* (March–April 1993): 30–38.
Wright, Henry H. *A History of the Sixth Iowa Infantry*. Iowa City IA: State Historical Society of Iowa, 1923.
Wynne, Ben. *A Hard Trip, A History of the 15th Mississippi Infantry, CSA*. Macon GA: Mercer University Press, 2003.
Young, Callie B. *From These Hills: A History of Pontotoc County*.
Young, L. D. *Reminiscences of a Soldier of the Orphan Brigade, June 26, 1916*. Paris KY: Louisville Courier-Journal Job Printing Company, 1918.

Zinn, John G. *The 33rd New Jersey in the Civil War, The Mutinous Regiment*. Jefferson NC: McFarland & Company, 2005.

Roster of the 2nd Ga. Battl., S.S., G.G.M. 35/1–2 (Winter/Spring 1995), vertical files, Chickamauga National Battlefield Park Library.

Internet

www.civilwararchive.com/CORPS/20thhook.htm (7 May 2006).

"128th New York Infantry Regt.," http://www.28thga.org/123ny_pictures_hq.html (4 April 2008).

"134th New York Infantry," http://www.dmna.state.ny.us/historic/reghist/civil/infantry-/134thInf/134thInfHistSketch.htm (7 May 2006).

"26th Alabama," http://www.rootsweb.ancestry.com/~alcw26/26thala.htm (20 March 2008).

www.dmna.state.ny.us/historic/reghist/civil/artillery/13thIndBat/13thIndBatTable.htm (13 April 2008).

"26th Wisconsin," http://www.russscott.com/~rscott/26thwis/26pgwk64.htm (10 November 2008).

"2nd Alabama Cavalry," http://www.archives.state.al.us/referenc/alamilor/2ndcav.html (21 December 2008).

"37th Mississippi Infantry," http://www.reynolds-genealogy.com/research/37th_mississippi_regiment.htm (15 October 2008).

"43rd Mississippi Infantry," http://43rdms.homestead.com/camel.html (27 August 2008).

"57th Alabama Flag," http://www.archives.state.al.us/referenc/flags/072.html (22 November 2008).

"57th Alabama Infantry," http://www.managementaides.com/my_interests/hispanic_america.htm (22 November 2008).

"6th Mississippi Infantry," http://sixthmsinf.tripod.com/index.htm (2 January 2009).

"78th Illinois Infantry," http://civilwar.ilgenweb.net/reg_html/078_reg.html (2 January 2009).

"Brookwood Hills Subdivision," http://www.buckhead.net/brookwood-hills/ (31 December 2008).

"Dahlonega Gold Ruch," www.dahlonegagagold.com/dghist.html (1 August 2008).

Davis, Burke. "The Civil War, Strange and Fascinating Facts," www.civilwarhome.com/casualties.htm (15 May 2008).

"Franklin, Tn." http://www.heritagepursuit.com/Franklin.htm (3 April 2008).

"Georgia Militia at Turner's Ferry, July 5, 1864," http://www.hmdb.org/marker.asp?marker=17022 (29 November 2009).

"History of the 28th Regiment, Pennsylvania Volunteers, Goldstream Regiment," http://www.pa-roots.com/~pacw/infantry/28th/28thorg.html. (7 May 2006).

"Indiana Regiments in the Civil War," http://www.indiana.edu/~liblilly/wpa/wpa_info.html. (16 June 2008).

"Kennesaw Mtn.," http://ourgeorgiahistory.com/ogh/Kennesaw_Mountain_National_Battlefield_Park (16 June 2008).

"Kennesaw Mtn.," http://www.nps.gov/kemo/index.htm (15 June 2008).

"The Letters and Papers of Charles Manning Furman," http://batsonsm.tripod.com/letters/letters9.html. (1 March 2008).

"McCarty, Bettie Louise, A History of Edward McCarty and His Descendants," http://www.peachtreebattlealliance.org/id52.html (10 January 2009).

Moore, Isaac V. "Our Confederate Ancestors, Co. E. 37th Ga." Edited by Ronald E. Jones, http://www.tennessee-scv.org/camp87/csa.htm (4 April 2002).

"O'Neal's Brigade, Col. Edward Asbury O'Neal," http://aotw.org/officers.php?officer_id=643; 26th Alabama Infantry, Flag (25 September 2006).

Overby, Charles A. "Georgia Gold," article in Gems and Minerals; www.goldmaps.com/east/georgia_gold_mines.htm (1 August 2008).

"Sumner Co., Tennessee in the Civil War," http://www.rootsweb.com/~tnsumner/sumnfg15.htm (1 March 2008).

Taylor, Samuel. "The Battle of Peachtree Creek." http://ngeorgia.com/history/peachtreecreek.html, (6 June 2003).

[AUTHOR], "Taylors's Rosters and Notes, Co. D, 16th South Carolina," http://www.geocities.com/BourbonStreet/Square/3873/franklin7d.html (27 August 2008).

"Texas in the Civil War," http://history-sites.com/mb/cw/txcwmb/index.cgi?noframes;read=8412 (10 February 2008).

"Timekeeping at the US Naval Observatory," http://tycho.usno.navy.mil/history.html (27 July 2008).

"Union Regimental Histories." http://www.civilwararchive.com/Unreghst/unnyinf9.htm (7 May 2006).

von Clausewitz, Carl. "On War," book 2, chapter 2, paragraph 24, http://en.wikipedia.org/wiki/Fog_of_war (19 April 2009).

"Weather," http://www.as.ysu.edu/~wbuckler/Weather/Readings/z_time_on_weather_maps.htm (27 July 2008).

Williams, David. "The Georgia Gold Rush, Twenty-Niners, Cherokees, and Gold Fever, Colombia, S.C.," www.goldrushgallery.com/dahlmint/show_men_pic15.html, (1 August 2008).

http://bioguide.congress.gov/scripts/biodisplay.pl?index'W000145.

Other

22nd Wisconsin, subject file PW-4, Kennesaw National Battlefield Park, Kennesaw, Georgia.

A. H. "A Memorial," 17 September 1896, The Drane House, French Camp, Mississippi.

Adjutant general, State of Illinois. "Report of the Adjutant General of the State of Illinois." In Jasper N. Reece and Isaac Hughes Elliot, editors, *History of One Hundred and Fifth Infantry*, 5:686–88. 5 volumes. Springfield IL: Phillips Bros., [1900].

Atlanta History Center, "Turning Point: The American Civil War" (exhibit).

Biggs, Greg. E-mail to author, 2, 7–8, 29–31 December 2008, in author's personal papers, Dalton, Georgia.

———. "The 'Shoupade' Redoubts: Joseph E. Johnston's Chattahoochee River Line," *Civil War Regiments, A Journal of the American Civil War* 1/3 (1990): 77–108.

Bird, Frank. Interview with author, May 2008.

"Brief History of Tupelo," *Clarion-Ledger/Jackson Daily News*, 22 Febraury 1987, 7–9.

Brown, Chuck. "The Atlanta Campaign, May 7 through September 3, 1864, with a Focus on the Dallas Line in Relation to Pickett's Mill" (map and time line).

Bunker, Robert M. Interview with author, July 2009.

Carlisle, Virginia Patterson, *Ye Olde Scrapbook: A Portrait of Choctaw County Before the World Changed*. Ackerman MS: Choctaw County Historical and Genealogical Society, Inc., [1987].

Clauss, Erol. "The Atlanta Campaign, July 18, 1864." Ph.D. dissertation, Emory University, 1965. Special Collections, Zack Henderson Library, Georgia Southern University, Statesboro, Georgia.

Cole, Steve. "Texas Confederate Cemetery in Clarke County, Miss.," *Our Heritage* 29/3 (April 1988): 1–5.

Covington, Tommy, compiler and editor. *Tippah County Heritage*. Volume 2. Ripley MS: Tippah County Historical Genealogical Society, 1994.

Cubbison, Douglas R. "Fireworks Were Plenty, The XV and XVI Army Corps at the Battle of Ruff's Mill, Georgia, July 3–5, 1864," Kenan Research Center, Atlanta History Center, Atlanta, Georgia.

Foote, Shelby. Interview. *The Civil War: A Film by Ken Burns*. Episode 2, "A Very Bloody Affair" (1990).

Georgia Historical Markers. Valdosta GA: Bay Tree Grove Publishers, 1973.

Harrrison, Patrick Morgan. "Confederate Dead at Canton, MS." Http://msgw.org/madison/Canton/index.htm.

Heery, George and Betty. Interview by author, 27 March 2008, tape recording, in author's personal papers, Dalton, Georgia.

"History of the Water Valley Rifles, Company F, 15th Mississippi Infantry." Supplement to the WPA Historical Research Project, Yalobusha County, 16 February 1937, Special Collections, J. D. Williams Library, University of Mississippi, Oxford.

Jones, Eugene W., Jr. *Enlisted for the War: The Struggles of the Gallant 24th Regiment, South Carolina Volunteers, Infantry, 1861–1865*. Hightstown NJ: Longstreet House, 1997.

Jones, Joseph. "Roster of the Medical Officers of the Army of Tennessee, Volume XXII, Richmond, Va. Jan.–Dec. 1894," pp. 165–274. In *Southern Historical Society Papers*. Volume 24. Richmond VA: Southern Historical Society, 1876–1943.

Julian, Allen P. "Operations through the Present Ridgewood Community, July 1864," MSS 130, box 4, folder 4, Wilbur G. Kurtz Collection, Kenan Research Center, Atlanta History Center.

Kaufman, Dave. "Riverchat," *Upper Chattahoochee Riverkeeper* **[VOL#/ISSUE#?]** (Fall 2002): 6–7.

Kaufman, David R. *Peachtree Creek: A Natural and Unnatural History of Atlanta's Watershed*. Athens: University of Georgia/Atlanta History Center, 2007.

Kincaid, Gerald Allen, Jr. "The Confederate Army: An Analysis of the Forty-Eighth Tennessee Volunteer Infantry Regiment, 1861–1865." Ph.D. dissertation, Ohio State University, 1980. Www.dtic.mil/cgi-bin/GetTRDoc?AD=ADA299772, 4 April 2013.

Kurtz, Wilbur G. "Atlanta in the Summer of 1864," *Inn Dixie Magazine* (January 1936).

———. "Battles of Atlanta," September 1895, MS 130, box 11, folder 6, Wilbur G. Kurtz Papers, Kenan Research Center, Atlanta History Center.

———. "Embattled Atlanta" (map), March 1930, MS 130, Wilbur G. Kurtz Papers, Kenan Research Center, Atlanta History Center.

———. "French's Division Hood's Left Flank," MS 15, Wilbur G. Kurtz Papers, Kenan Research Center, Atlanta History Center.

———. Typescript of markers, MS 130, box 38, Wilbur G. Kurtz Papers, Kenan Research Center, Atlanta History Center.

———. "Loring's Hill," box 55, folder 5, Wilbur G. Kurtz Papers, Kenan Research Center, Atlanta History Center.

———. "Peach Tree Dead," box 32, folder18, Wilbur G. Kurtz Papers, Kenan Research Center, Atlanta History Center.

———. "What James Bell Told Me about the Siege of Atlanta," 15 July 1935, MS 130, Wilbur G. Kurtz Papers, Kenan Research Center, Atlanta History Center.

Kurtz, Wilbur G., Sr. "Captain Thomas J. Key's Battery which was at the Battle of Peachtree Creek, July 20, 1864" (letter to members of the Atlanta Civil War Roundtable, 19 May 1955), MS 130, scrapbook 28, Wilbur G. Kurtz Papers, Kenan Research Center, Atlanta History Center.

Livingston, Melinda Burford, and Charles A. Rich. "A Treasure on the Trace—The French Camp Story." The Drane House, French Camp, Mississippi.

Long, Robert R. "A Brief History of the Battle of Peachtree Creek, July 20, 1864," in author's personal papers, Dalton, Georgia.

McCall, Phil, Private Isaiah Crook, 37th Ga. Smith's Brigade, prepared for 1998 Crook Reunion, courtesy Kennesaw Mountain Battlefield Park Library, vertical files.

McGavok Home and Cemetery records, subject files, Carnton Plantation Museum and Archives, Franklin, Tennessee.

McIntire, Carl. "Stories Reveal Old Greensboro's Bloody Legacy," *Mid-South Magazine*, 13 July 1975, 7–9.

McMurry, Richard M. "The Atlanta Campaign, December 23, 1863 to July 18, 1864." Ph.D. dissertation, Emory University, 1967, Zack Henderson Library, Georgia Southern University, Statesboro, Georgia.

Bibliography

Madry, Mrs. John Gray. "Battle of Peachtree Creek, July 20, 1864," MS 130, Wilbur G. Kurtz Collection, Kenan Research Center, Atlanta History Center, Atlanta, Georgia.

Mitchell, Margaret. *Gone With the Wind*. New York: Macmillan Company, 1936.

Morris, Roy, Jr., and Phil Noblitt. "The History of a Failure, Spring 1864: A Federal Army Tries to Slip through Georgia's Snake Creek Gap," vertical files, Crown Gardens and Archives, Dalton, Georgia.

Murphree, T. M. "History of Calhoun County," Special Collections, Calhoun County Library, Bruce, Mississippi.

Newspaper clipping of list of staff officers, Mississippi Department of Archives and History, Jackson, Mississippi, record group 9, vertical file 136.

Noblitt, Phil. "The Battle of Peachtree Creek," *America's Civil War* (September 1998): 39–43.

Van Nostrand, D. "How We Fight in Atlanta," 248. In Frank Moore, editor, *The Rebellion Record. A Diary of American Events*. Volume 11. New York: NP.

Orr, J. L. Proposed Senate bill on use of African Americans in Confederate military service, 30 January 1864. *Southern Historical Society Papers, New Series, No. XII, Volume L, First Congress, 4th Session*. Richmond VA: Southern Historical Society, 1953.

Osborne, Seward, Jr. "George Young: Forgotten Hero of Peach Tree Creek; North South Trader, Mar.–Apr. 1980; & Poem of The 143rd New York Vols.," Atlanta History Center, MS 612–F.

Papers of the Military Historical Society of Massachusetts, Vol VIII, The Mississippi Valley, Tennessee, Georgia, Alabama, 1861–1864. Wilmington NC: Broadfoot Publishing Company, 1989.

Popowski, Howard. "Battle of Dug Gap, May 8, 1864, Georgia Gilbraltar," Crown Gardens and Archives, Dalton, Georgia.

"Resaca Confederate Cemetery." United Daughters of the Confederacy, Georgia, 1993. Crown Gardens and Archives, Dalton, Georgia.

Rose, Kenny R. *Calhoun County, Mississippi: A Pictorial History*. Special Collections, Calhoun County Library, Bruce, Mississippi.

Simmons, Hugh. Letters to author, 20 and 22 August 2007, author's personal papers, Dalton, Georgia.

Stone, Larry. "Snake Creek Gap—Resaca," Crown Gardens and Archives, Dalton, Georgia.

———. "The Battle of Resaca (& Nance Springs)," Crown Gardens and Archives, Dalton, Georgia.

Stribbling Jimmy, compiler. "Roster of Members of the 31st Miss. Inf. Volume, Company D." In author's personal papers, Dalton, Georgia.

Thomas, Diane C. "City-Scape, Atlanta," The Magazine of the Urban South 22/4 (October 1982): 11–16.

Trammell, Randy. *Tilton. Georgia and the Civil War*. Dalton GA: self-published, 1998.

Twain, Mark, and Charles Dudley Warner. *The Gilded Age*. Chicago: American Publishing Company, 1873.

Warwick, Rick. "The Horrors of Battle of Franklin," Heritage Foundation of Franklin and Williamson County, July 2006, vertical files, The Carter House and Museum, Franklin, Tennessee.

Wetzel, C. Robert, "Mudheads," *Envoy* (newsletter), April 1999. Indianapolis: Emmanuel Christian Seminary.

William N. Nokes biographical information, Confederate file 134, Carter House and Museum, Franklin, Tennessee.

William Wing Loring subject file, Mississippi Department of Archives and History, Jackson, Mississippi.

WPA, "Records for Calhoun Co. Miss.," Mississippi Department of Archives and History, Jackson, Mississippi, record group 139, box 11, section 4, file 10654.

———. "Records for Choctaw Co. Miss.," Mississippi Department of Archives and History, Jackson, Mississippi, record 139, box 11, section 5, file 10661.

INDEX

Abernathy, John E. 173
Abernathy, 3rd Sgt. H. A. 242
Adams, General John 64, 176, 242, 350, 360
Adams's Mississippi brigade 24, 34, 35, 64, 65, 161, 350, 359, 360
Adams, Wilks 230
Adolphson, Steven J. 336, 343
Akeman, Lt. John 155
Alabama Street 50, 51
Alexander, David Henry 231
Alexander, Lt. Colonel 202
Alford, 2nd Sgt. Solomon B. 253
Alford, Churchwell (Church) 253, 254
Alford, Munroe P. 253, 254
Allen, Lt. Colonel Daniel B. 285
Allen, Sgt. Thomas C. 379, 380
Anderson, Captain David 202, 211
Anderson, Colonel John H. 60, 154
Andersonville, GA 28, 152, 175, 276
Anjaco Road 144, 153, 215, 219, 220
Ansley Park Golf Course 104, 105, 121
Archer, W. P. 192
Ardmore Circle 147, 148
Ardmore Park 113, 147, 148, 155, 192, 219, 222, 268, 417, 420
Ardmore Road 113, 144, 153, 217, 218, 219, 220
Armour Drive 121, 122
Arnn, William 267
Arnold, Major Henry L. 86
Arnold, Major W. R. 184
Arpege Way 91
Askew, Lewis (Lucius) Q. C. 119
Asmussen, Lt. Colonel C. H. 391, 392
Aten, Henry J. 2
Atkins, Thomas R. 213
Atlanta Constitution 400, 418
Atlanta History Center 298, 315
Atlanta Journal 422
Atlanta Medical College 50
Atlanta Memorial Park 86
Augusta Daily Chronicle 409
Ault, Sgt. Charles 210
Austin, Captain J. B. 367
Austin, Private (19th MI) 249
Aycock, John M. 242
Bailey, Mary 228
Bailey, Richard M. 231
Bailey, Robert M. 228
Bailey, Sgt. Harrison 197, 198
Baird, General Absalom 89, 90, 91, 357
Baird's division 89, 90, 357

Baker's brigade 23
Baker, Major John J. 202, 208, 211
Bainbury, Chester 421
Bald Hill (aka Leggett's Hill) 48
Baldwin, Captain Frank 208, 211
Baldwin, General William E. 279
Banks, Sergeant Robert Webb 326
Barclay, Captain Julius H. 46
Barfield, John 260
Barnard, George 250, 395
Barnes, 1st Sgt. Riley 184, 185
Barth, Major George W. 77, 123
Barton, James B. 231
Barrett, Colonel Wallace W. 77
Barrett, Sergeant John 151
Barry, Colonel William S. 279, 350
Barry, Captain Robert L. 333, 398
Barry's Tennessee (Lookout) Battery 333, 398
Bate, Major General William B. 55, 56, 57, 104, 106, 369, 370, 381, 407
Bate's division 23, 44, 55, 56, 57, 102, 104, 105, 106, 107, 108, 110, 121, 133, 158, 160, 222, 367, 369, 370, 378, 379, 381, 382, 385, 387, 388, 390, 406, 407, 408
Beauchamp, Dilmeda M. 263
Beauchamp, Zelabee 263
Beauregard, General P.G.T. 54
Beaverbrook Drive 90, 341
Bechstein, Lt. (82nd Illinois) 319
Bee, General Barnard 58
Belew, Ensign James V. 224
Bell, James 394, 395
Bell, Thomas Calvin 263
Belvedere, Drive 88, 305, 320
Benedict, Sgt. J. B. 256, 258
Bennett, Captain (Staff Officer, Williams Div.) 347
Berry, Charles M. 254
Berryhill, S. Newton 228, 415, 416
Berryhill, 1st Lt. William Harvey 360
Bethune, Lt. Colonel R. A. 184
Bethune, Lt. Colonel William C. 67, 162
Bevins, William E. 14, 377
Biddle, Captain James 356
Biggers, 4th Sgt. William H. 214
Bill, Colonel Charles Candy's horse 284
Bird, Jr., Francis (Frank) 394
Birmingham Standard 298
Bitsy Grant Tennis Center 87, 171, 187, 285, 286, 292, 294, 295, 297, 301, 302, 305, 314, 315, 347

Bivin, Captain Joseph A. 186
Black, Benjamin F. 242
Black, Major Samuel L. 72, 370, 407
Blackwell, Private John Y. 155
Blake, Colonel John W. 77, 78, 121, 122, 123
Blake's brigade 77, 101, 117, 119, 121, 122, 123, 124, 130, 131, 132, 387, 399
Blakeslee, Captain George H. 248, 249
Blair, Major General Francis P. 48
Blanch, Lt. Colonel Willis 78, 123, 131
Bloodgood, Lt. Colonel Edward 83, 166, 189, 203, 212, 216, 217, 226, 227, 395
Bloody Magnolia Spring 249, 250, 251
Blue, 1st Sgt. Jonathan Graham 253
Bobby Jones Golf Course 83, 86, 87, 216, 292, 420, 422
Bohler Road 69, 91, 341
Boughton, Colonel Horace 314, 315, 316, 317
Bowen, 1st Sgt. Oscar 260, 261, 262
Bradley, General Luther P. 79, 126, 127, 136
Bradley's brigade 42, 79, 119, 124, 125, 126, 127, 132, 133, 134, 135, 136, 394
Bragg, General Braxton 54, 405
Braswell, Robert 137
Braswell, Samuel 137
Braswell, Sgt. Major William 137
Braun, Xavier 267
Brewer, J. W. 227
Briant, Lt. Colonel Cyrus E. 335
Briar Vista School 110
Briarcliff Road 42, 44, 47, 361
Bridges, James E. 274
Brighton Road 75, 78, 97, 113, 117, 119, 122, 123, 124, 125, 126, 127, 131, 132, 133, 141, 384
Brock, Surgeon Jesse 284, 285
Brooks, Corporal William P. 273, 275
Brooks, Joseph G. B. 273, 275
Brookview Drive 341
Brookwood Hills Park (private) 420
Brookwood Hills Subdivision 78, 124, 422, 423
Broomhall, Myres W. 194
Broomhall, Sylvester P. 194
Brown, Chuck 2
Brown, Captain J. William 377
Brown, Corporal Edmund R. 74, 89, 306, 312, 313, 320
Brown, General John C. 47
Brown's brigade 23, 45
Brown's division 47
Brown, Quartermaster Sgt. James Freeman 383

Brown, Lt. J. D. 155
Brown, Lt. Colonel (61st Ohio) 317
Browning, Sergeant F. M. 109
Bryan, Major D. F. 69, 278
Bryant, Captain W. C. 28th Tennessee Infantry (Confederate) 154
Buck, Captain I. A. 17, 370, 373, 386
Buckhead, GA 20, 26, 27, 31, 32
Buckhead Road (Peachtree Road) 31, 35, 42, 57, 58, 59, 60, 75, 77, 78, 79, 82, 83, 97, 99, 101, 102, 104, 106, 110, 112, 114, 115, 117, 118, 119, 120, 122, 123, 124, 125, 126, 127, 129, 130, 132, 136, 139, 140, 141, 144, 146, 147, 150, 153, 156, 160, 192, 216, 219, 234, 260, 275, 356, 360, 367, 369, 370, 372, 373, 374, 375, 376, 382, 383, 384, 385, 386, 394, 399, 406, 417
Buckingham, Lt. Colonel Philo B. 262
Buckley, Dennis 255, 256, 257, 258
Buerstatte, Charles 271
Bull, Sergeant Rice 88, 89, 309
Bundy, Captain Henry 176, 177, 178, 283, 287, 288, 289
Bundy's battery 84, 170, 176, 177, 178, 183, 187, 193, 283, 286, 287, 288, 289, 290
Burdett, B. F. 422
Burnett, Major Thomas J. 3, 69, 278, 293
Burt, James A. 254
Bush, William J. 261
Butler, George W. 194
Butterfield, General Daniel 38, 84, 366
Cain, Giles Leroy 228
Camden Road 78, 113, 119, 122, 125, 130, 131
Cameron, 4th Sergeant Charles C. 194
Campbell, Henry 8,
Campbellton, GA 18, 27
Camp Chase, OH 213, 214, 243, 245, 254
Camp Douglas, IL 186, 195, 196, 242, 247, 254, 263, 336
Candy, Colonel Charles 169, 187, 281, 282, 284
Candy's brigade 169, 170, 171, 176, 177, 181, 183, 185, 187, 281, 282, 283, 284, 285, 286, 287, 288, 290, 292, 294, 295, 297, 299, 326, 346, 391
Cannon, J. P. 5, 36, 63, 176, 177
Cantey, General James 280
Cantey's (O'Neal's) brigade 24, 279, 280
Capers, Colonel Ellison 15, 140, 323, 347
Cardiac Hill 98, 118, 147, 216
Carey, Adjutant Seth C. 311
Carlin, General William P. 344
Carodine, 2nd Lt. William Bird 225
Carpenter, Wiley 194

Index

Carter, Jimmy, Presidential Library 50
Carter, Arthur B. 184
Carter, Colonel John C. 60
Carter's Tennessee (Wright's) brigade 72, 144, 145, 146, 148, 152, 153, 154, 155, 157, 159
Carter, Samuel 404
Casey's Hill 9, 351
Castel, Albert 145, 387
Cavalry Ford 28
Centennial Olympic Park 79
Chalaron, 1st Lt. Joseph Adolphe 379, 380
Chambless, E. F. 422
Chapin, Captain (136th NY) 256, 257
Chase, Colonel Henry 231, 235
Chastain, R. Boone 107
Chatfield, Lt. Colonel Harvey 296
Chattanooga Daily Rebel 158
Cheatham, Major General Benjamin F. 30, 55, 373, 407
Cheatham's corps 43, 44, 72, 230, 361, 371, 373, 407
Cheatham's division (Maney) 22, 55, 110, 143, 159, 164, 269, 369, 374
Cheshire Bridge Road 43, 121
Chew, Frank 249
Cincinnati Commercial 316
Clark, Captain Charles T. 135
Clark, Jerry 273
Clauss, Erol, 308
Clayton's brigade (Holtzclaw) 23
Clayton's division 46
Clayton Road 122
Clear Creek 9, 78, 100, 110, 113, 119, 120, 121, 122, 124, 125, 131, 132, 134, 160, 379, 380, 382, 394
Cleburne, Major General Patrick R. 48, 55, 60, 62, 147, 160, 269, 369, 370, 371, 372, 373, 374, 382, 385, 386, 407, 409, 410
Cleburne's division 22, 33, 48, 55, 56, 60, 75, 143, 160, 216, 269, 369, 370, 371, 372, 373, 374, 375, 377, 382, 385, 407, 408
Clifton Road 47
Cline, William 221, 346
Cobham, Colonel George A., Jr. 295, 296
Cobb, General Howell 115
Cobb, Gray 229
Cobb, Hillary C. 263
Cobb, Lucy Ann Parker 229
Cobb, Peter May 229
Cobb, William W. 229
Cobb, Winfred Wooten 229
Cobb's Artillery battalion 378
Cobb's Legion 367

Coburn, Colonel John 80, 191, 192, 200, 201, 202, 217, 219, 233
Coburn's brigade 79, 83, 86, 165, 191, 192, 200, 201, 202, 206, 207, 208, 209, 212, 213, 216, 217, 220, 225, 226, 233, 235, 244, 259
Cockerham, Thomas J. 194
Cockrell, General Francis M. 340, 341, 349, 350
Cockrell's Missouri brigade 24, 70, 71, 333, 340, 341, 349, 350, 351, 353
Colgrove, Colonel Silas 312, 319
Collier, Andrew Jackson 106, 234
Collier, Andrew Jackson house 97, 98, 112, 124, 141, 144, 145, 149, 260, 375, 386, 417, 423
Collier, George Washington 106
Collier, George Washington house 106, 423
Collier's (grist) Mill 79, 80, 84, 86, 87, 146, 147, 164, 167, 176, 178, 180, 182, 183, 192, 200, 204, 213, 216, 225, 231, 232, 233, 234, 238, 239, 248, 253, 273, 291, 295, 346, 389, 421, 422
Collier Ridge 144, 190, 192, 193, 195, 198, 201, 203, 204, 205, 206, 207, 208, 209, 211, 216, 217, 218, 219, 221, 223, 226, 232, 233, 234, 236, 239, 241, 246, 248, 249, 252, 256, 259, 260, 267, 270, 272, 273, 275, 283, 285, 286, 289, 291, 292, 294, 299, 300, 314, 315, 326, 328, 360, 368, 395, 397, 417, 418, 419, 421
Collier Road 69, 78, 79, 80, 82, 84, 85, 87, 88, 95, 112, 153, 156, 159, 165, 167, 169, 170, 171, 174, 175, 187, 189, 197, 199, 207, 209, 215, 216, 217, 218, 219, 220, 223, 234, 236, 252, 259, 266, 270, 273, 275, 280, 283, 291, 292, 294, 300, 314, 315, 316, 323, 326, 331, 333, 346, 351, 384, 391, 395, 397, 398, 417, 418, 421, 422
Collier Woods 106, 110, 143
Collins, 1st Lt. Robert Marvin 375, 376, 377
Collins, Walter 88
Colonial Homes condominiums 215, 216, 217
Conn, Lt. James P. 284
Conn, Robert E. 195
Connally, Major James A. 357
Connor, Lt. Colonel George W. 108
Connor, Edward T. 254
Connor, 5th Sgt. William M. 253
Connor, W. H. 270, 271, 398
Conoley, Colonel John F. 69, 278
Conrad, Colonel Joseph 78, 97, 98, 99, 119
Cooper, Captain J. A. 239
Cooper, James A. 246

Cooper, James Henry 195
Cooper, Thomas Littleberry 272
Cope, Adjutant Alexis 111
Cottage Lane 170, 291, 326
Cowan, J. H. 184
Cox, Acting Adjutant Charles H. 240
Cox, General Jacob D 9, 15
Crabb, James H. 209
Craft, 2nd Lt. W. H. 327
Craighead, Sergeant (1st & 3rd MO) 341
Craigue, James M. 242
Cram, Sergeant George F. 84, 85, 364, 365, 366
Crane, Lt. Colonel A. B. 210
Crawford, Captain William T. 209, 210
Cresson, Major Charles C. 285, 286
Crestlawn Cemetery 9, 63
Crist, Private Henry E. 165, 191, 200
Crook, Colonel D. C. 154, 155
Crook, Isaiah 49, 104, 107
Cross Creek Parkway 91
Cross Keys, GA 28, 361
Crossdale, Alfred 287
Crowel, Edward 256
Crowell, Tillman 246
Crowell, William J. 246
Crumpton, Washington Bryan 278, 282, 289, 290, 291, 322, 327, 328, 329, 347, 348
Crusselle, Tom 50
Cummings' brigade 23
Curtiss, Captain A. A. 256
Custis, 1st Lt. Cyrus E. 148, 181, 182, 183, 235, 236, 370
Cutter, George H. 1, 321
Cyclorama, Atlanta 48
D'Alvigney, Dr. Noe 50
Daboll, Captain Henry W. 310
Daerfler, Private George C. 152
Daugherty, Captain L. F. 357
Daves, James R. 194
Davis, Adjutant Claudius Virginius H. 197, 198, 199
Davis Circle 351
Davis, Major General Jefferson C. 35, 353, 354, 357
Davis' division 35, 89, 90, 91, 353, 354, 357
Davis, President Jefferson 5, 12, 29, 54, 403
Davis, Stephen 50, 109, 146
Davis, William P. 139
Deadrick, Captain J. G. 156
Deadrick, Major 155
Deas' brigade 23, 47
Dean Drive 90
Dean, Henry 211
Decatur Depot 367

Decatur, GA 17, 19, 27, 28, 41, 47, 48, 230
Decatur Road 47, 372, 377
Deerland Estate (home of J. J. Spalding) 147
DeFoor Avenue 351
De Gress, Captain Francis 47, 48
Dellwood Drive 205, 216, 218
Dewey, Lt. Ransom P. 339
Dickinson, C. H. 166
Dickinson, 1st Lt. Lewis 226
Dilger, Captain Hubert 90, 341, 349, 354, 355, 356
Dilger's battery 341, 349, 354, 355, 356
Dilworth's brigade 35, 91
Dixon, Captain Mumford H. 372
Dixon, Captain Robert M. 139
Doan, Lt. Colonel Azariah Wall 243
Dobbins, J. T. 298
Dobbs, 3rd Lt. Silas Mercer 274
Dodge, Major General Granville M. 6, 48
Doty, Captain John S. H. 339
Douglas, Thomas Jefferson, Sr. 228
Drane, Colonel James 66, 73, 94, 95, 161, 194, 225, 227, 247, 264, 275
Drake, Colonel Jabez L. 66, 161, 222, 265, 268, 269, 270, 271, 272
Drake, Lt. Colonel Edwin L. 378
Drullinger, Lieutenant Robert F. 46
DuBose, John W. 15, 16
Dudley, 3rd Sgt. James Jacob 273, 275
Duluth, GA 27
Duncan, William C. 263
Dunn, Captain Walter G. 286
Dunn, 1st Corporal E. E. 107
Dunn, Mathew Andrew 197, 265
Durand, Samuel A. 44
Durand's Mill 44
Durgin, Adjutant John C. 226
Dustin, Colonel Daniel 231
Dyer, Lt. Colonel Samuel M. 259, 260, 261
Early's Creek (aka Tanyard Branch) 79
Easterwood, Henry J. 214
Ector, General Mathew D. 70, 341, 349, 350, 351
Ector's Texas & North Carolina Brigade 70, 341, 349, 350, 351, 352, 353, 398
Edington, James M. 242
Edwards, George 352
Edwards, Thomas Jesse 228
Eighteenth Tennessee Infantry (Confederate) 45
Eighteenth U.S. Infantry 356
Eighth & Nineteenth Arkansas Infantry Consolidated 61
Eighth Georgia Battalion 57
Eighth Mississippi Infantry 57

Index

Eighth Tennessee Infantry (Confederate) 60, 155
Eighty-Eighth Illinois 77, 78, 101, 123, 126, 148, 152, 342
Eighty-Eighth Indiana 335
Eighty-Fifth Illinois Infantry 2
Eighty-Fifth Indiana Infantry 202, 203, 209, 210, 225
Eighty-Second Illinois Infantry 89, 314, 318, 319
Eighty-Second Ohio Infantry 314, 316, 317
Eighty-Seventh Indiana Infantry 357
Eleventh Michigan Infantry 356, 357
Eleventh Tennessee Infantry (Confederate) 154
Eleventh, Twelfth & Forty-Seventh Tennessee Infantry Consolidated 60
Elliott, Sergeant Fergus 286, 287, 288, 289
Ellis, Sarah 52
Ellis Street 49
Ellsworth Park 420
Elmore, Bruce 312, 317
Ely, Joseph W. 249
Elysian Way 91
Embry, Hiram house 87, 88, 304, 305, 306, 323, 331, 333, 334, 356, 357, 398
Emory University 47
Endsley, Captain H. M. 240
English, Lt. Pierce 289, 291, 322, 327
Este, Colonel George P. 91
Este's brigade 91
Evans, Captain John C. 249
Evans, John W. 184
Evans, William Jefferson 214
Evergreen Lane 170, 285, 295
Ewing, John M. 263
Faison, Captain Alexander 184
Fanning, James 256
Farmby, Captain John T. 197
Farrell, Colonel Mike 35, 353
Faulkner, Lt. Colonel Lester B. 216, 217, 256
Faulkner, Reuben P. 254
Featherston, General Winfield S. 64, 66, 74, 93, 95, 161, 162, 295, 346, 348, 349, 359, 360, 363, 364, 368, 369, 394, 395, 396, 410, 411, 412, 413, 414, 415, 419, 421
Featherston's Mississippi brigade 1, 24, 64, 66, 73, 95, 124, 144, 146, 147, 148, 149, 150, 152, 159, 161, 162, 163, 164, 165, 176, 177, 179, 180, 181, 183, 187, 189, 190, 191, 192, 193, 198, 199, 200, 202, 203, 204, 205, 206, 207, 209, 210, 214, 218, 219, 221, 222, 225, 226, 227, 231, 232, 233, 235, 236, 237, 238, 241, 244, 245, 248, 249, 252, 255, 258, 259, 260, 263, 264, 265, 268, 269, 270, 271, 274, 275, 281, 288, 293, 294, 300, 346, 348, 349, 359, 360, 363, 364, 368, 369, 385, 395, 396, 397, 400, 408, 410, 411, 412, 413, 414, 415, 417, 419, 421
Federal corps—
-IV 15, 26, 30, 31, 32, 34, 35, 37, 38, 44, 46, 64, 74, 80, 110, 121, 147, 149, 165, 190, 218, 220, 221, 223, 273, 305, 335, 364, 366, 381, 396, 406, 419
-XIV 26, 30, 31, 32, 34, 37, 38, 64, 67, 69, 70, 89, 305, 311, 320, 334, 350, 353, 354, 357, 393, 398, 399
-XV 9, 47, 48
-XVI 9, 48
-XVII 9, 48, 374
-XX 26, 31, 32, 34, 38, 39, 40, 64, 67, 74, 79, 86, 90, 124, 126, 149, 159, 176, 177, 180, 189, 206, 221, 269, 271, 273, 305, 308, 334, 335, 360, 363, 383, 391, 393, 394, 400, 402, 422
-XXIII 9, 33, 42, 46, 47, 360, 381, 406
Feiss, Sgt. Stephen 267
Fenton, E. B. 214, 215, 222, 223, 224
Ferrell, Captain C. C. 327
Ferguson's cavalry brigade 25, 26
Fields, John 113
Fields, Samuel 113
Fifteenth Kentucky Infantry (Federal) 335, 339, 340, 343, 344
Fifteenth Mississippi Infantry 35
Fifteenth Missouri Infantry (Federal) 76, 77, 78, 97, 101, 112, 119, 148, 150, 152
Fifteenth Ohio Infantry 111
Fifteenth & Thirty-Seventh Tennessee Infantry Consolidated 56, 109
Fifteenth U.S. Infantry 356
Fifth & Thirteenth Arkansas Infantry Consolidated 61
Fifth Confederate (Tennessee, Polk's brigade) Infantry 60
Fifth Connecticut Infantry 88, 301, 308, 309, 310, 311, 389, 400
Fifth Company, Washington Artillery battery 378, 379, 380, 381
Fifth Indiana Battery 46
Fifth Kentucky Infantry (Confederate) 56, 107
Fifth Ohio Infantry 170, 283, 286, 287, 290, 294
Fifth Tennessee (Confederate, Strahl's brigade) Infantry 145, 146, 155, 156
Fiftieth Tennessee Infantry (Confederate) 60
Fifty-Third Tennessee Infantry (Confederate) 69, 329, 345

Fifty-Fifth Alabama Infantry 67, 162, 180, 181, 183, 184, 185, 186, 190, 231, 258
Fifty-Fifth Ohio Infantry 39, 214, 218, 219, 265, 273
Fifty-First & Fifty-Second Tennessee Infantry Consolidated 60
Fifty-First Illinois 79, 126, 127
Fifty-Fourth Georgia Infantry 57, 138
Fifty-Second Georgia Infantry 46
Fifty-Seventh Alabama Infantry 67, 162, 180, 181, 183, 184, 185, 186, 188, 190, 231, 258
Fifty-Seventh Georgia Infantry 57, 121, 137, 138
Fifty-Seventh Indiana Infantry 78, 100, 110, 119, 121, 123, 130, 131, 132
Finley, General Jesse J. 56, 108
Finley's Florida brigade 23, 56, 106, 108, 110
Finley, Jefferson (James) R. 254
First Alabama Infantry 328
First & Fifteenth Arkansas Infantry Consolidated 60, 377
First & Fourth Florida Infantry Consolidated 56
First & Fourth Missouri Infantry (Confederate) 71
First & Third Florida Cavalry Consolidated (dismounted) 56
First & Third Missouri Cavalry Consolidated (dismounted) 71, 341
First Arkansas Mounted Rifles 344
First Corps (Alabama) Sharpshooters 69, 278, 291, 294, 296
First Georgia Infantry 57, 122, 138
First Georgia Confederate Infantry 57, 59, 112, 113, 114, 115, 116, 137, 141, 386
First Georgia (Battalion) Sharpshooters 57, 59
First Georgia State Line troops 46
First Illinois Light Artillery Battery H 47, 48, 50
First Illinois Light Artillery Battery M (Spencer's) 129
First Michigan Light Artillery Battery I (Smith's) 128, 130
First Mississippi Battalion Sharpshooters 66, 161, 166, 222, 227, 248, 264, 265
First New York Light Artillery Battery I 290, 307
First New York Light Artillery Battery M, 307
First Ohio Artillery Battery I (Dilger's) 90, 354, 355, 356
First Ohio Light Artillery Battery A (Goodspeed's) 78, 84, 128, 129
First Ohio Light Artillery Battery C (Stephens) 128, 130, 219, 220
First Wisconsin Infantry 22
Fitch, Major (21st WI) 342, 343
Flaherty, George W. 242
Flaherty, Thomas J. 242
Flat Shoals Avenue 9
Floyd House, Macon, GA 229, 299
Flynn, Lt. Colonel John 281, 289
Flynt, Lt. T. L. 375
Fondren, George H. 273, 274, 275
Fondren, Rufus K. 273, 274, 275
Forbes, Corporal John H. 90, 344, 355
Ford, Captain J. W. 340
Forrest, General Nathan B. 54
Fortieth Indiana 78, 117, 123, 399
Fortieth Mississippi Infantry 66, 161, 165, 183, 192, 209, 225, 231, 232, 233, 237, 238, 239, 240, 241, 248, 259
Fortune, James 175
Forty-Eighth Tennessee Infantry (Confederate) 328, 345
Forty-Fifth Alabama Infantry 61
Forty-Fifth Mississippi Infantry 11, 61
Forty-Fifth New York Infantry 319
Forty-First Tennessee Infantry 60
Forty-Fourth Illinois 77, 78, 148, 153
Forty-Ninth Alabama Infantry 66, 162, 173, 178, 179, 185, 186, 282
Forty-Ninth Tennessee Infantry (Confederate) 328, 329, 345
Forty-Second Illinois Infantry 79, 126
Forty-Second Indiana Infantry (Federal) 335, 342
Forty-Second Tennessee Infantry (Confederate) 328
Forty-Seventh Tennessee Infantry (Confederate) 154
Forty-Sixth Georgia Infantry 57, 61, 119, 138, 139, 384
Forty-Sixth Pennsylvania 309, 311, 318, 320, 332
Forty-Sixth & Fifty-Fifth Tennessee Consolidated Infantry (Confederate) 328, 329
Foster, Captain Samuel T. 52, 61, 143, 374, 377
Foster, 3rd Lt. William M. 253
Fountain, Frank 260
Fourat, Colonel Enos 163, 172, 173, 174, 175, 178
Fourteenth Texas Cavalry (dismounted) 70
Fourth Arkansas Infantry 344
Fourth Confederate, Sixth, & Ninth Tennessee Infantry Consolidated 60
Fourth Georgia Sharpshooters 56, 109

Fourth Kentucky Infantry (Confederate) 56
Fourth & Fifth Tennessee Infantry Consolidated 60
Fox, Lt. Colonel William F. 413, 414
Franks, Corporal James M. 195
French, Major General Samuel G. 2, 67, 70, 349, 350, 351, 352, 353, 398, 408
French's division 24, 63, 67, 70, 349, 350, 351, 354
Fuchs, Captain John William (Co. G or A, 26th WI) 267
Fuller, Corporal Benjamin H. 229
Fuller, Eliza Lauderdale 229
Fuller, Lucinda 229
Fuller, William F. 229
Furman, Captain Charles Manning 62, 117, 140
Gaines, Lt. Colonel J. F. 27
Garrett, Captain John 317, 318
Garrett, Franklin 8, 9
Gary, Lt. Asa H. 317
Gary, Captain Marco B. 130
Gates, Colonel 341, 350, 351, 352
Gault, Colonel Edward M. 46
Geary, General John White 38, 164, 167, 168, 169, 170, 172, 173, 175, 176, 226, 281, 282, 288, 294, 295, 299, 300, 304, 362, 395, 396
Geary's division 32, 38, 74, 83, 84, 86, 87, 91, 146, 147, 159, 161, 163, 166, 168, 170, 171, 176, 177, 178, 180, 181, 182, 183, 185, 187, 192, 198, 216, 237, 281, 286, 287, 291, 292, 297, 299, 300, 301, 302, 304, 305, 307, 308, 309, 311, 313, 315, 322, 325, 326, 346, 347, 362, 365, 391, 395, 396, 422
Gentry, Levi W. 263, 264
Georgia Railroad 9, 10
Georgia State Militia 14, 29, 30, 360
Gibbons, Major W. McD. 239
Gibson's brigade 23
Gilder, Abner B. 254
Gillespie, Major Francis Marion 94, 194, 224, 227, 228
Gillion, Samuel W. 242
Gilson, Asst. Surgeon A. J. 389
Gipson, William J. 52, 53
Gist, General States Rights 57, 58, 59, 125
Gist's brigade 23, 57, 58, 59, 61, 113, 117, 118, 119, 122, 124, 125, 131, 132, 138, 139, 140, 323, 384, 387, 394
Gladstone Road 320
Gleason, Colonel Newell 357
Glenbrook Drive 90, 332, 334, 341
Glenwood Avenue 9
Godwin, Lt. Colonel Aaron S. 328

Golfview Drive 205, 233, 236, 237, 249, 250
Gone With the Wind 421
Goodspeed, Captain Wilbur F. 78
Goodspeed's battery 84, 101, 102, 112, 117, 118, 123, 128, 129, 147, 150, 375
Gordon, General John B. 419
Gore, James William 229
Gore, John Ashford 229
Gourd, Sergeant Samuel 287
Govan, General Daniel C. 61, 406
Govan's Arkansas brigade 22, 61, 375, 408
Gove, Lt. Colonel David 309
Grammer, Benjamin F. 229
Grammer, Joseph W. 229
Granbury, General Hiram M. 60
Granbury's Texas brigade 23, 60, 61, 143, 374, 375, 407, 408
Grant Park 48
Grant, General U. S. 392
Gray, Lt. Charles W. 116
Gray, George B. 195
Gray, Reuben T. 214
Green, Abraham 228
Green Bone Creek 34
Green, Elizabeth 228
Green, Johnny 107
Green, 3rd Sgt. Henry W. 228
Gregory, 1st Sgt. John C. 196
Griffin, GA 155, 240
Griffin, 5th Sgt. Thomas A. "Bud" 229
Grinstead, Surgeon William 206, 400
Grissett, Lt. John P. 261
Grose's brigade 45
Gunter, Captain Pleasant Dickson 274
Gunter, Corporal Claiborn Preston 274
Gwynne, Lt. Colonel Andrew D. 155
Hagan, First Sergeant John W. 75
Hagar, Sgt. Phineas A. 208, 211
Hall, (33rd IN) 271
Hall, Captain James I. 157, 158, 222
Halleck, General Henry W. 363, 392, 393
Hallum, 3rd Lt. John C. 196
Halpin, Lt. Colonel William G. 340
Hamilton, Lt. Colonel Algemon S. 113
Hammond, Major Charles M. 78, 123
Hancock, 1st Corporal John R. 242
Hannon's Alabama cavalry brigade 27
Hapeman, Lt. Colonel Douglas 336, 337, 338, 339, 340, 341, 342, 343
Hardee, Lt. General William J. 12, 26, 30, 34, 42, 52, 53, 72, 104, 105, 106, 160, 247, 269, 304, 348, 349, 350, 363, 369, 370, 371, 372, 373, 378, 381, 382, 385, 386, 387, 396, 398, 401, 404, 405, 406, 407, 408, 409, 410

Hardee, Major John 52
Hardee, Joseph 52
Hardee's corps 22, 33, 34, 55, 56, 72, 75, 95, 108, 110, 151, 161, 165, 179, 221, 230, 304, 348, 363, 369, 370, 381, 382, 385, 386, 387, 388, 396, 398, 407, 408
Harman, Martin V. 243
Harper, Joel W. 246
Harrison, Colonel (& later President) Benjamin 80, 169, 183, 200, 201, 202, 217, 232, 233, 236, 237, 252, 419
Harrison's brigade 80, 85, 181, 182, 183, 190, 193, 200, 201, 202, 206, 216, 217, 218, 219, 231, 232, 233, 243, 244, 248, 257, 258, 364, 365, 366
Harrison, President William Henry 80
Hart, B. H. Liddell 362
Hartsfield, Mayor William B. 51
Hazen's Brigade 42
Held, Corporal John 267
Heery, Betty 250, 251
Heery, George 250, 251
Henderson, A. Jeff 107
Hendley, George D. 246
Hendley, Osborn W. 246
Hennesey, John 355
Hester, James Monroe 274
Hester, John Franklin 274
Hester, Joseph R. 274
Hester, Moses H. 107
Highland Avenue 9, 43, 44, 46, 50
Hightower, Sgt. Major Gustave G. T. 224, 225
Hindman, Major General Thomas C. 7
Hindman's division 23, 47
Hinman, Lt. Colonel Wilbur F. 76, 124, 125, 126, 128, 134, 136, 137
Hitchcock, Hiram 256
Hobart, Lt. Colonel Harrison C. 335
Hodgson, Kitty 249
Hoenig, George 270
Holcomb Bridge 27
Holland, Colonel Orlando S. 69, 278, 279, 280, 284, 325
Hollingsworth, Lt. 208
Hood, General John Bell 5, 6, 7, 8, 9, 12, 14, 16, 18, 22-24, 54, 92, 212, 326, 333, 357, 358, 360, 361, 362, 366, 369, 370, 371, 372, 373, 383, 385, 386, 387, 396, 397, 398, 401, 402, 403, 404, 405, 407, 408, 409, 410, 411
Hood's corps (Cheatham) 23, 361
Hooker, Major General Joseph 32, 33, 38, 67, 81, 169, 176, 182, 191, 269, 275, 294, 300, 304, 306, 312, 362, 366, 383, 389, 391, 392, 393, 394, 402, 414

Hopkins, Dr. Linton 249
Horn, Stanley 403
Hosler, 1st Lt. Rufus 221
Hotchkiss, Major T. R. 61, 372
Hotchkiss' Artillery battalion 62, 372
Howard, General Oliver O. 6, 15, 43, 46, 101, 142, 150, 167, 282, 381, 383, 392, 396, 406, 419
Howard, Lt. J. W. 146
Howell, Adjutant J. C. 184
Howell, Captain Evan P. 146, 147, 192, 398, 399, 417, 418
Howell's Georgia battery 146, 147, 148, 192, 398, 399, 417
Howell, Henry 249
Howell Mill Road 58, 62, 72, 73, 86, 87, 88, 89, 90, 91, 280, 305, 306, 315, 320, 321, 323, 331, 332, 333, 334, 335, 337, 354, 382, 397, 398, 399
Howell's Mill 26, 61, 80, 86, 90, 91, 139, 304, 305
Hoxton's artillery battalion 374, 382
Huddleston, Chaplin J. F. N. 240
Hudson, Private (37th Miss.) 327
Huff house 62
Huff, Jeremiah 62
Huff, Sarah 62, 332, 352, 399
Huffman, William C. P. 141
Hughes, Nathaniel Cheairs, Jr. 1, 52, 57, 104, 406, 408
Hull, Major Robert Newton 113
Hulme, Colonel Issac N. 328
Huntington Road 100, 131
Huron, Color Sgt. Frank H. 275, 276, 277
Hurst, Major Samuel H. 220, 221
Hutchins, Colonel Rue P. 335
Ide, Lt. 308
Ireland, Colonel David 169, 171, 290, 294, 295, 297, 300, 315
Ireland's brigade 171, 286, 290, 291, 292, 294, 295, 299, 300, 315, 346
Ishom's Ford 19, 27
Isom's Ferry 27
Ithaca Journal 298
Ives, Colonel Samuel S. 66, 67, 162
Ives, Washington M. 108
Ivy, Hardy 94
Ivy, Sarah Todd 94
Ivy Street 49, 94, 367
Ivy, Third Lt. Richard Nicholas 94
Jackson, Captain Moses 265, 269
Jackson, Colonel James 66, 162
Jackson, General John R. 57
Jackson's brigade 23, 57
Jackson, Lt. Colonel Allan H. 94, 174, 282
Jame's Bank 50

Index

James, F. M. 246
Jarvis, Joseph 152
Jenkins, Caradine (Jerry) T. 274
Jenkins, James S. 356
Jenkins, 2nd Lt. John 155
Jennings, Captain George L. 253
John Happy (pen name) aka Albert Roberts 109, 110, 158
Johns, Lt. Robert B. 226
Johnson, Alex 367
Johnson, Arch 367
Johnson, D. N. 367, 368
Johnson, General Richard W. 86, 87, 334, 335, 357, 399
Johnson's division 88, 89, 90, 91, 334, 337, 354, 357
Johnson Island, OH 195, 214
Johnson, John E. 298
Johnson, 2nd Sgt. Joel John 242
Johnson, Private Andy G. 156
Johnson Road 42, 62
Johnston, General Albert S. 53, 405
Johnston, General Joseph E. 4, 5, 6, 7, 8, 9, 10-12, 14-16, 29, 89, 197, 348, 396, 403, 405
Jolley, Orderly Sergeant Joseph 113
Jones, Colonel Jesse Stancel (Bushrod) 323, 324
Jones, Colonel Patrick H. 169, 170, 172, 281, 282, 296
Jones's brigade 169, 170, 176, 177, 281, 282, 283, 285, 286, 289, 294, 296, 297, 299, 305, 326, 346, 391
Jones, Captain Russell J., 114
Jones, Dr. Charles W. 357
Jones, Ensign S. W. 327
Jones, Major J. H. 184
Jones, Wyatt 326, 327
Juniper 366
Keiper, Gaskard 256
Kelly, Captain W. A. 262
Kelly, General J. H. 28
Kelly, J. H. (70th IN) 238
Kennerly, James A. 71
Kennett, Colonel Henry G. 231
Kennon, Emma Jane 118
Kern, John 11, 373
Kessler, Nicholas 77
Ketchum, Captain John R. 241
Key, Captain Thomas J. 62, 372, 374
Key's Arkansas battery 62, 147, 372, 374
Kimball, General Nathan 77, 78, 384
Kimball's brigade 76, 77, 112, 121, 122, 124, 143, 144, 148, 149, 150, 151, 152, 153, 159, 164, 217, 222, 384, 387
Kimbrell, Fred 272

King, General John H. 89, 356
King's brigade 90, 356
King, Jeremiah 261
Kirby, Colonel Isaac M. 46
Kollock, Frederick N. 299, 390
Knap's battery (Sloan's) 281
Knight, Isaac 175
Knipe, General Joseph F. 304, 311, 312, 313
Knipe's brigade 88, 304, 307, 308, 309, 310, 311, 313, 318, 319, 320, 332, 389, 400
Knox, Major Samuel E. 328
Kuechenmeister, Frank 267
Kurtz, Wilbur G. 148, 182, 370, 388, 421, 422
L. O. S. 192, 256
Lack, Ben 153
Lane, Colonel John Q. 77, 123
Law, Color-bearer Albert H. 208
Lawrence, Gilbert D. 317
Lawshe, Er 49
La Parc 91
La Vista Road 110
Lanius, Richard 261
Lastinger, America (Davis) 115
Lastinger, Elias 114
Lea, Lt. 199
Leaming, Lt. Colonel Henry 78, 123
Leatherman, Morgan 45
Lee, General Robert E. 403
Lee, General Stephen Dill 402, 419
Lee, Thomas W. 246
Lee, William L. F. 246
Legare, Corporal Oscar A. 379, 380
Leggett, General Mortimer 48
Leggett's division 48
Leggett's Hill (aka Bald Hill) 48
Lemonds, Lt. J. L. 145, 146
Lenox Road 42, 43
Lenox-Wildwood Park 44
Le Sage, Lt. Colonel John B. 314
Lever, John J. 195
Lewallen, Captain George Washington 263
Lewis, Captain Daniel 356
Lewis, General Joseph H. 56
Lewis' Kentucky (Orphan) brigade 23, 56, 106, 107, 108, 110
Lewis, Morris 344
Lewis, Noble 221
Ley, Bishop John 13
Lightsey, J. B., 326, 328
Limpert, George C. 201
Lincoln, President Abraham 392
Lindsey, Captain William H. 297, 325
Linewood Cemetery, Columbus, GA 225
Lipscomb, Dr. C. 377
Little, George 381

Lloyd, Lt. 168
Lofton, John R. 378
Logan, Major General John A. 48, 61, 392
Logie, Colonel William K. 309
Long, Robert 86
Longino, J. T. 197, 198
Longwood Drive 306
Lott, 1st Lt. D. F. 327
Loring, Hannah Kenan 64
Loring Heights Subdivision 388
Loring, Major General William W. 13, 17, 64, 65, 71, 161, 163, 164, 247, 269, 348, 349, 350, 359, 363, 364, 396, 397, 398, 401, 412
Loring, Reuben 64
Loring's division 24, 63, 64, 72, 73, 141, 161, 163, 164, 166, 239, 273, 348, 349, 359, 363, 364, 365, 388, 396, 397, 398, 400, 401, 408
Lovelace, Lt. Charles W. 333, 398
Lowe, 2nd Lt. Clay 378
Lowrey, General Mark P. 61, 373
Lowrey's Alabama & Mississippi brigade 11, 22, 61, 373, 407, 408
Luckie, Solomon 50, 51
Luckie Street 51
Lumsden's Alabama battery 381
Lyle, 1st Lt. Thomas J. 229
Lyon, 2nd Lt. Hezekiah H. 209
Lumpkin, Governor Wilson 52
MacArthur, General Douglas 149
MacArthur, Major Arthur, Jr. 78, 148, 149, 150
Mackay, Colonel Andrew J. 86
MacKay, Sergeant Charles W. 168
Mackall, General William W. 42, 372
Madison, GA 367, 368
Maddox, R. F. 419
Mageveny, Colonel Michael 60
Mageveny's Tennessee (fka Vaughan's) brigade 60, 144, 145, 148, 153, 154, 157, 159
Mahan, Lt. J. T. 341
Manahan, Adonoram Judson 214
Manahan, Captain John Franklin 213
Manahan, Thaddeus Aethelberg 213, 214
Maney, General George E. 55, 60, 72, 143, 144, 145, 369
Maney's brigade 22
Maney's Tennessee division (fka Cheatham's) 55, 56, 60, 93, 95, 108, 110, 113, 117, 136, 141, 143, 144, 145, 146, 148, 152, 153, 155, 156, 157, 159, 160, 164, 192, 218, 219, 220, 223, 260, 264, 268, 269, 369, 370, 371, 374, 384, 385, 388, 408, 410

Manigault, General Arthur M. 12, 13, 405
Manigault's brigade 23
Manner, John C. 274
Manning, James R. 243
Mannon, Lt. Colonel James M. 231
Massey, John C. 225
Masters, Captain (42nd IN) 335
Marcoot, Maurice 98, 99, 100, 101, 150
Marion Light Artillery (Florida) battery 374, 382
Markam, Reverend Thomas 413
Markham house 367
Marshall, Sgt. (Cleburne's courier) 370
Marshall, William, H. 45
Martin, Jim 153
Martin, Frank 373
Martin, Lt. Colonel William H. 377
Martin, William 152
Marvin, Captain Edward E. 301, 310, 311
Mathews, Captain C. H. 47
Mathis, Johnson 242
Matlock, Captain James T. 240
Matthews, James 261
Maurice, Major Thomas Davies 48
Maury, General Dabney H. 279
Maxwell, James R. 381
May, William 221
Maze, Captain 208
McAfee's Bridge 18, 27
McBride, Adjutant John R. 79, 80, 203, 204, 207, 208, 213
McCain, Major H. V. 186
McCarty, Sergeant Orange, Jr. 327
McCook, General Anson G. 89, 334, 335, 339, 342, 343, 344
McCook's brigade 90, 321, 334, 335, 337, 339, 340, 341, 342, 343, 344, 355, 393
McCuisiton, Mitchell H. 350, 351
McCullough, Colonel James 139
McCullough, 2nd Lt. John C. (Nute) 214
McCullough, Corporal Newton L. 253
McCully, John T. 213
McDaniel, William Thomas 240
McDermid, Angus 97, 115
McDougall, Colonel Archibald L. 309
McGowen, William A. 247
McGraw, Major John S. 130, 131, 132, 134
McGraw, 2nd Lt. Pleasant G. 263
McGroarty, Colonel Stephen J. 314, 317
McKee, Wiley T. 254
McKinley Road 88, 291, 301, 305, 306, 314, 315, 320
McLarty, 2nd Lt. Alexander W. 245
McLeroy, Lt. M. S. 186
McMahan, Edward L. 242, 243
McMahan, Corporal William L. 253

Index

McMahon, John T. 37, 39, 232, 255, 256
McMarks, Ezekiel 214
McMullen, Robert J. 254
McNair's brigade (Ector) 24
McNeilly, Chaplain James H. 13, 330
McPherson, General James B. 6, 9, 47, 360, 361, 362, 370, 372, 392, 402
McQueen, Axis 298
McQueen, M. D. 298
McRae, Floyd 249
McRae, William 261
Mead, Captain Francis 82, 166, 226
Mead, James 256
Mead, Commissary Sgt. Rufus 400
Meagher, Ensign Michael 197, 198
Mellon, Colonel Thomas A. 66, 161, 222, 260
Memphis Appeal 390
Mercer, General Hugh 57, 120
Mercer's Georgia brigade 23, 57, 120, 121, 122, 124, 125, 126, 127, 128, 131, 132, 133, 134, 135, 136, 137, 138, 150, 219, 384, 390, 394
Meredith, Captain William M. 240
Merrill, Lt. Colonel Samuel 231, 236, 237, 238, 239, 240, 241, 366
Merry, Sergeant Major Earl W. 356
Miles, Captain Abe 139
Miller, James T. 295
Miller, Corporal John W. 261
Miller, Lt. 177, 178
Miller's battery 178
Miller, Major Levin T. 202
Miller, Quartermaster Sgt. Finis E. 225
Mims, Bartholomew (Bart) W. 246, 247
Minter, Leroy 195
Mitchell's brigade 35, 91, 354
Mitchell, Margaret 421
Molt, William 179
Monroe Drive 121
Monterey Drive 320, 332
Montgomery, Lt. Colonel James H. M. 335
Montgomery, Jonathan 195
Montgomery Ferry Road 110, 121, 147, 234, 236, 384
Moody, Martin 152
Moore, Colonel Marshall F. 89, 354
Moore's brigade 23, 89, 90, 344, 354, 355
Moore, J.J. (John James) 241, 261
Moore, John Newton 240
Moore, Lt. Colonel David H. 127, 135
Moore, Lt. Samuel H. 347
Moore, Sergeant Isaac V. 108, 109
Moore's Mill 26, 68, 69, 80, 89, 91, 344, 345, 350
Moore's Mill Road 80

Moran, Michael 287
Moreland Avenue 9
Morgan, Colonel John Hunt 336
Morgan, Captain Otho H. 91
Morris, Nathan E. 109
Morris, William A. 214
Morrow, 3rd Lt. John C. 242
Mothershead, W. I. 293
Mt. Zion Church 58, 69, 278, 280, 300, 323, 331, 332
Mueller, Captain Robert 266, 267
Muller, Lt. (13th N.Y. Ind. Battery) 287, 288
Nail, Hyrum Marion 195
Nail, Mary 195
Nancy's Creek 25, 31, 32, 356
Napier, Captain Briggs Moultrie 116, 117
Naron, Captain George Washington 252, 253, 254
Naron, Eli Francis 254
Neal, Lt. A. J. 374, 382
Neighbor, Ensign M. 197
Neiphaus, Gerhard 267
Nelson, Colonel Noel L. 67, 162
Nelson, Sergeant James 193
Nesbitt, Lt. James A. M. 345
Newcomb, Captain E. H. 306, 347, 397
Newlin, Sergeant/1st Lt. William H. 75, 76, 150, 152
Newnan, GA 27
Newton, George 85, 181, 191, 233, 234, 235
Newton, Major General John 77, 101, 127, 129, 136, 360, 362, 383
Newton's division 42, 75, 76, 77, 97, 98, 102, 104, 119, 121, 125, 136, 142, 144, 147, 150, 151, 159, 160, 164, 165, 166, 216, 217, 218, 220, 221, 223, 260, 264, 265, 268, 356, 360, 362, 363, 369, 374, 375, 382, 383, 386, 387, 390, 394, 396, 399, 406
Nicholson, Bill 290, 291, 322, 348
Nineteenth Indiana Light Battery (Stackhouse's) 91, 356
Nineteenth Michigan Infantry 79, 202, 208, 211, 225, 226, 249
Nineteenth Tennessee Infantry (Confederate) 20, 60, 155, 156
Nineteenth U.S. Infantry 356
Ninety-Eighth Ohio Infantry 354
Ninety-Fourth Ohio Infantry 335
Ninety-Seventh Ohio Infantry 77, 78, 123, 126
Ninth Arkansas Infantry 69, 328, 331, 335
Ninth Kentucky Infantry (Confederate) 56, 107
Ninth Tennessee Infantry (Confederate) 157, 158

Ninth Texas Infantry 70, 350, 351
Nisbet, Colonel James Cooper 58, 59, 112, 115, 118, 119, 141, 373
Nisbet, Major John W. 59
Noble Creek Drive 341
Noblitt, Phil 269
Norfleet Park 420
Norfleet Road 87, 291, 301, 305, 306, 314, 315, 331
Norris, Captain John A. 354
North Avenue 381
Northcliffe Drive 90, 91, 92, 335, 341
North Decatur Road 47
North Highland Avenue 9, 44
Northside Drive 26, 32, 34, 73, 74, 86, 87, 88, 91, 167, 169, 170, 171, 280, 283, 285, 291, 292, 294, 302, 305, 306, 314, 315, 316, 323, 325, 326, 346, 391
Norwood, Lt. Colonel John H. 184
Nunnally, Peter 184
Oakland Cemetery (Atlanta, GA) 185, 272
Oatis, Major Martin A 66, 161, 193, 196, 197, 198, 199
O'Brien, Thomas S. 347
Ocmulgee Hospital (Macon, GA) 213, 214, 224, 229, 231, 242, 243, 254, 299
Old Marietta Road 62
Old Williams Road (North Decatur Road) 47
Oldham, Martin Van Buren 157,
Olmstead, Colonel Charles H. 122
Olyinska house 323
One Hundredth Illinois Infantry 78, 110, 119, 121, 123
One Hundred and Fifth Illinois Infantry 84, 181, 231, 233, 235, 236, 237, 238, 244, 258, 259, 364, 365, 366
One Hundred and First Illinois Infantry 314, 318
One Hundred and Fourth Illinois Infantry 90, 320, 321, 332, 334, 335, 336, 337, 338, 339, 340, 341, 342, 343, 344, 354, 399
One Hundred and Ninth Pennsylvania Infantry 171, 286, 287, 288, 289, 299
One Hundred and Second Illinois Infantry 181, 183, 190, 231, 232, 235, 237, 244, 252
One Hundred and Second New York Infantry 171, 296
One Hundred Eleventh Pennsylvania Infantry 171, 295, 296
One Hundred Fifty-Fourth New York Infantry 168, 171, 285
One Hundred Fifty-Fourth Tennessee Infantry (Confederate) 154, 157, 159
One Hundred Forty-First New York Infantry 309, 311
One Hundred Forty-Ninth New York Infantry 171, 296
One Hundred Forty-Seventh Pennsylvania Infantry 170, 283, 285, 286, 287, 299
One Hundred Forty-Third New York Infantry 312, 314, 315, 316, 317
One Hundred Nineteenth New York Infantry 169, 170, 283, 285, 299
One Hundred Thirty-Fourth New York Infantry 94, 170, 174, 282, 283, 285
One Hundred Thirty-Seventh New York Infantry 171, 297, 298
One Hundred Thirty-Six New York Infantry 38, 39, 80, 81, 83, 85, 95, 189, 192, 193, 209, 216, 217, 219, 231, 232, 238, 255, 256, 258, 395, 414
One Hundred Twenty-Fifth Ohio Infantry 79, 126, 127, 135, 136, 137, 275
One Hundred Twenty-Ninth Illinois Infantry 85, 181, 182, 231, 233, 235, 237, 238, 240, 244, 248
One Hundred Twenty-Third New York Infantry 88, 309, 311
O'Neal, Colonel Edward Asbury 67, 68, 187, 278, 279, 280, 291, 292, 293, 295, 346, 347, 348
O'Neal's Alabama & Mississippi (fka Cantey's) brigade 58, 67, 68, 69, 177, 187, 279, 280, 283, 288, 289, 291, 292, 293, 294, 295, 296, 297, 298, 300, 302, 307, 308, 314, 318, 322, 323, 324, 325, 326, 328, 331, 345, 346, 347, 348, 384, 396, 397
Opdycke, Colonel Emerson 125, 126, 127, 128, 132, 135, 383, 394
Opdycke, Lucy 125, 383
Orbreiter, John 45
Organ, Lt. John R. 284, 285
Orner, William H. (Hank) 208
Orr, Colonel (Congressman) Jehu A. 241, 247, 254, 273
Ott, Sgt. Bernhard 267
Ottley Drive 121
Otto, Captain John Henry 342, 345
Otts, 4th Sgt. Francis M. 245
Overbrook Drive 171, 286, 291, 292, 295, 302
Owens, Colonel Robert A. 328
Paces Ferry 27
Paces Ferry Road 69, 73, 332
Packer, Colonel Warren W. 301, 309, 310, 311
Page, 1st Lt. Alfred 344
Palisades Road 97, 98, 370, 373, 382

Index

Palmer, Major General John M. 67, 334, 382
Pardee, Colonel Ario 283, 287
Parks, Captain Henry F. "Thomas" 116
Patterson, Jimmy 261
Patton, Colonel William S. 279
Pea Vine Creek 30
Peachtree Battle Avenue 91
Peachtree Battle Circle 91
Peachtree Center Avenue (fka Ivy Street) 49, 94, 367
Peachtree Park Drive 130
Peachtree Road (& street) –see Buckhead Road
Peachtree Road Race 98
Peeples, Captain B. F. 145
Pennsylvania Light Artillery Battery E (Sloan's) 84, 170, 181, 182, 190, 193, 198, 205, 257, 258
Percy, Charles R. 380
Perry, Captain Henry F. 334, 355, 356
Pettus, General Edmund W. 44, 394
Pettus' brigade 44, 45
Phillips, George H. 139
Phister, Samuel 101
Pickett, Staff Officer W. D. 105, 106, 160
Piedmont Hospital 77, 79, 80, 106, 126, 147, 200, 215, 384
Piedmont Park 9, 44, 63, 104, 105, 381, 388
Piedmont Avenue 9, 44, 121
Pierson, Adjutant/First Lt. Stephen 94, 163, 172, 173, 174, 175, 176, 177, 178, 417, 418
Pinson, Aaron M. 146
Pitts, Cullen Lark 213
Plug Ugly (General A.S. Williams' horse) 304
Polk, General Leonidas 405
Polk, General Lucius 60
Polk's Arkansas & Tennessee brigade 22, 60, 131, 377, 378, 407, 408
Polk, 4th Corporal William C. 243
Porter, Sergeant R. W. 317
Prather, Corporal Francis M. 213
Pratt, 3rd Sgt. Alexander Henry 253
Preston, Major William 69, 324, 332, 333, 357, 398
Preston's Artillery battalion 69, 332
Preston, Sally "Buck" 333, 357, 358
Pritchard, Carol P. 242
Prude, 1st Lt. John W. 242
Pugh, Captain Cadwalader 226
Pulliam, Quartermaster/Commissary Sgt. James Terrill 225
Pulliam, John S. 225
Pulliam, Captain Thomas Jefferson 225, 363
Purcell, Madison 243

Purcell, Sgt. Mitchell C. 210
Quarles, General William A. 67, 328, 346
Quarles's Tennessee brigade 24, 67, 68, 69, 328, 329, 330, 345, 346, 347
Racine Boy 82, 83, 166, 368
Radcliffe Drive 90
Ragsdale house 349, 352
Ramsay, Captain Abiezar F. 260
Ramsay, Joseph W. D. 274
Randals, Major Benjamin 155
Raper, Corporal John T. 97, 122, 123, 130, 132, 133, 134
Rasberry, 1st Corporal Benjamin Franklin 213
Rasberry, Sgt. Joseph C. 213
Raspberry, Pinkney 195
Ratcliff, Adjutant (143rd New York) 317
Ratcliffe, 3td Lt. Warren E. 267
Rawlings, Thomas N. 261
Ray, Elizabeth 229
Ray, James M. 195, 229
Reagan, Charlie C. 243
Reagan, John T. 243
Redding, Captain Robert J. 138
Redland Road 200, 218, 226, 233, 234, 236, 237
Reed, Elizabeth Adele Jones "Bessie" (Napier) 116, 117
Reed, Wallace P. 50
Reed, William 116, 117
Reid, Harvey 83, 190, 205, 212, 213, 393
Rennolds, Edwin H. 145
Reuter, Franz 267
Reynolds, 1st Lt. John C. 244
Reynolds, General Daniel H. 69, 331, 332, 335, 342, 345, 348, 349
Reynolds, John (31st MS) 274
Reynolds, Major J. A. 177
Reynolds's Arkansas brigade 24, 34, 35, 67, 68, 69, 293, 294, 318, 321, 322, 331, 332, 335, 338, 339, 340, 341, 342, 343, 344, 345, 348, 349, 391, 396, 397, 408
Reynolds's North Carolina brigade 23
Reynolds, Colonel Thomas 399
Rice, First Lt. Ralsa 127, 128, 129, 135, 137, 275
Rice, Surgeon (Maney's/Cheatham's Division) Frank P. 49, 146, 159
Richards, Captain Cyrus Seymour White 195
Rivers, R. J. 324
Rives, Lt. Colonel Henry E. 79
Roberts, Albert (aka "John Happy") 109, 110
Roberts, John C. 333
Robertson, Rachel E. Countiss 230

Robertson, William B. 229, 230
Robin Hood Road 106, 110
Robinson, Colonel James S. 305, 314, 315
Robinson's brigade 89, 171, 291, 301, 305, 306, 307, 308, 309, 311, 312, 313, 314, 315, 316, 318, 319
Robinson, John Andrew (Robertson?) 263, 264
Robinson, 1st Sgt. Samuel H. 214
Robison, Lt. Isaiah 287
Roby, Captain Jacob W. 335
Rock Springs Road 46
Rogers, Major H. A. (9th TN) 157
Rorer, Lt. Colonel Walter A. 3, 4, 65, 66, 70, 71
Rose Hill Cemetery, Macon, GA 224, 231, 246
Rosecrans, General William 37
Ross, 1st Corporal James F. 230
Ross, Lt. William 118
Roswell, GA 19, 27, 28
Roswell Factory, GA 27
Rousseau, General Lovell H. 38
Roy, Thomas Benton 72, 371
Ruger, General Thomas H. 205
Ruger's brigade 305, 306, 308, 319, 320, 321
Rugg, Captain Harlan P. 310, 311
Russell, Augustus E. 270
Russell, Gideon B. 270
Russell, Sgt. Daniel William 269, 270
Russell, Tate, 270
Russell, 3rd Corporal Prince A. 270
Russell, W. B. 270
Salomon, Lt. Colonel Edwin S. 89, 314, 318, 319
Samuels, Colonel D. Todd 353
Sanders, James A. 254
Sandtown Road 18
Sasse, William 267
Sawyer, Private James 154
Scaife, William R. (Bill) 140, 141
Scales, Private (36th Ill.) 152
Schofield, General John M. 6, 9, 42, 360, 361, 362, 381, 406
Scott, General Thomas M. 64, 66, 161, 162, 346, 348, 396
Scott's Alabama & Louisiana brigade 24, 64, 66, 146, 147, 161, 162, 163, 164, 172, 173, 174, 175, 177, 178, 179, 180, 181, 182, 183, 186, 187, 190, 199, 205, 231, 235, 236, 238, 239, 278, 281, 282, 283, 286, 288, 289, 293, 294, 300, 322, 327, 346, 348, 359, 391, 396, 397, 400, 417
Scott, John H. 260

Scovill, Lieutenant Charles W. 78
Seaboard Coastline Railroad 215, 218
Sears, General Claudius W. 70, 279, 350
Sears's Mississippi brigade 24, 70, 89, 349, 350, 351
Second Arkansas Mounted Rifles 344
Second Corps Alabama Sharpshooters 297, 325
Second & Sixth Missouri Infantry (Confederate) 71
Second & Twenty-Fourth Arkansas Infantry Consolidated 61
Second Georgia Sharpshooters 57
Second Kentucky Infantry (Confederate) 56
Second Ohio Infantry 344
Second Tennessee Infantry (Confederate) 60, 131, 216, 378
Second United States Regulars 89
Sedden, Confederate Secretary of War James A. 7
Sedwick, Captain Dan. W. 232
Seeman, Captain John P. (Seaman) 266
Selden's Alabama Battery 332, 333, 357, 398
Selfridge, Colonel James L. 309, 319, 332
Seventeenth Alabama Infantry 3, 68, 69, 177, 278, 281, 291, 292, 293, 326
Seventh Florida Infantry 56
Seventh Indiana Light Battery (Morgan's) 91
Seventh, Tenth, Seventeenth & Eighteenth Texas Cavalry (dismounted) Consolidated 61, 377
Seventieth Indiana Infantry 80, 181, 231, 232, 233, 235, 236, 237, 238, 239, 240, 241, 244, 276, 366
Seventy-Eighth New York Infantry 296
Seventy-Fifth Illinois Infantry 46
Seventy-Fifth Ohio 265
Seventy-Fourth Illinois Infantry 77, 78, 148, 153
Seventy-Fourth Ohio Infantry 87, 88, 90, 344, 355
Seventy-Ninth Illinois Infantry 79, 126, 136
Seventy-Ninth Ohio Infantry 181, 182, 183, 190, 231, 232, 235, 238, 243, 244, 370
Seventy-Seventh Pennsylvania Infantry 46
Seventy-Third Illinois Infantry 75, 76, 78, 98, 99, 112, 119, 144, 148, 149, 150, 151, 152, 160
Seventy-Third Ohio Infantry 39, 214, 219, 220, 221, 346
Seventy-Third Pennsylvania Infantry 170, 285, 286, 299
Shapland, Corporal John 338
Shaw, General Albert D. 419

Index

Shaw, 1st Lt. William D. 359, 363
Shepherd, James D. 139
Sherman, General William Tecumseh 5, 6, 7, 14, 30, 31, 32, 33, 43, 47, 241, 326, 360, 361, 362, 363, 391, 392, 393, 394, 396, 402, 403, 405, 406, 420
Sherwood Forrest Subdivision 105, 106, 110, 121
Shields, Hugh 175
Shinn, Harmon C. 244
Shoal Creek 9
Shoup, Captain 378
Shurtleff, Dr. 373
Simmons, Hugh 186, 414
Simmons, James. M. 247
Sims, 3rd Sgt. Lycurgus 225
Sixteenth Alabama Infantry 61
Sixteenth South Carolina Infantry 57, 61, 117, 139
Sixteenth Tennessee Infantry (Confederate) 60, 153, 155
Sixteenth U.S. Infantry 356
Sixth & Seventh Arkansas Infantry Consolidated 61
Sixth Florida Infantry 56
Sixth Kentucky Infantry (Confederate) 56
Sixth Mississippi Infantry 35
Sixth & Fifteenth Texas Cavalry (dismounted) Consolidated 61, 375
Sixtieth New York Infantry 171, 286, 288, 290, 296, 299
Sixty-Fifth Georgia Infantry 57
Sixty-Fifth Ohio Infantry 76, 79, 124, 126, 136
Sixty-First Ohio Infantry 306, 314, 317, 318, 325, 397
Sixty-Fourth Ohio Infantry 79, 126, 136
Sixty-Ninth Ohio Infantry 356
Sixty-Third Georgia Infantry 57, 138
Sixty-Sixth Georgia Infantry 57, 58, 59, 112, 113, 115, 116, 117, 118, 141, 373, 383, 386
Sixty-Sixth Ohio Infantry 170, 281, 282, 283, 284
Skelton, William G. 247
Skinner, John Beale 243
Skinner, Richard La Fayette 243
Slaughter, Thomas B. 254
Sloan, Lt. Thomas S. 181
Sloan's (Knap's) battery 84, 147, 148, 170, 181, 182, 183, 190, 193, 198, 205, 237, 239, 257, 258, 281
Slocumb, Captain Cuthbert H. 379, 381, 398
Smith, Captain Luther R. 130
Smith, Captain Sidney B. 69, 278
Smith, Colonel Franklin C. 231

Smith, Colonel George A. 59, 112, 113, 141
Smith, Corporal Richard H. 297
Smith, Lt. (136th NY, Co. G) 256, 258
Smith, Private George T. (31st Miss.) 195
Smith, Colonel Orland 39
Smith, General Giles A. 48
Smith's (Giles A.) Federal division 48
Smith, General G.W. 30
Smith, General Thomas B. 56, 108
Smith's Georgia & Tennessee brigade 56, 106, 108, 109, 110, 131, 158
Smith, William Oliver 254
Snodgrass, Colonel John 67, 162
Soap Creek 27, 33
Spalding, J.J. house "Deerland" 147
Sparkman, Quartermaster Sgt. John W. 345
Sparks, Peter 399
Speed, A.A.G. Captain 227
Spencer, Captain George W. 129
Spring Street 9, 372
Springlake Park 420
Springlake Road 331
Spring Valley Road 169
Spring Valley Road Conservation Park 420
Spruill, Gabriel M. 247, 248
St. Mary's Hospial, LaGrange, GA 230
Stackhouse, Lt. William P. 91
Stacy, Isaiah David 230
Stacy, Miles Henry 230
Stacy, William M. 230
Stackhouse, 1st lt. William P. 356
Stamm, Charles 201, 266, 267
Standley, Captain George W. 197
Stanley's division 42, 43, 44, 45, 46, 110, 406
Stephens, Colonel M. D. L., 73, 228, 230
Stephens, Lt. Jerome B. 130, 219, 220
Stephenson, Philip Daingerfield 379, 380
Stevens, General Clement H. 57, 58, 113, 116, 117, 140, 394
Stevens' Georgia brigade 23, 57, 58, 112, 113, 115, 118, 122, 124, 131, 132, 140, 141, 141, 144, 145, 148, 373, 384, 385, 387
Stevens, Colonel P. F. 117
Stevenson's division 23, 43, 44, 45
Stevenson, T.A. 324
Stewart, Anderson A. 230
Stewart, Elizah D. 195
Stewart, Salina Tedford 230
Stewart, 3rd Corporal Jasper N. 230
Stewart, Lt. John W. 375
Stewart, William, Jr. 230
Stewart, Lieutenant General Alexander P. 11, 12, 16, 63, 351, 359, 360, 369, 382,

386, 396, 398, 404, 409, 410, 414, 415, 419
Stewart's corps 24, 33, 34, 55, 63, 71, 159, 162, 293, 300, 304, 325, 351, 386, 395, 398, 414
Stewart's division (Clayton) 23
Stigler, Major James M. 66, 161, 222
Stone, Frank 261
Stone, Henry 22,
Stone Mountain, GA 17, 19, 27, 367
Stoneman's federal cavalry 27, 28
Stovall's brigade 23, 46
Strahl, General Otho F. 60
Strahl's Tennessee brigade 22, 60, 144, 145, 146, 148, 155, 156, 159
Straw, Leyman B. 244
Strawn, Captain William 344
Stribbling, Jemima 230
Stribbling, Mark Mitchell 230
Stribbling, Mary Ann Chapman 230
Stribbling, Robert C. 230
Stuart, Dr. D. F. 377
Stuck, Matthias 240
Stuckey, 1st Lt. E. Samuel 297, 298
Sturdevant, Captain Ham 296
Sudderth, D. Glenn 421
Suggs, Rufus C. 214
Sullivan, Captain T. E. 138
Suman, Colonel Isaac C. B. 45
Summers, Burr 256
Sussex Park 44
Swindle, John Thomas 247
Talbot, Captain Bailey Montgomery 184, 187, 188
Talbot, Bailey Jr. 187, 188
Talbot, Mary Mullins 187, 188
Tanyard Branch 9, 79, 80, 81, 84, 87, 95, 146, 163, 164, 165, 174, 180, 181, 182, 183, 185, 186, 187, 216, 217, 218, 231, 233, 234, 236, 237, 238, 239, 248, 257, 258, 275
Tanyard Creek (fka Tanyard Branch) Park 84, 147, 170, 174, 180, 181, 183, 190, 192, 205, 258, 417, 420
Tatum, Color Corporal John T. 261
Taylor, Colonel Marion C. 335, 344
Taylor, James M. 274
Taylor, Lt. William V. 284
Tennyson Drive 90, 341
Tenth South Carolina Infantry 13,
Tenth Texas Cavalry (dismounted) 70, 351
Tenth Wisconsin Infantry 335, 339
Tharp, 2nd Corporal Daniel B. 245
Tharp, Simeon V. 245
The Prado 110
The Sherman Brigade-see Bradley's brigade

Third & Fifth Missouri Infantry (Confederate) 71
Third Confederate (Arkansas) Infantry 61
Third Connecticut Infantry 90
Third Kentucky Infantry (Federal) 79, 126
Third Maryland Detachment (Federal) 309
Third Mississippi Infantry 66, 161, 165, 210, 212, 222, 226, 248, 259, 260, 262, 270
Third Wisconsin Infantry 320, 321, 332
Thirteenth New York Light Artillery (Bundy's) 84, 170, 176, 287
Thirteenth Tennessee Infantry (Confederate) 154, 159
Thirtieth Alabama Infantry 45
Thirtieth Georgia Infantry 57, 59, 113
Thirtieth Tennessee Infantry (Confederate) 56, 109
Thirty-Eighth Indiana Infantry 334, 355, 356
Thirty-Eighth Tennessee Infantry 60, 155
Thirty-Fifth Alabama Infantry 66, 162, 173, 175, 178, 179, 185, 186, 282
Thirty-Fifth & Forty-Eighth Tennessee Infantry Consolidated 60
Thirty-Fifth Mississippi Infantry 279
Thirty-First Arkansas Infantry 345
Thirty-First Mississippi Infantry 1, 2, 66, 73, 81, 93, 94, 161, 163, 165, 166, 189, 192, 193, 194, 196, 197, 209, 212, 213, 224, 225, 226, 227, 231, 233, 237, 238, 241, 244, 245, 248, 252, 254, 255, 256, 257, 259, 263, 264, 273, 359, 364, 412, 413, 414
Thirty-First Tennessee Infantry 60
Thirty-First Wisconsin Infantry 319
Thirty-Ninth Alabama Infantry 47
Thirty-Ninth North Carolina Infantry 70, 351
Thirty-Second Mississippi Infantry 61
Thirty-Second Texas Cavalry (dismounted) 70, 351
Thirty-Seventh Georgia Infantry 56, 109
Thirty-Seventh Indiana Infantry 355
Thirty-Seventh Mississippi Infantry 68, 69, 177, 278, 279, 280, 281, 282, 283, 284, 289, 290, 291, 292, 325, 326, 327, 328, 346, 347
Thirty-Sixth Illinois Infantry 77, 78, 148, 149, 151, 152, 160
Thirty-Third Alabama Infantry 61
Thirty-Third Indiana 79, 191, 202, 203, 204, 207, 208, 209, 210, 213, 225, 270, 271, 398
Thirty-Third Massachusetts Infantry 39, 221, 393

Thirty-Third Mississippi Infantry 66, 161, 165, 221, 222, 241, 248, 264, 265, 266, 267, 268, 269, 270, 271, 272, 414
Thirty-Third New Jersey Infantry 38, 40, 94, 163, 169, 171, 172, 173, 174, 175, 176, 178, 179, 180, 183, 185, 281, 282, 300, 391
Thirty-Third Ohio Infantry 335, 342
Thirty-Third Tennessee Infantry 60
Thomas, General George 6, 7, 76, 77, 107, 129, 130, 132, 133, 134, 221, 360, 361, 362, 382, 386, 390, 392, 394, 402, 403, 405, 407
Thompson, "Chunky" 328
Thompson, Corporal Joseph Nicholas 175, 176
Thompson, J. M. 184
Thomson, Colonel David 314
Thornton, Sarah F. 1, 3
Thornton, Solomon M. 1, 3, 244, 245, 247
Traeumer, Adjutant George 267
Troup Hurt House 47, 48
Trout House 377
Trussell, James R. 196
Tschoepe, Moritz 150, 151
Tucker's brigade 23
Turley, Private Thomas B. 154
Turner, Captain J. W. 114
Tutt, William F. 380
Twelfth Louisiana Infantry 66, 67, 162, 173, 178, 180, 181, 183, 185, 186, 190, 231, 256, 258, 259, 300
Twelfth Tennessee Infantry (Confederate) 154
Twentieth Connecticut 39, 214, 215, 218, 219, 222, 223, 262, 265, 266, 268, 269, 270
Twentieth Mississippi Infantry 3,
Twentieth Tennessee Infantry 56, 109, 131
Twenty-Eighth Kentucky Infantry (Federal) 77, 78, 123
Twenty-Eighth Pennsylvania Infantry 170, 281, 282, 283, 286, 289, 294
Twenty-Eighth Tennessee Infantry (Confederate) 60
Twenty-Eighth Street 113, 117, 145, 146, 147, 156, 417
Twenty-Fourth & Twenty-Fifth Texas Cavalry (dismounted) Consolidated 61
Twenty-Fifth Georgia Infantry 57, 59
Twenty-Fifth Tennessee Infantry (Confederate) 154
Twenty-First Ohio Infantry 88, 356
Twenty-First Wisconsin Infantry 335, 342, 343, 345

Twenty-Fourth South Carolina Infantry 54, 57, 58, 62, 117, 304, 318, 323, 324, 325, 345, 347, 384
Twenty-Fourth Tennessee Infantry 60
Twenty-Fourth Wisconsin Infantry 78, 112, 119, 148, 149, 150, 151
Twenty-Ninth Alabama Infantry 68, 69, 278, 291, 294, 297, 298
Twenty-Ninth Georgia Infantry 57, 59, 75, 114, 115
Twenty-Ninth North Carolina Infantry 70, 351, 352
Twenty-Ninth Ohio Infantry 170, 281, 282, 286, 288
Twenty-Ninth Pennsylvania Infantry 171, 296, 299, 390
Twenty-Second Mississippi 66, 161, 165, 192, 193, 196, 197, 198, 199, 209, 212, 225, 226, 238, 244, 248, 249, 258, 259
Twenty-Second Wisconsin 80, 81, 82, 83, 85, 86, 95, 166, 189, 192, 202, 203, 207, 209, 211, 212, 213, 216, 217, 225, 226, 227, 249, 257, 258, 265, 368, 393, 395
Twenty-Seventh Alabama Infantry 63, 66, 162, 173, 176, 177, 178, 179, 185, 186, 282
Twenty-Seventh Illinois Infantry 79, 126
Twenty-Seventh Indiana Infantry 74, 88, 306, 310, 312, 313, 318, 319, 320
Twenty-Seventh, Thirteenth, & One hundred Fifty-Fourth Tennessee Infantry Consolidated 60
Twenty-Sixth Alabama Infantry 68, 69, 278, 279, 291, 294, 295, 296, 297, 325
Twenty-Sixth Georgia Battalion 58, 59
Twenty-Sixth Ohio Infantry 78, 97, 122, 123
Twenty-Sixth Wisconsin Infantry 201, 206, 214, 219, 227, 241, 265, 266, 267, 268, 270, 271
Twenty-Sixth Street 146, 147, 192, 234
Tyler, General R. C. 56
Tyler's (aka Smith's) brigade 23, 109
Tyrus, Captain Benjamin R. 375
Union Station Depot 367
Van de Graff, Adjutant William J. 225, 254, 255
Vaughan, General Alfred J, Jr. 60
Vaughan's Tennessee (aka Mageveny's) brigade 22, 60, 157
Vining Station 60, 196, 213, 229, 230, 242, 246, 253, 357
Vollmer, Charley 201
Wade, Burnal Henderson 263
Wagner, General George D. 121
Wagner's (Blake's) brigade 121, 130

Wakefield Drive 100, 123
Walker, Colonel Francis M. 60, 155
Walker's Tennessee (fka Maney's) brigade 60, 144, 148, 155, 156, 157
Walker, Colonel Irwin 13
Walker, Colonel Moses B. 91
Walker's (Moses' Federal) brigade 91
Walker, Lt. Colonel Thomas M. 296
Walker, Major General William H. T. 55, 57, 369
Walker's division 23, 55, 56, 57, 58, 97, 100, 102, 104, 108, 110, 112, 119, 121, 124, 126, 131, 136, 140, 141, 142, 144, 145, 151, 158, 160, 192, 222, 323, 345, 369, 371, 372, 374, 381, 382, 384, 385, 386, 388, 406
Walker, Scott 120
Wallace, Captain F. S. 325
Wallace, Colonel George P. 66, 161, 239
Walthall, Major General Edward C. 67, 69, 278, 327, 329, 345, 346, 348, 349, 351, 396, 397, 398
Walthall's brigade (Benton) 23
Walthall's division 24, 55, 58, 63, 66, 301, 323, 327, 332, 348, 349, 351, 352, 384, 390, 396, 397, 398, 400
Ward, General William 38, 81, 82, 84, 85, 86, 159, 191, 200, 201, 202, 203, 216, 217, 233, 360, 366, 368, 387, 395, 396
Ward's division 35, 38, 79, 82, 83, 86, 95, 128, 129, 130, 148, 150, 159, 165, 181, 182, 187, 189, 190, 191, 193, 199, 200, 201, 203, 205, 206, 207, 210, 213, 215, 216, 217, 218, 219, 221, 222, 249, 260, 265, 271, 275, 288, 297, 307, 311, 360, 364, 366, 368, 382, 395, 396, 397, 400, 407, 410, 414
Warner, Major Lewis D. 285
Warren, Lt. George W. 242, 341, 352
Washington Artillery battery (5th Co.) 378, 379, 380, 381, 398
Waterbury, Lt. (143rd New York) 317
Watkins, Colonel William M. 154
Watkins, Lt. Richard L. (Barry's Lookout TN Battery) 333
Watkins, Sam R. 145, 156, 387, 388
Watson, James K. 247
Way Hospital, Meridian, MS 225
Webber, Jacob 267
Weeden, Lt. Colonel John D. 66, 162
Weir, Lt. Colonel William W. 289, 327
Wellbourne Drive 44
Wellesley Drive 90
Wells, Captain E. T. 357
Wesson, James W. 263
West, Andrew J. 51

West, Captain Samuel A. 243
West Pace's Ferry Road 31
West, 2nd Lt. John 327
Westminster Drive 44
Wheeler, Major General Joseph 18, 24, 25, 34, 367, 372, 373, 419
White, Colonel John R. 329
White Columns 375, 388
White, Corporal James 263
White, Drummer Benjamin 107
White, 2nd Lt. Charles I. 226
Whited, Private George 154
Whitehall Street 50
Whitehead, Archibald 62
Whitehead house 62
Whitmore, Samuel 256
Why, Thomas 287
Wigfall, Senator Louis T. 15, 16,
Wildwood Park 44
Wildwood Road 44
Wiley, Bell I. 421
Wilkerson, Captain H. (1st & 3rd MO.) 341
Wilkerson, Captain William N. (9th OH) 190
Williams, Colonel Samuel C. 50
Williams, General Alpheus Starkey ("Pap") 38, 67, 169, 301, 302, 303, 304, 307, 311, 312, 319, 347, 397
Williams's (Alpheus Starkey) federal division 32, 35, 38, 67, 74, 86, 87, 89, 90, 159, 171, 285, 291, 297, 298, 299, 300, 301, 302, 304, 306, 307, 308, 309, 311, 312, 315, 321, 322, 324, 325, 331, 334, 337, 346, 347, 391, 397, 400, 422
Williams, General John S. 28
Williams's Kentucky cavalry brigade (Confederate) 28
Williamson, Captain Charles J. 116, 232
Williamson, Thomas J. 210
Willis, James 35
Wills, Charles W. 92
Wilson, 1st Sergeant James, Sr. 193
Wilson, Sergeant James 193
Wilson, James Lawson 231
Wilson Road 305, 306
Wilson, 3rd Corporal William J. Wilson 193
Wilson, William M. 338, 339
Wiltshire, Charles S. 195
Winegar's battery 307
Winkler, Major/Lt. Colonel Frederick C. 201, 266, 267
Witt, William A. 263
Wofford, Nathaniel S. 254
Womack, 1st Lt. William A. 245
Wood, Colonel James, Jr. 39, 200, 201, 212, 214, 215, 216, 217, 218, 219, 259, 268, 400

Index

Wood's brigade 80, 200, 201, 206, 212, 213, 214, 215, 216, 217, 218, 219, 220, 221, 222, 233, 259, 264, 265, 266, 268, 271, 273, 400
Wood's division 35, 42, 43, 44, 46, 76, 110, 111, 406
Wood, 1st Sgt. Thomas J. 242
Wood, Francis M. 242
Wood, J.P. 184
Woodbury, Captain John D., 308
Woodbury's battery 307, 308
Wormley, Sergeant (36th Ill.) 152
Worsham, Dr. J. W. 156
Worthington, Clark 153
Worthington, Sam 153
Worthy, Corporal William E. 263
Wright, Colonel (19th TN Confederate) 156
Wright, Lt. James M. 341, 342
Wright's Tennessee (aka Carter's) brigade 22, 60, 157, 159
Wycliffe Road 113, 117, 144, 153
Wyoming (County) Mirror 192
Young Colonel William F. (49th Tenn.) 329
Young, Colonel William H. (9th Tx.) 70, 350
Young, Lt. L. D. 104, 107, 108
Young, 1st Lt. George 314, 315
Youngblood, 2nd Corporal Claiborn J. 243
Youngblood, 3rd Corporal Andrew W. 243
Zimmer Drive 9, 44
Zinn, John C. 40